# Critical Readings on Piaget

*Critical Readings on Piaget* is a follow-up to *Jean Piaget: Critical Assessments*, a collection of eighty-three papers dealing with the critique of Piaget's work in psychology, education and philosophy during the period 1950–90. This new collection tracks developments in the most recent published work, with an integral guide and editorial commentary by Leslie Smith.

Starting with Piaget's epistemology, a major intellectual resource in developmental psychology and education, Leslie Smith sets out the main elements of Piaget's position in relation to 21 papers, dealing with equilibration, education, social development, reasoning development, number development and modal knowledge. A conclusion examines the psychological and educational assessment of Piaget's epistemology.

This collection of distinctive studies during the last five years provides high-profile and engaging examples from current research in this area. It will prove a useful and compact text for undergraduate and postgraduate students and researchers.

**Leslie Smith** is Senior Lecturer at the Department of Educational Research, Lancaster University. His interests lie in Piaget's theory and research and he is author of *Necessary Knowledge: Piagetian Perspectives on Constructivism* (1993) and editor of Piaget's *Sociological Studies* (1995) and *Jean Piaget: Critical Assessments* (1992).

# Critical Readings on Piaget

Edited by Leslie Smith

London and New York

First published 1996
by Routledge
11 New Fetter Lane, London EC4P 4EE

Simultaneously published in the USA and Canada
by Routledge
29 West 35th Street, New York, NY 10001
*Routledge is an International Thomson Publishing company*

© 1996 selection and editorial matter Leslie Smith; individual chapters
© respective contributor

Typeset in Times by J&L Composition Ltd, Filey, North Yorkshire

Printed and bound in Great Britain by
TJ Press (Padstow) Ltd, Padstow, Cornwall

*British Library Cataloguing in Publication Data*
A catalogue record for this book is available from the British Library

*Library of Congress Cataloguing in Publication Data*
A catalogue record for this book has been requested

ISBN 0–415–13317–3

*For Christine and Stephen*

I take this opportunity of saying how I understand the prefix "neo" and, more generally, the destiny of work which has been recast by its author's successors. That continuation can be linear, that is to say the theory is applied without adjustment to new facts or content. This is instructive but not necessarily fruitful. Usually, by contrast, the initial doctrine is extended in a fan, each branch of which is further from such-and-such a point from the linear trajectory and so finds itself locally "anti". Now the history of science shows that things usually take place like this starting from an initial doctrine which of course requires as many more adjustments as there are sciences where experimental findings play a dominant role. (This is even true in the historical development of logical theories.) But history also shows that, after this, at the end of this second phase where the initial doctrine is instrumental in its variegated renewal directed in a fan, there comes a third phase where the divergent branches of the fan give way to comparisons and syntheses. The upshot is a reorganization into a new overall conception and this constitutes the most authentic continuation of the initial works characteristic of the first of the three periods. Since we are not yet there and since my epistemology proscribes prophecies, it therefore follows that I could say nothing of the works to come nor what they will retain from my own attempts. But having previously been, as several American authors (Anthony and so on) have pointed out, the most criticized author in the history of psychology, and since I came through alive, I can only have some confidence in a future about which my knowledge will be none.

Jean Piaget, *Psychologie*, 1987

# Contents

# Contributors

**Philip Adey,** School of Education, King's College London

**Harry Beilin,** Developmental Psychology Program, City University of New York

**Trevor G. Bond,** School of Education, James Cook University of North Queensland

**Ann L. Brown,** School of Education, University of California at Berkeley

**Terrance Brown,** Chicago

**Peter Bryant,** Department of Experimental Psychology, University of Oxford

**James P. Byrnes,** Department of Human Development, University of Maryland

**Margaret Chalmers,** Laboratory for Cognitive Neuroscience and Intelligence Systems, University of Edinburgh

**Michael Chapman,** formerly Department of Psychology, University of British Columbia

**Kevin Crowley,** Psychology Department, Carnegie Mellon University, Pittsburgh

**Carol Foltz,** Department of Psychology, Temple University, Philadelphia

**Ernst von Glasersfeld,** Scientific Reasoning Research Institute, University of Massachusetts

**Usha Goswami,** Department of Experimental Psychology, University of Cambridge

**Paul L. Harris,** Department of Experimental Psychology, University of Oxford

**Christine Howe,** Centre for Research into Interactive Learning, University of Strathclyde

**Carl N. Johnson,** Program in Child Development and Child Care, University of Pittsburgh

**Richard F. Kitchener,** Department of Philosophy, Colorado State University

**Deanna Kuhn,** Teachers College, Columbia University

**Michelle L. McBride,** Department of Psychology, University of British Columbia

**Brendan McGonigle,** Laboratory for Cognitive Neuroscience and Intelligence Systems, University of Edinburgh

**Henry Markovits,** Départment du Psychologie, Université de Québec, Montréal

**David Moshman,** Department of Educational Psychology, University of Nebraska–Lincoln

**Willis F. Overton,** Department of Psychology, Temple University, Philadelphia

**Robert B. Ricco,** Department of Psychology, Temple University, Philadelphia

**Catherine Rodgers,** Department of Psychology, University of Strathclyde

**Michael Shayer,** School of Education, King's College London

**Robert S. Siegler,** Psychology Department, Carnegie Mellon University, Pittsburgh

**Leslie Smith,** Department of Educational Research, Lancaster University

**Catherine Sophian,** Department of Psychology, University of Hawaii

**Eugene V. Subbotsky,** Department of Psychology, Lancaster University

**Andrew Tolmie,** Department of Psychology, University of Strathclyde

**Jacques Vonèche,** Jean Piaget Archives, University of Geneva

# Tables

# Figures

# Foreword

The present collection is a follow-up to the companion series, which was a collection of eighty-three papers providing a critical commentary on Piaget's work during the period 1950–90 (Smith 1992 a–d). Its Foreword is included in this volume together with a chronological list of reprinted papers. They provide the starting-point for the present collection of papers, all of which have been published during the period 1990–95 or are published here for the first time. Thus the main aim of the present volume is to trace some of the distinctive contributions to Piagetian research during the last five years.

I have set out to model the present collection on its predecessor, notably by using many of its themes. The twenty-one papers which are included here have been selected because they are distinctive. They are not, of course, the only contributions to Piagetian research during this period but they are typical and engaging. It was not possible to pursue developments in all of the main sections from the previous series, still less to do this comprehensively in other areas.

I have also set out to contextualise the papers included here by reference to Piaget's epistemology. "All of the problems I have addressed are epistemological" (Piaget 1970b). It is essential to see any work in its own terms as a prerequisite of fair assessment, not so as to endorse this work but rather to ascertain what it amounts to. In Piaget's case, much remains to be done. This includes the translation of all of his published work, or the sixty books and five hundred papers listed in the catalogue of his writings (Jean Piaget Archives 1989; cf. Smith 1993a, p.xiii). It also should extend to Piaget's unpublished work (Vidal 1994). At that point, there is every opportunity to analyse systematically Piaget's several positions. Anyone who plans to take on the task of providing such a Piagetian inventory will have to heed the warning from one of the chief revisionists of the work of Piaget (1983, p.103).

Lastly, I have set out to offer a guided commentary on the papers. This could serve as an introduction. But it makes good sense to read the papers first and so my commentary appears last. The papers deserve to be read and thought over. In any case, I have not been able to do justice to what in every case is a subtle discussion. My commentary could also contribute to the continuing assessment of Piaget's work and so I have tried to raise some questions about central arguments as a starting-point for further scrutiny. In doing this, I have used my own work as a reference point for reasons of convenience rather than conviction.

Finally, my sincere thanks are due to Vivian Ward at Routledge for her welcome support which led to this collection.

Leslie Smith
Lancaster, August 1995

# Chronological table of reprinted papers

| Date | Author | Article/Chapter Number | Journal/Book Reference |
|---|---|---|---|
| 1990 | Usha Goswami and Ann L. Brown | Higher-order structure and relational reasoning: contrasting analogical and thematic relations. (10) | Cognition 36: 207–26. |
| 1990 | David Moshman | The development of metalogical understanding. (18) | In Willis Overton (ed.) Reasoning, necessity and logic, Hillsdale, NJ: Erlbaum. |
| 1991 | James P. Byrnes and Harry Beilin | The cognitive basis of uncertainty. (20) | Human Development 34: 189–203. |
| 1991 | Richard F. Kitchener | Jean Piaget: the unknown sociologist? (3) | British Journal of Sociology 42: 421–42. |
| 1991 | Robert S. Siegler and Kevin Crowley | The microgenetic method: a direct means for studying cognitive development. (8) | American Psychologist 46: 606–20. |
| 1991 | Eugene V. Subbotsky | A life-span approach to object permanence. (11) | Human Development 34: 125–37. |
| 1992 | Michael Chapman and Michelle L. McBride | Beyond competence and performance: children's class inclusion strategies, superordinate class cues, and verbal justifications. (17) | Developmental Psychology 28: 319–27. |
| 1992 | Christine Howe, Andrew Tolmie and Catherine Rodgers | The acquisition of conceptual knowledge in science by primary school children: group interaction and the understanding of motion down an incline. (6) | British Journal of Developmental Psychology 10: 113–30. |
| 1992 | Deanna Kuhn | Thinking as argument. (7) | Harvard Educational Review 62: 155–78. |
| 1992 | Leslie Smith | Judgements and justifications: criteria for the attribution of children's knowledge in Piagetian research. (19) | British Journal of Developmental Psychology 10: 1–23. |
| 1992 | Jacques Vonèche | Piaget's first theory of equilibrium (1918). (1) | In D. Maurice and J. Montangero (eds) Equilibrium and equilibration, Geneva: Jean Piaget Archives Foundation. |

| Date | Author | Article/Chapter Number | Journal/Book Reference |
|---|---|---|---|
| 1993 | Philip Adey and Michael Shayer | An exploration of the long-term far-transfer effects following an extended intervention program in the high school science curriculum. (5) | Cognition and Instruction 11: 1–29. |
| 1993 | Ernst von Glasersfeld | Learning and adaptation in the theory of constructivism. (2) | Communication and Cognition 26: 393–402. |
| 1994 | Carl N. Johnson and Paul L. Harris | Magic: special but not excluded. (12) | British Journal of Developmental Psychology 12: 35–51. |
| 1995 | Trevor G. Bond | Piaget and measurement II: empirical validation of the Piagetian model. (9) | Archives de Psychologie 63: 155–85. |
| 1995 | Terrance Brown | Values, knowledge, and Piaget. (4) | Abbreviated and edited version of a paper with the same title in E. Reed, E. Turiel and T. Brown (eds) Values and Knowledge, Hillsdale, NJ: Erlbaum, 1996. |
| 1995 | Peter Bryant | Children and arithmetic. (15) | Journal of Child Psychology and Psychiatry 36: 3–32. |
| 1995 | Carol Foltz, Willis F. Overton and Robert B. Ricco | Proof construction: adolescent development from inductive to deductive problem-solving strategies. (21) | Journal of Experimental Child Psychology 59: 179–95. |
| 1995 | Henry Markovits | Conditional reasoning with false premises: fantasy and information retrieval. (13) | British Journal of Developmental Psychology 13: 1–11. |
| 1995 | Brendan McGonigle and Margaret Chalmers | The ontology of order. (14) | Published this volume. |
| 1995 | Catherine Sophian | Representation and reasoning in early numerical development: counting, conservation, and comparisons between sets. (16) | Child Development 66: 559–77. |

# Foreword to *Jean Piaget: Critical Assessments*

## *Leslie Smith*

My aim has been to provide a collection of previously published papers in English which have contributed to the interpretation and appraisal of some main psychological themes in Jean Piaget's theory of intellectual development. In effect, this means viewing Piaget's theory through Piagetian research and commentary. The collection is a review of responses which have been made mainly, though not exclusively, by psychologists in their assessment of the acceptability of this aspect of Piaget's work.

By common consent, Piaget's work is demanding. His output was huge, spanning more than sixty years. Piaget was the author and editor of some eighty books and contributed some five hundred papers and reports (Foundation Archives 1989). His work was directed upon a cluster of complex problems which have been the preoccupation of philosophers and scientists for centuries. His interdisciplinary expertise was evident both because he drew upon recent advances in several disciplines and because of his novel contributions to those disciplines. The first impressions of the Piagetian corpus may appear so daunting that newcomers often look for a more comforting refuge in work which has been written about him by other developmentalists. This creates something of a paradox. The Piagetian literature is itself enormous, expanding, equally interdisciplinary and erudite. It makes more, not less, demands on developmentalists and, as such, is even more demanding still.

Making a suitable selection from the Piagetian literature is no easy task. A number of decisions led to the procedure used in this collection.

## IDENTIFY A SMALL NUMBER OF CORE ISSUES

The issues selected are as follows

1 *Understanding and Intelligence*
   Moral development; formal operational understanding; infant intelligence.

2 *Children's Thinking*
  Transitivity; inclusion; conservation.
3 *Education and Society*
  Culture; social co-operation; teaching.
4 *Intellectual Development*
  Genetic epistemology; developmental explanation; operational logic; equilibration.

The decision to focus upon these specific issues had its origin in a series of assessments of Piaget's work (for example, Sigel and Hooper 1968; Elkind and Flavell 1969; Vuyk 1981; Modgil and Modgil 1982; Mussen 1983; Sternberg 1987; Chapman 1988; Halford 1989). The selected issues are not exhaustive, since there are certainly other psychological issues in Piaget's theory and in Piagetian research. They are, however, paradigmatic since they are central issues which are illustrative of the genre.

## SELECT KEY PAPERS WHICH DEAL WITH EACH ISSUE

The eventual selection was made with due attention to the changes over the period 1950–90. A deliberate decision was taken not to rely on recent contributions for two reasons. First, just as there are standard themes in Piaget's work, so too there are standard responses and these responses have intrinsic interest. Early studies from this period exemplify the full range of responses, including replication, critique and interpretative extension. Second, the assessment of Piaget's theory is problematic and open to divergent interpretation. Studies which were at one time judged to offer valid criticism have in the sequel generated their own responses. Exclusive reliance on recent studies would beg questions about whether recent work should enjoy unquestioned priority as well as about its acceptability. A constraint was that the papers should be in English.

## CONCENTRATE ON THE WELL-FOCUSED CONTRIBUTIONS OF DISPUTANTS WHO ADDRESS THE SAME ISSUE

One, though not the sole, reason why Piagetian commentary is demanding is that the mutual relations of different contributions are not always clear. The intention was to select contributions which exhibited a degree of interdependence, including confirmation, modification and rejection.

## PLACE AN UPPER LIMIT ON THE CONTRIBUTIONS FROM ONE INDIVIDUAL

The intention was to limit each developmentalist to one contribution. One exception was in cases of multiple authorship. Another exception was the priority given to issue over author. Some issues were such that attention has been given to several contributions from one author. The overall effect has been to extend the number of contributors. One consequence has been that the work of those developmentalists who have been active either throughout most of the period or over a whole range of core issues has been underrepresented.

## DEFINE THE UNIVERSE OF CONTRIBUTORS AS ANYONE OTHER THAN PIAGET

While some of Piaget's writings are his own, others are jointly written with associates. Whilst some of Piaget's associates enjoy a high profile and have maintained distinctive interests, others are less well known. Thus a decision was needed either to exclude completely anyone associated with Genevan research (thus Jerome Bruner would have to be excluded) or to exclude only his more well-known associates (which of the following – all, some or none – would thus have to be excluded: Leo Apostel, Reuven Feuerstein, Annette Karmiloff-Smith, Eric Lunzer, Jan Smedslund?). There is some difficulty in drawing this distinction in a non-arbitrary and non-invidious way. In consequence, the decision was taken to exclude only those writings where Piaget was a sole or co-author.

## ENSURE A BROAD COVERAGE OF THE RANGE OF PERSPECTIVES USED IN THE PIAGETIAN LITERATURE

The central theme of the collection is the psychological aspects of Piaget's work. It is evident that this theme has led to the proliferation of perspectives and techniques. The intention has been to do justice to this diversity by the selection of salient examples of the available range. An example of a perspective is not, however, the perspective itself. This collection does not aspire to do justice to each of the alternative perspectives as well. The aim has been to review *Piagetian* commentary and criticism and not the alternative positions of other developmentalists.

## SELECT CONTRIBUTIONS MAINLY FROM JOURNALS RATHER THAN BOOKS

The justification for this restriction is that books are more readily available than journals. Yet some of the more illuminating contributions have appeared in journals, including journals which are difficult to locate even in specialist libraries.

The collection has two strands. One is a guided commentary, which includes a general introduction, introductory review of individual papers and concluding assessment. This commentary is offered neither as a complete review of Piaget's theory, still less of the Piagetian literature, but rather as a second opinion on the main papers in the collection. Thus the other strand is the more important strand, namely the papers themselves. The core issues can be read in any order of preference, provided they are all read. However, selective reading should start with the core issues which appear in volume 4. Within each core issue, the papers should probably be read in their present, roughly chronological order.

Roughly speaking, the collection amounts to the selection of my "first eighty papers to read on Piaget". Needless to say, the contributions included here are not the final ones to read.

## ACKNOWLEDGEMENT

My warm thanks are due to David Stonestreet, both for his initial invitation to compile this collection and for his encouragement and editorial support.

# Chronological table of reprinted articles in *Jean Piaget: Critical Assessments*

| Date | Author | Article | Journal/Book Reference |
|------|--------|---------|------------------------|
| **1951** | N. Isaacs | Critical Notice: *Traité de Logique* by Jean Piaget | *British Journal of Psychology* 42: 185–8 |
| **1959** | Martin D. S. Braine | The Ontogeny of Certain Logical Operations: Piaget's Formulation Examined by Nonverbal Methods | *Psychological Monographs: General and Applied* 73(5): 1–43 |
| **1961** | David Elkind | The Development of Quantitative Thinking: A Systematic Replication of Piaget's Studies | *Journal of Genetic Psychology* 98: 37–46 |
| **1962** | Bärbel Inhelder | Some Aspects of Piaget's Genetic Approach to Cognition | *Monographs of the Society for Research in Child Development* 27(2): 17–31 |
| **1962** | K. Lovell, B. Mitchell, and I. R. Everett | An Experimental Study of the Growth of Some Logical Structures | *British Journal of Psychology* 53: 175–88 |
| **1963** | Jan Smedslund | Development of Concrete Transitivity of Length in Children | *Child Development* 34: 389–405 |
| **1964** | T. S. Kuhn | A Function for Thought Experiments | Reprinted in T. S. Kuhn *The Essential Tension*, Chicago: University of Chicago Press 1977, pp. 240–65 |
| **1968** | Lawrence Kohlberg | Moral Development | In D. Sills (ed.) *International Encyclopedia of the Social Sciences*, vol. 10, New York: The Macmillan Company, pp. 483–94 |
| **1970** | Hans Aebli | Piaget, and Beyond | *Interchange* 1: 12–24 |
| **1970** | Jan Smedslund | Circular Relation between Understanding and Logic | *Scandinavian Journal of Psychology* 11: 217–19 |
| **1971** | P. E. Bryant and T. Trabasso | Transitive Inferences and Memory in Young Children | *Nature* 232: 456–8 |
| **1971** | Michael Cole and Jerome S. Bruner | Cultural Differences and Inferences about Psychological Processes | *American Psychologist* 26: 867–76 |

| Date | Author | Article | Journal/Book Reference |
|---|---|---|---|
| 1971 | Gerald Gratch and William F. Landers | Stage IV of Piaget's Theory of Infant's Object Concepts: A Longitudinal Study | Child Development 42: 359–72 |
| 1972 | Terrell Ward Bynum, James A. Thomas, and Lawrence J. Weitz | Truth-functional Logic in Formal Operational Thinking: Inhelder and Piaget's Evidence | Developmental Psychology 7(2): 129–32 |
| 1972 | Rochel Gelman | Logical Capacity of Very Young Children: Number Invariance Rules | Child Development 43: 75–90 |
| 1972 | Lawrence Kohlberg and Rochelle Mayer | Development as the Aim of Education | Harvard Educational Review 42(4): 449–96 |
| 1972 | Ted L. Rosenthal and Barry J. Zimmerman | Modeling by Exemplification and Instruction in Training Conservation | Developmental Psychology 6(3): 392–401 |
| 1973 | Charles J. Brainerd | Judgments and Explanations as Criteria for the Presence of Cognitive Structures | Psychological Bulletin 79(3): 172–9 |
| 1973 | Bénédicte de Boysson-Bardies and Kevin O'Regan | What Children Do in Spite of Adults' Hypotheses | Nature 246: 531–4 |
| 1974 | James McGarrigle and Margaret Donaldson | Conservation Accidents | Cognition 3: 341–50 |
| 1974 | Pierre Mounoud and T. G. R. Bower | Conservation of Weight in Infants | Cognition 3: 29–40 |
| 1974 | Susan A. Rose and Marion Blank | The Potency of Context in Children's Cognition: An Illustration through Conservation | Child Development 45: 499–502 |
| 1975 | Willem Doise, Gabriel Mugny, and Anne-Nelly Perret-Clermont | Social Interaction and the Development of Cognitive Operations | European Journal of Social Psychology 5: 367–83 |
| 1975 | Robert H. Ennis | Children's Ability to Handle Piaget's Propositional Logic: A Conceptual Critique | Review of Educational Research 45(1): 1–41 |

|  |  |  |  |
|---|---|---|---|
| 1975 | Annette Karmiloff-Smith and Bärbel Inhelder | If You Want to Get Ahead, Get a Theory | Cognition 3: 195–212 |
| 1976 | E. A. Lunzer, J. E. Wilkinson, and T. Dolan | The Distinctiveness of Operativity as a Measure of Cognitive Functioning in Five-year old Children | British Journal of Educational Psychology 46: 280–94 |
| 1976 | Ellen M. Markman and Jeffrey Seibert | Classes and Collections: Internal Organization and Resulting Holistic Properties | Cognitive Psychology 8: 561–77 |
| 1976 | Frank B. Murray and Sharon L. Armstrong | Necessity in Conservation and Nonconservation | Developmental Psychology 12(5): 483–4 |
| 1976 | M. Shayer, D. E. Küchemann, and H. Wylam | The Distribution of Piagetian Stages of Thinking in British Middle and Secondary School Children | British Journal of Educational Psychology 46: 164–73 |
| 1977 | George Butterworth | Object Disappearance and Error in Piaget's Stage IV Task | Journal of Experimental Child Psychology 23: 391–401 |
| 1977 | Deanna Kuhn and Joann Brannock | Development of the Isolation of Variables Scheme in Experimental and "Natural Experiment" Contexts | Developmental Psychology 13(1): 9–14 |
| 1977 | Peter C. Wason | The Theory of Formal Operations – A Critique | In B. Geber (ed.) Piaget and Knowing: Studies in Genetic Epistemology, London: Routledge & Kegan Paul, pp. 119–35 |
| 1978 | Charles J. Brainerd | The Stage Question in Cognitive-developmental Theory | The Behavioural and Brain Sciences 2: 173–82 |
| 1978 | Robbie Case | A Developmentally Based Theory and Technology of Instruction | Review of Educational Research 48(3): 439–63 |
| 1978 | Anton E. Lawson, Robert Karplus, and Helen Adi | The Acquisition of Propositional Logic and Formal Operational Schemata during the Secondary School Years | Journal of Research in Science Teaching 15(6): 465–78 |
| 1978 | Pierre Moessinger | Piaget on Equilibration | Human Development 21: 255–67 |

| Date | Author | Article | Journal/Book Reference |
|---|---|---|---|
| 1978 | Frank B. Murray | Teaching Strategies and Conservation Training | In A. Lesgold, J. Pellegrino, S. Fokkema, and R. Glaser (eds) *Cognitive Psychology and Instruction*, New York: Plenum Press, pp. 419–28 |
| 1978 | Robert S. Siegler | Cognition, Instruction, Development, and Individual Differences | In A. Lesgold, J. Pellegrino, S. Fokkema, and R. Glaser (eds) *Cognitive Psychology and Instruction*, New York: Plenum Press, pp. 389–403 |
| 1980 | Jerry Fodor | Fixation of Belief and Concept Acquisition | In M. Piattelli-Palmarini (ed.) *Language and Learning*, London: Routledge & Kegan Paul, pp. 143–9 |
| 1980 | Jacques Montangero | The Various Aspects of Horizontal *Décalage* | *Archives de Psychologie* 48: 259–82 |
| 1980 | Gerald Noelting | The Development of Proportional Reasoning and the Ratio Concept, Part I – Differentiation of Stages | *Educational Studies in Mathematics* 11: 217–53 |
| 1980 | Peter Tomlinson | Moral Judgement and Moral Psychology: Piaget, Kohlberg and Beyond | In S. Modgil and C. Modgil (eds) *Toward a Theory of Psychological Development*, Windsor: NFER, pp. 303–66 |
| 1981 | Pierre R. Dasen and Alastair Heron | Cross-cultural Tests of Piaget's Theory | In H. Triandis and A. Heron (eds) *Handbook of Cross-Cultural Psychology*, vol. 4, Boston: Allyn & Bacon, pp. 295–341 |
| 1981 | Reuven Feuerstein, Ronald Miller, Mildred B. Hoffman, Ya'acov Rand, Yael Mintzker, and Mogens Reimer Jensen | Cognitive Modifiability in Adolescence: Cognitive Structure and the Effects of Intervention | *Journal of Special Education* 15: 269–87 |

| 1981 | Herbert P. Ginsburg | Piaget and Education: The Contributions and Limits of Genetic Epistemology | In I. Sigel, D. Brodzinsky, and R. Golinkoff (eds) *New Directions in Piagetian Theory and Practice*, Hillsdale, NJ: Erlbaum, pp. 315–30 |
|---|---|---|---|
| 1981 | Robert Karplus | Education and Formal Thought – A Modest Proposal | In I. Sigel, D. Brodzinsky, and R. Golinkoff (eds) *New Directions in Piagetian Theory and Practice*, Hillsdale, NJ: Erlbaum, pp. 284–314 |
| 1981 | Derek Wright | The Psychology of Moral Obligation | Unpublished paper |
| 1982 | Leo Apostel | The Future of Piagetian Logic | *Revue Internationale de Philosophie* 142–3: 567–611 |
| 1982 | John H. Flavell | On Cognitive Development | *Child Development* 53: 1–10 |
| 1982 | Ernst von Glaserfeld | An Interpretation of Piaget's Constructivism | *Revue Internationale de Philosophie* 142–3: 612–35 |
| 1982 | Constance Kamii | Encouraging Thinking in Mathematics | *Phi Delta Kappan* 64: 247–51 |
| 1982 | Wolfe Mays | Piaget's Sociological Theory | In S. Modgil and C. Modgil (eds) *Jean Piaget: Consensus and Controversy*, London: Holt, Rinehart & Winston, pp. 31–50 |
| 1983 | Pierre Cormier and Yvon Dagenais | Class-inclusion Developmental Levels and Logical Necessity | *International Journal of Behavioral Development* 6: 1–14 |
| 1983 | Richard F. Kitchener | Developmental Explanations | *Review of Metaphysics* 36: 791–817 |
| 1983 | Michèle Robert | Observational Learning of Conservation: Its Independence from Social Influence | *British Journal of Psychology* 74: 1–10 |
| 1984 | Margaret Chalmers and Brendan McGonigle | Are Children More Logical than Monkeys on the Five-term Series Problem? | *Journal of Experimental Child Psychology* 37: 355–77 |
| 1985 | Renée Baillargeon, Elizabeth S. Spelke, and Stanley Wasserman | Object Permanence in Five-month-old Infants | *Cognition* 20: 191–208 |

| Date | Author | Article | Journal/Book Reference |
|------|--------|---------|------------------------|
| 1985 | Harry Beilin | Dispensable and Core Elements in Piaget's Research Program | *The Genetic Epistemologist* 13: 1–16 |
| 1985 | Graeme S. Halford and Frances M. Boyle | Do Young Children Understand Conservation of Number? | *Child Development* 56: 165–76 |
| 1986 | Paul L. Harris | Bringing Order to the A-not-B Error | *Monographs of the Society for Research in Child Development* 51 (Serial no. 214): 52–61 |
| 1986 | Scott A. Miller | Certainty and Necessity in the Understanding of Piagetian Concepts | *Developmental Psychology* 22(1): 3–18 |
| 1986 | Adrien Pinard | "Prise de Conscience" and Taking Charge of One's Own Cognitive Functioning | *Human Development* 29: 341–54 |
| 1987 | Terrance Brown and Lee Weiss | Structures, Procedures, Heuristics and Affectivity | *Archives de Psychologie* 55: 59–94 |
| 1987 | Robert L. Campbell and Mark H. Bickhard | A Deconstruction of Fodor's Anticonstructivism | *Human Development* 30: 48–59 |
| 1987 | François Y. Doré and Claude Dumas | Psychology of Animal Cognition: Piagetian Studies | *Psychological Bulletin* 102(2): 219–33 |
| 1987 | Barbara Hodkin | Performance Model Analysis in Class Inclusion: An Illustration with Two Language Conditions | *Developmental Psychology* 23(5): 683–9 |
| 1987 | Willis F. Overton, Shawn L. Ward, Ira A. Noveck, Jeffrey Black, and David P. O'Brien | Form and Content in the Development of Deductive Reasoning | *Developmental Psychology* 23(1): 22–30 |

| | | | |
|---|---|---|---|
| 1987 | Juan Pascual-Leone | Organismic Processes for Neo-Piagetian Theories: A Dialectical Causal Account of Cognitive Development | *International Journal of Psychology* 22: 531–70 |
| 1987 | Costas D. Porpodas | The One-question Conservation Experiment Reconsidered | *Journal of Child Psychology and Psychiatry* 28(2): 343–9 |
| 1987 | Leslie Smith | On Piaget on Necessity | In J. Russell (ed.) *Philosophical Perspectives on Developmental Psychology*, Oxford: Blackwell, pp. 191–219 |
| 1988 | Mark H. Bickhard | Piaget on Variation and Selection Models: Structuralism, Logical Necessity, and Interactivism | *Human Development* 31: 274–312 |
| 1988 | Michael Chapman and Ulman Lindenberger | Functions, Operations and *Décalage* in the Development of Transitivity | *Developmental Psychology* 24(4): 542–51 |
| 1988 | Philip M. Davidson | Piaget's Category-theoretic Interpretation of Cognitive Development: A Neglected Contribution | *Human Development* 31: 225–44 |
| 1988 | Karen Fuson, Barbara G. Lyons, Gerry G. Pergament, James W. Hall, and Youngshim Kwon | Effects of Collection Terms on Class-inclusion and on Number Tasks | *Cognitive Psychology* 20: 96–120 |
| 1988 | Michael Shayer, Andreas Demetriou, and Muhammad Pervez | The Structure and Scaling of Concrete Operational Thought: Three Studies in Four Countries | *Genetic, Social, and General Psychology Monographs* 114: 309–75 |
| 1989 | Caroline Lister, Chris Leach, Des McGraw, and Lucy Simpson | Similar-Sequence and Similar-Structure in Retarded and Non-retarded Children's Development | *British Journal of Educational Psychology* 59: 8–18 |
| 1989 | Sylvie Normandeau, Serge Larivée, Jean-Luc Roulin, and François Longeot | The Balance-scale Dilemma: Either the Subject or the Experienter Muddles Through | *Journal of Genetic Psychology* 150: 237–49 |

| Date | Author | Article | Journal/Book Reference |
|---|---|---|---|
| 1989 | M.-L. Schubauer-Leoni, N. Bell, M. Grossen, and A.-N. Perret-Clermont | Problems in Assessment of Learning: The Social Construction of Questions and Answers in the Scholastic Context | International Journal of Educational Research 13: 671–84 |
| 1990 | David Eames, Diane Shorrocks, and Peter Tomlinson | Naughty Animals or Naughty Experimenters? Conservation Accidents Revisited with Video-stimulated Commentary | British Journal of Developmental Psychology 8: 25–37 |
| 1990 | Rosalind Pears and Peter Bryant | Transitive Inferences by Young Children about Spatial Position | British Journal of Psychology 81: 497–510 |
| 1990 | G. Piéraut-Le Bonniec | The Logic of Meaning and Meaningful Implication | In W. Overton (ed.) Reasoning, Necessity and Logic: Developmental Perspectives, Hillsdale, NJ: Erlbaum, pp. 67–85 |
| 1990 | James Russell, Ian Mills, and Per Reiff-Musgrove | The Role of Symmetrical and Asymmetrical Social Conflict in Cognitive Change | Journal of Experimental Child Psychology 49: 58–78 |
| 1991 | Trevor Bond and Ian Jackson | The Gou Protocol Revisited: A Piagetian Contextualization of Critique | Archives de Psychologie 59: 31–53 |

# Chapter 1

# Piaget's first theory of equilibrium (1918)

## Jacques Vonèche

Partout l'idée en mission s'avance

Victor Hugo, *Voix intérieures*, 1837

### THEORETICIANS OF EQUILIBRIUM

Contrary to a particularly widespread idea, Piaget is not the only psychologist whose theory is grounded on the notion of equilibrium. Indeed, if we define equilibrium in a very simple way as a principle that affirms a relation between a system (or an organism) and its environment, so that any change in the environment produces an adjustment of the system in the sense that it tends to keep constant a certain number of conditions of existence of the system which are considered desirable if not vital for the system in question, then the theories of Spencer (1892), Freud (1923–25/1964), Watson (1929), Dewey (1933), Heider (1946) and Festinger (1957) are theories based on the principle of equilibrium.

Indeed, Spencer writes that:

> If the strengths of the connexions between the internal states are not proportionate to the persistences of the relations between the answering external agents, there will be a failure of the correspondence – the inner order will disagree with the outer order.
>
> (p. 409)

Now, this is a good definition of disequilibrium.

There is a striking resemblance between Dewey's conception of equilibrium in problem-solving and the way in which Piaget expresses himself. Here is Dewey's text:

> Suppose you are walking along where there is no regular path. As long as everything goes smoothly, you do not have to think about your walking; your already formed habit takes care of it. Suddenly, you find a ditch in your way. You think you will jump it (supposition, plan); but to make sure, you survey it with your eyes (observation) and you find

that it is pretty wide and that the bank on the other side is slippery (facts, data), you then wonder if the ditch may not be narrower somewhere else (idea) and you look up and down the stream (observation) to see how matters stand (rest of idea by observation). You do not find any good place and so are thrown back upon forming a new plan. As you are casting about, you discover a log (fact again). You ask yourself whether you could not haul that to the ditch and get it across the ditch to use as a bridge (idea again). You judge that idea as worth trying, and so you get the log and manage to put it in place and walk across (test and confirmation by overt action).

(p. 105)

The following is a psychological analysis given by Piaget at a time when he still had a car [Piaget's analysis was also presented in English in order to emphasise the parallel between the two extracts]. One is struck by the subtlety of the introspection.

In order better to understand the mechanism of this assimilation which has become deductive while remaining on the plane of sensorimotor opera-tions, let us again analyze a case of elementary practical invention observed in an adult and consequently capable of correct introspection. While driving an old automobile I am bothered by oil on the steering wheel which makes it slippery. Lacking time to stop I take out my handkerchief and dry the spots. When putting it in my pocket I observe that it is too greasy and look for a place to put it without soiling anything. I put it between my seat and the one next to me, as deeply as possible in the crevice. An hour later the rain forces me to close the windshield but the resulting heat makes me try to open it a little. The screws being worn out, I cannot succeed; it only stays wide open or completely shut. I try to hold the windshield slightly open with my left hand, but my fatigue makes me think that some object could replace my hand. I look around me, but nothing is in evidence. While looking at the windshield I have the impression that the object could be put, not at the bottom of the windshield (one pushed it at the bottom to open it), but by wedging it in the angle formed by the right edge of the windshield and the vertical upright of the body of the car. I have the vague feeling of an analogy between the solution to be found and a problem already solved before. The solution then becomes clarified. My tendency to put an object into the corner of the windshield meets a sort of motor memory of having just a few minutes before placed something into a crevice. I try to remember what it was, but no definite representation comes to mind. Then suddenly, without having time to imagine anything, I understand the solution and find myself already in the act of searching with my hand for the hidden handkerchief. Therefore the latter schema directed my search and directed me toward the lateral corner of the windshield when my last idea was a different one.

This trite observation demonstrates very well how a sensorimotor search can arouse schemata previously acquired and make them function independently of internal language and clear representation. The tendency to introduce an object into a slit, in this example, is modeled exactly on a schema remaining in an almost purely motor state, and the conjunction thus produced suffices to insure discovery of a solution. One therefore understands how a sensorimotor deduction is possible in the small child through simple practical evocation of the schemata and independently of a well-defined system of representations.

(1936/1952, p. 345)

Watson (1929) uses the model of equilibrium to explain how behaviour appears:

We shall see that there are common factors running through all forms of human acts. In each adjustment, there is always both a response or act and a stimulus or situation which calls out that response. Without going too far beyond our facts, it seems possible to say that the stimulus is always provided by the environment, external to the body, or by the movement of man's muscles and the secretions will be changed through action or through cognitive reorganization. If a change is not possible, the state of imbalance will produce tension.

(p. 39)

In the same way, Freud (1923–1925/1964), like the others, resorts to the equilibrium principle when he writes:

It seems a plausible view that this displaceable and neutral energy, which is no doubt active both in the ego and in the id, proceeds from the narcissistic store of libido – that it is desexualised Eros . . . From this, we can easily go on to assume that this displaceable libido is employed in the service of the pleasure principle to obviate blockages and to facilitate discharge.

(pp. 44–45)

Clearly for Freud, pleasure derives from an equilibrium between the organism and its environment, and between contradictory forces within the organism. In response to these forces, the organism puts its energy into certain forms of behaviour which alleviate the conflicts and make pleasure possible, that is, when it is at rest in an equilibrium free from tensions.

We shall see a little further on how close this is to Piaget's first theory of equilibrium. Now, Piaget had become familiar with Freud's ideas at a conference given by Flournoy to the *Associations chrétiennes de jeunes gens* in 1916 (Piaget 1945; Vidal 1989).

More recently, Heider (1946) has used the principle of equilibrium to explain the coherence of the social behaviour of an individual. He writes:

> A balanced state exists if all parts of a unit have the same dynamic character (i.e. if all are positive or negative), and if entities with different dynamic characters are segregated from each other. If no balanced state exists, then focus toward this state will arise. Either the dynamic characters will change, or the unit relations will be changed through action or through cognitive reorganization. If a change is not possible, the state of imbalance will produce tension.
>
> (p. 39)

This distinctly Gestaltist note is also found in Piaget's first theory of equilibrium.

The same idea of internal coherence by re-equilibrating is also a central principle of Léon Festinger's (1957) theory of cognitive dissonance, as is shown by the following lines:

> It has frequently been implied . . . that the individual strives toward consistency within himself. His opinions and attitudes, for example, tend to exist in clusters that are internally consistent.
>
> (p. 1)

> The existence of dissonance, being psychologically uncomfortable, will motivate the person to try to reduce the dissonance and achieve consonance. When dissonance is present, in addition to trying to reduce it, the person will actively avoid situations and information which would be likely to increase the dissonance.
>
> (p. 3)

## EVOLUTION OF THE NOTION OF EQUILIBRIUM IN PIAGET'S WORK

Contrary to the above-mentioned thinkers, Piaget does not use the concept of equilibrium to show that the organism has different states, but to explain how knowledge develops, i.e. why the organism has not only different states but also better ones. This is what Piaget calls the optimising or improving nature of equilibration.

Not only is Piaget not the only author to use the notion of equilibrium in psychology outside its common acceptation (e.g. an unbalanced person killed a passer-by) but, in addition, he did not have a single theory of equilibrium but several. We have distinguished with Inhelder and Garcia (1976) at least three successive forms of the theory.

Of these three forms, only the first is of interest to us here. The second theory formulated by Piaget in *Logique et Equilibre* (1957) was abandoned by its author shortly after publication, but remained the sole reference on this subject for more than twenty years. Piaget's central problem, at that time, was to explain the necessary, but not predetermined nature of the order of the sequences of cognitive development. To do this, he was animated by his own work on perception, on the encounters and couplings between the subject and his environment, and on what was understood at the time about game theory.

The main problem with this model, for Piaget, lay in the fact that it was too logico-mathematical – statistical even – in nature and that it overlooked the biological aspects of knowledge, in particular the principle of auto-regulation which is more than just a balance between physico-chemical forces; it necessarily involves a conservation of the parts by the whole and vice-versa. Now, as we shall see in the analysis of Piaget's first theory of equilibrium, this is precisely how he defined regulations right from the beginning.

The third theory published in the *Equilibration of Cognitive Structures* (1975/1985) tends to overcome these difficulties by emphasising the indissociability of compensations and constructions. For Piaget, any compensation of a perturbation by the organism necessarily implies progress since the perturbed activity has become perturbable, by the very fact that it has been compensated, which is the same as completing or improving it. This possibility of improving behaviour differentiates it from the purely physiological process of homeostasis, whence, from the outset, a tendency to constructions and to the production of novelties.

We shall not go into the mechanisms (e.g. negation, contradiction, abstraction, generalisation, integration) by which re-equilibrations take place. Nor shall we try to explain the theory of equilibrium. Nor shall we show why the notion of equilibrium is a central concept in Piaget's theory of the development of cognitive systems. We shall not even try to justify Piaget's basic formula, defended by some of his friends like Rolando Garcia, that equilibration theories involve structural discontinuity within a functional continuity. All you will find here is a historical study of the genesis of an idea that was central to the cosmic system of a young man aged twenty, and about which he wrote in a more or less autobiographical "novel" entitled *Recherche*.

## THE NOTION OF EQUILIBRIUM IN *RECHERCHE* (1918)

### Bergson's influence

This novel can be considered as being part of the spiritualist revival against the positivist materialism of the "stupid 19th century" as indicated in the opening chapters of the book which mention Charles Péguy, Cardinal Mercier, Pastor Monod, Auguste Sabatier, Ferdinand Buisson. But it is also in the line of critical rationalism represented by philosophers such as Léon Brunschvicg for example, and with French metaphysicians such as

Fouillée, Guyau, Boutroux and Lalande. What the young Piaget perceives remarkably well during the 1914–18 war is the crisis of European science, as Husserl called it, both as regards the nature of the relations between science and religion and the different forms of knowledge.

In his attempt to reconcile "a vague system" and "fragile metaphysical structures" with science, young Piaget found no better reference than Henri Bergson, the philosopher who had marked his youth with an indelible stamp.

Following in Bergson's footsteps, Piaget contrasts the physico-geo-metrical order of things, allowing mathematical generalisation and based mainly on repetition, with the vital order based on tendency, vital energy, creation and therefore transformation. Consequently, knowledge (which is life) will also concern transformations from one state to another. This idea will accompany Piaget throughout his life. Indeed, from his point of view, all that is not absolute must necessarily be transformed, for progress is situated in the transformation. Evolution is thus, as thought Bergson, always creative. It can only end in the moral absolute as far as man is concerned and in the vital absolute for animals.

The reader will have recognised here the resurgence, through Bergson, of the Aristotelian science of kinds. Piaget does not try to hide this:

> Sebastian, who had always been enthusiastic about Bergson's philo-sophy, did not accept any of its particular theses, but believed all the same that he prolonged it in its underlying logic. He was Bergsonian without duration, which is the limit for Bergsonism . . . What pleased him in particular was the way in which this philosophy had shown the possibility of rehabilitating the Greek kinds. Indeed, Bergson had bril-liantly understood that the time had come to reintroduce kinds into modern science. His whole psychology was deeply affected by this ulterior motive. His biology, which had stayed rather superficial and verbal, could also be interpreted in a similar way.
>
> Only, *Bergson did not define the kind* [italics added] and we don't see how he could have done so without seriously upsetting his system. All the work was left to be done then, and it was much more scientific in nature than philosophical. Aristotle, the genius of kinds, was a biologist: It was through biology that the construction should have taken place.
>
> (p. 53)

For Aristotle, as everyone knows, the law of falling bodies can be explained by the natural tendency of earthly bodies to return to their natural place, to wit, the earth. There is a comic version of this theory: the dormitive virtue of opium in Molière's work. There is also a contem-porary version: sociobiology.

For Bergson, the natural link between living bodies is life as a whole. Bergson called this effort towards life "vital energy". Vital energy is transmitted from one generation to another by the heredity of adaptations acquired by ancestors. This transformation of an adaptive change into a hereditary structure seems universal to Piaget, so much so that it encompasses logico-mathematical structures which are thought of as activities of adaptive classification. This leads him to consider intelligence as a form that is at once logical, biological and moral: logical because it is a normative structure of thought; biological because it is an adaptive organ of the individual; and moral because it is the logic of the subject's action.

Such a trilogy (we could almost say a trilogic) led Piaget very close to pragmatism; this was not surprising since, as everyone knows, William James had close links with Geneva and the French-speaking part of Switzerland, and since Piaget had read some of Edouard Claparède's essays on psychology. Indeed, when Piaget brings together the adaptive fact and the normative one, and in return, the norm of adaptation, he is to a certain extent flirting with pragmatism. But Piaget rejected pragmatism because he considered it as too relativistic; so he revived the science of kinds which gave him the notion of a quality opposed to that of quantity, as shown in the following passage:

## The science of kinds. Relation between the whole and its parts

In modern times, and especially since Descartes' universal mathematism, science has been confined to the study of quantity. A phenomenon has no value for the savant unless it can be measured and unless the quantities that it thus offers to experimentation are comparable to those of other phenomena. Biology and the sciences of the mind have, it is true, constantly introduced the quality into their field of study, but always with the idea that it is provisory and that sooner or later the quantity will be found to verify the thus established laws.

For the Ancients, on the contrary, everything was quality in natural science, and science as a whole was modelled on Aristotle's type of biology.

Where is the truth? I don't mean to be suspicious about the results of modern science, but I wonder if its exclusivism is not an abuse. By neglecting quantity, science has enabled philosophy to keep it for itself and you know how . . . it leaves the door open to metaphysics.

(p. 149)

But philosophy is wrong when it pretends that it knows quality itself. Only the relations between qualities are accessible and most philosophers would agree with this.

But it is precisely this kind of relationship that science has refused – perhaps not in reality, but by right. And this is why it is often arbitrary in the field of the living, be it organic life or psychological life. Now if, on the contrary, we introduce a positive theory of the quality, which only takes into account the relations of equilibrium and disequilibrium between our qualities, we have a life science founded on the ruins of metaphysics.

Therefore, it is very important to go deeper into these premises. First of all, the assumption on which this construction is based is that an original quality corresponds to each material movement as defined by its physical properties, and especially to each rhythmic movement. If you superpose two rhythms, you get two qualities. Combine two rhythms into a common rhythm and you will have a new quality which you cannot call original but about which you can say that the equivalent, the physical notation, is the result of the first two rhythms, and so on.

In addition, let us adopt from the outset the materialist hypothesis of an exact parallelism between the manifestations of the organism and those of consciousness. This means that consciousness is not an entity, nor even a force, but a glimmer that lights up the chemical mechanism of bodies without adding anything to it. Thus, it does not create anything; it informs about things. Perhaps this hypothesis is false but at least it has the advantage of excluding, from the start, any untoward intrusions of metaphysics. There will always be time, afterwards, to take the latter up again and discuss it.

This being said, let us now recall that *the manifestations of the living cell can all be reduced to movements and probably, as Le Dantec brilliantly suggested, to rhythmic movements. Thus, mechanical equilibria are at the basis of all the phenomena related to life, and in a parallel way, so are equilibria between qualities* [italics added]. Now the physical and mathematical meaning of these equilibria can be banal or on the contrary quite special – I don't intend to discuss this here – their qualitative and psychological meaning is of extreme interest and has been little remarked.

Indeed, owing to the very fact that a cell or a group of cells presents several different internal movements, the consciousness which translates these movements must present a minimum of distinct and original qualities. This is a first point. Second, there can be no consciousness of these qualities – thus these qualities cannot exist – if there is no relationship between them, if they are not, consequently, fused together within a total quality which contains them while at the same time maintaining them distinct. I would not for example be aware of the white of this paper nor of the black of this ink, if these two qualities were not fused together in my consciousness in a certain whole and if, despite this whole, they did not remain respectively one white and the other black. Here then is the second point and all the originality of the equilibria between qualities is here: There is equilibrium not only between discrete parts as it, and it alone exists in material equilibria whatever their nature, but between the parts – considered as distinct and original qualities – on the one hand, and a whole – considered as an overall quality resulting from these partial qualities – on the other. But this result is so special that it does not do away with the latter; it coexists with them and over them. When a mechanical resultant is composed of three different forces, these three forces have ceased to exist as such for they have given rise to a fourth force which sums them up because it implies all three. On the contrary, when a psychological resultant is composed of three qualities, the three continue to exist on their own, independently of the others in an original way, and yet they produced a common result which implies them! The difference is there, and it is so capital that it forms two types of scientific activity: that governed by laws and that governed by kinds. Consciousness has been described as allowing synthesis, coordination, and even selection, but no-one ever realised that the special nature of its activity lies in the *coexistence of independent, partial qualities and of an autonomous overall quality* [italics added]; this coexistence is an equilibrium which has no part in any material equilibrium.

This is why one felt obliged to see a "force" in consciousness, regardless of all methodological requirements, because there is nothing particularly original in a synthesis or in a selection, whereas a *sui generis* equilibrium like the one we have just outlined can be accounted for entirely by the mechanical play of the physical-chemical forces of life without doing away with any of the specificity of consciousness. *As such, the kind forces the mind to go from the whole to the parts, and not from the part to the whole as is the case for the physicist's mind* [italics added]. Auguste Comte remarked this, but he was far from drawing the right conclusions. Furthermore, unlike laws which allow a series of simple relationships between two terms or a very small number, kinds, because of the strange complication of the overall quality which acts continually on the parts and upsets the virtually simple relationships, are so complex that they can only be dealt with by probability calculus and only under certain conditions which I shall not go into here. Last, the simpler the laws, the clearer they are to the mind, whereas in the case of kinds, it is the most complex ones that are the clearest owing to their special equilibrium. This gives them an air of finality, even when it is not the case. It is this last point that has been best understood by philosophers, among whom Bergson, but they did not see the cause of it in this coexistence of a whole and its parts. Whatever the case, this equilibrium of the kind is likely to take on two elementary forms from the outset, and we shall see their variants later on. Or again, indeed, *the partial qualities are compatible with those of the whole* in which case *there is not only mutual tolerance, but also reciprocal conservation* [italics added]. My personality, for example, tends to conserve its partial qualities (the believer, the philosopher, etc.) in the same way that the latter tend to conserve the former. Or yet again, there is *incompatibility* and the *whole tends to conserve its unity at the expense of the parts and vice versa.*

(pp. 150–154)

As can be seen, Piaget places the notion of equilibrium at the heart of his cosmic system. This equilibrium is known as a relation between the whole and the parts, and between the parts. This is already an original idea, since at first sight, the relation between the parts and the whole and between the parts could appear to be a logical problem and nothing else. By transforming it into a question of equilibrium, Piaget links the logical side of things to the biological one from the outset. Indeed, for Piaget, insofar as the parts are compatible with the whole, the organisation is maintained, and there is conservation. But the equilibrium thus defined is a qualitative one which does not subsume the partial qualities in a total quality, thus making them disappear as would be the case in the quantitative domain, but conserves them with the result that this conservation generates a specific mode of scientific activity: the mode of kinds which is, so to speak, the opposite of the mode of laws.

From here on, everything is transformed but from an invariant principle which is equilibrium. It is in this way that life and matter come together. But this connection is less complete than the materialistic mechanists would have wished.

Indeed,

organic chemistry has knocked down the barriers which separated life from matter one after the other. The only thing left to define life is assimilation, the source of all organisation. The living being *assimilates* [italics added] i.e. reproduces, by the very fact that it is alive, a substance which is *identical* to itself [italics added]. It thus has an overall, *independent and stable quality* [italics added]. In addition, when assimilating, it undergoes the influence of the substances it assimilates, and therefore of the environment, and as such, it presents variations, a certain heterogeneity which constitutes partial qualities. Therefore, it is sufficient to postulate life, to assume that there is an equilibrium between qualities of the type we have just discussed, and our notion of kind seems a vain repetition, in the language of the quality, of the biology of Le Dantec. But this isn't so at all. Indeed, for this author, the action of assimilating and that of undergoing the influence of the environment, of varying, of "imitating external factors" are two opposite actions. The better I assimilate, the less I change. The more I vary, on the other hand, the less I am coherent, the less power I have to assimilate, the less personality I have. Le Dantec only envisages the second elementary form of equilibrium, where the whole and the parts are opposed. But this thesis is untenable. A being is all the more able to understand the external world, in other words to undergo its influence, "imitate it", that he is he himself more, that he has more individuality, i.e. that he "assimilates" better. These two approaches are not contradictory; they imply each other, and equilibrium such as Le Dantec knew it is only a deformation, a particular case, of this latter equilibrium which is that of the kind. The organisation is thus a kind and the parallelism between the equilibrium of qualities that consciousness implies and the reactions of the organism itself thus seems a fecund view. Let us summarise the main laws to be drawn from this conception and show how they govern the whole of biology.

First law: Any organisation tends to preserve itself as such. This law results directly from our definition since 'there is an equilibrium between an autonomous whole and its parts.

Second law: Of the two elementary types of equilibrium that result from the organisation, only the first results from the formula of this organisation, the second being a compromise between this first type and the subsequent action of the environment. These two elementary types are the ones already defined above, where the whole and the parts mutually conserve each other and where, on the contrary, they tend to exclude one another. Now the first derives, in fact, from the definition given, whereas the existence, within the organisation of a partial quality contrary to the overall qualities, can only come from an outside action: it is the environment which breaks the equilibrium of the original unity by continually forcing the organism to undergo new influences. Only this latter case is envisaged by Le Dantec.

Third law: All the possible equilibria are combinations of these first two. Let us take for example the other main type, the one we find in morality to characterise passion. The first type can be defined by the coordination of four cardinal actions: that of the whole on itself, of the whole on its parts, of the parts on themselves and of the parts on the whole. The second type can be defined by the coordination of the latter two (between themselves), and by the opposition of these two groups of action, which are in unstable equilibrium. As to the third type, the action of the whole on itself combines itself with the action of the part on the whole to fight against the other two. Now it is easy to see that such an equilibrium implies the existence of a secondary equilibrium of the second type in the whole itself.

Fourth law: All organic equilibria tend towards equilibrium of the first type. This law is the most important of all. Together with the definition of the organisation, it is the main point of the system. This is easily demonstrated by the existence of the third law: Since there are only two elementary types of equilibrium, if the second tends towards the first, any other type resulting from their combination will be cancelled out by the very fact of this reduction. Now, it is easy to see that the second type tends to equilibrate itself on the first.

All life is thus: An organisation in unstable equilibrium governed by a law of stable equilibrium towards which it tends. We shall therefore call ideal equilibrium equilibria of the first type and real equilibrium those of other types, even though any real equilibrium whatever the sort, supposes an ideal equilibrium that makes it possible and gives it its impulse according to defined laws.

Imagine now that all life came from an initial organisation like this. We must therefore admit that the environment has partly upset the equilibrium of this organism. The latter, broken into several parts, was too fragmented to preserve its unity in space, but not enough to lose the whole of its equilibrium. The organisation therefore found itself two-fold, though it is artificial to talk in such a way: On the one hand, a large whole encompassing parts that are separated in space, but nevertheless real. On the other hand, the parts themselves, each of which has become a new organised whole on its own. This large whole is the species, its parts the individuals and we can see here the indefinite variety that exists between a kind equilibrated on an intensive mode, in a state of high tension, so to say, like a personality, and looser kinds such as equilibria of biological species. But all remain kind and all differ from the mechanism of the "law".

Remember now that, as the environment continues to form an obstacle, equilibria are unformed and reformed in a continuous race towards stable equilibrium, and you have there the whole of evolution. It would be possible, on the basis of these premisses alone, to conciliate Lamarck and Darwin, and to deduce the known laws of biology. This conception of evolution was, in particular, that of the science of kinds, of Greek science. The loose equilibrium we just mentioned, is the series which penetrated Plato, these indefinite repetitions of the same type, which is the Idea. Whereas intensive equilibrium is the kind of Aristotle, it is the Form. We can see by this that Aristotle, who was a biologist, went to the extreme kind of "kinds", whereas Plato, who was a mathematician, stopped at an intermediate type between pure logic and vitality. But science has, by accident, taken up these notions, combining them with the chemism of inorganic science. The ideal equilibrium is Lamarck's Organisation, of which he has so well defined the "growing composition" and the "regular gradation", it is the organisation of Auguste Comte. It is also what Claude Bernard described under the name of "guiding idea". But let there be no misunderstanding. There is no metaphysics in this conception of evolution, as there was for the Greeks. There is no finality in the "guiding idea", for a series of equilibria is not a collection of final causes, and when the system tends towards equilibrium, it does not pursue a goal. Now, if qualitative equilibrium is quite special and it differs from physical equilibria, it is nonetheless mechanical both from the ideal point of view and from the real one. And if that is true, I challenge you to find the least bit of finality in the search for equilibrium which is what evolution is.

(pp. 155–159)

As can be seen from this last remark, the young Piaget wishes to keep his distance not only from Bergson and Le Dantec, but also from Fouillée (the guiding idea as a form of the key-idea) and Boutroux, although he adopts the distinction made by the latter between the "*constituted reason*" of science as science and the "*constituting reason*" of intelligence which constructs scientific knowledge. This distinction is too often overlooked today still, but it is essential if we wish to understand Piaget's approach in his genetic epistemology.

This passage also shows how the young Piaget likes to compare the mathematical Idea based on repetition as he puts it, not fearing to copy Bergson in this, and biological Form. We find this opposition again in the *Introduction à l'Epistémologie Génétique* (1950) in the form of a bipolarity between mathematical thinking "the most idealistic of all sciences" and biology which is "the most realistic". Logic is opposed to life and yet life has its logic and logic results from life. How?

## General organising principles of laws

From the outset, the young Piaget postulates an organising principle for life and an evolution for logic. Whence his insistence on the "growing composition" and the "regular gradation" of Lamarck. We understand why. In this way, and in this way only, everything depends on action and on the action of the individual to the extent that even before he became aware of the fact, Piaget had put psychology at the centre of his system. For it is the only science of action in its three-fold biological, logical and moral form:

This *a priori* could be expressed as follows: Act in such a way as to achieve the absolute equilibrium of the living organisation, both collective and individual, which is, finally, a fairly faithful translation of the famous Kantian formula.

(p. 177)

But it is also a way of underlining the social nature of this equilibrium. Now, from the outset, Piaget expresses the idea that "this moral equilibrium coincides with the ideal psychological equilibrium" (p. 188), that is, the social side of things is conceived of as a reduction of the individual one. This explains the future: Thinking goes from egocentrism to decentration; mental growth goes from the solipsism of the baby to the "absolute altruism and abstinence from all passion" (p. 178) characteristic of the adult at full maturity.

## Morality

In this conception, "evil is thus, in one sense or another, disequilibrium, either because it favours the end at the expense of the parts, or the parts at the expense of the whole" (p. 177), be this on the collective level or the individual one, with this difference however between the individual and the collective, that the individual not only forms an equilibrium between himself and his so to say individual parts but also between his own social tendencies and his own individual tendencies. This raises straightaway both the moral question and the need for a social psychology, both of which are going to preoccupy Piaget up until the Second World War. From *Recherche* on, Piaget tries to solve the opposition between Tarde and Durkheim which he sees as an opposition between the primacy of the individual over the collective, on the one hand, and the preeminence of the social over the individual, on the other. The solution is naturally "an equilibrium of qualities between the action of a whole on itself and on the parts – this is the second school [Durkheim] – and the action of these parts on themselves and on the whole – this is the first school [Tarde]" (p. 170). This solves the sociological question.

> We have just seen how the biological equilibrium of the qualities is the basis of psychology as far as the individual is concerned and of sociology as far as morality is concerned. We must now look into the connections between these two organisations . . .
>
> (p. 173)

## Aesthetics and religion

Having already examined the problem of morality, we must now go into that of aesthetics and religion. If we already know that ". . . the blossom of life is absolute altruism . . ." in pure Piagetian Bergsonism style, we cannot overlook the fact that, for Piaget, morality belongs to will, whereas aesthetics belongs to feeling.

For Piaget, art is a prolongation of life. "Beauty, like organisms, is a question of equilibrium, of order and, in the language of aesthetics, of harmony. Art, like life, is creation; known elements are continually recombined to organise a coherent whole" (p. 185). "Art organises, it constructs an ideal equilibrium. Beauty is the love of this equilibrium" (p. 186).

Religion is also a prolongation of life. It is Life itself in abundance. The absolute value which "necessarily goes beyond real existence" (p. 199) can only be incarnated by a transcendent God. But, by a movement of equilibrium which has by now become as familiar to the reader as to the author, this "absolute value is everywhere and in everything . . . " (p. 200). God is therefore also immanent.

A second movement corresponds to this equilibrium, and this is the opposition between the absolute of divine value and human misery, whose point of equilibrium is the incarnation of Christ and his sacrifice on the Cross. The god-made-man connects the divine absolute to the human relative and thus saves man from death.

Faith, for the young Piaget, leads to individual salvation but not to social salvation, which can only be obtained by a liberal socialism or in other words, by an internationalist, feminist, pacifist, federalist and cooperative "human socialism". This is so for several reasons: because in nationalism, the parts are favoured in comparison to the whole; because so long as women do not vote and are not elected, half of humanity is excluded; because war is opposed to universal harmony; because centralism favours the whole at the expense of the parts; and finally because cooperation alone conforms with the ideal equilibrium, since collectivism gives "terrible" advantages to the whole and "the bourgeois régime is abnormal and iniquitous because it in no way insures the equilibrium between individual possessions and society" (p. 210)

## Psychology

As can be seen, we are confronted with an extremely complete system, whose field of application is more or less equivalent to the universe. Strangely enough, here as in the case of the lacustrine lymnaea, Piaget speaks extremely little of psychology. As he was not interested (apart from a rapid observation [1914]) in the behaviour of these molluscs, despite the fact that they had been studied by Henri Piéron (1911), the space devoted to psychology and to the psychology of intelligence, which will later bring him to fame, is relatively limited in *Recherche*. Psychology prolongs biology, on the one hand, on the individual level, as does sociology on the collective one. Psychology is considered as a psychology of consciousness, considered as " . . . a pure internal translation of physical-chemical phenomena . . . " (p. 160) in the language of an ideal organisation that commands a real individual organisation. It is thus always the same principle of equilibrium between an ideal and its real instantiations which explains everything. We understand how Piaget, at the end of his life, came to subsume this first vision of equilibration under categories such as reality conceived of as one of many possibilities, and possibility as the producer of real or virtual novelties whose coordination and synthesis give rise to necessity.

The psychology of thinking is not very elaborate either. Indeed,

> the tendency of the organisation to conserve itself as such is at the basis of the principle of identity, from which the principle of contradiction can be deduced. As to the principle of sufficient reason, it is, as Fouillée showed, the result of an organisation "which maintains itself in its union with the whole".

(p. 163)

We find here the idea of conservation which will be developed in the way we know, and that of a logician's approach to the problems of thought, based on these three fundamental laws.

The next part of the text is once again inspired by Bergson: the spatial nature of thinking, but due here to a discursive approach arising from the awareness of the organisation by a process going from the whole to the parts.

Of greater interest is the assertion that reason is the synthesis of understanding ("Understanding is thinking acting on quantity" (p. 165)) and autistic thinking. "It [reason] owes to understanding its pursuit of what is universal and to autistic thinking its search for quality, but without the symbolism of the latter. Reason can thus know the organisation as a whole, uniting the kind and the law" (p. 165).

This passage calls for two remarks. First of all, the young Piaget was already familiar with the concept of autistic thinking, which we find in Bleuler's work on schizophrenia, before his departure for Zurich. In addition, when he speaks of symbolism, he uses the term in a rather curious way. It is doubtless this conception of symbolism that explains the internal position of the symbolic function in his genetic psychology. But it also enables us to understand how Piaget later considers that thinking goes from ego to alter or from autism to altruism.

In this passage from egotism, as Le Dantec called it, to socialised thinking, autistic thinking plays, for the young Piaget, the role of a sort of condensor into a single image of all sorts of disparate qualities. It is a form of thinking close to dreaming and its symbolism. It is neither the spatialising and depersonalising thinking stigmatised by Bergson, nor pure intuition. It is similar in some ways to the transduction of Stern, in that it is deeply linked to the concrete. But it is evident that, for the young Piaget, the psychology of intelligence that he develops later does not exist even in an embryonic form in this first theory of equilibrium, whereas his social psychology, which we should almost call moral psychology in its emphasis on the relation between action and value, is entirely present.

# CONCLUSION

In conclusion, we can say that the first theory of equilibration is a theory of the world seen as a big Living Being where matter and form are inseparably linked as quantity and quality, law and kind, fact and norm, immanence and transcendence, according to principles of equilibrium which are not purely mechanical as in Gestalt psychology – so close in some ways to the laws of equilibrium of the young Piaget – but which depend on dynamic interactions between the whole and parts and the parts between themselves. Contrary to the Gestaltists, for whom, following Leibniz, reality is finally the best possible world, Piaget's reality is only one possibility and certainly not the best, for the best has still and always to come. In this sense, Piaget's theory is an ecological theory, presenting both characteristics of modern ecology: The earth is living and we must, therefore, attack the problems concerning it from the point of view of the quality. But this is another dimension of Piaget's thinking, which would merit special attention and about which there is much to say.

What one should retain, on the other hand, from this first theory of equilibrium is that we are already confronted with an organismic genetic structuralism. The three terms: structure, genesis and organism are important and, in this order, ascendant.

Indeed, we can talk of structuralism because Piaget is interested above all in the relations between the whole and the parts. But this structuralism is not the logician's. There is no embryon of mereology, for example, nor should one consider this structuralism as mathematical; no group structure is apparent in this theory, for example. It cannot be considered as physical either: there is no parallelogram of forces, for example. Moreover, if it were physical, it would be a form of Gestalt. Curious structuralism then which is not even closed on itself by a closure principle.

More important, this structuralism is evolutionist, in a constant state of flux, pure springing forth of new qualities with each leap forward. It is directed towards a goal, a telos like an eschatology. This teleology which (the reader cannot resist this impression, despite Piaget's denial [see page 23]), serves as a theology to the young Piaget, anticipates retrospective causality and announces cybernetics and its pro- and retroactive systems.

Finally, this genetic structuralism is above all organismic. This is the most striking new element, as we have already said and repeated: Knowledge is to be considered as *living*. It is biological in its own right. Bergson's duration is transformed into something organic. To all the previous metaphors of knowledge that are productive in the sense of *homo faber*, Piaget opposes a radically different metaphor – that of the economics of life – in the same way as the theologians speak of the economics of salvation, that is, as a process which is at the same time individual, vital, true and chreodic – that is, a compulsory passage inserted in a duration or time with a direction.

It is in this sense that he accompanies the thinkers of modern ecology who belong, like him, to the posterity of Bergson and that he announces the science of the next century which will no longer try to reduce the organic to the inorganic, but to make Life the model of all thinking.

This culminating point in Piaget's thinking, which sums up the richness of his contribution to contemporary thinking, has often been misunderstood, doubtless because it is the newest, thus the most difficult to understand, but also because Piaget managed to express it in a paradoxical way. How can one put the organic in the same bed as logic? Is there not a fundamental contradiction in the idea of a genetic structuralism? How does action suddenly become endowed with a truth value at the moment of the passage to the semiotic function? The epistemological status of these points is unclear and probably contradictory. Whence the impression of a false way of thinking and one that may well be dangerous.

In reality, this is not so. But it seems urgent today to do a conceptual revision of the young Piaget's fundamental intuitions, since he stayed faithful to these intuitions throughout his life (this is shown by his last book on equilibration, written at the age of 80) and they are as prophetic in 1992 as they were in 1918, almost three quarters of a century later.

## ACKNOWLEDGEMENT

The author wishes to thank Professor H. E. Gruber for his pertinent remarks on a first version of this text.

## REFERENCES

Dewey, J. (1933) *How we think*, New York: D. C. Heath.

Festinger, L. A. (1957) *Theory of cognitive dissonance*, Stanford: Stanford University Press.

Freud, S. (1964) "The ego and the id", in S. Freud, *The standard edition of the complete psychological works of Sigmund Freud, vol. 19: The ego and the id and other works*, trans. J. Strachey, London: The Hogarth Press and the Institute of Psychoanalysis. (Original work published 1923–25.)

Heider, F. (1946) "Attitudes and cognitive organization", *Journal of Psychology* 21: 107–112.

Inhelder, B., Garcia, R. and Vonèche, J. (eds) (1976) *Epistémologie génétique et équilibration*, Neuchâtel, Paris: Delachaux et Niestlé.

Piaget, J. (1914) "Notes sur la biologie des Limnées abyssales", *Internationale Revue der gesamten Hydrobiologie und Hydrographie. Biologisches Supplement* 6 (Série 6): 1–15.

Piaget, J. (1918) *Recherche*, Lausanne: La Concorde.

Piaget, J. (1945) "Hommage à C. G. Jung", *Revue suisse de psychologie et de psychologie appliquée* 4(3–4): 169–171.

Piaget, J. (1950) *Introduction à l'épistémologie génétique, vol. 1: La pensée mathématique*, Paris: Presses Universitaires de France.

Piaget, J. (1952) *The origins of intelligence in children*, trans. M. Cook, New York: International Universities Press. (Original work published 1936.)

Piaget, J. (1957) "Logique et équilibre dans les comportements du sujet", in L. Apostel, B. Mandelbrot and J. Piaget, *Logique et équilibre* (pp. 27–117), Paris: Presses Universitaires de France.

Piaget, J. (1985) *The equilibration of cognitive structures: The central problem of intellectual development*, trans. T. Brown and K. J. Thampy, London, Chicago: University of Chicago Press. (Original work published 1975.)

Piéron, H. (1911) "Observations sur le comportement des limnées", in *La Mémoire*, Paris: Alcan.

Spencer, H. (1892) *The principles of psychology*, New York: D. Appleton.

Vidal, F. (1989) "Self and œuvre in Jean Piaget's youth", in D. B. Wallace and H. E. Gruber (eds) *Creative people at work* (pp. 189–207), New York, Oxford: Oxford University Press.

Watson, J. B. (1929) *Psychology from the standpoint of a behaviorist*, London: Lippincott.

Chapter 2

# Learning and adaptation in the theory of constructivism

*Ernst von Glasersfeld*

## ABSTRACT

Learning and adaptation are conceptually distinct and refer to different processes. Both concepts are incorporated in Piaget's *genetic epistemology* and in the more radical constructivist model of cognition that has sprung from it. Misinterpretation of the different roles the two terms play in that theoretical model is one of the reasons why the constructivist approach has often been misunderstood by educators. In this chapter I shall lay out the use of the two terms in the constructivist theory and give some indication of its application to learning and the practice of teaching.

## THE CONCEPT OF ADAPTATION

In everyday language the difference between the terms learning and adaptation is sometimes blurred because both refer to a fundamental requirement. If we were not adapted to our environment, we would be unable to survive, and if we could not learn, we would die of our mistakes. For the biologist, however, there is an important difference: adaptation refers to the biological make-up, the genetically determined potential with which we are born; and learning is the process that allows us to build up skills in acting and thinking as a result of our own experience.

Another way of bringing out this difference would be to explain that biological adaptation is the result of accidental mutations in the genes that determine possibilities of development, whereas learning can be engaged deliberately in view of goals that we or others choose. This means that learning is an activity that we, consciously or unconsciously, have to carry out ourselves. In contrast, the basic meaning of adaptation is not an activity of organisms or species. I am here not concerned with the much looser meaning of the word in everyday language, where it may refer also to deliberate modifications (e.g. we adapted our plan to the change in the weather). Adaptation, in the technical sense, merely ascribes to whatever organisms are alive today, the physical and behavioral characteristics that are necessary to survive and have offspring in their present environment.

What further tends to mislead about the biological meaning of the term adaptation is its definition as the outcome of a process called *natural selection*. This seems to relate the process to the deliberate, goal-directed selecting that is done, for example, by breeders of dogs or horses. Natural selection, in contrast, happens quite aimlessly as the result of changes in the environment which simply wipe out all those that do not have the characteristics necessary for survival. In this context one should emphasize the fact that the characteristics that enable an organism to survive a given environmental change have to be present in the organism *before* that change occurs; and since the theory of evolution holds that modifications of the genetic make-up must be caused by mutations, the adaptedness of living organisms can be credited only to accidental variations.[1]

Piaget started out as a biologist and began to investigate what he considered to be manifestations of "intelligence" (using the term in a wider sense than is usual). It began with his early discovery that mollusks of the same species were able to produce offspring that developed different and appropriately shaped shells, if they were transplanted from still to fast-flowing water or vice versa. It was a change of physical structure that did not involve a change in the mollusks' genetic make-up. He saw this as the effect of the environmental constraints that foreclosed all but the viable developmental possibilities of the organism. Hence it was a form of *adaptation* that was closer to learning – the natural selection that produced it did not eliminate other potential developmental pathways in the genome, but only in the individual mollusks in question. Their offspring, if placed in another environment, could develop different shells which, relative to the new constraints, were again adapted.

Seen in this way, the concept of adaptation could be incorporated in a theory of learning. In my view, this is the major contribution Jean Piaget has made to our understanding of cognition. Eventually this perspective led him to the conclusion that the function of intelligence was not, as traditional epistemology held, to provide cognitive organisms with "true" representations of an objective environment. Rather, he began to see cognition as generator of intelligent tools that enable organisms to construct a relative *fit* with the world as they experience it.

Though the notion of "fit" was borrowed from the biological concept of adaptation, it no longer contained the element of preformation or genetic determination in the cognitive domain. Here it was the product of intelligent construction, of the organism's own making, as the result of trial, error and the selection of what "works".[2] As the presence of various potential patterns of development enabled mollusks to grow shells that were adapted to the constraints of their actual environment, so the conceptual constructs of cognitive organisms could be developed to *fit* experiential requirements. Fit or viability in the cognitive domain is, of course, no longer directly tied to survival but rather to the attainment of goals and the mutual compatibility of constructs.

To make clear and emphasize the instrumental character of knowledge, be it on the level of sensory-motor activities or conceptual operations, I have always preferred the term *viability*. It seems more appropriate because, unlike "fit", it does not suggest an approximation to the constraints.

During the last two decades of his life, when Piaget had realized that his theory had much in common with the principles formulated by cybernetics,[3] he shifted his focus from the chronology of development in children to the more general question of the cognitive organism's generation and maintenance of *equilibrium*. In this regard, too, room was left for misunderstandings, because the term was not intended to have the same meaning on all levels of cognition. On the biological/physical level, an organism's equilibrium can be said to consist in its capability to resist and neutralize perturbations caused by the environment. On the conceptual level, however, the term refers to the compatibility and non-contradictoriness of conceptual structures.

## SCHEME THEORY

As a biologist, Piaget was well acquainted with the notion of *reflex* and he investigated the phenomenon in his children. Since infants manifest some such "fixed action patterns" as soon as they are born, they must be considered the result of genetic determination rather than learning. Whereas most developmental psychologists seemed satisfied with that explanation, Piaget focused on the fact that this genetic determination was likely to be the result of natural selection. In other words, he considered that these action patterns arose through accidental mutations and spread, because they, rather than others, had consequences that were conducive to survival. He therefore saw reflexes not as they are usually depicted in textbooks, viz:

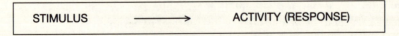

but as composed of three rather than two parts. The third part was the result of the activity that was crucial for the perpetuation of the reflex. On the basis of the organism's past experience, this result could be *expected*, and thus open the way to cognitive applications:

| 1<br>PERCEIVED<br>SITUATION | → | 2<br>ACTIVITY | → | 3<br>BENEFICIAL OR<br>EXPECTED<br>RESULT |
|---|---|---|---|---|

This addition was legitimate because, although reflexive action patterns are "wired in" and remain fixed for a certain time, they can eventually be modified or even dismantled by the organism's experience. Adults, for instance, no longer manifest some of the reflexes that helped them to find the mother's nipple when they were infants.

Piaget thus adopted the three-part sequence of the infant's reflex as the basic structure of goal-directed sensory-motor activity. He called it *action scheme (schème*[4]*)* and built on it, with the help of his concepts of *assimilation* and *accommodation*, a revolutionary learning theory.

The student of Piaget's writings, however, will not find this theory neatly formulated and described in any one place. Its development, presumably, took time and was spread in bits and pieces over a number of different publications (e.g. Piaget 1937, 1945, 1967). As Bärbel Inhelder, Piaget's constant and most important collaborator, remarked, "the notion of scheme has given and is still giving rise to different interpretations" (Inhelder and de Caprona 1992, p. 41). The interpretation I am presenting here has proven the most useful in our applications.

In the Piagetian action scheme, assimilation can be operative in two places. In part 1 it is involved in the recognition of a perceived situation as the sort with which the particular action is associated. Since no two experiential situations are ever exactly the same, the *recognition* of a situation entails being unaware of certain differences. If another observer – e.g. the psychologist who observes the child – notices such a difference, he or she will say that the child is assimilating the new situation to a specific past experience. From the point of view of the child, however, especially if it is a young child, there *is* no difference. The situation is simply perceived as the situation that led to a successful activity in the past. (As adults, of course, we frequently "assimilate" deliberately and mostly remain aware of doing it – e.g. when we are using a table knife as screwdriver, knowing full well that it is not a screwdriver and was not intended for that purpose.)

The second place of assimilation in an action scheme is in the recognition of part 3 as the result expected of the activity. If that result fits the expectation, that is, if the child remains unaware of the differences, the action scheme will be considered a success and will be strengthened as a repeatable pattern. In contrast, if the result of the activity is such that it cannot be assimilated to the expectation, there will be a discord and thus a *perturbation*. This perturbation may be disappointment or the surprise caused by an interesting novelty. In both cases it may open a path to *learning*.

## LEARNING AND TEACHING

The possibility of learning arises when the perturbation is serious enough to direct attention to the situation that triggered the activity. In that case one of the differences that were disregarded owing to the assimilation of the perceived situation, may now be noticed; and this, in turn, may lead to a modification of the perceptual requirements of the scheme or to the formation of a new one. Both would constitute an *accommodation*. Similarly, the failure of the original action scheme may point attention to the activity, which may again lead to a modification and thus to an accommodation.

I want to emphasize that I have so far spoken only of the sensory-motor level. A constructivist exposition of learning on the conceptual level would have to begin with Piaget's theory of *reflective abstraction* (Piaget 1977a, vols 1 and 2) which I have discussed elsewhere (cf., Glasersfeld 1991b). In this context, I can merely point out that the three-part model of the action scheme remains a powerful analytical tool in the domain of reflection, but there, obviously, the perceptual situation is replaced by a conceptual one, and the activity by a mental operation; and perturbations are no longer caused by unexpected perceptual results but by relational surprises, such as the breach of an expected regularity or an operational result that is incompatible with other conceptual structures.

The basic principle of the constructivist theory is that cognitive organisms act and operate in order to create and maintain their equilibrium in the face of perturbations generated by conflicts or unexpected novelties arising either from their pursuit of goals in a constraining environment or from the incompatibility of conceptual structures with a more or less established organization of experience. The urge to know thus becomes the urge to *fit*, on the sensory-motor level as well as in the conceptual domain, and learning and adaptation are seen as complementary phenomena.

If one accepts this principle, one can no longer maintain the traditional idea of knowledge as representing an "external" reality supposed to be independent of the knower. The concept of knowledge has to be dismantled and reconstructed differently. This is a shocking suggestion, and I have elsewhere laid out the reasons for such a radical step (Glasersfeld 1985). I have called my position *radical* constructivism to accentuate the changed concept of knowledge and to differentiate myself from those who speak of the construction of knowledge in the framework of a traditional epistemology. I want to emphasize, however, that radical constructivism is intended as a model, not as the description of a real world, let alone a metaphysical proposal. It is intended to be used as a working hypothesis whose value can lie only in its usefulness.

## APPLICATIONS AND SUGGESTIONS

In the past ten years the beginnings of a constructivist approach to teaching have been developed and applied in practice (Clement 1991; Cobb *et al.* 1992; Confrey 1990; Désautels and Larochelle 1989; Dykstra, D. I. 1991; Glasersfeld (ed.) 1991a; Steffe 1991). Some of these applications are now yielding longitudinal studies with elementary school classes followed over two or three years. The preliminary results are extremely promising in that they show children who are *learning to learn* (cf., Cobb *et al.* 1992b).

The teaching procedures that are based on the constructivist theory do not claim novelty or originality. Good teachers have always known all this and more, but they did not find it in the traditional dogma of instruction. They came to it by intuition or as a result of many trials and failures. Constructivism provides a model of cognition that leads directly to a method of teaching that credits the student with the power to become an active learner. Some tentative directives can be summarized as follows:

1 Training aims at the ability to repeat the performance of a given activity and it must be distinguished from teaching. What we want to call *teaching* aims at enabling students to generate activities out of the understanding *why* they should be performed and, ultimately, also how one can explain that they lead to the desired result.
2 Knowledge has to be built up by each individual learner, it cannot be packaged and transferred from one person to another.
3 Language is not a conveyor belt or means of transport. The meaning of words, sentences and texts is always a subjective construction based on the individual's experience.[5] Though language cannot "convey" the desired constructs to students, it has two important functions: it enables the teacher to orient the students' conceptual construction by means of appropriate constraints; and when students talk to the teacher or among themselves in groups, they are forced to reflect upon what they are thinking and doing.
4 Students' answers and their solutions of problems should always be taken seriously. At the moment they are produced, they mostly make sense to the student even if they are wrong from the teacher's point of view. Ask students how they arrived at their answer. This helps to separate answers given to please the teacher from those that are the result of understanding or misunderstandings.
5 Only a problem the student sees as his or her own problem can focus the student's attention and energy on the genuine search for a solution.

6 Rewards (i.e. the behaviorists' external reinforcements), be they material or social, foster repetition, not understanding.
7 Intellectual motivation is generated by overcoming an obstacle, by eliminating a contradiction, or by developing principles that are both abstract and applicable. Only if students have themselves built up a conceptual model that provides an explanation of a problematic situation or process, can they develop the desire to try their hand at further problems; only success in these attempts can make them aware of their power to shape the world of their experience in a meaningful way.

This sample of constructivist directives is far from complete, but it illustrates the thrust of our effort. Without distorting it too much, one could say that constructivism does not invent a new didactic method, but it shows the teacher what *not* to do, and it suggests an attitude of respect towards the student. If we want to teach thinking, we must have the faith that students are able to think and we must provide them with opportunities to do it. Where this has been practised, it has tended to show that both teachers and students can come to profit from their interactions and at the same time find them enjoyable.

## NOTES

1 This is in no way changed by recent hypotheses that environmental stress or "pressure" may accelerate the rate of mutations, because the mutations as such are still random events.
2 In principle this is what Campbell (1960) called "blind variation and selective retention"; I would only add that, in the cognitive domain, the blindness is sometimes tempered and partially overcome by analogical thinking.
3 Cf. Cellérier *et al.* 1968, and Piaget 1977.
4 Piaget occasionally used the word *schéma* to designate standardized patterns or simplified representations but never in the same sense as *schème*; hence Piaget's meaning is wholly obscured if the second term is translated as "schema".
5 This must not be understood as a negation of the role of social interaction which causes the unceasing "adaptation" of individual meanings.

## REFERENCES

Campbell, D. T. (1960) "Blind variation and selective retention in creative thought as in other knowledge processes", *Psychological Review* 67(6): 380–400.
Cellérier, G., Papert, S. and Voyat, G. (1968) *Cybernétique et Épistémologie*, Paris: Presses Universitaires de France.
Clement, J. (1991) "Nonformal reasoning in experts and in science students: The use of analogies, extreme cases, and physical intuition", in J. F. Voss, D. N. Perkins, and J. W. Segal (eds) *Informal reasoning in education* (pp. 345–362), Hillsdale: Lawrence Erlbaum.
Cobb, P., Yackel, E. and Wood, T. (1992) "A constructivist alternative to the representational view in mathematics education", *J. for Research in Mathematics Education* 23: 2–23.

Cobb, P., Wood, T., Yackel, E. and Perlwitz, M. (1992b) "A follow-up assessment of a second grade problem-centered mathematics project", *Educational Studies in Mathematics* 23(5): 483–504.

Confrey, J. (1990) "A review of the research on student conceptions in mathematics, science, and programming", in C. Cazden (ed.) *Review of research in education*: 3–56, Washington: American Educational Research Association.

Désautels, J. and Larochelle, M. (1989) *Qu'est-ce que le savoir scientifique?* Québec: Presses de l'Université Laval.

Dykstra, D. I. (1991) "Studying conceptual change: Constructing new understandings", in R. Duit, F. Goldberg and H. Niedderer (eds) *Research in physics learning: Theoretical issues and empirical studies*, Kiel: IPM, Universität Kiel.

Glasersfeld, Ernst von (1985) "Reconstructing the concept of knowledge", *Archives de Psychologie* 53: 91–101.

Glasersfeld, E. von (ed., 1991a) *Radical constructivism in mathematics education*, Dordrecht: Kluwer.

Glasersfeld, E. von (1991b) "Abstraction, re-presentation, and reflection", in L. P. Steffe (ed.) *Epistemological foundations of mathematical experience*: 45–67, New York: Springer.

Inhelder, B. and de Caprona, D. (1992) "Un parcours de recherche", in B. Inhelder and D. de Caprona (eds) *Le cheminement des découvertes de l'enfant*, Lausanne: Delachaux et Niestlé.

Piaget, J. (1937) *La construction du réel chez l'enfant*, Neuchâtel: Delachaux et Niestlé.

Piaget, J. (1945) *La formation du symbole chez l'enfant*, Neuchâtel: Delachaux et Niestlé.

Piaget, J. (1967) *Biologie et connaissance*, Paris: Gallimard.

Piaget, J. (1977a) *Recherches sur l'abstraction réfléchissante, vols 1 & 2*, Paris: Presses Universitaires de France.

Piaget, J. (1977b) "Appendix B", in B. Inhelder, R. Garcia and J. Vonèche (eds) *Épistémologie génétique et équilibration*: 90–92, Neuchâtel: Delachaux et Niestlé.

Steffe, L. P. (ed. 1991) *Epistemological foundations of mathematical experience*, New York: Springer.

# Chapter 3

# Jean Piaget: the unknown sociologist?[1]

*Richard F. Kitchener*

## ABSTRACT

Piaget's sociological theory is not widely discussed among sociologists, partly because much of it is contained in untranslated French works. In this chapter I summarize several aspects of Piaget's sociological views, especially his social exchange theory, and briefly indicate its relevance to several current theories in sociology and social psychology.

Rejecting both Durkheim's sociologist holism and Tarde's individualism, Piaget advances a sociological *relativism* (relationalism) in which all social facts are reducible to social relations and these, in turn, are reducible to *rules, values,* and *signs*. Piaget's theory of social values takes the form of a social exchange theory characterized first in an abstract, logical way – its structural aspect – and second its developmental aspects. Piaget claims social exchange requires normative principles of reciprocity and that individual social development results in such an equilibrium because rationality itself is social in nature and based upon social co-operation. These views, in turn, derive from his orthogenetic view concerning the course of evolution: development can be characterized as an increase in equilibrium manifested both in individual action and in social interaction.

## INTRODUCTION

A sociologist might read a score of books on sociological theory before encountering the name of Jean Piaget. For although Jean Piaget is widely known for his theory of cognitive development, his name is not a household word among most sociologists. Textbooks on sociological theory typically do not mention his name or discuss his ideas. When Piaget is discussed, it is usually his theory of moral development and symbolic interactionism that is mentioned.[2] Several sociologists[3] are also aware that Piaget has written an influential book on structuralism[4] and must be counted as an important structuralist thinker.[5] But that Piaget himself has articulated a distinctive structuralist sociology has apparently escaped the attention of most sociologists.[6]

My aim in this paper, therefore, is twofold: (1) to point out that Piaget has written a substantial work – *Études sociologiques* – explicitly devoted to sociology and social psychology but a work virtually unknown to sociologists,[7] and (2) to articulate, in a very brief and cursory way, the major outlines of this sociological view.

## PIAGET'S *ÉTUDES SOCIOLOGIQUES*

Part of the reason Piaget's sociological views are not better known to English-speakers is the fact that his most systematic and mature views on sociology are contained in a still untranslated collection of writings on sociology – his *Études sociologiques*. The first edition (1965) of this work contains four reprinted articles[8] and an excerpt from his 1950 *magnum opus*.[9] The second edition (1977) contains several additional articles.[10] These works (together with several others)[11] form the basis of his complete sociological theory, a rich and complex theory having fundamental similarities to exchange theory,[12] to symbolic interactionism,[13] to functionalism,[14] to Habermas' theory of communicative competence,[15] and to certain versions of structuralism.[16] In addition, his theory has important implications for the sociology of science[17] with significant similarities, for example, to Merton's [18] normative approach to the sociology of science. A full-length study of Piaget's sociology would obviously have to discuss these and related issues.[19]

## SOCIOLOGICAL HOLISM VERSUS INDIVIDUALISM

### The classical debate

The historical setting of Piaget's sociological views concerned a classical sociological debate over the nature of social facts – holism vs individualism. Emile Durkheim, whose influence on Piaget can hardly be overestimated,[20] maintained a position sometimes called *sociological holism*: social facts are irreducible wholes since the (social) whole has properties none of the individual members possess. These holistic properties, which modify, influence, or constrain the individual members, emerge as a result of the individual members uniting or associating together.

> Whenever certain elements combine and thereby produce by the fact of their combination, new phenomena, it is plain that these new phenomena reside not in the original elements but in the totality formed by their union . . . If, as we may say, this synthesis constituting every society yields new phenomena, differing from those which take place in

individual consciousness, we must, indeed, admit that these facts reside exclusively in the very society itself which produces them, and not in its parts, i.e. its members. They are, then, in this sense, external to individual consciousness, considered as such, just as the distinctive characteristics of life are external to the mineral substances composing the living being. These new phenomena cannot be reduced to their elements without contradiction in terms, since by definition, they presuppose something different from the properties of these elements.[21]

Durkheim's sociological holism has a complex basis, but part of the reason he introduced such holistic entities as "the collective conscience" was his belief that the moral order provides the basis for society and that no individualistic theory, e.g. rational self-interest, could account for the origin and justification of society. Only an irreducible social theory could do this and morality had precisely this function: individuals engage in social interaction, according to Durkheim, because of super-individual norms (feelings of obligation), which guide this behavior and provide necessary sanctions. Durkheim believed the moral order, in turn, resulted from social constraint or socialization in which adults and other authorities instilled such standards into the youth. As we will see, this appeal to social constraint is fundamentally rejected by Piaget in favor of a different set of social relations – social cooperation.

Opposed to Durkheim's holism (or *sociologism*) was the *individualism* (and psychologism) of Gabriel Tarde, who denied sociological emergence and holism and claimed that society is merely an aggregate of individuals. Thus sociology was reducible to psychology, since the subject-matter of sociology is really the beliefs and desires of individuals "under the different names of dogmas, sentiment, laws, wants, customs, morals, etc."[22] "Psychology studies their interrelations in the single mind; sociology studies their relations between minds."[23] Thus sociology deals with desires and beliefs of individuals transmitted to other individuals by means of imitation, which is the central principle needed to account for such transmission of ideas.[24]

## Piaget's relationalism

Although it remains unclear whether Tarde was really a sociological individualistic or not (since he also wrote about an "inter-individual" psychology), the important point vis-à-vis Piaget is the dilemma posed by the two positions of holism vs individualism and Piaget's attempted resolution, which he calls *sociological relativism (relationalism)*. Contrary to individualism, the whole is not the simple addition of the individual properties of the members forming the whole, but neither is it (contrary to holism) an emergent (non-predictable) entity somehow existing over and above (and hence independently of) the individual parts. Rather, the social whole is the resulting addition of all the *relations* between the individual members, e.g. relations of constraint, cooperation, social role-taking, etc. Thus, if we knew all the interactions between individuals we would have *composition laws*[25] which would allow us to explain the social whole by showing how the whole is formed from individual parts as a result of these composition laws. This *relationalism* is a central feature of Piaget's sociology, psychology, and his genetic epistemology in general[26] and is drawn in opposition to Durkheim's holism and Tarde's individualism. In contemporary terms, it is the debate over "methodological individualism" and the foundations of sociology.[27] Rejecting both the view that an individualistic psychology is adequate as an account of social entities and the view that there are irreducible social wholes, Piaget offers a dialectical resolution in which inter-individual relations can explain all social entities.

## THE SOCIAL EXCHANGE OF VALUES

According to Piaget, all social facts can be reduced to interactions between individuals. Furthermore, all fundamental types of inter-individual interaction consist of either *rules, values*, or conventional *signs*; these correspond (respectively) to the cognitive, the affective and the symbolic aspects of individual behavior. Although Piaget begins his social theory with a discussion of the values of exchange, it turns out that such values (and signs) require normative rules to provide a rational foundation, just as the affective and symbolic realms require a cognitive grounding.

Values, according to Piaget, originate from the individual's interests (desires). But in interacting with other persons, who have their own values, one will come to exchange values with them. As a result, values become systematized into larger regulatory structures that tend towards a reversible equilibrium.

In the paradigm case of a social exchange of values between two individuals (A and B), there are four components: (1) an *action* performed by A towards B ($r_a$), (2) a *satisfaction* received by B as a result of this action ($s_b$), (3) a *debt* incurred by B towards A ($t_b$), and (4) the *payment* of this debt by A to B ($v_a$). Suppose, for example, that A gives a university lecture to a class. This action, we may suppose, is satisfying to a student B. This satisfaction, in turn, produces a debt on the part of B towards A, an obligation to repay A in kind. The payment of this debt might take the form of a monetary payment to A (an *actual value*), or, say, a promise to tell other students about A's class lectures (a *virtual value*). In this latter case, A can count on B to spread the word about the quality of A's lectures and this is a "valorization" of A by B. As a result, A will receive something of value from B. Although there are several important relations between these components, two equations in particular stand out – those representing states of equilibria (where $v_a = r_a$ and $s_a = v_a$). In the case where A is valued by B in proportion to the service rendered towards B, we have an equilibrium since $v_a = r_a$, i.e. if $(r_a = s_b)$ and $(s_b = t_b)$ and $(t_b = v_a)$, then $(v_a = r_a)$. In the case of virtual values, we have an equilibrium in the following case: if $(v_a = t_b)$ and $(t_b = r_b)$ and $(r_b = s_a)$, then $(s_a = v_a)$.

## Equilibrium

The social exchange of values can thus be represented by an abstract, qualitative model in which one can define an equilibrium. But the above representation is a static or synchronic way of understanding equilibrated value exchange. A much more fundamental issue concerns the question "why is this equilibrium maintained?" Why do A and B respect the equivalence? To ensure an equilibrium in which values are really conserved over time, one must bring in *norms* of obligations (rules).

One can see why the existence of norms of obligation is required if we contrast a *virtual exchange of values* (an exchange of values over time) with an *actual exchange of values*. In the case of an actual exchange of values, e.g. an exchange of goods in the open market place, there is no need for norms of obligation since everyone can immediately see, during the actual exchange of goods, what obligations have been incurred and paid. This *perceived* or *intuitive reciprocity* (as Piaget calls it), is an example of a kind of thought or intelligence he calls pre-operational, one relying exclusively on currently perceived matters of fact. Such a way of thinking can attain a certain degree of equilibrium, but it is inadequate precisely in those cases where intuitive matters of fact are not sufficient, viz. where one is reasoning about non-present, non-perceptual states of affairs. This requires a different (and higher) type of reasoning in which *rules* or *norms* of reasoning are required, e.g. concerning the transitivity of relations. Rules of reasoning are thus normative obligations binding upon the individual; such rules of reasoning ensure that values will be conserved over time and hence that equilibrium will be maintained.

Piaget is obviously drawing upon a presumed similarity here between *object constancy* and *value constancy*: in order to guarantee that objects are conserved in thought over time and maintain their identity (even when they disappear from view), certain types of mental operations of transformations are necessary. Similarly, in the case of a virtual exchange of values there is the analogous situation of *value constancy*, which requires a normative operation (a rule). In short, reasoning in general requires normative principles of inference and the most adequate one is *normative reciprocity*,[28] i.e. that norm governing all relevant points of view in which the reciprocal duties and rights of each party to the other parties are specified in an impartial and disinterested way. With normative reciprocity we have reached an ideal state of equilibrium.

If the principle of normative reciprocity is operating, "value conservation" will occur since it will coordinate the means and ends of all concerned parties from an objective and disinterested, third person point of view. Consequently, in such a situation one person can no longer treat the other person merely as a means towards one's own self-interest but also, as Kant required, as an end in itself to whom one has responsibilities even if this entails the necessity of sacrificing one's own personal interest. In normative reciprocity "both individuals evaluate things reciprocally, as a function of the other and not merely from a personal point of view".[29] Values are thus conserved over time because norms involving, say, the relation of a debt incurred to that of an obligation to repay the debt, apply with equal validity to all points of view. Normative reciprocity thus involves abandoning egoism and taking up "the disinterested or moral point of view".[30] The principle of normative reciprocity defining this moral point of view constitute norms of moral reasoning involving the exchange of values over time. A necessary condition for an equilibrated social exchange of values, therefore, is a set of moral norms that function as normative principles of inference binding on all parties. It is thus the principle of normative reciprocity that explains why the social exchange of values takes the particular ideal structural form it does.

### Intellectual exchange of ideas

One way to illustrate what Piaget has in mind here is to consider an intellectual discussion or dialogue – an intellectual exchange of ideas – which is an example of inter-individual action and a social exchange of values. If Piaget is correct, norms are required to guarantee an equilibrated intellectual discussion and to support the ethics of reasoning.

Suppose that A asserts a proposition and thereby *communicates* a judgment to B ($r_a$). Suppose B *agrees* with A and thus *attributes validity* to A's proposition ($s_b$). As a result of B's recognition of the validity of this proposition, B becomes *committed* to conserving this accord of A and B ($t_b$). Finally this results in A's *valorization*, i.e. this confers a value or validity upon A's proposition ($v_a$). Since $t_b$ in turn leads to $r_b$, which leads to $s_a$, we have: $r_a \rightarrow s_b \rightarrow t_b \rightarrow r_b \rightarrow s_a$.

What guarantees equilibrium here? According to Piaget, there are three necessary and sufficient conditions for an equilibrated exchange of intellectual values. First, A and B must possess a *common scale of values* rendering the evaluations of A comparable to the evaluations of B. This in turn involves: (a) the possession of a *language*, (b) an agreement concerning the *meaning* of terms, and (c) an agreed upon set of *criteria* (or standards of reference) relating these terms. Secondly *an equality of values* is required, an agreement about values (e.g. $r_a = s_b$), and the recognized obligation of conserving earlier agreed upon propositions. This in turn requires normative rules which Piaget terms *rules of communication*.[31] They consist of several principles: (a) the principle of *identity*, which "maintains a proposition in an invariant way during the course of further exchanges"; and (b) the principle of *contradiction* which "conserves [a proposition's] truth or its falsity without the possibility of affirming it and denying it simultaneously".[32]

Finally, the possible actualization (at any time) of the virtual values is necessary (i.e. the possibility of returning to earlier recognized validities). Here we have *reversibility* and this entails a *reciprocity* of points of view ($r_a = r_b$, $s_a = s_b$, etc.).

The upshot of this discussion, therefore, is this: the exchange of qualitative values and the exchange of intellectual values can be said to be in *equilibrium* on the condition that there is a norm obliging us to conserve these respective values. What this shows, therefore, is that morality (moral norms) and logic (logical norms) are really much closer than most people suspect and in fact are isomorphic to each other – they are two aspects of one and the same thing (a system of equilibrated operations characterized as a *grouping*).[33] Thus there is a parallelism between the intellectual exchange of values (cognition) and the affective exchange of values (ethics).

## Social exchange theory

Piaget's theory of social exchange is thus similar in certain ways to modern social exchange theory, but it is also different. The basic way in which it differs from that of Pareto[34] and Homans[35] is that it is based on a Durkheimian conception of social exchange – one based on morality – rather than on an economic model of rational self-interest or individual reward. On this point Piaget seems to be basically in agreement with Blau[36] and with Blau's distinction between economic exchange and social exchange (although Piaget would reject both Blau's *emergentism* [in favour of relationalism] and Blau's model of social exchange based on power and unilateral respect [in favor of equality and cooperation]).

Most modern social exchange theories are based upon a model of the egoistic individual trying to maximize his/her gain. Piaget rejects this conception: self-interest cannot underlie the principle of reciprocity or justice and neither can utilitarianism or classical capitalism. On the other hand Lévi-Strauss' theory of social exchange has much in common with Piaget's theory, especially with regard to the claim of Lévi-Strauss that "generalized exchange presumes equality".[37] Piaget parts company with Lévi-Strauss, however, and with Durkheim and Mauss over the issue of the relevance of psychology to social exchange theory and the issue of sociological holism versus sociological individualism. As should be apparent, Piaget's theory of social exchange is not individualistic but neither is it a version of sociological holism. Instead, it is a social exchange theory based on inter-personal relations.

A question that has not been adequately discussed concerns normative reciprocity itself, a question about its origin and development. *How do individuals come to accept such a normative principle?* As we might expect, Piaget's answer – cooperation – is formulated in response to that of Durkheim's answer – constraint. Consequently, as Piaget sees it, the issue is whether social constraint or social cooperation is a better explanation of the development of normative reciprocity. As part of Piaget's program of genetic epistemology, any answer to such a question will have to appeal to the empirical question of how individuals actually develop in their social relations. Hence we must look to the evolution and development of inter-individual social relations, for it is here that we will find the answer. Before doing so, however, one preliminary point must be made concerning a question that invariably arises in discussions about sociological holism vs. sociological individualism, namely, is rationality, logic and intelligence social or individual in nature?

## THE SOCIAL NATURE OF RATIONALITY

Piaget is often criticized for denying the importance of the social dimension and hence for having a purely "individualistic" theory of intelligence and rationality. Such a view is often ascribed to psychological versions of exchange theory. As our discussion of Piaget's relationalism should have made clear, such an interpretation is mistaken. But, on the other hand, rationality is neither a matter of sociological wholes. On the contrary, rationality consists of a set of relations between individuals of a particular kind – equilibrated relations taking the form of a logical grouping. In particular, Piaget has consistently maintained what I will call the *correspondence thesis*: the equilibrium present in inter-individual (social exchange) and that present in individual action is one and the same thing. Hence neither individual rationality nor social rationality is the correct answer to our question concerning the nature of rationality. However, the social dimension is certainly essential for the development of equilibrium. In particular, certain kinds of social relations (namely, cooperation) are necessary for the development of those equilibrated structures found in social exchange and the mature thinking of individuals.

### Role theory

Piaget has often insisted that the social is a necessary condition for the development of intelligence, knowledge, and rationality. For example social life is a necessary condition for the development of logic. We believe therefore that social life transforms the individual with regard to his very nature, changing an autistic state into one of personality.[38]

Elsewhere he says:

human knowledge is essentially collective and social life constitutes one of the essential factors in the formation and increase of pre-scientific and scientific knowledge.[39]

This claim has been defended in several of Piaget's early works[40] in which he argued, in a manner similar to that of James, Dewey, Cooley, Mead and Baldwin, that rationality and objectivity presuppose other social agents. If one were really autistic or egoistic, and thus unaware of others, one would also be unaware of oneself: *Self-consciousness presupposes the consciousness of others*. Furthermore, in the absence of self-consciousness, no objectivity would be possible, since objectivity entails the distinction between the self (the merely "subjective") and not-self (the "objective"). Being objective means, among other things, not confusing these two perspectives. This requires an awareness that what one thinks may not coincide with what is true. Lacking such a distinction, the individual will fail to recognize his/her own thought for what it is and will instead take it to be automatically real. Thus

In order to be objective, one must have become conscious of one's "I". Objective knowledge can only be conceived in relation to subjective, and a mind that was ignorant of itself would inevitably tend to put into things its own pre-notions and prejudices, whether in the domain of reasoning, of immediate judgment, or even of perception. An objective intelligence in no way escapes from this law, but, being conscious of its own "I", it will be on its guard, it will be able to hold back and criticize, in short it will be able to say what, roughly, is fact and what is interpretation.[41]

*Objectivity thus presupposes self-consciousness* and the latter, in turn, presupposes the awareness of other selves. Likewise, logic itself (along with the giving of reasons for things) depends upon the awareness of other persons, for otherwise (in the absence of other persons and divergent points of view), there would be no need to defend one's own point of view. "Only under the pressure of argument and opposition will he seek to justify himself in the eyes of others . . . "[42]

Anyone who thinks for himself exclusively and is consequently in a perceptual state of belief, i.e. of confidence in his own ideas, will naturally not trouble himself about the reasons and motives which have guided his reasoning. Only under the pressure of argument and opposition will he seek to justify himself in the eyes of others and thus acquire the habit of watching himself think, i.e. of constantly detecting the motives which are guiding him in the direction he is pursuing.[43]

Thus when forced to give reasons to someone else for what one believes, the subject develops the ability to evaluate his/her own reasons by taking up the other person's point of view and evaluating his/her own ideas from that perspective. External dialogue thus gives rise to internal dialogue. As several individuals[44] have noted, such a view is similar to that of Cooley's[45] "looking glass self" and also to Mead's[46] and Baldwin's[47] views that the self emerges through social interaction and social role-taking (although Piaget's concern here is much less with the development of the self and the notions of "me" versus "I").

There are important differences, of course, between Piaget and symbolic interactionism just as there are important similarities. For example, Piaget stresses symbolic mediation (especially language) less than individuals such as Mead do and has much in common with Cooley's more "individualistic" social psychology. But the similarities are impressive to a striking degree and perhaps warrant labelling Piaget a "symbolic interactionist".

## COGNITIVE DEVELOPMENT AND SOCIAL DEVELOPMENT

Piaget's claim that social interaction is the basis for the child's abandonment of egocentrism is well-known and underscores his point that the social is a necessary condition for the development of knowledge. But Piaget also claims that a particular type of social relation, viz. cooperation, is the particular form of social interaction necessary for the development of knowledge. In fact, *cooperation generates reason.*[48]

### Stages of social development

As is well-known, Piaget characterizes cognitive development in terms of a series of stages – sensori-motor, pre-operational, concrete-operational, and formal-operational – each of which has a certain increasingly greater degree* of equilibrium. When one has reached this final stage, one has attained a state of relatively full equilibrium in which there is a set of (reversible) operations, performed on propositions possessing the logical structure of a "grouping". According to Piaget, social development also occurs via a series of stages, which correspond to the stages of cognitive development.

During the *sensori-motor* period (0–2 years), for example, there is virtually no socialization: other people are merely the physical locus of pleasure and pain, and Piaget characterizes this stage as that of pure *individualism* or *autism*. In the second, pre-operational period (2–7 years) there is the beginning of socialization and the appearance of language, but the individual has not yet distinguished his/her own point of view from that of others, and this lack of differentiation Piaget labels *egocentrism* ("the unconscious [*inconsciente*] confusion of one's own point of view with that of others").[49] This stage of egocentrism has the same cognitive characteristics as that of pre-operational thought, which centers on the immediate appearances of things. Furthermore, in this stage the social relation of *constraint* is dominant.

During the *concrete-operational* period (7–12 years) there are significant changes: the individual distinguishes his/her own point of view from that of others, there is a co-ordination of different points of view, discussion emerges, and *cooperation* appears. For the first time, as a result of this "decentering of the subject", a truly social point of view can be said to emerge and it corresponds to the parallel cognitive stage in which concrete logic, a logic of operations, appears.

During the final period of *formal operations* (12–15 years), this logical process culminates in the abstract ability to deal with propositions. It is at this stage that socio-cultural influences become dominant and the individual increasingly assimilates his/her culture. Ignoring this latter stage, the first three stages can be characterized in terms of the stage-sequence: *autism–constraint–cooperation*.

The progress of social development thus corresponds, stage by stage, to logico-cognitive development; indeed, the individual and the social "constitute two indissolvable aspects of one and the same reality, at the same time social and individual".[50] Logical development corresponds to social development not only in terms of an isomorphism between the respective stages but also with regard to the underlying developmental dynamics involving the principle of equilibrium: there is an orthogenetic tendency towards increasing equilibrium in logic (individual equilibration) isomorphic to the orthogenetic equilibrium found in the social, moral and affective domains. The equilibrium of logical thinking, characterized by a grouping of operations, is isomorphic to the underlying logical structure of social cooperation, which can also be characterized as that of a "grouping" involving inter-individual actions. Hence "a grouping is the form common to the equilibrium of individual actions and interindividual interactions, because there are not two ways of equilibrating actions, and action on others is inseparable from acting on objects".[51]

cooperation itself consists of a system of operations of such a sort that the activities of the subject exercised on objects and on the activities of the other subject reduces in reality to one and the same integrated system (*system d'ensemble*) in which the social aspect and the logical aspect are inseparable in form as well as content.[52]

This "underlying reality" is itself a general logic (a form of equilibrium) characterizing the general coordination of actions.[53]

## "Cooperation is co-operation"

To illustrate Piaget's claim that cooperation involves a system of interactions having an equilibrated structure, consider the following example. Two individuals, on opposite banks of a river, are each building a pillar of stones across which a plank will go as a bridge.[54] If these two individuals are cooperating with each other, what is the logical structure of this cooperation? Piaget's answer is that *"cooperation is co-operation"*, i.e. each is operating in mutual accord with the other so that the actions of both parties are adjusted to each other by means of new operations. Each party is adjusting his/her own actions in relation to the actions of the other. Some of these actions are: (1) *similar* to each other and thus *correspond* to each other with regard to their common characters (e.g. each is making a pillar of the same form and in the same vertical direction). This correspondence is itself a higher-order operation performed on other actions; (2) Some actions are *reciprocal* or *symmetrical* (e.g. both parties are orienting the vertical slopes of the pillars so as to face each other and to be inclined in opposite directions). Reciprocity (like correspondence) is also an abstract operation on actions; (3) Finally, some operations may be *complementary*, e.g. one of the banks of the river is higher than the other, thus requiring a supplementary action on the part of one of the parties. (Performing the complement of something is itself an operation.) Thus not only are the two parties each individually acting in certain ways, but their actions themselves possess a certain logical structure, a series of operations – *correspondence, reciprocity, addition* or *subtraction* of complementary actions, etc. – characterized as a group or grouping of operations. It is precisely this logical form that makes cooperation equilibrated.

## The primacy of cooperation

It is a central claim of Piaget's sociological views that individual social development proceeds through a series of stages – autism – constraint – cooperation – of increasing logical and social adequacy. Thus, contrary to Durkheim, Freud and others, the social relation of *constraint* can not adequately account for the development and structure of equilibrated thinking.

*Constraint* is a form of social relations involving an authority (e.g. parents, teachers), who, by virtue of their power, enforce social agreement via some sanction. But this is inadequate as an explanation of the moral or logical order. In a relation of constraint, in which there is a unilateral relation of power, individuals are not equal. Consequently there is no reciprocity between the two points of view, nor is there reversibility. Consequently, there is no normative obligation present in constraint, only *de facto* power and coercion. (All of this is different in the case of cooperation, for here individuals are equal, there are reciprocal points of views, and reversibility is present.)

Autism and constraint are not fundamentally different, according to Piaget,[55] since both are cases of affirming a proposition or belief without proof! In autism, the individual affirms his/her own opinion, whereas in social constraint, (s)he merely affirms the authority's opinion. In both cases, therefore, there is mere affirmation of a belief without any justification. Hence, in social constraint (as in autism), there is no felt need to *prove* or *justify* one's opinion to others since (from this point of view) authorities need no backing. The need to justify one's beliefs or actions emerges only under the particular social conditions of equality – when other individuals are seen as equals and no longer as power-wielding authorities to be obeyed. It is precisely in this social context that the need for evidence arises, since with regard to truth equals have no special privileged authority.[56]

Social pressure and the sanctions of family, school and peer group cannot account for the nature of rationality and objectivity whether in matters epistemic or moral. Hence "the sociological thesis," in which sociological constraint is invoked as the explanation of why individuals are moral, is inadequate. But then so is "the individualistic thesis," according to which logic is constructed from solitary individual activities.[57] Logic does not arise merely from the activity either of isolated individuals or from social constraint, but rather from the interactions (relations) between individuals.[58]

## Habermas on communicative competence and social development

If Piaget is a social exchange theorist, he is not a typical one; indeed, as I have suggested, his model of social exchange is much closer to that of Durkheim and Mauss than it is to, say, Homans and Blau. His theory of social exchange is a rational, equilibrated one in which morality and logic (i.e. reason) prevail over egoism and self-interest. This can be seen most clearly in the case of a communicative exchange of ideas, for it is precisely in the case in which one individual A is communicating to another individual B that shows the necessity for the type of equilibrated reciprocity found in what Piaget calls "rules of communication." If there are such normative rules of communication, one can perhaps without great distortion say communication is a rational affair.

For several decades Jürgen Habermas has been charting a similar project – to lay the foundations for a theory of communicative action[59] that will provide for a theory of rationality that is, like Piaget's, both philosophically adequate and empirically grounded. Indeed, the influence of Piaget's genetic epistemology on Habermas is explicitly pervasive;[60] indeed "only the genetic structuralism worked out by Piaget, which investigates the development logic behind the process in which structures are formed, builds a bridge to historical materialism . . . it offers the possibility of bringing different modes of production under abstract developmental-logical viewpoints."[61] Piaget's genetic epistemology is thus most perspicacious as a model of the growth of rationality.[62]

Such a theory of communicative action "clarifies the normative foundations of a critical theory of society."[63] It does so (partly) by providing a "rational reconstruction"[64] of the history of social systems in "internalist" (not merely "externalist") terms,[65] by showing that certain types of societies are epistemically better than others, better in terms of their epistemic, moral and social problem-solving power.[66] Consequently one can speak of an *evolution* (or better: *development*) of societies in which one can order them linearly according to a "stage law" sequence by means of a "developmental logic."[67]

Stressing "the correspondence thesis" we earlier ascribed to Piaget, Habermas maintains that societies develop according to the developmental logic of a stage theory in a way isomorphic to the epistemic, moral and ego development of individuals. This occurs, following the stage theories of Piaget, Kohlberg and Loevinger, by means of a process of "decentration" of the individual subject, a process in which the distorting cognitions of the purely subjective and individual ego gives way to more rational and objective cognitions of the "decentered" subject. This occurs by means of a stage-series of epistemic constructions of every more abstract and universal "relational" structures in which there is an increasing normative reciprocity (operational transformation) concerning all points of view and not merely that of the subject. In such a cognitive scheme there is justice and equality instead of egoism. As Habermas puts it: "I speak of *communicative actions* when social interactions are co-ordinated not through the egocentric calculation of success of every individual but through co-operative achievement of understanding among participants."[68] Thus just as the principle of normative reciprocity (equilibrated social interaction) characterizes the development of individuals, so we can also use this same principle to rank hierarchically the various socio-economic relations of production, technology, and social structure of different social systems involving power relations and types of social integration, e.g. neolithic, early civilized and modern societies. As Piaget would put it, in such a sequence of social systems, one finds a progressive increase in the degree of equilibrium reached by each level of society and this degree of equilibrium can be partially cashed out in terms of epistemic and moral adequacy of their social problem solving potential. Hence there is not merely individual development (ontogenesis); there is also social development (sociogenesis).

Building upon the speech act theory of Austin and Searle and the "conversational pragmatics" of Grice, Habermas has attempted to construct a theory of communicative competence. His program is to develop a theory of rationality based not upon the solitary, Cartesian knower but upon the social relations of interaction – the "exchange relations" found in the act of communication. Although he explicitly disavows any attempt to ground rationality on incorrigible foundations, he does attempt to ground rationality on a quasi-transcendental basis by specifying those conditions that are necessary presuppositions for an act of communication to occur. When an individual A says something to individual B, A is making the claim that what A says is intelligible, true, justified, uttered sincerely, etc. Furthermore, A is claiming that good reasons can be provided for each of these claims. But if so, this claim presupposes universal (impersonal) criteria of evaluation.[69]

The very act of communication thus presupposes certain ideal epistemic conditions involving truth, objectivity and rationality, which correspond to correlative moral and socio-political conditions, namely, the aim of communication is a certain ideal situation in which rationality and objectivity prevail, in which there is unlimited discussion, mutual understanding, open communication free from domination and distortion, etc. But such conditions presuppose, as Piaget has maintained, a social situation of cooperation instead of domination and constraint, and this in turn presupposes equality and, we might add, democratic freedom. Communicative competence thus presupposes not only ideal standards of rationality, but also a particular kind of social and political structure – the emancipated society of Habermas' "critical social theory." We have thus come full circle, having returned to his "reconstruction of historical materialism" based, not surprisingly, upon a developmental approach. This is not to say, however, that Habermas has utilized all the relevant aspects of Piaget's theory; in fact, there is little of Piaget's particular sociological theory, especially that found in his *Études sociologiques*, that Habermas does utilize. How Habermas' theory would be modified, if Piaget's sociological theory were given serious attention, remains an interesting and intriguing question.[70]

## CONCLUSION

In summary, what has Piaget shown? First of all, that the social plays a necessary role in the development of knowledge and logic. Piaget is not an individualist: the Cartesian solitary knower, separate from social interaction with others, cannot construct an equilibrated logic. In order for an individual to be able to construct a formal logic, one must be able to give evidence (proof, justification) for what one claims. But this requires social interactions with others who force the individual to defend his/her point of view. Furthermore, the giving of reasons entails a social perspective in another way: if something is to count as a good reason for a belief or statement, universal principles are necessarily involved, principles going beyond mere egoism or individualism.

Consistent with his criticism of the inadequacy of sociological individualism, one cannot account for social facts, social relations and social institutions by assuming an individualistic model of egoistic, rational self-interest. Mere economic rationality, therefore, the economic exchange or values captured in the social equilibrium models of most exchange theorists, is inadequate as a model of rationality: since this simple economic model involving value exchange lacks underlying normative principles, one can only attain at best a partial equilibrium (a mere *regulation*) but not the more adequate and complete equilibrium of a *grouping*. Hence the pure economic model, based on profit maximization, must be abandoned in favor of a model of cooperation between equals and normative reciprocity.

If sociological individualism (elementarism) is incorrect, so is sociological holism. The collective moral order is not an emergent property, constraining and compelling the actions of individuals. Instead, moral principles (like logical ones) are principles inherent in certain kinds of social relations between individuals, those structural relations characterizing the type of operations and transformations normatively possible between individuals.

Piaget is clear about how the social exercises its influence: it does not occur by means of imitation, internalization, introjection, or socialization. As a cognitivist and constructivist, he believes that any social influence (just as any environmental influence) must be mediated via one's cognitive structures which are constructed by the individual. This cognitive construction is not arbitrary or variable, however, for the social environment imposes strong constraints upon such a construction. In a very illuminating passage Piaget sums up his views by saying

> between organic maturation, which furnishes mental potentialities but without providing a psychological structure ready-made, and social transmission, which furnishes the elements and the model of a possible construction but without imposing it as a finished product, there exists an operatory construction, which translates the potentialities offered by the nervous system into mental structures. But it effects this translation only as a function of interactions between individuals, and consequently is under the accelerative or inhibitive influence of different actual types of social interactions.[71]

Kant's critical philosophy revolved around reason. But Kant distinguished Pure Reason (Logic) and Practical Reason (Ethics) and argued that they are inextricably connected. Piaget's genetic epistemology, translated into appropriate evolutionary dress, can be seen as making essentially this same point. For following nineteenth-century evolutionary thinkers such as Spencer and Comte, Piaget believes the course of development (in all spheres) can be characterized by a principle of *orthogenesis* – a tendency towards increasing equilibrium (progress). Such a principle is both rational and good. There are, however, two forms of this equilibrium: Logic (Pure Reason) and Ethics (Practical Reason). These are two forms of one and the same underlying principle of rationality (equilibrium). One can thus see Piaget's overall program as a type of evolutionary Kantianism (or better: Hegelianism). As such it is rooted in the Enlightenment tradition of freedom, rationality and progress. This principle of increasing equilibrium (orthogenesis) constitutes the source of his particular views on sociology.

There is much to criticize in such a sociological theory but before such criticism can be made, it is necessary to first understand what this sociological theory is. Although several individuals have claimed Piaget has no sociological views or "underestimates the social," I believe their claims are wrong (or certainly exaggerated). Indeed, most of them are simply unaware that Piaget even has a richly worked out (but unknown) sociology. I have attempted to sketch the views of "Piaget, the unknown sociologist," and to show why such views might be worth studying.

[*Editor's note*: Since this paper was written, *Études sociologiques* has been published in English as *Sociological Studies*, London, Routledge, 1995.]

## NOTES

1  I wish to thank the assessors of *The British Journal of Sociology* for their helpful suggestions concerning an earlier version of this manuscript.
2  For example, D. Martindale, *The Nature and Types of Sociological Theory*, Boston: Houghton Mifflin, 1960, pp. 64–369, does mention Piaget as a symbolic interactionist. In the monumental *Theories of Society: Foundations of Modern Sociological Theory* (Parsons *et al.* (eds), New York: Free Press, 1961), there are occasional references (K. Naegeli, "Some Observations on the Scope of Sociological Analysis," pp. 3–29; J. R. Pitts, "Introduction," pp. 685–716; J. R. Pitts, "Process of Socialization," pp. 821–22) to Piaget's *The Moral Judgment of the Child*, trans. M. Gabain, New York: Free Press, 1965 [originally published 1932] along with two excerpts from his early works.
3  T. Bottomore, "Structure and History," in Blau, *Approaches to the Study of Social Structure*, New York: Columbia University Press, 1975, pp. 159–71; F. E. Katz, "Structural Autonomy and the Dynamics of Social Systems," in Rossi, *Structural Sociology*, New York: Columbia University Press, 1982, pp. 99–121; R. Merton, "Structural Analysis in Sociology," in Blau, *Approaches to the Study of Social Structure*, New York: Columbia University Press, 1975, pp. 21–52; I. Rossi, "Relational Structuralism as an Alternative to the Structural and Interpretative Paradigm of Empiricist Orientation," in Rossi, *Structural Sociology*, New York: Columbia University Press, 1982, pp. 3–21; I. Rossi, *From the*

Sociology of Symbols to the Sociology of Signs: Toward a Dialectical Sociology, New York: Columbia University Press, 1983.

4 Jean Piaget, *Structuralism*, trans. C. Maschler, New York: Harper, 1971 (originally published 1968).

5 Although Rossi ("Relational Structuralism as an Alternative to the Structural Interpretative Paradigm of Empiricist Orientation") is concerned to distinguish a "relational structuralism" from other types of structuralism, and although he is certainly correct that Piaget is a relational structuralist, it remains somewhat unclear precisely what this relational structuralism is. I have tried to clarify this in my "Holistic Structuralism, Elementarism, and Piaget's Theory of Relationalism," *Human Development*, vol. 28, 1985, pp. 281–94.

6 T. Bottomore and R. Nisbet, "Structuralism," in Bottomore and Nisbet, *A History of Sociological Analysis*, New York: Basic Books, 1978, pp. 557–98, recognize the importance of Piaget's structuralist sociology and cite his *Études sociologiques*, Geneva: Droz, 1965. Unfortunately, they do not discuss it in any detail.

7 It is also unknown to most social psychologists and developmental psychologists. See my "Piaget's Social Psychology," *Human Development*, vol. 11, 1981, pp. 253–78.

8 J. Piaget, "Essai sur la théorie des valeurs qualitatives en sociologie statique," *Publication de la Faculté des sciences économiques et sociales de l'Université de Genève*, Geneva: Georg, 1941; "Les relations entre la morale et la droite," *Publications de la Faculté des sciences économiques et sociales de l'Université de Genève*, Geneva: Georg, 1944; "Les opérations logiques et la vie sociale," *Publications de la Faculté des sciences économiques et sociales de l'Université de Genève*, Geneva: Georg, 1945; "Pensée egocentrique et pensée sociocentrique," *Cahiers internationaux de sociologie*, vol. 10, 1951, pp. 34–49.

9 J. Piaget, *Introduction à l'épistémologie génétique, Vol. III: La Pensée biologique, la pensée psychologique et la pensée sociologique*, Paris: Presses Universitaires de France, 1950.

10 J. Piaget, "Logique génétique et sociologie," *Revue philosophique*, vol. 57, 1928, pp. 167–205; "L'individualité en histoire," in *L'individualité 3$^{me}$ semaine internationale de Synthèse*, Paris: Alcan, 1933; "Le développement chez l'enfant de l'idée de partie et des relations avec l'étranger," *Bulletin Internationaux des sciences sociales* (Paris: UNESCO), vol. 3, 1951, pp. 605–21; "Problèmes de la psycho-sociologie de l'enfance," in Gurvitch, *Traité de sociologie*, vol. 2, Paris: Presses Universitaires de France, 1960.

11 J. Piaget, *The Language and Thought of the Child*, trans. M. Gabain, New York: Meridan Books, 1955 (originally published 1923); *Judgment and Reasoning in the Child*, trans. M. Warden, Totowa, N.J.: Littlefield, Adams & Co., 1959 (originally published 1924); *The Child's Conception of the World*, trans. J. R. A. Tomlinson, Totowa, N.J.: Littlefield & Adams, 1969 (originally published 1926); *The Moral Judgment of the Child; Les relations entre l'affectivité et l'intelligence dans le développement mental de l'enfant*, Paris: Centre de Documentation Universitaire, 1954; *Comments on Vygotsky's Critical Remarks Concerning the Language and Thought of the Child and Judgement and Reasoning in the Child*, Cambridge: MIT Press, 1962.

12 P. M. Blau, *Exchange and Power in Social Life*, New York: Wiley, 1964; E. Foa and U. Foa, *Societal Structures of the Mind*, Springfield, IL: C. C. Thomas, 1974; G. C. Homans, *Social Behavior: its Elementary Forms*, New York: Harcourt, Brace & World, 1961; C. Lévi-Strauss, *The Elementary Forms of Kinship*, Boston: Beacon, 1969 (originally published 1949); M. Mauss, *The*

*Gift*, trans. I. Cunnison, New York: Free Press, 1954 (originally published 1925); J. W. Thibaut and H. H. Kelley, *The Social Psychology of Groups*, New York: John Wiley, 1959. For the most part, writers on exchange theory (J. K. Chadwick-Jones, *Social Exchange Theory*, London: Academic, 1976; P. P. Ekeh, *Social Exchange Theory*, Cambridge: Harvard University Press, 1974; A. Heath, *Rational Choice and Social Exchange*, Cambridge: Cambridge University Press, 1976; M. J. Mulkay, *Functionalism, Exchange and Theoretical Strategy*, London: Routledge & Kegan Paul, 1971) are unaware of Piaget's theory of exchange. For one of the few discussions of Piaget and certain aspects of exchange theory see P. Moessinger, "Piaget et Homans, même Balance?," *Canadian Psychological Review*, vol. 19, 1978, pp. 291–5 and "Interpersonal Comparisons in Piaget's Interpersonal Equilibrium," *Canadian Journal of Behavioral Science*, vol. 11, 1979, pp. 153–9.

13 G. H. Mead, *Mind, Self and Society*, Chicago: University of Chicago Press, 1934; C. H. Cooley, *Human Nature and the Social Order*, New York: Scribner, 1902.

14 R. Merton, *Social Theory and Social Structure*, New York: Free Press, 1968; T. Parsons, *The Social System*, Glencoe, IL: Free Press, 1951 and *Societies: Evolutionary and Comparative*, Englewood Cliffs, N.J., Prentice-Hall, 1966. For a comparison of Piaget and Parsons, see C. W. Lidz and V. M. Lidz, "Piaget's Psychology of Intelligence and the Theory of Action," in Loubser *et al., Explorations in General Theory in Social Science: Essays in Honor of Talcott Parsons*, New York: Free Press, 1976, pp. 195–239.

15 Habermas, *The Theory of Communicative Action, Vol. 1: Reason and the Rationalization of Society*, trans. T. McCarthy, Boston: Beacon Press, 1984 (originally published 1981); *The Theory of Communicative Action, Vol. 2: Life World and System: a Critique of Functionalistic Reason*, trans. T. McCarthy, Boston: Beacon Press, 1987 (originally published 1981).

16 E. Durkheim, *The Division of Labor in Society*, New York: Free Press, 1947 (originally published 1893); Lévi-Strauss, *The Elementary Forms of Kinship*. For a discussion of Piaget and structuralism see H. Gardner, *The Quest for Mind: Piaget, Lévi-Strauss, and the Structuralist Movement*, New York: Random House, 1974; Rossi, *op. cit.*

17 R. F. Kitchener, "Genetic Epistemology and the Prospects for a Cognitive Sociology of Science; a Critical Synthesis," *Social Epistemology*, vol. 3, 1989, pp. 153–69.

18 R. Merton, *The Sociology of Science: Theoretical and Empirical Investigations*, Chicago: University of Chicago Press, 1973, pp. 254–80.

19 I know of no such study. I am currently working on such a project, tentatively entitled: *Genetic Epistemology and the Social Foundations of Knowledge*.

20 In his "Autobiography" (in Boring *et al., A History of Psychology in Autobiography*, vol. IV, Worcester, Mass.: Clark University Press, 1952, pp. 237–56) Piaget explicitly acknowledges the important influence not only of Durkheim but also of Comte, Spencer and Tarde. To this list surely must be added Marx and Pareto. There are no current works that adequately discuss the strong similarities between Durkheim and Piaget and the important role Durkheim played in Piaget's development. The theme common to both is Kantianism – the sociological version of Durkheim vs. the psychological version of Piaget (see my *Piaget's Theory of Knowledge: Genetic Epistemology and Scientific Reason*, New Haven, CT: Yale University Press, 1986). In particular two similar themes stand out: the attempt to explain the origin of

Kant's categories and the attempt to estabish Kant's principles of morality on scientific grounds.

21 E. Durkheim, *The Rules of Sociological Method*, New York: Free Press, 1938, pp. xlvii, xlv, xliv (originally published 1895).

22 G. Tarde, *The Laws of Imitation*, trans. E. C. Parsons, New York: Holt, 1933, p. 28 (originally published 1890).

23 Martindale, *op. cit.*, p. 306.

24 Tarde's notion of imitation strongly influenced Piaget (*Plays, Dreams and Imitation in Childhood*, trans. C. Gattegno and F. M. Hodgson, New York: W. W. Norton, 1962 [originally published 1946]).

25 Piaget, *Structuralism, op. cit.*

26 I have discussed this further in "Holism and the Organismic Model," *Human Development*, vol. 25, 1982, pp. 233–49 and "Holistic Structuralism, Elementarism and Piaget's Theory of Relationalism."

27 For a collection of articles on this debate see John O'Neill (ed.), *Modes of Individualism and Collectivism*, London: Heinemann, 1973.

28 On normative reciprocity in general see Alvin W. Gouldner, "The Norm of Reciprocity," *American Sociological Review*, vol. 25, 1960, pp. 161–78: Lévi-Strauss, *op. cit.*, Mauss, *op. cit.*

29 Piaget, "Essai sur la théorie des valeurs qualitatives en sociologie statique," *op. cit.*, p. 123.

30 For this concept see K. Baier, *The Moral Point of View*, Ithaca: Cornell University Press, 1958.

31 *Introduction à l'épistémologie génétique, op. cit.*, p. 270.

32 *Ibid.*

33 A "group" is a set of the operations – closure, association, inversion, and identity – performed on elements. A "grouping" has the additional operation of tautology.

34 V. Pareto, *The Mind and Society*, New York: Harcourt, Brace & Co., 1935 (originally published 1916).

35 *Op. cit.*

36 P. M. Blau, "A Theory of Social Integration," *American Journal of Sociology*, vol. 65, 1960, pp. 545–56; *Exchange and Power in Social Life*; "Interaction: Social Exchange," in Sills, *International Encyclopedia of the Social Sciences*, vol. 7, New York: Macmillan, 1968.

37 *Op. cit.*, p. 266.

38 "Logique génétique et sociologie," *op. cit.*, p. 204.

39 *Introduction à l'épistémologie génétique, op. cit.*, p. 187.

40 *The Language and Thought of the Child*; *Judgment and Reasoning in the Child*; *The Moral Judgment of the Child*; *The Child's Conception of the World*; *The Construction of Reality in the Child*, trans. M. Cook, New York: Ballatine, 1971 (originally published 1937).

41 *The Child's Conception of Physical Causality*, trans. M. Gabain, Totowa, NJ: Littlefield, Adams & Co., 1969, pp. 241–42 (originally published 1927).

42 *Judgment and Reasoning in the Child*, p. 137.

43 *Ibid.*

44 H. E. Barnes and H. Becker, *Social Thought from Lore to Science*, vol. 2, New York: Heath, 1938; M. Deutsch and R. M. Krauss, *Theories of Social Psychology*; T. M. Kando, *Social Interaction*, St. Louis, MO: C. V. Mosb, 1977; Martindale, *The Nature and Types of Sociological Theory*.

45 *Op. cit.*

46 *Mind, Self and Society*.

47  J. M. Baldwin, *Social and Ethical Interpretations in Mental Development*, New York: Macmillan, 1897.
48  "Logique génétique et sociologie," *op. cit.*, p. 191.
49  "Pensée egocentrique et pensée sociocentrique," *op. cit.*, p. 39.
50  "Les opérations logiques et la vie sociale," *op. cit.*, p. 158.
51  J. Piaget, *Introduction à l'épistémologie génétique, op. cit.*, p. 265.
52  *Ibid.*, p. 264.
53  "Les opérations logiques et la vie sociale," *op. cit.*, p. 170; *Introduction à l'épistémologie génétique, op. cit.*, p. 204; "Problèmes de la psycho-sociologie de l'enfance," *op. cit.*, p. 234.
54  *Introduction à l'épistémologie génétique, op. cit.*, p. 263.
55  "Logique génétique et sociologie," *op. cit.*, p. 191.
56  *Ibid.*, pp. 195–7.
57  "Les opérations logiques et la vie sociale,' *op. cit.*, p. 159.
58  "Problèmes de la psycho-sociologie de l'enfance," *op. cit.*, p. 234.
59  *Op. cit.*
60  Although this is widely known, few individuals have discussed this influence. See, however, Michael Schmid, "Habermas' Theory of Social Evolution," in Thompson and Held, *Habermas: Critical Debates*, Cambridge, MA: MIT Press, 1982, pp. 162–80, and Anthony Giddens, "Reason without Revolution? Habermas' *Theorie des kommunikativen. Handelns*," in Bernstein, *Habermas and Modernity*, Cambridge, MA: MIT Press, 1985, pp. 95–121. I am not aware of any full-length discussion of Habermas and Piaget.
61  Habermas, "Toward a Reconstruction of Historical Materialism," in his *Communication and the Evolution of Society*, Boston: Beacon, 1979, p. 169.
62  In addition to Piaget's general developmental theory, Habermas consistently cites the important work of Lawrence Kohlberg (e.g. "From Is to Ought," in Mischel, *Cognitive Development and Epistemology*," New York: Academic, 1973, pp. 151–26), Jane Loevinger (e.g. "The Meaning and Measurement of Ego Development," *American Psychologist*, vol. 21, 1966, pp. 195–206), and Erik Erikson (e.g. *Childhood and Society*, New York: W. W. Norton, 1963) as providing supplementary developmental theorizing for an adequate philosophical account of moral development and ego development. It is the work of these latter thinkers, however, rather than the distinctive sociological theory of Piaget that Habermas seems to have appropriated. Indeed, besides an occasional passing reference to Piaget's theory of moral development and the latter's early work, I have found no explicit reference to Piaget's *Études sociologiques*.
63  Habermas, *The Theory of Communicative Action, Vol. 1: Reason and the Rationalization of Society, op. cit.*, pp. 396–7.
64  For a discussion of "rational reconstruction" in the context of developmental theories see my "Developmental Explanations," *Review of Metaphysics*, vol. 36, 1983, pp. 791–818.
65  On "internalist" vs. "externalist" history of science in the context of Piaget's theory, see my *Piaget's Theory of Knowledge*, ch. 7.
66  On similar attempts to use problem solving power to show progress in the history of science, see I. Lakatos, *Philosophical Papers*, vol. 1, Cambridge: Cambridge University Press, 1980, pp. 8–101, and Lawrence Laudan, *Progress and its Problems*, Berkeley: University of California Press, 1978.
67  See J. Habermas, "Moral Development and Ego Identity," "Historical Materialism and the Development of Normative Structures," and "Toward a Reconstruction of Historical Materialism," in his *Communication and the Evolution of Society*, Boston: Beacon Press, 1979, pp. 69–94, 95–129, 130–77 respec-

tively; "Können komplexe Gesellschaften eine vernünftige Identität ausbilden?," "Zum Theorienvergleich in der Soziologie: am Beispiel der Theorie der sozialen Evolutionstheorie," and "Geschichte und Evolution," in his *Zür Rekonstruktion des Historischen Materialismus*, Frankfurt: Suhrkamp, 1976, pp. 92–118, 129–43, and 200–59 respectively; "Stichworte zür einer Theorie der Sozialisation," "Notizen zum Begriff der Rollenkompetenz," in his *Kultur und Kritik*, Frankfurt: Suhrkamp, 1973, pp. 118–94, 195–231 respectively; and "Einleitung," in Döbert, Habermas and Nunner-Winkler, *Die Entwicklung des Ichs*, Köln: Keipenheuer & Wirsch, 1977, pp. 9–30.

68 "A reply to My Critics," in Thompson and Held, *Habermas: Critical Debates*, Cambridge, MA: MIT Press, 1982, p. 264. Cf., his remarks ("Moral Development and Ego Identity", p. 88): "I shall proceed on the assumption that 'moral consciousness' signifies the ability to make use of interactive competence for *consciously* processing morally relevant conflicts of action . . . the consensual resolution of an action conflict requires a viewpoint that is open to consensus, with the aid of which a transitive ordering of the conflicting interests can be established. But competent agents will . . . be in agreement about such a fundamental point of view only if it arises from the very structures of possible interaction. The reciprocity between acting subjects is such a point of view. In communicative action a relationship of at least incomplete reciprocity is established with the interpersonal relation between the involved parties. Two persons stand in an incompletely reciprocal relation insofar as one may do or expect x only to the extent that the other may do or express y (e.g. teacher/pupil, parent/child). Their relationship is completely reciprocal if both may do or expect the same thing in compatible situations (x = y) (e.g. the norms of civil law) . . . [The expression "normative reciprocity"] is not entirely apt, since reciprocity is not a norm but is fixed in the general structures of possible interaction. Thus the point of view of reciprocity belongs *eo ipso* to the interactive knowledge of speaking and acting subjects.

69 Cf. his remarks ("What is Universal Pragmatics?," *op. cit.*, pp. 2–3): " . . . anyone acting communicatively must, in performing any speech action, raise universal validity claims and suppose that they can be vindicated [or redeemed: *einlösen*]. Insofar as he wants to participate in a process of reaching understanding, he cannot avoid raising the following – and indeed precisely the following – validity claims. He claims to be:

a  *Uttering* something understandably;
b  Giving [the hearer] *something* to understand;
c  Making *himself* thereby understandable; and
d  Coming to an understanding *with another person*.

The speaker must choose a comprehensible (*verständlich*) expression so that speaker and hearer can understand one another. The speaker must have the intention to communicate a true (*wahr*) proposition (or a propositional content, the existential presuppositions of which are satisfied) so that the hearer can share the knowledge of the speaker. The speaker must want to express his intentions truthfully (*wahrhaftig*) so that the hearer can believe the utterance of the speaker (can trust him). Finally, the speaker must choose an utterance that is right (*richtig*) so that the hearer can accept the utterance and speaker and hearer can agree with another in the utterance with respect to a recognized normative background. Moreover, communicative action can continue undisturbed only as long as participants suppose the validity claims they reciprocally raise are justified.

The goal of coming to an understanding (*Verständigung*) is to bring about an agreement (*Einverständnis*) that terminates in the intersubjective mutuality of reciprocal understanding, shared knowledge, mutual trust, and accord with one another. Agreement is based on recognition of the corresponding validity claims of comprehensibility, truth, truthfulness, and rightness."

70  In *The Theory of Communicative Action, Vol. 1: Reason and the Rationalization of Society*, pp. 101, 409 (footnote) Habermas begins to address the issue of the connection between Piaget's "exchange theory" and his theory of communicative competence by distinguishing purposive action in general from communicative action. But these remarks remain sketchy at best and call out for explication.

71  *Introduction à l'épistémologie génétique, op. cit.,* p. 197.

# Chapter 4

# Values, knowledge, and Piaget[1]

*Terrance Brown*

Piaget was both passionate and ambivalent about values throughout his career. In his earliest works, he often seemed concerned with little else. Not only are there poems of tender feeling concerning the beauty of the first snow in winter and the wish to lead a lover to summits above the human plane, but there is also, in *La Mission de l'Idée*, a plaint against the poverty of the real (Vidal 1994). A bit later, in an autobiographical novel written as his adolescence ended, Piaget (1918) appeared to be more enthusiastic about reality when he resolved to create a biological theory of Good and Evil. Fifteen or so years later, this project developed scientific teeth with the publication of *The Moral Judgment of the Child* (1932/1965), a pioneering study from which much of the modern research on moral development derives, and it was still fitfully alive in the early 1950s when Piaget published a study on patriotic feeling (Piaget 1951/1976) and gave his lectures on *Intelligence and Affectivity* (Piaget 1953–1954/ 1981). As time went on, however, Piaget's focus underwent a subtle shift. Where once he had believed that Good and Evil were universal, objective, and capable of being known, he came to believe that all values except logicomathematical necessity and empirical truth are subjective, diverse, and difficult to study. Where once he imagined that evaluation led to higher forms of knowledge, he came gradually to the conclusion that evaluation, while preliminary to all knowledge construction, can neither lead to nor modify knowledge in any way (Piaget 1953–1954/1981, 1965/1971, 1966). In the end, Piaget no longer expressed interest in subjective forms of value and, in one of his rare self-contradictions, even attempted to displace the problem onto another discipline, i.e. neurology (Bringuier 1977/1980).

Despite his apparent change of mind, one can find in Piaget's ever more negative and restrictive statements about the role and the importance of values many of the elements needed to formulate a naturalistic theory of evaluation. The reason, in my view, that Piaget's grudging, nascent theory was never fully realized was because he did not achieve for evaluative phenomena what he achieved for sensation and motricity: an accurate functional analysis.

Reviewing the written record, it becomes apparent that Piaget argued the question of values in two incompatible ways. On the one hand, he argued that subjective values are a method of philosophy used to tackle complex problems unamenable to exact solution, in which case they produce, at best, possible rather than true positions. On the other hand, he argued that subjective values are the product of the affective system and, as such, determine the content of motivation without playing any role in constructing even approximate solutions. Because the first of these arguments itself contains an ambiguity, the trouble does not end there. As a philosophical method, subjective values are both a means of knowledge and, in certain cases, a content of it. As a means of knowledge, the fact that individual knowers have different subjective values leads to disagreement and, therefore, to beliefs that do not qualify as knowledge. As a content of knowledge, when other subjects are taken as the "object" of knowledge, their subjective values must be evaluated objectively.

Piaget tried to get around these difficulties by saying that, while psychologists might have to deal with subjective values or even "lived experience", epistemologists do not. By properly delimiting problems, they need consider two things only: (1) the "epistemic subject" from whom all values except objective values have been abstracted, and (2) how scientific thought "proceeds from a state of less knowledge to a state of knowledge judged superior" (Piaget 1950, p. 18). I wonder, however, whether it is as easy as all that. While it would be illegitimate to question Piaget's personal disinterest in people's lived experience (Piaget 1968/1970), it is not illegitimate to ask whether his conception of the epistemic subject is adequate for a theory of knowledge. By his own admission, subjective values play a role in discovery. Are they, therefore, as indispensable as Piaget believed?

What is regrettable about all of this is that Piaget was so close to solving the riddle of why people have feelings. Had he been truer to himself, he would have realized that the answer to that question lies, as he had shown in the case of intelligence and knowledge, in biology taken in the sense of natural history, in the sense of Darwin. Had he stuck with his original inspiration, he would have created a natural place for values within the theoretical edifice he had erected. That edifice, after all, had its foundations in the functional analogies between organic and psychosocial evolution. But Piaget was, in the case of values, motivation, and affectivity, frightened off by the legacy of his history: by his parents' personalities, by the chaos of the First World War, by his adolescent abhorrence of uncertainty, by his disappointment with philosophy, and, significantly, by his distrust of Charles Darwin (Brown 1980). In the end, his own subjective feelings, his own affective evaluations led, as he himself might have predicted, to a theory of knowledge that is impoverished and distorted. In what follows, I argue that that would not have had to be the case.

## A PIAGETIAN CONCEPTION OF VALUES AND EVALUATION

Selecting and reorganizing Piaget's various assertions concerning values (Piaget 1950, pp. 14–15; Piaget 1965/1971, pp. 11–12; Piaget 1953–1954/ 1981; Piaget 1967/1995, pp. 97–133), one arrives at the list that follows.

1 Evaluation in terms of subjective criteria is a method of philosophy, i.e. the reflective analysis preliminary to all knowledge construction.
2 Evaluation is a function of the affective system. Awareness of evaluative activities comes in the form of feelings. Values can be studied in terms of tastes, preferences, interests, choices, decisions, judgments, motivations, and feelings.
3 Infants are provided with a system of values by biological evolution. These are the rudimentary forms out of which all other values are constructed.
4 Value structures result from the intellectualization of values and constitute a form of knowledge.
5 There are both subjective and objective values; logical necessity and truth are objective values.
6 Subjective evaluation is heuristic in nature.
7 Subjective values are both intra and interpersonally diverse and lead to conflicts.
8 Values are domain-specific, e.g. there are intellectual values, values regulating social exchanges, etc.
9 Values are somehow related to motivation, bound up with personality, and central to interpersonal exchanges.

Good as far as it goes, Piaget's list remains descriptive rather than explanatory for the simple reason that, even reordered in this way, it lacks any feeling of necessity. This is quite surprising from a man who insisted throughout a very long career that the empiricist renunciation of causality was wrong. The essence of explanation, according to Piaget, was that it lent necessity to compositions of events that at the descriptive level remained contingent (Piaget 1963/1968; 1971/1974). And more surprising still is the fact that he himself had pioneered an approach that could have given his description of values and affectivity the very feeling of necessity it lacks. But, as I said before, Piaget seemed unwilling to do for values and evaluation what he did for knowledge. He was unwilling to draw functional analogies between mental and biological functioning insofar as values were concerned. For that reason, they were not fully and consistently integrated into his conception of intelligence but remained sequestra on the fringes of cognition. My task, then, in creating an explanatory theory of values is to frame Piaget's description of evaluative phenomena within his own interpretive framework.

## The hierarchy of teleonomic frameworks

Stated in the simplest terms, Piaget's theory distorts the evolution of knowledge because he could not free himself from the morphism with biology as far as selection was concerned. In consequence, he did not grasp how, when problems are enormously complicated, as most adaptive problems are, people make adaptive choices. One way they choose, according to Piaget, is by matching the results with the goals of thought or action. Another way they choose is by assessing the consistency of new possibilities with what is already believed or known. The first of these methods can assure adaptation only insofar as the goal itself is adaptative. Piaget never examined how the adaptivity of goals is determined. Because he never dealt with that issue straight-on, he ends up making the somewhat paradoxical claim that intention (goal-corrected action) is the criterion of intelligence but that goals are selected after-the-fact and never are intelligent. For goal selection to be intelligent would require that adaptation be anticipated, something unknown in biological evolution.

Piaget was able to sustain his belief that selection in terms of success or coherence might be possible because, in line with his principles of "impoverishment" and "renunciation" (Piaget 1950, pp. 14–15), he bracketed motivational issues and limited his investigations to the solution of rather simple problems, e.g. how to judge equivalence of volume when liquid is poured from one container to another. For such problems, once the goal is accepted by the subject, objective evaluation of means in terms of progress toward that goal or coherence with what is already known seems possible (although careful scrutiny of children's problem-solving procedures even casts doubt upon that intuition (Blanchet 1986)). But most of the problems human beings face are not so simple. Consider, for example, the decision hierarchy facing a college student sitting on the edge of the bed each morning: Is life worth living? If so, how should I live it? What sort of person do I want to be? Do I really want to be a teacher? Should I marry Sally? Do I want kids? How many? How would I raise them? What should I have for breakfast? Did Brown really mean what he said about values? Should I change my major? Is that Webern? People call that beautiful? What should I do today? Should I call my mother? Can I pay this bill? When should I leave for class? Where are my bus tokens? Where are my shoes?

On the one hand, this list can be viewed from the motivational point of view: why did the student ask these and not other questions? On the other it can be viewed from the point of view of the great differences in scale involved and the attendant differences in complexity of the decisions required. For any theory of knowledge to be complete, both perspectives must be considered. Insofar as Piaget dealt with the first perspective at all, he did so at the very end of *Possibility and Necessity* (Piaget 1981/1987, 1983/1987) where he reframes the basic motivational idea inherent in his theory of equilibration (Piaget 1975/1985) in terms of presentative and procedural systems. Although this final formulation remains subject to the objections raised above, it does indicate that Piaget's attempts to understand possibility and necessity forced him to readmit the psychological subject in both its statistical and "lived experience" forms back into his epistemological theory.

From the perspective of the widely varying complexity of adaptive problems, one sees that the questions at the beginning of the student's list have, at least as long as human history has been recorded, eluded rigorous response, while the questions at the lower levels are answered rather easily. In other words, Piaget's idea that problems can be solved in terms of success or coherence applies only at the lower levels of this hierarchy. At the upper levels, decisions cannot be made on the basis of Piaget's selective criteria and the selection of means proceeds, as does selection of the goals themselves, on the basis of subjective evaluative criteria. It is at this point that a theory of affectivity enters.

## Affectivity as a system of evaluative heuristics

In a prophetic but neglected book, *The Biological Origins of Human Values*, Pugh (1977) demonstrated why rigorously logical decisions are impossible in most of the situations adapting organisms face and why, therefore, accounts of human intelligence cannot be based on logical rationality alone. Instead, Pugh argued, intelligence is a "value-directed" system, a key feature of which is the use of heuristics for estimating adaptive value and *selecting* among possibilities of action or thought. In mathematics, heuristics have been employed in conceptualized form for centuries; in intuitive form, they have been around forever. They have also played a central role in artificial intelligence since its inception. So the idea that intelligence makes use of heuristics is nothing new. What was original about Pugh's hypothesis was that he attributed the heuristics at the core of human intelligence to the affective system. Rather than suggesting, as Piaget had done, that affectivity has to do with the energetics of behavior without influence on its structure, Pugh posited that, in fact, affectivity provides a method for inventing provisional or "good-enough" knowledge structures. Further, Pugh interpreted feelings as the conscious manifestation of evaluative activity and demonstrated that the affective heuristics needed to solve complex problems are multiple, particular to various levels of the goal–subgoal hierarchy, specific to different tasks, and often contradictory. He provided a provisional classification of the types of values needed to engineer intelligence and struggled with the problem of how value conflicts are resolved. Although he appreciated that a developmental theory was necessary both for constructing the knowledge base that value-governed systems employ and for developing what he called "secondary" values, he did not provide one.[2]

### Pugh and Piaget

Making reasonable allowance for differences in lexicon, Piaget's and Pugh's descriptions of evaluative phenomena virtually converge. Piaget in his better moments and Pugh consistently saw affective evaluation as a heuristic method used in solving complex problems; both recognized that feeling was the way in which the results of evaluative activity appear in consciousness; both acknowledged that feelings vary in intensity; both agreed that values are diverse, conflictual, and domain specific; both believed that certain values are inborn and that other values develop from these rudimentary affects. But Pugh was less anxious and less pessimistic than Piaget. Up until *Possibility and Necessity*, Piaget focused on the incertitude and chaos of subjective values and saw them as an obstacle to be surmounted in the march toward objectivity. Although he finally granted them positive value, he continued to conflate evaluative and energetic functions. In contrast, Pugh focused on the speed and efficiency of values and saw them as an important tool in creating probability that might eventually lead to objectivity and certainty. Obviously, Piaget's and Pugh's interpretations differed in a fundamental way. It is instructive to examine how.

Neither in his theory of equilibration nor in his notion of procedural schemes did Piaget conceive affectivity as the functional analogue of selection in biological evolution. In clearer moments, he saw that feelings were an expression of values and assigned affectivity the role of deciding which assimilations would be performed. In murkier moments, he conflated, as many theorists of emotion still do, the evaluative-motivational role of affectivity with the energizing role of arousal. This confusion is evident in his unfortunate metaphor: "affectivity would play the role of an energy source on which the functioning but not the structures of intelligence would depend. It would be like gasoline, which activates the motor of an automobile but does not modify its structure" (Piaget 1953–1954/ 1981, p. 5).

The great shortcoming of Piaget's functional analysis of affectivity is that it does not appreciate the need for a surrogate selective system that makes use of subjective values and that occupies an intermediary position between biological and rational selection. He only admits psychological selection of the latter type in which evaluation is accomplished "objectively" either by success and consistency with existing schemes (procedural selection) or by necessity and truth (presentative or operatory selection). Moreover, Piaget did not consider rational selective criteria to be affects (although he always spoke of the feeling or "*sentiment*" of necessity). For him, the *objective* qualities of necessity and truth were simply the psychological realization of the functional stability that explains survival. It was an important part of his explanation of why reality and knowledge structures correspond.

For his part, Pugh realized that affects fulfill the selective function in mental evolution and recognized that truth and necessity are feelings. He also observed, correctly, that the latter are rather rare commodities, that one does not jump from ignorance to certainty in one fell swoop, and that it is not possible to reproduce adaptive functions psychologically in the direct way that Piaget imagined. In biology, manifold new possibilities are created at the time of reproduction, but it takes lifetimes or even generations to play out their full effects and determine their ultimate value in reproductive or survival terms. If the whole functional idea of intelligence is to speed up evolution, direct analogues of biological selection like necessity and truth, which also take enormous amounts of time, can play only a limited part in psychological creation. For that reason, Pugh interposed a heuristic selective system between biological selection and "exact" or "rigorous" or "real" psychological selection. He envisioned affectivity as an elaborate system of surrogates for adaptive value that is used to approximate solutions to complex adaptive problems. Although he agreed that values play a role in motivation, he did not believe that affectivity's role was simply to fuel the structures of intelligence as they grind out exact solutions. For Pugh, affectivity was not energy. It was structure; it was knowledge; it was an instrument of intelligence; it was a system of tricks and ruses that intelligence uses to discover partial or provisional equilibria, to create structures that will work until truth and necessity are found.

All of this leads to a curious situation. On the one hand, Piaget created a theory of how empirical and formal knowledge develop, while Pugh greatly clarified the functional role that values play in constructing knowledge. On the other hand, Piaget's and Pugh's theories taken together do not tell us how values themselves develop. Piaget did, however, provide a clue. In fact, his account of the intellectualization of feelings into normative scales of values and his work on possibility and necessity led him to the brink of understanding the way in which values participate in the developmental processes of intelligence and how they are constructed. Unfortunately he never integrated these two lines of thought. I, therefore, attempt to do so now.

## Affective transforming schemes and affective development

Piaget's point of departure in explaining development of any kind was the Wallace–Darwin theory of organic evolution. In that view, biological, psychological, and social entities are constructed through the interaction of organisms, people, societies, and environments in every conceivable combination. Physical, psychological and social structures vary and are functionally selected. That being the case, explaining affective development requires that the structures of affectivity be identified, that their functions be specified, and that some version of variation and selection be invoked.

### Schemes of action

Recall in this respect that in Piaget's theory the source of all knowledge is action, and that action results from assimilation of information to "schemes of action". Schemes of action are a form of knowledge, but only of "knowing how". They are structured, but in the sense of feedback regulations, not in the sense of "operations".

> There is, of course, an immense class of structures which are not strictly logical or mathematical, that is, whose transformations unfold in time: linguistic structures, sociological structures, psychological structures, and so on. Such transformations are governed by laws ("regulations" in the cybernetic sense of the word) which are not in the strict sense "operations," because they are not entirely reversible (in the sense in which multiplication is reversible by division or addition by subtraction). Transformation laws of this kind depend upon the interplay of anticipation and correction (feedback) . . .
>
> (Piaget 1968/1970, pp. 15–16)

Cognitive functioning, Piaget further argued (Piaget and Inhelder 1963/1969), has both figurative and operatory aspects. The figurative aspect is linked to consciousness. Its function is to monitor the results of action. The operatory aspect is unconscious (but in many cases can be consciously conceptualized). Its function is to organize action. Since different systems of knowing become evident during development, one needs to look at how figurative and operative aspects interact in each system.

### Sensorimotor schemes

On the sensorimotor level, the feedback loop between figurative and operative aspects of knowledge might be schematized, as in Figure 4.1. In that figure, *Perceptual Consciousness* corresponds to the figurative aspect of sensorimotor functioning and the *Scheme of Sensorimotor Action* corresponds to the

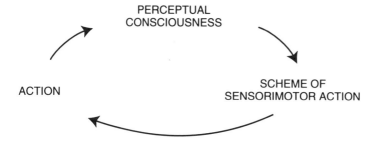

*Figure 4.1* Sensorimotor assimilation

operative aspect. By comparing or transforming what is perceived, sensori-motor schemes control the flow of perceptual consciousness.

There are, however, other kinds of consciousness and other kinds of action.

### Semiotic-operational schemes

A central tenet of Piaget's theory is that thought is "internalized action". With the advent of the semiotic function, the child becomes capable of representing himself, the world, and his actions on and in the represented world. The great advantage of semiotic-operational reduplication of the sensorimotor world is that actions can be tried out in the represented world before they are actually carried out. This allows mistakes to be corrected in advance – Ashby's definition of operations. By analogy with Piaget's term sensorimotor, which indicates both the figurative and operative aspects of assimilation to knowledge structures in the preverbal period, I use the term semiotic-operational to designate assimilation to knowledge mediated by signs and symbols. I then posit a feedback loop between figurative and operative aspects of semiotic-operational knowledge as schematized in Figure 4.2.

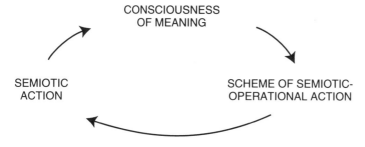

*Figure 4.2* Semiotic-operational assimilation

In this figure, the figurative aspect of semiotic-operational assimilation takes the form of the conscious awareness of meanings. It is how we "see" represented rather than perceived objects and events. The operative aspect of semiotic-operational assimilation acts on meanings, and the flow of semiotic consciousness is controlled by its "actions".

### Affect-transforming schemes

Piaget said relatively little about affective "structures" and, apparently, had no notion of affective schemes. I start then from the two simple facts: (1) Piaget admitted that feelings were conscious; (2) Piaget believed that objective values result from action. Suppose, therefore, that subjective values present in consciousness in the form of feelings and that such conscious presentations result from what I shall call "affect-transforming actions." Further, suppose that such actions are regulated by affect-transforming schemes, and that the functioning of such schemes exhibits figurative and operative aspects. We would then arrive at the schematization shown in Figure 4.3.

This figure recognizes that feeling is a form of consciousness that, although present in the sensorimotor period, is not perceptual in nature. Further, it suggests that feelings can be acted on by affect-transforming schemes, just as perceptions can be acted on by sensorimotor schemes. Affective-transformational schemes would, then, control the flow of affective consciousness or feeling. On Pugh's hypothesis that feelings are surrogates for adaptive values, that they dichotomize into bad and good, and that intelligence is set up to search out and intensify good feelings, then affective-transforming schemes, by always creating better feelings, more often than not drag adaptation in their wake.

Feeling, the figurative aspect of affective functioning, differs from perception in two essential ways. The first difference may be illustrated as follows. If I look twice at a tree, I twice perceive a tree, but I do not

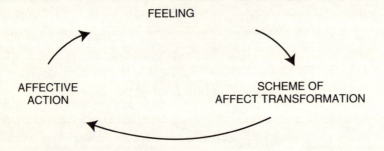

*Figure 4.3* Affect-transforming assimilation

necessarily feel the same way about the tree each time I see it. When it is hot and I am seeking shade, the tree is "seen" as a welcome haven; when my kite is caught in its upmost branches, it is seen as a nuisance to be cut down. Feeling, then, has something to do with me, the subject, in relation to the tree; it is not a property of the tree.

The second way in which feeling differs from perception is that it can arise from semiotic-operational meanings while perceptions cannot. For example, interest, fear, hesitation, anger, joy, etc – a whole range of feelings and emotions – can be provoked by something that I learn about symbolically, as, for example, by reading. Such feelings are direct, immediate, and real. They are not different from the feelings stimulated by sensorimotor action. In contrast, meanings cannot provoke perceptions. The "perceptual" experience I have when imagining a tree is decidedly different from my experience in perceiving it. I conclude, therefore, that here too affectivity reflects something about me in relation to a symbolized "reality." The reason that feelings can be experienced directly as a result of semiotic-operational assimilation is that I am present in the situation.

With regard to the operative aspect of affective functioning, it is at first a bit confusing to discover that whatever it is that transforms feelings appears to be the same as whatever it is that transforms perceptions or meanings.

One maneuver necessary for resolving this apparent paradox lies in recognizing that assimilation is never purely sensorimotor or semiotic-operational. It always and without exception involves affect-transforming assimilation as well. (That is why Piaget [1953–1954/1981] said that there is no such thing as purely cognitive or purely affective behavior.) When, therefore, I assimilate inky little figures on a piece of paper into knowledge structures that permit their comprehension, I also assimilate the meaning assigned by that assimilation into knowledge structures that permit value to be assigned.

A second maneuver necessary for understanding feeling transformation lies in maintaining strict analogies between sensorimotor, semiotic-operational, and the affect-transforming assimilation proposed in Figure 4.3. (For the sake of simplicity, I shall consider only the analogy with sensorimotor functioning, but it is not difficult to make the analogy to semiotic-operational functioning as well.) Recall that in the sensorimotor assimilation, schemes of action transform perceptions in two ways. Either they transform the subject's physical relation to the object (changes in perspective), or they transform the object (causal action). By analogy, affect-transforming schemes transform feeling in two ways. Either they switch the point of view – the value structure – from which something is evaluated, or they transform the situation being evaluated through direct action. In both cases, the maneuvers employed may range from the very simple to the highly complex. The change in perspective might be so simple as to decide that "it is not really all that important to have a haircut before the weekend", thus relieving unpleasant stress. Or it might be as complicated and painful as giving up the superordinate value that all physical events must be determined (cf., Born 1971). Similarly, direct affect- transforming action may be so simple as turning the shower valve toward "COLD" to relieve unpleasant warmth or as complex as Medea murdering her children to mitigate her fury and assuage the pain of Jason's infidelity.

Schematic as they are, the notion of affect-transforming schemes makes clear how affective consciousness is regulated. If space permitted, I would examine the important implications that this idea has for epistemologies of psychology and sociology. All that I can point out here is that all perceptual and all semiotic information is assimilated to affective structures. Akin to Piaget's presentative structures, those structures allow value to be assigned both qualitatively and quantitatively. The resulting values are afferents to a control system that composes affective, perceptual, and semiotic information into intentional schemes of action. Such actions are organized around the principle of optimizing positive feeling, not around the principle of optimizing equilibrium. Because positive feeling is a heuristic surrogate for equilibrium, this orients action toward optimizing equilibrium – *but that is a secondary effect*. Objective values are only one among many value structures. When they are invoked and action formulated under their aegis, true or necessary knowledge may result. But confusion and failure are also possible, in which case other value systems will have to be employed. As a general rule, objective evaluation is achieved only for action on relatively simple "objects" like electrons or numbers. It is much harder to apply it to complicated objects like actions or people.

### *Affective development*

There can be no doubt that something about affectivity develops. Babies who vehemently spit out anchovies come, in the decay of middle age, to crave *tapénade* and crackers. Yuppies once swathed in fur volunteer as dowagers to care for homeless cats. Senators committed to the "right to choice," turn up ten years later at demonstrations for the "right to life." How, then, are such changes effected?

I fear that what I have to say about affective development is a bit anticlimactic. Clarifying affective concepts and positing affect-transforming schemes simply leads back to (but also profoundly changes) Piaget's developmental theory.

> *It appears to us that in explaining cognitive development, whether accounting for the history of science or psychogenesis, the concept of improving or optimizing equilibration imposes itself as fundamental . . .*
> *Since every reequilibration involves actions with a teleonomic character, we must explain how goals, new as well as old, are chosen and*

*account for how the means used to reach a goal are improved or why the means applied succeed. In this regard, the distinction between three broad forms of equilibrium provides the beginnings of a solution . . . the equilibrium of coordinations between the subject and objects, the equilibrium of coordinations between schemes and subsystems of schemes, and the general equilibrium between the whole and its parts . . .The third type of equilibrium appears to orient the finality of actions. In effect, it is always when a lacuna turns up, and because of the perturbations that are either its source or its result, that a new endeavor is undertaken. The finality of that endeavor therefore arises from the system as a whole in its incomplete state and tends to complete it by differentiating it. Relationships between subject and object and coordinations among schemes of the same rank, on the other hand, provide means whose particular goals are subordinated to the goal determined by the need for equilibrium between the whole and its parts.*

(Piaget 1975/1985, p. 139)

The only change that I would make is to revise Piaget's conception of the third type of equilibration as follows:

*The third type of equilibrium appears to orient the finality of actions. In effect, it is always when positive desires or bad feelings turn up that a new endeavor is undertaken. The finality of that endeavor therefore arises from affective structures and works always to increase positive feeling. Relationships between subject and object and coordinations among schemes of the same rank, on the other hand, provide means whose particular goals are subordinated to the goal determined by the need for feeling good. If that is achieved, equilibrium between the whole and its parts will usually follow.*

Apart from these minor but theory-shaking changes, I would leave Piaget's account of equilibration unaltered. I would even posit that Piaget gave unwitting voice to the accuracy of these revisions when, in his *Autobiographie* (1976), he wrote "Fundamentally, I am an anxious person whom work alone assuages" (p. 21, fn. 17). His search was obviously for affective not cognitive equilibrium. I would also posit that Piaget suspected the role affectivity plays in equilibration in his syncretic fusion of feeling and motivation, although he never grasped exactly how it worked. But contrary to his intuitions and in the manner of the philosophers he mistrusted, he made a *subjective evaluation* that people – whom he always confused with epistemic subjects – must, above all else, be rational. That was his great mistake.

Piaget's theory of equilibration is realizable – one can build an equilibrating machine with blood and bones – only when one sees clearly that human intelligence cannot aim at equilibrium directly because it takes too much knowledge, too much intellectual power and too much time to evaluate possibilities after-the-fact in terms of necessity and truth. In fact, logical necessity and its bedfellow empirical truth arise from the functioning of a more general and affectively-organized system. The construction of true or necessary knowledge arises from value-guided evolutions in which a rigid, narrow set of values is made to play the deciding role. Because of its enormous cost, construction in this manner is not practical in many cases, most of which have to do with the profoundest concerns of the human race. But nature found a way around this difficulty. By making feelings surrogate indices of adaptation and by creating a system organized around the superordinate value of feeling good, intelligence can, most of the time, advance toward adaptive equilibrium while at the same time having no exact knowledge of it.

## NOTES

1 This is an abbreviated and edited version of a chapter in E. Reed, E. Turiel and T. Brown (eds) *Values and Knowledge*, Hillsdale, NJ: Lawrence Erlbaum Associates (1996).
2 The relevance of Pugh's ideas to Piaget's epistemology has been extensively argued in Brown and Weiss 1987; Brown 1990; and Brown 1994.

## REFERENCES

(Where two dates separated by a slash are given, the first date refers to the original date of publication.)

Blanchet, A. 1986 "Rôle des valeurs et des systèmes des valeurs dans la cognition", *Archives de Psychologie* (Geneva) 54: 251–270.
Born, M. 1971 *The Born–Einstein, Letters*, trans. Irene Born, New York: Walker.
Bringuier, J-C. 1977/1980 *Conversations with Jean Piaget*, trans. Basia Gulati, Chicago: University of Chicago Press.
Brown, T. 1980 "Foreword", in *Jean Piaget, Adaptation and Intelligence: Organic Selection and Phenocopy*, trans. S. Eames, Chicago: University of Chicago Press.
Brown, T. 1990 "The Biological Significance of Affectivity", in N. L. Stein, B. Leventhal and T. Trabasso (eds) *Psychological and Biological Approaches to Emotion*, Hillsdale, NJ: Lawrence Erlbaum Associates.
Brown, T. 1994 "Affective Dimensions of Meaning", in W. F. Overton and D. S. Palermo (eds) *The Nature and Ontogenesis of Meaning*, Hillsdale, NJ: Lawrence Erlbaum Associates.
Brown, T. and Weiss, L. 1987 "Structures, Procedures, Heuristics, and Affectivity", in *Archives de Psychologie* (Geneva) 55: 59–94.
Piaget, J. 1918 *Recherche*, Lausanne: Édition La Concorde.
Piaget, J. 1932/1965 *The Moral Judgment of the Child*, trans. Marjorie Gabain, New York: Free Press.
Piaget, J. 1936/1952 *The Origins of Intelligence in Children*, trans. Margaret Cook, New York: International Universities Press.

Piaget, J. 1950 *Introduction à l'Épistémologie Génétique 1: La Pensée Mathématique*, Paris: Presses Universitaires de France.

Piaget, J. 1951/1976 "Le Développement, chez l'Enfant, de l'Idée de Patrie et des Relations avec l'Étranger", in *Revue Européenne des Sciences Sociales et Cahiers Vilfredo Pareto*, 36–39: 124–147, Geneva: Droz. (Originally published in *Bulletin International des sciences sociales III*, 1951, no 3: 605–650.)

Piaget, J. 1953–1954/1981 *Intelligence and Affectivity: Their Relationship during Child Development*, translated and edited by T. A. Brown and C. E. Kaegi, Palo Alto, California: Annual Reviews.

Piaget, J. 1963/1968 "Explanation in psychology and psychophysiological parallelism", in P. Fraisse and J. Piaget (eds) *Experimental Psychology: Its Scope and Method, I: History and Method*, trans. Judith Chambers, New York: Basic Books.

Piaget, J. 1965/1971 *Insights and Illusions of Philosophy*, trans. Wolfe Mays, New York: World.

Piaget, J. 1966 "Débat: Psychologie et Philosophie", *Raison Présente*, 1: 4me trimestre.

Piaget, J. 1967/1995 *Sociological Studies*, L. Smith (ed.), Hillsdale, NJ: Lawrence Erlbaum Associates.

Piaget, J. 1968/1970 *Structuralism*, trans. Chaninah Maschler, New York: Basic Books.

Piaget, J. 1971/1974 *Understanding Causality*, trans. Donald and Marguerite Miles, New York: W. W. Norton.

Piaget, J. 1975/1985 *The Equilibration of Cognitive Structures*, trans. T. Brown, Chicago: University of Chicago Press.

Piaget, J. 1976 "Autobiographie", in *Revue Européenne des Sciences Sociales et Cahiers Vilfredo Pareto*, 36–39: 1–43, Geneva: Droz.

Piaget, J. 1981/1987 *Possibility and Necessity: The Role of Possibility in Cognitive Development*, trans. Helga Feider, Minneapolis: University of Minnesota Press.

Piaget, J. 1983/1987 *Possibility and Necessity: The Role of Necessity in Cognitive Development*, trans. Helga Feider, Minneapolis: University of Minnesota Press.

Piaget, J. and Inhelder, B. 1963/1969 "Mental Images", in P. Fraisse and J. Piaget (eds) *Experimental Psychology: Its Scope and Method, VII: Intelligence*, trans. Thérèse Surridge, New York: Basic Books.

Pugh, G. E. 1977 *The Biological Origins of Human Values*, New York: Basic Books.

Vidal, F. 1994 "Piaget Poète. Avec Deux Sonnets Oubliés de 1918", in *Archives de Psychologie* 64: 3–7.

# Chapter 5

# An exploration of long-term far-transfer effects following an extended intervention program in the high school science curriculum

*Philip Adey and Michael Shayer*

Pupils in eight schools were given special lessons within their science curriculum based on notions of cognitive conflict, metacognition and bridging, set in the context of the schemata of formal operations. These special lessons replaced regular science lessons once every 2 weeks for 2 years. Results of tests given immediately after the intervention and 1 and 2 years later, standardized with respect to pretest scores of experimental and control pupils, indicate that the intervention led to immediate gains in Piagetian measures of cognitive development and to gains in experimental groups' achievement in science, mathematics, and English language measured 2 and 3 years after the end of the intervention program. Groups most affected included the boys who started the program in Year 8 (Grade 7) and the girls who started in Year 7 (Grade 6). There were stronger effects on girls' gains in English achievement and on boys' gains in science and mathematics achievement. We explore possible explanations for the results in terms of underlying domain-specific or domain-general cognitive structures.

During the late 1960s and 1970s, there was considerable interest in the Piagetian model of stepwise cognitive development. Educationalists used it both to seek explanations for the difficulties encountered by students in learning and as a basis for the design of more effective instruction (e.g. Karplus 1978; Lawson, Blake and Nordland 1975; Renner *et al.* 1976; Shayer 1978). At the same time, academic psychologists were questioning the mechanisms of cognitive development and both the construct and the empirical validity of domain-general stages proposed by the Genevan school (Brainerd 1978; Brown and Desforges 1979). This is not the place to review whether the change in fashion against the Genevan model was justified. We merely note our opinion that the British version of the critical position (Brown and Desforges 1979) was shown to be selective in its use of the literature and empirically unjustified (see Shayer 1979, and the reply by Desforges and Brown 1979). Whatever one's position is in this debate, it is relevant to recognize that the work reported here grew out of results obtained at Chelsea College, London, in the 1970s based on a broadly Piagetian paradigm.

At that time, we conducted a national survey to determine levels of cognitive development using a large representative sample of the adolescent population (Shayer, Küchemann and Wylam 1976; Shayer and Wylam 1978). At the same time, we developed an instrument for the analysis of curricula in terms of the cognitive demands made on learners (the "Curriculum Analysis Taxonomy" in Shayer and Adey 1981) and applied it to curricula then in use. The coordination of these two pieces of evidence provided some explanation for what had been the empirical experience of many science teachers – that the demands made by much of the material then used in schools was beyond the reach of most pupils.

We thus came to the question that had been bothering American instructors theoretically for some years: Can cognitive development be accelerated? In 1975, Niemark wrote:

> One of the more surprising gaps in the reported research concerns what Piaget has called "The American Question": the possibility of accelerating cognitive development through specific training . . . When more is known about the course of normal development and the variables which affect it, it is quite likely that sophisticated training research will begin in earnest. Piaget's prediction would be that all such attempts are doomed to failure.
>
> (pp. 584–585)

In 1980, following discussion with the Clarkes, who had earlier surveyed the whole field of intervention studies (Clarke and Clarke 1976), Shayer worked with a number of studies using different intervention models, summarized in Shayer (1987). One of these was a small-scale replication of Feuerstein's Instrumental Enrichment program (Feuerstein, Rand, Hoffman and Miller 1980). The reported effect sizes in relation to controls (Shayer and Beasley 1987) were large, including a figure of 1.2 $SD$ on a battery of individual interview Piagetian tasks and 1.1 $SD$ on Raven's Matrices. With this intervention model, however, teachers found it difficult to relate the improved thinking skills of the students, achieved in the context of subject-free intervention lessons, to the specifics of the school curriculum. No effects on school achievement were found at immediate posttest.

At the same time, there was something of a rush of cognitive acceleration studies reported from North America and Australia (e.g. Case 1974; Kuhn and Angelev 1976; Lawson and Snitgen 1982; Rosenthal 1979), reviewed in Adey (1988) and Goossens (1989). Now, when the Piagetian star has waned somewhat and the majority of cognitive psychologists are emphasizing domain-specific skills rather than a general underlying cognitive structure, the question of cognitive acceleration may seem meaningless or at best irrelevant. Nevertheless, some continue to dig for the possibility of general thinking skills that are amenable to influence and enhanced development. Nickerson, Perkins and Smith (1985) expressed the search in a form of Pascal's wager:

> If (teaching thinking) cannot be done, and we try to do it, we may waste some time and effort. If it can be done, and we fail to try, the inestimable cost will be generations of students whose ability to think effectively will be less than it could have been. So we are better advised to adopt the attitude that thinking can be taught, try hard to teach it, and let experience prove us wrong if it must.
>
> (p. 324)

We started from both this viewpoint that the possibility of teaching general thinking skills was worth pursuing and the viewpoint that what has recently been referred to as "higher order thinking skills" (Resnick 1987) is well characterized by Inhelder and Piaget's descriptions of formal operations. Again, this is not the place to reopen debates on the validity of the Inhelder–Piaget account of formal operations, but it is worth noting that the characteristic performance of children on the Inhelder tasks has always replicated the original findings and can be regarded as a fact requiring explanation.[1] Although Piaget's propositional calculus can be handled in a general form, his use of it as an explanatory model is invariably contextualized. This may infuriate logicians (Parsons 1960), but it does lead to a consistent descriptive model of thought, as Papert (1961) demonstrated. If further justification for pursuing the Piaget model is required, it may be found in a challenge given to Shayer by Alan Clarke. "If you want to go on using a Piagetian model," he said, "bear in mind that one of the best ways of studying a phenomenon is to try to change it." If the intervention model is incoherent, no successful change can come from it. Thus, by acting on the belief that the Piagetian account of formal operations is a satisfactory description of general higher order thinking skills, the best test is to look for evidence that, both in terms of the model (Piagetian tests) and inferred consequences if the model is true (school achievement in science and other subjects), the results are in accord with the prediction.

Funding was obtained in 1980 from the Social Science Research Council (SSRC) to investigate the possibility of promoting formal operational thinking in 11- to 14-year-olds. A pilot study conducted in one school led to further SSRC funding to involve teachers in a sample of ordinary state high schools in Britain. The Cognitive Acceleration Through Science Education (CASE) projects were based at the (then) Chelsea College Centre for Science and Mathematics Education, University of London.

The results of the experiment, especially as they relate to science education, have been reported piecemeal as they occurred (Adey and Shayer 1990; Shayer and Adey 1992a, 1992b, 1993). Here we provide more detail of the instructional strategies employed, summarize these results in a uniform manner, try to fill in the overall picture that emerges, and (by looking especially at the language development) draw implications for models of the mind (Adey and Shayer 1994).

## CONTEXT

In approaching a high school principal with a proposal to introduce a set of activities that might or might not help pupils to develop higher order thinking skills, there are (at least in Britain) two negative answers: (a) "It will interfere with preparation for external examinations" and (b) "I am not going to rewrite the timetable to provide a new space for thinking lessons." The riposte to answer (a) is to offer to work with the younger pupils, before they get near the end-of-school examination, and that to answer (b) is to embed the new activities in an existing subject. In any case, if an intervention model can be interpolated within the context of an existing body of widely used teaching skills and content, both students and teachers are helped immediately to apply new thinking skills to that context. Given successful application within such a context, accompanied by an emphasis on the generalizable skills, chances should be much increased of the students' improved cognition subsequently affecting performance in other contexts. Although it has been shown that the Piagetian account of concrete and formal operations can usefully be applied to the context of history (e.g. Hallam 1967; Jurd 1973) and English comprehension and social studies (Fusco 1983), the field of science learning was chosen for micropolitical reasons. These include our own familiarity with the foundations of science teaching and because in the United Kingdom the science teaching fraternity has shown the greatest interest in the application of learning theories to the curriculum. It also seemed that, whether or not Inhelder and Piaget (1958) intended the schemata of formal operations to be free of domain constraints, they do look very scientific and are initially easier to "sell" to science teachers than, say, to language teachers.

## THE BASES OF THE INTERVENTION ACTIVITIES

We thus set about designing a set of activities, set in a scientific context and using the schemata of formal operations as a guiding framework. We considered that the chances of achieving domain-general improvements in higher order thinking skills would be maximized by addressing all 10 of Piaget's schemata. Reviews of the literature (Adey 1988; Goossens 1989) on cognitive acceleration suggested certain features that should maximize an intervention program's chances of bringing about long-term effects on the general ability of learners, including:

1 The introduction, through concrete activities, of the terminology of relationships and the context in which a problem is presented. Goossens (1989) called this *perceptual readiness*, but we now prefer the term *concrete preparation*.
2 The presentation of problems that induce *cognitive conflict*.
3 The encouragement of *metacognition*.
4 The *bridging* of thinking strategies developed within the context of the special lessons to other areas.

We may say that concrete preparation is the "setup", cognitive conflict the "sting", metacognition makes the thinking process conscious in the learner, and bridging provides a wide range of applications. The set of activities developed is called *Thinking Science* (Adey, Shayer and Yates 1989).

## Concrete preparation

Formal operations operate only on a situation that has first been described by the subject in terms of descriptive concrete models. Thus, concrete preparation involves establishing that students are familiar with the technical vocabulary, apparatus and framework in which a problem situation is set. The first few activities concentrate on the key ideas of *variables* and *relationships between variables*. The terms are introduced in a way that requires only concrete operational processing. For example, the teacher displays a selection of books on the table: "In what ways are these different from one another?" she asks. Answers typically include "color", "size", "hard- or soft-back". "These are ways in which the books *vary* from each other. We call color, size, etc. *variables*." Pupils are then shown a collection of shapes (Figure 5.1). "What are the variables here?" Typically 11-year-olds have no difficulty in establishing that shape, color, and size are variables. Now we move on: "Can you see any way in which any of these variables go together?" Some more probing questions and verbal or nonverbal prompting lead pupils from specific statements ("the triangles are red; the squares are blue") to the more general recognition that "color goes with shape". After further similar examples, the term *relationship* is

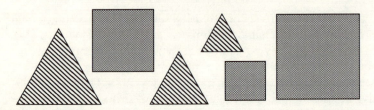

*Figure 5.1* What are the variables here?

*Figure 5.2.* What are the variables? What relationship is there among them?

introduced. There is a relationship between the variables color and shape. Cartoon examples give practice in recognizing relationships between variables in terms such as, "as the number of sausages goes up, their size goes down" (see Figure 5.2). Within the same sequence, it is also important to recognize when there is no relationship. For example, with a set of loaded but opaque colored jars, there is a relationship between color and size (big ones are blue; small ones are red), but pupils find that the weight of the jars bears no relationship to either color or size.

Where there is a relationship, pupils can be encouraged to use the relationship to make predictions. In the squares and triangles activity, the teacher may ask, "Now, if I produce another triangle that follows the same pattern, what color will it be?" Where there is no relationship, no prediction can be made. Knowing the color of the jar does not help you to decide what its weight is.

Other terms introduced early in the scheme, *input variable* and *outcome variable*, are used instead of the more formal terms *independent* and *dependent* variables, respectively.

The examples given illustrate some CASE activities that provide concrete preparation for the whole *Thinking Science* scheme. In addition, almost every activity starts with a conceptual readiness phase for that particular activity, as will be shown. Note that the strategy here is to give the student confidence in the use of the technical vocabulary in a situation requiring only concrete modeling, before he or she needs to apply it in a context requiring formal modeling.

## Cognitive conflict

This term is used to describe an event or observation that the student finds puzzling and discordant with previous experience or understanding. All perceptions are interpreted through the subjects' present conceptual framework. When current conceptualization fails to make sense of an experience, constructive mental work by students may lead to accommodation and a change in their conceptual framework. Kuhn, Amsel and O'Loughlin's (1988) investigation of the coordination of new evidence with existing cognitive schemata confirms that instances of cognitive conflict do not automatically produce a "Road to Damascus" conversion to a new conceptualization. Younger and less able pupils often appear unaware of a conflict or at least are not bothered by it. But if there is no conflict, there is no chance of accommodation. In Vygotsky's (1978) words:

> Learning which is oriented toward developmental levels that have already been reached is ineffective from the viewpoint of a child's overall development. It does not aim for a new stage of the developmental process but rather lags behind this process . . . The only "good learning" is that which is in advance of development.
>
> (p. 82)

The following two examples illustrate activities designed to induce conflict.

1 *Floating and sinking jars*: Two sets of jars are prepared (see Figure 5.3). Five jars, A through E, are all the same size but are loaded to have different masses. Six jars, 1 through 6, are each successively smaller than the one before, but they all have the same mass. Jar 1/A is common to both sets. The jars are opaque and labeled only with their number or letter. Pupils have worksheets showing the jars arranged in a matrix. They are invited to weigh each jar and then drop it into a large bowl of water. On the worksheets, they record each jar's weight and whether it floats or sinks. The discussion centers first on Jars A through E. What conclusions can be drawn? Only two variables, weight and buoyancy, are involved, so students can develop a simple concrete model relating the two: "Heavy things sink; light things float". Similarly, a focus on Jars 1 through 6 leads to another concrete model: "Small things sink; big things float" (they know that pins sink and ships float, so this accords with experience, albeit rather selected experience). Next, Jar X is produced. It is established that it is the same size as Jar 3 (a floater) and the same weight as Jar C (also a floater). Students must predict what they think will happen when Jar X is put in water. Application of the two concrete models already developed leads to the prediction that Jar X will float. When put into the water, it sinks. Thus, there is conflict between perceptual experience and the concrete operations used so far. Concrete operations do not provide an explanation for the sinking of Jar X. A three-variable, formal model is required, employing the notion of "weight for a certain size".

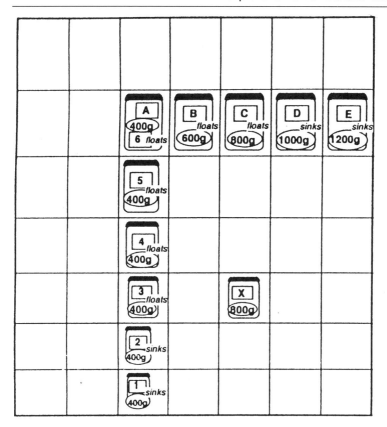

*Figure 5.3* Will Jar X float or sink?

2 *Wheelbarrow*: Introductory discussion and demonstration (the conceptual readiness phase) establishes the parallel between a notched stick and the wheelbarrow as lever systems (Figure 5.4). Students record and tabulate the force at the "handle" as successive loads are added. With about six pairs of values completed, they draw the straight line graph relating the two on a given grid. From this, they are asked to make predictions about what the force would be with extra loads, which are not available. The first predictions can be read off by simple extrapolation of the graph, but then the graph paper runs out. A concrete strategy is no longer available. This is the point of conflict, requiring the invention of a more sophisticated view of the relationship – that involving the constant ratio of load to effort. They have to go beyond the conceptual support of the graph and construct a more general mathematical model through which they can extrapolate. Cognitive operations on the data must become formalized to achieve a successful solution to the problem.

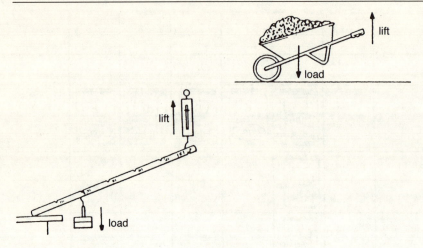

*Figure 5.4* The wheelbarrow as a lever system

We aimed to maximize the permanent effect on subjects of conflict situations by (a) effective concrete preparation and (b) repeated, sometimes small, doses of conflict over an extended period. Note that these small doses were given in many different contexts with the underlying implication that such treatment would lead to accelerated development of a general cognitive structure. This contrasts with the conflict situations presented by curriculum materials founded in the Alternative Conceptions Movement (ACM; see e.g. Children's Learning in Science Project 1987). An ACM style teaching sequence devotes considerable time to setting up and, it is hoped, to resolving cognitive conflict about one concept. The ACM aim is the development of that concept rather than the development of general thinking skills. The CASE aim was less specific and potentially more widely generalizable. Our expectation was not that after the floating and sinking activity pupils would have a grasp of density (some did; some did not), but that they would develop their repertoire of general ideas – in this case that of compound variables – that provide explanatory power. Such higher order thinking skills are developed so that new problems in completely different contexts can be treated effectively.

## Metacognition

It is now widely accepted (Nickerson *et al.* 1985; Perkins and Salomon 1989) that students are more likely to develop wide-ranging thinking skills if they are encouraged to think about their own thinking, to become aware of the strategies of their own thinking and actions. This is what is meant by *metacognition*. In a *Thinking Science* lesson, the teacher asks pupils to talk both with the teacher and with each other about difficulties and successes they have with problems, not just saying "That was difficult", but also explaining "what was difficult about it, and how did I overcome the difficulty?" Students become accustomed to reflecting on the sort of thinking they have been engaged in, to bringing it to the front of their consciousness, and to making of it an explicit tool that may then be available for use in a new context. Using words to describe reasoning patterns is another aspect of metacognition. The aim is for CASE students not only to be better equipped to recognize a proportionality problem, for example, when they see one but also to be able to say, "That's a proportionality problem!", and so open the door to a particular set of solution strategies. This is a special application of what Vygotsky (1978) described as the use of language as a mediator of learning. The language of reasoning mediates meta-learning.

It is not easy to illustrate this metacognitive element from *Thinking Science* activities, because it is more a feature of the teacher's strategy introduced through staff development programs than of the printed materials. One example illustrates how a worksheet can act as a starting point for metacognitive speculation, although, in prosecuting the activity, the teacher plays an essential role in building on this starting point:

> *Classification*: Students go through a set of simple exercises such as putting animals into groups (according to their own criteria), arranging a variety of foodstuffs on the shelves of a larder, and sorting chemicals by color and by solubility.

Finally (see Figure 5.5), students are asked to consider the classifications that they have done and to reflect on which was the most difficult for them and why and on which was the easiest and why. They compare their

---

**6. Thinking Back**

Put a tick by the classification activity you found easiest.
Put a cross by the one you found most difficult.

Why was the one you ticked the easiest?
Why was the one you crossed the most difficult?

Has everyone ticked and crossed the same ones as you?

Write a sentence about a friend, using the word *characteristic*.

Why do you think that it is useful to be able to classify things?

---

*Figure 5.5* The last of a series of classification activities. Note that the British English *tick* is equivalent to the US English *check*

feelings with other groups and discuss why some groups found some activities difficult and others found the same ones easy.

## Bridging

The explicit bridging to other contexts is the final link in this chain of developing, abstracting, and generalizing reasoning. During inservice introductions to *Thinking Science*, teachers engaged in exercises to develop their own links between the *Thinking Science* activities and their regular science curriculum and pupils' experiences in everyday life. During visits by members of the project team to schools, further opportunities for bridging were explored in the context of each school's curriculum and environment. This can be illustrated with one activity concerned with probability:

> *Tea tasting:* Some people think that tea tastes different if you put the milk in before or after the tea. One student volunteer leaves the room while five cups of tea are prepared, some with milk first, others with tea first. She or he returns and tastes each cup, reporting "tea first" or "milk first" on each. The problem before the class is, how many out of five must she or he get right before the students believe that she or he really can tell the difference? (American readers may wish to substitute Coke® vs. Pepsi®, although that is much easier.) Typically, 11- and 12-year-olds may consider that three out of five or four out of five would be convincing. Next, everyone spins five coins many times, producing a large number of spins. In a concrete way, the children discover the percentage of times all five coins show heads, just by chance. The conflict arises as they realize that there is no simple answer to the question "How many rights is convincing?" Even 100 out of 100 could occur by chance. There is no deterministic answer, only a probabilistic one. The bridging occurs through discussion of, for example, the relationship between smoking and lung cancer. Not everyone who smokes will get lung cancer. Not everyone who does not smoke will avoid it. The idea of a probabilistic relationship between a cause and effect is given meaning.

## DEVELOPMENT OF THE INTERVENTION, EXPERIMENT, AND TESTS

Activities were drafted and taught by the research team (the authors and Carolyn Yates) to two classes of 12-year-olds in an ordinary London comprehensive secondary school. A total of 30 such activities, each designed to last about 60 to 70 minutes, were thus devised, pretested, revised and duplicated.

Nine schools representing a variety of environments in England were chosen in consultation with Local Education Authorities' science advisers who were asked to recommend what they considered to be ordinary mixed comprehensive schools typical of their locality. In some cases, advisers directed us to schools that they felt would "do a good job" for us and in others to schools that they felt needed some help. A total of 24 classes of pupils of average ability[2] in these schools were selected and randomly assigned to experimental and control conditions, with experimental and control classes in each school. Some control classes were taught by the same teacher as the experimental classes; others were taught by different teachers. Four classes were of the 11+ age group (UK Year 7, US Grade 6), eight of 12+ (UK Year 8, US Grade 7). These separate cohorts are referred to simply as the "11+" and "12+" groups.

In 1985, the 12 experimental classes started to receive a *Thinking Science* lesson in place of a regular science lesson about once every 2 weeks. Classes in this age group typically receive two or three science lessons per week, so the *Thinking Science* lessons could have taken as much as 25 per cent of the normally allotted science time. The *Thinking Science* activities were introduced to teachers through a series of 1-day workshops and followed up by visits to the schools during which lessons were observed and discussed with the teacher. We did not expect the psychological foundation of the proposed teaching strategies to become readily accessible to teachers through the printed material alone.

One school withdrew after two terms, and another, working under especially difficult circumstances, failed to deliver the intervention even approximately as planned. We report results here for the 10 experimental classes (four 11+ and six 12+) in seven schools that continued with the program, more or less as intended, for 2 years. After the 2-year intervention program, students were no longer maintained in identifiable experimental and control groups but were mixed together as they chose options for the subjects they continued to study. In the case of three of the 11+ classes, the end of the intervention coincided with the end of the middle school period, and pupils were dispersed to a number of different high schools. The experimental design and testing program is illustrated in Figure 5.6.

Testing occasions were *pretest*, before the intervention began; *posttest*, immediately after the 2-year intervention; *delayed posttest*, 1 year after the end of the intervention; and the *General Certificate of Secondary Education (GCSE)* taken 2 (for those who started at 12+) or 3 (for those who started at 11+) years after the end of the intervention. We have no reason to suppose that those who moved from the schools in which we were able to trace them for testing, or who missed particular tests, did so because they had been experimental or control pupils.

To test cognitive development, we used demonstrated group Piagetian

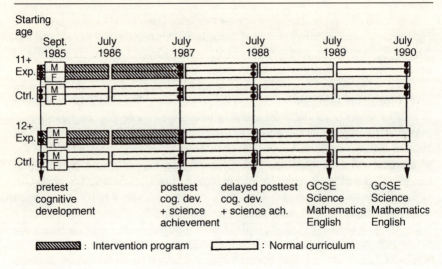

*Figure 5.6* The experimental design and testing program

Reasoning Tasks (PRTs). These tasks were developed as Science Reasoning Tasks (Shayer, Wylam, Küchemann and Adey 1978) in the 1970s for the Concepts in Secondary Science and Mathematics project's large-scale survey of the school population and have been widely used since. Information on the validity and reliability of PRTs is available in Shayer, Adey and Wylam (1981). There were originally six PRTs that yielded scores within a common scale ranging from *preoperational* (1) to *mature formal operational* (3B). Since their development and before the analyses reported here, PRT data were reanalyzed using Rasch scaling to give a finer estimate of person level. Now the total number of items correct on a given PRT can be converted directly into a decimal score on the scale ranging from *early preoperational* (1) to *mature formal operational* (10), with a standard error of about 0.4. Table 5.1 shows some PRT titles, including those used in this experiment and the ranges within which each operates. When two PRTs were used, the mean was taken.

Science achievement was assessed at posttest by a common achievement

*Table 5.1* Some Piagetian reasoning tasks

| Name of Task | Range | Use in CASE Experiment |
| --- | --- | --- |
| 1 Spatial relations | 1 to 5 | Not used in CASE |
| 2 Volume and heaviness | 2 to 7 | Pretest |
| 3 Pendulum | 5 to 10 | Pretest and posttest |
| 4 Probability | 3 to 10 | Posttest and delayed posttest |

test that the teachers agreed fairly reflected the objectives of their science curricula for the previous year. At the delayed test, each school's end-of-year science test or mean of module tests was used. By definition, these tests, thus, covered the objectives of each school's curriculum. They were converted to percentages before further treatment.

The GCSE is now the examination taken in England and Wales by most 16-year-olds as a school-leaving examination and/or as a selection test for further education. There are four different regional examining boards and, within each board, a number of syllabus options. Schools may choose the regional board they wish to use for each subject. For instance, a school may decide to enter some pupils for one, two, or occasionally three out of chemistry, physics, or biology, others for double certificate general science, others again for single general science, and these examinations may be set by the same or by different regional boards. Norm-referenced grades are awarded in all GCSE examinations on a scale ranging from A through G and unclassified, eight grades in all, moderated across boards to ensure equivalence of standards. For the purpose of treatment here, they were mapped onto an equal-interval scale with values 7 down to 0.

## TREATMENT AND PRESENTATION OF RESULTS

Post and delayed cognitive development scores could be reported simply as raw gains over pretest scores, comparing control and experimental groups. The common science achievement test could be reported as a comparison between experimental and control means, although this ignores any difference between starting ability levels as assessed by the pretest. However, the variety of tests used among different schools for the delayed achievement measures and for the GCSE made it impossible to make such simple comparisons. For these measures, the method of *residualized gain scores* was used (Cronbach and Furby 1970).

The method depends on the fact that PRT scores are fair predictors of subsequent academic success. For each particular achievement test or GCSE exam, we compute the predictive relationship between pre-PRT score and achievement (regression of achievement test score on pre-PRT) for the control group that took that particular test. Then, for each corresponding experimental subject, we use the same regression equation to predict from their pre-PRT score what achievement test score they would obtain, if there were no difference between the experimental and control groups. Finally, we compare the experimental subjects' scores predicted on this assumption with the actual scores they obtained. The difference is the residualized gain score (rg score). For any group of students, the mean rg score is a measure of the extent to which their development or learning has been different from the initially matched control group.

For convenience of comparisons, all results are reported in terms of rg scores. Note that rg scores build in comparison with controls and that, by definition, the mean rg score of a control group must be zero.

Results are presented separately for the two groups, 11+ and 12+ (as explained earlier, these represent the ages at which pupils started the intervention program). Results are broken down further by gender. For each experimental group, the number of subjects ($n$), their mean rg score ($M$), the standard deviation of the rg score ($\sigma$), and the probability that the mean score is significantly different from that of the corresponding control group ($p <$) are shown. For significant differences, the effect size ($e$) is also shown in units of standard deviation of the control group ($\sigma_c$). The distribution of the rg scores for the experimental group is shown as a histogram.

In many of the distributions, we claim evidence of bimodality. This is based on computing the cumulative $\chi^2$ values for the numbers occurring at each interval compared with those expected on the basis of normal distribution. A sharp rise in the significance of the $\chi^2$ value indicates that a second peak in the distribution is significant.

## RESULTS

### 1985 Pretests

Pretest scores for each group are shown in Table 5.2. There are no significant differences between any of the subgroups within an age range, but the 11+ group was generally more able than the 12+ group, because the mean scores of the two age groups are similar despite their age difference.

Table 5.2 Pretest scores

| Age Group | Boys | | Girls | |
|---|---|---|---|---|
| | Experimental | Control | Experimental | Control |
| 11+ | | | | |
| N | 39 | 55 | 31 | 35 |
| M | 6.04 | 5.94 | 6.26 | 6.00 |
| σ | 0.88 | 1.06 | 0.69 | 0.57 |
| 12+ | | | | |
| N | 65 | 76 | 59 | 64 |
| M | 6.09 | 6.20 | 6.01 | 6.10 |
| σ | 0.75 | 1.06 | 0.89 | 0.93 |

## 1987 Immediate posttests

*PRT posttests*

These are the tests of cognitive development given immediately after the end of the 2-year intervention program. The results are summarized in Figure 5.7.

Clearly, the 12+ boys made highly significant gains in levels of cognitive development compared with controls. Further analysis reveals that, for this 12+ boys group, the distribution of gain scores is bimodal. That is, one group made little or no better gain than the controls, and another group had gains far greater than the controls. The distribution of scores for the 11+ girls is also bimodal, although overall their gain was not significantly greater than that of the corresponding control group.

*Science achievement posttest*

This was the common science achievement test given in many of the schools immediately after the intervention. At this point, no significant differences emerged between any of the experimental and control groups, although it should be noted that the experimental group lost about 25 per cent of its science curriculum time to the *Thinking Science* intervention lessons, so it may be considered a virtue that this group's achievement

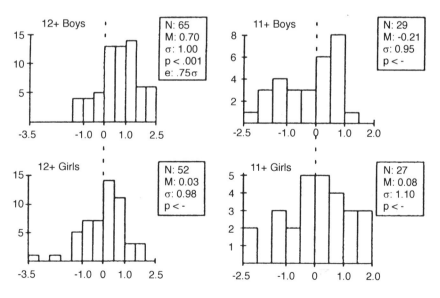

*Figure 5.7* Post-PRT residualized gain scores for experimental groups: means, distribution, etc.

remained at the same level as that of the controls. It is not reasonable to expect an intervention program that addresses underlying cognitive functioning to show an immediate effect on academic achievement, because only after completing the intervention do the subjects have an opportunity to apply their newly acquired thinking skills in new learning. Thus, measures of achievement should not be expected to show improvement until some time after the end of the intervention.

## 1988 Delayed posttests

### PRT delayed posttest

This was the measure of cognitive development given 1 year after the end of the intervention program. Data from this test are summarized in Figure 5.8. One year after the end of the intervention, none of the experimental groups showed any overall difference from the control groups in these measures of cognitive development. The gains that were present immediately after the intervention apparently dissipated. There is, however, some evidence of bimodality in the distribution of the 12+ boys and the 11+ girls that is very marked in the former group. As shown later, this particular result seems to be anomalous in the whole pattern of data that emerges.

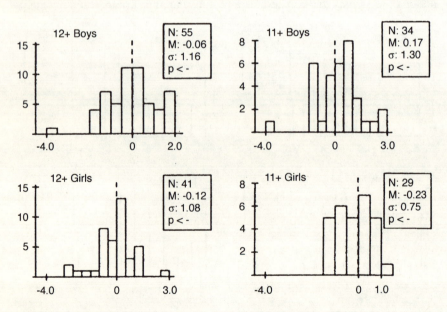

Figure 5.8 Delayed post-PRT residualized gain scores for experimental groups: means, distribution, etc.

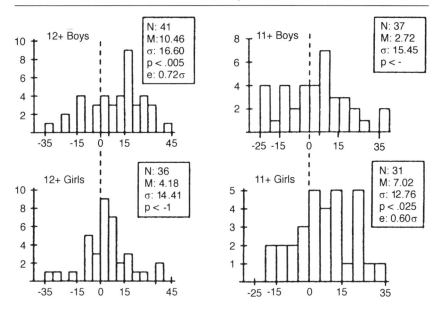

*Figure 5.9* Delayed postscience residualized gain scores for experimental groups: means, distribution, etc.

## Delayed science achievement

These were the schools' own tests, very different in nature from the Piagetian measures already reported. At this point, the CASE intervention was over, and the schools were asked to provide end-of-year examination results that tested the students on the science they learned during the year following the intervention. In most cases, the students were no longer in classes that could be identified with previous experimental and control groups but were mixed and taught by different teachers. Pupils in most of the 11+ groups had actually moved from middle school to high school and so were in a completely different environment. Figure 5.9 provides a direct comparison between ex-CASE and control students of their ability to benefit from the same instruction. The 12+ boys again showed a very strong effect and the bimodality noted previously. The 11+ girls also showed a significant effect, confirming the suspicion raised already about an effect with this group. Note that all groups showed positive effects, although they did not reach statistical significance for 12+ girls or 11+ boys.

## 1989–1990: GCSE examinations

The six 12+ classes completed their Year 11 (US Grade 10) at secondary school and took the GCSE examinations in June 1989, two years after the

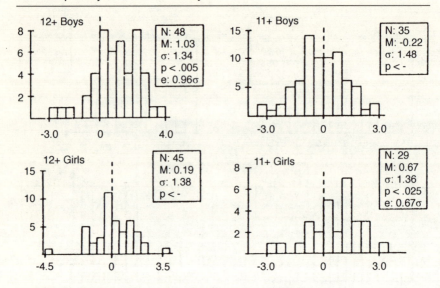

*Figure 5.10* Residualized gain in grades of experimental group on General Certificate of Secondary Education: science

end of the CASE intervention program. The three 11+ classes took their GCSE in 1990, three years after the end of the intervention program. We analyzed GCSE results for science (amalgamated results for whichever combination of chemistry, physics, biology, and integrated science an individual took), mathematics, and English. Results for science are shown in Figure 5.10. The effect on the 12+ boys group was even stronger than in the delayed test results just reported. This group averaged one grade higher than controls, after individual pretest differences are taken into account. This represents an effect size of 1 *SD*, achieved 2 years after the end of the CASE intervention program. The 11+ boys and the 12+ girls showed no significant effects, although the girls who started the experiment aged 11+ showed a significant effect. Their science grades improved, compared with controls, by $\frac{2}{3}$ *SD*. Thus, the hints from data reported earlier that there was some effect with the 11+ girls finally showed up strongly in externally set and marked national examinations of science achievement, 3 years after the end of the intervention. By any standard, this must be counted as a long-term effect. In both of the groups that showed significant effects, bimodality of distribution appeared again, indicating that some benefited far more than others from the *Thinking Science* experience.

So far, the data provide evidence consistent with the hypothesis that the strategies incorporated into the teaching and materials of *Thinking Science* promote the long-term development of general thinking ability within the domain of science, which can be applied to a wide variety of new learning within that domain. Even allowing for the inconsistency of the effect across

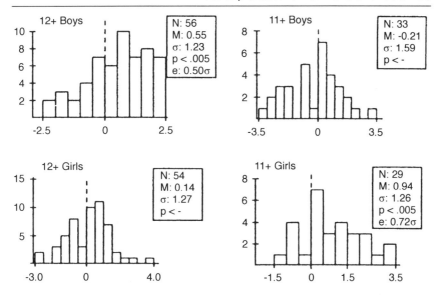

*Figure 5.11* Residualized gain in grades of experimental group on General Certificate of Secondary Education: mathematics

different individuals, this already provides substantial support for a parti-cular approach to the long-term improvement of learning in science through the development of general science thinking ability. We discuss the age and gender differences after results for other subjects are presented.

Results from the other domains throw more light on the underlying psychological model. Figure 5.11 shows the results for GCSE mathe-matics. The results follow a similar pattern to those in science, with significant effects achieved in the 12+ boys' and 11+ girls' groups. The former result is weaker than that for science but is consistent with a possible "knock-on" effect of the mathematical nature of many of the *Thinking Science* activities on achievement in mathematics itself, although the longevity is again remarkable. For the 11+ girls, the effect was stronger than for science (over 0.7 *SD*) and was longer lasting even than for the 12+ group. This could be taken as evidence for the effect of the intervention on general underlying cognition. We return to this discussion later. For both groups, there was again evidence of bimodality of distribution of gains. For a completely different domain, we turn to the GCSE English data. Before presenting results, it is worth looking at some tasks typical of a GCSE English examination:

1 A tape recording of some dialogue is played twice, and a transcript is provided. Students are given 50 minutes to write assessments of some of the characters portrayed, to describe the views of one of them on a

particular issue discussed in the dialogue, and to write their own response to these views.

2 Three excerpts from guidebooks describing the same place but written in very different styles are presented. The student is given 45 minutes to write two pieces: one describing the place from a historical perspective and one providing technical information useful for a group making a school visit to the place.

3 Students are given 1 hour to write a free composition of about 600 words based on the students' choice of one out of five topics. Each topic is stimulated by a title, an opening sentence, a picture, or the topic of one of the earlier questions.

The skills required in these tasks include analysis and comprehension, as well as imagination, creativity, and style. Enhanced achievement in such an English test following an intervention set in a science context must be described as *far transfer* of an effect from one domain to another very different domain.

Now, consider the experimental groups' residualized gain in grades on GCSE English shown in Figure 5.12. These results show significant effects in three out of the four groups. As before, there were effects in the 12+ boys and the 11+ girls, although they were rather weak in the former.

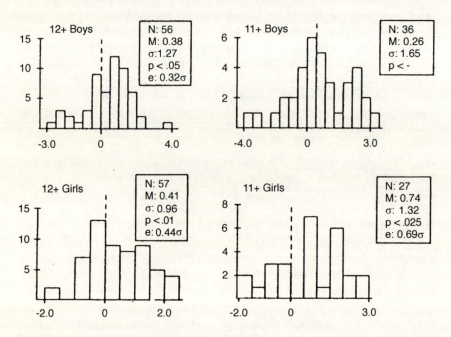

*Figure 5.12* Residualized gain in grades of experimental group on General Certificate of Secondary Education: English

Additionally, there was an effect in the 12+ girls' group. Even the one group that showed no overall effect, the 11+ boys, showed very marked bimodality of distribution and would have shown a significant effect if just one of two very low-scoring individuals had scored at the average for the group.

## Possible explanations

Evidence of long-term far transfer has potential importance for models of cognition; therefore, it is necessary to explore in more detail possible explanations for these results.

1 *Confidence?* The suggestion is sometimes made that the intervention boosts the confidence of students in their own abilities and that this, in turn, improves learning across domains. It seems unlikely, however, that confidence developed within science would affect performance in other domains (see the gender-difference work in physical and biological sciences; e.g. Hadden and Johnstone 1983; Kelly 1981; Ormerod and Duckworth 1975). In any case, a global notion of "confidence" is vacuous as a causal explanation for improved learning without a mechanism by which confidence influences learning, which brings us back to some sort of cognitive model. At the risk of sounding like behaviorists rejecting mentalistic concepts, we will not consider this line further.

2 *Language training?* An apparently simple explanation of how pupils who followed the *Thinking Science* program subsequently performed better in English is that of a direct training effect. This supposes that, although the program was set in a science context, it encouraged reasoned discussion among pupils exploring the meaning of new vocabulary in the search for explanations of physical events. This enrichment of language use is then supposed to persist (in memory?) and show up in enhanced performance in general English tests 2 and 3 years later. We find it implausible that a language-development effect that is almost incidental to the aims of the program and is set in a science context could be so long-lived and become generalized. A more deep-rooted explanation seems to be necessary.

3 *Language develops language?* Perhaps the intervention enhances linguistic development so that the new linguistic skills open the way for improved subsequent learning in language. Such a self-promoting system or "virtuous circle" would be characteristic of development, as contrasted with learning, and as such would be consistent with the hoped-for outcomes of the experiment. This explanation still relates particularly to the development of a domain-specific function, as something parallel to but not integral with the development of scientific and mathematical proficiencies.

4 *General cognitive development?* Results from the English GCSE are also consistent with the possibility that the CASE intervention, by directly addressing the promotion of the development of underlying cognitive structures, raises students' general intellectual processing power and thus enables them to make better use of all the learning experiences provided by their schooling. This is the most general level of cognitive explanation and the one for which long-term far transfer is cited as necessary evidence.

In summary, we seriously consider two hypotheses at different levels of generality: (a) parallel development in linguistic and mathematical–scientific domains and (b) general intellectual development. We use differences in effects on different age and gender groups in trying to construct possible explanations but admit to some hesitation in this: 11+ and 12+ groups were not different only with respect to starting age. Those in the 11+ group were somewhat more able generally, and many of them were in middle schools that provide a rather different learning milieu from secondary schools. There are thus at least two potentially confounding factors militating against simple 11+ versus 12+ comparisons.

With this proviso in mind, it is consistent with either hypothesis (a) or (b) that the girls make the predominant contribution to the overall gains in language learning. In the first hypothesis (a), it is claimed that girls have a greater propensity for language and make the most of the linguistic opportunities within the intervention program. If the general cognitive development hypothesis (b) is favored, the claim is that students apply their enhanced intellectual power in learning domains that are of greatest interest to them and that the domains of interest tend toward science and mathematics for boys and language for girls.

The difference in effects with 11+ and 12+ groups is not readily explained by hypothesis (a). Why should 11- to 13-year-old boys be less susceptible to the development of domain-specific scientific thinking strategies than 12- to 14-year-old boys? Why should 11- to 13-year-old girls be more susceptible to the development of domain-specific scientific thinking strategies than 12- to 14-year-old girls? We suggest that only if one uses hypothesis (b) (based on general intellectual enhancement), includes a maturational factor, and adds the long-established evidence on the faster intellectual development of girls over boys at this age can an adequate explanation be provided. Using hypothesis (b), we can say that at 11, the intervention struck a chord with the girls' earlier emerging higher level cognitive processing system but failed to resonate with the boys, who were still mostly limited to concrete operational reasoning. Just a year later, the boys had reached the emergent phase that the girls were in previously and so were ready to make the most of the intervention experiences. Why the 12-year-old girls seemed to have passed the period of most effective intervention is another question, and we can only speculate that the answer may be found in the evidence on girls' affective disillusion with things that appear scientific when they reach Years 8 and 9 (Grades 7 and 8).

**Further analyses**

To explore the suggested possibilities further, our analyses focus on the immediate posttest of cognitive development, because this is the best measure we have of underlying cognitive structure and the development in that structure that took place during the intervention. Any explanation based on the idea of cognitive structure should refer back to this measure.

First, we must answer two technical questions.

● How widely distributed among the experimental classes were pupils who made the greatest gains?

We consider as "high gainers" the nineteen 11+ pupils and the thirty-one 12+ pupils who showed the highest residualized gains on the PRT posttest, who formed the top three bars of the distribution histograms of those scores (see Figure 5.7). Table 5.3 shows the percentage of each of the experimental classes that were high gainers. The percentage of high gainers in any one class ranges fairly evenly from 15.4 to 45.5, with no outstandingly good or poor results. This argues in favor of the effect being due to the general CASE strategy rather than to its particular expression through one or two exceptional teachers.

● Were the high gainers those who started either with a low score (and, therefore, had much to make up) or with a high score (who might be thought to be "ready" for the CASE-type activities)?

The answer is shown in Figure 5.13. The high gainers highlighted in the distribution of PRT posttest gains are also highlighted in the distribution of PRT pretest scores. Clearly, high gainers come from a wide range of starting levels, which is supported by the absence of any correlation between starting level and gain.

Now, we must consider three additional questions, which cannot be answered so simply.

● Do gains in cognitive development predict gains in academic achievement?

*Table 5.3* Distribution of high gainers among experimental classes

| | Age Group | | | | | | | | | |
|---|---|---|---|---|---|---|---|---|---|---|
| | 11+ | | | | 12+ | | | | | |
| Class identity | 51 | 52 | 61 | 91 | 31 | 32 | 71 | 81 | 92 | 111 |
| % high gainers | 15.4 | 42.9 | 33.3 | 40.0 | 18.8 | 20.0 | 28.6 | 19.0 | 45.5 | 22.7 |

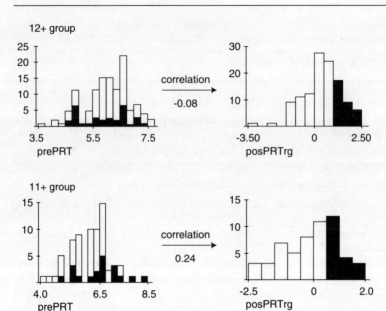

*Figure 5.13* Pretest levels of cognitive development of those who made the greatest gains to posttest PRT

Table 5.4 shows the correlations between post-PRT rg scores and the various measures of academic achievement. If the *Thinking Science* intervention program enhances cognitive development, and if enhanced cognitive development facilitates learning in all academic subjects, one would expect pupils making the greatest gains during the intervention program to be the same as those who subsequently show the greatest gains in measures of academic achievement. In other words, there should be significant correlations between post-PRT gains and gains in academic achievement.

*Table 5.4* Correlations between rg scores of PRT posttest, science-delayed posttest, and GCSE

|  |  | GCSE rg Score | | |
|---|---|---|---|---|
|  | Delayed Science rg | Science | Math | English |
| Post-PRT rg |  |  |  |  |
| 11+ boys | 0.52 | 0.47 | 0.41 | 0.45 |
| 11+ girls | 0.62 | 0.73 | 0.61 | 0.22[a] |
| 12+ boys | 0.39 | 0.33 | 0.67 | 0.38 |
| 12+ girls | 0.32 | 0.28 | 0.30 | 0.24[a] |

[a] Number does not reach a significance of < .05.

Table 5.4 shows that this is generally the case: Immediate gains in the posttest measure of cognitive development successfully predict all GCSE gains achieved by boys 2 and 3 years after the intervention, and they also predict gains made by girls in science and mathematics. However, there appear to be only weak nonsignificant correlations between girls' immediate gains in cognitive development and their subsequent gains in English GCSE. That this occurs in both 11+ and 12+ groups independently suggests that it is not a chance effect.

A possible explanation is that both boys and girls must approach learning and examinations in science and mathematics in an analytical way, and the PRT tests of cognitive development are good measures of analytical thinking. But boys and girls approach language tasks in different ways: boys still rely mainly on analytical methods, whereas girls predominantly use a different cognitive function that is not well tapped by the PRTs. Whatever this different function may be, it seems to be positively affected by the intervention, because girls who have experienced *Thinking Science* do, in fact, make gains in English scores. Our cognitive instruments, however, are less useful for detecting growth of this function.

- What happened to the gains in cognitive development during the year following the intervention?

If we use the word *development* to indicate a nonreversible change that provides the potential to improve further learning, the hypothesis of enhanced underlying cognitive development is not served by data indicating that gains are not maintained (Figure 5.8). Table 5.5 shows the correlations between delayed PRT rg scores, immediate post-PRT rg scores, and the measures of academic achievement. There is little unusual about the data for the 12+ boys or girls. Correlation coefficients are generally higher than the corresponding values for the immediate post-PRT gains, as one would expect for tests taken 1 year nearer to the academic achievement measures. Correlations with English GCSE are

*Table 5.5* Correlations between rg scores of delayed PRT posttest, PRT posttest, science-delayed posttest, and GCSE

| | Post-PRT rg | Delayed Science rg | GCSE rg Score | | |
|---|---|---|---|---|---|
| | | | Science | Math | English |
| Delayed PRT rg | | | | | |
| 11+ boys | 0.49 | 0.36 | 0.44 | 0.46 | 0.45 |
| 11+ girls | 0.27[a] | 0.34 | 0.28[a] | 0.25[a] | 0.24[a] |
| 12+ boys | 0.65 | 0.63 | 0.40 | 0.64 | 0.45 |
| 12+ girls | 0.40 | 0.29[a] | 0.53 | 0.47 | 0.29 |

[a] Number does not reach a significance of $< .05$.

low, as we found with the post-PRT gains and for which we have already offered a possible explanation. In the 12+ groups, only the low correlation with the delayed science gains differs from expectation.

For the 11+ groups, the data are distinctly odd. Correlation values for delayed PRT gains are not higher than they were for post-PRT gains; and, in the girls' case, there are no significant correlations between delayed PRT gains and GCSE gains. In reviewing this element in the whole story some years after these delayed PRTs were administered, it is worth noting that three out of four 11+ classes were in middle schools. This meant that the *Thinking Science* intervention program was completed at the end of the pupils' stay in those schools and that the delayed tests were given after the pupils had spent 1 year in new (to them) high schools. The school change and becoming accustomed to new friends, new teachers and new working methods may have caused a hiatus in the normal progress of cognitive development. If so, for the 11+ group, we can set aside the apparently aberrant delayed PRT gain scores and point to the ultimate long-term success in GCSE gains as the most important evidence for the eventual real effect of the intervention program on academic achievement.

For the 12+ group, this explanation is not available, but here, except for the absence of difference between the experimental and control groups' delayed PRT gain scores, the pattern of correlations is inconsistent with the view that (a) the intervention has caused an enhanced development of cognitive operations and (b) this enhanced development has improved academic achievement in a range of domains. We believe that explaining the aberrant result would require a further longitudinal study in which the same measures of cognitive development were administered each year for at least 3 years and related to academic achievement.

● How can we explain the bimodality in many of the distributions?

It seems clear from the distributions of gain scores that some pupils from the 11+ and 12+ groups, boys and girls, have made great gains in achievement compared with controls, whereas others have made little or no gain. Even regarding tests on which the greatest mean gains were achieved, only two subgroups can be interpreted: Subgroup 1, consisting of perhaps one third of the group, made gains of 2 SD or more; Subgroup 2, the remainder, made little or no greater gain than the controls.

We strongly suggest that this effect can be explained in terms of learning styles: The whole *Thinking Science* approach suited some students better than it did others. Unfortunately, the design of the experiment, including limitations of time and money, did not allow us to carry out the in-depth classroom observations and interviews with pupils that might have elucidated this suggestion further. We recognize this as a limitation of the study.

## CONCLUSION

Evidence has been presented of substantial and long-lasting effects on general academic achievement of a cognitive acceleration program that concentrates on cognitive conflict, metacognition and bridging and that uses the schemata of formal operations as a framework for the development of activities. In particular, boys starting at 12+ and girls starting at 11+ showed strong and actually increasing effects over the period following the intervention program. The gender differences observed may be due to the different conjunction of the intervention program with critical periods for girls' and boys' cognitive development.

Two hypotheses rooted, respectively, in domain-specific and in general models of cognition have been explored: (a) that the intervention program influenced one underlying general cognitive structure, the enhanced development of which permitted improved learning in all academic domains and (b) that the intervention acted independently on two intellectual structures (e.g. a spatial-numerical one and a linguistic one), each of which in turn led to improved performance in its own domain. The evidence does not allow one to choose with a high degree of confidence between these two hypotheses, and the apparent loss of cognitive advantage by the experimental group 1 year after the intervention is a puzzling feature. Nevertheless, the gains in English remain a reality in need of explanation, and to science-teachers-turned-psychologists, who in this project worked through science teachers and the science curriculum, it seems unlikely that our intervention directly influenced language behavior more effectively than language teachers and language curricula did.

Which of the results presented do we expect to be replicable? New work in Korea and in England, currently in preparation for publication, provides replication of the immediate gains in cognitive development following a CASE intervention. In addition, we are confident that CASE or similar work in ordinary public high schools can bring about a long-term gain in academic achievement across a range of subject areas. We are less confident about the apparent age and gender differences and the point at which the intervention is most effective. This and a careful longitudinal tracking of cognitive development using measures consistent from year to year remain areas in need of further investigation.

We believe that we have responded to Alan Clarke's challenge. An intervention heavily dependent on Piaget's account of operational thinking has produced large effects on theory-independent national school examinations. We believe that the strongest contender for an explanation of these results is that of a general cognitive processor that has been positively influenced by the CASE intervention. If we have succeeded in raising the head of such a contender an inch above the parapet without it being blown off, we hope that will be sufficient encouragement for others to investigate its viability further. Come back, Piaget: much (but not all) is forgiven.

## NOTES

1 Although Kuhn, Amsel and O'Loughlin (1988) criticized Piaget's logical explanation of formal operations, they accepted that (a) there is a developmental aspect in the growth of scientific thinking and (b) the Inhelder–Piaget schemata have provided a rich source for a broadly consistent body of empirical studies into the development of thinking.
2 A typical but by no means universal pattern for a six- or seven-form entry comprehensive high school in Britain is to assign children with learning difficulties to a remedial group, and sometimes to select especially able children for a second group, and to form four or five equivalent mixed-ability groups from the remainder.

## REFERENCES

Adey, P. S. (1988) "Cognitive acceleration – Review and prospects", *International Journal of Science Education* 10: 121–134.
Adey, P. S. and Shayer, M. (1990) "Accelerating the development of formal thinking in middle and high school students", *Journal of Research in Science Teaching* 27: 267–285.
Adey, P. S. and Shayer, M. (1994) *Really raising standards: Cognitive intervention and academic achievement*, London: Routledge.
Adey, P. S., Shayer, M. and Yates, C. (1989) *Thinking science: The curriculum materials of the CASE project*, London: Thomas Nelson & Sons.
Brainerd, C. J. (1978) *Piaget's theory of intelligence*, New York: Prentice-Hall.
Brown, G. and Desforges, C. (1979) *Piaget's theory: A psychological critique*, London: Routledge & Kegan Paul.
Case, R. (1974) "Structures and strictures: Some functional limits to cognitive growth", *Cognitive Psychology* 6: 544–574.
"Children's Learning in Science Project" (1987) *CLIS in the classroom*, Leeds: University of Leeds Centre for Studies in Science and Maths Education.
Clarke, A. M. and Clarke, A. D. B. (1976) *Early experience: Myth and evidence*, London: Open Books.
Cronbach, L. and Furby, L. (1970) "How should we measure change, or should we?" *Psychological Bulletin* 74: 68–80.
Desforges, C. and Brown, G. (1979) "The educational utility of Piaget: A reply to Shayer [with final comment by Shayer]", *British Journal of Educational Psychology* 49: 277–281.
Feuerstein, R., Rand, Y., Hoffman, M. and Miller, M. (1980) *Instrumental enrichment: An intervention program for cognitive modifiability*, Baltimore: University Park Press.
Fusco, E. T. (1983) *The relationship between children's cognitive level of development and their responses to literature*, unpublished PhD thesis, Hofstra University, Hempstead, NY.
Goossens, L. (1989, September) *Training scientific reasoning in children and adolescents: A critical review and quantitative integration*, paper presented at the Third European Conference for Research on Learning and Instruction, Madrid.

Hadden, R. A. and Johnstone, A. H. (1983) "Secondary school pupils' attitudes to science: The year of erosion", *European Journal of Science Education* 5: 309–318.

Hallam, R. N. (1967) "Logical thinking in history", *Educational Review* 119: 182–202.

Inhelder, B. and Piaget, J. (1958) *The growth of logical thinking from childhood to adolescence*, London: Routledge & Kegan Paul.

Jurd, M. (1973) "Adolescent thinking in history-type material", *Australian Journal of Education* 17: 2–17.

Karplus, R. (1978) *Teaching for the development of reasoning*, unpublished manuscript.

Kelly, A. (1981) "Science achievement as an aspect of sex roles", in A. Kelly (ed.) *The missing half: Girls and science education*: 73–84, Manchester: Manchester University Press.

Kuhn, D., Amsel, E. and O'Loughlin, M. (1988) *The development of scientific thinking skills*, San Diego: Academic.

Kuhn, D. and Angelev, J. (1976) "An experimental study of the development of formal operational thought", *Child Development* 47: 697–706.

Lawson, A. E., Blake, A. J. D. and Nordland, F. (1975) "Training effects and generalization of the ability to control variables in high school biology students", *Science Education* 59: 387–396.

Lawson, A. E. and Snitgen, D. A. (1982) "Teaching formal reasoning in a college biology course for preservice teachers", *Journal of Research in Science Teaching* 19: 233–248.

Nickerson, R. S., Perkins, D. N. and Smith, E. E. (1985) *The teaching of thinking*, Hillsdale, NJ: Lawrence Erlbaum Associates.

Niemark, E. (1975) "Intellectual development during adolescence", in F. D. Horowitz (ed.) *Review of child development research*, Vol. 4, pp. 541–594, Chicago: University of Chicago Press.

Ormerod, M. B. and Duckworth, D. (1975) *Pupils' attitudes to science: A review of research*, Slough: National Foundation for Educational Research in England and Wales.

Papert, S. (1961) *The growth of logical thinking: A Piagetian viewpoint*, unpublished manuscript, Geneva: Archives Jean Piaget.

Parsons, C. (1960) "Critical notice", *British Journal of Psychology* 51: 75–84.

Perkins, D. N. and Salomon, G. (1989) "Are cognitive skills context-bound?" *Educational Researcher* 18: 16–25.

Renner, J. W., Stafford, D. E., Lawson, A. E., McKinnon, J. W., Friot, F. E. and Kellogg, D. H. (1976) *Research, teaching, and learning with the Piaget model*, Norman: University of Oklahoma Press.

Resnick, L. B. (1987) *Education and learning to think*, Washington, DC: National Academy Press.

Rosenthal, D. A. (1979) "The acquisition of formal operations: The effect of two training procedures", *Journal of Genetic Psychology* 134: 125–140.

Shayer, M. (1978) "Nuffield combined science: Do the pupils understand it?" *School Science Review* 211: 210–223.

Shayer, M. (1979) "Has Piaget's construct of formal operational thinking any utility?" *British Journal of Educational Psychology* 49: 265–267.

Shayer, M. (1987) "Neo-Piagetian theories and educational practice", *International Journal of Psychology* 22: 751–777.

Shayer, M. and Adey, P. S. (1981) *Towards a science of science teaching*, London: Heinemann Educational.

Shayer, M. and Adey, P. S. (1992a) "Accelerating the development of formal thinking in middle and high school students, II: Post-project effects on science achievement", *Journal of Research in Science Teaching* 29: 81–92.

Shayer, M. and Adey, P. S. (1992b) "Accelerating the development of formal operational thinking in high school pupils, III: Testing the permanency of the effects", *Journal of Research in Science Teaching* 29: 1101–1115.

Shayer, M. and Adey, P. S. (1993) "Accelerating the development of formal operational thinking in high school pupils, IV: Three years on after a two year intervention", *Journal of Research in Science Teaching* 30: 351–366.

Shayer, M., Adey, P. S. and Wylam, H. (1981) "Group tests of cognitive development – Ideals and a realization", *Journal of Research in Science Teaching* 18: 157–168.

Shayer, M. and Beasley, F. (1987) "Does instrumental enrichment work?" *British Educational Research Journal* 13 (2): 101–119.

Shayer, M., Küchemann, D. E. and Wylam, H. (1976) "The distribution of Piagetian stages of thinking in British middle and secondary school children", *British Journal of Educational Psychology* 46: 164–173.

Shayer, M. and Wylam, H. (1978) "The distribution of Piagetian stages of thinking in British middle and secondary school children, II – 14- to 16-year-olds and sex differentials", *British Journal of Educational Psychology* 48: 62–70.

Shayer, M., Wylam, H., Küchemann, D. E. and Adey, P. S. (1978) *Science reasoning tasks*, Slough: National Foundation for Educational Research.

Vygotsky, L. S. (1978) *Mind in society*, Cambridge, MA: Harvard University Press.

# Chapter 6

# The acquisition of conceptual knowledge in science by primary school children

## Group interaction and the understanding of motion down an incline

*Christine Howe, Andrew Tolmie and Catherine Rodgers*

It is widely accepted that primary school children will approach science with strong "alternative conceptions" about the variables at play which, unless directly challenged, will circumscribe learning. Extensive discussion concerning the form the challenges should take has led to the conclusion that learning will be maximized if children explore their conceptions while working with peers whose alternative conceptions are different. At present, however, there is little research to support this, and the small amount that does exist says little about the process by which learning is effected. The current study attempted to redress this in the context of motion down an incline. Individual pre-tests were administered to 113 8- to 12-year-old children to establish their alternative conceptions. On the basis of their pre-test responses, and in order to establish adequate controls, the children were put into groups of four according to whether their conceptions were different or similar. The children worked in their groups on tasks designed to elicit the exploration of alternative conceptions, and were subsequently post-tested. The pattern of pre- to post-test change gave some support to the notion that learning is maximized when alternative conceptions differ. However, it gave few grounds for thinking that learning involves the internalization of conceptions that the groups jointly construct. Rather, it suggested a process of private conflict resolution, for which the catalyst was discussion held during the groups but continuing long after their completion.

In the past, research into the acquisition of conceptual knowledge in science by primary school children was seldom contemplated. Educationalists were mainly concerned with the secondary age range, and when conceptual knowledge was studied by psychologists, the logical and social domains were the central focus. Recently, however, there has been a change, and it is not hard to see why. After a decade of debate, the

National Curriculum (Department of Education & Science 1989) has stipulated that "the knowledge and understanding of science" be taught from the first years of schooling. Thus, primary teachers have been charged with finding appropriate methods, and there was a widely held impression that research with the secondary age range would have little to tell them. It was known that prominent reviews like McDermott (1984) were documenting widespread failure to get conceptual knowledge across, with students often entering university with only the vaguest grasp of fundamental notions. Hence, it was felt that little could be gleaned from secondary practice apart from a need for different methods. Further research would be needed for positive suggestions, and this is what produced the momentum for the recent research.

Much of the research has been inspired by the view that children will come to primary school science not as "blank slates", but with strong alternative conceptions about the issues at stake. Thus, the problem, as articulated by Hewson and Hewson (1983), will not so much be to write in the received wisdom as to change ideas in the appropriate direction. The proposed solutions vary depending on the precise nature of the conceptual knowledge under scrutiny. However, when it is understanding of the relevant variables, a popular approach has been one that involves children in making their alternative conceptions explicit and subjecting these to empirical test. It is a solution that has already been incorporated into published teaching materials and, in that sense, is readily translatable to classroom usage. However, resource limitations mean that the materials will almost certainly be presented to children in groups, and this has been a consideration in the recent research. It has been hypothesized that given group presentation, the composition of the groups is by no means irrelevant. On the contrary, if the groups comprise children whose alternative conceptions differ, their interaction will be such as to maximize learning.

The motivation for the hypothesis is partly the theorizing of Piaget. This is because Piaget (e.g. Piaget 1972) clearly saw alternative conceptions about the variables which science makes relevant as the kind of ideas that advance by equilibration. As is well known, Piaget (1985) not only believed equilibration to be activated when opposing but incomplete conceptions give rise to internally experienced conflict. He also saw interaction over conceptions between children with differing and incomplete perspectives as a context where such conflict should arise (Piaget 1932). Piaget, however, never tested his ideas empirically, and it was left to Doise and his associates to take things further. Their studies in the logical and spatial domains (now summarized in Doise and Mugny 1984) and the follow-ups by, for example, Ames and Murray (1982), Berkowitz, Gibbs and Broughton (1980), Damon and Killen (1982) and Weinstein and Bearison (1985) have added further weight to the hypothesis in science.

Glancing at the research which the hypothesis has stimulated, it might appear as if the advantages of groups where alternative conceptions differ has already been shown. In studies which required children to explicate, discuss and test their conceptions about the variables at play, Champagne, Gunstone and Klopfer (1983), Forman and Cazden (1985), Forman and Kraker (1985), Nussbaum and Novick (1981) and Osborne and Freyberg (1985), obtained results which are seemingly positive, giving the impression of ample support. On closer scrutiny, however, there are a number of problems. In some cases, the guarantees that the alternative conceptions differed were far from convincing. In others, the interaction was subject to the interpolation of "expert" ideas (usually, though not always, from teachers), and this may have been producing the effects rather than the exchanges between the children. When these difficulties were avoided, the studies rarely had control groups of children with similar conceptions to differentiate the effects of group composition from the effects of empirical testing, and they seldom considered whether the beneficial outcomes survived over time.

An attempt to avoid such problems while researching the basic issue has, however, been reported by Howe, Tolmie and Rodgers (1990). It involved two studies, both concerned with knowledge of the variables relevant to flotation. In both, children aged 8 to 12 were pre-tested to establish their alternative conceptions, and grouped such that these conceptions were either different or similar. The children worked in their groups on tasks designed to elicit the discussion and empirical appraisal of alternative conceptions, and a few weeks later they were post-tested. In both studies, the children who worked in groups where alternative conceptions differed showed significantly greater progress from pre- to post-test, providing support for the hypothesis in the context of flotation. Flotation is, however, only one of the topics which, under the National Curriculum, primary school children will have to master, and it is not clear that similar outcomes would be obtained elsewhere.

The generalizability to other contexts is particularly unclear given the nature of the differing groups in Howe et al.'s (1990) study. Consistent with earlier research, Howe et al. found their subjects differing firstly in which of the countless possible irrelevant variables they habitually invoked, and secondly in whether the irrelevant variables were supplemented with relevant ones. Consequently, it was this kind of difference that their differing groups reflected. Reviews like Driver, Guesne and Tiberghien (1985) and Piaget (1930, 1974) make it clear that 8- to 12-year-olds differ in a similar fashion with other topics. Nevertheless, there are exceptions and studies by Ferretti, Butterfield, Cahn and Kerkman (1985), Inhelder and Piaget (1958) and Stead and Osborne (1981) suggest that motion down an incline is one of these. According to these studies, 8- to 12-year-olds differ little over irrelevancies, for object weight is the only irrelevant variable commonly referred to. Equally, they differ little over supplementation with relevancies, for all the relevant variables are habitually acknowledged. Where 8- to 12-year-olds do differ is over how they deploy the relevant variables. Some are confused about how the variables operate, thinking for example that a steep angle inhibits motion. Others avoid confusion, but cannot coordinate the variables into an integrated model. A third group (usually at the upper end of the age range) can coordinate, and only have the details left to derive.

Given the contrasts with flotation, it would be helpful to see whether grouping such that alternative conceptions differ has beneficial effects with motion down an incline, and this was one aim of the study reported in this chapter. In this sense, the study attempted to replicate Howe et al. with a contrasting topic. Replication was not, however, the study's only aim for, assuming the effects of group composition to be mediated through interaction, it sought also to supplement Howe et al. on the process by which this occurs. Doise and Mugny (1984) would seem to anticipate a process whereby group-generated conflict stimulates the joint construction of a superior conception which is then individually internalized. However, neither of Howe et al.'s studies supported this. In one, children whose group performance was worse than their pre-test were as likely to advance from pre- to post-test as children whose group performance was better. In the other, pre- to post-test change was positively correlated with group performance, but children whose performance was in opposition to other group members were as likely to advance as children whose performance was joint. Asking what factors other than internalization are precipitated by interaction, Howe et al. noted that it could be the continuation of changes made privately within the group. Alternatively (or in addition), it could be the adoption of changes made after the group's completion. If the latter, it could be with reference solely to the interaction or it could involve information solicited later. Recognizing these possibilities, the study aimed to shed light on each.

## METHOD

### Design

Pre-tests were administered to 113 8- to 12-year-old children to assess their alternative conceptions about the variables relevant to motion down an incline. Using the pre-tests, 84 of the children were assigned to groups of four such that alternative conceptions were either different or similar. Some six weeks later, the children worked in their groups on a task designed to elicit the explication, discussion and empirical testing of alternative conceptions. After completing the task, 25 per cent were given immediate post-tests to estimate private change within the group. All 84 were given delayed post-tests around four weeks later. These post-tests were designed not simply to assess conceptual change, but also to investigate the solicitation of information after the task.

## Subjects

The children were all pupils at the same inner Glasgow primary school. They were randomly selected from four age bands: primary four (8 to 9 years), primary five (9 to 10 years), primary six (10 to 11 years) and primary seven (11 to 12 years). Roughly equal numbers were chosen from each age band. Out of the total sample, 38 per cent of the children were of Asian origin, primarily from the Indian subcontinent.

## Apparatus

The pre-tests, group task and post-tests all used four toy vehicles. These were two lorries, identical in appearance but different in weight; and two cars, identical in both appearance and weight, the latter being between that of the lorries. Thus, there were vehicles of what will be called "light", "middle" and "heavy" object weights.

The vehicles were used with four parallel slopes which were supported by a vertical frame. The slopes were 1 m in length and 6 cm in width, and rested on pegs inserted into the frame. These pegs could be positioned 8.7, 19.3 and 42.4 cm from the ground to incline the slopes at "low", "middle" and "steep" angles. Three gates were located at 10, 59 and 80 cm from the top of each slope. These gates could be open or closed to produce "high", "middle" and "low" starting positions. Two of the slopes were covered with identical surfaces, the third with a lower friction surface and the fourth with a higher. Thus, the apparatus also allowed for "high", "middle" and "low" surface friction.

The slopes terminated, via short flexible extensions, on a mat which was divided into "near", "middle" and "far" areas.

## Materials

**(a) Pre- and post-test interview schedules**   The apparatus permitted the manipulation of the three variables which are relevant to motion down an incline (angle, starting position and surface friction) and the one which though irrelevant was known from the literature cited earlier to be favoured by children (object weight). Within the pre- and post-tests, manipulation of the variables formed the basis for interview schedules which examined understanding of their independent and coordinated operation. There were two schedules, one for the pre-test and immediate post-test and one for the delayed post-test. They differed in content but both provided six opportunities to respond on each of the relevant variables and eight to respond on the irrelevant. They did this through six three-stage and five single-stage items.

The three-stage items presupposed that a middle-friction slope had been set up with the middle angle and middle starting position, and that one of the cars (i.e. a middle-weight vehicle) had been allowed to roll down and come to rest in the middle area. This constituted the "standard display". The first stage of each item presupposed that another slope had been adjusted, such that it (or the vehicle to be rolled down it) differed from the standard on one of the variables but was identical on the others (e.g. the middle-friction slope with the middle angle and the middle-weight vehicle but the low starting position). The second and third stages presupposed further adjustments, such that there were differences from the standard on two of the variables (e.g. the middle-friction slope with the middle-weight vehicle but the steep angle and the low starting position) and then on three (e.g. the middle-friction slope with the heavy-weight vehicle, the steep angle and the low starting position). At each stage, subjects were asked to predict whether the vehicle would travel to the same area as in the standard, the near area or the far, and to explain their answers. It was assumed that subjects would reveal their alternative conceptions about the variables through the explanations they gave. Object weight was manipulated on all six items, with two of the manipulations at each of the stages. The other variables were manipulated on four items, with at least one of the manipulations at each of the stages.

The single-stage items were presented between the three-stage ones. They described real-world instances like two skateboarders, one on a gentle, icy slope and the other on a steep, ice-free slope, and two lorries, both free-wheeling on the same slope but one empty and the other loaded with bricks. Here, subjects were asked to predict which (if any) would travel furthest from the foot of the slope, and to explain their answers. Again, it was assumed that alternative conceptions would be revealed through the explanations. Two of the items manipulated object weight. The other three manipulated two of angle, starting position and surface friction.

The delayed post-test schedule concluded with three additional items. These required subjects to say whether they could find out more about rolling down slopes from, respectively, books, other people and direct observation, and if so whether they had tried to do this after the group task.

**(b) Group task instruction book**   Using a method shown by Howe *et al*. (1990) to be particularly successful at eliciting discussion, the group task comprised an individual phase followed by a collaborative one. For the individual phase, the apparatus was to be used with sets of six cards. The cards presupposed the standard display. They each asked subjects to tick whether the same area, the near area or the far area would be reached after a change from the standard on one variable.

For the collaborative phase, the apparatus and cards were to be used with a book which provided detailed instructions on how to proceed. An extract is reproduced in Appendix I. The book presented six three-stage and five single-stage items. These items were similar in form but different in content from those appearing in the pre- and post-tests. For each of the three-stage items, the book invited subjects to create a display which differed from the standard on one variable. For guidance, the book provided an illustration of the display to be created, omitting the "static" elements (i.e. the slopes that were not to be adjusted and the areas on the floor) to avoid clutter. Then the book requested subjects to compare the responses on the relevant cards and, when these responses differed, to come to an agreement. Once subjects had agreed a prediction, they were invited to test it, and agree an explanation when the outcome was different from what they expected. After doing this, they were asked to agree and test predictions and agree explanations given changes from the standard on two and then three variables, again following text which provided illustrations of the displays to be created. For the single-stage items, the book simply asked subjects to agree predictions and explanations.

## Procedure

**(a) Pre-test**   For the pre-test, the children were taken individually into a vacant classroom. After a brief introduction, the interviewer set up the standard display, and presented the items orally. When presenting the three-stage items, the interviewer always altered the apparatus as required by the schedule before asking the questions. Once the children had answered, they were occasionally allowed to roll the vehicles down. This was purely in the interests of interviewer–subject harmony and, to avoid influencing conceptions prior to the group task, it was only permitted when the correct area had been predicted. The interviewer recorded the children's responses in note form during the pre-test, and at the end indicated an assessment of their English. Five children were excluded from further participation because their English was deemed inadequate.

**(b) Scoring and grouping**   The responses made by the remaining children were used to assess their alternative conceptions. Assessment began by identifying the explanations given first for the angle manipulations, then for the starting position, then for the surface friction and finally for the object weight, and scoring these with reference to Table 6.1. To check reliability, the responses from a randomly chosen 25 per cent of the pre-tests were scored by two judges. Their agreement was 87.9 per cent.

*Table 6.1* Principles of scoring

| Score | Angle/starting position/surface friction | Object weight |
|---|---|---|
| 1 | Variable not considered or confusion about how it operates, e.g. increasing angle or decreasing surface friction will decrease distance travelled. | Variable not considered. |
| 2 | Understanding of how variable operates but inability to coordinate variable with another, e.g. increasing angle or decreasing surface friction will increase distance travelled. | Variable believed to be important but not coordinated with another variable, e.g. increasing weight will increase distance travelled. |
| 3 | Understanding of how variable operates and coordination with another variable, e.g. increasing angle will reduce the effects of increasing surface friction. | Variable believed to be important and coordinated with another variable. |
| 4 | Full understanding of how variables coordinate, e.g. distance travelled is directly related to starting position height, increasing angle will decrease the effects of surface friction when the latter is held constant. | Variable excluded as irrelevant, e.g. object weight makes no difference. |

Using the scores, 27 children were categorized as "Level I". These children not only failed to coordinate, scoring 1 or 2 for at least 50 per cent of their responses. They were also uncertain about how one or more of the relevant variables operated, scoring 1 for at least 50 per cent of their responses to angle, starting position and/or surface friction. A further 44 children were categorized as "Level II". These children also failed to coordinate when judged by the above criterion. However, they were clear about how the relevant variables operated, scoring 2 or more for at least 50 per cent of their responses to angle, starting position and/or surface friction. A total of 37 children were categorized as "Level III". These children scored 3 or more (though a score of 4 was rare) for at least 50 per cent of their responses to all four variables, indicating clarity about how the factors operate and some coordination. Consistent with the results of Ferretti *et al.* (1985) and Inhelder and Piaget (1958), there was some tendency for level to increase with age band, although this was not statistically significant ($\chi^2(6) = 11.68$, n.s.).

Using the ascribed levels, the children were grouped into foursomes as shown in Table 6.2. In forming the groups, steps were taken to ensure, firstly, that the members of each group came from the same school class and, secondly, that the members of each D group differed as much as possible in ways apart from level while the members of each S group

Table 6.2 Groups as a function of pre-test level

|  |  | Differing | Similar |
|---|---|---|---|
| Low | Low D | Six groups each containing two Level I children and two Level II children (i.e. $N = 24$) | Three groups each containing four Level I children (i.e. $N = 12$) |
|  |  | Low S | Three groups each containing four Level II children (i.e. $N = 12$) |
| High | High D | Six groups each containing two Level II children and two Level III children (i.e. $N = 24$) | |
|  |  | High S | Three groups each containing four Level III children (i.e. $N = 12$) |

differed as little as possible. Thus, the D groups always had two children who thought heavy vehicles would travel further, and two who thought that light vehicles would do this. The S groups were always homogeneous over object weight. The low D groups always had Level I children who differed over the variable/s of which they were uncertain. The low S groups always had Level I children who were similar.

Such considerations meant that some pre-tested children had to be excluded from the group task. Had age and sex also been considered, subject wastage would have become acute. Accordingly, these factors were ignored. Despite this, there were no significant sex differences between the low D children and the low S ($\chi^2(1) = 2.12$, n.s.) nor between the high D children and the high S ($\chi^2(1) = 0.08$, n.s.). Equally, there was no significant age difference between the low D children and the low S ($t(46) = 0.83$, n.s.). The age difference between the high D children and the high S was, however, statistically significant ($t(46) = 2.56$, $p < .05$), with the high D children being on average 7 months younger than the high S.

**(c) Group task**   The group task was presented by an experimenter who had not been involved in either the pre-testing or the scoring and grouping, and who was ignorant of the type of group at the time of the task. This experimenter took the children in their groups to the classroom used for pre-testing, reassured them about a video-camera that was recording throughout, and explained the task. She then set up the standard display. Once the car had come to rest, she gave each child a set of cards, and invited them to make the predictions. The need to work independently was emphasized, and the experimenter demonstrated the display referred to on the cards (without, of course, rolling the vehicles) prior to each prediction.

Once the predictions had been made, the experimenter produced the book, and took the children through the text until they had completed the second three-stage item. She did not give feedback on the decisions, but checked that the reading was manageable and the procedure (especially the need to discuss and agree) had been grasped. For subsequent items, the children were on their own. When they had finished, the experimenter returned and, once more without giving feedback, enquired about some of the decisions. In total, the group task lasted between 45 and 75 minutes.

**(d) Post-test**   Prior to the task, one child in each group had been randomly chosen for the immediate post-test. This child was given a set of cards marked with a sticker. At the end of the task, the children were asked to look for the sticker, and the "winner" invited to "do the task again". Since most children were disappointed to lose, it was clear that enthusiasm for the task was in no sense diminished by its lengthy duration.

The immediate post-test was presented the afternoon following a morning group task or the morning following an afternoon one. It kept to the same procedure as the pre-test, except that it was conducted by the group task experimenter. The pre-test interviewer did, however, present the delayed post-test which was administered to all 84 group participants. The procedure for the delayed post-test was the same as for the pre-test and the immediate post-test. Scoring of the immediate and delayed post-tests was done in ignorance of the children's groups, and, like the pre-test, was with reference to Table 6.1.

## RESULTS

It will be remembered that one aim of the study was to see whether grouping such that alternative conceptions differ has the beneficial effects with motion down an incline that Howe *et al.* (1990) reported for flotation. These beneficial effects were in terms of the progress that individual children made towards the received wisdom of science when they were tested some weeks after a group task. Thus, it was learning in an individual and not necessarily immediate sense that was the primary concern, and in the context of the present study, this meant focusing on learning as defined by pre- to delayed post-test change. Before proceeding, however, it was necessary to decide whether the pre- and delayed post-test scores would have to be analysed separately for each variable or whether they could be combined across variables. Accordingly, the mean scores for angle, then starting position, then surface friction and finally object weight were computed for each child's pre- and delayed post-test. Each pre-test mean was subtracted from the corresponding delayed post-test mean to produce a

*Table 6.3* Change from pre-test to delayed post-test

| | Mean pre-test score[a] | Mean delayed score[a] | Mean change pre- to delayed post-test |
|---|---|---|---|
| *Low D children* | | | |
| Level I | 1.91 (.25) | 2.52 (.38) | +.61 |
| Level II | 2.34 (.18) | 2.84 (.11) | +.50 |
| All low D | 2.12 (.30) | 2.68 (.32) | +.56 |
| *Low S children* | | | |
| Level I | 2.02 (.28) | 2.38 (.28) | +.36 |
| Level II[b] | 2.40 (.13) | 2.69 (.19) | +.29 |
| All low S | 2.21 (.29) | 2.54 (.29) | +.33 |
| *High D children* | | | |
| Level II | 2.40 (.08) | 2.72 (.21) | +.32 |
| Level III | 2.71 (.16) | 2.78 (.18) | +.07 |
| All high D | 2.56 (.20) | 2.75 (.20) | +.19 |
| *High S children* | | | |
| Level II[b] | 2.40 (.08) | 2.69 (.21) | +.29 |
| Level III | 2.67 (.13) | 2.82 (.17) | +.15 |
| All high S | 2.54 (.19) | 2.76 (.19) | +.22 |

[a] SD in parentheses.

[b] Low S Level II children ≡ high S Level II children.

measure of change. Seven one-way ANOVAs were carried out to see whether the amount of change differed between variables for, respectively, the Level I children in the low D groups, the Level I in the low S, the Level II in the low D, the Level II in the low S/high S, the Level II in the high D, the Level III in the high D and the Level III in the high S. The results for the Level II children in the low S/high S groups proved significant ($F (3,33) = 5.08$, $p < .01$) with more change for angle and surface friction than for starting position or object weight. However, as there were no other significant results, a composite measure seemed warranted. Therefore, the means across, firstly, all pre-test scores and, secondly, all delayed post-test scores were computed for each child, and the former subtracted from the latter as the measure of change.

Once computed, the scores were organized as indicated by Table 6.3, and level × condition ANOVAs carried out on first the low children and then the high. By separating the analyses in this fashion, it was possible to avoid problems resulting from having the same Level II children in both the low S and the high S groups. With the low children, there was no significant level effect and no significant interaction, but there was a significant condition effect ($F (1,44) = 10.25$, $p < .01$). Thus, regardless of whether they had started at Level I or Level II, the children in the D groups progressed more. This was of course consistent with benefits accruing from grouping such that alternative conceptions differ. With the high children on the other hand, there was a significant level effect ($F$ (1,44) = 14.67, $p$ < .001), but there was neither a significant interaction nor a significant condition effect. Here then, regardless of condition, the Level II children progressed more. The absence of a significant condition effect cannot have been an artefact of the age difference between the conditions documented earlier. The correlations between pre- to delayed post-test change and age were +.05 (n.s.) and −.14 (n.s.) for the high D and the high S children respectively.

In addition to comparing the learning in the differing and similar groups, the study also had the aim of clarifying the process by which learning is effected. Its particular concern was whether learning could have been through the internalization of superior conceptions which the groups constructed jointly, and if not, when and how change was effected. To resolve the first issue, it was decided to analyse the group task interactions at the one point where the children were explicitly invited to construct joint conceptions, namely the point at which they were asked to agree explanations of outcomes that were at variance with their predictions. It was recognized that the children were not precluded from constructing joint conceptions at other points. However, preliminary scrutiny of the videotapes had revealed that when joint constructions occurred, it was only at the explicitly signposted points.

The issue under scrutiny seemed to imply two separate questions: (1) how superior are the explanations that individual group members construct? and (2) how many other group members accept each explanation? Accordingly, the relevant interactions were located on the videotapes, and an attempt was made to identify the explanations to which each child was subscribing. These explanations were then scored using Table 6.1 and a count was made of the number of other group members by whom they were accepted. It was not always easy. The children did not advance explanations at every stage, and (despite the utilization of verbal and non-verbal information) it was not always clear who was accepting and who was not. For purposes of analysis, ambiguous cases were discarded, and when what can be called mean "within-group performance" and "number of agreements" scores were computed for each group member, it was the remaining instances that were considered. The way this operated in practice can be clarified with reference to Appendix II which presents interactions that contrast over both the number of agreements and the explicitness of the explanations. The scores were obtained by a single judge. However, to check her reliability, the children in four randomly chosen groups were independently scored by a second judge. The consensus between the two judges was 80 per cent over within-group performance and 66 per cent over number of agreements.

Treating the consensus as acceptable, the pre-test scores obtained by the group participants were subtracted from the within-group performance scores to produce measures of "within-group change". As Table 6.4 shows, the values were largely negative, indicating that, far from being superior to the initial conceptions, the conceptions elaborated in interpretation of outcomes were characteristically inferior. However, the children's within-group change scores were based on some conceptions that were accepted by other group participants and some that were not. Since, as Table 6.4 intimates, the overall level of acceptance was not particularly high, it is possible that the scores when conceptions were agreed were better than the scores when conceptions were not agreed. If this were the case, it might still be legitimate to argue for jointly constructed conceptions being superior. To investigate further, within-group change was correlated with number of agreements. As Table 6.4 shows, the overall results were not encouraging. With the S children, the correlations were negative, suggesting that these children performed better when they failed to agree. With the D children, the correlations were positive, but they only reached statistical significance with the low D. Moreover, even here, there is little suggestion that the internalization of jointly constructed conceptions was involved in learning. As Table 6.4 shows, the correlations between within-group and pre- to delayed post-test change were never more than weakly positive. Given the generally regressive nature of

*Table 6.4* Correlates of within-group change

|  | Mean within-group change | Mean number of agreements | Correlations between within-group change and number of agreements | Correlations between within-group change and pre- to delayed post-test change |
|---|---|---|---|---|
| *Low D groups* |  |  |  |  |
| Level I | +.14 | 1.62 | +.71** | +.45 |
| Level II | −.18 | 1.44 | +.52 | −.01 |
| All low D | −.02 | 1.53 | +.59** | +.38 |
| *Low S groups* |  |  |  |  |
| Level I | +.11 | 1.96 | −.11 | +.56 |
| Level II[a] | −.21 | 2.27 | −.13 | −.56 |
| All low S | −.05 | 2.12 | −.28 | +.33 |
| *High D groups* |  |  |  |  |
| Level II | −.31 | 1.81 | +.09 | +.01 |
| Level III | −.52 | 1.78 | +.19 | +.20 |
| All high D | −.42 | 1.80 | +.14 | +.34 |
| *High S groups* |  |  |  |  |
| Level II[a] | −.21 | 2.27 | −.13 | −.56 |
| Level III | −.51 | 2.35 | −.77** | +.24 |
| All high S | −.36 | 2.31 | −.55** | +.22 |

** $p < .01$.

[a] Low S Level II children ≡ high S Level II children.

within-group change coupled with the generally positive nature of pre- to delayed post-test change, this means that there must have been many children who advanced from pre- to delayed post-test despite group performances that were worse than their pre-test.

In view of these results, it would be hard to argue that learning involved the internalization of conceptions that were jointly constructed within the groups. However, this leaves unclear whether learning involved conceptions that were privately constructed at that time. In order to investigate this, mean scores across immediate post-test responses were obtained for the children who participated in this part of the study. The pre-test means were subtracted from these scores to produce measures of pre- to immediate post-test change. Correlations were calculated between pre- to immediate post-test change and pre- to delayed post-test change, firstly for the low children and secondly for the high. The small numbers of children receiving immediate post-tests precluded subdivision within the low and high groups. The correlations were +.53 ($p < .1$) for the low children and +.63 ($p < .05$) for the high, suggesting that private construction while the groups were in progress may have been relevant. This accepted, it was unlikely to be the whole story as can be seen from the mean pre-test, immediate post-test and delayed post-test scores shown in Table 6.5. These scores were compared using one-way ANOVAs. As they proved significant ($F (3,33) = 12.36$, $p < .001$ for the low children, and $F (3,33) = 18.83$, $p < .001$ for the high), post hoc comparisons were made using the Scheffé test (Kirk 1968). As Table 6.5 makes clear, the immediate post-test scores did not differ significantly from the pre-test, but were significantly lower than the delayed post-test. This suggests that much of the progress took place once the group tasks were over.

Granted post-group progress, the issue is whether the crucial information was generated within the groups or solicited afterwards. The interviews at the end of the delayed post-tests suggest that it must have largely been the former. Only 19 children reported looking for further information, and for some the outcome was of dubious value. For example, 11 of the 19 claimed to have made direct observations, mostly via skateboarding or constructing

*Table 6.5* Immediate post-test related to pre-test and delayed post-test

| Group | Pre-test | Immediate post-test | Delayed post-test |
|---|---|---|---|
| Low | $2.20_a$ (2.17) | $2.38_a$ | $2.66_b$ (2.61) |
| High | $2.55_a$ (2.54) | $2.46_a$ | $2.72_b$ (2.75) |

*Note.* Means in the same row whose subscripts differ are significantly different ($p < .05$).

Unbracketed means are derived from the children who were given the immediate post-test. Bracketed means are derived from the whole sample.

slopes but one irrelevantly by varying the weights attached to balloons. Eight claimed to have consulted other people (mainly parents) but in one case this was to be told that object weight was critical. Four claimed to have read relevant books, but for one this was an account of car manufacture and for another it was the antics of Rudolph the Diesel! It is not then surprising that the children who reported looking for further information were no more likely than the other children to show above average pre- to delayed post-test change ($\chi$ (1) = .82, n.s.).

## DISCUSSION

The starting point for the study was the alternative conceptions which, according to the literature, children aged 8 to 12 display over motion down an incline. With this age group, conceptions almost always include all the relevant variables and only one irrelevant one. Where there are differences is over how the relevant variables operate and whether these variables are coordinated into an integrated model. This provided the starting point for the study in that it contrasts with the alternative conceptions which children in the same age group display for flotation. Thus, it raised the question of whether research with motion down an incline would substantiate the evidence which Howe *et al.* (1990) provide for flotation that when children work in groups to discuss and test their alternative conceptions, progress is maximized when the conceptions differ. Finding out was one of the study's major aims and in the event, its results were mixed. They were consistent with Howe *et al.* in that the low D children showed significantly greater pre- to delayed post-test progress than the low S. They were inconsistent in that the high D children did not show significantly greater pre- to delayed post-test progress than the high S.

Seeking to explain the mixed results, two possibilities warrant attention. The first is that although working in groups where alternative conceptions differ does not invariably maximize learning, it is one of the conditions that must be fulfilled. The second is that although working in groups where alternative conceptions differ may be helpful, it is by no means necessary. Evidence for the first can be drawn from the fact, made clear by Table 6.3, that besides failing to differ from the high S subjects, the high D children also progressed less than the low D. Of course, it could be argued that the high D performance was subject to ceiling effects or the tendency of relatively high scores to regress statistically towards the mean. However, this can only be part of the story. The mean pre-test score of the most advanced children in the high D groups, the Level III, was 2.71. Seeing from Table 6.3 that the mean pre- to delayed post-test change in the low D groups was only +.56, 2.71 seems sufficiently far from the ceiling of 4. In addition, the poor performance of the high D children relative to the low D was only partly caused by the Level III subjects. It was due also to the fact, apparent from Table 6.3, that the Level II children in the high D groups progressed less than the Level II children in the low D, a difference that was statistically significant ($t$ (22) = 2.50, $p$ < .05). This finding is of general theoretical interest because, being indicative of children learning more with lower performing peers than they did with higher, it is problematic for theories that rely on modelling. In the present context, it is strong evidence that the deflation of the high D performance resulted, in part at least, from a condition (or conditions) additional to differing conceptions which only the low D groups managed to meet.

The most obvious candidate for the condition/s is that the combination of conceptions should reflect the low D groups rather than the high D. Perhaps, remembering what Level II plus Level I amount to, groups where alternative conceptions differ help when the combination involves differences over how the relevant variables operate. Perhaps, remembering what Level II plus Level III amount to, they do not help when the combination involves differences over whether the relevant variables are coordinated. If this were the case, extensive limits would be placed on the benefits to be gained from group composition. Assuming that, as children get older, the differences between them are increasingly likely to be over coordination, extrapolation from primary to higher educational levels would be rendered unsafe. Indeed, limits would also be indicated for the primary level itself, since research reported by Clough and Driver (1986), Kaiser, McCloskey and Profitt (1986), Piaget (1974) and Strauss (1981) suggests that the differences in 8- to 12-year-olds' conceptions of air, heat and free-fall are also partly in degrees of coordination. However, before the limits are taken as read, recent work by Thorley and Treagust (1987) needs to be noted. Working with science students at an Institute of Technology, these authors investigated the effects of group interaction on the understanding of mechanics and electricity. From the descriptions they provide, the interactions were almost certainly between individuals who differed over whether the relevant variables were coordinated, and they appear to have been beneficial.

Thorley and Treagust's data are far from conclusive, and in any event they relate to an older age group. Nevertheless, they do raise the possibility that the additional condition/s may be something other than a combination of conceptions. Thinking what else might be involved, the requirement that the task have a particular form cannot be overruled. To see why, it should be noted that the differences within the low D groups were such as to guarantee disagreement over the predictions expressed on cards. After all, the predictions made by children who think steep angles inhibit are bound to conflict with those made by children who think steep angles help. However, as the predictions related to displays that changed one variable from the standard, the differences within the high D groups were not such as to guarantee disagreement over the predictions on cards. This meant that the high D children were not obliged by the group task instructions to discuss the predictions whereas the low D children were, and this may have been important. It is a conversational convention (Levinson 1983) that when disagreement occurs, stances have to be justified and it is hard to think how the predictions in the present study could have been justified without reference to conceptions. Thus, in being obliged to discuss their predictions in a context of disagreement, the low D children were being offered an additional opportunity to interact over conceptions. The high D children were restricted to interaction in the context of jointly explaining outcomes. The difference may have been crucial, particularly when the examples of interaction over explanations already presented in Appendix II are compared with the lively exchanges over prediction differences in the following example:

(*The children had just put the heavy-weight vehicle at the middle starting position on the middle-friction slope inclined at the middle angle.*)

> *Moien* [*reads from text*]: If you all ticked the same box, go on to the next page. If you did not, try to agree where the lorry will roll to.
> *Barnaby*: I think it's the same square.
> *Imran*: I think the same square, the same square.
> *Emily*: But Moien did the further square. I did the same square.
> *Barnaby*: I think it's because it's not on a steep slope.
> *Moien*: But it's heavy on it.
> *Barnaby*: I think it'll go to the middle one.
> *Emily*: Shall we try it?
> *Barnaby*: No we've got to agree. I think it'll go to the middle one. It'll go to the middle one because it's not on a very steep slope.
> *Moien*: But it's got weight on it.
> *Imran*: It's the slope that's important, and where it starts from.
> *Barnaby*: The weight doesn't matter.
> *Emily* [*to Moien*]: Will you change your mind?
> *Moien*: I suppose so.

If discussion in the context of prediction disagreement was important, it would suggest a condition additional to group composition whose implications are not unduly restrictive. Tasks which guarantee contrasting predictions when the differences are over coordination could, after all, be readily designed. In addition, however, it would indicate that the resolution of conception disagreements was in no way essential. Earlier, it was pointed out that the "joint construction" of conceptions only occurred after predictions had been tested, meaning that the resolution of conception differences cannot have taken place at the prediction stage. The example shows why this was. The children advanced conceptions of underlying variables to support their predictions, but they did not see the reconciliation of these conceptions as required for the agreement of predictions. However, once it is recognized that the centrality of prediction formulation implies the non-centrality of conception resolution, the question is raised as to whether further evidence can be found for the latter. It probably can be when it is noted from Table 6.4 that the "number of agreements" scores were not very high. Remembering that these scores were computed from interactions after predictions were tested, it can be inferred that even though joint construction did occur at this stage, it was still infrequent, meaning that even here there was some considerable failure to resolve conception disagreements. Yet failure to agree cannot have inhibited learning, particularly when, as Table 6.4 shows, the mean number of agreements was lowest with the low D children who learned the most. Indeed, the low D children produced significant positive correlations between number of agreements and within-group change but insignificant correlations between within-group change and pre- to delayed post-test change. This also suggests that it was not the resolution of conception disagreements that mattered for growth.

Of course, if the resolution of conception differences is by no means essential, it follows that learning cannot have proceeded by the internalization of conceptions which the groups jointly constructed. However, this notion was found wanting on other scores. It was not just the low D children who produced insignificant correlations between within-group and pre- to delayed post-test change. It was all the children. Moreover, with the low D children as indeed with the others, overall within-group change was regressive while pre- to delayed post-test change was positive. Thus, there are additional reasons for concluding that learning cannot have involved the internalization of jointly constructed conceptions, and this is of course important. It is, as intimated earlier, contrary to what Doise and Mugny (1984) appear to imply. Moreover, it is also problematic for theorists who look to Vygotsky (e.g. 1987) for an all-embracing analysis of development and learning, for here too the notion of internalization plays a crucial role. It is true that Tudge (1990) departs from Vygotsky in proposing that what is internalized from social interaction will not necessarily be progressive. It is also true that Forman (1989) sees the internalization process as mediated and perhaps undermined by decontextualization. Nevertheless, these writers share with Vygotsky the conviction that when a child operates independently "he continues to act in collaboration . . . This help – this aspect of collaboration – is invisibly present. It is contained in what looks from the outside like the child's independent solution of the problem" (Vygotsky 1987, p. 216).

Of course, rejecting internalization in the context of the present study does not entail rejecting it in every context. Garton (1984) has pointed out that most work in the Vygotskian tradition is concerned with practical problem solving. It may be, as Forman and Cazden (1985) intimate, that internalization operates in practical contexts but not in conceptual. This is certainly an issue for further research. Pending such research, it should be noted that, working with conceptual topics in non-science domains, Emler and Valiant (1982), Mackie (1980) and Roy and Howe (1990) have obtained results that are also hard to reconcile with an internalization process. Thus, there are clearly some areas where the effects of group interaction cannot be by way of internalization, and it is appropriate to look for an alternative process. From the results of the present study, the most plausible candidate seems to be a process which involves the private resolution of conflicts between conceptions made salient by the group interactions. The fact that pre- to immediate post-test change was positively correlated with pre- to delayed post-test change, coupled with the fact that learning seems to have been largely on the basis of within-group information, seems to signal the impact of group experiences. At the same time, the fact that pre- to immediate post-test change was less than pre- to delayed post-test change suggests that the experiences created conflicts to be resolved rather than solutions to be remembered. What the indications are, then, is a learning process which makes conceptual growth implicit, and this of course also concurs with the notion that discussion in the service of prediction resolution is all important. However, regarded more generally, the implied process squares equally with the emphasis which, as noted earlier, Piaget (1985) places on "internally experienced conflicts" and gradual equilibration, suggesting that in some contexts at least such notions remain relevant to developmental theory. Finally, to conclude with the educational issue with which the chapter began, the process would, if similar effects were found in ordinary classroom contexts, have profound implications for the pacing of teaching.

## ACKNOWLEDGEMENTS

The research reported in this paper was supported by ESRC grant C00232426. Thanks are due to the ESRC and also to the schools who participated in the research and its pilot study.

## REFERENCES

Ames, G. J. and Murray, F. B. (1982) "When two wrongs make a right: Promoting cognitive change by social conflict", *Developmental Psychology* 18: 894–897.
Berkowitz, M. W., Gibbs, J. C. and Broughton, J. M. (1980) "The relation of moral development to developmental effects of peer dialogues", *Merrill-Palmer Quarterly* 26: 341–357.
Champagne, A. B., Gunstone, R. and Klopfer, L. E. (1983) 'Effecting changes in cognitive structure amongst physics students", paper presented to American Educational Research Association, Montreal.
Clough, E. E. and Driver, R. (1986) "A study of consistency in the use of students' conceptual frameworks across different task contexts", *Science Education* 70: 473–496.
Damon, W. and Killen, M. (1982) "Peer interaction and the process of change in children's moral reasoning", *Merrill-Palmer Quarterly* 28: 347–367.

Department of Education & Science (1989) *Science in the National Curriculum*, London: HMSO.

Doise, W. and Mugny, G. (1984) *The social development of the intellect*, Oxford: Pergamon.

Driver, R., Guesne, E. and Tiberghien, A. (1985) *Children's ideas in science*, Milton Keynes: Open University Press.

Emler, N. and Valiant, G. (1982) "Social interaction and cognitive conflict in the development of spatial co-ordination skills", *British Journal of Psychology* 73: 295–303.

Ferretti, R. P., Butterfield, E. C., Cahn, A. and Kerkman, D. (1985) "The classification of children's knowledge: Development of the balance-scale and inclined-plane tasks", *Journal of Experimental Child Psychology* 39: 131–160.

Forman, E. A. (1989) "The role of peer interaction in the social construction of mathematical knowledge", in N. Webb (ed.) *Peer interaction, problem-solving and cognition: Multidisciplinary perspectives*, Oxford: Pergamon.

Forman, E. A. and Cazden, C. B. (1985) "Exploring Vygotskian perspectives in education: The cognitive value of peer interaction", in J. V. Werstch (ed.) *Culture, communication and cognition: Vygotskian perspectives*, Cambridge: Cambridge University Press.

Forman, E. A. and Kraker, M. J. (1985) "The social origin of logic: The contribution of Piaget and Vygotsky", in M. W. Berkowitz (ed.) *Peer conflict and psychological growth*, San Francisco: Jossey-Bass.

Garton, A. F. (1984) "Social interaction and cognitive growth: Possible causal mechanisms", *British Journal of Developmental Psychology* 2: 269–274.

Hewson, M. G. and Hewson, P. W. (1983) "The effect of instruction using students' prior knowledge and conceptual change strategies on science learning", *Journal of Research in Science Teaching* 20: 731–743.

Howe, C. J., Tolmie, A. and Rodgers, C. (1990) "Physics in the primary school: Peer interaction and the understanding of floating and sinking", *European Journal of Psychology of Education* V: 459–475.

Inhelder, B. and Piaget, J. (1958) *The growth of logical thinking from childhood to adolescence*, New York: Basic Books.

Kaiser, M. K., McCloskey, M. and Profitt, D. R. (1986) "Development of intuitive theories of motion", *Developmental Psychology* 22: 67–71.

Kirk, R. E. (1968) *Experimental design procedures for the behavioural sciences*, Belmont, CA: Brooks Cole.

Levinson, S. C. (1983) *Pragmatics*, Cambridge: Cambridge University Press.

Mackie, D. (1980) "A cross-cultural study of intra-individual and inter-individual conflicts of centrations", *European Journal of Social Psychology* 10: 313–318.

McDermott, L. C. (1984) "Research on conceptual understanding in mechanics", *Physics Today* 37: 24–32.

Nussbaum, J. and Novick, S. (1981) "Brainstorming in the classroom to invent a model: A case study", *School Science Review* 62: 771–778.

Osborne, R. and Freyberg, P. (1985) *Learning in science*, Auckland: Heinemann.

Piaget, J. (1930) *The child's conception of physical causality*, London: Routledge & Kegan Paul.

Piaget, J. (1932) *The Moral judgement of the child*, London: Routledge & Kegan Paul.

Piaget, J. (1972) *The principles of genetic epistemology*, New York: Basic Books.

Piaget, J. (1974) *Understanding causality*, New York: Norton.

Piaget, J. (1985) *The equilibration of cognitive structures*, Chicago: Chicago University Press.

Roy, A. W. N. and Howe, C. J. (1990) "Effects of cognitive conflict, socio-cognitive conflict and imitation on children's socio-legal thinking", *European Journal of Social Psychology* 20: 241–252.

Stead, K. and Osborne, R. (1981) "What is friction? – Some children's ideas", *Australian Science Teachers' Journal* 27: 51–57.

Strauss, S. (1981) *U-shaped behavioural growth*, New York: Academic Press.

Thorley, N. R. and Treagust, D. F. (1987) "Conflict within dyadic interactions as a stimulant for conceptual change in physics", *International Journal of Science Education* 9: 203–216.

Tudge, J. (1990) "Vygotsky, the zone of proximal development, and peer collaboration: Implications for classroom practice", in L. C. Moll (ed.) *Vygotsky and education: Instructional implications and applications of sociohistorical psychology*, New York: Cambridge University Press.

Vygotsky, L. S. (1987) "Thinking and speech", in R. W. Rieber and A. S. Carton (eds) *The collected works of L. S. Vygotsky*, New York: Plenum.

Weinstein, B. D. and Bearison, D. J. (1985) "Social interaction, social observation and cognitive development in young children", *European Journal of Social Psychology* 15: 333–343.

## APPENDIX I: EXTRACT FROM GROUP TASK TEXT

(The extract gives the text for the *first* stage of the *first* item. The text became progressively briefer to avoid labouring instructions that are well understood.)

### The lowest gate

To start off, close the lowest gate on slope B and put the car behind it. Now, each of you must find your Card 1. Do this before reading on.

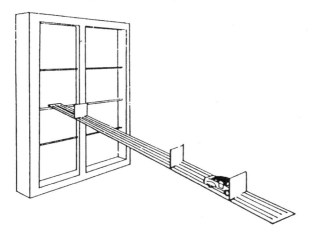

Have you done this? If you have, look at what each of you has ticked. Did you all think that the car would roll to the *nearer* square? If so, go on to the next page. If not, read on.

Did all of you think that the car would roll to the *same* square as the other car? If so, go on to the next page. If not, read on.

Did all of you think that the car would roll to the *further* square? If so, go on to the next page. If not, read on.

Did some of you think that the car would roll to the *nearer* square, and some of you think that it would roll to the *same* square as the other car or the *further* square? Look at the car together, and talk about which square the car will roll to. When you have agreed, go on to the next page.

Have you agreed? When you are ready, pull the gate up so that the car can roll down the slope. Watch carefully to see where it stops.

What happened? Did things turn out the way you all thought? If so, go on to the next page. If not, read on.

Talk very carefully about what happened. Try to agree why the car stopped where it did. Make sure that everybody in the group says what they think. Then talk about the different ideas until you agree which are right. Take your time and do not go on until you all think the same way.

Do you all agree why the car stopped in that square? If you do, turn to the next page.

## APPENDIX II: GROUP TASK SCORING

### High agreement

*(The children had been incorrect regarding the heavy-weight vehicle on the low-friction slope with the middle starting position and the middle angle.)*

> *George* [*reads from text*]: Try to agree why the lorry stopped where it did. Then go on to the next page.
> *David*: We can't go on to the next page then. We've got to agree.
> *Sam*: It's because it's got a smooth track.
> *David*: 'Cos it's got a smooth track.
> *Others*: Yes.
> *Sam*: Good on you all, you agreed with me.

(Each child was awarded a "within-group performance" score of 2 for understanding how surface friction operates without coordination and a "number of agreements" score of 3 for seeming to concur with everyone.)

### Low agreement

*(The children had been incorrect regarding the heavy-weight vehicle on the middle-friction slope with the high starting position and the low angle.)*

*Andrew* [*reads from text*]: If the lorry stopped where you thought, go on to the next page. If not, try to agree why it stopped where it did. Do not go on until you all agree.
*Abrar*: It's because there's not much hill.
*Sirinder*: Because I got it correct.
*Kemal*: No you didn't because you agreed with us.
*Sirinder*: No I didn't. It's because you made me agree.
*Kemal*: No I didn't.
*Others*: Yes you did.
*Andrew*: It's because it's a long slope.
*Abrar*: It's because it's not much of a hill. The peg's down.
*Sirinder*: I agree.
*Kemal*: I thought it would go further.

(Andrew was awarded a "within-group performance" score of 2 for recognizing the relevance of starting position without coordination. His "number of agreements" score was 0 in that nobody seemed to concur with him. Abrar and Sirinder were also awarded "within-group perform-ance" scores of 2, this time for recognizing the relevance of angle without coordinating. Their "number of agreements" scores were 1 for concurring with each other. Kemal was too inexplicit to be coded.)

# Chapter 7

# Thinking as argument

*Deanna Kuhn*

*In attempting to define intelligence in real-world contexts, psychologists have focused primarily on the kinds of thinking that people do in work-related environments. In this chapter, however, Deanna Kuhn describes another form of thinking that should be central to efforts to describe real-world intelligence: thinking as argument. It is in argument, the author maintains, that we find the most significant way in which higher order thinking and reasoning figure in the lives of most people. Kuhn describes her research, which examines the extent to which a process of reasoned argument underlies the beliefs people hold and the opinions they espouse about important social issues. Her results indicate that argumentive reasoning ability does not differ systematically as a function of sex or age (from adolescence through the late sixties), but is strongly related to education level. Kuhn believes that social contexts, such as the classroom, are the most promising arena for practicing and developing argumentive thinking skills.*

In their respective ways, both philosophers and psychologists are searching for more satisfactory conceptions of intelligence. Philosophers (Cherniak 1986; Harman 1986) have become concerned about how limitations of the human information-processing system may constrain theories of rationality, a concern that has led them to pay increasing attention to psychological inquiry into the nature of human cognition. Psychologists (Baron 1988; Gardner 1983; Sternberg 1985) have sought to remedy what they have come to regard as overly narrow conceptions of intelligence, arguing that intelligence must encompass a broader range of abilities and be defined in relation to contextual factors.

The efforts of those seeking new ways to assess intelligence originate from a wide range of psychological traditions, including judgment and decision theory (Baron 1985, 1988), structurally oriented developmental psychology (Gardner 1983), and psychometric and information-processing approaches (Sternberg 1985). Yet all of these efforts are united by the conviction that intelligence must be identified in the real-life contexts in which it occurs. Researchers have become hesitant to judge people's thinking abilities by their performance on problems conceived of and presented to them by psychologists. Instead, it is argued, we need to identify the problems that arise in people's lives and the kinds of thinking they have developed to deal with them.

Empirical studies of practical or real-world intelligence have thus far focused largely on the thinking that people do in work contexts (Perlmutter, Kaplan and Nyquist 1990; Scribner 1986; Sternberg and Wagner 1986; Wagner and Sternberg 1985, 1986). This has been a sensible starting point. Work is a major and often challenging part of most people's lives and hence one in which people's best, most complex thinking is likely to be observed. Yet, for many – perhaps most – people, work may not be the arena in which the ability to think well ultimately matters the most. In this article, I describe the investigation of a non-work-related kind of real-world thinking. I claim not only that this kind of thinking lies at the heart of what we mean – or should mean – by real-world intelligence, but also that no other kind of thinking matters more – or contributes more – to the quality and fulfillment of people's lives, both individually and collectively.

Social, rather than cognitive, psychologists have come closest to an examination of this kind of thinking in their study of attitudes and opinions (McGuire 1969; Tesser and Shaffer 1990). Traditionally, however, attitudes have been conceived of as points on a unidimensional continuum, and research attention has focused on the variables that influence movement in one direction or the other on that continuum. This same conception dominates opinion-survey and poll-taking activities in our culture more broadly: Is the President doing a good job? Should sex education take place in schools? Social psychologists now know that an attitude is much more than a point on a continuum, and yet, as any politician is aware, the point-on-a-continuum conception continues to prevail in our culture. Paradoxically, we expend a great deal of money and effort to assess exactly *what* people think on a whole range of social issues, but devote very little to understanding *why* they think this way; that is, what the reasoning is behind the opinions they profess. Implicit in all opinion surveys is the assumption that the views people hold are *reasoned* views – that a process of weighing pros and cons, or positive and negative evidence, has at least at some level of consciousness gone into an opinion; otherwise, the opinions that we undertake to assess with such precision seem scarcely worthy of the attention. And yet we have little real evidence that this is the case.

To what extent does a process of rational argument underlie the beliefs people hold and the opinions they espouse? It is this very basic sense of thinking well that I address in this article. Rather than debate the historical reasons why psychologists have paid relatively little attention to such an important kind of thinking and have tended instead to approach thinking largely as problem-solving, I will simply note, using the psychologist's terminology, that the thinking to be examined here is open-ended, ill-structured, and deeply embedded in a rich, complex knowledge base. As such, it threatens to be intractable. A major goal of the research described in this chapter has been to develop a way to conceive of such thinking that makes it more approachable – namely, thinking as argument.

It is in argument that we are likely to find the most significant way in which higher order thinking and reasoning figure in the lives of most people. Thinking as argument is implicated in all of the beliefs people hold, the judgments they make, and the conclusions they come to; it arises every time a significant decision must be made. Hence, argumentive thinking lies at the heart of what we should be concerned about in examining how, and how well, people think.

## STUDYING ARGUMENTIVE THINKING

### Rhetorical and dialogic argument

To examine thinking as argument, we must first establish a distinction, and then an identity, between two kinds of argument. The dictionary definition of an argument is "a course of reasoning aimed at demonstrating the truth or falsehood of something" (*American Heritage Dictionary* 1981). I will refer to an argument in this sense as a *rhetorical* argument. We think of an argument more commonly in its second sense – as a dialogue between two people who hold opposing views. Each person offers justification for his or her own view, and, at least in a skilled argument, each attempts to rebut the other's view by means of counterargument. I will refer to an argument in this sense as a *dialogic* argument.

Though connections are rarely made between these two kinds of arguments, they bear a close relationship to one another in terms of certain fundamental cognitive skills that are entailed in both. In a dialogic argument, one must at a minimum recognize an opposition between two assertions – that on surface appearance, at least, both are not correct. One must then relate supporting and refuting evidence to each of the assertions, and ideally, if the argument is to move toward resolution, be able to weigh all of the evidence in an integrative evaluation of the relative merit of the opposing views.

What is less often noted is that these same skills are entailed in more implicit form in a rhetorical argument, though the rhetorical argument may appear less complex. An argument supporting an assertion is empty, indeed superfluous, unless there is an alternative – an opposing assertion. Once two or more contrasting assertions are in place, cognitively speaking, the challenge of relating evidence to them poses itself. Presumably, the weighing of positive and negative evidence leads to favoring one assertion over its alternatives. Indeed, it is just such a weighing process that is implicit when we speak of a *reasoned* argument. Thus, any reasoned or rhetorical argument in support of an assertion implicitly contains a full dialogic argument.

## Scope of the research

The identity between rhetorical and dialogic arguments provides a framework for exploring the less externally observable rhetorical argument. Are the elements of dialogic argument evident when we probe the thinking underlying people's beliefs and opinions? And is the presence or absence of these elements indicative of the quality of people's thinking?

To investigate these questions, I asked people their opinions or, more formally, their causal theories on three topics: (1) What causes prisoners to return to crime after they are released? (2) What causes children to fail in school? (3) What causes unemployment? These topics were chosen as examples of significant social issues that people have occasion to think and talk about. They are also topics about which people are able and willing to make causal inferences without a large base of technical knowledge. Nevertheless, they involve phenomena of which the true causal structure is complex and uncertain.

Following the framework of the dialogic argument, our interview team asked subjects for evidence to support their theories, and then probed them regarding alternative theories, counterarguments, and rebuttals. We also asked a number of questions that addressed the subjects' epistemological reflections on their own thinking – for example, about certainty ("How sure are you about what causes ———————? "), alternative viewpoints ("Could more than one point of view be right about this? "), and expertise ("Do experts know for sure what causes ———————? "). At a second session, we presented some evidence of our own related to two of the topics, and asked subjects to interpret it. (See Kuhn 1991 for a full report of the research.)

## Participants

The 160 subjects who participated in our research were selected to represent people from across the life span, beginning with adolescents (ninth graders) and including young adults in their early twenties, middle-aged adults in their forties, and older adults in their sixties. Within each age group, as well as among males and females, we interviewed people of two different educational levels – generally those with a high school education and those with at least some college education. This difference was prospective among the adolescent group.

The teenaged participants came from four New York City high schools. Those in the higher education group came from two private schools serving a middle- to upper-middle-class population; more than 90 per cent of these students go on to four-year colleges. Those in the lower education group came from two parochial schools (one girls' and one boys') serving a lower- to lower-middle-class population; most of these students finish high school, but 60 per cent do not go on to further education, and the remaining 40 per cent enroll in community colleges or vocational schools. The racial composition of all of the schools was mixed African-American, Hispanic, Asian, and White, though the proportion of African-American and Hispanics was slightly higher in the parochial schools.

The young adults in the higher education group were university students in their junior or senior years. Those in the lower education group attended a combined business-training institute and beauty school; they either possessed a high school diploma or were required to earn an equivalency certificate concurrent with their training. The racial composition was African-American, Hispanic, Asian, and White in both schools, though the proportion of African-Americans and Hispanics was higher at the business institute.

The female participants in their forties from the two educational levels were either attendees at a New York City YWCA job re-entry program or administrative employees at a suburban junior high school. The male participants in their forties from both educational levels came from the suburban neighborhood in which one of the interviewers lived, and were solicited through personal contacts; they had varied occupations. In the case of both sexes, assignment to educational group was based on self-report. Participants in the higher education group had completed at least two years of college, and those in the lower education group had completed at least tenth grade, although almost all had completed high school. Racial composition was a mix of African-American, Hispanic, and White in roughly equal numbers in both educational groups.

Participants in their sixties of both sexes were members of a YMCA social group in a middle-class neighborhood in Queens, New York City. All were retired and had previously worked in a range of occupations. Those in the higher education group had completed at least two years of college and those in the lower education group had completed at least the tenth grade. All participants in this age group were White.

Also included was a group of experts of three different types – experienced parole officers, who were regarded as having expertise in the return-to-crime topic; experienced teachers, who were regarded as having expertise in the subject of school failure; and philosophers (specifically, Ph.D. candidates working on their dissertations in the philosophy department at Columbia University), who were regarded as having expertise in reasoning.

## Evidence to justify theories

I will not dwell here on the subjects' theories, though they were fascinating, since they were not our primary concern. It is important to note, however, that people tended to hold their theories with certainty; from one-half to three-quarters (across topics) claimed that they were sure or very sure that their theories were correct. Thus, we were asking people questions to which they felt they knew the answers.

Our primary interest was in the arguments people offered to support their theories. We began simply, by asking the question, "How do you know that this is the cause?" (followed by a number of probing questions along this same line). People also answered this question quite readily; no one said, "I don't know why I think so – I just think it's the cause."

What kind of evidence could we expect lay people with no special knowledge of or interest in these topics to offer? For each topic, roughly 40 per cent of subjects (averaged across topics) offered what we classified as genuine evidence. Such evidence is not conclusive, compelling, or even necessarily very convincing evidence. Rather, it is simply evidence that: (a) is differentiated from the theory – an important criterion, as I will show; and (b) bears on the theory's correctness.

Table 7.1 summarizes the different kinds of genuine evidence that were observed. The examples provide an idea of what genuine evidence looked like, in the subjects' own language. About half of the genuine evidence responses fall into the category of covariation, in which variation in the alleged cause corresponds to variation in the outcome. However, other kinds of reasoning recognizable from the experimental literature also appear, such as counterfactual reasoning, discounting, and analogy (see Baron 1988, for a literature review).

Instead of successful genuine evidence, I focus here on unsuccessful responses, beginning with those in a category we called nonevidence. Nonevidence took a number of forms, but the most striking was one in which the phenomenon itself is taken as sufficient evidence that it is produced by the cause the subject advocates. For example, one subject, Joe, indicated poor nutrition as the cause of school failure.

*Interviewer*: What evidence would you give to show this?

*Joe*: The points that they get in school. The grades that they get in school to show . . . [pauses]

*Interviewer*: What would that show?

*Joe*: That they are lacking something in their body. That the kids who were failing lack something in their body.

In other words, the outcome itself presumes the cause.

While Joe's response is clearly an example of nonevidence, other

## Table 7.1 Genuine evidence

| I. | Covariation evidence | |
|---|---|---|
| Ia. | **Correspondence.** Evidence notes simply a correspondence between antecedent and outcome. | (20Cms) [family problems] Well, if someone makes a study of cases of students where failures, dropouts . . . students who drop out of school . . . and sees where they have family problems, perhaps that would be solid evidence to prove what I believe. |
| Ib. | **Covariation.** The idea of covariation becomes explicit, and the evidence incorporates both comparison and quantification. | (60Cfs) [lack of parental support] Let's say the reading scores that are being published right now, and it somehow has a reflection on the [geographical] area they are in. The good ones are being in areas where parents take an interest, and the bad ones appear where there are many single-parent families, where perhaps they don't even have a home. |
| | | (TCmc) [unemployment] You could probably take a survey and find out the percentage of people who get jobs who have been convicts. I'm sure it's very low. |
| Ic. | **Correlated change.** Change in the outcome co-occurs with change in the antecedent. | (TCfs) [drugs] I guess people who have drugs and might not be doing so great in school, and so if they knew they took drugs they could see what happened when they weren't on drugs and, you know, prove it or whatever. |
| II. | Evidence external to the causal sequence itself | |
| IIa. | *Positive* | (40Nfc) [bad environment] It is not uncommon to hear that when someone is arrested that they have had previous charges in the same place for a similar crime. (What does this show?) I think it does show that it is in fact true that it's the environment. |
| IIb. | *Negative* (counterfactual) | (40Nmc) [prison's failure to rehabilitate] Their habit patterns. All outward appearances in every case that I have known or even heard of has not changed. If they had had their head properly shrunk, everything about them would have changed, from their haircut right on through. |
| III. | Indirect evidence | |
| IIIa. | *Analogy* (particular to particular) | (20Cmc) [return to a familiar way of life] I think if you look at it in terms of, well, an occupation, whether crime could be an occupation or not . . . most people generally stay in an occupation their whole life, and it's very hard for them to change. |
| IIIb. | *Assumption* (general to particular) | (20Cmc) [desire for material rewards] People that don't have things . . . I mean, everybody wants things, especially in this country. This is a consumer society. People want to accumulate things, and that's not true of everywhere. People just want basic things, and if you don't have them, and you don't know how to get them, then you can take them. |

| IIIc. | Discounting (elimination of alternatives) | (40Nfc) [unemployment] Well, I don't believe that anyone is just born that way . . . that they like crime, that they like going to prison. So if they could get a good job, I don't believe anyone would turn to crime. |
| IIId. | Partial discounting (discounting of alternative factor at one level or end of its range of operation only) | (40Cfs) [family background] The background of the parent is something important, because you find some very intelligent children with IQs of 140. And yet they have no family with background. You put them in a very expensive school, they cannot sustain themselves. |

Note: Shown in parentheses are subject identity – age group (T, 20, 40, 60), education group (C for college, N for noncollege), sex (form), and topic (c for crime, s for school). The subject's causal theory is indicated in brackets.

responses were somewhat harder to classify. Another subject, Frank, believed problems at home, specifically divorce, to be the cause of school failure.

*Interviewer*: How do you know that this is what causes children to fail in school?

*Frank*: Well, it's like mostly when the mother and father are divorced they can have psychological problems, you know, and they can't actually function in school.

*Interviewer*: Just to be sure I understand, can you explain exactly how this shows that problems at home are the cause?

*Frank*: Well, the kid, like, concentrates on how he's going to keep his mother and father together. He can't really concentrate on schoolwork.

*Interviewer*: If you were trying to convince someone else that your view is right, what *evidence* would you give to try to show this?

*Frank*: Well, let's see, I would take some kids maybe if their mother and father got divorced and show how it affects them mentally, you know. It makes them less alert in class.

*Interviewer*: Can you be very specific, and tell me some particular facts you could mention to try to convince the person?

*Frank*: Sometimes they have editorials in newspapers or on TV, you know, and maybe it could be a friend of yours that it happens to.

*Interviewer*: Is there anything further you could say to help show that this is the cause?

*Frank*: Not at the moment.

*Interviewer*: Is there anything someone could say or do to *prove* that this is what causes children to fail in school?

*Frank*: Yes. It could be, you know, partly, they could be the persons that have problems at home, and can't really handle it.

A similar form of response was offered by another subject, Kathryn, on the crime topic. Her theory was that prisoners return to crime because they prefer life in prison.

*Interviewer*: How do you know that this is the cause?

*Kathryn*: I think because if they commit crime they're getting attention. They'll be – the prisoner, you know, in prison – they'll be taken care of, they'll be given food and all this, and they get attention. They come out and everybody, you know . . . he was a prisoner, so that they stay away from him; they're scared and everything. So they decide that the only way they're going to be, that they'll have attention or they're going to be cared for is if they're in prison.

*Interviewer*: If you were trying to convince someone else that your view is right, what evidence would you give to try to show this?

*Kathryn*: The evidence I would give is that when they are in prison, they're secure. They're sure that, you know, no one's going to hurt them. Well, they're not sure no one's going to hurt them, but, you know, they know they're secure. They've got a place to eat, a place to sleep. But if they come out into the world and, you know, with unemployment and people not wanting to take anybody in that was an ex-con or something, when people reject them because of their past, they're sure to go back into the crime just to go back to their jail cell and stay in it.

*Interviewer*: Can you be very specific, and tell me some particular facts you could mention to try to convince the person?

*Kathryn*: Well, some facts could be that when they're in there, they'd want to make friends with other cons and stuff like that, and when they're out here, they've got to start all over again, and it's real hard for people who committed a mistake, for other people to accept that they've paid for it and everything. And then when they're out here people reject them and they look at them, you know, like they're scared of them. They don't want to stay in the world if they think everywhere they go people are going to be looking at them and feeling, you know, real insecure when they're around. So they'd rather be where people, you know, they're all the same.

We classified Frank's and Kathryn's responses as *pseudoevidence*, defined simply as a scenario, or script, depicting how the phenomenon might occur. In contrast to genuine evidence, pseudoevidence cannot be sharply differentiated from the theory it purports to support. Hence, responses to "What causes X?" do not differ greatly from responses to "How do you know that this is so?" or "What evidence can you give to show this?" In Kathryn's case, the content of her explanation is rich enough that she is able to make an intuitively convincing case for the *plausibility* of the cause she specifies, yet she fails to provide any genuine evidence that this cause is operating when the phenomenon occurs. Her own words, in fact, establish that, for her, the function of evidence is to establish such plausibility: "The evidence I would give is that when they are in prison they're secure." This "evidence" does not prove that desire to return to prison *is* the cause; it merely enhances its plausibility as a possible cause.

At its best, then, pseudoevidence enhances the plausibility of a causal sequence. At its most minimal, pseudoevidence simply illustrates the causal sequence, in which case it can be characterized as evidence by illustration or example. Some of our subjects' comments, such as the following from Nancy, explicitly equate evidence with examples:

> *Interviewer*: If you were trying to convince someone else that your view is right, what *evidence* would you give to try to show this?

> *Nancy*: Well, I could give examples of people I heard about that it happened to, and I could ask them questions about what they've seen in their own classes.

> *Interviewer*: Just to be sure I understand, can you explain exactly how this would show that this is the cause?

> *Nancy*: Because if I could give examples, they couldn't disprove my examples since they really happened.

For Nancy, it is not only examples that are "proven" simply by their occurrence; it is the theory itself. Again, the examples *are* the evidence to prove the theory.

In demonstrating the plausibility of a theory, pseudoevidence scripts like those of Frank and Kathryn elucidate causal *mechanism*, and there is much in the causal reasoning literature to suggest that mechanism is a perfectly appropriate means of causal explanation (Amsel, Langer and Loutzenhiser 1991; Antaki 1988; Hilton 1988). Might not we then simply regard pseudoevidence and genuine evidence as alternative explanatory styles? I would claim that the difference between the two is more fundamental and important than a simple matter of style. In the causal reasoning and attribution literature, subjects are asked to identify the causal factor that produced a specific past event, making the criterion of plausibility a relevant one (Hilton and Slugoski 1986): Could this cause have produced the outcome? In the context examined here, in contrast, subjects were asked to justify an assertion that, *in general*, X is the cause of Y. In this context, genuine evidence can be regarded as superior to pseudoevidence because it is more definitive.

What are the grounds for this claim? First, plausibility is neither a necessary nor a sufficient condition for the correctness of a causal theory. Causal theories that initially appeared very implausible have later been proven correct; for example, the germ theory of disease (Einhorn and

Hogarth 1986). Conversely, highly plausible theories have been disconfirmed. Furthermore, a causal relation between two factors can be demonstrated in the absence of any plausible theory connecting them; for example, when a substance is found to be beneficial in treating a disease in the absence of an understanding of how it works.

"Good" pseudoevidence, therefore, might heighten our interest in testing a causal theory, but it does not indicate whether the theory is correct. Because pseudoevidence can never conflict with a theory, it cannot really be considered evidence at all. Instead, pseudoevidence is more appropriately regarded as part of the theory itself. It is reasonable to assume that, in proposing their theories, all of our subjects envisioned some mechanism whereby the alleged cause produced its effect. When they elaborated upon their description of this mechanism by offering pseudoevidence, they were elaborating the theory, not providing evidence bearing on its correctness. Again, even the most plausible theories can be wrong.

## Alternative theories

A salient question thus becomes: Can subjects who offer only pseudoevidence envision an alternative to this scenario? Following the framework of the dialogic argument, we looked at this question next.

The subject was asked, "A person whose view is different from yours – what might they say is the cause? " Some subjects presented an alternative theory without difficulty. Others offered what appeared to be an alternative, but then immediately agreed with it – "That could be part of it too" – in effect incorporating the alternative cause into their own theory. They did not conceive of anything that was *not* a cause. Other subjects tried unsuccessfully to generate an alternative and instead produced something very similar to their own theory. But most interesting were the subjects who declined; for example:

I don't know what someone else would say. I have no idea.

I don't know what they would say. I'd really have to get someone else's point of view. 'Cause I imagine my thoughts run in this direction and that's about it.

I don't know what they might say is the reason. I don't think I'm wrong.

Or, significantly, the hypothetical other's view is simply assimilated to their own:

I think they'll say the same thing I'd say. I think the majority think the way I do.

Averaged across topics, the percentage of subjects able to generate alternative theories was about 60 per cent. This figure was higher than the 40 per cent who generated genuine evidence, but importantly, there is a significant association between the two: an average of 52 per cent of the subjects who generated alternative theories also offered genuine evidence; in contrast, an average of only 26 per cent who did not generate alternative theories offered genuine evidence. This association makes the meaning of pseudoevidence even clearer. In not generating alternatives, subjects who relied on pseudoevidence did not ask it to perform the very function it cannot undertake – to address the correctness of a theory relative to other theories with which (if the subject considered the possibility) it might compete.

Subjects who generated neither genuine evidence nor alternative theories thus took their theories for granted, as statements about the way the world is. They did not reflect on their theories as objects of cognition – as claims needing to be evaluated in the light of alternatives, as well as evidence. To truly evaluate a theory, one must not only reflect on it as an object of cognition, but reflect on it relative to its alternatives. Only by considering alternatives – by seeking to identify what is not – can one begin to achieve any certainty about what is.

## Counterarguments

Evaluating a theory against alternatives implies that it could be true or false – that is, it indicates an acceptance of its falsifiability. We looked at the issue of falsifiability in the study of counterarguments ("What could someone say to show that you were wrong?"). Would subjects comprehend the evidence that falsified their theory if they were to encounter it? The success rate here was about 50 per cent, but again, we focused on unsuccessful responses. Table 7.2 summarizes the various forms of successful counterarguments.

The most common reason that attempted counterarguments were unsuccessful was that they left the original causal theory in place – they did not constitute an argument against it. For example, Dean offered the following counterargument to the theory that lack of parental support causes school failure:

*Dean*: Well, the parents can use a lot of arguments that I am wrong. They would say they try their best under the circumstances, naturally, because they claim first comes to make a living, to sustain their house, and taking care of the children. But maybe they haven't got the opportunity to give them as much as they would like to give them. But that's a lot of cause of failure a lot of times.

*Interviewer*: What evidence might this person give to try to show that you were wrong?

*Dean*: The evidence would be that they try their best. They try to do everything that is possible, but sometimes it is just impossible to do it.

*Table 7.2* Successful counterarguments

| I. | Noncovariation arguments | |
|---|---|---|
| Ia. | Arguments against causal sufficiency. Antecedent is present and outcome fails to occur. | (60Nms) [lack of family support] He could possibly point out to me that here is a kid who succeeded while the family was let's say drunkards or separated and there was no inspiration at home. |
| Ib. | Arguments against causal necessity. Antecedent is absent and outcome still occurs. | (40Cms) [lack of family support] I think they would have to prove it with hard fact, that would show that not just one child but a large cross section of the population was failing and, you know, the parents were very heavily involved. |
| Ic. | Arguments against causal sufficiency and necessity. | (40Cms) [family problems] They could point out examples, specific examples that particular children failed and their family situation was very . . . what we consider a strong, stable family situation. They could also conversely point out a child doing well but yet the family is fragmented. |
| II. | Discounting arguments | |
| IIa. | Full discounting. Existence of the antecedent is denied. | (60Cms) [poor educational system] The fact that they are really consistently introducing and carrying out a practical program, an intelligent program, a progressive program in the schools. |
| IIb. | Partial discounting. The antecedent is denied for some subset of cases. | (TNms) [negative attitude toward school] He would show me some other students who have these . . . have good marks, and ask them why do you study hard. And they will say because the school is good. |

Clearly, Dean had addressed the factors responsible for his alleged cause (the cause of the cause), rather than offering an argument *against* its causal status. Possibly, subjects like Dean take the correctness of their theory for granted to the extent that they can only question *why* the causal antecedent exists, not whether it exists or plays a causal role.

Other subjects claimed to be open to the possibility of counterarguments, but were unable to envision any. For example:

*Bill*: Well, they would have to come up with a different viewpoint on the whole subject. I don't know what they could say.

*Interviewer*: Could someone prove that you were wrong?

*Bill*: Oh, sure. I'm flexible.

*Interviewer*: Is there any fact or evidence which, if it were true, would show your view to be wrong?

*Bill*: Sure.

*Interviewer*: What would it be?

*Bill*: I have no idea.

Some of the subjects who attempted a counterargument simply offered an alternative theory as a counterargument; for example, "They would say it's not the parents, it's the school that causes kids to fail." Counterarguments of this form leave the original theory unexamined.

Another form of unsuccessful counterargument does address the theory, but does not focus on the evidence that would be critical in evaluating it. Harriett believed, for example, that stress causes return to crime. She offered the following counterargument:

> *Harriett*: I have no idea [what they could say]. I don't know how they could say that there is no stress [here] in New York. I can't imagine. Even sitting on the bus . . . Why isn't the bus moving faster? I'm looking at my watch and saying this man is sitting in the office waiting for me, and this was stress. It was all built up in me.
>
> *Interviewer*: What evidence might this person give to try to show that you were wrong?
>
> *Harriett*: They couldn't, unless they live in a dream world.
>
> *Interviewer*: Could someone prove that you were wrong?
>
> *Harriett*: If they can prove it, I'd love to know it. No, I don't think so.

Harriett makes an inferential error identical to that found in much of the experimental reasoning literature (see Baron 1988, for a review). Her reasoning is based entirely on positive cases (of antecedent and outcome). It is the absence of negative cases (stress without return to crime or return to crime without stress), not the presence of positive ones, that is critical in establishing support for a theory.

Despite the critical role of falsifying cases, our subjects not only failed to consider them, like Harriett, but showed considerable resistance to the idea of falsifying evidence. As one subject put it:

> If I knew the evidence that I'm wrong, I wouldn't say what I'm saying.

Other subjects were even more adamant that there could be no counterarguments to their theories. Their responses are especially interesting because they offer an idea (more than does supporting evidence) of how subjects regard their own theories by demonstrating exactly what about the theory a subject sees as uncontestable. For example, Marilyn's theory regarding school failure centered on family problems:

> *Interviewer*: Suppose now that someone disagreed with your view that this is the cause, what might *they* say to show that you were wrong?
>
> *Marilyn*: They will never prove me wrong. I stand firm. I am a parent. I have two children, and they're not going to prove me wrong.
>
> *Interviewer*: What evidence might this person give to try to show that you were wrong?

*Marilyn*: I'm not really interested. All I have are the results that I put into it, and it's worked thus far, and I'm not changing my stance. And they're not going to prove anything to me, because if they do, to me they're just very narrow people who want things exactly the way they want. It's not going to work out that way.

*Interviewer*: Could someone prove that you were wrong?

*Marilyn*: No, they're not going to prove a darn thing to me. This is my career.

*Interviewer*: Is there any fact or evidence which, if it were true, would show your view to be wrong?

*Marilyn*: No. I'm a parent. I've lived it. Absolutely. My experiences may not coincide with somebody else's. Maybe their life was a lot easier. So they will be speaking from their experience. But don't step on my turf.

Marilyn's response reflects a sense of ownership of her theory that undermines its independent existence, leaving it uncontestable. In such cases, the argument or point of view "belongs" to the subject and, as such, is not available for independent examination. To challenge the theory is to challenge the subject's own self.

## Rebuttals

Rebuttals are critical because they complete the structure of an argument. They integrate argument and counterargument (or original and alternative theory). Only 25 per cent of subjects (averaged across topics) offered an integrative rebuttal. (Table 7.3 summarizes the various forms of successful integrative rebuttals.) Others offered a more limited form of rebuttal in which they simply provided a counterargument to an alternative theory, thereby leaving the original theory unexamined. Some simply argued by assertion – for example, "They said it's the school, I'd say no, it's the parents" – thus leaving both original and alternative theories unexamined. Still others simply declined:

*Interviewer*: What could you say to show that this other person was wrong?

*Lois*: I don't think I'd even try.

*Interviewer*: Why not?

*Lois*: He wants to believe it, that's fine. I'm not argumentive.

## Epistemological theories

As Lois's reply suggests, implicit theories of knowledge and knowing underlie subjects' argumentive reasoning. Our major findings regarding

*Table 7.3* Integrative rebuttals

| I. | Rebuttals of counterarguments | |
|---|---|---|
| Ia. | *Qualitative rebuttal.* The counterargument is rebutted on qualitative grounds that undermine its force, thereby restoring force to the original theory. | (40Cms) [poor home environment] (*What evidence might this person give to try to show that you were wrong?*) Evidence that shows that their early environment was not the way I said it was in cases of failures – for instance, that the people were wealthy or that the situation was other than the way I said it. But I think there are subtle forms of deprivation. The fact that somebody is wealthy does not mean that they pay attention to their children or set a good example. |
| Ib. | *Quantitative rebuttal.* The instances that constitute the counterargument are alleged to be of low frequency. | (40Cfc) [return to same environment] Every once in a while you hear of someone who really did better themselves while they were in prison. They went to school or they wrote a book or whatever, but that's one in a million, is my guess. |

| II. | Rebuttals involving alternative theories | |
|---|---|---|
| IIa. | *Arguments against causal sufficiency of the alternative theory.* The alternative cause is not sufficient to produce the outcome, as long as the original cause is absent. | (40Cms) [lack of motivation] [alternative theory: "enticements" of earning money and taking drugs] In terms of what you might call enticements of life, I would revert back to my basic premise that if you have the desire for learning and value learning, then even if you might to some degree take up the other enticements, you'd still maintain enough interest in learning to not fail. |
| IIb. | *Arguments against causal necessity of the alternative theory.* The outcome occurs in the absence of the alternative cause, as long as the original cause is present. | (40Cfc) [lack of motivation] [alternative theory: "joining gangs" and poor home life] Well, I could show that there are students who are failing and they're not in gangs and they have a fine home life, but they just don't seem to try for some reason. |
| IIc. | *Arguments against relative importance of the alternative theory.* The alternative cause may be contributory but to a lesser extent than the original cause. | (60Nmc) [innate character] [alternative theory: poor environment] While environment plays an important part, I think even more important is the importance of that innate quality of goodness. |
| IId. | *Arguments that attempt to reconcile original and alternative theories.* Original and alternative causes are linked into a single causal chain. | (60Nmc) [lack of economic opportunity] [alternative theory: "antisocial" personality] I've heard arguments where they said certain people are basically antisocial. But there again you come right back to what made them antisocial, and you come back with they never had the real opportunities to get into the mainstream of today. |

subjects' epistemological theories, summarized in Table 7.4, resemble those of other investigations of naive epistemological theories, beginning with Perry's (1970) pioneering work (Kitchener and Fischer 1990; Kramer and Woodruff 1986). Most interesting is the rich insight into subjects' epistemological beliefs obtained solely from responses to the three simple questions shown at the top of Table 7.4. (Assignment to epistemological level was based only on these questions about expertise, with the questions

Table 7.4 Epistemological theories

| | Do experts know for sure what the cause is? | Would it be possible for experts to find out for sure if they studied this problem long and carefully enough? | How sure are you of your view, compared to an expert? | Questions about proof |
|---|---|---|---|---|
| *Absolutist* Knowledge is objective, certain, and simply accumulates. | (20Nms) If they're experts, they know. | (40Cfs) Yes, if they have all the facts to draw conclusions. | (60Nfc) Not as sure. There again, I have to get my statistics and do some research and have some facts, which, as I say, I haven't thought about it. I mean, I have my feelings and thoughts, but I don't have the facts. | (40Cms) (*Is there anything you could say or do to prove that this is the cause?*) I'm probably very susceptible to, you know, acceptance of almost any proof on that. I think if somebody took a study from some place like a university like Yale or Columbia, or somebody of that nature, it would be believed. |
| *Multiplist* Knowledge is subjective, dictated only by personal tastes and wishes of the knower. | (TCfc) I don't think anybody knows for sure really, because there really isn't one right answer. There's not one right answer really for anything. | (60Nms) I don't think anything is sure. Things change. Just because an expert says something. There are so many experts, and that goes for doctors too. They have been wrong in so many instances. They are always changing. | (TCfs) The same. My opinion can stand just as high as theirs. | (TCfs) (*Would you be able to prove this person wrong?*) No, you can't prove an opinion to be wrong. (*Why not?*) Because an opinion is something which somebody holds for themselves. You can't change their opinion or alter it. They have their own opinion. <br><br> (40Cfs) (*Could someone prove that you were wrong?*) They could prove I'm wrong if they can give me good examples, but I can still hold my opinion. |
| *Evaluative* Knowledge is an open-ended process of evaluation and judgment. | (20Cms) Well, I think they're close. I mean, nothing's for sure, but I'm sure they have good ideas about why people fail. | (40Cmc) I don't know if it's provable. In other words, the situation is such that we probably are going to get to a point where it is still a matter of judgment which opinion would be right or wrong. | (20Cms) Confronted by an expert, I might be less sure than I am, because he can marshall all kinds of evidence and argue in an entirely different manner. I'm arguing from just a personal kind of perspective. But, by the same token, I would be reluctant to change my position unless a substantially varied, lucid and documented argument were presented to me. | (40Cmc) (*Would you be able to prove this person wrong?*) Perhaps to my satisfaction, not necessarily to his. I think it's more a matter of convincing by arguments, and whatever, than it is by any indisputable proof that you are wrong. |

about proof, shown in the fourth column, merely corroborative). About half of our subjects (averaged across topics) were classified as absolutists, who regard knowledge as certain and accumulative. This is a rather remarkable percentage, in view of the topics involved. Fully half of a population of average adolescents and adults believe that complex questions, such as why prisoners become repeat offenders, can be answered with complete certainty. Another roughly 35 per cent of the sample were classified as multiplists, or relativists. They typically noted that even experts disagree; therefore, nothing is certain, and all opinions are of equal validity. Everyone has a right to their opinion, multiplists maintain, and hence all opinions are equally right. In this way, both absolutists and multiplists leave the knowing process out of their judgments. Only 15 per cent of subjects fell into the evaluative epistemological category, in which knowing is regarded as a process that entails thinking, evaluation, and argument.

This epistemological naïveté may be an important factor in the limited argumentive reasoning ability that people display. People must see the point or the value of argument if they are to engage in it. If one accepts the absolutist view of knowledge as entirely certain and accumulative, or the multiplist view of knowledge as entirely subjective, argument becomes superfluous. Without an epistemological understanding of the value of argument, people may lack the incentive to develop and practice the skills examined here.

## Evaluation of evidence

Finally, the evidence (for the crime topic) that we presented to subjects is shown in Table 7.5. We presented two types of evidence, underdetermined and overdetermined, for both the crime and the school failure topics. The underdetermined evidence did little more than restate the phenomenon in the context of a specific instance, with few clues as to its cause. The overdetermined evidence, in contrast, explicitly referred to three broad families of causes, without favoring any of them. Subjects commonly assimilated both kinds of evidence to their own theories. "This pretty much goes along with my own view", was the prototypical response, and, again, subjects expressed certainty regarding these judgments.

If evidence is simply assimilated to a theory, any ability to evaluate its bearing on the theory is lost. More broadly, this loss implies a lack of firm differentiation between what derives from one's own thought and what derives from external sources (Kuhn 1989a). In such cases, one lacks control over the interaction of theory and evidence in one's own thinking.

## Results across subject groups and topics

Results across subject groups are easily summarized, since they were consistent for all of the skills. Skill levels show virtually no statistically

*Table 7.5* Evaluation of evidence

### Underdetermined Evidence (Crime Topic)

Pete Johnson is someone who has spent a good portion of his adult life in prison. He was first convicted of a crime at age 14, when he took part in the theft of a newspaper stand. He began serving his first prison sentence at age 18, after being convicted on several charges of auto theft and robbery. He remained in a medium-security state prison until the age of 20. After he was released on parole, he returned to live with his mother in the same neighborhood where he had grown up and began to look for a job. After 3 months out of jail, he took part in the robbery of a grocery store. He was caught and convicted and returned to prison. Since then, Pete has served 3 more prison sentences for different crimes, with only brief periods out of prison between sentences.

### Overdetermined Evidence (Crime Topic)

A study was done of 25 prisoners who were about to be released from prison. All had served more than one prison sentence; some were in prison for the third or fourth time. All had been in prison for the past 3 years or longer, mostly for crimes of armed robbery.

A social worker investigated the prisoners' life histories. All had unhappy early lives with many personal and family problems. None had good school records. They tended to be uninterested in school, to do poorly, and to drop out without finishing. Almost all became involved in crime at an early age.

A government official did a study of their prison life. The prison was badly overcrowded; each prisoner shared a cell with 2 or 3 others. Because of crowded conditions, prisoners were able to have periods of exercise and outdoor recreation only infrequently. No prisoner received job training.

Another social worker followed their lives outside prison during the 6 months following their release. The majority had been unable to find jobs since they had been released. Some applied to training programs, but there were long waiting lists with only a few openings. Many hadn't found suitable housing.

significant differences by sex or by age. However, there are consistent, sizeable differences by education group at every age level, as illustrated in Table 7.6, for two of the major skills for the school failure topic.

The other important result is the degree of generality observed across the three topics. Although many subjects exhibited a skill on some topics and not on others, the number of subjects who exhibited a particular skill either on all topics or on no topics was significantly greater than would be expected by chance, if performance across topics were independent. This outcome is critical, because it suggests that we have identified forms of thinking that transcend the particular content or contexts in which they are expressed. However imperfectly, we have tapped something about the *way* people think, above and beyond what they are thinking about. The performance of the expert participants supports this conclusion. The philosophers

*Table 7.6* Percentages of subjects generating genuine evidence and alternative theories for the school failure topic

| | Genuine evidence | | | | |
| --- | --- | --- | --- | --- | --- |
| | *Teens* | *Twenties* | *Forties* | *Sixties* | *Total* |
| Noncollege | 10 | 35 | 45 | 25 | 29 |
| College | 65 | 80 | 65 | 55 | 66 |
| | Alternative theories | | | | |
| | *Teens* | *Twenties* | *Forties* | *Sixties* | *Total* |
| Noncollege | 75 | 55 | 45 | 55 | 58 |
| College | 75 | 95 | 80 | 75 | 81 |

*Note*: Total N = 160.

reasoned well overall, as we expected, but the domain expertise of the others did not influence reasoning ability. Parole officers reasoned no better about the crime topic than they did about the other topics, nor did teachers reason better about the school topic.

## DEVELOPING ARGUMENTIVE THINKING SKILLS

### Individual and developmental variation

In earlier work (Kuhn, Amsel and O'Loughlin 1988), we looked at similar phenomena among younger subjects (third, sixth and ninth graders), using structured material in which theories and evidence were highly constrained and explicitly laid out for subjects. Under these conditions, we did observe age-group differences, but performance improved only up to ninth grade. At this age, education level again takes over as the variable that predicts performance, as we found in the research described in this chapter. Although the two contexts are not strictly comparable, subjects appear to perform somewhat better under the more structured conditions. This fact and, even more directly, the less-than-perfect generality of skills across topics in the work described here underscore the fact that these skills are not present or absent in any absolute sense. Developmentalists now think of skill acquisition in terms of a continuum, rather than as a fixed point. Virtually all cognitive skills will be displayed initially in only a very few contexts in which there is high environmental support. They are then gradually extended to a broader range of contexts that will eventually include those in which only minimal environmental support is provided (Fischer and Farrar 1988). Hence, an individual's skill level should be regarded as covering some range on a continuum, with the specifics of the context dictating the extent to which the skill will appear.

Although it is possible that we could have devised a more supportive context that would have enhanced the performance of our subjects, this fact in no way diminishes the importance of our findings. Assuming a skill acquisition continuum extending from implicit to full, explicit mastery, we are concerned with the upper, explicit range of the continuum. Psychologists have paid much less attention to this part of the continuum than they have paid to the early origins of skills (Kuhn 1989b). If, in a comfortable, neutral setting, someone asks us to justify what we claim is highly certain to be true regarding an important social issue, are we able to offer a reasoned argument to support our claim? It is this skill, not a lesser or more implicit one, that we would like and expect individuals to have.

The variability in such skills among an average population is perhaps the single most important finding of the research described here. Some people display these skills readily and without difficulty, others scarcely at all. How can this variability be accounted for?

Before turning to the central factors of age and education, some comment should be made regarding gender. A wide range of literature suggests that men and women may think differently. In many contexts, women are portrayed as less capable of rational decisionmaking than men, a depiction that often has critical practical consequences; for example, in legal deliberations regarding patients' rights to terminate life-support systems (Miles and August 1990). Whether or not such gender differences in fact exist, our results establish that they do not derive from, or build upon, differences in basic cognitive skills of argument. It is, of course, ill-advised in scientific investigation to draw any, much less definitive, conclusions on the basis of negative findings, yet our findings are valuable in suggesting where *not* to look in explaining sex differences. No evidence from our investigation suggests that one sex is any more disposed or competent to engage in argumentive thinking than the other.

With respect to age, we first need to consider the systematic change observed in early adolescence (Kuhn, Amsel and O'Loughlin 1988). How should this change be interpreted? The large developmental literature on Piagetian formal operations (Inhelder and Piaget 1958) supports the claim that early adolescence is the age at which the ability to reflect on one's own thought first emerges, as does the developmental theory of Vygotsky (1962), who regarded metacognitive thought as absent until at least late childhood. Though the Piagetian work on formal operations can be criticized for paying insufficient attention to the content of the theories subjects reason about, the hypothesis that thinking about one's own thought does not emerge until late childhood or early adolescence appears to be correct (Kuhn 1989a).

The research by Kuhn *et al.* (1988) showed that it is very difficult to induce subjects younger than early adolescents to think about their theories and about how evidence might bear on them. Children hold implicit theories about the world, but they largely think *with* these theories, not *about* them; hence they do not exercise control over the revision these theories undergo as new evidence is encountered. Children have weak metacognitive skills, in the most fundamental of the many senses in which psychologists have used this term in recent years. Many adolescents and adults in the Kuhn *et al.* (1988) studies do much better than children, and can clearly differentiate between theories and evidence and reflect on how the two bear on one another. Other adolescents and adults do not, however, which results in the same inter-individual variation observed in the research described in this article.

## Education and thinking

The associations we observed between educational level and performance appear consistently within each of the age groups, even though the skills involved are not usually an explicit part of the school curriculum at any age level. It is especially significant that the skill differences appear among adolescents when educational differences are only prospective and – most important of all – that we see no further development in skill when we might most expect and hope for it; that is, between early adolescence and early adulthood. Together these findings suggest that there are some very broad, general kinds of experience associated with education – not all of which take place inside school – that are responsible for these performance differences. Within school, it is possible that the academic experience encourages the attitude that assertions need to be justified and alternatives considered. But whatever these benefits are, they are conferred early, certainly by the end of junior high school, and we see no further development in these respects.

Our findings further imply that promotion of such attitudes and skills does not occur equally across all school environments. In our study, ninth graders in an academically and socially advantaged school environment manifested them to a significantly greater extent than ninth graders in a non-college-oriented school. On the positive side is the message that school environment makes a difference; on the negative side, however, is the disheartening finding that school makes no *further* difference beyond the junior high school years, at least with respect to the kinds of cognitive skills of interest here.

Increasingly, developing the ability to think well has been promoted as a central aim of education. The goal is an easy one to endorse, as the enthusiasm surrounding it attests, but to define exactly what it means to think well is a more difficult undertaking. If good thinking is to be a meaningful goal of education, we must first define with some precision exactly what it means to think well and, by implication, to be an educated person. This task is critical at a time of increasing pressure on educators at all levels to specify in concrete terms the expected outcomes of education and to document the extent to which these outcomes are realized. In this respect, the research described here contributes to defining what it means, cognitively speaking, to be an educated person, or at least what it means to define an educated person as one who thinks well.

To convey such a definition in a sentence or two, we might contrast two kinds of knowing, although they are in fact poles of a continuum on which most knowing lies. At one pole, knowing prevails because the knower never has considered otherwise; at the other pole, knowing is an ongoing *process* of evaluation, which the ever-present possibility of new evidence and new arguments leaves always uncompleted. Central to this process is reflection on one's own thinking – *metacognition* in its most basic and important sense – and beneath its surface is the structure of argument examined in this article. It is this structure that must be in place for someone to hold a reasoned belief or make a reasoned judgment, which we can think of as the building blocks of educated thinking.

## Thinking as a social activity

Only with such definitions clearly in mind can we address the question of how school environments might be designed to maximize the development of thinking. If, as already suggested, cognitive skills exist in implicit form before they appear more explicitly, the educational challenge becomes to a large degree one of reinforcing and strengthening skills already present in implicit form, rather than instilling skills that are absent. The difference is important, for once a skill is in place, in even rudimentary form, the most obvious method of strengthening it is practice.

As I have discussed elsewhere (Kuhn 1989b, 1990), despite the long history of advocacy for this method in educational theory, many educational programs designed to teach thinking skills focus on teaching students *about* good thinking, rather than engaging them in the practice of thinking. In the case of the thinking skills discussed in this chapter, it is not difficult to envision how students might be engaged in the practice of thinking. Their own theories on familiar social-science topics could serve as starting points, as illustrated by the argument research described here. Students could be asked for evidence to justify their theories, and their thinking could then be probed using the argumentive framework of alternative theories, counterargument and rebuttal introduced earlier.

Such activities, however, would differ in an important way from our research interviews, since they would take place in a social context. Because of the link between dialogic and rhetorical (or social and internal) argument, social argument is an ideal vehicle for developing the kinds of thinking described in this chapter. Social dialogue offers us a way to externalize the internal thinking strategies we would like to foster within the individual, an externalization that serves not only the researcher's objective of analysis, but also the practical objective of facilitation.

Social interaction offers a natural corrective to the egocentrism of individual minds. The critical impact·of social interaction on individual thought has long been noted by developmental theorists, beginning with Baldwin (1895, 1906), who invoked early social interaction as an explanation for how the child comes to define him- or herself in the course of development. The reactions of others serve as a mirror that allows the child to discover who he or she is. We thus develop a self through interaction with others.

It has less often been noted that a similar process operates on the plane of ideas. We try out our individual theories in social discourse, which serves as a corrective to what our theories have failed to take into account. In this way, the diversity of the social world enhances and corrects individual thought. This holds true for the whole range of human discourse, from the simplest everyday conversation to the evolution of scientific theories. In the case of the cognitive skills examined here, individuals who conceive of no other view than their own on a topic need only to participate in argumentive discourse on the topic, and this deficit will soon be remedied.

## Environments for thinking

Argumentive dialogue thus externalizes argumentive reasoning and offers the exposure to contrasting ideas and the practice that may facilitate its development. Where might the opportunities for such practice lie? We might assume that schools would offer students a great deal of practice of just this sort. But does school experience in fact offer the opportunity for the kind of exchange of ideas and argumentive discourse that would enhance development of argumentive thinking? In one sense, the answer is yes; in another sense it is no. The answer is yes in the sense that from the earliest years, schooling provides a social environment of peers. In the informal social interaction that is a major part of school experience, ideas are tested and inevitably challenged; thus social experience serves as the natural challenge to individual thought.

In a second deeper sense, however, the answer is no; schools do not provide this opportunity, or at least do not provide it optimally. Informal social dialogue only occasionally leads students to think explicitly about their ideas – to reflect on their own thought. More formal educational experiences may foster this reflection with – at best – limited effectiveness. Even in the best schools, what may appear to be genuine group debates about an issue are usually heavily controlled by the teacher (Edwards and Mercer 1987; Billig et al. 1988). The teacher already possesses the understanding of an issue that he or she wishes students to attain. In seemingly "open" discussion, the teacher shapes students' answers until they finally "spontaneously generate" the answer the teacher is seeking. Students who "think well" in such discussions are likely to be those most sensitive to the teacher's communicative cues. Most often missing, even in the best of such "discovery-based" pedagogies, is genuine, open debate of complex, unanswered questions.

Educators may be reluctant to introduce such issues in the classroom because they are seen as involving values or morality; in particular, the educator may feel uneasy about promoting the idea that such questions can have more than one acceptable answer. One can encourage thinking in schools, however, without entering into the complex debate on whether moral education should occur in schools. The three topics employed in our argument research are examples of important, complex issues that could be debated appropriately in a classroom setting. They entail questions about causes and effects – about the way the world is, rather than the way it should be – and the realization that such questions have more than one possible answer arises inevitably in group discussion. Once alternative theories have been generated, and the fact that things could be otherwise is recognized, the framework is in place for the remainder of the argumentive structure examined in this chapter.

A remaining question is whether the generation and deliberation of alternative viewpoints in dialogic arguments are sufficient conditions for the development of competent argumentive reasoning. Can higher forms of reasoning emerge from the interaction of disparate perspectives at a lower level? Or is some modeling or scaffolding of the more competent form necessary? While these questions can only be answered definitively by means of careful research, it seems that the less directive method, in which people simply engage in extended practice of dialogic argument, warrants systematic observation and analysis. For the most part, this work remains to be done.

In concluding, it is worth noting that the timing of educational efforts may have important consequences. A provocative study by Krosnick and Alwin (1989) indicates that political attitudes are highly susceptible to change during late adolescence and early adulthood, but immediately thereafter this susceptibility drops sharply and remains low during the remainder of the life span. The findings described in this chapter are suggestive of some of the reasons that attitudes and opinions may be rigidly held during most of the adult life span. They also help to identify the thinking skills that turn an unexamined opinion into a reasoned one. These are thinking skills that can enhance the control people exercise over their lives and, as such, they merit the attention of both researchers and educators.

# REFERENCES

*American Heritage Dictionary* (1981), Boston: Houghton Mifflin.

Amsel, E., Langer, R. and Loutzenhiser, L. (1991) "Causal inquiry and the acquisition of expertise in law and psychology", in R. Sternberg and P. Frensch (eds) *Complex problem solving: Principles and mechanisms*, Hillsdale, NJ: Erlbaum.

Antaki, C. (1988) "Structures of belief and justification", in C. Antaki (ed.) *Analyzing everyday explanation*, London: Sage.

Baldwin, J. M. (1895) *Mental development in the child and the race*, New York: Macmillan.

Baldwin, J. M. (1906) *Social and ethical interpretations in mental development*, New York: Macmillan.

Baron, J. (1985) *Rationality and intelligence*, New York: Cambridge University Press.

Baron, J. (1988) *Thinking and deciding*, New York: Cambridge University Press.

Billig, M., Condor, S., Edwards, D., Gane, M., Middleton, D. and Radley, A. (1988) *Ideological dilemmas: A social psychology of everyday thinking*, London: Sage.

Cherniak, C. (1986) *Minimal rationality*, Cambridge, MA: Bradford/MIT Press.

Edwards, D. and Mercer, N. M. (1987) *Common knowledge: The development of understanding in the classroom*, London: Methuen.

Einhorn, J. and Hogarth, R. (1986) "Judging probable cause", *Psychological Bulletin* 99: 3–19.

Fischer, K. and Farrar, M. (1988) "Generalizations about generalization: How a theory of skill development explains both generality and specificity", in A. Demetriou (ed.) *The neo-Piagetian theories of cognitive development: Toward an integration*, North-Holland: Elsevier.

Gardner, H. (1983) *Frames of mind: The theory of multiple intelligences*, New York: Basic Books.

Harman, G. (1986) *Change in view: Principles of reasoning*, Cambridge, MA: MIT Press.

Hilton, D. J. (1988) "Logic and causal attribution", in D. J. Hilton (ed.) *Contemporary science and natural explanation*, New York: New York University Press.

Hilton, D. and Slugoski, B. (1986) "Knowledge-based causal attribution: The abnormal conditions focus model", *Psychological Bulletin* 93: 75–88.

Inhelder, B. and Piaget, J. (1958) *The growth of logical thinking from childhood to adolescence*, New York: Basic Books.

Kitchener, K. and Fischer, K. (1990) "A skill approach to the development of reflective thinking", in D. Kuhn (ed.) *Contributions to human development: Vol. 21. Developmental perspectives on teaching and learning thinking skills*, Basel, Switzerland: Karger.

Kramer, D. and Woodruff, D. (1986) "Relativistic and dialectical thought in three adult age groups", *Human Development* 29: 280–290.

Krosnick, J. and Alwin, D. (1989) "Ageing and susceptibility to attitude change", *Journal of Personality and Social Psychology* 57: 416–425.

Kuhn, D. (1989a) "Children and adults as intuitive scientists", *Psychological Review* 96: 674–689.

Kuhn, D. (1989b) "Making cognitive development research relevant to education", in W. Damon (ed.) *Child development today and tomorrow*, San Francisco: Jossey-Bass.

Kuhn, D. (ed.) (1990) *Contributions to human development: Vol. 21. Developmental perspectives on teaching and learning thinking skills*, Basel, Switzerland: Karger.

Kuhn, D. (1991) *The skills of argument*, New York: Cambridge University Press.

Kuhn, D., Amsel, E. and O'Loughlin, M. (1988) *The development of scientific thinking skills*, Orlando, FL: Academic Press.

McGuire, W. (1969) "The nature of attitudes and attitude change", in G. Lindzey and E. Aranson (eds) *Handbook of social psychology* (2nd edn.), Reading, MA: Addison-Wesley.

Miles, S. and August, A. (1990) "Courts, gender, and 'the right to die' ", *Law, Medicine and Health Care* 18: 85–95.

Perlmutter, M., Kaplan, M. and Nyquist, L. (1990) "Development of adaptive competence in adulthood", *Human Development* 33: 185–197.

Perry, W. (1970) *Forms of intellectual and ethical development in the college years*, New York: Holt, Rinehart & Winston.

Scribner, S. (1986) "Thinking in action: Some characteristics of practical thought", in R. Sternberg and R. Wagner (eds) *Practical intelligence: Nature and origins of competence in the everyday world*, New York: Cambridge University Press.

Sternberg, R. (1985) *Beyond IQ: A triarchic theory of human intelligence*, New York: Cambridge University Press.

Sternberg, R. and Wagner, R. (eds) (1986) *Practical intelligence: Nature and origins of competence in the everyday world*, New York: Cambridge University Press.

Tesser, A. and Shaffer, D. (1990) "Attitudes and attitude change", *Annual Review of Psychology* 41: 479–523.

Vygotsky, L. S. (1962) *Thought and language*, Cambridge, MA: MIT Press.

Wagner, R. and Sternberg, R. (1985) "Practical intelligence in real-world pursuits: The role of tacit knowledge", *Journal of Personality and Social Psychology* 49: 436–458.

Wagner, R. and Sternberg, R. (1986) "Tacit knowledge and intelligence in the everyday world", in R. Sternberg and R. Wagner (eds) *Practical intelligence: Nature and origins of competence in the everyday world*, New York: Cambridge University Press.

# Chapter 8

# The microgenetic method
## A direct means for studying cognitive development

*Robert S. Siegler and Kevin Crowley*

*Progress in understanding cognitive developmental change mechanisms requires methods that yield detailed data about particular changes. The microgenetic method is an approach that can yield such data. It involves (a) observations of individual children throughout the period of the change, (b) a high density of observations relative to the rate of change within that period, and (c) intensive trial-by-trial analyses intended to infer the processes that gave rise to the change. This approach can illuminate both qualitative and quantitative aspects of change, indicate the conditions under which changes occur, and yield otherwise unobtainable information about short-lived transition strategies. The cost in time and effort of such studies is often high, but the value of the information about change can more than justify the cost.*

The essence of development is change. However, determining how change occurs is very difficult. Historically, this difficulty has limited both theoretical and empirical progress in understanding cognitive development. As Flavell (1984) commented,

> Serious theorizing about basic mechanisms of cognitive growth has actually never been a popular pastime, now or in the past. It is rare indeed to encounter a substantive treatment of the problem in the annual flood of articles, chapters, and books on cognitive development.
>
> (p. 189)

In the past few years, however, considerable progress has been evident. Deepening recognition of the importance of understanding change has led to increasingly precise theorizing about the mechanisms that produce it. This emphasis is reflected in the titles of several recent edited volumes: *Mechanisms of Cognitive Development* (Sternberg 1984), *Mechanisms of Language Acquisition* (MacWhinney 1987), and *Transition Mechanisms in Child Development: The Longitudinal Perspective* (de Ribaupierre 1989). Descriptions of a number of the most promising current models of cognitive developmental change mechanisms and an analysis of what they share in common is provided in Siegler (1989b).

One reason why progress in understanding these mechanisms has been so long in coming has been the difficulty of devising effective methods for studying the topic. As Appelbaum and McCall (1983) noted, "In contrast to other specialties, the study of development is the study of *change* . . . But developmental psychology has often not been truly developmental, and therefore it has not seriously faced the methodological issues unique to its definitional purpose" (p. 415).

Again, however, movement is apparent. The challenges of studying change are increasingly being accepted. This trend is not unrelated to the theoretical progress being made in understanding basic mechanisms. Studies that examine changes *while they are occurring* suggest ideas about the mechanisms that produce the changes and also provide data against which to evaluate the plausibility and power of potential mechanisms. The theoretical progress, in turn, creates greater demand for revealing methods that can resolve points of disagreement among alternative models and that can indicate directions in which models need to be extended.

The main purposes of this chapter are to describe a method that seems particularly well suited to studying change, to review the progress that has been made using it, and to advocate its increased use. Different investigators have used different labels, but the most common is the *microgenetic method*.

## THE MICROGENETIC METHOD

Three key properties define the microgenetic approach: (a) Observations span the entire period from the beginning of the change to the time at which it reaches a relatively stable state. (b) The density of observations is high relative to the rate of change of the phenomenon. (c) Observed behavior is subjected to intensive trial-by-trial analysis, with the goal of inferring the processes that give rise to both quantitative and qualitative aspects of change. The rationale underlying the approach and its history and uses to date are examined in this section.

### Rationale

Most developmental methods only indirectly assess change. They are more like snapshots than movies. This criticism has often been leveled at cross-sectional designs, but it applies equally to most longitudinal approaches. Observing a given child at ages 6, 8, 10, and 12 tells us more about stability of individual differences than does observing different children of each age at a single point in time. However, ordinarily it tells us no more about the process that produced the changes.

The crucial variable is not whether the design is longitudinal, but rather is *the density of observations during the period of change relative to the rate of change of the phenomenon*. This can be illustrated by thinking of depictions of tornadoes or hurricanes descending on a town. Photographs of an area before and after a cataclysm allow appreciation of the extent of damage and often elicit a "wow" reaction. To comprehend the process that wreaked the damage, however, requires observation of the effects at much more frequent intervals. A movie is ideal, but even a sequence of still photos, taken before, after, and at frequent intervals during the storm, yields a much finer understanding of the change than do before-and-after shots. Especially important, observation and measurement of ongoing changes allows analysis of the relation between the damage being done and changes in cloud formations, barometric pressure, wind patterns, and other causal influences.

The situation is the same in trying to understand the less cataclysmic process of cognitive change. Suppose we wanted to study development of understanding of liquid quantity conservation. Suppose further that individual children took roughly one month to progress from thinking that the taller liquid column must contain more water, to being unsure, to realizing that simply pouring the water does not change its quantity. Examining understanding of liquid quantity conservation at ages five, six, seven, and eight would indicate how many children understood the concept at each age. It also might prove informative concerning their reasoning before they understood the importance of the transformation. However, regardless of whether the design was cross-sectional or longitudinal, such a study would reveal little about how the change occurred. The density of observations during the period of change would simply be too low relative to the rate of conservation acquisition.

Dense sampling of behaviors over time has an obvious cost in terms of time, effort, and money. This cost makes it essential that the period of intense sampling substantially coincides with the period during which the rate of change is relatively rapid. Ideally, the observations would begin shortly before the change began and would continue until a point of relative stability was reached.

With changes that are closely age linked, the combination of a relatively dense distribution of observations and a high degree of overlap between the period of observation and the period of rapid change allows much more direct observation of the process of change than is typical. For example, binocular depth perception (stereopsis) consistently emerges in infants between 12 and 24 weeks of age. This regularity led Shimojo, Bauer, O'Connell and Held (1986) to test the stereo acuity of infants at 1-week intervals from ages 4 to 26 weeks. The study revealed that the developmental function for individual infants was much steeper than for the group as a whole. Typically, an infant moved in 1 or 2 weeks from extremely poor to asymptotic levels of stereo acuity. Only a dense distribution of observations that was well targeted to the period of change would have produced this information.

Most changes, particularly those occurring after infancy, are not so tightly bound to particular ages, though. For example, children typically acquire conservation of liquid quantity between ages six and nine, but the variability of the age of acquisition is measured in years rather than weeks. Under this circumstance, it is prohibitively expensive to observe at frequent intervals while awaiting the change.

The need for dense sampling, combined with the long period of time over which age-related changes typically occur, creates serious difficulties for observing ongoing cognitive growth. However, investigators using microgenetic methods have developed two strategies for meeting the challenge. One is to choose a task from the everyday environment, hypothesize the types of experiences that typically lead to changes in performance on it, and provide a higher concentration of such experiences than would otherwise occur. An alternative approach is to present a novel task and to observe children's changing understanding of it within a single session or over multiple sessions. Both of these approaches have proved capable of yielding high-quality data about how change occurs.

It might be objected that such studies involve examinations of change over minutes, days, weeks, or months, rather than years, and that they therefore address issues of learning but not those of development (see Liben 1987). Several considerations lessen the force of this argument, however. Most important, having high-quality information about some types of change is surely better than not having such information about any type of change. As Werner (1948) hypothesized, there may be important commonalities underlying changes that occur on radically different time scales. The more precise the understanding that we can gain of any set of changes, the better our chance of theoretical progress in identifying such commonalities and thus of understanding long-term, as well as short- and medium-term, changes. In addition, distinguishing neatly between phenomena that reflect development and phenomena that reflect learning has proved no easier than distinguishing between phenomena that reflect genetics and those that reflect environment. The sources of difficulty in separating the contributions of the two factors are largely the same. Development and learning, like genetics and environment, are so complexly intertwined that usually no clear separation of their influence is possible. Further, as the term *readiness* suggests, many of the most striking "developmental" phenomena involve differences in learning at different ages (as in the difference in learning of syntax at different ages, documented by Johnson and Newport 1989). Regardless of whether microgenetic methods are viewed as providing information about learning or development, they allow us to compare the range of experiences that trigger a given change at different ages.

The third defining characteristic of microgenetic methods – in addition to observations that span the entire period of rapid change and a high density of observations within that period – is intensive analysis of both qualitative and quantitative aspects of change. Training experiments and skill-acquisition studies both have involved observation of changes within and across sessions. However, they typically have been limited to descriptions of quantitative changes in speed and/or accuracy. Failure to analyze qualitative as well as quantitative shifts has limited the contribution of such studies to an understanding of change. Consider the impact of failing to assess the types of qualitative changes involved in changes in strategy use. Some improvements in speed and accuracy are due to construction of new strategies; some are due to shifts in the relative frequency of existing strategies; some are due to more efficient execution of the existing strategies. Intensive analysis of strategy use can differentiate what each of these sources of change contributes and when it makes the contribution. This potential for yielding more differentiated descriptions of particular changes is what makes microgenetic methods so promising a source of data about how change occurs.

## History

The concept of microgenetic methods and the rationale for using them go back at least as far as two of the forefathers of developmental psychology, Heinz Werner and Lev Vygotsky. As early as the mid 1920s, Werner was performing what he termed *genetic experiments*, that is, experiments aimed at depicting the unfolding of successive representations that made up psychological events (e.g. Werner 1925). For example, he described how repeated presentation of highly similar tones led to increased perceptual differentiation of the tonal space. Although his own microgenetic studies focused on change within a single stimulus presentation or a single experimental session, he also noted that the approach could be applied to processes that continued over hours, days, or weeks (Werner 1948).

Vygotsky (1978) cited approvingly Werner's arguments favoring genetic experiments, and argued more generally for studying concepts and skills "in the process of change" (p. 65). He condemned the more usual practice of examining procedures whose development was essentially complete, commenting "Previous investigators have studied reactions in psychological experiments only after they have become fossilized" (p. 68). As an alternative to such desiccated research strategies, Vygotsky advocated studying changes as they occur within and across experimental sessions.

In the ensuing years, a variety of investigators who agree on little else have advocated increased use of this approach. Consider the following testimonials from Piagetian, Vygotskyan, and information-processing-oriented researchers:

> The most appropriate method for tracing the evolution of a process such as this is a method which permits the subject to have the opportunity for

repeated learning experiences in order to activate his existing schemes and to increase the opportunity for interaction between these schemes and the emergent schemes which result from interaction with the problem environment. The unfolding of the subject's behavior during these repeated sessions constitutes what might be termed a microgenesis, or in other words, a telescoping of the much longer time span of macrogenetic development. (Inhelder *et al.* 1976, p. 58; translated from French)

When it is possible to utilize microgenetic analysis, it has the great advantage of allowing the investigator to observe the genetic roots and the final form of a strategy within a single session. When one observes a subject during all phases of strategy development, one can better identify the transitional processes and limit explanations. (Wertsch and Stone 1978, p. 9)

When questions about transition processes are central, the microgenetic approach seems to be the method of choice. (Siegler and Jenkins 1989, p. 103)

It is not difficult to see why the method would appeal to those interested in understanding the process of change, regardless of their theoretical orientation. The microgenetic approach can reveal the steps and circumstances that precede a change, the change itself, and the generalization of the change beyond its initial context.

Consider an example of the type of information the method can yield regarding the steps preceding a change. Karmiloff-Smith (1984) noted a consistent pattern in microgenetic experiments she had conducted. Representational growth frequently followed success rather than failure. That is, children often stopped using approaches that had been producing success on the task and began using alternative approaches instead. Only direct observation of ongoing change could have yielded this type of information.

Next, consider an example of how the approach can yield information about the change itself. Lawler (1985) intensely observed his daughter's understanding of arithmetic, tic-tac-toe, LOGO, and other skills in the half year following her sixth birthday. He noted a number of insights and discoveries in the course of her learning and found that they tended to occur when two or more competing conceptualizations were suddenly realized to be sufficient to solve the same problem. As he put it, "The elevation of control was *not* necessity driven, but rather derived from the surprising confluence of results where no such agreement between disparate structures was expected" (p. 63). This view, quite different from the usual stereotype of discovery, illustrates the type of nonintuitive ideas that can emerge from intensive observation of changes.

Now, consider an example of the way in which the microgenetic approach can inform our understanding of how changes are generalized beyond their initial contexts. Kuhn and Phelps (1982) examined 10- and 11-year-olds' experimentation strategies over an 11-week period (one session/week). They found that even after children discovered a systematic experimentation strategy, they continued to use a variety of unsystematic strategies as well. This was true of literally every subject in their study. Schauble (1990) reported similar results with the same age group over 8 weekly sessions on a different scientific reasoning problem, and found that the variability was present within as well as between subjects, and at times even within the same subject on a single trial. This variability was paralleled by variability of beliefs about the causal status of variables in the problems. Often, children performed a valid experiment to test the effect of a variable, recognized that the results indicated that the variable had no effect, yet later in the session indicated that the variable did matter. Schauble described such beliefs as "appearing finally to fade rather than conclusively being rejected" (p. 52). Again, it is difficult to see how such information about change could have been obtained without intensive observation of the process.

The microgenetic approach can further understanding of these three phases of the change process in social as well as solitary contexts. It has proved particularly helpful for investigating the interactions through which teachers and learners, or learners working together, acquire new competencies. In one such study, Saxe, Guberman and Gearhart (1987) examined how mothers teach their preschoolers to play number games. They found that both lower and middle-class mothers adjusted task presentations to their children's level of success on the task. If the child succeeded, the mother proceeded to a higher level goal, which involved less support for the child's problem solving. If the child failed, the mother proceeded to a lower level goal, which involved more direct guidance of the child's efforts. Again, only direct observation of changes during the course of the interaction could produce such finely nuanced descriptions. (See Forman 1989; Wertsch and Hickmann 1987; and Wood and Middleton 1975, for related accounts of how social interaction contributes to cognitive growth. Also see Catan 1986, for a more extensive history of microgenetic methods.)

## Current status

With all of these testimonials and positive examples, one might expect microgenetic experiments to be extremely prevalent. In fact, they are not. There seem to be between 10 and 20 such studies on cognitive development, depending on the stringency of the definition of the term *microgenetic study*.

The reason for the relative paucity of such experiments is not hard to grasp: They are difficult and time consuming to conduct. Subjects generally must be tested individually to obtain the type of detailed data that is essential for trial-by-trial analyses of performance. Determining when changes occur for each subject requires poring over the videotaped record of performance, transcribing large numbers of verbal statements, and classifying each trial with regard to the approach the subject used. When the validity of strategy classification is an issue, as it often is, converging measures from accuracy and solution time data are also needed to validate the strategy assessments. In addition, the amount of time required for children to make a given change often is difficult to anticipate, highly variable across individuals, and heavily dependent on the fit between the capabilities of the children tested and the demands of the task.

Even if these data collection, coding, and experimental design problems are overcome, complex statistical and presentational issues remain. Analyses of repeated measures data, especially repeated measures categorical data, introduce many difficulties and often demand choosing the lesser evil rather than formulating an ideal solution (Appelbaum and McCall 1983; Landis and Koch 1979). The demand of many statistical tests for large numbers of subjects conflicts directly with the practical demand of using samples small enough to allow trial-by-trial analyses of the data. Integrating verbal protocol data, which can convey the flavor of changes, with quantitative data, which provide a more aggregated depiction of the changes, poses challenges of its own. Given all of these difficulties, it is in some ways surprising that any such studies exist.

More than simply existing, however, the prevalence of such studies appears to be growing. One reason is that the availability of high-quality, relatively inexpensive videocassette recorders has made them easier to conduct. Another is that expanding knowledge of the typical course of development has made possible better informed estimates of the most appropriate age groups. However, the most important reason, we believe, is that it is increasingly evident that the value of the data yielded by such studies more than compensates for the logistic and methodological complexities that they entail.

On the logic that the best recommendations for a method are the types of data that it yields and the issues that it allows us to address, we next describe in some detail the issues and findings in one microgenetic study – Siegler and Jenkins's (1989) study of four- and five-year-olds' discovery of the *min* strategy for adding numbers.

## A MICROGENETIC STUDY OF STRATEGY DISCOVERY

### Background

The min strategy is an approach to adding that involves counting up from the larger addend the number of times indicated by the smaller addend. For example, a child using the min strategy to solve 2 + 5 would start at 5 and count upward 2 counts (the child would think "5, 6, 7"). Some kindergartners and most first, second, and third graders know and use this strategy (Ashcraft 1982, 1987; Carpenter and Moser 1982; Geary and Brown 1991).

Groen and Parkman (1972) hypothesized that young children consistently use the min strategy to solve single-digit addition problems. Their main evidence was that the size of the smaller addend was an excellent predictor of first graders' mean solution times on different problems. That is, they found that problems such as 6 + 3, 3 + 6, and 4 + 3 all had similar mean solution times and that problems such as 7 + 2 elicited shorter times and problems such as 5 + 4, longer ones.

To account for this finding, they proposed the min model. Within this model, children would set a counter to the number corresponding to the larger addend and count on from there the number of times indicated by the smaller addend. The time to set the counter was assumed to be constant across problems. Thus, variation among problems in solution times was predicted to be a linear function of the number of counts upward, that is, of the size of the smaller (minimum) addend.

Subsequent findings, based primarily on chronometric data, seemed to support this analysis. Consistent with the main prediction of the model, size of the smaller addend was found by a number of investigators to be the best predictor of first and second graders' solution times. It was also found to be a very good predictor in absolute terms, accounting for between 60 per cent and 75 per cent of variance in solution times in a number of experiments (Ashcraft 1982, 1987; Kaye, Post, Hall and Dineen 1986; Svenson 1975). These studies included children with learning disabilities as well as children without such problems, and children in Europe as well as children in North America (Svenson and Broquist 1975). The model also was found to fit individual children's solution times as well as group averages (Groen and Resnick 1977; Kaye et al. 1986; Svenson 1975).

The one discordant note came from mathematics educators' descriptions of what children said they did to solve addition problems (e.g. Carpenter and Moser 1982; Fuson 1982). The children reported using a variety of strategies, with some describing five or more distinct approaches.

The divergence between these self-reports and the min model suggested two alternatives. One was that the children's verbal reports were inaccurate. Even adults' verbal reports are often misleading (Nisbett and Wilson 1977); young children might have yet greater difficulty (Brainerd 1973). The other possibility was that the verbal reports were accurate, and that the results of the chronometric analyses did not in fact imply consistent use of the min strategy.

To distinguish between these alternatives, Siegler (1987) presented kindergartners, first graders, and second graders simple addition problems and collected both solution times and verbal reports of strategy use immediately following each problem. The results replicated the findings of both the chronometric and the verbal protocol studies. Consistent with the chronometric studies, the min model was the best predictor of median solution times on each problem, accounting for 76 per cent of the variance in the times. Consistent with the protocol studies, children reported using not only the min strategy but also the sum strategy (representing the first addend, representing the second addend, and then counting from one to the sum of the addends), decomposition (e.g. $9 + 4 = 10 + 4 - 1$), retrieving answers from memory, and guessing. The diversity of strategy use characterized individual children as well as the group; most children reported using at least three strategies. Overall, children reported using the min strategy on only 36 per cent of trials.

Thus, the question remained: Were children consistently using the min strategy to add, or were they using multiple strategies? To find out, solution times on each problem were divided according to the strategy that children were classified as using on the basis of their verbal report and the videotape of their nonverbal behavior during the problem.

Separating solution times according to the strategy classifications yielded a clear pattern. On trials in which children were classified as using the min strategy, the min model was an even better predictor of solution times on each problem than in past studies or in this data set as a whole. Size of the smaller addend accounted for 86 per cent of the variance in solution times. In contrast, on trials in which they used a different strategy, the min model was not a good predictor of solution times in either absolute or relative terms. It never accounted for as much as 40 per cent of the variance and never was either the best or the second best predictor of solution times for any of the other strategies. These and a variety of other data converged in indicating that children used multiple strategies and that they used them on the problems where they said they did. (See Siegler 1987, for a statistical analysis of why the min model was such a good predictor of the overall solution times when the strategy was used only on a minority of trials.)

These findings provided essential background information for the microgenetic experiment on acquisition of the min strategy. They indicated that some five-year-olds and almost all six-year-olds knew the min strategy. This suggested that four- and five-year-olds would be a good population for examining its acquisition. The findings also provided convergent validation for the combination of videotaped records of ongoing problem solving and immediately retrospective verbal reports as a method for assessing strategy use on each trial. Finally, the findings provided a context for understanding the data yielded by the new experiment. For example, knowing that second graders, who presumably had been using the min strategy for at least a year, continued to use a variety of other strategies as well as the min approach, provided a different perspective on variability in strategy use following the initial discovery than if the second graders had used the min strategy on 100 per cent of trials. More generally, microgenetic experiments seem most likely to succeed in areas in which previous studies indicate appropriate age groups, assessment techniques, and descriptions of typical development that provide context for interpreting findings.

## The microgenetic experiment

The Siegler and Jenkins (1989) experiment included two main parts: a pretest and an 11-week practice period. In both parts, children were tested individually and their strategy use was assessed on each trial. Strategy assessment involved a combination of videotaping and asking the child immediately after each trial how he or she had solved the problem. When overt behavior indicated how the child had solved the problem, it provided the basis of strategy classification on that trial. When overt behavior was ambiguous or absent, the immediately retrospective reports provided the basis of classification. Converging evidence for the validity of strategy assessments obtained in this way has been provided by solution time and accuracy data (Siegler 1987, 1989a). Obtaining the self-reports also has been found not to influence the strategy use itself, as indicated by highly similar frequencies and patterns of overt strategic behavior when verbal reports are and are not requested (McGilly and Siegler 1990).

The pretest was used to select four- and five-year-olds who did not already know the min strategy but who possessed some skill in adding numbers. Children were presented simple addition problems with addends 1–5. They were asked after each trial how they had solved the problem. In another part of the pretest, they were asked repeatedly to recommend possible ways of adding numbers to a hypothetical younger child until they said they did not know any more ways to recommend. Data were also collected on the children's counting and magnitude comparison skills. (See Siegler and Jenkins 1989, for a more detailed presentation of this and other aspects of the study.)

The children who were selected to participate in the practice phase were those who did not report counting from a number greater than one on any of the pretest problems, did not give evidence of doing so on the videotapes of their ongoing problem-solving activities, and did not recommend any such strategy to the hypothetical younger child. To guarantee reasonable prior knowledge of addition, children also needed to answer correctly at least 50 per cent of the problems.

This selection procedure resulted in 10 children being selected for participation in the practice period. These children correctly answered 78 per cent of the addition problems on the pretest. The sum strategy (counting from 1) was their most frequent approach; they used it on 43 per cent of the pretest addition problems.

The 11-week practice period involved approximately three sessions per week for each child. In general seven problems were presented in each session. The only exception was the session (if any) in which the child first used the min strategy. In that session, the experimenter presented several further problems to probe the nature of the child's understanding at the time of the discovery. Previous evidence (Groen and Resnick 1977; Resnick and Ford 1981) indicated that children ordinarily invent the min strategy simply on the basis of solving addition problems, rather than being taught it by teachers or textbooks. This led to the expectation that the experimental conditions would be effective in eliciting the discovery and that they would approximate the conditions under which children typically construct the min strategy.

All but two of the children in this sample completed the 11-week practice period. One child did not finish because she took the situation so seriously that she became upset when she answered incorrectly. The other child failed to finish for the opposite reason; he gave extensive evidence of not trying. Furthermore, a minor epidemic of flu and colds resulted in children completing varying numbers of sessions (18–34) and trials (130–244). Both attrition and absenteeism are problems that are likely to arise in many long-term microgenetic studies. Including more subjects and more sessions than the minimum expected to be necessary seems essential for success in such circumstances.

The original plan was to present repeatedly the problems with addends 1–5 until all of the children discovered the min strategy. The logic followed that of Case's (1985) theory: Discovery of new strategies would occur most often when processing was highly automatized and substantial processing resources were available. This approach was effective to an extent. After seven weeks of the practice period, five of the eight children had made the discovery, in the sense of using the new strategy at least once. However, they tended to use it only occasionally.

This led to adoption of a necessity-is-the-mother-of-invention perspective. To create a need to use the min strategy, the experimenter presented *challenge problems* during Week 8. These were problems such as 2 + 21, that is, problems with one large and one small addend. These challenge problems provided both a carrot and a stick for using the min strategy – the carrot because such problems could be solved quite easily by counting from the larger addend, the stick because the children's other strategies, such as the sum strategy and retrieval, could not be easily executed on them. Finally, in the period following the challenge problems (Weeks 9–11), children were presented a mix of problems, ranging from 2 + 1 to 22 + 4, with all gradations of difficulty in between.

## Overview of findings

Microgenetic experiments can yield the same types of data on speed and accuracy as more conventional designs, as well as other data that are unique to them. The more typical data are especially useful for establishing overall levels of performance.

Summed over the 11-week practice phase, the accuracy of individual children ranged from 76 per cent to 98 per cent correct; the mean was 85 per cent. All children usually advanced the correct answer on small addend problems (problems with both addends no greater than 5), with individual children's percentage correct ranging from 81 per cent to 100 per cent. Performance on large addend problems (those with at least one addend above 5) was more variable, with individual children's accuracy ranging from 42 per cent to 94 per cent. Percentage correct on the small addend problems, the only ones that were presented throughout the experiment, changed substantially over the course of trial blocks (blocks of five sessions each), improving from 80 per cent correct in children's first trial block to 96 per cent correct in their final one.

Children used a number of strategies to solve problems. The most frequent ones are illustrated in Table 8.1. Across all children, the sum strategy and retrieval were the approaches used most often, with the two strategies being employed on 34 per cent and 22 per cent of trials, respectively. As might be expected, there was some movement over trial blocks toward greater use of the more advanced strategies (retrieval and the min strategy) and less use of the less advanced approaches (guessing and the sum strategy).

More striking, however, was the variability in children's strategy use. Variability was apparent at two levels. One was in the number of strategies used by each child. As shown in Table 8.2, each child used at least five strategies. The second type of variability was the relative frequency of use

*Table 8.1* Percentage use, percentage correct, and median reaction time (RT) for each strategy

| Strategy | Percentage use | Percentage correct | Mdn RT |
|---|---|---|---|
| Sum | 34 | 89 | 10.8 |
| Retrieval | 22 | 89 | 5.0 |
| Short-cut sum | 17 | 85 | 13.2 |
| Finger recognition | 11 | 92 | 6.4 |
| Min | 9 | 86 | 9.0 |
| Guess | 2 | 20 | 9.9 |
| Count-from-first | 1 | 40 | 15.6 |
| Unknown | 4 | 71 | – |
| Total | 100 | 85 | 9.4 |

*Source*: Data are from *How Children Discover New Strategies* (p. 60), by R. S. Siegler and E. Jenkins, 1989, Hillsdale, NJ: Erlbaum. Copyright 1989 by Lawrence Erlbaum Associates. Reprinted by permission.

Table 8.2 Percentage use of each strategy by each child

| Child | Sum | Retrieval | Short-cut sum | Finger recognition | Min | Guess | Count from first | Unknown |
|---|---|---|---|---|---|---|---|---|
| Brittany | 43 | 6 | 9 | 19 | 21 | 1 | – | – |
| Christian | 31 | 10 | 27 | 25 | 1 | – | – | 2 |
| Danny | 65 | 1 | 6 | 13 | – | – | – | 14 |
| Jesse | 0 | 23 | 68 | 1 | 2 | – | – | 4 |
| Laine | 69 | 5 | 1 | 6 | 1 | 17 | – | – |
| Lauren | 40 | 40 | 8 | – | 6 | – | – | 6 |
| Ruth | 13 | 42 | 9 | 8 | 17 | 2 | 6 | 1 |
| Whitney | 5 | 61 | 5 | 5 | 18 | 2 | – | 3 |
| Total | 34 | 22 | 17 | 11 | 9 | 2 | 1 | 4 |

Note: The notation "–" indicates the strategy was never used. The notation "0" indicates that it was used, but on less than 0.5% of trials.

Source: Data are from How Children Discover New Strategies (p. 61), by R. S. Siegler and E. Jenkins, 1989, Hillsdale, NJ: Erlbaum. Copyright 1989 by Lawrence Erlbaum Associates. Reprinted by permission.

of each strategy by different children. Use of the sum strategy ranged from 0 per cent to 69 per cent, use of retrieval from 1 per cent to 61 per cent, use of finger recognition from 0 per cent to 25 per cent, and so on. This variability could not be explained entirely as the result of more knowledgeable children using the more advanced approaches, such as retrieval. There was some relation between knowledge and use of the more advanced strategies, but it was far from perfect. The child who used retrieval on the greatest percentage of trials ranked seventh among the eight children in percentage correct. The child who produced the highest percentage correct was only fourth highest in percentage use of retrieval. This was not an isolated finding. There were exceptions to even the most regular relations in the study; the extensive data collected on each subject made it difficult to dismiss these exceptions as random occurrences or reflections of measurement error. Such results from this and other microgenetic studies indicate that theoretical accounts need to explain the variability as well as the consistencies that characterize performance and change.

The central focus of the study was not on speed, accuracy, or overall strategy use, however, but rather on discovery of the new strategy. It is here that the advantages of microgenetic methods are greatest. Next we describe the discovery itself, precursors that led up to it, and generalization beyond its initial use.

## Discovering a new strategy

The largest risk in conducting a microgenetic study is that the change of interest may not occur in the available time. Fortunately, this problem did not arise here. Over the 11 weeks, seven of the eight children made the discovery. The time that they required varied greatly. The first discovery occurred in the 2nd session of the experiment, on the particular child's 8th trial. The last discovery occurred in the 30th session, on the 209th of the 210 trials that that child encountered. Other discoveries were spaced rather evenly in between.

### Quality of the discoveries

Microgenetic studies allow observation of discoveries, as they are being made, and thus can convey a qualitative sense of the discovery process. The following protocol was taken from the trial on which one five-year-old girl first used the min strategy. (The names of children cited here and throughout the article are aliases.)

E: OK Brittany, how much is 2 + 5?
B: 2 + 5 – [whispers] 6, 7 – it's 7.
E: How did you know that?
B: [excitedly] Never counted.

*E:* You didn't count?

*B:* Just said it – I just said after 6 something – 7 – 6, 7.

*E:* You did? Why did you say 6, 7?

*B:* 'Cause I wanted to see what it really was.

*E:* OK, well – so, did you – what – you didn't have to start at one, you didn't count, 1, 2, 3, you just said 6, 7?

*B:* Yeah – smart answer.

This protocol fits well with the common prototype of discovery, which is probably Archimedes shouting "eureka" following his insight in the bathtub concerning how to test whether the king's crown was pure gold. This prototype entails awareness of what has been done, realization that it is important, and excitement at making the discovery.

Other children's discoveries showed none of these properties, however. Consider Whitney's protocol:

*E:* How much is 4 + 3?

*W:* 5, 6, 7, I think it's 7.

*E:* 7, OK, how did you know that?

*W:* Because I'm smart and I just knew it.

*E:* Can you tell me, I heard you counting. I heard you. Tell me how you counted.

*W:* I just – I didn't count anything – [*long pause*] I just added numbers onto it.

*E:* Can you tell me how you added numbers?

*W:* No.

*E:* Come on Whitney – come on, we have to do this, OK?

*W:* OK [*in a bored voice*], 3, add one makes 4, add one makes 5, add one makes 6, add one makes 7, add one more makes 8.

*E:* Wait, but how did you know what 4 + 3 was?

*W:* 'Cause I did what I just showed you. I just used my mouth to figure it out.

Unlike Brittany, Whitney showed little awareness of what she had done (she first said that she just knew it, and the counting that she reported in the protocol was not the counting that was recorded on the videotape). She also displayed little affect during or immediately after her first use of the new strategy.

Whitney's and Brittany's protocols were not atypical; indeed, we quoted them because they were representative. The most insightful first uses of the strategy showed surprising understanding of why the new strategy was desirable. For example, Ruth explained why she had counted from 4 on 4 + 3 by saying that "I don't have to count a very long ways if I start from 4, I just have to do 3 more." At the other extreme, some children insisted that they had retrieved the answer from memory, despite the videotapes containing audible counting from the larger addend. Thus, strategy discoveries clearly entail a wide range of degrees of awareness, insight into implications, and affective reactions.

### The role of impasses in discoveries

What types of problems give rise to discoveries? One common view is that discoveries generally occur on difficult problems that cannot be solved in other ways. This view is often labeled *impasse driven learning*.

Discoveries of the min strategy were inconsistent with this view, however. The problems on which discoveries were made were quite representative of the total set of problems that children encountered: 2 + 5, 5 + 2, 4 + 1, 3 + 9, 1 + 24, and 4 + 3 (twice). Apparently, discoveries can occur in the course of solving easy problems, difficult problems, or problems of middling difficulty. Further, most of the discoveries came on problems that, earlier in the experiment, the particular child had solved correctly without any apparent difficulty.

These findings were directly at odds both with traditional views of learning and with a number of current artificial intelligence and theoretical linguistics models of strategy construction (e.g. Newell's, 1990, SOAR model; VanLehn's, 1988, RT2 model; Wexler and Cullicover's, 1980, and Berwick's, 1987, syntax acquisition models). VanLehn succinctly stated the basic assumption of these models regarding how new procedures are learned: "Learning occurs only when an impasse occurs. If there is no impasse, there is no learning" (pp. 31–32).

There is no question that changes often do take place in response to impasses and failure. However, it is becoming increasingly evident that in many situations, changes occur under other circumstances as well. For example, children initially solve class inclusion problems by counting the number of objects in the total set, counting the number of objects in the larger subordinate set, and then comparing the results of the two counts. Although this approach typically yields perfect performance, older children do not use it. Instead, they base their conclusions on the logic that the superordinate set must necessarily have more objects (Markman 1978). Similarly, in number conservation, young children solve problems by counting and comparing the number of objects in the two rows. Again, despite this approach yielding consistently correct performance, older children shift away from it. They base answers on the reasoning that just spreading out or contracting a row could not change the number of objects (Siegler 1981). In map drawing, children shift without any negative feedback or impasse from simple correct notations to ones with more redundancy (Karmiloff-Smith 1984). In language use, they shift from consistent correct use of verbs such as *dropped* and *fell* to incorrect use, again without any apparent external pressure. After noting several such cases, Bowerman

(1987) concluded "Our theory of language acquisition is going to have to explain what causes grammars to change even when children receive no overt evidence that there is anything wrong with their current grammars" (p. 459).

These observations point to a basic inadequacy in prevailing approaches to cognitive development. Flavell (1971) noted that one shortcoming of stage theories was that within them, "the individual spends virtually all of his childhood years 'being' rather than becoming" (pp. 426–427). The criticism applies not just to stage theories but to all approaches that depict change in terms of static states punctuated by occasional episodes of change. Assuming that thinking changes only under duress – or only when some maturational constraint has been satisfied – relegates change to a conditional status. Yet, the examples of conceptual development, language development, and development of problem-solving skills that were cited in the previous paragraphs suggest that it may be more accurate to view change, rather than static states, as the norm. Other types of evidence point in the same direction. The ubiquity of the practice law (Newell and Rosenbloom 1981) has been found to reflect a continuous stream of qualitative and quantitative changes that occur across extremely diverse content domains (Agre and Shrager 1990; Cheng 1985; Hirst, Spelke, Reaves, Caharack and Neisser 1980). The success of self-modifying artificial intelligence models, such as Holland, Holyoak, Nisbett and Thagard's (1986) genetic algorithm, rests in large part on change being integral to the overall program. Similarly, the success of Klahr and Wallace's (1976) production system models depended critically on their detecting regularities in the time line even when there was no external pressure to do so. The large amount of subject-to-subject variability observed in this and other microgenetic studies in every part of the strategy construction process is a natural, though not a necessary, concomitant of this perspective.

One desirable consequence of viewing variation and change as integral parts of ongoing cognitive activity is that it makes explaining cognitive growth far less problematic. Mechanisms that produce a steady stream of variations would provide the raw material from which innovations could emerge. Mechanisms of selection would then differentially maintain those innovations that produced useful outcomes. Consistent with this analysis, the best-worked-out recent models of cognitive development have included variation-producing mechanisms. Three examples are MacWhinney, Leinbach, Taraban and MacDonald's (1989) model of language acquisition, Holland et al.'s (1986) model of the development of encoding, and Gentner's (1989) model of the development of analogical reasoning. Each of these illustrates how variation-producing mechanisms might operate. Recent findings in developmental neurophysiology also have demonstrated that initial overproduction and subsequent pruning of synapses is involved in many age- and experientially related changes in cognitive functioning (e.g. Goldman-Rakic 1987; Greenough, Black and Wallace 1987; Hutten-locher 1979). Viewing change as continual, rather than sporadic or periodic, promises to lead to more viable accounts of cognitive development.

*Discoveries that were not made*

Just as the microgenetic design yielded data about the nature of discoveries that were made, it also yielded evidence about discoveries that were not made. The situation was reminiscent of the classic conversation in *The Memoirs of Sherlock Holmes*:

> *Holmes:* But there was the curious incident of the dog in the nighttime.
> *Watson:* The dog did nothing in the nighttime.
> *Holmes:* That was the curious incident.

In Siegler and Jenkins (1989), the curious incident was that not one child ever used a strategy that violated the principles underlying addition. Several potential illegitimate strategies were superficially similar to legit-imate approaches and therefore could easily have been tried. For example, children might have tried counting the first addend twice, or counting on from the second addend the number of times indicated by the larger addend, regardless of whether it was first or second. In fact, not one child used these or other illegitimate strategies on even one trial. This raised the question, Why not?

*Goal sketches*

Siegler and Jenkins (1989) suggested one potential answer to this question: The strategy generation process was constrained by a *goal sketch*, which specified the hierarchy of objectives that a satisfactory strategy needed to meet. In general, such a hierarchical structure would direct searches of existing knowledge toward procedures that could meet the goals. In so doing, it also would direct searches away from illegitimate procedures. The goal sketch for addition might be realized as a pair of productions:

P1:  IF your goal is to add two numbers and you know the number that quantita-
     tively represents their sum
     THEN state that number.

P2:  IF your goal is to add two numbers and you do not know the number that
     quantitatively represents the two sets
     THEN set as subgoals
       1. To symbolically represent each addend in the original problem.
       2. To quantitatively represent the objects in the combined symbolic rep-
          resentation.

This goal sketch would exclude illegitimate strategies. For example, both of the aforementioned illegitimate strategies would be ruled out because they did not include a representation of each addend, as specified in the first subgoal of P2.

The goal sketch also has another empirical implication: Children who possess such knowledge should recognize the superiority of strategies that meet the goals over strategies that do not. Such discrimination should be evident even among children who do not know either the legitimate or the illegitimate strategies, if they possess the goal sketch and perceive the relation of the novel strategies to it. Consistent with this implication, Reeve and Humpal (1989) reported that five-year-olds who did not yet use the min strategy nonetheless judged it superior to other strategies that violated the goals of addition.

The goal sketch described earlier by P1 and P2 reflects only the inherent logic of the task, addition. It also seems likely, however, that goal sketches can be expanded to include circumstantial constraints when the situation calls for them. For example, in Gelman and Gallistel's (1978) order invariance experiment, children were asked to obey the usual rules of counting and also to conform to the experimenter's request to assign a specific number to a specific object. The request might be to count a row of five objects in such a way that the left-most object was labeled 4. By age five, most children succeeded in meeting both the standard rules of counting and these further stipulations. This finding, together with five-year-olds' consistent discrimination between those counting procedures that violate counting principles and those procedures that are odd but legitimate (Briars and Siegler 1984; Gelman, Meck and Merkin 1986), suggests that five-year-olds' goal sketches for counting are permeable to the demands of the particular situation and reflect the basic hierarchy of goals in the domain. This seems likely to be a property of goal sketches in many domains.

Although they clearly are not the only mechanism involved, goal sketches also may contribute to construction of new, legitimate strategies. Findings from Siegler and Jenkins (1989) illustrate this point. Even before children discovered the min strategy, they gave evidence of possessing most components of it. These included identifying the larger of two numbers, reversing the addend order, counting on from numbers greater than one, and simultaneously keeping track of two sets of counts (essential for stopping at the right point in the min strategy). The one component that appeared to be missing was the realization that a number can be represented quantitatively by simply restating the number and using it to represent the quantity associated with it. Although this seems a simple realization, Secada, Fuson and Hall (1983) found that many children lacked it and that the lack was associated with absence of the min strategy.

If children did not possess this knowledge, how might they acquire it? The goal-sketch construct suggests that one fruitful place to look is to components of existing strategies. The reason is that these components of existing strategies are directed at meeting the same goals that components of the new strategy must meet – that is, the goals and subgoals within the goal sketch.

Consistent with this analysis, changes during the Siegler and Jenkins (1989) study in children's execution of existing strategies appeared critical for construction of the missing component. As children gained practice using the sum strategy, they increasingly represented the value of each addend by putting up that number of fingers without counting them out. For example, if asked to solve 4 + 2, they simply raised four fingers, rather than counting 1, 2, 3, 4. In the course of the study, children also became increasingly adept at recognizing the number of fingers they had put up. That is, on a problem like 3 + 1, once they had put up three fingers on one hand and one on the other, they increasingly often said "4" without any apparent counting. This suggests that through the process of composition (Anderson 1983), children who already possessed P3 and P4 might generate the missing production, P5.

P3:   IF your goal is to quantitatively represent N,
      THEN put up N fingers.

P4:   IF your goal is to quantitatively represent N and you have put up N fingers,
      THEN say "N" to represent the quantity.

P5:   IF your goal is to quantitatively represent N,
      THEN say "N" to represent the quantity.

Creation of the knowledge represented in P5 seems to have removed the last obstacle to children using the min strategy. Once P5 was created, it would meet the subgoal within the goal sketch of providing a means of representing a number quantitatively, and thus could be used in the construction of the min strategy. (See Siegler and Jenkins 1989, for a more extensive discussion of the strategy construction process.)

Regardless of the correctness of the particular account, this analysis has several general implications. First, individual mechanisms such as the goal sketch may influence both which strategies are discovered and which are not. Second, construction of appropriate new strategies seems to require both conceptual knowledge akin to that represented in the goal sketch and knowledge of procedures that serve as components of strategies for meeting the goals. Third, components of existing strategies may often be a useful source of components for new strategies because they are directed at meeting the same goals. Fourth, microgenetic methods can yield data that are valuable for constraining hypotheses about mechanisms. Only by densely sampling strategy use prior to and during construction of the new approach could we have learned anything about which components presented the final obstacles to the discovery, about improvements in existing strategies that may have made possible construction of an essential component within the new strategy, or about children never using illegitimate strategies.

## Precursors of the discovery

### The role of impasses

As noted earlier, children did not usually discover the min strategy on problems that were unusual or difficult relative to other problems they encountered in the experiment. Most discoveries came on problems that they previously had solved correctly through application of other addition strategies. The possibility remained, however, that children's discoveries were still being driven by impasses – not on the discovery problem but on problems encountered immediately preceding the discovery. If this were the case, the prior impasses may have stimulated cognitive activity that, over the course of several problems, coalesced into the new strategy.

The relevant data, performance on problems earlier in the same session in which the discovery was made, did not support this interpretation. The preceding problems were not unusually difficult; 88 per cent were small addend problems, versus 72 per cent for all sessions combined. Children did not usually fail on them; they answered 75 per cent correctly, versus 85 per cent for the experiment as a whole. Furthermore, one child contributed three of the four errors; the others were correct on more than 90 per cent of the preceding trials. All of the children were correct on the trial immediately before the discovery.

The one unusual feature of children's performance just before the discovery was very long solution times. Children took twice as long to solve problems in the same session but before the discovery as on problems in general (medians of 18 vs. 9 seconds). In addition to long solution times, these preceding trials were often marked by verbalizations that indicated partial execution of a strategy, followed by long pauses and/or strange statements that resisted straightforward interpretation. The unusual protocols, combined with the increased solution times, suggest that immediately before the discovery, children began to experience increased cognitive activity, which culminated in creation of the new strategy. However, because the problems children encountered just before the discovery were representative in difficulty of the overall set of problems, and because children performed quite accurately on them, the problems did not present impasses in any usual sense of the term.

### Transition strategies

A number of investigators have suggested that the *count-from-first* strategy mediates the transition between the sum and min approaches (Groen and Resnick 1977; Neches 1987; Resnick and Neches 1984; Secada *et al.* 1983). A child who used this count-from-first strategy would solve 2 + 4 by counting "2, 3, 4, 5, 6" and would solve 4 + 2 by counting "4, 5, 6."

This seemed a very plausible candidate for a transition strategy because it included one, but not the other, of the two main innovations of the min strategy. Like the min strategy, it involved beginning to count at a point corresponding to one of the addends rather than always beginning at the number *1*. Unlike the min strategy, however, it involved always counting from the first addend, regardless of whether it was larger or smaller than the second. Once children realized that they always obtained the same answer on a + b as on b + a, and that less counting was needed when the larger addend was first, they would complete the transition to the min strategy.

Groen and Resnick (1977) searched for evidence for this strategy in their chronometric study of early addition. In particular, they examined whether the size of the second addend was ever the best predictor of solution times, as would occur if counting from the first addend was the dominant strategy. This pattern was not evident in any child's performance. Nonetheless, Groen and Resnick correctly noted that a chronometric analysis, such as the one they used, would not detect such a transition strategy if it was used only briefly or sporadically. On this logic, Neches (1987; see also Resnick and Neches 1984) made the count-from-first strategy the key transition approach within a very elaborate computer simulation of acquisition of the min strategy. Much of the simulation was devoted to accounting for how children made the transition from the sum strategy to counting from the first addend and to how they then made the transition from counting from the first addend to the min strategy.

The trial-by-trial data yielded by Siegler and Jenkins's (1989) micro-genetic experiment, however, demonstrated conclusively that counting from the first addend does not in general mediate discovery of the min strategy. Only one of the eight children ever counted from the first addend on trials in which it was not also the larger addend. That child only began using the strategy *after* she had already used the min strategy. Thus, the hypothesized transition strategy was in fact transitional for none of the eight children.

The microgenetic data suggested that a different strategy, the *short-cut sum* strategy, may be critical to the transition. Like counting from the first addend, it contains some but not all of the innovations of the min approach. The particulars are different, though. It is like the sum strategy in that it involves starting at one and counting all of the numbers between one and the sum of the addends. It is like the min strategy in that representation of the second addend and its addition to the running total take place simultan-eously. Thus, on 4 + 2, a child using the short-cut sum strategy would count "1, 2, 3, 4 – 5, 6" rather than "1, 2, 3, 4 – 1, 2 – 1, 2, 3, 4, 5, 6," as the sum strategy would dictate, or "4, 5, 6," as the min strategy would dictate.

Use of the short-cut sum strategy emerged prior to use of the min strategy in all seven children who discovered the min strategy during the experiment. For five of them, it emerged no more than two sessions before they discovered the min strategy: Two first used it two sessions before they first used the min strategy, one first used it one session before, and two first used it earlier in the same session in which they discovered the min strategy. Interestingly, because the short-cut sum strategy, like the traditional sum approach, produces solution times proportional to the sum of the addends, there is no obvious way that chronometric or accuracy data could ever have led to its identification, regardless of how often it was used. In sum, the data illustrate how microgenetic approaches can both disconfirm hypotheses about transition strategies and suggest alternative ones.

## Generalization of the discovery

Discovery of the min strategy did not quickly lead to its widespread generalization. Even children who eventually generalized the strategy quite widely used it only occasionally at first. For example, the two children who eventually used the strategy on the highest percentages of trials of any participant used it on only 7 of 84 and 2 of 49 trials following their discoveries. Again, this ran counter to the eureka stereotype, in which discovery of a new approach leads to its immediate application.

The finding raises the issue of what it means to say that someone has made a discovery. One possibility is to reserve the term for uses in which the person can adequately explain the logic underlying the new acquisition. Adopting this standard would not appreciably change the pattern described earlier, though. None of the children used the min strategy much before they encountered the challenge problems (the problems such as 2 + 21 that were presented in Week 8), despite several children having clearly explained the advantages of the min strategy on the trial on which they first used it. More generally, defining discovery in this way evades the issue of what such uses without explanations signified.

Another possibility is to define use of a new strategy as a discovery only if initial uses lead to extensive subsequent use. However, this could also lead to large problems. One problem is arbitrariness; how much subsequent use is enough to conclude that a strategy has been discovered? Another problem, again, is evasion of the issue. If the first use is not the discovery, what is it?

A more useful conceptualization may be to recognize that discovery of a strategy is frequently just the first step toward its mastery. Only as people use new concepts and strategies, and experience their consequences, do they fully comprehend their advantages, disadvantages, and conditions of applicability.

Children may be especially susceptible to the limited insight that this perspective implies. However, adults – even the most innovative scientists – are also far from immune. Wegener (1929/1966), the father of plate tectonic theory, described his theory as originating in 1910 or 1911, as a result of his being struck at that point "by the congruence of the coastlines on either side of the Atlantic" (p. 1). Yet Giere (1988) noted that a fellow graduate student recalled that Wegener was struck by this same congruence, and talked about it often, in 1903. Giere commented, "If that is so, the idea lay fallow in Wegener's brain for a long time before 1911" (p. 230). With great scientists, as with children, understanding of one's own ideas often may come only with their use.

*The role of impasses*

As discussed earlier, impasses were not evident either on the trial in which the min strategy was first used or on the trials leading up to the discovery. However, they played a critical role in children's generalization of the strategy.

Recall that in the eighth week of the practice period, children were presented challenge problems such as 22 + 3. Such problems did not facilitate discovery of the min strategy; none of the three children who had not previously used the min strategy did so in response to this set of challenge problems. However, the problems did have a large impact on generalization of the strategy among the five children who had used the min approach previously. Use of the strategy, which had been below 20 per cent of trials on which the children counted, immediately jumped to 60 per cent of the challenge problems on which counting occurred (Figure 8.1). The use

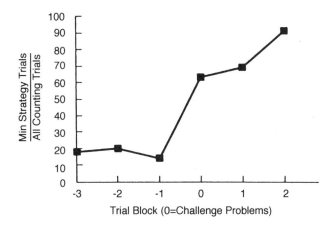

*Figure 8.1* Min strategy use before and after challenge problems

Note: Data are from children who used min strategy before the challenge problems.
Source: From *How Children Discover New Strategies* (p. 74), by R. S. Siegler and E. Jenkins, 1989, Hillsdale, NJ: Erlbaum. Copyright 1989 by Lawrence Erlbaum Associates. Reprinted by permission.

continued to increase in the last three weeks of the experiment, eventually reaching 90 per cent of trials on which children used counting strategies. The change was also evident when consideration was limited to the small addend problems that were used predominantly early in the study and mixed among other problems later. Here, use of the min strategy increased from less than 20 per cent of counting trials in each of the trial blocks before the challenge problems to 45 per cent after them. The change was striking in four of the five individual children; the fifth rarely used the min strategy either before or after the challenge problems.

These findings suggest that impasses play an important role in learning, but not necessarily the role that usually has been attributed to them. Impasses may be especially effective in promoting the use of strategies that have already been discovered but that have been used only occasionally. In particular, the impasses could lead to more elaborate encoding and memory representations of the strategies themselves, the problems on which they are used, and the sources of difficulty posed by the problems. This elaborated encoding would heighten the accessibility of these previously rare approaches, which in turn would increase subsequent use of them.

This view suggests that the automaticity perspective and the necessity-is-the-mother-of-invention perspective are not incompatible. As suggested by Case (1985), among others, it may generally be easier to construct strategies in the context of well-known content. As suggested by Newell (1990) and VanLehn (1988), among others, impasses may promote learning. The difference may be in the point within the discovery-generalization sequence at which attention is focused. Initial discovery may occur most often on simple problems; subsequent generalization may occur most dramatically when problems present obstacles that can only be overcome through use of the new strategy. Here, as in many cases, the Siegler and Jenkins (1989) data are not definitive – too few subjects, nonrandom sequencing of easy and difficult problems, design limited to a single discovery and a single age group – but they do demonstrate the potential of microgenetic studies to provide critical information for refining theoretical analyses of such issues as the role of impasses in discovery and generalization.

## CONCLUSIONS

The studies described in this chapter illustrate some of the benefits of studying change as it occurs. Such studies can convey both quantitative and qualitative aspects of change. They can indicate the conditions under which changes are most frequent and allow observation of short-lived transition strategies that would not be detected within chronometric or other more aggregated analyses. They can yield conclusive data about strategies that are not used, as well as about ones that are. They can convey a sense of the process as well as the products of social interaction. These types of data should contribute to improved future theorizing about change mechanisms.

Especially encouraging, microgenetic experiments have yielded closely parallel results across quite diverse changes. One such finding involves the halting and uneven use of newly acquired competencies. Even after children discover sophisticated scientific experimentation strategies, they often continue to use less sophisticated ones as well (Kuhn, Amsel and O'Loughlin 1988; Kuhn and Phelps 1982; Schauble 1990). When they discover a new problem-solving method with the help of their mothers, they may later fall back on shared control rather than continuing to exert sole responsibility for its execution (Wertsch and Hickmann 1987). New concepts about the workings of gears are applied in a similarly sporadic fashion (Metz 1985), as are new strategies for adding numbers (Siegler and Jenkins 1989).

Another common finding of microgenetic studies is that innovations occur following successes as well as failures. Discoveries have been found to follow successes, rather than impasses or errors, in many children's map drawing and language use (Karmiloff-Smith 1984), arithmetic (Siegler and Jenkins 1989), pictorial representations (Inhelder *et al.* 1976), and scientific experimentation strategies (Kuhn *et al.* 1988; Kuhn and Phelps 1982; Schauble 1990). These findings point to the importance of observing in a variety of domains the frequency and types of variation produced without apparent external motivation. They also point to the importance of investigating internal motivations for cognitive change, such as interest (Renninger and Wozniak 1985) and desire for meta-procedural understanding (Bowerman 1982; Karmiloff-Smith 1984). More generally, they point to the need for understanding in detail the mechanisms that produce cognitive variation in the absence of external pressure.

These two commonly observed phenomena may at a deeper level constitute two realizations of the same phenomenon: Cognition and cognitive growth are far more variable than our models typically suggest (Griffin and Cole 1984; Kessen 1984; Klahr and Wallace 1976). People often use multiple strategies where they have been depicted as using only one. The most accurate children tend to use more advanced strategies, but sometimes do not. Long solution times precede many, but not all, children's discoveries. Discoveries are made following successes as well as failures, and are often used sporadically once they are made. Unambiguous documentation of this variability may provide the impetus for future models that will account for it and explain its role in producing change. Stimulating such models may prove to be one of the most enduring contributions of microgenetic methods.

## ACKNOWLEDGEMENTS

The research for this chapter was supported by grants from the Speneen Foundation, the McDonnell Foundation, the Mellon Foundation, and the National Institute of Health (Grant HD 19011), as well as by a National Institute of Mental Health Predoctoral Fellowship.

Thanks to David Klahr and Leona Schauble for their helpful reading of an earlier draft, and to Mark Ashcratt, Dun Foss, and an anonymous reviewer for their constructive reviews. Correspondence concerning this chapter should be addressed to Robert S. Siegler, Psychology Dept, Carnegie Mellon University.

## REFERENCES

Agre, P. and Shrager, J. (1990, July) *Routine evolution as the microgenetic basis of skill acquisition*, paper presented at the meeting of the Cognitive Science Society, Cambridge, MA.

Anderson, J. R. (1983) *The architecture of cognition*, Cambridge, MA: Harvard University Press.

Appelbaum, M. I. and McCall, R. B. (1983) "Design and analysis in developmental psychology", in P. H. Mussen (ed.) *Handbook of child psychology: Vol. 1. History, theory, and methods* (pp. 415–476), New York: Wiley.

Ashcraft, M. H. (1982) "The development of mental arithmetic: A chronometric approach", *Developmental Review* 2: 213–236.

Ashcraft, M. H. (1987) "Children's knowledge of simple arithmetic: A developmental model and simulation", in C. J. Brainerd, R. Kail and J. Bisanz (eds) *Formal methods in developmental psychology* (pp. 302–338), New York: Springer-Verlag.

Berwick, R. C. (1987) "Parsability and learnability", in B. MacWhinney (ed.) *Mechanisms of language acquisition* (pp. 345–365), Hillsdale, NJ: Erlbaum.

Bowerman, M. (1982) "Starting to talk worse: Clues to language acquisition from children's late speech errors", in S. Strauss (ed.) *U-shaped behavioral growth* (pp. 101–145), San Diego, CA: Academic Press.

Bowerman, M. (1987) "Commentary", in B. MacWhinney (ed.) *Mechanisms of language acquisition* (pp. 443–466), Hillsdale, NJ: Erlbaum.

Brainerd, C. J. (1973) "Order of acquisition of transitivity, conservation, and class inclusion of length and weight", *Developmental Psychology* 8: 105–116.

Briars, D. and Siegler, R. S. (1984) "A featural analysis of preschoolers' counting knowledge", *Developmental Psychology* 20: 607–618.

Carpenter, T. P. and Moser, J. M. (1982) "The development of addition and subtraction problem-solving skills", in T. P. Carpenter, J. M. Moser and T. A. Romberg (eds) *Addition and subtraction: A cognitive perspective* (pp. 9–24), Hillsdale, NJ: Erlbaum.

Case, R. (1985) *Intellectual development: Birth to adulthood*, San Diego, CA: Academic Press.

Catan, L. (1986) "The dynamic display of process: Historical development and contemporary uses of the microgenetic method", *Human Development* 29: 252–263.

Cheng, P. W. (1985) "Restructuring versus automaticity: Alternative accounts of skill acquisition", *Psychological Review* 92: 414–423.

de Ribaupierre, A. (1989) *Transition mechanisms in child development: The longitudinal perspective*, Cambridge, MA: Harvard University Press.

Flavell, J. H. (1971) "Stage-related properties of cognitive development", *Cognitive Psychology* 2: 421–453.

Flavell, J. H. (1984) "Discussion", in R. J. Sternberg (ed.) *Mechanisms of cognitive development* (pp. 187–209), New York: Freeman.

Forman, E. (1989) "The role of peer interaction in the social construction of mathematical knowledge", *International Journal of Educational Research* 13: 55–70.

Fuson, K. C. (1982) "An analysis of the counting-on solution procedure in addition", in T. P. Carpenter, J. M. Moser and T. A. Romberg (eds) *Addition and subtraction: A cognitive perspective* (pp. 67–81), Hillsdale, NJ: Erlbaum.

Geary, D. C. and Brown, S. C. (1991) "Cognitive addition: Strategy choice and speed-of-processing differences in gifted, normal, and learning disabled children", *Developmental Psychology* 27: 398–406.

Gelman, R. and Gallistel, C. R. (1978) *The child's understanding of number*, Cambridge, MA: Harvard University Press.

Gelman, R., Meck, E. and Merkin, S. (1986) "Young children's numerical competence", *Cognitive Development* 1: 1–29.

Gentner, D. (1989) "The mechanisms of analogical transfer", in S. Vosniadou and A. Ortony (eds) *Similarity and analogical reasoning* (pp. 199–241), London: Cambridge University Press.

Giere, R. N. (1988) *Explaining science: A cognitive approach*, Chicago: University of Chicago Press.

Goldman-Rakic, P. S. (1987) "Development of cortical circuitry and cognitive function", *Child Development* 58: 601–622.

Greenough, W. T., Black, J. E. and Wallace, C. S. (1987) "Experience and brain development", *Child Development* 58: 539–559.

Griffin, P. and Cole, M. (1984) "Current activity for the future: The zo-ped", in B. Rogoff and J. V. Wertsch (eds) *Children's learning in the "zone of proximal development"* (pp. 45–64), San Francisco: Jossey-Bass.

Groen, G. J. and Parkman, J. M. (1972) "A chronometric analysis of simple addition", *Psychological Review* 79: 329–343.

Groen, G. and Resnick, L. B. (1977) "Can preschool children invent addition algorithms?" *Journal of Educational Psychology* 69: 645–652.

Hirst, W., Spelke, E. S., Reaves, C. C., Caharack, G. and Neisser, U. (1980) "Dividing attention without alternation of automaticity", *Journal of Experimental Psychology: General* 109: 98–117.

Holland, J. H., Holyoak, K. J., Nisbett, R. E. and Thagard, P. R. (1986) *Induction: Processes of inference, learning, and discovery*, Cambridge, MA: MIT Press.

Huttenlocher, P. R. (1979) "Synaptic density in human frontal-cortex-developmental changes and effects of aging", *Brain Research* 163: 195–205.

Inhelder, B., Ackerman-Vallado, E., Blanchet, A., Karmiloff-Smith, A., Kilcher-Hagedorn, H., Montagero, J. and Robert, M. (1976) "The process of invention in cognitive development: A report of research in progress", *Archives de Psychologie* 171: 57–72.

Johnson, J. S. and Newport, E. L. (1989) "Critical period effects in second language learning: The influence of maturational state on the acquisition of English as a second language", *Cognitive Psychology* 21: 60–99.

Karmiloff-Smith, A. (1984) "Children's problem solving", in M. Lamb, A. L. Brown and B. Rogoff (eds) *Advances in developmental psychology* (Vol. 3, pp. 39–89), Hillsdale, NJ: Erlbaum.

Kaye, D. B., Post, T. A., Hall, V. C. and Dineen, J. T. (1986) "The emergence of information retrieval strategies in numerical cognition: A developmental study", *Cognition and Instruction* 3: 137–166.

Kessen, W. (1984) "Introduction: The end of the age of development", in R. J. Sternberg (ed.) *Mechanisms of cognitive development* (pp. 1–17), New York: Freeman.

Klahr, D. and Wallace, J. G. (1976) *Cognitive development: An information processing view*, Hillsdale, NJ: Erlbaum.

Kuhn, D., Amsel, E. and O'Loughlin, M. (1988) *The development of scientific thinking skills*, San Diego, CA: Academic Press.

Kuhn, D. and Phelps, E. (1982) "The development of problem-solving strategies", in H. Reese and L. Lipsitt (eds) *Advances in child development and behavior* (Vol. 17, pp. 2–44), San Diego, CA: Academic Press.

Landis, J. R. and Koch, G. G. (1979) "The analysis of categorical data in longitudinal studies of development", in J. R. Nesselroade and P. B. Baltes (eds) *Longitudinal research in the study of behavior and development* (pp. 233–261), San Diego, CA: Academic Press.

Lawler, R. W. (1985) *Computer experience and cognitive development: A child's learning in a computer culture*, New York: Wiley.

Liben, L. S. (1987) *Development and learning: Conflict or congruence?* Hillsdale, NJ: Erlbaum.

MacWhinney, B. (1987) *Mechanisms of language acquisition*, Hillsdale, NJ: Erlbaum.

MacWhinney, B., Leinbach, J., Taraban, R. and MacDonald, J. (1989) "Language learning: Cues or rules?" *Journal of Memory and Language* 28: 255–277.

Markman, E. M. (1978) "Empirical versus logical solutions to part–whole comparison problems concerning classes and collections", *Child Development* 49: 168–177.

McGilly, K. and Siegler, R. S. (1990) "The influence of encoding and strategic knowledge on children's choices among serial recall strategies", *Developmental Psychology* 26: 931–941.

Metz, K. E. (1985) "The development of children's problem solving in a gears task: A problem space perspective", *Cognitive Science* 9: 431–471.

Neches, R. (1987) "Learning through incremental refinement procedures", in D. Klahr, P. Langley and R. Neches (eds) *Production system models of learning and development* (pp. 163–219), Cambridge, MA: MIT Press.

Newell, A. (1990) *Unified theories of cognition: The William James lectures*, Cambridge, MA: Harvard University Press.

Newell, A. and Rosenbloom, P. S. (1981) "Mechanisms of skill acquisition and the law of practice", in J. R. Anderson (ed.) *Cognitive skills and their acquisition* (pp. 1–55), Hillsdale, NJ: Erlbaum.

Nisbett, R. E. and Wilson, T. D. (1977) "Telling more than we can know: Verbal reports on mental processes", *Psychological Review* 84: 231–259.

Reeve, R. A. and Humpal, L. (1989, April) *The development of the ability to recognize the efficacy of a count-on strategy as a function of counting behavior*, paper presented at the meeting of the Society for Research in Child Development, Kansas City, MO.

Renninger, K. A. and Wozniak, R. H. (1985) "Effect of interest on attentional shift, recognition, and recall in young children", *Developmental Psychology* 21: 624–632.

Resnick, L. B. and Ford, W. W. (1981) *The psychology of mathematics for instruction*, Hillsdale, NJ: Erlbaum.

Resnick, L. B. and Neches, R. (1984) "Factors affecting individual differences in learning ability", in R. J. Sternberg (ed.) *Advances in the psychology of human intelligence* (pp. 275–323), Hillsdale, NJ: Erlbaum.

Saxe, G. B., Guberman, S. R. and Gearhart, M. (1987) "Social processes in early number development", *Monographs of the Society for Research in Child Development* 52 (2, Whole No. 216).

Schauble, L. (1990) "Belief revision in children: The role of prior knowledge and strategies for generating evidence", *Journal of Experimental Child Psychology* 49: 31–57.

Secada, W. G., Fuson, K. C. and Hall, J. W. (1983) "The transition from counting-all to counting-on in addition", *Journal for Research in Mathematics Education* 14: 47–57.

Shimojo, S., Bauer, J., O'Connell, K. M. and Held, R. (1986) "Pre-stereoptic binocular vision in infants", *Vision Research* 26: 501–510.

Siegler, R. S. (1981) "Development sequences within and between concepts", *Monographs of the Society for Research in Child Development* 46: 1–74.

Siegler, R. S. (1987) "The perils of averaging data over strategies: An example from children's addition", *Journal of Experimental Psychology: General* 116: 250–264.

Siegler, R. S. (1989a) "Hazards of mental chronometry: An example from children's subtraction", *Journal of Educational Psychology* 81: 497–506.

Siegler, R. S. (1989b) "Mechanisms of cognitive development", *Annual Review of Psychology* 40: 353–379.

Siegler, R. S. and Jenkins, E. (1989) *How children discover new strategies*, Hillsdale, NJ: Erlbaum.

Sternberg, R. J. (1984) *Mechanisms of cognitive development*, New York: Freeman.

Svenson, O. (1975) "Analysis of time required by children for simple additions", *Acta Psychologica* 39: 289–302.

Svenson, O. and Broquist, S. (1975) "Strategies for solving simple addition problems: A comparison of normal and subnormal children", *Scandinavian Journal of Psychology* 16: 143–151.

VanLehn, K. (1988) "Towards a theory of impasse-driven learning", in H. Mandl and A. Lesgold (eds) *Learning issues for intelligent tutoring systems* (pp. 19–41), New York: Springer-Verlag.

Vygotsky, L. S. (1978) *Mind and society: The development of higher mental processes*, Cambridge, MA: Harvard University Press.

Wegener, A. (1966) *The origin of continents and oceans* (trans. J. Biram), New York: Dover. (Original work published 1929.)

Werner, H. (1925) "Über mikromelodik und microharmonik [Musical micromelodies and microscales]", *Zschr. Psychol* 98.

Werner, H. (1948) *Comparative psychology of mental development*, New York: International Universities Press.

Wertsch, J. V. and Hickmann, M. (1987) "Problem solving in social interaction: A microgenetic analysis", in M. Hickmann (ed.) *Social and functional approaches to language and thought* (pp. 251–266), San Diego, CA: Academic Press.

Wertsch, J. V. and Stone, C. A. (1978) "Microgenesis as a tool for developmental analysis", *Laboratory of Comparative Human Cognition* 1: 8–10.

Wexler, K. and Cullicover, P. W. (1980) *Formal principles of language acquisition*, Cambridge, MA: MIT Press.

Wood, D. J. and Middleton, D. (1975) "A study of assisted problem-solving", *British Journal of Psychology* 66: 181–191.

# Chapter 9

# Piaget and measurement II
## Empirical validation of the Piagetian model

*Trevor G. Bond*

Piaget's theorizing can be seen to exist in three distinct tiers (in a form which parallels theory building in biology; see e.g. Maderson 1982). In the first tier Piaget collected data concerning the occurrence of certain observed behaviours amongst children of various ages. In the second tier he imposed upon those observed behaviours a classificatory system in which he characterized some behaviours as formal operational, some as concrete operational, and still others as pre-operational. In the third tier he attempted to theorize his behavioural accounts, classifications and the progression of the subject towards intellectual maturity by relying on a meta-system based on principles drawn from logic and mathematics. Where critics express some reservations concerning the validity or applicability of Piagetian theory, that often occurs at the formal operational stage. At least part of this concern derives, directly or indirectly, from Piaget's use of an idiosyncratic logico-mathematical model to describe significant features of the underlying structure of thinking at this stage.

In *De la logique de l'enfant à la logique de l'adolescent* (LELA, Inhelder and Piaget 1955) Piaget tried for the first time to match experimental evidence from Inhelder's investigations of adolescents' reasoning with the sophisticated logico-mathematical model he had previously painstakingly described in *Traité de logique* (Piaget 1949). Each chapter of LELA reported a different experimental situation together with protocols of children's attempts to solve the problems presented by Inhelder and her colleagues. Following this, Piaget analysed the children's responses to show that the reasoning of children who solve the problems could be represented by logical operations from *Traité de logique*. Further, he argued that those who could not resolve the problems used less sophisticated logical thinking patterns. At the same time Piaget's work on other aspects of thinking made a major impact on educational psychology in the United States.

Subsequently, in 1958, LELA appeared in an English translation entitled *The growth of logical thinking from childhood to adolescence: An essay on the construction of formal operational structures* (GLT, Inhelder and Piaget 1958). For the first time Piaget introduced a general classificatory scheme whereby the behaviours described in his earlier works (e.g. Piaget and Inhelder 1948; Piaget and Szeminska 1941) could be allocated to the stages he used in GLT and *The early growth of logic in the child* (Inhelder and Piaget 1964). In typical Piagetian fashion this work was never explicitly undertaken, either at the theoretical level or at the level of behavioural descriptions.

Researchers with a long-term interest in the area of formal operational thought – of whom Shayer in the UK and Lawson in the US are singularly productive and useful examples – have documented a wealth of evidence in support of the Piagetian descriptions of the behaviours characteristic of formal thought (i.e. tier two). However, there remains as influential as ever a body of argument – take, for example, the work of Ennis (1975, 1976) – which denies the value of appropriateness of Piaget's idiosyncratic logico-mathematical model for the formal operations stage. It is often argued that if the logico-mathematical model for the stage is invalid, then all of Piaget's work at the formal operational stage is also invalid (see e.g. Brainerd 1976; Seltman and Seltman 1985; Weitz 1971). However, these important and fundamental attacks on Piagetian theory have drawn an unexpected response (or, more significantly, lack of response) from the large group of researchers concerned with the more practical issues of formal operational thinking. The criticism of the logical model remains largely unacknowledged, perhaps on account of the fact that the logical model itself is disregarded as an integral component of formal thought. Apparently, the utility of the remaining two levels of the theory (the behavioural descriptions and their classification into formal/concrete operational thought), unburdened by the necessity to answer critics of the model, provides sufficient research opportunities and rewards, as well as classroom applications.

This situation epitomises the difficulty in attempting to construct and maintain a position between that of the pragmatic educational researcher and that of the purist genetic epistemologist as theoretician. The demise of the logico-mathematical model for the formal operational stage would be a, perhaps regretted, but nevertheless trivial inconvenience for the Piaget-oriented practising psychologist; for the Piagetian constructivist epistemologist, it would be a lamented, even irredeemable, loss with fatal consequences for a large portion of Piagetian theory.

It is suggested, however, that the complete dismissal of the Piagetian logico-mathematical model is premature. The work of Leiser (1982) and Smith (1987) at the logico-mathematical level, as well as that of the present author (Bond 1978, 1980), indicated that even at its most damning, the evidence of the critics is equivocal and the debate should not yet be concluded. The current chapter is directed to ascertaining whether empirical evidence may be so construed as to support the notion of the validity of this central aspect of Piaget's theory – the logico-mathematical model for the formal operations stage. While it is recognized that Piaget's is a peculiarly empirical epistemology, the focus of the empirical dimension of the present research was a test more in keeping with the empiricist research tradition which currently dominates psychological research and thinking in the US, the UK and Australia.

The present author has claimed elsewhere (Bond 1978) that the first two reviews of GLT were quite prophetic of the reception that Piaget's theory of formal operational thinking received in the ensuing three decades. As the following survey of events reveals, the tenor of critics' arguments and reactions has continued, essentially unchanged, to reflect a sharp division of perspective.

The prominent developmental psychologist, Bruner, reviewed GLT in an article entitled, "Inhelder and Piaget's *The growth of logical thinking* I. A psychologist's viewpoint" in *The British Journal of Psychology* (Bruner 1959). He lauded what he described as Piaget's genius in the "special approach to observation" necessary to "the task of establishing correspondences between logical structures and psychological operations of thinking . . . The approach consists of designing intellectual tasks that internalize thought into action in such a way that one is able to infer the logical assumptions on which the action was based and the nature of the logical system or 'structure d'ensemble' from which these assumptions were derived" (Bruner 1959, p. 363). In response to his own test of the adequacy of the theme of GLT, "Does Piaget's formal descriptions of pre-operational (sensori-motor) thinking, thinking by concrete thinking, and thinking by interpropositional or formal operations do the job?", Bruner replied: "Let me show my bias from the outset by urging that it does so remarkably well, but that it could do so remarkably better", with his reservation based upon Piaget's continued use of some static concepts – "particularly the rather turgid notion of equilibrium . . ." (p. 368).

Parsons's review in the very next issue of the same journal, "Inhelder and Piaget's *The growth of logical thinking* II. A logician's viewpoint" heralded the beginning of a number of analyses of Piaget's work by academics claiming particular interest or expertise in the area of logic which were critical of his (mis)-use of aspects of propositional logic as a model for adolescent thinking. Parsons's criticism of Piaget's use of his logico-mathematical model to describe the abilities consonant with formal operational thought may be succinctly summarized: "Although Piaget uses the standard notation of the propositional calculus, it turns out that he vacillates somewhat in his interpretation . . ." (Parsons 1960, p. 75) and ". . . it is not an interpretation in the sense in which that work is ordinarily used in logic, since the theorems (tautologies) of truth-functional logic are not always true under it" (p. 77). The conclusion that he draws from his critique is, "What fails to make logical sense can hardly make psychological sense in a study of intellectual development" (p. 78).

The tenor of these original critical reviews of GLT is apparently maintained even three decades later; the responses of the Genevans to the criticisms of the use of a logic-related model for formal operational thought seem to remain largely ignored.

Piagetian Papert intended that there should have been an adequate rebuttal of Parsons's attack and submitted an article entitled "*The growth of logical thinking* III. A Piagetian viewpoint" to the publisher of the previous reviews but the paper was not accepted. Papert firstly admits "that Piaget is not easy to read when he discusses logical and mathematical matters. His use of formulae is loose, highly unorthodox and sometimes superficially inconsistent" (Papert 1961, p. 1). He vitiated Parsons's claims that Piaget's logic does not stand up to the rigour of the logician's gaze by pointing out the role of propositional logic in Piaget's work; Piaget's "claim is that he can use the notation and methods of logic (and of certain mathematical systems) in order to systematize and, finally, to understand the thought processes of his subjects" (Papert 1961, p. 2). He further asserts that the Piagetian logical model can be self-consistent and, moreover, it avoids the paradoxes of material implication that mar the classical view of the syllogism.

In reply to Parsons's query (p. 81), "One can associate with the first order functional calculus a much more complicated algebra than general first order Boolean algebra . . . Why is this richer structure not included in the 'algebra as calculus' to which 'the logic of the real subject is isomorphic'?", Papert replies in a way that crystallizes the differences in the approaches of Piaget and Parsons: "The answer is that Piaget includes certain Boolean operations in the 'algebra as calculus' because he has seen subjects use these operations and not on account of any purely formal associations. The 'richer structure' in question is not included simply because its operations are not observed; its connection with the logic is purely formal" (p. 17).

In later years Piaget contended that Parsons's criticisms of his logico-mathematical model for the formal operations stage had been adequately refuted by Papert (Piaget 1967, p. 273). Although Piaget, with his usual cavalier disregard for the conventional practice of citation of references, does not provide a source for his contention, "S. Papert a répondu, (a) que notre usage est cohérent (non contradictoire) et caractérise un 'mode d'interprétation' ou 'd'emploi' comme un autre, ce qui est donc légitime en psychologie; (b) que son intérêt logique est d'éviter les implications 'paradoxales'" (Piaget 1967, p. 273), it is most likely that Piaget is referring to Papert's "Sur la logique Piagétienne" (Papert 1963). Obviously, Papert intended that this paper should constitute a defence of Piaget's use of logic and a rebuttal of the logicians, Parsons in particular:

"Cet article doit son existence aux critiques sévères que l'on fait sans cesse à l'adresse du *Traité de logique* et d'autres ouvrages de Piaget où il emploie la logique des propositions dans l'analyse des données expérimentales. Au cours d'une discussion avec notre ami C. Nowinski à propos de Charles Brainerd, le dernier à se livrer à attaque, une formule heureuse a été suggérée: 'Ce que les logiciens reprochent à Piaget est justement ce qu'il a fait de mieux'. C'est en poursuivant cette pensée que nous avons été amenés à réunir ici quelques idées sur 'la genèse de la logique chez Piaget' " (Papert 1963, p. 106).

In this paper he presented an elegant argument which delineated the differences between the logical model adopted by Piaget and that based on quantification theory commended by Parsons (1963). He contended that the very weaknesses identified by the critics were exactly what makes Piaget's model so appropriate for representing the development from concrete to formal thought: "La faiblesse de Piaget, en tant que système formel, deviendrait sa grande vertu, en tant qu'hypothèse psychologique. (En effet il est difficile de savoir si ce sont les enfants ou Piaget que Parsons prend à partie en faisant cette critique.)" (p. 110) – [It is difficult to know whether it is the children or Piaget that Parsons takes to task in making this critique.] He then followed this with step by step analyses of classical, then Piagetian, logic to demonstrate the critical differences between them and moreover to stress the suitability of the Piagetian model to its explicit function of representing the processes of adolescent thinking.

It is hard to imagine which of the Papert articles could have had the lesser effect in stemming the criticisms of the American logicians: an English language paper that was not published or a French language article published in the usual Genevan collection.

Whatever the answer, it is apparent that Piaget (at least) considered that the critics had been answered satisfactorily by Papert and later by himself (Piaget 1967).

The first word in replication studies of the GLT research was provided by Lovell (1961), while the latest and perhaps definitive word was provided some years later by another group of British researchers led, over an extended period, by Shayer (Shayer, Küchemann and Wylam 1976; Shayer and Wylam 1978). The research by Lawson into aspects of formal operational thinking makes him the most productive researcher in this field in the USA. Typically his work (individually and with colleagues) has provided substantiation of the behavioural descriptions of experimental problem-solving among formal operational thinkers devised by Inhelder and Piaget and the corresponding stage level ascriptions (see e.g. Lawson 1977; Lawson and Blake 1976). Although his papers have tended to leave untouched the philosophical and theoretical components of Piaget's theory, two of his later papers are particularly relevant to the questions being pursued in the present chapter.

Lawson, Karplus and Adi (1978) examined the acquisition of propositional logic and three other formal operational schemata amongst 507 students from 11.5 to 20.0 years. After the administration of a seven item test of these concepts (apparently related to the same psychological parameters as the classical Piagetian tasks) it was concluded, using factor analysis, "that the formal operational schemata and propositional logic are in fact separate psychological factors" (Lawson *et al.* 1978, p. 472). The authors contended that the concept "hypothetico-deductive thought" is more accurate and adequate and that "it is assumed here that (propositional logic) plays essentially no role" in the hypothetico-deductive process. This research did not assess performance on any of the classical Inhelder tasks *per se* and the choice of propositional logic items for this test appears to have been somewhat unfortunate; one involves the Wason four card selection task which has until recently remained an inexplicable problem for many researchers (see Overton, Ward, Noveck, Black and O'Brien 1987) whilst the other involves Piaget-like reasoning couched in a rather complicated experimental situation. The propositional logic problems proved to be substantially more difficult than the other test items and Lawson acknowledged the argument that the two-factor solution might have revealed artifactual factors – "factors that arise due to varying levels of item difficulty" (Lawson *et al.* 1978, p. 472), thereby casting serious doubt on the appropriateness of the statistics being used. What then is the significance for Piagetian theory of research that is based on tests and statistical models which have, at best, a tangential or even accidental relationship with the key elements of the theory?

The other paper by Lawson that is particularly relevant to the issues being addressed in this research attempted to determine if such Piagetian formal operational skills as combining variables, controlling variables, and proportions represent "a structural unit of a unified whole" (Lawson 1979, p. 67). The results of 28 secondary school students' (aged 11.9–13.2 years) performance on the chemical combinations, bending rods and equilibrium in the balance tasks were subjected to factor analysis, producing "one principal component that accounted for 76.6 per cent of the variance of the task scores" (p. 70). However, Lawson dismissed Piaget's system of 16 binary operations and the INRC group as underlying this considerable agreement across task performance claiming "numerous investigators have found Piaget's system of propositional logic based upon 16 binary operations wanting both empirically and theoretically" (p. 71). (The present author's published response to this paper (Bond 1980) will be more fully considered later.)

Discussions with Piagetian scholars in the US, the UK and on the Continent have indicated the impact of the work of Weitz and his doctoral supervisors on perceptions of the validity of the Piagetian logical model. Although the research is reported in a number of places (Weitz, Bynum and

Thomas 1972; Weitz, Bynum, Thomas and Steger 1973), it is evident that the original source material for the articles is a doctoral dissertation by Weitz (1971). (It may be noted that not one of the Piagetians who had cited the Weitz work in our discussions had read the original thesis.) Primarily, the investigation was a conceptual and empirical analysis of the development and use of the sixteen binary operations of propositional logic. Interestingly, Weitz traced the development of the sixteen binary operations from Venn diagrams (1971, pp. 15–18) using a method identical to that of Piaget (GLT, pp. 274ff.; 1953, pp. 30ff.) and explained by Mays (Piaget 1953, pp. xi ff.). Although he cited the article by Parsons in his literature review and was advised by "two logicians at the State University of Albany, Professors Bynum and Thomas" (Weitz 1971, p. 50), Weitz commented "that Piaget's sixteen binary combination system should not be dismissed but should be further investigated" (p. 87). From that point on, however, the value of the reported investigation is, at best, questionable; a thorough re-examination of this apparently influential work may be found in Bond and Jackson (1991) with associated commentary in Smith (1992) and Bideaud, Houdé and Pedinelli (1993).

The most vigorous long-standing critic of Piaget's investigations relevant to the logical capacities of children has been Ennis (1962, 1969, 1975). In the last of these papers Ennis mounted a well-referenced 40 pages attack on Piaget's propositional logic, especially the operation of implication. It is worth noting, *en passant*, that the likely source of the conflict between Ennis's and Piaget's positions is the fact that Piaget had been examining the development of thinking in children and ascribed to it some operations based on some principles of logic whereas Ennis's *œuvre* has been concerned with the examination of children's ability to handle the classical problems of traditional logic.

Brainerd's (1976) paper "On the validity of propositional logic as a model for adolescent intelligence" attempted to demonstrate by theoretical argument that the Piagetian approach was wrong-headed in principle because it contradicted a number of established laws concerning the relationships between the branches of classical logic. He further presented some preliminary data based on the use of certain forms of classical logical connectives by early primary school children to substantiate his claims.

The present author inadvertently stumbled across the problem of asserting the validity of Piaget's logico-mathematical model for formal operational thought while attempting to develop a satisfactory pencil and paper group test (the BLOT test) as an alternative to the time consuming *méthode clinique* interview technique. Rather than using the first and second tier behavioural and stage descriptions as the starting point for the test development, the BLOT owes its derivation to those very logical parameters from GLT that have been the object of continued critical attention. Inasmuch as performance on the BLOT correlated well with performance on three classical Piagetian tasks expressed as a combined ranking ($r_s$ = .93, $p$ < .0005, N = 30), there appeared to be some implications for the validity of the Piagetian model (Bond 1976a).

Incorporating a reanalysis of the initial test development and additional, subsequently collected data, this author's reply to the criticisms of Brainerd, entitled "Propositional logic as a model for adolescent intelligence – additional considerations" (Bond 1978) used Piagetian sources, primarily *Logic and psychology* (Piaget 1953) to show that Piaget had already abandoned the use of axiomatic or classical logic for some of the very same reasons as Brainerd had (later) suggested, claiming that "axiomatic logic is useless for the particular purpose we have in mind" (p. 23), and arguing in support of his position as follows: the order inherent in axiomatization reverses in certain respects the genetic order of the construction of operations. For example, from the axiomatic standpoint the logic of classes is to be deduced from that of propositions, whilst from the genetic point of view propositional operations are derived from the logic of classes and relations (p. 24). Piaget, however, interpolated between psychology and axiomatic logic a *tertium quid* and adopted the term "psycho-logic" from Isaacs's (1951) review of *Traité de logique* related to both psychology and logic "in the same way as mathematical physics is related to pure mathematics and experimental physics" (1953, p. 25). In light of the explanation Piaget provided in *Logic and psychology*, it is patently incorrect to assert, as Brainerd and others have done, that the axioms and rules of inference of the propositional logic branch of modern abstract logic are used by Piaget as his model of cognitive development (cf., Bond 1978).

A further reanalysis of the data from the initial test concurrent validation reported above (i.e. the BLOT v *méthode clinique* data; N = 30) along lines suggested by Lawson (Lawson 1979) provided results which corresponded to an extraordinary extent with Lawson's factor analysis of performance across three classical tasks (Bond 1980). Whereas Lawson dismissed the potential role of the 16 binary operations and the INRC four groups as an explanation of the "psychological link" he found between the tasks, the present author extended the same factor analytical principles from Lawson's article to uncover equally powerful linkages among three parallel tasks and BLOT (which was based directly on the 16 binary operations and INRC model). While Lawson's article provided evidence in support of the lower two levels of the Piagetian formulation it appears that, using the same criteria of acceptability, the reply (Bond 1980) provided the same measure of support for those two levels as well as for the integrity of the metatheoretical logical model. Admittedly, the small sample size in the "validation" analyses (N = 30) restricted the amount of weight that these results could bring to bear on the argument.

It is interesting to note the role that Johnson-Laird's research (see e.g. Johnson-Laird 1983) has played in the criticism of the Piagetian logical model for the formal stage. His earlier criticism of Piagetian theory and his later dismissal of the logico-mathematical model as a suitable explanatory device for reasoning processes evolved from his research using the selection task. The "selection task", also known as the "four-card" of "AD47" problem, a task based on the logical operation of denial or implication, has been used to assert that formal operational reasoning was rarely demonstrated even by the intellectually gifted (see Johnson-Laird, Legrenzi and Legrenzi 1972; Wason and Johnson-Laird 1972) or did not relate to other classical measures of formal thought (see dell'Aquila, di Gennaro and Picciarelli 1985; Lawson *et al.* 1978, referred to above, and critical comment by Shayer and Adey 1981, p. 62). Both outcomes were claimed to deny the validity of the Piagetian model.

The summary of Johnson-Laird's criticism appears encapsulated in his assertion that "The relationship between his [Piaget's] theory and observations is consequently problematical. This flaw runs through all of his work like a geological fault: it seems that one can step easily from hypothesis to data, but at any moment these two massive bodies of dogma and description are threatened by total dislocation" (Johnson-Laird 1983, p. 25). Johnson-Laird's premature dismissal of the Piagetian model relies heavily on his interpretation of Piaget's statement that "reasoning is nothing more than the propositional calculus itself" (GLT, p. 305) (see Johnson-Laird 1983, pp. 24–34). Smith argues that differences between aspects of Piaget's use of logical forms and those common in textbook logic seem "to have been lost on certain critics (Johnson-Laird, 1983), who are perhaps over-reliant on inadequate translation" (Smith 1987, p. 344). Smith offers: "reasoning is nothing more than the calculus embodied in the propositional operations (Inhelder and Piaget 1955, p. 270/* 1958, p. 305)" as a more faithful translation of the oft quoted passage (where Smith's use of an asterisk signals his dissatisfaction with the original translation).

The selection task is held by Johnson-Laird to be an embarrassment to Piaget's logico-mathematical model of formal operational thought; Johnson-Laird does not provide evidence of the specific target of his criticisms, waving airily at some 600 pages of Piagetian text (GLT and Beth and Piaget 1966). Certainly the various versions of the selection task provide evidence about form and content interactions in Piagetian style thinking which do not appear to be adequately explicated in GLT. Clearly, empirical data need to be collected in order to shed some light on the performance aspect of this part of the Piagetian competence model (see here both Begg 1987 and Overton *et al.* 1987). Underlying the Johnson-Laird argument is an apparently naïve view that competence in formal operational thinking then requires immediate transfer to all performance situations.

The Seltman and Seltman (1985) review of genetic epistemology added little of consequence to the critique of Piaget's logical model of the formal operations stage in order to come to the unsophisticated realist conclusion that "the existence of his structures . . . is baseless" (*ibid.* p. 112). It is clearly worth noting that in attempting to provide a critique entitled *Piaget's logic*, the authors made much of the well-rehearsed arguments of Parsons and Ennis but failed to refer at all to the rebuttal of self-acknowledged Piagetian Papert (1963) and conveniently avoided reference to Piaget's own comments on the "Critiques des logiciens" (Piaget 1967). Perhaps their misconceptions of Piaget's work derive from their acknowledged starting point from which they "saw Piaget simply as a developmental psychologist with leanings toward epistemology" (1985, p. vii). It must be recognized that their complaint about the shifting meaning of p and q in GLT is justified but this of itself does not invalidate the events underlying Piaget's discussion given that his expressed intention was to use logic as a calculus in a model of operational thought characteristic of certain situations. The model does not seek to reflect the quotidian events of adolescent thinking. It is further admitted that the binarity of the Piagetian model by virtue of its reductive nature leaves unanswered the question of degree of alteration that may be made to a physical system to have it more closely approach equilibrium. It does fail to model the wide array of precise adjustments that may be made in, say, the equilibrium in the balance problem (*ibid.* pp. 101 ff.). However, surely the point is not "that the INRC group, as defined by Piaget, cannot be reconciled with the balance situation as given and certainly not in its full potentialities" (*ibid.* p. 105) but whether the INRC four group is a reductive binary set of correspondences which can be reconciled adequately with the balance problem – although not in its entirety nor exhaustively.

Seltman and Seltman's antipathy to the rationalism underlying Piaget's genetic epistemology is perhaps best summarized in their assertion that ". . . a propositional interpretation can be abstracted by the experimenter and put into propositional logical form. There is, however, no guarantee that this *actually represents* even the subject's propositional logical thought" (1985, p. 98, emphasis added). This quintessential expression of *naïve* realism could stand as an object lesson in philosophical *naïveté* and epitomizes the philosophical chasm that separates the Piagetian viewpoint from that of many of his critics.

In contrast to the difficulties encountered by Parsons, Brainerd, Ennis and the like in making sense of the system of sixteen binary operations, the Butch and Slim sub-test of the British Intelligence Scales provided a useful and meaningful interpretation of that portion of the model. Butch and Slim are two bank robbers who are questioned together by the police; subjects select from four cards in front of them those which correspond to claims about the commission of a robbery. Research by Ward (1972), Ward and Pearson (1973), Airasian, Bart and Greaney (1975) and Jansson (1978) provide results which support the role of the sixteen binary operations in Piagetian theory (Bond and Jackson 1991).

After well over a decade of silence on matters formal operational, the Genevans released an English language "Discussion on recent research on the formal operational stage" as a postscript to the first of a new series of books entitled *Cahiers de la Fondation Archives Jean Piaget*. It was compiled by two members of the Foundation's staff, Monnier and Wells. The paper defended the orthodox Piagetian view of formal operations by illustrating "Piaget's point of view with extracts from his own works rather than to reformulate his ideas ourselves" (Monnier and Wells 1980, p. 204).

Leiser (1982) appeared to point the way out of the difficulties encountered in the interpretation of Piaget's logical model for the formal operations stage. He asserted (as did Papert) that the appropriate interpretation of the logical formulae from GLT depended on the situation in which the formulae were found. "I submit that the two interpretations that we saw correspond to different states of knowledge. The Parsons–Ennis interpretation becomes relevant after the subject has reached the state of complete knowledge, in which he has identified all the combinations of values allowed by the apparatus . . . The epistemic interpretation is relevant as long as the subject is in a state of partial knowledge" (Leiser 1982, p. 93). He then claimed that neither of the interpretations made sense of all the relevant passages but that "both can be combined in a consistent interpretation when attention is paid to the functional context of the subject's use of logical operations in this book" (p. 87). Certainly, Leiser's interpretation is attractive, makes explanatory sense of GLT and, more importantly, vitiates the criticisms of Parsons and Ennis. The following year Braine (an acknowledged advisor to Leiser (1982, p. 87, footnote) in a review with Rumain (Braine and Rumain 1983) pointed out that although Leiser's interpretation did nullify the previous criticisms, it encompassed another, new paradox ("The formulas that are supposed to be inverses are not the negation of each other") which made the Leiser view also unsustainable (Braine and Rumain 1983, p. 315).

Smith (1987) proposed an elegant solution to the vexatious problem of finding an adequate interpretation of Piaget's logic. He emphasized that Piaget's logic is not the usual textbook variety: "It is worth restating, however, that Piaget's logic cannot simply use the standard interpretation of propositional logic . . . The standard interpretation presupposes that an understanding of the relevant possibilities is already possessed. Inhelder and Piaget, by contrast, wish to show how that understanding is acquired" (Smith 1987, p. 348). Again, in accord with a common thread of the constructivist approach evident in both Papert and Leiser, Smith asserted that "Central to the proposed interpretation is a concern with the epistemological question 'Which one operation fits an individual's current set of observations?' . . . The issue in a given case is to ascertain which possibilities have been instantiated in that case. On the basis of these observations, a conclusion is drawn as to which one operation applies with respect to the observation made by that individual" (1987, p. 351).

Smith's approach adheres closely to the premises underlying GLT: that the logic of adolescents' thinking is different from the logic of children's thinking (Smith retranslated the title of GLT as *From childhood logic to adolescence logic*) and that the task undertaken in GLT was to describe those differences and to show how the more advanced type develops from its less advanced analogue. Smith claimed that, not only did his interpretation of the model avoid the problems of all previous interpretations, but his explanation was further consistent with aspects of more recent statements of Piaget's constructivism (Piaget 1983, 1986) (see Smith 1992).

The status of Piaget's description of the formal operational period at the present time appears to be as follows: the descriptions of behaviours demonstrated by children while attempting to solve Inhelder's (and similar) problems are indeed substantially similar to those outlined in GLT. The second tier of formal operational theory, Piaget's ascriptions of these behaviours to stages is, by and large, substantiated by the replication studies, although there is a need for minor reallocations of stages for some tasks and the incidence of formal operational thinking is substantially less than Piaget had implied. At the third, meta-theoretical, tier the evidence is quite equivocal. Although some evidence has been adduced to support the validity of the Piagetian logical model, many researchers, with prominent Piagetians amongst them, concede that evidence to the contrary is substantial and has not been adequately refuted to this point.

This produces somewhat of a paradox in itself: if tiers one and two of formal operational theory are supported, then what of the status of the tier three metatheory, when Piaget has used tier three principles on the tier one behaviours to produce the tier two stage classifications? Inhelder's ingenious situations, designed to highlight the process of experimental induction actually used by children *in situ*, provided the data for the behavioural descriptions (tier one). During the collaborative analysis of these data, Piaget brought to bear the analytical tools he had developed in his *Traité de logique* (1949), and *Essai sur les transformations des opérations logiques. Les 256 opérations ternaires de la logique bivalente des propositions* (1952b). It was the analysis and interpretation of the tier one behavioural descriptions using the logical model of tier three which brought about the hierarchical ordering which is the substance of tier two. Piaget's procedural strategy here amplifies what was clearly for him the logically prerequisite nature of the metatheory in tier three for the stage classifications that form the basis of tier two. The collaborative approach adopted for this work by Inhelder and Piaget is described in the Preface to GLT (GLT, pp. xxi–xxiv) and reaffirmed in Inhelder's autobiography (Inhelder 1989, p. 223).

Smith (1987) argues a hard line on this issue: "So the criticism that

Piaget's logical model lacks logical sense has prior importance. If the criticism is valid, it cuts the ground from those who continue to investigate merely empirical issues, whether to support or reject the Genevan account" (p. 342). In terms of Piaget's description of the theory, Smith's "prior importance" claim must hold sway; but that is not to deny the possibility of another formula's being used on the same behavioural data to produce the same stage classifications (as neo-Piagetians once claimed for the construct "M-space" or as latter-day Piagetians suggest is the inevitable consequence of reconsiderations published in Piaget and Garcia (1987)). It · does not however negate the argument of those whose exclusive concern is for the utility of certain segments of the Piagetian conception of formal operational thinking rather than for its theoretical validity. No doubt the complete Piagetian description of formal thinking rests on Smith's "prior importance" claim; but the use of, say, the testing procedures and stage classifications suffers under no such constraint. Correspondingly, if the Piagetian model for formal operational thought can be empirically and/or theoretically demonstrated then it would seem as though Piaget's contention concerning the critical role of the model for his theory should also have prior claim.

## An empirical test

In order to provide an empirical test of the relationship between behavioural descriptions and logico-mathematical model, it is first necessary to establish the adequacy of the measures chosen to represent the theoretical tiers that constitute the major dimensions of the problem.

The Piagetian reasoning tests of Shayer *et al.* (Wylam and Shayer 1978) specifically address the elicitation of the behaviour from the Inhelder tasks as set out in GLT and described in tier one of the theory. An important criterion used in the development of the tests was that in each test the child should have two separate opportunities to display each of the critical behaviours described in GLT. Furthermore, the original scoring procedures were designed to impose on each child's performance one of Piaget's classificatory ordering levels (i.e. the second tier) based on the Piagetian criteria taken directly from GLT. Shayer recommended the use of PRTIII – Pendulum for the present project because his experience with the PRTs and the original Inhelder tasks demonstrated that this test provided the best spread of ability levels appropriate to early adolescence (personal discussions, 1987).

While Shayer (1978, 1979; Shayer and Adey 1981) showed that the PRTs have more than satisfactory face, construct and predictive validity, of particular importance in this context is the concurrent validity of these testing procedures with the original Inhelder/Piaget *méthode clinique* interview technique. An independent review of the tests (Hartley 1984, p. 677) provided the following summary: "Comparisons were made between Science reasoning test data (for Tasks III to VII), and the assessment on these tasks conducted through individual interviews. The numbers of pupils involved were small (between 15 and 24 per task); the group test always preceded the interview by a period of one week to one month. The mean differences (assuming the stages are placed on a seven-point equal-interval scale) were approximately one-fifth of a stage on average and showed no systematic variation . . . However, the small numbers of pupils involved limit the authority of these conclusions." For PRTIII – Pendulum in particular, Shayer and Adey (1981, p. 37) reported the following results: KR20 internal consistency .83, test-retest correlation .79 (N = 560) and task-interview correlation .71 (N = 24). Of course the small task-interview sample size qualifies Shayer's conclusion, "There is no systematic difference between subjects' Piagetian levels when assessed by SRTs or by individual interview in the Genevan manner" (Wylam and Shayer 1978, p. 13); it was precisely this restriction on the numbers of students that might reasonably be assessed using the time-consuming *méthode clinique* technique that prompted Shayer to develop the set of demonstrated class tasks.

This, in turn, provided the opportunities and techniques for a far more rigorous and powerful empirical testing of Piaget's theory of formal operational thinking than was previously possible. The availability of the Inhelder experiments in a valid class-task form allowed for the collection of considerably larger data sets (by group testing) than would be feasible with the demanding procedures of the one-to-one *méthode clinique* interviews. As well, the precision of the results generated by Rasch analysis of PRT data allowed for more demanding quantitative testing of hypotheses developed from Piaget's theory of formal operational thought. Central to the current issues is that while the PRTIII provides a measure of concrete and formal operational thinking in terms of the tier one behavioural descriptions, it does not contain any items which could possibly be construed as directly representing the logical model of Piaget's theory.

Unlike any other test which purports to measure formal operational thinking, Bond's Logical Operations Test was designed to represent each and every one of the logical schemata of the formal operations stage. In GLT, Piaget's recourse to a mathematical model based on his interpretation of principles drawn from symbolic logic (the third tier of the theory) is explicated in Chapter 17 "Concrete and formal structures" (pp. 272–333). This delineation of the formal thought structures (tier three), rather than the behavioural descriptions and their ordering (tiers one and two), was the starting point for BLOT item development (Bond 1976b, 1978, 1980). BLOT consists of 35 items in multiple choice format which are designed as instantiations of the calculus of the sixteen binary operations of truth functional logic and the INRC four-group of operations from Piaget's logical model. None of Inhelder's experimental situations from GLT is represented in any form, so there are no items which could be construed as representing the behavioural descriptions. The report of the test development (Bond 1976) indicated that BLOT has construct validity as well as a test-retest reliability correlation of .91 ($p$ < .001, N = 91 random sub-sample from N = 899) for an interval of greater than six weeks (1976, p. 149) (while the issue of concurrent validity with three *méthode clinique* tasks, Pendulum, Chemicals and Balance has been canvassed elsewhere (Bond 1976b, 1980) with a small sample (N = 30), it is primarily the dissatisfaction with the authority of results from such sample sizes that motivated the selection of the PRTIII for the current investigation).

In order to demonstrate how the items in BLOT reflect the scope of the tier three logico-mathematical model described by Piaget in GLT, Tables 9.1 and 9.2 have been constructed to reflect each item's semantic and logical content along with the appropriate reference from GLT for the logical specifications for that item.

It is the chief contention of the present chapter that Piaget's logical model is an integral part of the theory of formal operational thought and that performance on PRTIII – Pendulum (representing the behavioural descriptions of the theory) and on BLOT (representing the logical model of the theory) is related in ways which confirm, or in its minimal form, fail to disconfirm, Piagetian theory. As a consequence of the line of reasoning developed by Hacker, Pratt and Matthews (1985), Rudinger (1987), Bond (1980, 1995) and Hautamäki (1989) it is also an important contention of this chapter that a probabilistic measurement model which has premises consistent with those of the data to be measured would provide a more felicitous test of the fit between model and data than would an equivalence measurement model.

## METHOD

### Sample

Children who comprised the whole of the third-year draft of a rural secondary school in England made up the sample. As a consequence, all subjects were aged in their fifteenth year (ages 15.0–15.11 years). Complete data sets exist for one hundred and fifty subjects (N = 150).

### Tests

*Piagetian reasoning task III – Pendulum (PRTIII)*

The Pendulum PRT "investigates the pupil's ability to sort out the effects of three variables: how the length, weight and push of a pendulum

Table 9.1 BLOT content: Sixteen binary operations

| Q | Operation | Asserted | Denied | Symbol |
|---|-----------|----------|--------|--------|
| 3 | Implication | $(p.q)\lor(\bar{p}.q)\lor(\bar{p}.\bar{q})$ | $(p.\bar{q})$ | $(p{\supset}q)$ |
| 4 | Incompatibility | $(p.\bar{q})\lor(\bar{p}.q)\lor(\bar{p}.\bar{q})$ | $(p.q)$ | $(p/q)$ |
| 9 | Conjunction | $(p.q)$ | $(p.\bar{q})\lor(\bar{p}.q)\lor(\bar{p}.\bar{q})$ | $(p.q)$ |
| 10 | Disjunction | $(p.q)\lor(p.\bar{q})\lor(\bar{p}.q)$ | $(\bar{p}.\bar{q})$ | $(p\lor q)$ |
| 11 | Conjunctive Negation | $(\bar{p}.\bar{q})$ | $(p.q)\lor(p.\bar{q})\lor(\bar{p}.q)$ | $(\bar{p}.\bar{q})$ |
| 12 | Affirmation of $p$ | $(p.q)\lor(p.\bar{q})$ | $(\bar{p}.q)\lor(\bar{p}.\bar{q})$ | $p\,[q]$ |
| 13 | Reciprocal Exclusion | $(p.\bar{q})\lor(\bar{p}.q)$ | $(p.q)\lor(\bar{p}.\bar{q})$ | $(p\lor vq)$ |
| 15 | Reciprocal Implication | $(p.q)\lor(p.\bar{q})\lor(\bar{p}.\bar{q})$ | $(\bar{p}.q)$ | $(q{\supset}p)$ |
| 25 | Complete Negation | $(o)$ | $(p.q)\lor(p.\bar{q})\lor(\bar{p}.q)\lor(\bar{p}.\bar{q})$ | $(o)$ |
| 26 | Complete Affirmation | $(p.q)\lor(p.\bar{q})\lor(\bar{p}.q)\lor(\bar{p}.\bar{q})$ | $(o)$ | $(p^{*}q)$ |
| 27 | Negation of $p$ | $(\bar{p}.q)\lor(\bar{p}.\bar{q})$ | $(p.q)\lor(p.\bar{q})$ | $\bar{p}\,[q]$ |
| 28 | Non-implication | $(p.\bar{q})$ | $(p.q)\lor(\bar{p}.q)\lor(\bar{p}.\bar{q})$ | $(p.\bar{q})$ |
| 29 | Affirmation of $q$ | $(p.q)\lor(\bar{p}.q)$ | $(p.\bar{q})\lor(\bar{p}.\bar{q})$ | $q\,[p]$ |
| 30 | Equivalence | $(p.q)\lor(\bar{p}.\bar{q})$ | $(p.\bar{q})\lor(\bar{p}.q)$ | $(p = q)$ |
| 31 | Negation of $q$ | $(p.\bar{q})\lor(\bar{p}.\bar{q})$ | $(p.q)\lor(\bar{p}.q)$ | $\bar{q}\,[p]$ |
| 32 | Negation of Reciprocal Implication | $(\bar{p}.q)$ | $(p.q)\lor(p.\bar{q})\lor(\bar{p}.\bar{q})$ | $(\bar{p}.q)$ |

Table 9.2 BLOT content: INRC four-group and other schemata

| Q | Schema | Operation |
|---|--------|-----------|
| 16 | INRC | Reciprocal (to negate Identity) |
| 17 | INRC | Identity (to negate Reciprocal) |
| 18 | INRC | Negation (to negate Correlative) |
| 19 | INRC | Reciprocal (to cause disequilibrium) |
| 20 | INRC | Negation (to cause disequilibrium) |
| 21 | INRC | Correlative & Negation → equilibrium |
| 22 | INRC | Reciprocal & Negation → disequilibrium |
| 23 | INRC | Correlative & Identity → disequilibrium |
| 1 | Mechanical Equilibrium | Negation (to negate Identity) |
| 2 | Mechanical Equilibrium | Reciprocal (to negate Identity) |
| 5 | Multiplicative Compensation | Multiplicative compensation |
| 14 | Probability | Probability |
| 24 | Co-ordination of two systems of reference | Correlative & Identity → disequilibrium |
| 33 | Probability | Probability |
| 34 | Co-ordination of two systems of reference | Reciprocal (to negate Identity) |
| 35 | Co-ordination of two systems of reference | Correlative (negate Negation) |
| 6 | Correlations | $(p.q) \vee (\bar{p}.\bar{q}) > (p.\bar{q}) \vee (\bar{p}.q)$ |
| 7 | Correlations | $(p.q) \vee (\bar{p}.\bar{q}) > (p.\bar{q}) \vee (\bar{p}.q)$ gives partial support |
| 8 | Correlations | Remove $(p.\bar{q}) \vee (\bar{p}.q)$ |

determine the period of oscillation. Of course only the length is important, but the student has to overcome strong intuitive feelings to realize this. To be successful the pupil must be able to design experiments which control the appropriate variables, and make deductions from the demonstrated evidence. The task is based on chapter 4 of Inhelder and Piaget's *The growth of logical thinking*" (Wylam and Shayer 1978, p. 9). The apparatus consisted of two hanging strings (long and short) from which either of two weights is hung. A stopclock is used to time 30 second intervals while pupils count the number of swings. After each teacher-demonstrated experiment the children record their responses to questions on their task answer sheets. The results of the survey (Shayer and Wylam 1978) and other analyses discussed earlier (Shayer 1979) confirmed the validity of the PRTs as measures of formal thinking. More recent research with PRTs using Rasch analysis techniques (Bond 1978; Hacker *et al.* 1985; Hautamäki 1989; Shayer *et al.* 1988) further emphasized their utility and validity.

## *Bond's logical operations test (BLOT)*

Bond's logical operations test is an item-by-item operationalization of each of the schemata of the formal operations stage including the sixteen binary operations and the INRC four-group (from GLT) in multiple-choice format. Further use of BLOT by Morley (1979), Christiansson (1983) and by Smith and Knight (1992) as well as the reanalysis of the (N = 30) subsample data using techniques adopted by Lawson (1979) underline the validity and utility of BLOT (Bond 1980; Bond and Jackson 1991).

## Administration and analysis

Administration of the test instruments took place during the week of the scheduled end of term examinations for the school. Whole science-class groups of pupils were assessed on the two tests. The primary data collected during this research were, in the main, subjected to analysis using PC-CREDIT (Masters and Wilson 1988), a computer program designed to apply the Rasch procedure UCON (Wright and Masters 1982; Wright and Stone 1979) to data according to the Rating Scale model and the Partial Credit model. UCON is the unconditional maximum likelihood estimation procedure developed by Wright and Panchapakesan (1969) to test for fit of dichotomously scored items to the basic Rasch model. Masters' (1980) extension of the Rasch model to include the analysis of items with one or more intermediate levels of performance is included as one of the options in the CREDIT program.

Table 9.3 Rasch analysis of BLOT items

| Q | Item Estimates (logits) difficulty | error | Fit Statistics v | q | t | Q | Item Estimates (logits) difficulty | error | Fit Statistics v | q | t |
|---|---|---|---|---|---|---|---|---|---|---|---|
| 1 | -.77 | .26 | .99 | .17 | -.03 | 19 | .47 | .20 | 1.01 | .09 | .15 |
| 2 | -.70 | .26 | 1.01 | .16 | .13 | 20 | -.84 | .27 | .91 | .17 | -.46 |
| 3 | .74 | .20 | .98 | .08 | -.23 | 21 | 2.34 | .20 | 1.27 | .10 | 2.65 |
| 4 | .00 | .22 | 1.00 | .11 | .03 | 22 | -1.06 | .29 | .91 | .19 | -.41 |
| 5 | -.98 | .28 | .98 | .19 | -.06 | 23 | .35 | .21 | 1.06 | .10 | .66 |
| 6 | -2.42 | .48 | 1.06 | .40 | .28 | 24 | .22 | .21 | .89 | .10 | -1.09 |
| 7 | -.64 | .25 | .98 | .16 | -.11 | 25 | .51 | .20 | 1.07 | .09 | .81 |
| 8 | .85 | .19 | .91 | .08 | -1.09 | 26 | .78 | .20 | .90 | .08 | -1.28 |
| 9 | .18 | .21 | 1.07 | .10 | .67 | 27 | -.91 | .27 | .85 | .18 | -.84 |
| 10 | -.19 | .23 | .92 | .12 | -.66 | 28 | 1.64 | .19 | 1.12 | .08 | 1.42 |
| 11 | .18 | .21 | 1.02 | .10 | .25 | 29 | -.46 | .24 | .94 | .14 | -.41 |
| 12 | -1.76 | .37 | .70 | .28 | -1.13 | 30 | 1.07 | .19 | 1.19 | .08 | 2.27 |
| 13 | 1.00 | .19 | 1.16 | .08 | 1.99 | 31 | .18 | .21 | 1.07 | .10 | .70 |
| 14 | -.70 | .26 | 1.15 | .16 | .97 | 32 | 1.14 | .19 | .96 | .08 | -.50 |
| 15 | 1.00 | .19 | .97 | .08 | -.41 | 33 | -.52 | .25 | 1.10 | .15 | .69 |
| 16 | -.30 | .23 | 1.13 | .13 | 1.01 | 34 | -.41 | .24 | 1.00 | .14 | .06 |
| 17 | .39 | .20 | .87 | .09 | -1.45 | 35 | -.30 | .23 | .93 | .13 | -.54 |
| 18 | -.05 | .22 | .90 | .12 | -.86 | | | | | | |

# RESULTS

The data from students' (N = 147) performance on BLOT were subjected to Rasch analysis using the UCON procedure (following the routine practice the three students with perfect BLOT scores of thirty-five were excluded from the analysis by the program).

The results of that analysis are shown in Table 9.3. Item difficulties are spread along a logit scale centred on zero (see Figure 9.1) from –2.42 for item 6 (the easiest item) to +2.34 for item 21 (the most difficult item). The estimates of the fit of items to the Rasch model and hence to its underlying construct of unidimensionality are contained in the column headed "Fit Statistics – $t$". Inspection of these results indicates that the vast majority of BLOT items (33 from a total of 35) fit the Rasch model (fit statistics in the range from –2 to +2 i.e. at the conventional $p < .05$, in terms of a transformed $t$ statistic (Wright and Stone 1979), are generally deemed to be acceptable) with item 30 ($t = 2.27$) and item 21, the most difficult item ($t = 2.65$), having the least satisfactory fit to the measurement model. At the 95% confidence level, five items in 100 (i.e. between one and two out of 35 items) would be expected not to fit the model just on sampling fluctuations alone.

## Rasch analysis of PRTIII performance

Data from the students' performance on the PRTIII were subjected to the same statistical procedure with the results shown in Table 9.4, and Figure 9.2 (one student with a perfect score of 13 on the PRT and six students with scores of zero were disregarded in the analysis). Item difficulties span a range from –3.21 logits for the easiest item, 1, to + 3.43 logits for item 2, the most difficult of the PRTIII items (Rasch analysis adopts an arbitrary zero point for each scale, usually at the mid-point of each test's difficulty range). All the PRTIII items fit the Rasch model well with the $t$ statistic ranging from + 1.55 to –1.77, comfortably within the acceptable levels. Item 7 has the least satisfactory fit to the Rasch model with an acceptable $t$ statistic of –1.77.

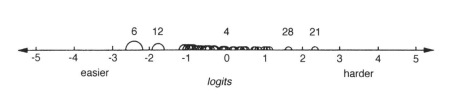

Item Estimates - BLOT
error bands shown

Figure 9.1 BLOT items shown along difficulty continuum

*Table 9.4* Rasch analysis of PRTIII items

| Item Estimates (logits) | | | Fit Statistics | | |
|---|---|---|---|---|---|
| Q | difficulty | error | v | q | t |
| 1 | −3.21 | .30 | 1.29 | .19 | 1.48 |
| 2 | 3.43 | .44 | .92 | .35 | −.10 |
| 3 | .81 | .22 | 1.18 | .11 | 1.55 |
| 4 | −.61 | .21 | .94 | .10 | −.54 |
| 5 | −.37 | .21 | .93 | .10 | −.68 |
| 6 | .95 | .23 | 1.18 | .11 | 1.53 |
| 7 | −.77 | .21 | .83 | .10 | −1.77 |
| 8 | −2.84 | .27 | 1.11 | .16 | .73 |
| 9 | .54 | .22 | 1.05 | .11 | .45 |
| 10 | −.81 | .21 | 1.01 | .10 | −.09 |
| 11 | .67 | .22 | .85 | .11 | −1.37 |
| 12 | −.41 | .21 | .97 | .10 | −.89 |
| 13 | 2.63 | .33 | .80 | .23 | −.89 |

Item Estimates - PRTIII
error bands shown

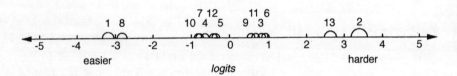

*Figure 9.2* PRTIII items shown along difficulty continuum

## The critical test – test score equating using latent trait theory

In order to apply the most stringent statistical test to the claim that both the PRTIII and the BLOT were measuring the same underlying unitary variable, Rasch person ability estimates on the two tests for each student were plotted against each other. Figure 9.3 also contains paired 95 per cent quality control lines which illustrate the extent to which the 150 student points conform to the model expectation of person-ability invariance. In plots which are used to evaluate the invariance of person-ability across two tests, the 95 per cent lines show how satisfactorily the person points follow the expected identity line (after Wright and Stone 1979, p. 94).

Common-person equating is not a usual procedure of Rasch analysis but relies on the logic of equating item-difficulty estimates of test items from two independent samples. The procedure is demonstrated in Chapter 5 of *Best test design* (Wright and Stone 1979) and is further outlined in Masters

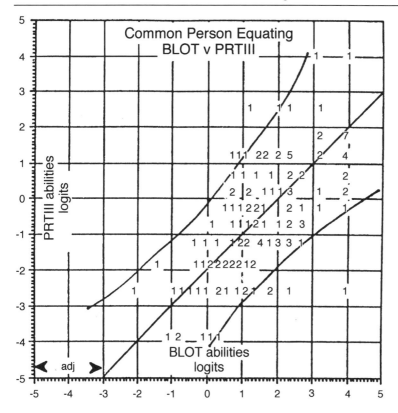

*Figure 9.3* Common-person equating BLOT *v* PRTIII

and Beswick (1986). It was advocated by Masters (personal communication, 1987) and takes advantage of a key principle of Rasch analysis: that
the logic of the analytical procedures for determining person-ability and
item-difficulty estimates is identical and completely interchangeable. The
application of that process for BLOT and PRTIII scores relies heavily on
the exposition by Masters and Beswick (1986, pp. 32 ff.).

The only difference between the two measurement scales resulting from
the independent Rasch analyses of the BLOT and PRTIII will be a
difference in scale origin which can be adjusted for by comparing the
mean abilities B.x and B.y. The ability estimates of students taking both
BLOT and the PRTIII are plotted on the corresponding X and Y axes in
Figure 9.3 with numerals showing the number of students plotted at each
position. A diagonal line of slope 1.0 is drawn through the group means B.x
and B.y. This is not a regression line: it is the expected relationship
between X and Y. In the complete absence of measurement error (an
unachievable situation), all points would be expected to lie on this

diagonal line. The intercept on the X axis is the adjustment that must be made to the BLOT estimates to bring them to the scale of the PRTIII ability estimates. In this case the BLOT estimates require a –2 logits adjustment ("adj" in Figure 9.3) to bring them to the PRTIII scale (i.e. the PRTIII is two logits more difficult than BLOT).

The availability of estimates of the measurement errors associated with each student's measures enables a confidence band to be drawn around the diagonal line according to the formulae in Wright and Stone (1979, pp. 94– 95). This band is widest at the extremes (very low and very high scores) where students' achievements on BLOT and PRTIII are measured least precisely. When the data conform to this model, approximately 95 per cent of observations fall within this band. To the extent that the observed spread of points exceeds the modelled variation, the data misfit the model and the "equating" of X and Y measures is considered to be of dubious validity (after Masters and Beswick 1986).

In an article directly addressed to the theoretical validity and empirical utility of the common-person method of equating two (or more) tests, Masters claimed: "This study shows that an equating based on Rasch abilities can produce the same results as an equating based on Rasch difficulties. It also brings out an advantage of common-person equating: when form equating is based on abilities . . . , an explicit and rigorous test of the underlying assumption of unidimensionality is a natural extension of the equating procedure . . . The most explicit check on this (unidimensionality) assumption is to test the invariance of the ability estimates with measures on more than one form" (Masters 1985, p. 80).

The ability identity plot shows that the vast majority (140 +) of person points do indeed lie within the 95 per cent quality control band. Of course with a sample size of N = 150 it would be expected seven or eight points might lie outside the 95 per cent lines based on sampling variations alone. Within the parameters set by the foregoing discussion the results of the comparative analyses are unequivocal. That all of the data fit so well to the various analytical procedures based on the Rasch model attests to the data's essential compliance with the underlying unidimensionality construct that is explicitly prerequisite for satisfying the demands of this model. Consequently, the Piagetian description of the relationship between the three tiers of the formal operational stage in GLT has withstood these quite specific and stringent tests of its validity.

Central to the claims made in the present research is that unidimensionality of data as expressed by fit to the Rasch model is the most suitable statistical representation of Piaget's concept of the *structure d'ensemble* incorporated in the structure of each stage of his cognitive developmental theory. The robust nature of the fit statistics for the BLOT and the PRTIII supports the strong claim that formal operational thinking skills are unidimensional and this provides appropriate empirical validation of Piaget's theoretical construct, the *structure d'ensemble* at the formal operations stage. That the data from BLOT and the PRTIII taken together fit the Rasch model (thereby satisfying its underlying unidimensionality premise) is quite remarkable. While each test was designed to be a valid group measure of formal operational thinking skills based on specifications derived explicitly from GLT, the obvious similarities end there.

Shayer's development of the PRTIII was based exclusively on the experimental situation reported by Inhelder and Piaget in Chapter 4 of GLT: "The oscillation of a pendulum and the operations of exclusion" and sought to assess performance on the basis of the behaviours described therein. The format of the PRTIII is that of a 13 item demonstrated class-task, and assessment is based on the requirements of tier two of Piagetian theory at the formal stage. The present author's development of BLOT proceeded almost simultaneously but entirely independently (and, incidentally, half a world away), based entirely on the specifications of the logico-mathematical model of the formal operations stage alluded to throughout GLT but specifically delineated in Chapter 17: "Concrete and formal structures", and sought to assess performance in terms of the bases of the logical operations described therein. The format of the BLOT is that of a 35 item multiple choice test and assessment is based on the specifications laid down for tier three of Piagetian theory at the formal stage.

It has been a primary contention of the case being developed in this chapter that the most plausible explanatory link between performance on the PRTIII and the BLOT is that which is explicated in GLT; that success in solving the experimental tasks is based on the use of formal operational thought whose model is currently best represented by the sixteen binary operations and the INRC four-group. Shayer's comments on the importance and relevance of the BLOT to this crucial test of Piagetian theory are summarized thus: "It is therefore of some interest that Trevor Bond has in fact constructed a multiple choice test embodying in combinatorial form all the sixteen operations distinguished in the use of formal thought (BLOT). This means that an empirical test can be carried out of Piaget's logical model against the Inhelder/Piaget behavioural description model of formal tasks" (Shayer 1989, p. 327).

## IMPLICATIONS

This is not the first time that aspects of Piagetian theory have been put to empirical test, and nor is it the first time that Piagetian theory has passed such a stringent test. Even at the stage of formal operations the theory has been quite robust when a fair and reasonable test of underlying premises has been applied. The nationwide testing by Shayer's team in the UK using a battery of PRTs has provided powerful corroboration of the Piagetian tier one and tier two behavioural descriptions on an unprecedented sample size of over 14,000 children. Several implications for the application of testing strategies to Piagetian theory follow from the success of the current research, and by obvious association from the work of Shayer *et al.* (1976).

While many may claim to have put Piagetian theory to an empirical test it is only possible to substantiate that claim when it is demonstrated that the measures collected in the study effectively correspond with, or somehow express, the very essence of the Piagetian principles under scrutiny and that those measures have substantial claims for reliability and for face, construct and concurrent validity. In particular, the use of the *méthode clinique* situations by Inhelder and Piaget (1955) to uncover the scope of formal thought appears as a stroke of genius but the interpretation of the best features of those tasks into reliable and valid PRTs has provided the tools for the present rigorous testing of the Piagetian model. It is argued that the PRTs succeed because each demonstrated class task incorporates opportunities for every subject to display exactly those responses identified in GLT as critical indices of performance on that task. Unfortunately other adaptations of the Inhelder tasks (e.g. Karplus, Karplus, Formisano and Paulsen 1977; Karplus and Peterson 1970; Tisher 1971) and other tests often using measures of formal thought which do not stand up to the rigorous validity requirements listed above, cannot be considered as providing equitable empirical testing.

Correspondingly the apparent adequacy of BLOT as a reliable and valid test of the logico-mathematical component of formal thought derives from the author's apparently successful attempt to develop test items in direct correspondence with the specifications of the model described by Piaget in GLT. Inasmuch as other tests of the logical components of formal thinking do not reflect the details of the model specifically outlined by Piaget then they do not provide a valid test of Piaget's claims. In particular the research of Lawson (Lawson *et al.* 1978), Brainerd (1976), Weitz (1971), and Ennis (1975, 1976), based on the syllogisms of classical logic, are not directly about the Piagetian model. It is blatantly wrongheaded to devise a test which misrepresents the constructs under examination and then to impute fault on the part of the construct and the theory when the test results prove inadequate.

The PRTs and BLOT were developed according to principles derived from the test development procedures current at that time (although the PRTs did have the advantage of Shayer's discrimination analysis). Yet, subsequent re-examination of those tests using Rasch analysis not only strengthens the claims of these tests as valid measures of formal thought but underlines the important role of measurement models in Piagetian research. A crucial line in the argument that has supported the development of the current research has been generated by concerns about the sorts of measurement models that have been and should be adopted in the analyses of data produced by Piagetian research. The major implication here is that a felicitous empirical test of the Piagetian model cannot be undertaken with a statistical test derived from a measurement model that is antithetical to the Piagetian premises being investigated.

Consequently, there exists a *prima facie* case for the adoption of tests from the family of Rasch models for research in this area. Shayer's Rasch scaling of the formal operational stage behaviours has already added considerable psychometric detail to the Genevan description of this stage. These statistical techniques are currently being used to investigate the nature and extent of horizontal *décalage* at the formal operations stage and to shed light on the relationship between the solution of two (AD47 and Post office) variations of Wason and Johnson-Laird's (1972) selection task and BLOT and PRT performance. The latter project should inform as to whether the selection tasks fit in a corresponding way to the same uni-dimensional construct as the BLOT and PRTIII. Further it should provide an empirical estimation of the difficulty interval between the two selection tasks themselves as well as their relationship to the Piagetian substages. These findings should help clarify the import of selection task performance for formal operational theory.

Throughout this demonstration, an attempt was made to acknowledge a number of competing theoretical demands from one of a number of perspectives which could tend to invalidate the major research findings. Firstly then, under the widely recognized falsificationist convention, the rejection or non-rejection of research hypotheses is all that is permitted. Consequently a conclusive confirmation can never thereby be realized and it is necessary always to accept highly indirect support for any canvassed theoretical arguments. It followed that support for any particular Piagetian theoretical principle under investigation could be demonstrated in a most indirect way only.

But the foremost consideration has been the need to maintain informed sensitivity to the requirements of Piagetian theory whilst recognizing that attempting to provide an empirical test of the theory was quite foreign to Piaget's rationalist orientation. Further, it was accepted that the presence of this empiricist/rationalist dichotomy demanded the closest possible adherence to the nuances of Piagetian theory. This was essential if the outcomes of the research were to be even considered as relevant to orthodox Piagetians on the one hand yet methodologically sound by empiricists on the other.

It is acknowledged that an empirical test of this kind is quite irrelevant to Piagetian genetic epistemology; equally then, critics of that position may argue that Piagetian theory is consequently untestable. However, if the current controversy surrounding the role of the structure of formal operational thought and its behavioural concomitants is going to develop into something more than a series of parallel but largely unconnected discussions from seemingly irreconcilable philosophical viewpoints, and if there is ever to be any sort of *rapprochement* between the structuralist and empiricist paradigms for the study of adolescent thought, then rationalist Piagetians must find some empirical component to their model while the empiricists must accept that testing and analytical procedures must not violate the theoretical integrity of the Piagetian model.

That the requirements of the empiricist and rationalist paradigms are at odds should not deter the researcher from considering the data collected in the course of the present study. Although these paradigms guide not only the questions being asked but the nature of the data being collected, it has been the undisguised intention of the present author for this research to straddle the gulf between two philosophical worlds in a manner that makes the results of the research compelling to both and able to be ignored by neither.

## SUMMARY

*The research reported in this chapter provides a rigorous statistical test of Piaget's logico-mathematical model of the stage of formal operational thinking. It does so within an immediate empiricist framework in order to provide a test suitable to the needs of practising psychologists while at the same time acknowledging the philosophical parameters of Piaget's genetic epistemology. One hundred and fifty British secondary school students' performances on two measures of formal operational thinking were subjected to Rasch analysis. Ability on the separation of variables task – pendulum was measured on Shayer's PRTIII whilst the BLOT was used to assess students' use of the operations outlined by Piaget in GLT as forming the basis of his logico-mathematical model for formal operational thinking. For each test the underlying ability was inferred as unidimensional and the two sets of data taken together were shown to fit the Rasch model (p < .05). These results were interpreted as* prima facie *empirical evidence for the* structure d'ensemble *of formal thought and of the appropriateness of the Rasch measurement model for Piagetian research. It was argued that the probabilistic model provides a conceptually faithful statistical interpretation of the* structure d'ensemble *which is consonant with other key Piagetian principles. Implications for Piagetian theory, measurement and education were canvassed.*

## ACKNOWLEDGEMENTS

The author wishes to acknowledge the suggestion of Michael Shayer to carry out this empirical test, the advice of Ian Jackson in philosophical matters and the assistance of Leslie Smith with problems of translation from the French.

# REFERENCES

Airasian, P. W., Bart, W. M. and Greaney, B. J. (1975) "The analysis of a propositional logic game by ordering theory", *Child Study Journal* 5: 13–24.

Begg, I. (1987) "Some", *Canadian Journal of Psychology* 41: 62–73.

Beth, E. W. and Piaget, J. (1966) "General psychological problems of logico-mathematical thought", in *Mathematical epistemology and psychology* (pp. 163–191), Dordrecht: Reidel.

Bideaud, J., Houdé, O. and Pedinelli, J.-L. (1993) *L'homme en développement*, Paris: Presses Universitaires de France.

Bond, T. G. (1976a) *The development, validation and use of a test to assess Piaget's formal stage of logical operations*, Honours thesis, James Cook University of North Queensland.

Bond, T. G. (1976b) *BLOT: Bond's logical operations test*, Townsville: T.C.A.E.

Bond, T. G. (1978) "Propositional logic as a model for adolescent intelligence – additional considerations", *Interchange* 9: 93–100.

Bond, T. G. (1980) "The psychological link across formal operations", *Science Education* 64: 113–117.

Bond, T. G. (1991, November) *Assessing developmental levels in children's thinking: Matching measurement model to cognitive theory*, paper presented at the Annual Conference of the Australian Association for Research in Education, Gold Coast.

Bond, T. G. (1995) "Piaget and measurement I: The twain really do meet", *Archives de Psychologie* 63: 71–87.

Bond, T. G. and Jackson, I. A. R. (1991) "The Gou protocol revisited: A Piagetian conceptualization of critique", *Archives de Psychologie* 59: 31–53. (Reprinted in L. Smith (ed.) (1992) *Jean Piaget: Critical Assessments*, London: Routledge.

Braine, M. D. S. and Rumain, B. (1983) "Piaget's logic and the stage of formal operations", in J. H. Flavell and E. M. Markman (eds) *Handbook of child psychology, vol. III: Cognitive development* (pp. 263–234), New York: Wiley.

Brainerd, C. J. (1976) "On the validity of propositional logic as a model for adolescent intelligence", *Interchange* 7: 40–45.

Bruner, J. (1959) "Inhelder and Piaget's *The growth of logical thinking* I – a psychologist's viewpoint", *British Journal of Psychology* 50: 363–370.

Christiansson, D. J. (1983) *An investigation of the relationship between cognitive developmental stage and quantitative skills in college students*, doctoral dissertation, University of the Pacific.

Dell'Aquila, C., Di Gennaro, M. and Picciarelli, V. (1985) "The logic of hypothesis testing and the control of variables formal schema: Is there a link?" *European Journal of Science Education* 7: 67–72.

Ennis, R. H. (1962) "A concept of critical thinking", *Harvard Educational Review* 32: 81–111.

Ennis, R. H. (1969) "Piaget's logic", *Working Papers in Educational Research* 2.

Ennis, R. H. (1975) "Children's ability to handle Piaget's propositional logic: A conceptual critique", *Review of Educational Research* 45: 1–41.

Ennis, R. H. (1976) "An alternative to Piaget's conceptualization of logical competence", *Child Development* 47: 903–919.

Hacker, R. G., Pratt, C. and Matthews, B. A. (1985) "Selecting *Science reasoning tasks* for classroom use", *Education Research and Perspectives* 12: 19–32.

Hartley, J. R. (1984) *CSMS Science reasoning tasks*, in H. Goldstein and P. Levy (eds) *Tests in education* (pp. 670–680), London: Academic Press.

Hautamäki, J. (1989) "The application of a Rasch model on Piagetian measures of stages of thinking", in P. Adey (ed.) *Adolescent development and school science* (pp. 342–349), London: Falmer.

Inhelder, B. (1989) "Bärbel Inhelder", in G. Lindzey (ed.) *A history of psychology in autobiography: Vol. 8* (pp. 208–243), Stanford: Stanford University Press.

Inhelder, B. and Piaget, J. (1955/1958) *De la logique de l'enfant à la logique de l'adolescent / The growth of logical thinking from childhood to adolescence: An essay on the construction of formal operational structures*, Paris: Presses Universitaires de France/London: Routledge & Kegan Paul.

Inhelder, B. and Piaget, J. (1964) *The early growth of logic in the child. Classification and seriation*, London: Routledge & Kegan Paul.

Isaacs, N. (1951) "Review of *Traité de logique*", *British Journal of Psychology* 42: 185–188.

Jansson, L. C. (1978, March) *Logical reasoning learning hierarchies*, paper presented at the Conference of the American Educational Research Association, Toronto.

Johnson-Laird, P. N. (1983) *Mental models*, Cambridge: Cambridge University Press.

Johnson-Laird, P. N., Legrenzi, P. and Legrenzi, M. S. (1972) "Reasoning and a sense of reality", *British Journal of Psychology* 63: 395–400.

Karplus, R., Karplus, E., Formisano, M. and Paulsen, A. (1977) "A survey of proportional reasoning and control of variables in seven countries", *Journal of Research in Science Teaching* 14: 411–417.

Karplus, R. and Peterson, R. W. (1970) "Intellectual development beyond elementary school II: Ratio, a survey", *School Science and Mathematics* 70: 813–820.

Lawson, A. E. (1977) "Relationships among performances on three formal operational tasks", *Journal of Psychology* 96: 235–241.

Lawson, A. E. (1979) "Combining variables, controlling variables and proportions: Is there a psychological link?" *Science Education* 63: 67–72.

Lawson, A. E. and Blake, A. J. D., (1976) "Concrete and formal thinking abilities in high school biology students as measured by three separate instruments", *Journal of Research in Science Teaching* 13: 227–235.

Lawson, A. E., Karplus, R. and Adi, H. (1978) "The acquisition of propositional logic and formal operational schemata during the secondary school years", *Journal of Research in Science Teaching* 15: 465–478.

Leiser, D. (1982) "Piaget's logical formalism for formal operations: An interpretation in context", *Developmental Review* 2: 87–99.

Lovell, K. (1961) "A follow-up of Inhelder and Piaget's *The growth of logical thinking*", *British Journal of Educational Psychology* 52: 143–153.

Maderson, P. F. A. (1982) "The role of development in macroevolutionary change", in J. T. Bonner (ed.) *Evolution and development* (pp. 279–312), Berlin: Springer-Verlag.

Masters, G. N. (1980) *A Rasch model for rating scales*, doctoral dissertation, University of Chicago.

Masters, G. N. (1985) "Common-person equating with the Rasch model", *Applied Psychological Measurement* 9: 73–82.

Masters, G. N. and Beswick, D. G. (1986) *The construction of tertiary entrance scores: Principles and issues*, Melbourne: Center for the Study of Higher Education, University of Melbourne.

Masters, G. N. and Wilson, M. R. (1988) *PC-CREDIT* (Computer program), Melbourne: Center for the Study of Higher Education, University of Melbourne.

Monnier, C. and Wells, A. (1980) "Discussion of recent research on the formal operations stage", *Cahiers de la Fondation Archives Jean Piaget, n° 1*, 203–242.

Morley, K. A. (1979) *The development of spatial ordering concepts in geography at the secondary school level*, Honours thesis, James Cook University of North Queensland.

Overton, W. F., Ward, S. L., Noveck, I. A., Black, J. and O'Brien, D. P. (1987) "Form and content in the development of deductive reasoning"; *Developmental Psychology* 23: 22–30.

Papert, S. (1961) *"The growth of logical thinking III*: A Piagetian viewpoint", unpublished manuscript, Archives Jean Piaget, Genève.

Papert, S. (1963) "Sur la logique Piagétienne", in L. Apostel, J. B. Grize, S. Papert and J. Piaget (eds) *La filiation des structures* (pp. 107–129), Paris: Presses Universitaires de France.

Parsons, C. (1960) "Inhelder and Piaget's *The growth of logical thinking II*: A logician's viewpoint", *British Journal of Psychology* 51: 75–84.

Piaget, J. (1949) *Traité de logique. Essai de logistique opératoire*, Paris: Colin.

Piaget, J. (1952) *Essai sur les transformations des opérations logiques. Les 256 opérations ternaires de la logique bivalente des propositions*, Paris: Presses Universitaires de France.

Piaget, J. (1953) *Logic and psychology*, Manchester: Manchester University Press.

Piaget, J. (1967) "Logique formelle et psychologie génétique", in *Actes du colloque international sur les modèles et la formalisation du comportement*, Paris: CNRS.

Piaget, J. (1983) *Le possible et le nécessaire: Vol. 2*, Paris: Presses Universitaires de France.

Piaget, J. (1986) "Essay on necessity", *Human Development* 29: 301–314.

Piaget, J. and Garcia, R. (1987) *Vers une logique des significations*, Genève: Murionde.

Piaget, J. and Inhelder, B. (1948) *La représentation de l'espace chez l'enfant*, Paris: Presses Universitaires de France.

Piaget, J. and Szeminska, A. (1941) *La genèse du nombre chez l'enfant*, Neuchâtel: Delachaux/Niestlé.

Rudinger, G. (1987, September) *Analysis of developmental patterns and sequences in cognitive development*, paper presented at the nineteenth advanced course, Foundation Archives Jean Piaget, Université de Genève.

Seltman, M. and Seltman, P. (1985) *Piaget's logic*, London: George Allen & Unwin.

Shayer, M. (1978) *A test of the validity of Piaget's construct of formal operational thinking*, doctoral dissertation, University of London.

Shayer, M. (1979) "Has Piaget's construct of formal operational thinking any utility?" *British Journal of Educational Psychology* 49: 265–276.

Shayer, M. (1989) "Formal operations: Its validity and application to science teaching", in P. Adey (ed.) *Adolescent development and school science* (pp. 327–328), London: Falmer.

Shayer, M. and Adey, P. (1981) *Towards a science of science teaching*, London: Heinemann.

Shayer, M., Küchemann, D. E. and Wylam, H. (1976) "The distribution of Piagetian stages of thinking in British middle and secondary school children", *British Journal of Educational Psychology* 46: 164–173.

Shayer, M. and Wylam, H. (1978) "The distribution of Piagetian stages of thinking in British middle and secondary school children II: 14 to 16 year olds", *British Journal of Educational Psychology* 48: 62–70.

Shayer, M., Demetriou, A. and Parvez, M. (1988) "The structure and scaling of concrete operational thought: three studies in four countries", *Genetic, Social and General Monographs* 114: 309–75. Reprinted in L. Smith (ed.) *Jean Piaget: Critical Assessments*, London: Routledge.

Smith, L. (1987) "A constructivist interpretation of formal operations", *Human Development* 30: 341–354.

Smith, L. (1992) *Jean Piaget: Critical assessments*, London: Routledge.

Smith, L. (1993) *Necessary knowledge*, Hove: Erlbaum.

Smith, L. and Knight, P. (1992) "Adolescent reasoning tests with history content", *Archives de Psychologie* 60: 225–242.

Tisher, R. P. (1971) "A Piagetian questionnaire applied to pupils in a secondary school", *Child Development* 42: 1633–1636.

Ward, J. (1972) "The saga of Butch and Slim", *British Journal of Educational Psychology* 43: 267–289.

Ward, J. and Pearson, L. (1973) "A comparison of two methods of testing logical thinking", *Canadian Journal of Behavioural Science* 5: 385–398.

Wason, P. C. and Johnson-Laird, P. N. (1972) *Psychology of reasoning: Structure and content*, Cambridge: Harvard University Press.

Weitz, L. J. (1971) *A developmental and logical analysis of Piaget's sixteen binary operations*, Ann Arbor: University Microfilms.

Weitz, L. J., Bynum, T. W. and Thomas, J. A. (1972) "Truth-functional logic in formal operational thinking: Inhelder and Piaget's evidence", *Developmental Psychology* 7: 129–132.

Weitz, L. J., Bynum, T. W., Thomas, J. A. and Steger, J. A. (1973) "Piaget's system of sixteen binary operations: An empirical investigation", *Journal of Genetic Psychology* 123: 279–284.

Wright, B. D. and Masters, G. N. (1982) *Rating scale analysis*, Chicago: MESA Press.

Wright, B. D. and Panchapakesan, N. (1969) "A procedure for sample-free item analysis", *Educational and Psychological Measurement* 29: 23–48.

Wright, B. D. and Stone, M. H. (1979) *Best test design*, Chicago: MESA Press.

Wylam, H. and Shayer, M. (1978) *CSMS science reasoning tasks*, Windsor: NFER.

# Chapter 10

# Higher-order structure and relational reasoning

## Contrasting analogical and thematic relations

*Usha Goswami and Ann L. Brown*

## ABSTRACT

A popular explanation of younger children's success in analogy tasks is that lower-level associative reasoning strategies are used. Younger children are said to have a primarily associative understanding of analogy, with the ability to coordinate sets of relations largely emerging later in development (Goldman, Pellegrino, Parseghian and Sallis 1982; Sternberg and Nigro 1980). One way of testing the associative claim is to pit young children's emergent analogical abilities against thematic (associative) relations, which are known to play an important role in the knowledge structures of young children. The present experiments presented 4-, 5- and 9-year-old children with **a:b::c:d** analogies in a picture choice format, offering a choice between Analogy and Thematic responses. Only the Analogy responses were correct in terms of the higher-order structure of the analogies. The results showed that the Analogy responses were consistently preferred to the Thematic responses by children of all ages. It is concluded that analogy is an important building block for learning from an early age.

## INTRODUCTION

Recently, a number of studies of the analogical abilities of young children have challenged the generally accepted notion that reasoning by analogy is a developmentally sophisticated skill. This notion arose from two sources: from the performance of children in intelligence tests such as the Stanford–Binet, and from the theoretical work of Piaget (Inhelder and Piaget 1958; Piaget, Montangero and Billeter 1977). Piaget proposed that analogical reasoning was the hallmark of formal operational thinking, emerging in early adolescence, and a large body of work has found evidence apparently consistent with this developmental position (e.g. Gallagher and Wright 1977; Levinson and Carpenter 1974; Lunzer 1965; Sternberg and Nigro 1980). More recently, however, studies of problem solving by analogy

(Brown and Kane 1988; Brown, Kane and Echols 1986; Brown, Kane and Long 1989; Holyoak, Junn and Billman 1984), of the use of analogy in learning tasks such as reading and spelling (Goswami 1986, 1988a, 1988b), and even of performance in the difficult "item" or classical (**a:b::c:d**) analogies used in intelligence testing (Alexander, Wilson, White and Fuqua 1987; Goswami, 1989; Goswami and Brown 1990) have provided evidence against the notion that very young children are unable to reason by analogy.

This recent work has not gone unchallenged. It is still possible to maintain a pessimistic view of young children's analogical skill by appealing to associative reasoning (e.g. Gentile, Tedesco-Stratton, Davis, Lund and Agunanne 1977; Sternberg and Nigro 1980). Sternberg and Nigro suggested that for children below 11–12 years of age given verbal analogies of the form *narrow:wide::question: (trial/statement/answer/ask)*, "solution is primarily but not exclusively associative" (p. 36). The suggestion is that the high degree of association between *question* and *answer* frequently results in the selection of the correct response by younger children. Similar effects of association have been noted by Goldman *et al.* (1982), also using a verbal analogy format: They note that their research "strongly indicate(s) some type of simpler associative understanding of analogy" (p. 558). Further support for the role of association is found in the work of Gallagher and Wright (1979), and Achenbach (1970, 1971). Willner (1964) has shown that almost 60 pert cent of the classical item analogies used in IQ tests such as the Stanford–Binet can be correctly associatively "solved" by presentation of the **c** term alone (e.g. subject is given *shoe:* [*arm, table, foot, lamp*], responds "foot." The corresponding analogy item is *hat:head::shoe:?*).

A strong test of the claim that even very young children can reason by analogy would thus be to pit children's emergent ability to reason by analogy against their strong preference for reasoning by association. This preference for associative reasoning has also been documented in the developmental literature on thematic relations. A number of studies have shown that in picture sorting tasks designed to test categorising skills, younger children often choose to relate items by thematic or associative relations in preference to category relations (Markman and Hutchinson 1984; Nelson 1977; Smiley and Brown 1979). Younger children prefer to pair *dog* with *bone* rather than with other animals, or *fish* with *net* rather than with other fish (although these preferences may depend on task instructions: see Bauer and Mandler 1989; Waxman 1990).

We set out to provide a strong test of the analogy claim by designing classical analogies in which the most common associate of the **c** term was the *wrong* response in terms of the analogy. Children were provided with two different kinds of relations on which a response could be based. One relation was thematic (e.g. *dog:bone*). The other relation was that specified by the higher-order structure provided by the analogy. These were familiar relations such as "lives in" (e.g. *bird:nest::dog:kennel*). If children are able to reason by analogy in this paradigm in spite of the attractive thematic relation alternatives pitted against the analogical relations, this would be strong evidence for analogical competence in young children.

The analogies were administered in a multiple choice picture format. To test our assumption that the thematic responses were attractive alternative solutions to the analogies, we designed a control condition in which children were only given the **c** term in each analogy with the different distractors, and were asked to choose the picture that went best with the **c** term picture. This was the task used by Willner (1964). We expected that children would be equally likely to choose the analogical response (e.g. *kennel*) to match the **c** term (e.g. *dog*) in this condition as the thematic response (e.g. *bone*).

We included two additional distractor pictures in the analogy and control tasks. One of these was a mere appearance match choice. This was included to test Gentner's (1989) theory that analogical responding in younger children and other novices is frequently based on surface similarity. For the example given, the mere appearance match response would be another *dog*. The other distractor was an object from the same category as the **c** term (e.g. *cat*). A category distractor was included because category relations are those most commonly pitted against thematic relations in the experimental literature (Markman and Hutchinson 1984; Nelson 1977; Smiley and Brown 1979).

## EXPERIMENT 1

### Method

*Subjects*

Sixty children took part in the study. There were 20 4-year-olds (mean age 4 years 6 months, range 4;0–4;11), 20 5-year-olds (mean age 5 years 5 months, range 5;1–5;9), and 20 9-year-olds (mean age 9 years 9 months, range 8;6–10;5). The mean PPVT (Peabody Picture Vocabulary Tables) scores for each group were 110.7, *SD* 13.3 (4 years); 96.9, *SD* 10.9 (5 years); and 102.1, *SD* 14.4 (9 years) respectively.

*Procedure*

The children were seen twice for two separate sessions. In one session they received the Analogy condition, in the other the Thematic Control condition. In each condition the children were required to select one picture from four alternatives, either to complete a sequence of four pictures (Analogy condition) or to form a pair with a single picture (Thematic Control). There were ten picture sequences in each condition.[1] Children were required to justify their choice on each trial, and were asked whether any of the other pictures would also be appropriate to finish the sequence. Justifications of further choices were also required.

## Conditions

*Analogy condition*: In the Analogy condition children were presented with a sequence of three pictures, and were asked to choose a fourth to complete the sequence from a range of four alternatives. The first three pictures comprised the **a:b::c:?** part of the analogy, and were placed in front of the child so that the **a** and **b** pictures were next to each other, and the **c** picture was separated by a 10 in. gap. The child was required to select the picture to go next to the **c** term of the analogy, forming a second pair of pictures related in the same way as the **a:b** pair (see Figure 10.1).

The task was introduced as a game about choosing pictures. The experimenter said "We are going to play a game about choosing pictures. I'm going to put two pictures down on this side, then a third picture over here, and you have to figure out which picture we need to finish the pattern." The children were asked to name the first three pictures in the sequence to ensure that there was no confusion about the objects depicted, and were also asked to name the four pictures presented as alternative solutions. If the child hesitated or was uncertain, the experimenter named the pictures for the child. The ten analogies were presented in a randomised order for

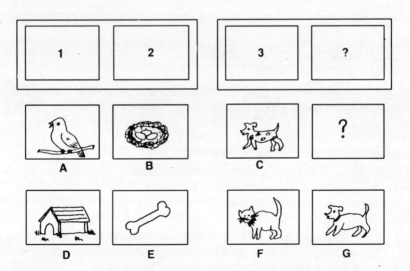

*Figure 10.1* The stimuli and distractors for the analogy bird:nest::dog:kennel

each child, and the four distractors were laid out in a randomised order in each trial.

Prior to presentation of the alternative solution pictures, the children were asked to predict which picture they would need to finish the pattern. Predictions were required to see whether children could complete the analogies without the aid of the pictures. After completion of each sequence, the children were also asked whether any of the other pictures could fit the analogy, and if so, why.

There were four alternative choices to finish the **a:b::c:?** sequence. These were:

D  The correct answer
E  A strong thematic associate of the **c** term
F  A category match for the **c** term
G  A mere appearance match for the **c** term

For example, for the analogy *pencil:pencil eraser::chalk:chalkboard eraser*, the correct (D) response was *chalkboard eraser*, the thematic associate (E) response was *chalkboard*, the category match (F) response was *paints*, and the mere appearance match (G) response was *crayons*.

Depending on the solution strategy used by the children, a number of different responses are possible. Children who can use the higher-order structure provided by the analogy should select response D, the Analogy response. Children who rely on associative reasoning to solve analogies should choose response E, the Thematic response. This response would be predicted by the associative hypothesis. Children who rely on surface similarity to solve analogies, a possibility suggested by Gentner (1989), should choose response G. Selection of response F would imply category matching, and would not be predicted by any of the theories of analogy being compared here. A full list of the stimuli used is given in Table 10.1.

*Thematic Control condition:* The Thematic Control condition was intended to provide a measure of thematic responding, and was identical to the Analogy condition except that the **a:b** part of the picture sequence was not presented. Children were simply given the **c** term used in the different analogies, and were asked to choose which of the four alternative solution pictures fitted best with the **c** picture. They were asked to justify their choice, and were then asked whether any of the other pictures would also fit, and if so, why. Children were expected to be more willing to allow alternative responses in the Thematic Control condition, where there is no "correct" answer, than in the Analogy condition, where the correct answer is constrained by the higher-order structure of the problem.

The response choices were exactly as in the Analogy condition. However, it was expected that response E (the Thematic response) would be as frequently selected as the Analogy response in the Thematic Control

*Table 10.1* Analogical sequences and response alternatives used in the experiment

| (a:b::c:d) Analogy | Thematic (E) | Category (F) | Mere Appearance (G) |
|---|---|---|---|
| spider:web::bee:hive | honey | ant | fly |
| pencil:pencil eraser:: chalk:chalkboard eraser | chalkboard | paints | crayons |
| dog:dog basket::baby:crib | bottle | kitten | doll |
| train:tracks::boat:water | sailor | car | canoe |
| dress:hanger::coat:hook | hat | sweater | coat |
| bird:nest::dog:kennel | bone | cat | dog |
| gloves:hands::shoes:feet | socks | boots | shoes |
| cow:milk::hen:egg | feather | duck | rooster |
| king:crown::policeman:police hat | police-car | fireman | policewoman |
| bird:plane::fish:boat | net | crab | fish |

*Note*: Pictures used in the Thematic Control condition are choices C, D, E, F, G in each case.

condition, as it was a strong thematic associate of the **c** term. Other possible responses are selection of response G, which would imply matching on the basis of surface similarity, and selection of response F, which would be evidence for category matching.

*Order of conditions*

The main comparison of interest was between the children who received the Analogy condition first and those who received the Thematic Control condition first. However, in order to see whether there would be any transfer effects, all the children received both the conditions, but half of the children received the Analogy condition first, and the other half received the Thematic Control condition first. Children who had already selected the Analogy response in the analogy task were expected to form a learning set in favour of the Analogy response, and thus to show a tendency to stick to the Analogy response in the Thematic Control condition, where the task format provided no consistent basis for preferring one response over another.

**Results**

The results showed that children of all ages were able to solve the analogies correctly. The percentage of children scoring above a criterion of six or more analogies solved correctly ($p < .019$, Binomial test; $p < .001$ for the 5-year-olds who received nine trials) was 100 per cent at age 9, 65 per cent at age 5, and 60 per cent at age 4. This is an impressive level of performance in the **a:b::c:d** task given usual performance levels reported in the literature.

The mean number of choices of each response by age and order of condition is given for each condition in Table 10.2. As well as responses D (Analogy), E (Thematic), F (Category) and G (Mere Appearance match), it was necessary to include a separate response category for children who maintained that the Analogy and Thematic responses were both equally correct, and refused to choose between them. This tendency was most marked in the Control condition, where no "correct" basis for matching was provided.

The important effects to notice are the high proportion of Analogy responses in the Analogy condition for both order groups, and the stronger tendency to select the Analogy response in the Control condition for the children who had already received the Analogy condition.

To examine whether children were significantly more likely to select the Analogy response in the Analogy condition than in the Control condition, a between-subjects analysis comparing those children who received the Analogy condition first with those who received the Thematic Control condition first was carried out. The analysis was a 3 × 2 (Age [4, 5, 9 years] × Condition [Analogy and Thematic Control]) Analysis of Variance, taking the number of times that response D (the Analogy response) was selected as the dependent variable.

The analysis showed a significant interaction between Age and Condition, $F(2,54) = 4.20$, $p < .02$. Post-hoc tests (Newman–Keuls) showed that the interaction was due to significantly more Analogy responses being selected in the Analogy condition than in the Control condition at each age ($ps < .01$). However, significantly more analogies were solved by the 9-year-olds than by the 5-year-olds ($p < .01$), while the performance of the 5-year-olds and the 4-year-olds did not differ significantly. Thus there is an improvement in the analogy task with age.

Inspection of Table 10.2 shows that, whereas children in both order groups chose the Analogy response most frequently in the Analogy condition, those children who received the Control condition second chose the Analogy response in this condition more frequently than those children who received the Control condition first. To examine whether this transfer effect was significant, a 3 × 2 × 2 (Age × Order of Conditions × Condition) Analysis of Variance with repeated measures on condition was carried out, again taking the number of times that response D (the Analogy response) was selected as the dependent variable. The analysis showed a three-way interaction between Age, Order and Condition, $F(2,54) = 12.13$, $p < .02$.

Post-hoc tests (Newman–Keuls) showed that the interaction was caused by a transfer effect in the two older groups only. The 9-year-olds chose the Analogy response significantly more frequently in the Control condition

*Table 10.2* Number of times each response selected out of 10*

| Order | Condition | Response | | | | |
|---|---|---|---|---|---|---|
| | | Analogy (D) | Thematic (E) | Both (D/E) | Category (F) | Mere App (G) |
| **9-year-olds:** | | | | | | |
| A/Con. | Analogy | 9.40 (0.70) | 0.20 (0.63) | 0.00 (0.00) | 0.00 (0.00) | 0.40 (0.51) |
| | Control | 6.20 (3.32) | 2.10 (2.18) | 0.50 (0.71) | 0.40 (0.97) | 0.80 (1.03) |
| Con./A. | Analogy | 9.20 (1.23) | 0.60 (1.26) | 0.00 (0.00) | 0.00 (0.00) | 0.20 (0.42) |
| | Control | 3.90 (1.45) | 3.10 (1.66) | 1.30 (1.83) | 0.10 (0.32) | 1.60 (2.41) |
| **5-year-olds:** | | | | | | |
| A/Con. | Analogy | 6.55 (1.61) | 2.78 (1.31) | 0.00 (0.00) | 0.33 (0.75) | 0.33 (0.54) |
| | Control | 8.22 (1.20) | 1.55 (0.94) | 0.11 (0.35) | 0.00 (0.00) | 0.11 (0.35) |
| Con./A. | Analogy | 6.55 (1.61) | 2.22 (1.81) | 0.00 (0.00) | 0.67 (0.78) | 0.56 (1.20) |
| | Control | 3.22 (2.25) | 3.00 (2.22) | 2.89 (3.06) | 0.33 (0.54) | 0.56 (0.94) |
| **4-year-olds:** | | | | | | |
| A/Con. | Analogy | 5.90 (1.60) | 2.90 (1.52) | 0.00 (0.00) | 0.40 (0.52) | 0.80 (0.63) |
| | Control | 5.10 (1.52) | 2.70 (1.77) | 0.80 (1.23) | 0.80 (0.79) | 0.50 (0.71) |
| Con./A. | Analogy | 4.10 (2.28) | 2.70 (1.25) | 0.10 (0.32) | 1.20 (1.03) | 1.90 (1.60) |
| | Control | 3.20 (1.62) | 2.30 (1.25) | 0.40 (0.97) | 0.70 (0.95) | 3.30 (2.21) |

*Scores for the 5-year-olds were multiplied by 10/9 to give scores out of 10.
*Note*: Standard deviations in parentheses.

after receiving the Analogy condition than before receiving the Analogy condition, $p < .01$: a straightforward transfer effect. This transfer effect was even more marked in the 5-year-olds: they not only showed the same pattern, $p < .01$, they actually chose the Analogy response more frequently in the Control condition than in the Analogy condition if the Control condition was received second, although this effect was not significant. The 4-year-olds' data show a trend towards a transfer effect, but this failed to reach significance.

It should be noted that no evidence was found for an increasing preference for the Category distractor (response F) with age. Such an increase (at least in the Control condition) might have been expected given that previous studies (e.g. Smiley and Brown 1979) have documented a shift from thematic to category responding with age in a similar task. However, this difference may not be surprising given more recent evidence (Bauer and Mandler 1989) that children as young as 16 months can sort by categories if task instructions are unambiguous. Furthermore, our task differed from that of investigators such as Smiley and Brown in that four rather than two response alternatives were offered, two of which were associatively related to the c term (the Thematic and Analogy responses). The presence of more than one associative response may have affected the choice pattern of the older subjects.

These findings are supported by additional analyses carried out with the justification and prediction data.

*Prediction data*

Analyses of the prediction data confirmed the finding that some children of all ages were able to solve the analogies correctly, and that the ability to do so improved with age. If a child is able to correctly predict the solution picture to an analogical sequence before seeing any of the picture choices, this is strong evidence that the analogy is understood, and that the child is arriving at the correct answer by extracting the relation between the **a** and **b** terms, and constructing the same relation between the **c** term and their chosen response. The percentage of correct (D response) predictions made by children of each age group expressed as a proportion of the total number of predictions made was 87 per cent (9-year-olds), 54 per cent (5-year-olds) and 35 per cent (4-year-olds) respectively.

The numbers show that the ability to correctly predict the solution of the analogies improves steadily with age. Comparison of the prediction data with performance in the picture choice task shows that simply asking younger children verbally to solve analogies underestimates the competence of the youngest age group tested (the 4-year-olds). These children only predicted correctly on 35 per cent of occasions, yet were able to choose the correct solution successfully on 50 per cent of the analogies (averaging the group means across order groups), a performance level which does not differ from that of the 5-year-olds.

It is notable that most of the incorrect responses in the younger groups were predictions based on thematic relations. These accounted for 66 per cent of incorrect responses at age 4 and 72 per cent at age 5: The most frequent were *chalk–chalkboard, dog–bone, shoes–socks, policeman–police, car–robber*, and *fish–water*. Verbal questioning, the technique used in most of the experiments supporting the associative hypothesis, clearly leads younger children to produce verbal associations as responses. Many of the children went on to choose the correct solution to the analogy once the picture choices were displayed, even though children were not informed that their predictions were wrong. Whether the prediction was correct or incorrect, the experimenter put out the pictures and said "So which picture do we need to finish the pattern?"

The picture choice data show a similar pattern: The most frequent incorrect responses were based on association (choice of the Thematic Relation response) at all ages, with the exception of the 4-year-olds who received the Control condition first. The latter were the only group who preferred the Mere Appearance distractor to the Thematic distractor. This finding contrasts with the Goswami and Brown (1990) study of analogies based on causal relations, in which errors based on mere appearance responding were far more frequent than errors based on associative responding. Thus we have evidence that children will base incorrect responses in analogy tasks on both association (Goldman *et al.* 1982; Sternberg and Nigro 1980) and mere appearance (Gentner 1989).


*Justification data*

The finding that children at all ages were able to reason analogically is further supported by the justifications that children gave to explain their picture choices. Some of these spontaneously referred to the need to match the relations depicted in each half of the analogy. Such justifications included " 'Cause trains go on railroad tracks and boats go in water" (*train:track::boat:water*; Joshua, age 4 years 2 months), " 'Cause babies sleep in cribs. Dogs sleep in their own beds" (*dog:dog basket::baby:crib*; Lissa, age 4 years 11 months), "Because a spider . . . well, it's kind of hard to explain . . . a spider lives in a spider web and a bee lives in a hive" (*spider:web::bee:bee-hive*; Sarah, age 10 years 5 months), "Because a dress hangs on a hanger and a coat hangs on hooks" (*dress:coathanger::coat:hook*; Jamie, age 9 years 9 months).

The spontaneous references to the similarity of the relations linking the terms on both sides of the analogy were most common in the 9-year-olds. Many of the younger children required further probing to make their understanding of parallel (analogical) relations explicit. For example, Kelly, age 4 years 3 months, having verbally predicted "Honey" as the solution to the analogy *spider:web::bee:?*, picked the beehive to complete the picture sequence.

Table 10.3 Percentage of choices for which children denied that there could be another correct answer, given initial selection of a single response

| Age | Analogy | Thematic Control |
|---|---|---|
| 9 years | 89 | 24 |
| 4 years | 60 | 18 |

E: Why did you pick that one?
C: Because the others don't go there.
E: But why does the beehive go there? Could you tell me about the pictures?
C: Because the bee supposed to go in the beehive.
E: And what about the spider?
C: 'Cause the spider supposed to go in the spider web.

As this example makes clear, it is not necessarily the case that initial failure to mention the relations on both sides of the analogy means that both relations have not been taken into account in selecting a response.

The age effect (the older children solving more analogies correctly than the younger children) is further supported by an analysis of how likely children were to agree that there could be another right answer in the Analogy and Thematic Control tasks. Table 10.3 presents a comparison of the percentage of trials in each condition for which children maintained that there was no other correct answer, calculated as a proportion of the trials for which only a single answer was initially selected. Only the 9-year-olds and the 4-year-olds are compared, as this further probe ("Would any of the other pictures fit?") was unfortunately omitted with the 5-year-olds.

Inspection of the table shows that the 9-year-olds were much more likely to defend their choice of response D (the Analogy response) in the Analogy condition than the 4-year-olds. However, even the performance of 4-year-olds is impressive: They are clearly more likely to defend their choice of the Analogy response than to allow the possibility of other answers. In contrast, children of both ages were very ready to allow the possibility of more than one answer in the Thematic Control condition: Here a large majority of the children thought that there could be other correct answers. Thus while the older children are more certain about the analogies, both age groups recognize that there is no higher-order structure which makes one response preferable in the Control condition. This is strong evidence that even the youngest children were using the higher-order structure provided by the analogy as a basis for responding in the Analogy condition.

## Discussion

This experiment provides clear evidence that even very young children can reason by analogy in the face of competing associative relations, and at an age when analogical solutions are supposed to be largely determined by reasoning by association (Goldman *et al.* 1982; Sternberg and Nigro 1980). The task was designed to provide a strong test of the competence hypothesis, by pitting emergent analogical reasoning against thematic (associative) reasoning. Although no preference between Analogical and Thematic responses was found in the Control condition, the Analogical responses were strongly preferred to the Thematic responses in the Analogy condition, where the higher-order structure constrained solution choice. It is notable that in spite of the strict controls used, a higher success rate was found in this task than in any previous examinations of young children's analogical ability in the **a:b::c:d** task.

A different theoretical claim is that younger children may focus on surface similarity cues when solving analogies (Gentner 1988, 1989; Gentner and Toupin 1986). In this experiment, surface similarity cues could not be used as a basis for responding, as there was no resemblance between the **c** and **d** terms used in the analogies (e.g. *bee:hive, baby:crib*). Gentner (personal communication, July 1988) has pointed out that her theory would predict that shared appearance between the **b** and **d** terms might be important. However, here too there was no resemblance between the items used (e.g. *web–hive, tracks–water, milk–egg*; although it could be argued that there was some resemblance for *dog basket–crib*, and *pencil eraser–chalkboard eraser*). Recent evidence that younger children can also succeed in problem solving analogy tasks in the absence of surface similarity cues (Brown and Kane 1988) rules out a mere appearance matching explanation of younger children's analogical competence.

The experimental procedure used here highlights two methodological shortcomings of previous experiments in the literature that may have seriously underestimated younger children's analogical competence. The first is a widespread reliance on verbal or written presentation of the analogy problems (Gallagher and Wright 1977; Goldman *et al.* 1982; Levinson and Carpenter 1974; Lunzer 1965; Sternberg and Nigro 1980), consequently requiring a verbal or written response from the child. Our prediction data demonstrated that requiring younger children to produce a spoken response to an analogical problem tends to produce verbal associations to the **c** term rather than a consideration of the relations between the terms depicted in the analogy. Written techniques probably have the same effect, as these are in effect reading tasks: The child verbalises the problem. The use of pictures to present the analogical problems enables the competence of much younger childrent to be properly tested (see also Piaget *et al.* 1977) as shown by the discrepancy between the verbal predictions and the actual pictures chosen to complete the analogies by our younger subjects.

The second shortcoming of previous studies is the assumption that justifications that spontaneously mention the relations in both halves of the analogy provide an index of analogical ability (Gallagher and Wright 1977, 1979; Goldman *et al.* 1982; Levinson and Carpenter 1974). Our further probing shows that this is not necessarily the case. Young children are notoriously poor at verbalising the basis for their responses in all kinds of cognitive tasks (Brown, Bransford, Ferrara and Campione 1983), and so assertions that the better verbalisations of older children provide an index of analogical ability are misplaced.

The main puzzle in Experiment 1 concerns the performance of the youngest children. The 4-year-olds might have been expected to show the strongest thematic preferences and the strongest transfer effect, yet in the Control condition (when received first) they were more likely to select the Analogy response or the Mere Appearance match response than the Thematic response, and the trend towards a transfer effect did not reach significance.

One possibility is that these discrepancies are due to the overwhelming effect for young children of being presented with a large number of distractors (Brown 1973). We decided to look at a second group of 4-year-olds in the same Analogy and Control tasks, but to offer the children a choice of only two responses, the Analogy response and the Thematic response (D and E respectively).

## EXPERIMENT 2

### Method

*Subjects*

Twenty-two 4-year-olds took part in the study. The mean age of the group was 4 years 7 months, range 4;2–5;0. The mean PPVT score for the group was 111.7, *SD* 13.1.

*Procedure*

This was exactly as in Experiment 1, except that the children were only offered a choice between responses D (Analogy) and E (Thematic) in both the Analogy and the Control conditions. Half of the children received the Analogy condition first, and half received the Control condition first. Prediction and justification data were collected as in Experiment 1.

### Results

The number of times that the children selected the Analogy and Thematic responses in the two conditions is shown in Table 10.4, separated by order of receiving the conditions. There was a clear preference for the Analogy

Table 10.4 Number of times each response selected out of 10 in Experiment 2

| Order | Condition | Response | |
|---|---|---|---|
| | | D (Analogy) | E (Thematic) |
| A/Con. | Analogy | 6.82 | 3.18 |
| | | (1.17) | (1.17) |
| | Control | 7.09 | 2.91 |
| | | (1.92) | (1.92) |
| Con./A. | Analogy | 6.45 | 3.55 |
| | | (1.92) | (1.92) |
| | Control | 5.36 | 4.64 |
| | | (1.29) | (1.29) |

Note: Standard deviations in parentheses.

response over the Thematic response in the Analogy condition for both order groups. Children were also more likely to select the Analogy response in the Control condition when this was received second: In fact, the data look very similar to those of the 5-year-olds in Experiment 1.

To test whether the analogy effect was significant, a between-groups analysis was first conducted, as in Experiment 1. This was a one-way Analysis of Variance using the difference scores obtained by subtracting the Thematic responses from the Analogy responses (D–E) in the two conditions as the dependent variable. The analysis showed a main effect of condition, $F(1,20) = 7.71$, $p < .01$. This shows that the children were significantly more likely to prefer the Analogy response over the Thematic response in the Analogy condition (mean difference = 3.64) than in the Control condition (mean difference = 0.73). Hence the children were clearly making analogies.

To test whether the transfer effect was significant, a within-groups Analysis of Variance was conducted (as in Experiment 1) again using the difference scores (D–E) as the dependent variable. The analysis was $2 \times 2$ (Order $\times$ Condition), with repeated measures on condition. If the transfer effect is robust, an interaction between Order and Condition would be expected. This interaction failed to reach significance, $F(1,20) = 1.61$. Instead, the analysis showed a main effect of Order, $F(1,20) = 5.97$, $p < .02$. This was due to the mean difference score across the two conditions being larger for the children who received the Analogy condition first (3.9) than for the children who received the Control condition first (1.8). This order effect cannot be unambiguously attributed to a transfer effect: All that can be concluded is that receiving the Analogy condition first had a significant effect on the number of Analogy responses chosen in the experiment. However, some of the justifications offered for selecting the Analogy response a second time in the Thematic Control condition do suggest that some degree of transfer was occurring: Lucas' justification for selecting the coat hook to go with the coat was "Because I did it last time."

*Prediction data*

Children's ability to correctly predict the response to the Analogy sequences was again scored. If children are able to work out the correct solution to the analogy sequences before seeing the picture choice alternatives, this is good evidence that they are reasoning by analogy. The 4-year-olds in the Analogy condition correctly predicted the Analogy response on 35 per cent of predictions, which is slightly better than in Experiment 1. Many of the incorrect predictions were again verbal associates of the **c** term: 61 per cent of the incorrect predictions were of this type. As in Experiment 1, the most frequent thematic predictions were *honey* (bee), *chalkboard* (chalk), *socks* (feet), and *water* (fish). It was also the case that, as in Experiment 1, many children who made incorrect predictions about the solution of the analogies went on to choose the correct picture to complete the analogies: 35 per cent of predictions concerned the Analogy response, but 66 per cent of picture choices were of the Analogy response. Again, younger children tend to produce verbal associations to the **c** term if they are questioned verbally.

*Justification data*

The justifications given by the 4-year-olds who successfully reasoned by analogy again showed that the children were attending to the relation that linked the two halves of the analogies. Here is an example from Lauri (4;3):

C: [Looking at the first three pictures] Cow gives milk. Chicken gives . . .
   eggs. [Prediction]
E: Let's take a look at our pictures . . . The egg. And why did you pick that
   egg?
C: Because chickens lay eggs and cows lay milk.

Such relational reasoning occasionally resulted in errors when children focused on the wrong relation to solve the analogy. Hence Lucas (4;7), looking at the first three terms of the analogy *bird:nest::dog:?*

C: Bird lays eggs in her nest. Dog . . . dogs lay babies, and the babies are
   . . . um . . . and the name of the babies is puppy!
E: Let's take a look at our pictures.
C: I don't have to look. And the name of the baby is puppy. [Child then
   induced to look at pictures, and selects "kennel".]

Some children spontaneously mentioned both halves of the analogy when justifying their responses, as shown by Megan (4:11), solving the analogy *bird:plane::fish:?*:

E: What might go in our last box?
C: [Predicts] Seaweed.
E: Let's take a look . . . [child selects *boat*] . . . And why does the boat go there?
C: Because birds and airplanes both fly, and fish and boats both go on water.

However, as found previously, most younger children required further probing to reveal this understanding. If children's ability to reason about parallel (analogical) relations had been scored only on the occasions when they spontaneously mentioned them, as did Megan, performance would have appeared to be dismal.

## Discussion

Reducing the number of possible responses to two (Analogy and Thematic) clarifies the performance of the 4-year-olds considerably. Without the extra distractors, the 4-year-olds are shown to behave in a very similar manner to 5- and 9-year-olds. Although the 4-year-olds appear to be slightly more successful at solving analogies in this paradigm than in the first experiment (the Analogy response is chosen on 66 per cent of trials [averaging across groups] compared with 50 per cent of trials previously), this is not the case: Once the scores are corrected for guessing, performance in both paradigms is equivalent.

However, the transfer effect that has become more marked is still not significant. In Experiment 1, the 4-year-olds chose the Analogy response on 51 per cent of control trials following experience of the Analogy condition: Here the figure is 71 per cent of trials. Children are clearly remembering the correct response from the Analogy condition and using it as a basis for deciding which of two equally attractive alternatives "fits best" with the c term in the Control condition.

The prediction and justification data show a very similar pattern to Experiment 1. The 4-year-olds are not very good at predicting the correct solution to the analogies, tending to produce verbal associations to the c term, but once they are shown the possible completion pictures for the analogies, performance improves dramatically. Their justifications show that they have a very clear understanding of why the Analogy response is correct. Four-year-olds require more prompting than older children in order to display this understanding (see also Brown and Kane 1988), and so the utilisation of a non-verbal response (picture selection) is very important for demonstrating competence.

## OVERALL DISCUSSION

The current experiments provide strong evidence for analogical ability in very young children. The emergent analogical reasoning skills for 4- and 5-year-olds remained robust in spite of attractive associative relations that could have provided a basis for responding in the analogy task. Children can succeed in classical analogy tasks long before the period of formal operations as long as the relations on which the analogies are based are familiar to them (Goswami 1989; Goswami and Brown 1990). Goswami and Brown have shown that even 3-year-olds can solve classical analogies if these are based on early-developing knowledge structures such as physical causal relations (e.g. *melting* and *cutting*), whereas Goswami (1989) used perceptual analogies based on proportions to show that relational complexity significantly affects analogical responding in children aged from 4 to 8 years.

These experiments have also shown that the use of verbal techniques encourages associative responding in younger children, thus seriously underestimating analogical ability. Even very young children can ignore association and respond to higher-order structure if more sensitive tasks are used. Given that younger children have the ability to reason by analogy, research should now focus on the question of how analogies can be used in teaching and learning, a question that has already received some attention in the area of reading and spelling (Brown, Campione, Reeve, Ferrara and Palincsar 1991; Bryant and Goswami 1987; Goswami 1986, 1988a, 1988b).

The growing literature on children's ability to reason analogically in problem-solving tasks supports our finding that even very young children can reason successfully by analogy (e.g. Brown 1989; Brown and Kane 1988; Brown et al. 1986; Brown et al. 1989; Holyoak et al. 1984). For example, Brown (1989) has shown that 3-year-olds can reason that the porcupine fish (which can double its size and raise spikes to deter predators) and the hawkmoth caterpillar (which can look like a poisonous snake to deter predators) have evolved analogous solutions to the problem of avoiding predation. As long as children understand the relations on which analogies are based, they seem capable of transfer. Apparent failure to use analogies by very young children (e.g. in Deloache's [1987, 1989] recent studies requiring children to locate a large toy in a real room by using the location of a small toy hidden in a model of the room to direct search) may be due to a failure to fully understand the representational relations on which the analogy is based (e.g. that the spatial relations in the model correspond to the spatial relations in the room). We would argue that recent results with both classical and problem analogies indicate that reasoning by analogy is an important building block in learning from a very early age.

## ACKNOWLEDGEMENTS

We would like to thank Stephanie Lyons-Olson, Anne Slattery and Mary-Jo Kane for help with collecting and transcribing the data, and the children and teachers of The Montessori School, The Caring Place, The Children's House, The First Step, and Leal School, Champaign-Urbana, Illinois: of the Montessori Schools at Cedar, Francisco and Scenic Avenue, and the Child Study Center, Berkeley, California: and of Dunn's Kiddie Care, Bowling Green, Ohio. We also thank Donald Laming and Peter Bryant for statistical advice. This work was supported by NICHD grant no. 06864 to Ann Brown, and research fellowships from Merton College, Oxford and the Commonwealth Fund of New York to Usha Goswami.

## NOTE

1 Owing to an experimenter error, the 5-year-olds only received nine picture sequences in each condition.

## REFERENCES

Achenbach, T.M. (1970) "Standardisation of a research instrument for identifying associative responding in children", *Developmental Psychology* 2: 283–291.

Achenbach, T.M. (1971) "The children's associative responding test: A two-year follow-up", *Journal of Educational Psychology* 61: 340–348.

Alexander, P.A., Willson, V.L., White, C.S. and Fuqua, J.D. (1987) "Analogical reasoning in young children", *Journal of Educational Psychology* 79 (4): 401–408.

Bauer, P.J. and Mandler, J.M. (1989) "Taxonomies and triads: Conceptual organisation in one- to two-year olds", *Cognitive Psychology* 21: 156–184.

Brown, A.L. (1973) "Mnemonic elaboration and recency judgements in children", *Cognitive Psychology* 5: 233–248.

Brown, A.L. (1989) "Analogical learning and transfer: What develops?" in S. Vosniadou and A. Ortony (eds) *Similarity and analogical reasoning* (pp. 364–412), Cambridge: Cambridge University Press.

Brown. A.L., Bransford, J.D., Ferrara, R.A. and Campione, J.C. (1983) "Learning, remembering and understanding", in J.H. Flavell and E.M. Markman (eds) P.H., Mussen (series ed.) *Handbook of child psychology, 4th ed., Vol. 3: Cognitive development* (pp. 515–529), New York: Wiley.

Brown, A.L., Campione, J.C., Reeve, R.A., Ferrara, R.A. and Palincsar, A.S. (1991) "Interactive learning, individual understanding: The case of reading and mathematics", in L.T. Landsmann (ed.) *Culture, schooling and psychological development*, Norwood, NJ: Ablex.

Brown, A.L. and Kane, M.J. (1988) "Preschool children can learn to transfer: Learning to learn and learning by example", *Cognitive Psychology* 20: 493–523.

Brown, A.L., Kane, M.J. and Echols, C.H. (1986) "Young children's mental models determine analogical transfer across problems with a common goal structure", *Cognitive Development* 1: 103–121.

Brown, A.L., Kane, M.J. and Long, C. (1989) "Analogical transfer in young children: Analogies as tools for communication and exposition", *Applied Cognitive Psychology* 3: 275–293.

Bryant, P.E. and Goswami, U. (1987) "Phonological awareness and learning to read", in J. Beech and A. Colley (eds) *Cognitive approches to reading*, New York: Wiley.

Deloache, J.S. (1987) "Rapid change in the symbolic functioning of very young children", *Science* 238: 1556–1557.

Deloache, J.S. (1989) "Young children's understanding of the correspondence between a scale model and a larger space", *Cognitive Development* 4: 121–139.

Entwhistle, D.R. (1966) *The word association norms of young children*, Baltimore, MD: Johns Hopkins University Press.

Gallagher, J.M. and Wright, R.J. (1977) *Children's solution of verbal analogies: Extension of Piaget's concept of reflexive abstraction*, paper presented to the Society for Research in Child Development, New Orleans.

Gallagher, J.M. and Wright, R.J. (1979) "Piaget and the study of analogy: Structural analysis of items", in J. Magary (ed.) *Piaget and the helping professions (Vol. 8)*, Los Angeles: University of Southern California.

Gentile, J.R., Tedesco-Stratton, L., Davis, E., Lund, N.J. and Agunanne, B.A. (1977) "Associative responding versus analogical reasoning by children", *Intelligence* 1: 369–380.

Gentner, D. (1983) "Structure-mapping: A theoretical framework for analogy", *Cognitive Science* 7: 155–170.

Gentner, D. (1988) "Metaphor as structure-mapping: The relational shift", *Child Development* 59: 47–59.

Gentner, D. (1989) "The mechanisms of analogical learning", in S. Vosniadou and A. Ortony (eds) *Similarity and analogical reasoning* (pp. 197–241), London: Cambridge University Press.

Gentner, D. and Toupin, C. (1986) "Systematicity and surface similarity in the Development of analogy", *Cognitive Science* 10: 277–300.

Goldman, S.R., Pellegrino, J.W., Parseghian, P.E. and Sallis, R. (1982) "Developmental and individual differences in verbal analogical reasoning", *Child Development* 53: 550–559.

Goswami, U. (1986) "Children's use of analogy in learning to read: A developmental study", *Journal of Experimental Child Psychology* 42: 73–83.

Goswami, U. (1988a) "Orthographic analogies and reading development", *Quarterly Journal of Experimental Psychology* 40A: 239–268.

Goswami, U. (1988b) "Children's use of analogy in learning to spell", *British Journal of Developmental Psychology* 6: 21–33.

Goswami, U. (1989) "Relational complexity and the development of analogical reasoning", *Cognitive Development* 4: 251–268.

Goswami, U. and Brown, A.L. (1990) "Melting chocolate and melting snowmen: Analogical reasoning and causal relations", *Cognition* 35: 69–95.

Holyoak, K.J., Junn, E.N. and Billman, D.O. (1984) "Development of analogical problem-solving skill", *Child Development* 55: 2042–2055.

Holyoak, K.J. and Koh, K. (1987) "Surface and structural similarity in analogical transfer", *Memory and Cognition* 15: 332–340.

Inhelder, B. and Piaget, J. (1958) *The growth of logical thinking from childhood to adolescence*, New York: Basic Books.

Levinson, P.J. and Carpenter, R.L. (1974) "An analysis of analogical reasoning in children", *Child Development* 45: 857–861.

Lunzer, E.A. (1965) "Problems of formal reasoning in test situations", in P.H.

Mussen (ed.) *European research in child development, Monographs of the Society for Research in Child Development* 30 (2. Serial number 100): 19–46.

Markman, E. and Hutchinson, J. (1984) "Children's sensitivity to constraints on word meaning: Taxonomic versus thematic relations", *Cognitive Psychology* 16: 1–27.

Nelson, K. (1977) "The syntagmatic-paradigmatic shift revisited: A review of research and theory", *Psychological Bulletin* 84: 93–116.

Piaget, J., Montangero, J. and Billeter, J. (1977) "Les correlats", in J. Piaget (ed.) *L'Abstraction réfléchissante*, Paris: Presses Universitaires de France.

Smiley, S.S. and Brown, A.L. (1979) "Conceptual preference for thematic or taxonomic relations: A non-monotonic age trend from preschool to old age", *Journal of Experimental Child Psychology* 28: 249–257.

Sternberg, R.J. and Nigro, G. (1980) "Developmental patterns in the solution of verbal analogies", *Child Development* 51: 27–38.

Waxman, S.R. (1990) "Linguistic biases and the establishment of conceptual hierarchies: Evidence from preschool children", *Cognitive Development* 5: 169–94.

Willner, A. (1964) "An experimental analysis of analogical reasoning", *Psychological Reports* 15: 479–494.

# Chapter 11

# A life span approach to object permanence

*Eugene V. Subbotsky*

**KEY WORDS**

Adult beliefs · Life span · Magic · Object permanence · Permanence parameters · Violations of parameters.

**ABSTRACT**

The development of the concept of object permanence is traced in infants, children, and adults. In infancy this development takes the form of a gradual change in understanding of objects' identity parameters – the cues that, if altered, lead to a sense that the object's identity has changed. Studies are reviewed which suggest that by 2 years of age, children have a full understanding of the identity parameters of physical objects. Among older children and adults, the development of object permanence has been studied in two respects – (a) studies of pathological distortions in the understanding of permanence parameters, and (b) studies of the conditions under which notions of object permanence can be destroyed. Attention is focused on the second line of studies, particularly those in which the phenomenon on an object's nonpermanence is demonstrated to preschoolers and to adults. Under two conditions, children and adults alike evidence belief that an object can spontaneously turn into something else, that a physical object can be created "from nothing", and that a physical object can disappear. These results suggest that the concept of object permanence, even in the case of physical objects, is not attained in some final form by the age of 2.

Over the last decades, a good deal of research has been devoted to understanding the development of the concept of the stable object. The concept is one of great theoretical importance. It is a foundation of human consciousness, underlying early concepts of space, time, and causality. Development of the object concept is also implicated in subsequent cognitive development, for example in the acquisition of relational words (Wachs 1975; Tomasello and Farrar 1984, 1986).

It is perhaps redundant to include the modifier "stable" in referring to the development of a concept of the stable object, because in principle one cannot speak of an unstable object. Anything that is perceived or contemplated has some degree of stability. Therefore, an empirical approach to the problem is possible only as an investigation of the subjective stability of an object to the subject observing it. The main objective of empirical research has been to distinguish permanence parameters – parameters of the object which, if changed, cause the object itself to be regarded as changed – from parameters which, if changed, allow the object's existence to remain stable. Hence, investigation of the development of the stable object concept may more accurately be regarded as investigation of the development of understanding of permanence parameters.

## The development of object permanence in infancy

The development of the object concept was discussed initially by Piaget (1936, 1937), who described its development over the course of 6 stages. In the first two stages (0–3 months), the concept exists only as a primitive associative-emotional schema. During this period, an object has two permanence parameters – its affective meaning for the infant, and the presentation of the object in the infant's perceptual field.

In the third stage (approximately 3–7 months), some precursors of object permanence appear. But the infant's belief in the object's permanence exists solely as a function of activity with the object. If the object disappears from the infant's perceptual field without having been acted on in some way (such as being regarded or manipulated), the infant behaves as if the object has disappeared. The permanence parameters themselves – affective meaning and perceptual presence – do not change at this stage.

At stage 4 (approximately 8–12 months), infants can retrieve a hidden object even if they have not been actively involved with it previously. The permanence parameters themselves have changed, "perceptual presence" having been replaced by "location in space". This development is important, as objects no longer lose their existence when occluded. However, if an object that was initially hidden and retrieved at point A is transferred to point B and again occluded, the infant will continue to search at A (the AB̄ error). The object, according to Piaget, is tied to the spatial location where it was initially discovered.

Identification of an object with its initial location disappears at stage 5 (approximately 12–17 months). The infant now searches for an object where it was last, not first, hidden, but only so long as the move to point B takes place in plain view. Finally at stage 6 (from 18 months), the child has no problem with hidden transpositions. The object may be hidden, but it is "conserved" in representational form. The object is now permanent and independent of its immediate location in space and time and with respect to activity.

A central claim made by Piaget, then, is that by 2 years of age the child acquires the ability to attribute permanent existence to sensorimotor objects. Central to this attribution is a rule stating that the object retains its existence after it disappears from the perceptual field – a "permanence" rule. An infant below this age, in contrast, uses a "nonpermanence' rule in identical situations. Implicit in a permanence rule are the assumptions that (a) an object cannot turn into nothing or be created from nothing, (b) an object can't turn into another object, and (c) an object can't be changed (destroyed or reconstructed) by pure mental effort, without material tools or actions.

Piaget's theory of the development of object permanence, and the presuppositions on which it is built, have been questioned by a number of authors. It is not my intention here to undertake a comprehensive review of the theoretical or empirical literature on object permanence. Several such reviews already exist, for example those by Harris (1975, 1985) and Schuberth (1983). Here, I focus on studies having to do with violations of the permanence rule.

The pioneering work is by Bower (1971, 1974), who conducted experiments using "transformed" objects. In these studies, a moving object disappeared behind one side of a screen and a different object appeared from behind the screen, at the point where the original object would be expected to reappear. Infants of less than 16 weeks of age were not surprised by this phenomenon and continued to watch the new object as if it were the original one. Infants of 4 months and above, in contrast, expressed surprise and searched for the missing object where it had vanished.

Bower's findings suggest that a complex change in the permanence parameters takes place at about 4–5 months of age (Piaget's stage 3). Spatial location and trajectory, parameters that dominate until this age, are replaced by the features of an object. What was, for the 3-month-old, a bounded volume of space in a particular place or on a particular path of movement becomes for the 4- to 5-month-old a bounded volume of space, shape, and color. According to Bower, Piaget's "phenomenal presence" parameter loses its significance, with the implication that object permanence is attained far earlier than Piaget suggested.

A further study of the dynamics of permanence parameters involving violations of the permanence rule was conducted by Cossette-Ricard (1983). The author analyzed the manual and visual search behaviors of 5- to 15-month-old infants. In one particularly interesting situation, infants watched a toy car, moving at constant speed, as it disappeared behind a screen and then (after an appropriate time interval) reappeared not at the other side of this screen but at the other side of a second, adjacent screen, without the car having been seen passing between the two screens. The youngest infants (5–9 months) either stopped watching or simply visually followed the new car, ignoring the gap in the car's trajectory. Older infants (15 months) visually searched for the original car, indicating they regarded the reappearing car as a different object from the original.

These findings indicate emergence of a completely new permanence parameter – the spatiotemporal contiguity of an object. The spatiotemporal contiguity of an object (whether mobile or stationary) becomes a necessary condition for its permanence. Contiguity is an attribute that allows one to differentiate the same object at different points in space and time from other objects that appear identical (duplicates). Whereas younger infants appear not to consider a violation of an object's spatiotemporal contiguity to be a violation of its permanence, older infants treat such a violation as proof that a reappearing object is a duplicate rather than the original.

Gratch (1982; Meider and Gratch 1980) examined a condition in which infants visually followed an object as it moved back and forth on a track, with an occluding screen at the center. In this situation, 5-month-olds anticipated the object's reappearance, but only infants of 16 months expressed surprise when the object reappeared in changed form. These findings contradict Bower's claim that 5-month-olds have representational capacities and provide support for Piaget's position.

Different results, however, were obtained by Baillargeon and her colleagues (Baillargeon 1987; Baillargeon *et al.* 1985). Infants were habituated to a screen that moved back and forth through a 180-degree arc. A box was then placed behind the screen. In the experimental conditions, the screen was either impeded in its motion by the box (a possible event) or it moved through the space occupied by the box (an impossible event). Some infants as young as 3.5 months looked reliably longer at the impossible than at the possible event. These results support the view that young infants believe that objects continue to exist even when occluded and are impermeable to a solid object.

Another variant is an experiment in which there occurs an unexpected change in a hidden object. In one study (Le Compte and Gratch 1972), infants repeatedly found an object hidden in a box. The object was then placed in the box, covered, and, when uncovered, proved to be a different object. Nine-month-olds were surprised by this occurrence but did not attempt to search for the original object or to make sense of the "mechanism" of the box. Infants of 18 months, in contrast, both searched for the original object and tried to understand how the box worked. Similar results were obtained by Ramsay and Campos (1975, 1978). These findings support the view that at stage 4 infants are able to differentiate a new object from an old one using featural cues (shape, size, color, etc.), but are not yet capable of representing the missing object. Active representation does not appear until stage 6.

## Object permanence in childhood

Piaget mentioned but did not investigate the object concept as it moves out of the sensorimotor domain and into the domain of objects that are not accessible to direct manipulation, such as heavenly bodies, the wind, and so forth. He suggested, however, that the development of a stable object concept is not completed until age 10 or 11 (Piaget 1937, 1976). Nevertheless, researchers generally have assumed that the permanence parameters that constitute stability for the 2-year-old – the features of the object (size, shape, and color), its spatiotemporal contiguity, and the fact that placing some opaque object in front of it does not cause its disappearance from anything other than the perceptual field – remain constant throughout the life span. This assumption of constancy across the life span is taken as obviating the need for further study of object permanence, at least when dealing with manipulation of objects. Researchers studying children above age 2 have been more likely to study not conservation of objects but conservation of qualities of objects (quantity, mass, weight, length, volume).

Despite the assumption of constancy of permanence parameters across the life span, there are certain conditions under which young children accept violations of the permanence rule, even though the permanence parameters themselves are not obviously violated. Such conditions most commonly occur in the sphere of "magical" beliefs, e.g. when a magician pulls objects "out of thin air". Similarly, nonpermanent, imaginary objects may acquire the "real" status of physical objects (Harris *et al.* 1988).

These phenomena are inconsistent with the view that the nonpermanence rules that prevail in the young infant disappear by 2 years of age, to be replaced by permanence rules. Contrary to this view, I suggest that permanence and nonpermanence rules (a) emerge in the child's consciousness at the same time, (b) coexist in categorical opposition to one another, and (c) continue to exist in opposition to one another throughout the life span. Viewing the problem in this way avoids the difficulty of explaining the transition from complete nonpermanence (which a priori cannot be challenged by experience because "experience" itself is based on a conception of permanence) to permanence. These two ways of assimilating the world – permanence and nonpermanence – are learned as oppositions, following which they coexist both within a single domain of a child's experience and across different domains. Specifically, permanence rules may dominate in the domain of everyday reality, whereas nonperformance rules may dominate in the domain of unusual experience, such as dreams, fairy tales, and fantasy play. Under some conditions, however, nonpermanence rules may transcend the borders separating the two domains.

To test the latter hypothesis, a method must be developed in which the same phenomenon in everyday reality can be assimilated by the child in different ways – either in terms of permanence rules or in terms of nonpermanence rules. An initial group of experiments (Subbotsky 1985) was devoted to examining the permanence rule that it is impossible to exert a force upon an object directly by mean of thought, e.g. "magical" words, commands, etc. Insofar as the child's beliefs (or disbeliefs) involve magical practice, the experiments in fact address the child's conception of natural causality.

In one of these experiments, 4- to 6-year-old children were first questioned verbally, to determine whether the child admitted the possibility of the direct action of thought on an object in the sphere of everyday reality. The experimenter asked two questions: (1) Can drawings be changed into what they depict? (2) Can a drawing of an elephant be changed into a real elephant if you say a magic word?

The child was then told this story:

*The Magic Box*
A little girl, Masha, received a box for a present. The box had the magical capacity to change drawings of objects into the objects themselves. To do this, it was necessary to put a drawing in the box and say the magic words "alpha beta gamma" aloud. At first, Masha did not believe this, but when she tested the box, she became convinced of its magical properties.

The child was requested to retell the story and then was asked, "Why does the box change the pictures into objects?" The purpose of this question was to determine whether the child admitted the possibility of the direct action of thought on an object within the domain of a story.

A few days later, the child returned and was asked, "Do you want me to show you the same magic box that was given to Masha?" The experimenter then gave the child a pretty box and drawings depicting a ring, brooch, cigarette lighter, fountain pen, spider, and wasp. He then showed the child some of these same objects, which were allegedly obtained from the box, following which he said, "I'm going to do some things; meanwhile, you can play. If you want, you can use the box." The experimenter reminded the child of the magic words and then left.

The child's behavior was observed through an opening in a screen. It was assumed that their behavior would reveal the way children had assimilated the phenomena. If at a "background" level, i.e. at the level of latent, "subordinated" norms, children admitted the possibility of direct action of thought on an object, they would in this particular situation try to produce the alleged function of the box. If they did not admit this possibility, they would handle the box and objects only by rational means, since the attempt to transform pictures into objects would be dismissed as meaningless. In the former case, two further interpretations are possible: (a) The child's assimilation of the phenomena spontaneously shifts into another sphere – that of fantasy – and the child simply pretends that the box has magic properties. (b) This shift does not take place and the child really does anticipate that the picture will be transformed.

A postexperimental interview was included to distinguish between these two interpretations. When the experimenter returned, he asked the child, "Well, did you try to change the pictures? Did you succeed?" If children had truly anticipated the transformation to occur, their statements should contain elements of disappointment and reference to their own failure. If children's actions had been of a pretending nature, they would not be disappointed.

Results showed that all 5- and 6-year-olds and 75 per cent of 4-year-olds verbally denied the possibility of the direct action of thought on an object in the sphere of everyday reality in the initial segment of the interview. When asked why, some were unable to give any justification. Others referred to the material of which the object was made ("A drawing of an elephant can't be changed into a living elephant because it's paper and it's drawn"). The most typical answer of the older children was to say that magic was impossible in real life. When asked where magic could be found, they gave such answers as "in stories", "in church", or "in animated films".

In the experimenter's absence, in contrast, about 90 per cent of children in each age group tried to transform the pictures into objects. Children typically put the drawings of the wasp and spider aside, saying, "I don't want a spider or a wasp; they're terrible". They then placed one of the other drawings in the box (typically the ring or brooch for girls and the cigarette lighter or fountain pen for boys), closed it, and pronounced the magic words. Many made a gesture over the box or made circular hand movements as they pronounced the words. They then opened the box, looked with bewilderment at the drawings, and shrugged their shoulders or exclaimed with surprise, "It didn't happen!" Many children then repeated the attempt. After a second failure, some stopped trying and began to play with the objects, while others stubbornly continued their efforts, changing the cards or their position in the box, varying the loudness of their voices in pronouncing the magic words, using different gestures, etc.

When the experimenter returned, all of the children who had tried to transform the pictures expressed surprise and disappointment. Many asked the experimenter to show them the right way to do it. However, only a few children (7–23 per cent across age groups) accepted the experimenter's invitation to try again in his presence. The adult's presence apparently embarrassed the child and represented a tangible obstacle to magical practice.

A second group of studies (Subbotsky 1988) was devoted to examining the permanence rules that objects cannot be created from nothing or turn into nothing. Children of 4–6 years of age observed (a) sudden disappearance of a physical object, (b) one object inexplicably turning into another, and (c) a new object created "from nothing".

One study focused on disappearance of an object. At an initial session, children in the experimental condition were questioned verbally:

> Look, I put a piece of paper in this empty box.
>
> (1) Is it possible that instead of the paper a nice postage stamp appears in the box? Why? Is it possible in a fairy tale?
>
> (2) If I take this empty box, close the lid, and then open it, is it possible that a postage stamp appears in the box? Why? Is it possible in a fairy tale?
>
> (3) If I put a postage stamp in the empty box, close the lid, and then open it, is it possible that there is nothing in the box? Why? Is it possible in a fairy tale?

At a second session, the child was presented a box and told that the box was one that had featured in a fairy tale. It possessed magical characteristics – specifically, it could turn an object into something else when the object was placed inside it. The box was a small wooden one, in which a metal plate separates from one of the inside walls and sinks to the bottom when the box is closed. The box was constructed in such a way that this plate cannot be discovered by any sort of manipulation of the box. The child was asked if he or she would like to turn a postage stamp into some attractive object (a ring, pen, etc.) and keep this object as a reward. The experimenter then left the room and secretly observed the child's behavior.

When the child placed the stamp in the box, closed it, and then reopened it, the stamp had disappeared. When the experimenter returned, he asked the child to explain what had happened.

Children assigned to a control condition omitted the first session. In the second session they were presented the same postage stamp and box but the postage stamp was presented as a reward to the child for some work that had been done. It was then suggested to the child that he or she put the stamp in the box while another task was performed. When, after completing the task, the child returned to the box to collect the stamp, it was discovered that the box was empty.

If children interpret disappearance of the stamp in terms of a permanence rule, they should be surprised and search for the stamp. If they believe that objects can magically disappear or transform themselves, there should be no evidence of surprise.

Results from the first session were that virtually all of the experimental children admitted that physical objects could indeed appear from thin air, vanish, or spontaneously transform themselves – but only in the context of fairy tales and not in real life. In spite of these beliefs, in the second session most of the children in the experimental condition behaved as though magical transformations or disappearances often occurred in their every-day lives. When the stamp disappeared, they envinced no surprise, and they did not even try to find it. Instead of searching inside or outside the box, children typically tried to reproduce the event, as in a fairy tale, by closing and reopening the box several times. In contrast, children in the control condition were extremely surprised by the disappearance and searched for the object that had disappeared.

The implication of these results is that, under certain conditions, a nonpermanence rule continues to regulate children's behavior, even in the case of objects that are physically present and easily manipulable. The crucial factor appears to be the context, defined in this case by the instruction the children are given. If these instructions indicate that the experimenter believes in nonpermanence, children likewise behave in accordance with it. In the absence of such instructions (control condi-tion), children interpret disappearance in terms of a permanence rule.

In another variation of these experiments, children observed a piece of paper change into a postage stamp. In this case, children were even more likely to revert to a nonpermanence rule. This difference may be due to the fact that in real life one does often see one object turn into another, e.g. ice into water, in contrast to total disappearance or sudden appearance of an object. This variant of nonpermanence is thus more "real" for children, and they consequently more easily admit its existence in the domain of real life than they do other variants of nonpermanence that have no "real-life" analogs.

The preceding results support the hypothesis that the nonpermanence rule does not simply disappear from the mind of a 2-year-old. Instead, it is forced into different spheres of activity – into the realms of fairy tales, fantasy, dreams, and so on. This idea is not new, of course. Starting with Piaget, similar points have been made. What is new is the fact that under certain conditions young children attribute nonpermanence not only to natural phenomena such as the wind or moon, but also to manipulable physical objects.

## Object permanence in adulthood

Compared to the wealth of research on the early development of object permanence, surprisingly little research exists on adults' representations of object existence and permanence. Although Piaget made some occasional remarks on the subject, the best known work with adults is that by Michotte (1962). Michotte carefully explored the perceptual conditions under which subjects attributed permanence to phenomenal objects. He demonstrated that adult subjects were inclined to consider an object as "the same" (identical to itself) if only one of 4 characteristics (shape, size, color, and spatial location) had been changed. However, if two or more characteristics were changed simultaneously, subjects were likely to report that one object had been replaced by another. Thus, from an adult's perspective an object's identity is established not by its separate qualities, but by their combination or gestalt.

Warren (1977) demonstrated that an object which moved and changed its shape simultaneously was perceived as being permanent only if these changes made sense – for example, as a door opening and closing when a square and a trapezoid were repeatedly substituted for one another. If a "sensible" interpretation could not be found, subjects perceived two separate alternating objects.

While extremely interesting, these results are nevertheless tied to the phenomenal world of visual perception and provide no answer to the question: Are there conditions under which an adult will feel that a real physical object is nonpermanent? Equally interesting research on pathological subjects who lack object constancy (Bell and Richmond 1984; Riddoch and Humphreys 1986; Wells and Glickauf-Hughes 1986) likewise fail to answer this question.

To address this question, I investigated the possibility of nonpermanence in adult subjects, ranging in age from 17 to 43 (mean age 26.2), most of them university educated (Subbotsky 1991). Subjects were told that the purpose of the experiment was to investigate their judgments of the existence of material objects. The experimenter pointed to a postage stamp lying on a table next to a box (the same one used in the previously described experiments) and asked, "What is this?" and then, "Does this postage stamp exist? Why do you think so?" The aim of these questions was to establish subjects' reasons for attributing existence to material objects in their perceptual field.

The subject was next asked to put the stamp into the box and close the box. The following questions were then asked: "Does the postage stamp still exist?" "Why do you think so?" "You can't see it or touch it – why do you think it still exists?" The aim of these questions was to establish subjects' reasons for attributing existence to material objects when out of their perceptual field.

Next, the experimenter brought his hands close to the box from either side. He looked intently at the box, with apparent great effort (reflected by a facial expression of concentration and strain, and trembling hands). After a few seconds, he took away his hands and asked, "Do you believe this postage stamp disappeared from the world or turned into another postage stamp?" Subjects were then asked to estimate on a 0–100 per cent probability scale, the probability with which they believed either of these events to have occurred. Subjects were instructed that 100 per cent probability meant that they were absolutely sure the event happened, 0 per cent probability meant that they were absolutely sure it didn't happen, and 50 per cent probability meant that they admitted equally both possibilities. The aim of this question was to determine whether subjects would admit the possibility of mental transformation of an object, in the absence of material contact.

The subject was then asked to remove the stamp from the box and put it on the table. Upon opening the box, the subject found a transformed object (that had been hidden between the plate and inside wall of the box). The experimenter asked the following questions: "What is it?" "Is it the same object that you put into the box or is it another object?" "Do you notice any change in the object?" After the subject's replies, the experimenter attempted to elicit an explanation of what had happened. There were three experimental conditions, representing three variations of object transformation, with 15 subjects experiencing each condition. In the first (reconstruction), a torn and crumpled stamp became new; in the second (destruction), a new stamp became torn and crumpled; and in the third (transformation), there appeared a bigger stamp having a different picture and color.

If subjects interpreted the transformation phenomenon in terms of a permanence rule, they ought to insist that (a) this was a new object, (b) the original object (or its remnants) still existed somewhere, and (c) the new object had somehow been substituted for the original one. If, instead, subjects interpreted the original and new objects as the same object that had simply changed its appearance, they would have to explain how this transformation occurred in the absence of any obvious physical influence. They either had to find some natural causal explanation, retaining the permanence rule, or they had to admit that the object had been transformed by "mental effort", that is, resort to a nonpermanence rule.

Following their own explanations of what had happened, the experimenter asked the subject to judge the probabilities of three explanations: (a) "I have an ability to change (destroy, renew, or transform) small material objects with my 'will effort', without touching them." (b) "I hypnotized you and substituted the stamp while you were asleep. I also suggested to you a posthypnotic amnesia, so that you couldn't remember what had happened." (c) "It was just a trick."

Finally, subjects were asked to estimate the probability of existence of certain unexplained, mysterious phenomena – (a) unidentified flying objects as cosmic stations of unearthly civilizations, (b) parapsychological phenomena, (c) the "abominable snowman", (d) the "Loch Ness monster", (e) an omnipotent intellect who created the universe and is responsible for its laws, and (f) the continuation of the human soul after death. The purpose of these questions was to ascertain the probability of existence an individual was inclined to attribute to unusual, enigmatic phenomena and to compare this probability to that attributed to the mental transformation of material objects.

Results of this research indicated first that all subjects recognized the stamp as existing. As the basis for this judgment they referred to (a) the fact that the stamp was in their perceptual field ("I can see it, touch it, etc."); (b) the fact that the experimenter could also see it; (c) the fact that such objects had been encountered many times in their past experience. Subjects also recognized the stamp as continuing to exist after it was put into the box. The reasons offered were (a) the clarity and distinctness of the experience of placing it in the box ("I put it there myself; I remember very clearly"); (b) the fact that its placement inside the box lacked the capability of transforming it ("Nothing happened – no physical event that could change it or destroy it"); and (c) the fact that there were no gaps in the subject's consciousness and attention ("I've been watching the box attentively, and I saw that you didn't touch it").

Following the experimenter's attempt to influence the object by "will effort", the majority of subjects denied the possibility of its disappearance or transformation. Mean subjective probability (sum of all subjects' judged probabilities divided by the number of subjects) ranged from 3.6 per cent (transformation condition) to 9.6 per cent (destruction condition).

In the reconstruction condition, upon opening the box almost half of subjects (43 per cent) failed to notice any transformation and recognized it only after the experimenter pointed it out. Over all conditions, if subjects interpreted the change as the substitution of a new object, they were clearly making use of a permanence rule to explain the event. If, in contrast, they believed the object to be the same object despite it transformation, the subject had to explain the phenomenon, possibly using a nonpermanence rule. Mean subjective probabilities (that the object is the same object despite its transformation) were highest (62 per cent) in the destruction condition, lower (21 per cent) in the reconstruction condition, and negligible (7 per cent) in the transformation condition.

Spontaneous explanations of the change were mostly based on a permanence rule. For example, subjects mentioned the possibility of a chemical or mechanical process that had taken place in the box. Only a few subjects made reference to the mental effort of the experimenter. However, once the three explanations were proposed by the experimenter (see above), subjects' responses were different. Mean probabilities ranged from 32 per cent (transformation condition) to 52 per cent (destruction condition) that the change was accomplished by the experimenter's mental effort. The hypnosis explanation (15–41 per cent across conditions) and the "trick" explanation (29–36 per cent) were less popular. Finally, the mean probability for mysterious phenomena (36 per cent) was almost exactly that of the mean for will power, averaged across the three conditions (40 per cent).

Subjects often expressed a desire to encounter the impossible or super-natural ("I'd like this (transformation of the stamp) to be possible"; "I wish this phenomenon to exist, because it broadens the limits of reality"). There was a definite impression that a significant number of subjects experienced something like a "need" to encounter phenomena that transcend the boundaries of everyday reality.

## CONCLUSIONS

The results that have been described indicate the following conclusions. First, belief in the possibility of nonpermanence of physical objects is not unique to the minds of young children, but can also be found in adults. Second, this belief reveals itself most clearly after the apparent observation of nonpermanence and a "nonpermancence-admitting" instruction from an experimenter, i.e. the experimenter sanctions the nonpermanence belief. Third, the probability of belief in nonpermanence is similar to the probability of belief in other enigmatic phenomena beyond the bounds of everyday reality.

An implication of these results is that development of the object concept is not completed by age 2. A great deal of research has been devoted to analyzing the various changes or stages that children pass through in the first 2 years of life in the course of arriving at object permanence. However, it would clearly be unwise to conclude that the only developments in later years have to do with understanding the stability and permanence of objects such as the wind and the moon (that cannot be manipulated). One line of research has examined delays and deficits in attaining the concept of the stable object in "exceptional" or pathological populations. A second line of research, the focus of this paper, has been concerned with the conditions under which notions of objects permanence can be destroyed in normal subjects. As one might expect, subjects may judge nonpermanence if some permanence parameters (such as "feature of an object" or the "ecological validity of an object") are violated (Michotte 1962; Warren 1977). In this case, however, subjects retain the "permanence rule", dismissing the nonpermanence phenomenon as "nothing but a trick".

There are, however, conditions under which nonpermanence of physical objects is accepted both by children and adults, even in the absence of violation of permanence parameters. The conditions are most likely to be met when the subject observes nonpermanence in the company of an experimenter who admits to the possibility of nonpermanence. One might suppose that subjects may simply be unwilling to contradict the expressed views of the experimenter ("He has said that these magical things happen, and he's in a more powerful position, than me . . . so I perhaps shouldn't argue with him"). However, the possibility of such an interpretation is diminished by the fact that children were left to act privately in the absence of the experimenter or other people and so were free to follow either permanence or nonpermanence rules. In the case of adults, this interpretation is likewise unlikely for three reasons: (1) the status of the experimenter and the adult subject were similar; (2) the hypothesis of "will power" influence was only one of three possible interpretations; and (3) "magical" interpretation of any event is more socially disapproved than approved in a modern society.

Additional factors relating to the attribution of nonpermanence have to do with specific features of the form of the changes witnessed (destruction, transformation, or creation), and the subjects' "personal interest" in the phenomenon. The phenomenon is accepted much more readily if it fits the subject's pragmatic needs. For example, children proved more ready to accept nonpermanence when the box created a reward from "thin air", than when the box turned the reward previously obtained from the experimenter "into nothing" (Subbotsky 1988). Better understanding of these factors (for example, their influence on typical decision making processes) is to be examined in future research.

## ACKNOWLEDGEMENT

The author thanks Jonathan Tudge for his careful reading of the manuscript and thoughtful and constructive comments.

## REFERENCES

Baillargeon, R. (1987) "Object permanence in 3.5- and 4.5-month-old infants", *Developmental Psychology* 23: 655–664.

Baillargeon, R., Spelke, E.S. and Wassermann, S. (1985) "Object permanence in five-month-old infants", *Cognition* 20: 191–208.

Bell, J. and Richmond, G. (1984) "Improving profoundly mentally retarded adults' performance on a position discrimination", *American Journal of Mental Deficiency* 89: 180–186.

Bower, T.G.R. (1971) "The object in the world of the infant", *Scientific American* 225: 30–38.

Bower, T.G.R. (1974) *Development in infancy*, San Francisco: Freeman.

Butterworth, G. and MacPherson, F. (1984) "Sensorimotor intelligence in severely/ profoundly mentally handicapped children", *International Journal of Rehabilitation Research* 7: 82–84.

Cossette-Ricard, M. (1983) "L'identité de l'objet chez le jeune enfant", *Archives de Psychologie* 9: 261–325.

Dowson, G. and McKissick, F.C. (1984) "Self-recognition in autistic children", *Journal of Autism and Developmental Disorders* 14: 383–394.

Gratch, G. (1982) "Responses to hidden persons and things by 5-, 9-, and 16-month-old infants in a visual tracking situation", *Developmental Psychology* 18: 232–237.

Harris, P.L. (1975) "Development of search and object permanence during infancy", *Psychological Bulletin* 82: 332–344.

Harris, P. (1985) "The development of search", in P. Salapatek and L.B. Cohen (eds) *Handbook of infant perception*, New York: Academic Press.

Harris, P.L., Marriott, C. and Whittal, S. (1988) "Monsters, ghosts and witches: Testing the limits of the fantasy–reality distinction in young children", paper presented at the European Conference on Developmental Psychology, Budapest.

Le Compte, G.K. and Gratch, G. (1972) "Violation of a rule as a method of diagnosing infants' levels of object concept", *Child Development* 43: 385–396.

Meider, M. and Gratch, G. (1980) "Do 5-month-olds show object conception in Piaget's sense?" *Infant Behavior and Development* 3: 265–282.

Michotte, A. (1962) *Causalité, permanence et réalité phénoménales*, Paris: Publications Universitaires de Louvan, Editions Béatrice – Nauwelaerts.

Piaget, J. (1936) *La naissance de l'intelligence chez l'enfant*, Neuchâtel–Paris: Delachaux et Niestlé.

Piaget, J. (1937) *La construction du réel chez l'enfant*, Neuchâtel–Paris: Delachaux et Niestlé.

Piaget, J. (1976) *La formation du symbol chez l'enfant*, Neuchâtel–Paris: Delachaux et Niestlé.

Ramsay, D.S. and Campos, J.J. (1975) "Memory by the infant in an object notion task", *Developmental Psychology* 11: 411–412.

Ramsay, D.S. and Campos, J.J. (1978) "The onset of representation and entry into stage 6 of object permanence development", *Developmental Psychology* 14: 79–86.

Riddoch, M.J. and Humphreys, G.W. (1986) "Neurological impairments of object constancy: The effect of orientation and size disparities", *Cognitive Neuropsychology* 3: 207–224.

Schuberth, R.E. (1983) "The infant's search for objects: Alternatives to Piaget's theory of concept development", in L.P. Lipsitt and C.K. Rovee-Collier (eds) *Advances in infancy research* (vol. 2), Norwood, NJ: Ablex.

Subbotsky, E.V. (1985) "Preschool children's perception of unusual phenomena", *Soviet Psychology* 23: 91–114.

Subbotsky, E.V. (1988) (Preschool child's conceptions of object permanence: real and verbal behavior.) Vestn. Mosk. University, Ser. 14, Psikhol., no. 3, pp. 56–69.

Subbotsky, E.V. (1991) "Existence as a psychological problem: Object permanence in adults and preschool children", *International Journal of Behavioral Development* 14, 1: 67–82.

Tomasello, M. and Farrar, M.J. (1984) "Cognitive bases of lexical development: Object permanence and relational words", *Journal of Child Language* 11: 477–493.

Tomasello, M. and Farrar, M.J. (1986) "Object permanence and relational words: A lexical training study", *Journal of Child Language* 13: 495–505.

Wachs, T.D. (1975) "Relation of infants' performance on Piaget scales between 12 and 24 months and their Stanford–Binet performance at 31 months", *Child Development* 46: 929–935.

Warren, W.H. (1977) "Visual information for object identity in apparent movement", *Perception and Psychophysics* 21: 264–268.

Wells, M. and Glickauf-Hughes, C. (1986) "Techniques to develop object constancy with borderline clients", *Psychotherapy* 23: 460–468.

# Chapter 12

# Magic
## Special but not excluded

*Carl N. Johnson and Paul L. Harris*

In three experiments, children's ability to identify examples of magic and their credulity towards magic were studied. In Experiments 1 and 2 children were asked to distinguish between two equivalent outcomes: one outcome was brought about in an ordinary causal fashion whereas the other violated a familiar physical principle. Taken together, the two experiments show that children aged 3 to 5 years systematically judge the latter type of outcome as magical. Nonetheless, Experiment 3 showed that some young children have a credulous stance towards magical outcomes. Having checked that each of two boxes was empty, children aged 3, 5 and 7 years were asked to pretend that one of the two boxes contained a potentially attractive entity (either a fairy or an ice cream). Most children could be allocated to one of two groups: sceptical children who mostly ignored the boxes when left alone, and insisted that they were empty; and credulous children who typically opened a box and acknowledged that they had wondered if the pretend entity was inside it. Overall, the three experiments show that most young children know what counts as magic but vary in their credulity.

Early work on the child's concept of causality implied that young children scarcely think of magical outcomes as a special category. Instead, they assume that many ordinary, mechanical or physical phenomena are brought about in a quasi-magical fashion. For example, Piaget (1928) claimed that 3- and 4-year-old children often attribute the movements of inanimate objects to their own bodily movements. They assume that such gestures can influence external objects with no spatial intermediary. Piaget claimed that even 8-year-olds think that objects move according to human purpose rather than independent physical laws.

Subsequent research has questioned this account. Huang (1930) presented children aged 4–10 years with various "strange" phenomena. For example, children were shown water in a glass tube with a piece of paper covering the mouth. When the tube was inverted the water did not spill. Despite this apparent violation of gravity, children rarely offered magical explanations. Instead, they sought plausible physical explanations (e.g. "The paper sticks to the tube because it is wet"; "There is some glue on the rim of the tube", etc.). In an extensive review, Huang (1943) concluded that children's dominant mode of explanation is in terms of physical causes; their explanations may be naïve or incorrect but they rarely invoke magic.

Similar conclusions were reached by Margaret Mead (1932) in a study of Manus children. Although Manus adults routinely invoked magic to explain everyday mishaps, Manus children typically eschewed this mode of explanation. Thus, asked to say why a canoe might go adrift, they referred to the security of the mooring; only adults speculated about acts of sorcery.

This critique of Piaget's early claims suggests that children typically discount magic as a plausible explanation for everyday phenomena. In line with this critique, more recent work on children's causal notions has tended to ignore Piaget's thesis and to focus instead on discovering just what causal or mechanical principles children understand at different points in development (Gelman and Baillargeon 1983). The child is depicted as a naïve scientist armed with a theory that despite its shortcomings falls firmly into the category of common sense physics.

However, this portrayal of the young child as a budding scientist who avoids any form of magical explanation ignores certain fundamental issues. Even if children rarely invoke magic as an explanation for everyday events, it seems likely that they must still develop a category of metaphysical or magical phenomena. This will allow them to bracket off certain outcomes as special or magical, precisely because they do not fit in with everyday expectations.

There are several reasons for this hypothesis. First, most cultures, including contemporary Western culture, routinely describe various super-natural beings to young children. God, Santa Claus and the tooth fairy are all supposedly capable of supernatural feats that defy most versions of folk physics. It would be surprising if young children remained entirely oblivious of the alleged existence of such beings and their special powers. Second, studies of children's collective beliefs show that they do lend credence to magical forces, and indeed many of these ideas are passed on from one generation of children to the next independent of adults (Opie and Opie 1959). Third, many young children are afraid of supernatural creatures. For example, they are fearful of monsters despite parental reassurance that such creatures do not exist (Jersild 1943). Moreover, children sometimes endow such creatures with special capacities for penetrating an otherwise safe environment (Harris, Brown, Marriott, Whittall and Harmer 1991). Their normal grasp of object displacement and permanence appears to be set aside when coping with such creatures. Finally, children's spontaneous comments suggest that at around 4 or 5 years of age they do not simply think of magic as an empty category. They comment on what could be done by someone with magical powers. For example, the following exchanges were located through the records of spontaneous speech located in Childes (MacWhinney and Snow 1985). The first took place between Walter (aged 4 years 11 months) and his father. Father: "I think I'll stay up real late this year and see if I can see Santa when he comes to our house". Walter: "Santa gots real magical powers. If you look up . . . he'll be up . . . down. If you look down . . . he'll be up". The second occurred between Adam (aged 4 years 7 months) and his mother. Adam: " . . . Hey, look, my fingers are cutters. See . . . it's magic, isn't it?" Mother: "I didn't know you had scissor fingers". Adam: "I didn't cut it with my fingers". Mother: "How did you?" Adam: "No way. It's just magic. . . . I'm a magic boy. I can make anything go away. I'm magic. Look, I made it small, didn't I?"

Taken together, these various pieces of evidence suggest that even if young children do not inappropriately invoke magical explanations, they have an interest and perhaps a belief in the existence of magic. Magical phenomena may not pervade their everyday world but they do penetrate it from time to time.

In three studies, we probe children's conception of magical phenomena more systematically. We begin by asking whether children make any kind of distinction, however rudimentary, between outcomes that have occurred with and without magic. Given that children rarely invoke magical explanations (Huang 1930), we anticipated that children would not invoke magic to explain phenomena that are consonant with everyday causal principles. On the other hand, we also expected children to have some positive concept of magic so that they should readily identify phenomena that do count as magic.

In selecting "magical" phenomena, we were guided by the assumption that children will be especially likely to judge an outcome as magical if it is realized in a way that is not consonant with firmly held physical or causal principles. We identified four such principles: (a) inertia – inanimate objects do not move spontaneously; (b) constancy – inanimate objects do not spontaneously transform their shape or identity; (c) permanence – inanimate objects do not spontaneously disappear, or cease to exist; (d) non-creation – inanimate objects do not spontaneously come into existence. Notice that violations of these principles cover many of the (apparent) outcomes that feature in magic shows, especially for young children. Violation of these particular principles clearly does not exhaust the category of magic as held by adults. For example, most adults judge alleged feats of mind-reading or precognition as magic. Our aim was rather to utilize principles of "naïve physics" that are likely to be universally understood by young children (Wellman and Gelman 1992).

Children were told about eight pairs of outcomes. For each pair, one outcome was brought about in a routine fashion (e.g. paints were used to make a picture on some paper) whereas the other was brought about in a magical fashion (e.g. a picture appeared on some paper, all by itself). Children were asked whether each outcome could happen or whether it would be magic. Among the eight magical outcomes, there were two that violated each of the principles described above.

We also assessed children's sensitivity to another common feature of magic, especially in primitive cultures (e.g. Evans-Pritchard 1937). Magic is often seen as the deliberate product of a human intention (benign or malevolent) that realizes its goal via extraordinary powers; special acts (e.g. uttering a spell; staring or thinking intently) are aimed at the to-be-affected entity. To assess children's sensitivity to the role of such acts, children were asked about magical outcomes that occurred with and without any special action by the self.

## EXPERIMENT 1

### Method

#### Subjects

Subjects were 14 young children (mean age 4 years 5 months; range 3 years 9 months to 5 years 1 month) and 14 older children (mean age 6 years 2 months; range 5 years 4 months to 7 years 5 months). They were tested in state schools in Oxfordshire, UK.

#### Procedure

Children were first engaged in a preamble to clarify the meaning of the word "magic". Children were told about four different outcomes (eating ice cream; making an ice cream jump into one's hand; riding a bicycle; a bicycle that went along the road by itself), and asked whether each outcome could happen with or without magic. Correction and explanation were given for these questions where necessary.

There were eight pairs of test items (i.e. 16 items in total). For any given pair of items there was a distinct set of props (e.g. a marble placed in one of two boxes). Children were first shown these props and then asked to consider two different outcomes – an ordinary, non-magical outcome, such as moving the marble with their hands from one box to another, and a magical outcome such as moving the marble from one box to another by thinking hard rather than by handling the marble. After describing each item, the experimenter immediately asked whether the outcome could take place in the manner described or whether it would be magic. For example, with respect to moving the marble by hand, the experimenter asked: "Could you move the marble with your hands like that or would it be magic?" With respect to moving the marble by thinking hard, the experimenter asked: "Could you move the marble by thinking like that or would it be magic?"

Four of the eight pairs involved an action by the child (as in the pair just described); the remaining four pairs did not involve any action by the child. Within each set of four pairs, there were four different types of outcome: movement (as in the case of the marble), change of identity, disappearance and creation. The magical outcome for these four different pairs violated the principles of inertia, constancy, permanence and non-creation respectively (as defined earlier). Details of the props, the type of outcome, the actions involved, and the form of questioning are given in Appendix 1.

Each child was tested on all eight pairs. Order of pair presentation was decided by shuffling eight cards. Children received the ordinary and magical items of a given pair one after the other. An additional set of cards was shuffled to determine whether the ordinary or the magical item should be presented first for a given pair.

## Results

For each item children were scored in terms of whether or not they claimed that the outcome could only occur by magic. Initial inspection showed that there was no systematic variation across the four types of outcome (i.e. movement, change of identity, disappearance and creation). Accordingly, children's scores were summed across these four types of item. The mean number of responses that invoked magic (out of a maximum of four) is shown in Table 12.1 as a function of age (younger vs. older), item (ordinary vs. magical) and involvement (child involved vs. not involved).

Table 12.1 shows that irrespective of age and involvement of the child, children were much more likely to invoke magic for the magical items than' the ordinary items. A three way ANOVA of age (2) × item (2) × involvement (2) confirmed the main effect of item ($F(1,26) = 23.88$, $p < .0001$). No other main effect or interaction proved significant.

*Table 12.1* Mean number of responses (out of four) invoking magic as a function of age, item (ordinary vs. magical) and involvement

| | Child involved | | Child not involved | |
|---|---|---|---|---|
| Age | Ordinary | Magical | Ordinary | Magical |
| Younger | 1.86 | 3.07 | 2.00 | 2.93 |
| Older | 1.57 | 3.86 | 1.86 | 3.79 |

## Discussion

Both age groups distinguished systematically between ordinary and magical outcomes. This distinction was influenced neither by the type of outcome (e.g. disappearance compared with movement) nor by whether the child was mentioned as a potential agent in the outcome.

## EXPERIMENT 2

Experiment 2 was designed to refine the methods used in Experiment 1 and to test whether younger children, namely 3-year-olds, can discriminate ordinary from magical events. Although Experiment 1 showed that young children can discriminate magical from everyday events, performance was limited by a tendancy to overextend the category of magic. This over-extension may have resulted from the fixed order in which the response choices were presented. Children were always asked whether the given event could happen or whether it was magic, with the magic option mentioned last. If children "echoed" the last-mentioned option, this would lead to correct judgements for magical items but an overextension of this magic category for regular items. To avoid this bias, a non-verbal pointing procedure was used in Experiment 2.

A second limitation of Experiment 1 was that children were asked to distinguish between events that could happen versus those that were magic. Hence, the category of magic was implicitly defined as something that cannot happen. To avoid this implication, events in Experiment 2 were presented as having already occurred, and children were asked to say whether they were caused by a "Magic Fairy", described as only doing things by magic, versus "Jack" (or "Jill"), a child described as only doing things the regular way.

## Method

### Subjects

Subjects were 16 3-year-olds (mean age 3 years 8 months; range 3 years 3 months to 3 years 11 months) and 16 4-year-olds (mean age 4 years 6 months; range 4 years 3 months to 4 years 10 months). Subjects were drawn from a preschool serving upper-middle-class families in a suburb of Pittsburgh.

### Procedure

Each child was initially introduced to two characters, Jack (Jill for girls) and Magic Fairy, depicted in drawings: "This is Jack who is a little boy just like you. Jack can do lots of regular things, but he can't do anything magical. But this is Magic Fairy. Magic Fairy does everything magical. Magic Fairy never bothers doing things the regular way. Now I'm going to tell you about some things that happened and I want you to guess who did them. You tell me whether Jack did it or whether Magic Fairy did it".

Following this introduction, children were given four pre-training items, two magic and two ordinary (see Appendix 2). Errors on the pre-training were corrected with the reminder that the Magic Fairy does special magic things, while Jack does regular, ordinary things.

Paralleling Experiment 1, each subject was then presented with eight changes of state of four types: two involving movement, two change of identity, two disappearance and two creation. In each case children were presented with the change of state, caused by everyday means and also by magical means. Hence, children were presented with a total of 16 outcomes. Within each type of change of state, one magical outcome was presented as spontaneous whereas the other magical outcome was presented as caused by wishing or verbal commands (see Appendix 3).

Item order was randomized across subjects. The order of presentation and questioning about magic versus ordinary items was counterbalanced: each subject was presented and questioned about half of the eight items in a magic–ordinary sequence, the other half in an ordinary–magic sequence.

## Results

As in Experiment 1, scores were summed across the four item types (movement, change of identity, disappearance and creation) because there was no systematic variation in performance. The mean number of responses attributed to Magic Fairy is shown in Table 12.2 as a function of age (3 years vs. 4 years), item (ordinary vs. magical) and involvement. (spontaneous magic vs. magic invoked by words or wishes).

Table 12.2 shows that both age groups were very accurate. In contrast to Experiment 1, there was little tendency for children to overextend magic to include the ordinary events. A three-way analysis of variance confirmed that only the overall effect of item was statistically significant ($F(1,30) = 208.25$, $p < .0001$).

## Discussion

Experiments 1 and 2 show that young children can make a clear distinction between two types of outcome: ordinary versus magical. Granted that children can identify magical outcomes as such, we may ask a further question. Do young children think of the category of magical outcomes as an empty category, one that only embraces events that cannot happen in everyday life? Alternatively, do they believe that magic can sometimes

Table 12.2 Mean number of responses (out of four) attributing the event to the Magic Fairy, as a function of age, item (ordinary vs magical) and involvement

| Age | Verbal/wish | | Spontaneous | |
|---|---|---|---|---|
| | Ordinary | Magical | Ordinary | Magical |
| 3 years | 0.75 | 3.56 | 0.63 | 3.44 |
| 4 years | 0.63 | 3.44 | 0.19 | 3.81 |

occur? We attempted to answer this question in Experiment 3 which examined children's credulity with respect to a magical outcome.

## EXPERIMENT 3

Harris *et al.* (1991) asked 4- and 6-year-old children to first check that a box was empty and then to imagine that there was a creature inside it. When children were left alone, they were more likely to approach and investigate this empty box than a control box in which they had not imagined anything. Children behaved as if the imagined entity might magically appear inside the box even though they had established that it was empty shortly before. The present study was designed to replicate and extend these findings. One important goal was to examine the link between children's investigation of the box and their replies in a structured interview. Specifically, it was predicted that those children who opened the box would be credulous. They would admit to wondering about its contents and the possibility of a magical transposition. Conversely, children who ignored the box would be sceptical: they would insist that the box had remained empty given the physical and spatial constraints.

A second goal was to assess whether the nature of the imagined entity influenced children's credulity or scepticism. Half the children in each age group were asked to imagine an ice cream and the other half were asked to imagine a fairy inside one of the boxes. It was anticipated that the fairy might be more readily associated with magical transpositions than the ice cream. Subbotsky (1985, 1994) has shown that preschool children anticipate otherwise impossible appearances and disappearances in the context of fairy tales.

## Method

### Subjects

Three age groups of children were tested, 3-, 5- and 7-year-olds. Each age group comprised 24 children. Three-year-olds ranged from 3 years 0 months to 3 years 11 months; 5-year-olds from 5 years 0 months to 5 years 11 months; and 7-year-olds from 7 years 0 months to 7 years 11 months. Children were recruited from schools and preschools in the area of Oxford (UK) serving a broad socio-economic range.

## Materials

Each child was taken into a quiet room containing two wooden boxes (each 1 metre cubed). Each box had a hinged lid; one lid was coloured white and the other black. A concealed timer recorded each separate raising of each lid. The lids were sprung so that they remained open only when held open. Thus, the experimenter could keep track of children's investigation of each box when she was absent from the room. The boxes were placed approximately 2 feet apart.

## Procedure

On entering the room, the female experimenter said: "Shall we play a game of pretend? I bet you're good at pretend games." Half the children were then given the pretend box instructions followed by the neutral box instructions (see below). The remaining children heard the instructions in the reverse order. Half the children within each age group were assigned to the fairy condition and half to the ice cream condition. Finally, within each subgroup the association between lid colour and pretend versus neutral box was systematically varied. The instructions for the pretend box were as follows:

*Pretend box (ice cream).* "Now we'll go and see if there's anything in that box with the black/white lid. Look carefully right into the box to see if it's empty. Now come and sit here between the boxes." After the child and experimenter had established that the box was empty, the child was seated and the experimenter proceeded: "Now, let's pretend that the box with the black/white lid has some ice cream inside it" (pointing to the appropriate box). "Have you pretended that there's some ice cream in the black/white box? Now pretend that it's chocolate ice cream. Now pretend that the ice cream is in a bowl ready to eat. OK. Have you pretended all that? How big is the ice cream? Is it a big bowl of ice cream like that . . . " (holding hands 12 inches apart), " . . . or is it a small bowl of ice cream like that?" (holding hands 1 inch apart). (This question was aimed at ensuring that children did imagine some ice cream in the box.)

Finally, the experimenter asked: "Is there really some ice cream in the black/white box, or are you just pretending that there's some ice cream?" Children who failed to reply or said that there really was ice cream in the box (19 per cent) were reminded that the box had been empty when they looked inside it.

*Pretend box (fairy condition).* The procedure was similar to that used for the ice cream condition. The experimenter looked in the appropriate box with the child, and confirmed that it was empty. Then, when the child was sitting between the boxes, she said: "Now let's pretend that the box with the white/black lid has a fairy inside it" (pointing to appropriate box). "Have you pretended there's a fairy in the white/black box? Now pretend that she's dancing round and round. Now pretend that she's waving her magic wand. OK. have you pretended all that? How big is the fairy? Is she a big fairy like that . . . " (holding hands 12 inches apart), ". . . or is she a little fairy like that?" (holding hands 1 inch apart). As for the ice cream condition, this question was intended only to ensure that children did imagine a fairy in the box.

After the child expressed his/her opinion about the imaginary fairy, the experimenter asked: "Is there really a fairy in the white/black box or are you just pretending that there's a fairy?" Again, the minority of children who failed to give a correct reply (16 per cent) were corrected.

*Neutral box instructions.* The instructions for the neutral box were the same for both the fairy and ice cream conditions. The experimenter said: "Now we'll go and see if there's anything inside that box with the black/white lid. Look carefully right into the box to see if it's empty. Now come and sit here between the boxes . . . " When the child was seated, she continued: "Was the box empty when we looked inside it?" After confirming that the box was empty, the experimenter said: "OK. We won't pretend that there's anything in the box with the black/white lid. Let's just leave it empty".

After instructing the child about both boxes, the experimenter said that she had to leave for two minutes to get a gift (a picture) for the child. She added: "You don't need to sit still but don't go out of the room, will you?" The experimenter left and started the timer for a two-minute period.

*Interview after experimenter's return*

On her return, the experimenter asked the children two warm-up questions (Questions 1–2) and then more detailed questions about their thoughts and actions in her absence (Questions 3–5).

*Question 1*: "Did you look inside one of the boxes while I was away?"

*Question 2*: "And which box did you look inside?"

*Question 3A*: (This question was put to children who acknowledged opening either box) "And what did you think when you went to open the box? Did you think the box was empty or did you think to yourself: 'I wonder if there's some ice cream/a fairy inside'?"

*Question 3B*: (This question was put to children who denied opening either box) "Were you sure the box was empty, or did you wonder if there was some ice cream/a fairy inside?"

*Question 4A*: (This question was put to children who admitted wondering whether a box contained some ice cream/a fairy in reply to questions 3A or 3B, whether or not they had looked inside it) "How did you think the ice cream/a fairy got inside the box?"

*Question 4B*: (This question was put to children who denied wondering whether a box contained some ice cream/a fairy irrespective of whether they had looked inside it) "How did you know there wasn't any ice cream/a fairy in the box?"

*Question 5*: (This was a memory check for all children) "Do you remember when we looked in the boxes together before I went out? Did you see some ice cream/a fairy in the boxes?"

## Results

### Approach to the boxes

Children were scored for the latency and frequency with which they opened each box within the two-minute period. (Children who failed to open a given box were assigned a default latency score of 120 s, i.e. the total duration of the timed period.) Mean scores are shown in Table 12.3 as a function of age (3 years vs. 5 years vs. 7 years), condition (ice ceam vs. fairy) and box (pretend vs. neutral). The interview replies of two 3-year-olds and one 7-year-old showed that they mistakenly regarded the neutral box as the box to which they had directed their initial pretence. Their scores for the pretend and neutral box were therefore switched in line with this error.

Table 12.3 shows that children tended to investigate the pretend box more quickly and more frequently than the neutral box. To check this conclusion, a three-way ANOVA of age × condition × box was carried out for each measure.

The analysis of latency showed that children were quicker to open the pretend box than the neutral box (box, $F(1,66) = 6.06$, $p < .016$). This difference was greater for children in the fairy condition than the ice cream condition, so that the interaction of condition × box approached significance ($F(1,66) = 3.78$, $p < .06$). Finally, latency to approach the boxes varied with age ($F(2,66) = 3.26$, $p < .045$). Tukey's tests showed that 7-year-olds were slower to approach the boxes than 5-year-olds ($p < .05$) but the other pairwise comparisons were not significant.

Analysis of the frequency with which each box was opened showed that children opened the pretend box more often than the neutral box ($F(1,66) = 8.86$, $p < .004$). No other effect was significant.

*Table 12.3* Mean scores as a function of age, condition (ice cream vs. fairy) and box (pretend vs. neutral) for (a) latency to open box; and (b) total number of times that box was opened

|  |  | Fairy | | Ice cream | |
|---|---|---|---|---|---|
|  |  | *Pretend* | *Neutral* | *Pretend* | *Neutral* |
| Latency | 3 years | 48.45 | 83.80 | 58.72 | 67.81 |
|  | 5 years | 40.26 | 43.04 | 62.64 | 59.40 |
|  | 7 years | 69.29 | 85.63 | 92.11 | 92.67 |
| Number of openings | 3 years | 2.17 | 1.33 | 1.75 | 1.00 |
|  | 5 years | 1.75 | 1.25 | 4.25 | 3.33 |
|  | 7 years | 1.25 | 0.92 | 0.50 | 0.58 |

Thus, children were quicker to open the pretend box than the neutral box and they opened it more often.

*Interview after experimenter's return*

*Questions 1 and 2*: Most children accurately stated whether they had opened a box, and if so which one(s). On question 1, only one 3-year-old erred (as shown by the timer). On question 2, three 3-year-olds, two 5-year-olds and three 7-year-olds made errors; five made errors of omission (they indicated one box, but had opened both); two indicated the wrong box; and one claimed to have opened a box, but the time showed that he had not.

*Questions 3A and 3B*: In questions 3A and 3B, children were asked about the existence of the pretend item, irrespective of whether they had looked in a box. Replies were allocated to one of three categories: *credulous*, *unsure* and *sceptical*. If children said that they wondered whether the pretend entity might be inside the box, they were scored as *credulous*. If they explicitly claimed to be unsure or vacillated between belief in the pretend item and belief that the box was empty (e.g. "I think it's empty but there might be", or "I didn't open it 'cos I thought there wasn't but now I think there might be"), they were scored as *unsure*. Finally, if they claimed that the box was empty, they were scored as *sceptical*. Sixteen subjects from each age group (eight from each condition) were scored by two judges. They agreed for 46 out of 48 decisions (96 per cent). The two disagreements were resolved through discussion. The remaining subjects were scored by a single judge. This three-way classification was then related to whether children did or did not open the pretend box.

Table 12.4 shows the number of credulous, unsure and sceptical children who did or did not open the pretend box as a function of condition (fairy vs. ice cream). Inspection of the bottom row of Table 12.5 shows that

*Table 12.4* Number of children falling into three different belief categories who did or did not investigate (+ vs. −) the pretend box

| | Fairy | | | | | | Ice cream | | | | | |
| | Credulous | | Unsure | | Sceptical | | Credulous | | Unsure | | Sceptical | |
| | + | − | + | − | + | − | + | − | + | − | + | − |
|---|---|---|---|---|---|---|---|---|---|---|---|---|
| 3 years | 6 | 0 | 0 | 0 | 3 | 3 | 6 | 3 | 0 | 0 | 2 | 1 |
| 5 years | 6 | 2 | 1 | 1 | 2 | 0 | 7 | 0 | 0 | 0 | 0 | 5 |
| 7 years | 6 | 0 | 0 | 0 | 1 | 5 | 2 | 1 | 1 | 3 | 2 | 3 |
| | 18 | 2 | 1 | 1 | 6 | 8 | 15 | 4 | 1 | 3 | 4 | 9 |

credulous children mostly opened the pretend box, whereas sceptical children were more likely to ignore it. This link between opening the box and interview stance occurred for the ice cream and fairy condition. Chi-square tests (with unsure children excluded) showed that a higher proportion of credulous compared with sceptical children opened the pretend box in each condition ($\chi^2(1) = 6.69$, $p < .01$, for the fairy condition; $\chi^2(1) = 5.57$, $p < .02$, for the ice cream condition).

*Questions 4A and 4B*: Children were asked to explain their claim that the imagined entity might be in the box or could not be there. Explanations were allocated to four categories: *none:* no informative explanation offered (e.g. "I don't know"); *magical:* reference to the presence/absence of magic, or spells (e.g. "A witch made a spell on her (the fairy) and made her get in there", "Because you don't have a magic wand"); *mental:* reference to the efficacy/inefficacy of a mental state (e.g. "By imagining it", "Because I wanted it", "'cos it's just pretending"); *physical/spatial:* reference to the possibility/impossibility of entering the box or to its previously empty state (e.g. "Came through a window and flew in the box when I opened it but I didn't see her 'cos she's teeny", "It can't happen – it was empty before").

Table 12.5 shows the number of credulous, unsure and sceptical children giving each type of explanation as a function of condition. (The distribution of replies showed no systematic variation with age so that Table 12.5 was simplified by omitting age as a variable.) Inspection of Table 12.5 shows that credulous children differed in the pattern of explanations they offered compared with sceptical children. Irrespective of condition, credulous children often referred to the possibility of magical causation, whereas sceptical children chiefly referred to physical/spatial factors and rarely mentioned magical causation. A chi-square test confirmed that the proportion of children who gave a magical explanation (rather than any other type of explanation) was larger among credulous than among sceptical children ($\chi^2(1) = 7.67$, $p < .01$).

It is worth noting that the coding system may have underestimated the

Table 12.5 Number of children offering four categories of explanation as a function of condition (fairy vs. ice cream) and belief

| | Credulous | | | Unsure | | | Sceptical | | |
|---|---|---|---|---|---|---|---|---|---|
| | Fairy | Ice cream | Total | Fairy | Ice cream | Total | Fairy | Ice cream | Total |
| None | 2 | 6 | 8 | 0 | 0 | 0 | 3 | 2 | 5 |
| Magical | 8 | 6 | 14 | 1* | 0 | 1 | 0 | 1 | 1 |
| Mental | 0 | 2 | 2 | 0 | 2 | 2 | 0 | 0 | 0 |
| Physical/ spatial | 10 | 5 | 15 | 2* | 2 | 4 | 11 | 10 | 21 |

* One unsure child (aged 5 years) who offered both a magical and a physical/spatial explanation appears twice in the table.

frequency of magical thinking among credulous children. They gave explanations such as: "It (the ice cream) got through a hole in the bottom of the box" or "She (the fairy) flew through the window and got under the lid because she's so tiny". Although such explanations were coded as physical/spatial since magic was not explicitly mentioned, children may nonetheless have assumed a magical component to the causal chain they described.

*Question 5:* Children were asked whether they had seen a fairy or some ice cream when they checked the boxes at the beginning of the experiment. For each of the six combinations of age and condition (fairy vs. ice cream) 10 or more children (out of 12) replied correctly. There was little indication, therefore, that children had forgotten the outcome of their initial check.

## Discussion

The results of Experiment 3 show that when some children imagine an outcome it leads them to wonder whether such an outcome has actually occurred even if its occurrence would be magical. Children had seen that the boxes were empty, and before the experimenter left they mostly agreed that they were only pretending there was something in one of them. Yet some children in each age group then acted as if that box might contain the entity in question. Three pieces of evidence support this claim. Children were quicker to open the pretend box and opened it more often than the neutral box. Second, most children who said that they wondered if the imagined entity might be in the box had opened it while the experimenter was absent. Children who denied that the imagined entity was in the box were more likely to have left it unopened. Third, some credulous children justified the possible presence of the entity by invoking magical causation whereas this mode of causal explanation was rarely mentioned by sceptical children.

These three pieces of evidence suggest that most children adopted either a credulous or a sceptical stance. Credulous children wondered if the imagined entity might be in the box, tested that possibility by opening it, and sometimes invoked magic by way of explanation. Sceptical children denied that the imagined entity could be in the box, did not check whether it was, and justified their scepticism in terms of ordinary spatial or physical considerations. A small residual group wavered between credulity and scepticism. These findings raise several interesting issues: the exact nature of the credulous stance; the possible existence of stable individual differences; and the surprising absence of clear-cut age changes.

It might be objected that credulous children did not really anticipate a magical creation or transposition, rather they suspected that the experimenter might trick them while she was absent, somehow arranging for the imagined entity to enter the box. However, when children invoked the possibility of magic, they attributed it to the imagined entity, not to the experimenter. Only one child ever suggested that the experimenter might play any role. In this respect, our results are similar to those reported by Rosengren, Kalish, Hickling and Gelman (1994) and by Chandler and Lalonde (1994). Young children are certainly capable of discovering and diagnosing the experimenter's use of a piece of trick apparatus if they are given an opportunity to explore it – as in Chandler and Lalonde's initial study. However, there is little indication that children assume from the outset that a magical outcome must necessarily be the result of adult trickery. Note that even with strong hints that trickery had taken place (the use of a magician's robe) Chandler and Lalonde found in their second study that much older children (ranging from 9 to 13 years) all accepted that a ball of clay could change its weight following a change of shape. Moreover, almost half the children exposed to the magician, and most of those exposed to the priest or the psychologist, persisted in their credulous non-conservation responses. For better or worse, then, young children do not routinely suspect conjuring or trickery by the experimenter.

An alternative interpretation of our results is that children were simply extending the game of make-believe that the experimenter had proposed by opening the relevant box in her absence. However, in that case, one would not expect a link between opening the box and credulity; opening the box for a make-believe entity would be perfectly compatible with a sceptical stance.

How should we explain children's credulity? One possibility is that children are prone to confusion about the realm of the imagination. They assume that objects can "transmigrate" from fantasy to reality (Harris *et al.* 1991). Children's justifications offer little support for this interpretation. Children did occasionally imply that such mental feats were possible. For example, asked to explain how the ice cream might have got inside the box, one 7-year-old explained: "By imagining it — but I didn't try that hard". Yet confusion about the power of the imagination was not widespread in the interview.

A different explantation fits the evidence better. It rests on two linked assumptions. First, a state of affairs that can be easily brought to mind is deemed more likely than one that cannot be easily brought to mind. Research with adults has demonstrated this so-called availability heuristic (Tversky and Kahneman 1973). Given that children have imagined an entity in the pretend box, we may assume that this possibility is easily brought to mind and judged as more likely than it might otherwise be. Hence, children will be disposed to think that the imagined object might be in the pretend box, but not that it might be in the control box.

The second assumption borrows from the intriguing research of Subbotsky (1985, 1991, 1994). He argues that young children accept that extraordinary transformations might occur, even if they are usually wary of admitting such beliefs to adults. For example, having listened to a story in which various magical outcomes are described (e.g. a box that changes the identity of an object placed inside it) children seek to reproduce such outcomes themselves, if given an opportunity. Subbotsky proposes that although children accept the laws of object permanence, they never entirely discard the counter-hypothesis, namely that objects can suddenly come into existence or change their identity. Such a hypothesis remains latent or dormant, and can be reactivated under appropriate circumstances.

Combining these two assumptions, we arrive at the following interpretation of both the credulous and the sceptical stance. Children imagine an object in the pretend box, and the ensuing availability of that idea makes it more plausible that such an object is in the box. Children can further gauge the likelihood of that possibility in the light of two principles – the non-creation principle or the latent alternative principle of magical creation. For some children it is the former principle that prevails. These are the sceptical children who do not bother to look in the pretend box, and justify their scepticism by referring to the physical and spatial impossibility of an empty box suddenly containing anything. For some children it is the principle of magical creation that prevails, or to put it more cautiously, that cannot be completely suppressed. For them it is worth checking the pretend box. Having looked in it and discovered that it is empty, many credulous children explain their stance by referring to the power of magic. Thus, these twin assumptions do not imply that children are confused about the generative power of the imagination. Instead, they imply that the imagination provides a breeding ground for magical fantasies: these fantasies may be opposed by the child's common-sense principles, or bolstered by latent magical principles. These assumptions also imply – with some plausbility – that it is not just an act of pretence that will lead some children to accept or even expect magical or supernatural outcomes. Any activity that increases the mental availability of such outcomes will have a similar effect. Thus, reading a fairy tale, watching a cartoon, or participating in a religious ceremony might be equally efficacious.

As noted earlier, most children may be described as either credulous or sceptical. An important question for future research is whether such individual differences are stable across different settings. For example, if children were tested repeatedly with different imaginary creatures, would they show a stable response of either credulity or scepticism? Speculating further, are credulous children likely to be among the minority of children who make friends with an imaginary companion or exhibit a persistent fear of monsters or ghosts (Jersild 1943)? Whatever the outcome of such research, the twin assumptions described above offer a way of conceptualizing individual differences. Specifically, individual differences could arise at two different points. First, credulous children might differ from sceptical children in their vulnerability to availability effects. Second, credulous children might find it particularly difficult to inhibit activation of the latent hypothesis of magical creation. Although its activation is appropriate in some circumstances (e.g. for understanding fairy stories or miracles), credulous children may have difficulty in inhibiting it when dealing with the everyday world. In either case, we speculate that differences may be linked to well-documented individual differences in imagination and fantasy proneness (Myers 1983). Children who enjoy a particularly vivid imagination would presumably be more prone to both generate a salient imaginative representation (such as the fairy in the box) and to activate fantasy scenarios from long-term memory.

Finally, it is interesting to note that credulity was quite common even at 7 years. Only in the ice cream condition was there some indication of an age change: compared with 7-year-olds, a higher proportion of 3-year-olds were credulous. This suggests that scepticism may triumph first with respect to everyday objects. With respect to supernatural creatures such as fairies, monsters or even deities, scepticism may never attain a complete victory. This makes sense because children can constantly validate the laws of object permanence in the case of ordinary physical objects: their current location can usually be predicted from a knowledge of their immediate prior location or displacement. Such validation is impossible in the case of supernatural creatures. Their current location is unpredictable. The implication is that in the case of supernatural entities the mental contest between the non-magical principles and latent magical thinking is less one-sided.

## In conclusion

Our experiments show that young children distinguish systematically between magical and non-magical outcomes. Nevertheless, children vary in their credulity towards magic. Finally, by characterizing some young children as credulous, or prone to magical thinking, we do not wish to imply that the sceptical stance is somehow more rational or more mature. In his defence of Christian faith, Pascal pointed out that, in the absence of evidence to the contrary, there is nothing irrational about a wager that God exists.

## ACKNOWLEDGEMENTS

Portions of this paper were presented at the biennial meeting of ISSBD, Minneapolis, 3–7 July 1991 and at the BPS Developmental Section Conference, Cambridge University, 13–16 September 1991. We thank Jill Ceralvolo, Donna Rechin, Rachel Grimwood and Kate Oliver for help in gathering data for Experiments 2 and 3. Hugh Jones, Szabolcs Kiss and Mary Whalen made helpful comments on the manuscript.

## REFERENCES

Chandler, M.J. and Lalonde, C.E. (1994) "Surprising, magical and miraculous turns of events: Children's reactions to violations of their early theories of mind and matter", *British Journal of Developmental Psychology* 12: 83–96.

Evans-Pritchard, E.E. (1937) *Witchcraft, Oracles and Magic Among the Azande*, Oxford: Clarendon Press.

Gelman, R. and Baillargeon, R. (1983) "A review of some Piagetian concepts", in J. H. Flavell and E.M. Markman (eds) *Handbook of Child Psychology*, vol. III, pp. 166–230, New York: Wiley.

Harris, P.L., Brown, E., Marriott, C., Whittall, S. and Harmer, S (1991) "Monsters, ghosts and witches: Testing the limits of the fantasy–reality distinction in young children", *British Journal of Developmental Psychology* 9: 105–123.

Huang, I. (1930) "Children's explanations of strange phenomena", *Psychologische Forschung* 14: 63–183.

Huang, I. (1943) "Children's conception of physical causality: A critical summary", *Journal of Genetic Psychology* 63: 71–121.

Jersild, A. T. (1943) "Studies of children's fears", in R. G. Barker, J. S. Kounin and H. F. Wright (eds) *Child Behavior and Development*, New York: McGraw-Hill.

MacWhinney, B. and Snow, C. (1985) "The child language data exchange system", *Journal of Child Language* 12: 271–296.

Mead, M. (1932) "An investigation of the thought of primitive children, with special reference to animism", *Journal of the Royal Anthropological Institute* 62: 173–190.

Myers, S.A. (1983) "The Wilson–Barber inventory of childhood memories and imaginings: Children's form and norms of 1337 children and adolescents", *Journal of Mental Imagery* 7: 83–94.

Opie, I. and Opie, P. (1959) *The Lore and Language of Schoolchildren*, Oxford: Oxford University Press.

Piaget, J. (1928) "La causalité chez l'enfant", *British Journal of Psychology* 18: 276–301.

Rosengren, K.S., Kalish, C.W., Hickling, A.K. and Gelman, S.A. (1994) "Exploring the relation between preschool children's magical beliefs and causal thinking", *British Journal of Developmental Psychology* 12: 69–82.

Subbotsky, E.V. (1985) "Preschool children's perception of unusual phenomena", *Soviet Psychology* 23: 91–114.

Subbotsky, E.V. (1991) "A life-span approach to object permanence", *Human Development* 34: 125–137. Reprinted as Chapter 11, this volume.

Subbotsky, E.V. (1994) "Early rationality and magical thinking in preschoolers: Space and time", *British Journal of Developmental Psychology* 12: 97–108.

Tversky, A. and Kahneman, D. (1973) "Availability: A heuristic for judging frequency and probability", *Cognitive Psychology* 5: 207–232.

Wellman, H.M. and Gelman, S.A. (1992) "Cognitive development: Foundational theories of core domains", *Annual Review of Psychology* 43: 337–375.

## Appendix 1: Test items for Experiment 1

1 Items involving child

*Boxes and marble: movement*

Props: Here are two boxes. Watch while I put this marble in this box.

*Everyday*. Now what if I let you take the marble out of that box and move it to the other one. Could you move the marble with your hands like that or would it be magic?

*Magical*. Now what if you moved the marble from that box to the other one without touching it – just by thinking very, very hard. Could you move the marble by thinking like that or would it be magic?

*Play-Doh: change of identity*

Props: Here's a ball of Play-Doh.

*Everyday*. Now what if I gave you the ball of Play-Doh and you rolled it and changed it into a sausage shape. Could you change the Play-Doh by rolling it like that or would it be magic?

*Magical*. Now what if you looked at the ball of Play-Doh and you looked very, very hard without touching it and changed it into a sausage shape. Could you change the Play-Doh by looking at it like that or would it be magic?

*Sweets: disappearance*

Props: Here's some sweets.

*Everyday*. Now what if you ate the sweets so that you made them all gone. Could you make the sweets all gone by eating them like that or would it be magic?

*Magical*. Now what if you whispered to the sweets without touching them and you made them all gone. Could you make them all gone by whispering like that or would it be magic?

*Pencil and paper: creation*
Props: Here's a pencil.

*Everyday.* Now what if I gave you some paper and you drew a picture of your house. Could you make a picture by drawing like that or would it be magic?

*Magical.* Now what if you loked at the piece of paper and you looked very, very hard without touching it and you made a picture of your house. Could you make a picture by looking at the paper like that or would it be magic?

2 Items independent of the child

*Car: movement*
Props: Here is a toy car.

*Everyday.* Now what if I took this car and pushed it across the table. Could I move the car like that or would it be magic?

*Magical.* Now what if the car started moving across the table all by itself. Could the car move all by itself like that or would it be magic?

*Wood: change of identity*
Props: Here is some wood.

*Everyday.* Now what if I cut the wood and made a box with it. Could I make box by cutting it like that or would it be magic?

*Magical.* Now what if the wood cut itself and made a box all by itself. Could the wood make a box by cutting itself like that or would it be magic?

*Dirt on cup: disappearance*
Props: Here's some dirt on a cup.

*Everyday.* Now what if I got a towel and rubbed the cup and made the dirt go away. Could I make the dirt go away by rubbing it like that or would it be magic?

*Magical.* Now what if the dirt went away all by itself. Could the dirt really go away by itself like that or would it be magic?

*Paints: creation*
Props: Here's some paper.

*Everyday.* Now what if I got some paints and made a painting on the paper. Could I really make a painting on the paper like that or would it be magic?

*Magical.* Now what if a painting came onto the paper all by itself. Could a painting really come onto the paper all by itself like that or would it be magic?

## Appendix 2: Pre-training items for Experiment 2

1 "One day a little frog was sitting by the water and all of a sudden the frog turned into a prince. Who made him turn into a prince? Was it Magic Fairy or Jack?"

2 "One day a little frog was sitting by the water and someone caught him

with their hands. Who caught him with their hands? Was it Magic Fairy or Jack?"

3 "One day somebody made a wish and turned a pine cone into a real live kitty. Who turned a pine cone into a real live kitty? Was it Magic Fairy or was it Jack?"

4 "One day somebody petted a real live kitty. Who petted a real live kitty? Was it Magic Fairy or Jack?"

## Appendix 3: Test items for Experiment 2

1 Items involving a spontaneous change
   *Two toy cars: movement*
      One day, Jack and Magic Fairy had two toy cars. One of them made their car go across the floor all by itself without pushing it; the other pushed their car across the floor. Who made the car go across the floor all by itself, without pushing it? Who pushed the car across the floor?
   *Two piles of blocks: change of identity*
      One day, Jack and Magic Fairy had two piles of blocks like these. One of them made their pile into a little house without touching the blocks; the other one picked up their blocks and built a little house. Who made the blocks turn into a house without touching them? Who picked up the blocks and made a house?
   *Two candies: disappearance*
      One day, Jack and Magic Fairy had two candies like these. One of them made their candy disappear without touching it; the other one picked up their candy and ate it. Who made the candy disappear without touching it? Who picked up the candy and ate it?
   *Pencils: creation*
      One day, Jack and Magic Fairy had two pencils like these. One of them made the pencil draw all by itself without touching it; the other one picked up a pencil and used it to make a drawing. Who made the pencil draw all by itself? Who picked up the pencil and made the drawing?
2 Items involving a wish/command
   *Two dishes: movement*
      One day, Jack and Magic Fairy finished their snack and were supposed to take their dishes into the kitchen. One of them picked up their dish and took it into the kitchen; the other said, "Dish go" and the dish went into the kitchen all by itself. Who picked up their dish and took it to the kitchen? Who said, "Dish go" and made their dish go to the kitchen all by itself?
   *Two balls of Play-Doh: change of identity*
      One day, Jack and Magic Fairy had two balls of Play-Doh like these. One of them rolled the Play-Doh with their hands into a hot-dog shape; the other said, "Hot dog, hot dog" and made the Play-Doh turn into a

hot-dog shape without touching it. Who made the hot-dog shape by using their hands to roll the Play-Doh? Who made a hot-dog shape by saying, "Hot dog, hot dog"?

*Two dirty cups: disappearance*

One day, Jack and Magic Fairy had two dirty cups like these. One of them got a sponge and washed their cup and made it all clean; the other one made a wish and cleaned their cup without touching it. Who cleaned their cup with a sponge? Who cleaned their cup by wishing it clean?

*Drawing paper: creation*

One day, Jack and Magic Fairy had two pieces of paper like these. One of them got a brush, some paint and painted a picture; the other one made a wish and a picture popped onto the paper all by itself. Who made the picture by painting it? Who made the picture by wishing it?

# Chapter 13

# Conditional reasoning with false premises

## Fantasy and information retrieval

*Henry Markovits*

Previous studies (Dias and Harris 1988, 1990; Markovits and Vachon 1989) have established that young children can correctly respond to certain conditional reasoning problems with empirically false premises, when these are presented in a fantasy context. Such results have been interpreted as indicating that young children possess logical reasoning competence which must be protected from interference with their empirical knowledge. However, Markovits (1993) has proposed a model of reasoning in which context effects are considered in the light of both developmental and information retrieval processes. This predicts that presenting empirically false premises in a fantasy context should improve performance on the valid logical form *modus ponens* among young adolescents. It also predicts that presenting empirically true premises in a fantasy context should decrease performance on the invalid logical form affirmation of the consequent. A total of 89 12-year-olds and 117 14-year-olds were given two reasoning problems involving either true or false premises. These problems were embedded in either a fantasy or a realistic context. Results were consistent with the predictions made by the model.

Logical reasoning with premises that are empirically false is one of the prototypical examples of hypothetico-deductive reasoning, and is a key component of reasoning competence. Accounting for this kind of reasoning must be a critical aspect of any theory of reasoning. This is particularly interesting since the tension between empirical knowledge and logical principles is a key point in the development of logical reasoning abilities (Markovits and Bouffard-Bouchard 1992; Moshman and Franks 1986). Some recent work has permitted a better idea of how both children and adolescents perform on conditional reasoning problems with premises that are empirically false.

Conditional reasoning involves reasoning on the basis of some given "if then" relation. It is the cornerstone of deductive reasoning and is probably the form that has been the most intensively studied in the psychological literature. Basic conditional reasoning involves four logical forms. *Modus ponens* is the logical principle that involves reasoning with the premises "P implies Q, P is true" and leads to the logically correct conclusion "Q is true". *Modus tollens* involves reasoning with the premises "P implies Q, Q is false" and leads to the logically correct conclusion "P is false". These two are valid logical forms, since they both lead to a single, logically correct conclusion. Affirmation of the consequent involves reasoning with the premises "P implies Q, Q is true". Denial of the antecedent involves reasoning with the premises "P implies Q, P is false". Neither of these forms leads to a single, logically correct conclusion. They are thus invalid logical forms.

The data on conditional reasoning with empirically false premises concern reasoning with both valid and with invalid forms. Several studies have examined young children's ability correctly to resolve simple valid forms with false premises. Hawkins, Pea, Glick and Scribner (1984) found that 5-year-olds had a strong tendency to make what Markovits and Vachon (1989) subsequently referred to as "inversion" errors. This kind of error involves reasoning of the following kind:

If it rains, then the street will become dry.
It is raining.
The street will become wet.

This type of error indicates that the reasoner has difficulties in accepting empirically false premises without interference from their real-world knowledge. Such errors occur both with young children (Dias and Harris 1988; Hawkins *et al.* 1984) and adolescents (Markovits and Vachon 1989). Of critical importance in this context are studies (Dias and Harris 1988, 1990; Markovits and Vachon 1989) that show that young children make many fewer inversion errors on valid logical forms when empirically false conditionals are presented verbally in a fantasy context that has concrete support.

One approach to understanding these results would claim that the basic competence required for logical reasoning is present in both children and adolescents, but that the expression of this competence is interfered with when subjects' empirical or pragmatic knowledge is accessed, leading to the kinds of erroneous responses found with false premises in realistic context. This is the point of view of Hawkins *et al.* (1984) and of Dias and Harris (1988, 1990). It also corresponds (at least in a general sense) to Braine's analysis of conditional reasoning in which factors such as invited inferences, which are a form of pragmatic knowledge, are used to explain reasoning errors in children who are assumed to possess at least basic inference schemas (Braine 1990; Rumain, Connell and Braine 1983). This general approach would then assume that presenting reasoning problems in a fantasy context would serve to insulate the reasoning process from interference and facilitate use of existing logical competence. It would thus predict that presenting empirically false conditionals, of the kind referred to above, in a fantasy context would result in generally more "logical" reasoning.

This general approach to reasoning and context implies the existence of a clear division between reasoning competence and contextual factors which may globally promote or hinder the expression of this competence. However, there is evidence that reasoning and context may not be as independent as this view would assume. One way of understanding this interdependence is based on a model of conditional reasoning (Markovits 1988; Markovits and Vachon 1989, 1990) that combines both a Piagetian developmental approach with an information processing model (Johnson-Laird's, 1983, mental models). In a recent article (Markovits 1993), the current author has presented this model in detail, including a complete description of the analysis of reasoning with false premises. The following provides a résumé of the critical arguments.

Briefly, this model assumes that reasoners construct an initial mental model of the major premises of a reasoning problem and then add in the information contained in the minor premise in order to generate possible conclusions. A critical aspect of how conditional reasoning problems are treated involves the kind of model that is generated of conditional premises of the form "if P then Q". For example; consider the conditional relation "If a rock is thrown in a window, then the window will break". An *incomplete* model of this relation would involve only the elements directly represented in the premise:

rock thrown in window – window broken

Subjects starting with this model would respond correctly to the valid forms *modus ponens* and *modus tollens*. However, they would respond incorrectly to the invalid forms, affirmation of the consequent and negation of the antecedent. For example, if given the minor premise "the window is broken", the above model would provide the unique conclusion that a rock was thrown through the window (a commonly found biconditional error to affirmation of the consequent).

A *complete* model of the conditional relation would incorporate at least one other alternative of the form "if A then Q", in the following manner:

chair thrown at window – window broken
rock thrown at window – window broken

A subject starting with this model could correctly respond to both the valid and the invalid forms. For example, if given the minor premise "the window is broken", the above model could provide the logically valid conclusion that "it is not certain that a rock was thrown into the window", since it also provides for the possibility that the window was broken because a chair was thrown into it.

Now, there is evidence that, among adolescents, generation of a complete model depends on subjects' retrieval of appropriate real-world knowledge (Cummins, Lubart, Alksnis and Rist 1991; Markovits and Vachon 1990). The probability of correctly responding to the invalid logical forms varies with the degree of access to this knowledge. How would this analysis be applied to reasoning of the kind that has been discussed here? The first assumption is that, if less competent reasoners are presented with a relation of the kind "if a feather is thrown through a window, the window will break", they will tend to spontaneously incorporate into their model of this relation their knowledge about the real world, as follows:

feather thrown into a window – window not broken
feather thrown into a window – window broken

Presented with a minor premise such as "a feather is thrown into a window", they will tend to respond about half of the time that "the window will not break", which corresponds reasonably well to previous empirical results. For example, Dias and Harris (1988) found a 44 per cent rate of such inversion responses to *modus ponens* on verbally presented problems in a concrete context with 4-year-olds, and Markovits and Vachon (1990) found a 37 per cent inversion rate with 10-year-olds with written problems. A fantasy context would act as a cognitive filter reducing access to real-world knowledge (and to subject's long-term memory [LTM]) and thus reduce the probability of a factually correct, but logically inconsistent, relation being incorporated into the model. This would reduce the number of inversion responses and improve performance on the valid logical forms, which corresponds to the obtained results with very young children using concrete situations and verbal presentation of premises. Young adolescents who are beginning to reason on a more abstract level (Markovits and Vachon 1990) also produce inversion responses to reasoning problems with false premises, when these are presented without any concrete support (Markovits and Vachon 1989). Embedding these problems in a fantasy context should decrease inversion responses compared with a realistic context.

However, this model also provides for a much more interesting and somewhat counter-intuitive prediction. Suppose that an empirically true premise is presented in a fantasy context. According to our basic hypothesis, the fantasy context would act as a cognitive filter reducing access to LTM. Access to LTM is required to generate appropriate alternative relations in order to produce a complete model of the major premises. Therefore, presenting a conditional reasoning problem with factually true premises in a fantasy context should reduce the number of correct responses to the invalid forms, as compared with a realistic context.

The present study examined the performance of adolescents aged 12 and 14 (who are in the first and third years of Quebec high school, respectively) on conditional reasoning problems presented in either a realistic or a fantasy context. This is a critical age level for reasoning of this kind since previous results (Markovits and Vachon 1989) indicate that these subjects are both prone to making spontaneously a certain number of inversion errors and are also beginning to respond spontaneously correctly to invalid logical forms on reasoning problems that are presented with no concrete support. Specifically, performance on the valid form *modus ponens* and the invalid form affirmation of the consequent will be looked at. These two forms were chosen because the two negative logical forms, *modus tollens* and negation of the antecedent, present somewhat complicated patterns. In addition, pre-testing suggested that the efficacy of context may diminish if too many problems are presented. It was decided to limit the logical forms to the two most likely to provide a clear measure of the predicted effects.

## METHOD

### Subjects

A total of 197 subjects at high school level were examined. Of these, 89 (average age = 143 months: 44 girls, 45 boys) were in Secondary 1, and 108 (average age = 165 months: 49 girls, 59 boys) were in Secondary 3. The subjects were native French speakers and were students at a private college.

### Materials and procedure

Eight test booklets each containing two conditional reasoning problems were constructed. The initial page of each booklet contained the following instruction: "For each of the following pages, read the story carefully and answer the question by checking off the correct answer at the bottom of the page. FOR EACH STORY, YOU MUST SUPPOSE THAT EVERY-THING THAT IS WRITTEN IS TRUE." On the second page a short story was presented in which a conditional relation of the form "If *P* then *Q*" was followed by a question corresponding to *modus ponens*. On the third page of the booklet a different story was presented followed by a question corresponding to affirmation of the consequent.

The conditional relations were either factually true or factually false (the ones used here were adapted from Markovits and Vachon 1989). In order to minimize the possible effects of content variations, the true and false premises had identical consequents and only the antecedents were changed.

The two true conditions used here were:

(1) If one hits glass with a rock, the glass will break.
(2) If one soaks a sweater in soapy water, the sweater will become clean.

The two false conditionals were:

(1) If one hits glass with a feather, the glass will break.
(2) If one soaks a sweater in mud, the sweater will become clean.

Four stories were used in this study. Two of these described a realistic context and two of them described a fantasy context. The first of the realistic contexts was the following:

Francine has just dirtied her new sweater. She would like it to be clean so that she can wear it tonight. However, she doesn't know how to go about doing this or what products to use. In order to get some clear information, she phones Mr Whitecity who is an expert in cleaning. Mr Whitecity gives Francine a book which describes how to clean different kinds of things. In this book is written that it is absolutely certain that IF ONE SOAKS A SWEATER IN SOAPY WATER, THE SWEATER WILL BECOME CLEAN.

Note that when the false premise is presented the final sentence would read: IF ONE SOAKS A SWEATER IN MUD, THE SWEATER WILL BECOME CLEAN.

The corresponding fantasy version is the following:

Imagine that a witch has opened a recreation centre for children. Jules goes there. At the entrance, he wiggles his nose and OUF! here he is in a mysterious world. While going through this new world, Jules sees wizards that are walking around upside down. Super! Jules says a magic formula so that he can walk around in the same way. But he made a mistake. Balls of greyish water are thrown on his brand new clean sweater. Jules would like it to be as clean as before. He doesn't know how to clean the sweater. Jules calls on a wizard who is an expert in cleaning. The wizard tells him that it is absolutely certain that IF ONE SOAKS A SWEATER IN SOAPY WATER, THE SWEATER WILL BECOME CLEAN.

The second realistic context was:

Today, Jacques had a class outing. His teacher took him to visit a factory where they make windows. This was the first time that Jacques saw how glass was produced and he was very attentive to the teacher's explanations. An employee of the factory explained in detail how they make windows. He gave Jacques a sheet of paper on which was written the characteristics of the glass used to make windows. On this sheet was written, among other things, that it is absolutely certain that IF ONE HITS GLASS WITH A ROCK THE GLASS WILL BREAK.

Note that when the false premise is presented the final sentence would read: IF ONE HITS GLASS WITH A FEATHER, THE GLASS WILL BREAK.

The corresponding fantasy context is:

Imagine that Julie is playing with a new video game. She pushes the start button and POUF! she finds herself inside the game. Julie is now the new hero of the game and she must go out and battle against the enemy. She looks around her for a spaceship and she sees a man who is floating on a cloud while walking on his hands. On his feet, he has a huge hat. He explains to Julie that the spaceship that she must use for her mission is underneath a blue tree. He also gives her some advice about her mission against the enemy. He tells her that it is absolutely certain that IF ONE HITS GLASS WITH A ROCK, THE GLASS WILL BREAK.

At the end of each context, a statement is added to the effect that either the antecedent (for *modus ponens*) or the consequent (for affirmation of the consequent) is true. Subjects are then presented with three possible responses as to the inference that can be made and asked to choose the correct answer. For example, in the case of the first realistic context for *modus ponens*, this was done by adding to the context the following:

Later on, you see Francine who is soaking her sweater in soapy water. You can say:

(a) that it is certain that her sweater will become clean.
(b) that it is certain that her sweater will not become clean.
(c) that it is not certain whether her sweater will become clean or not.

Each test booklet contained two problems: the first always corresponded to *modus ponens*, while the second always corresponded to affirmation of the consequent. A first version was formed by combining realistic contexts with true premises. The second was formed by combining realistic contexts with false premises. The third contained fantasy contexts with true premises, while the fourth contained fantasy contexts with false premises. Within each of the four types of booklet, the two contexts were systematically interchanged (but not the logical forms), leading to eight versions in all.

## RESULTS

Table 13.1 presents the proportion of the various responses to *modus ponens* and to affirmation of the consequent as a function of the type of major premise (true or false), context (fantasy or realistic) and age.

*Table 13.1* Percentage of the various responses to *modus ponens* (MP) and to affirmation of the consequent (AC) as a function of the type of premise (true or false), context (realistic or fantasy), and age

| Logical form | Age | Response | True premise | | False premise | |
|---|---|---|---|---|---|---|
| | | | Realistic | Fantasy | Realistic | Fantasy |
| | | | (N=23) | (N=21) | (N=23) | (N=22) |
| MP | 12 | 'Q is true' | 60.8 | 71.4 | 39.1 | 68.1 |
| | | 'Q is false' | 4.3 | 0.0 | 43.4 | 13.6 |
| | | Uncertain | 34.7 | 28.5 | 17.3 | 18.1 |
| | | | (N=21) | (N=25) | (N=32) | (N=30) |
| | 14 | 'Q is true' | 80.9 | 84.0 | 46.8 | 50.0 |
| | | 'Q is false' | 0.0 | 4.0 | 31.2 | 13.3 |
| | | Uncertain | 19.0 | 12.0 | 21.8 | 36.6 |
| | | | (N=23) | (N=21) | (N=23) | (N=22) |
| AC | 12 | 'P is true' | 39.1 | 52.3 | 34.7 | 68.1 |
| | | 'P is false' | 4.3 | 9.5 | 43.4 | 13.6 |
| | | Uncertain | 56.5 | 38.0 | 21.7 | 18.1 |
| | | | (N=21) | (N=25) | (N=32) | (N=30) |
| | 14 | 'P is true' | 23.8 | 52.0 | 12.5 | 43.3 |
| | | 'P is false' | 0.0 | 4.0 | 31.2 | 6.7 |
| | | Uncertain | 76.1 | 44.0 | 56.2 | 50.0 |

## Inversion responses

The first major hypothesis makes specific predictions about the relative number of inversion responses with false premises in fantasy and realistic contexts. In order to examine this, a three-way ANOVA with the production (or not) of an incorrect inversion response (i.e. "Q is false") to *modus ponens* as dependent variable and age, premise type and context as independent variables was performed. This indicated significant main effects for premise type ($F(1,189) = 23.81$, $p < .0001$) and context ($F(1,189) = 7.68$, $p < .01$) and a significant premise type $\times$ context interaction ($F(1,189) = 6.20$, $p < .02$). There were more inversions produced overall with false than with true premises and more inversions produced in the real than in the fantasy context. A Newman–Keuls procedure with $p = .05$ was used for *post hoc* analyses of the premise type $\times$ context interactions. This indicated that, as predicted, there were significantly more inversions with false premises in the realistic context than in the fantasy context, while no such difference was found with the true premises (due to the fact that there were almost no inversions produced with the latter). These results indicate that embedding false premises in a written fantasy context without concrete support does reduce inversions and thus reduces interference between logical reasoning and empirical knowledge in young adolescents.

## Uncertainty responses

The second hypothesis predicts that there should be a relative decrease in correct uncertainty responses to affirmation of the consequent with true premises when these are embedded in a fantasy context as compared to a realistic context. In order to examine this, a three-way ANOVA with the production (or not) of an uncertainty response to affirmation of the consequent as dependent variable and age, premise type and context as independent variables was performed. This indicated significant main effects for age ($F(1,189) = 10.20$, $p < .002$), premise type ($F(1,189) = 5.56$, $p < .02$) and context ($F(1,189) = 4.42$, $p < .04$). More uncertainty responses were produced by the older than by the younger subjects. In addition, more uncertainty responses were produced in the realistic than in the fantasy context, and more with true than with false premises. Thus, these results confirm the hypothesis that embedding premises in a fantasy context reduces production of correct uncertainty responses to affirmation of the consequent. Although the corresponding interaction term was not statistically significant ($F(1,189) = 2.31$, $p < .13$) inspection of the data suggests that this effect tended to be greater with true than with false premises.

There is, however, one factor that could affect the interpretation of these results. The theoretical analysis presented in support of these hypotheses assumed that a fantasy context should act as a cognitive filter by reducing access to LTM. However, as a reviewer has pointed out, embedding premises in a fantasy context might also have the effect of reducing the likelihood of subjects accepting the premises as true since, in the contexts used here, everyday "facts" are often contradicted. If such a factor does operate, then it should be visible in performance on *modus ponens*, for which an uncertainty response is not correct. In fact, examination of Table 13.1 does indicate a tendency to give uncertainty responses to *modus ponens*, although there is no indication that this is context dependent (none of the differences between realistic and fantasy contexts are statistically significant). Thus, there is no clear evidence that fantasy differentially affects subjects' tendencies to accept premises as a basis for reasoning.

Nonetheless, a second analysis examined uncertainty responses to affirmation of the consequent as a function of response to *modus ponens*. More specifically, in order to eliminate any possible effects of a tendency to give uncertainty responses, the proportion of correct uncertainty responses to affirmation of the consequent was examined for those subjects who gave the logically correct response to *modus ponens*. This is shown in Table 13.2. Although this reduces the subject base for comparison, inspection of this table indicates that the pattern of results is similar to that previously obtained. A three-way ANOVA with the production (or not) of an uncertainty response to affirmation of the consequent as dependent variable and

*Table 13.2* Percentage of uncertainty responses to affirmation of the consequent for subjects who gave a correct response to *modus ponens*
as a function of type of premise (true or false), context (realistic or
fantasy) and age

| Age | True premise | | False premise | |
|---|---|---|---|---|
| | *Realistic* | *Fantasy* | *Realistic* | *Fantasy* |
| 12 | 42.9 (14) | 26.7 (15) | 22.2 (9) | 13.1 (15) |
| 14 | 76.5 (17) | 47.6 (21) | 66.7 (15) | 53.3 (15) |

*Note*: Total number of subjects is shown in parentheses.

age, premise type and context as independent variables was performed.
This indicated significant main effects for age ($F(1,113) = 15.44$, $p < .001$)
and context ($F(1,113) = 4.78$, $p < .03$). More uncertainty responses were
produced by the older than by the younger subjects. In addition, more
uncertainty responses were produced in the realistic than in the fantasy
context. These results support the hypothesis that fantasy does (among
other effects) inhibit production of correct uncertainty responses to affirmation of the consequent, even among subjects who respond correctly to
*modus ponens*.

## DISCUSSION

These results generally confirm the two specific hypotheses. First, presenting written conditional reasoning problems involving empirically false
premises in a fantasy context reduces interference from empirical knowledge that results in inversion responses of the kind "If it rains, then the
street will be dry. It has rained, thus the street will be wet". Previous results
have shown that very young children, who make this kind of error with
concrete, verbally presented premises, do not do so when given the
premises in a fantasy context (Dias and Harris 1988, 1990; Markovits
and Vachon 1990). Young adolescents of the age examined here make
similar inversion errors with written premises (Markovits and Vachon
1990), and these results indicate that embedding false premises in a
(written) fantasy context can insulate them from interference by empirical
knowledge in the same way as has been found with young children using
more concrete methods. However, these and previous results have also
shown that 12- and 14-year-olds are also beginning to respond to invalid
logical form affirmation of the consequent with the correct response of
uncertainty. The results of this study also show that embedding premises in
a fantasy context reduces the related proportion of correct uncertainty
responses to affirmation of the consequent produced by subjects, even
when an explicit correction is made for more generalized context effects.

Thus, while the insulating effect of fantasy diminishes inversion errors, it simultaneously decreases the probability of correctly responding to invalid logical forms.

It must be noted that the effect of fantasy found here relied on the creation of a strange other-world context. This is consistent with results obtained by Hawkins *et al.* (1984) and Markovits and Vachon (1989) with young children. There is a question as to whether the obtained results are due specifically to this form of context or to a more general factor, as found by Dias and Harris (1988, 1990). The latter results seem to indicate that, with young children, the effects of material presentation can be understood as being mainly due to induction of a "make-believe" attitude that enables children to accept contrary-to-fact premises as a basis for deduction. The fantasy context used here had the same enabling effect on young adolescents, and it seems reasonable to assume that the same basic mechanism is responsible, although possibly at another level of reasoning. The question of the specificity of the context is important in another way. A reviewer has suggested that the reduction in uncertainty responses found with the fantasy context may be due to subjects' considering that in a strange world only data that are explicitly given (i.e. the specific premises) can be considered relevant. This would result in a biconditional interpretation of the premises that could account for the observed differences. A critical point is whether such a biconditional interpretation involves reduced access to real-world information (as would be claimed here) or whether it can be understood as an overall effect of context on logical rule selection (biconditional or conditional). While the latter interpretation cannot be ruled out, it is inconsistent with previously cited data (Cummins *et al.* 1991; Markovits and Vachon 1990) that indicate that access to real-world knowledge accounts for content differences in biconditional responding with true premises. It is also not clear how such an explanation would account for the developmental decrease in biconditional responding found here across both realistic and fantasy contexts, since it would postulate essentially different types of processes in the differing contexts.

These results are thus consistent with the notion that understanding the interaction between reasoning and context cannot be done in a global manner. The effect of context can be usefully analysed within a framework of information retrieval and specific real-time procedures. More specifically, this permits a clearer understanding of the cognitive problems posed by reasoning with empirically false premises. The initial difficulty that confronts a reasoner involves representing the premises without interference from their knowledge about the real world. This requires that the subject construct an internal model that does not include information resident in LTM that contradicts the (empirically false) premises. Failure to do so results in a high level of inversion responses of the form "If it rains, then the street will be dry. It rains, thus the street will be wet".

Insulating the process of model construction from LTM can be done either by embedding the premises in a fantasy (or possibly other kinds of) context, or spontaneously by the subject (possibly by adopting an appropriate mind-set). In fact, the progressive decrease in the production of inversion responses to false premises presented in isolation (Markovits and Vachon 1989) suggests an increasing ability in early adolescence to filter access to LTM during the process of model construction.

The necessity of limiting access to LTM during construction of a model of given (empirically false) premises is important in order to eliminate interference from the subject's real-world knowledge. However, knowledge stored in LTM also permits an understanding of the nature of the invalid logical forms. Specifically, given the problem "If it rains, then the street will be dry. The street is dry", subjects appear to arrive at an uncertain response ("It may or may not have rained") by generating examples of the sort "If it is sunny, then the street will be dry" (Cummins *et al.* 1991; Markovits and Vachon 1990). Insulating model construction from LTM would at the same time limit access to information critical to understanding the uncertainty of the invalid logical forms. This analysis is consistent with the effects of fantasy on responding to affirmation of the consequent with true premises observed in this study. It is also consistent with the observation in this study and in a previous one (Markovits and Vachon 1989) that performance on the invalid forms is generally lower with false than with true premises. In the case of empirically false premises, the subject must spontaneously limit access to LTM during model construction, and this would simultaneously tend to reduce access to information required to respond with uncertainty to the invalid forms.

Thus, with empirically false premises, easy access to LTM is at the same time helpful and harmful at different stages of the reasoning process. It is this tension between the need to prevent interference between empirical knowledge and premises and the need to use empirical knowledge in the reasoning process that creates the developmental pattern found in young adolescents.

The results of this study permit an extension of the positive effects of fantasy on reasoning with false premises to adolescents. They also support the model insofar as this effect is coupled with a decrease in correct responding to the invalid forms. It is important to note that demonstrating the latter effect requires that subjects have the ability to respond correctly to the invalid logical forms on true premises to a sufficient extent (Markovits and Vachon 1989). This has not been shown with younger subjects. The question of whether pre-adolescents can spontaneously respond correctly to the invalid forms and, if so, under what conditions, remains open. The developmental model that I have presented (Markovits 1993) claims that young children should be able to respond correctly to the invalid logical forms if these are presented with content that allows ready access to specific concrete counter-examples. Any extension of the present results to younger children's reasoning requires verification of this claim, and this is in fact the subject of a subsequent study.

## ACKNOWLEDGEMENTS

Preparation of this manuscript was supported by grants from the National Science and Engineering Council of Canada (NSERC) and from the Fonds pour la Formation de Chercheurs et l'Aide à la Recherche (FCAR). I would like to thank the students and staff of the Collège Stanislaus for their participation in this study. I would also like to thank Guilaine Nantel, Nadia Pion and François Lemaître for help with construction of the materials and data collection.

## REFERENCES

Braine, M.D.S. (1990) "The natural logic approach to reasoning", in W.F. Overton (ed.) *Reasoning, necessity, and logic: Developmental perspectives*, Hillsdale, NJ: Erlbaum.

Cummins, D.D., Lubart, T., Alksnis, O. and Rist, R. (1991) "Conditional reasoning and causation", *Memory and Cognition* 19: 274–282.

Dias, M.G. and Harris, P.L. (1988) "The effect of make-believe play on deductive reasoning", *British Journal of Developmental Psychology* 6: 207–221.

Dias, M.G. and Harris, P.L. (1990) "The influence of the imagination on reasoning", *British Journal of Developmental Psychology* 8: 305–318.

Hawkins, J., Pea, R.D., Glick, J. and Scribner, S. (1984) " 'Merds that laugh don't like mushrooms': Evidence for deductive reasoning by preschoolers", *Developmental Psychology* 20: 584–594.

Johnson-Laird, P.N. (1983) *Mental models*, Cambridge: Harvard University Press.

Markovits, H. (1988) "Conditional reasoning, representation, and empirical evidence on a concrete task", *Quarterly Journal of Experimental Psychology* 40A: 483–495.

Markovits, H. (1993) "The development of conditional reasoning: A Piagetian reformulation of mental models theory", *Merrill-Palmer Quarterly* 39: 133–160.

Markovits, H. and Bouffard-Bouchard, T. (1992) "The belief-bias effect in reasoning: The development and activation of competence", *British Journal of Developmental Psychology* 10: 269–284.

Markovits, H. and Vachon, R. (1989) "Reasoning with contrary-to-fact propositions", *Journal of Experimental Child Psychology* 47: 398–412.

Markovits, H. and Vachon, R. (1990) "Conditional reasoning, representation, and level of abstraction", *Developmental Psychology* 26: 942–951.

Moshman, D. and Franks, B.A. (1986) "Development of the concept of inferential validity", *Child Development* 57: 153–165.

Overton, W.F. (1990) "Competence and procedures: Constraints on the development of logical reasoning", in W.F. Overton (ed.) *Reasoning, necessity and logic: Developmental perspectives* (pp. 1–34), Hillsdale, NJ: Erlbaum.

Rumain, B., Connell, J. and Braine, M.D.S. (1983) "Conversational comprehension processes are responsible for reasoning fallacies in children as well as adults", *Developmental Psychology* 19: 471–481.

# Chapter 14

# The ontology of order[1]

## Brendan McGonigle and Margaret Chalmers

## INTRODUCTION

Our general aims are to contribute to a characterisation of intelligent systems from an ontological perspective afforded by systems theory and by our cognitive research programme at Edinburgh which has featured human and non-human primate investigations into what many have regarded as core cognitive competences *viz.* relational learning (Bryant 1974; Lawrenson and Bryant 1972; McGonigle and Jones 1978; Reese 1968), transitivity (Bryant and Trabasso 1971; Halford 1993; Inhelder and Piaget 1964; McGonigle and Chalmers 1977; Trabasso 1977), and ordering skills (Lashley 1960; Terrace and McGonigle 1994). As a logical extension, the programme has more recently extended into cognitive modelling (e.g. Harris and McGonigle 1994) and robotics (McGonigle 1990). In this we have taken the view that good characterisations of complex intelligent systems in particular should lead to testable designs for artificial agents (Donnett and McGonigle 1991; Nehmzow and McGonigle 1993). However, the flow is not one way: instead it is becoming more and more apparent that a symbiotic relationship between research on real and artificially intelligent systems is the most fruitful way forward – a domain which we would term *synthetic* intelligence.

From this standpoint McGonigle and Chalmers (1995a) have recently argued that truly complex behaviour, regulated autonomously by the agent, cannot be installed in an artificial agent, only its pre-conditions. In common with complex biological agents, artificially intelligent agents will need prolonged periods of everyday problem solving to promote cognitive growth. In this, complex systems differ from simple reactive agents whose behaviours are already well engineered by evolution. This should not be taken to imply, however, that complex systems are less well endowed by their evolutionary heritage. On the contrary, as argued by McGonigle and Chalmers (1995a), for example, the more complex the species, the *richer and more resourceful* are its lower ontological bounds. In short, there is arguably a strong positive correlation between the affluence of the wetware and the space of possibilities for individual development. The simpler the agent in design terms, on the other hand, the less potential it has for knowledge gain and the less autonomy it will achieve as a consequence. However, adaptive resource does not appear to vary in quantitative terms only. Simpler biological systems appear to regulate their affairs by means of reflex, cybernetic-like mechanisms based on a tight coupling between input and output. In complex biological agents, whilst many behaviours are organised this way, other key adaptive behaviours are exhibited where this principle of tight coupling is breached. In these circumstances, as T. C. Schneirla pointed out many years ago, there is utterly no point in attempting to explain such complex behaviours as an emergent phenomenon of populations of basic reflexes. As robotics is now illustrating very clearly, tightly coupled behaviours are very useful in a variety of circumstances, but they are not the basic building blocks of complex systems, more what McGonigle (1990) has described as "first strike" behaviours, a preamble only to later development. The latter process is not, nevertheless, a matter of "learning" *per se*. As Lashley (1960) pointed out, learning enters the evolutionary process early; however, what really counts is *what* is learnt. Here, much will depend on the nature of the design or system primitives themselves as part of the agent's adaptive resource. In the case of simple learning by association, based on spatial and temporal contiguity, evolution appears to have discovered a simple, useful constraint by keeping the inductive space as small as possible. Few irrelevant events can distract from any contingency based solely on the very short (optimal) time and space intervals involved in connecting stimulus and stimulus and stimulus and response. Just as crucially, given that such bonds between objects or events are based on the frequency of such co-occurrences, their material relationships can be quite *arbitrary*. However, as we shall argue in this chapter, a significant evolutionary and epistemological advance comes from the perception of material relationships between objects. In a critical sense it is *necessary* knowledge at its most fundamental, conceived here as the grasp of at least some of the connectives between objects in the world which enforce non-arbitrary consequences on the agent. This does not, of course, imply an immediate awareness of entailment and "truth", but it provides, we argue, an important layer of adaptation and assimilation of world knowledge which entrains a cognitive growth profile quite unlike that based on associative and arbitrary connectives alone (Terrace and McGonigle 1994).

Finding the primitives to flesh out the ontological floor of a given system has been by no means easy, however. A good example of this can be seen in the long history of comparative, developmental, and linguistically based approaches to the vexed issues inherent in our understanding of relational competences – a qualitative move away from arbitrary associationism – and expressed in language through the acquisition of comparative terms such as e.g. "bigger" and "smaller" etc. (Kuenne 1946; Reese 1968;

Bryant 1974). However, it is clear that important species' differences centre on precisely this layer of competence. As Herrnstein (1989) has pointed out:

> abstract relations differentiate most sharply among animals. It has been noted that we see the largest gaps in comparative performance at the level of abstract relations. It may not be surprising that the means for dealing with just the transient contingencies of reinforcement has had lower evolutionary priority than the means for the enduring ones represented by concepts or by open-ended categories. But once a species has a foothold at the level of abstract relations, the possibilities are unbounded.

In this chapter we shall review some of the comparative and developmental work carried out in our lab programme at Edinburgh, since 1969, designed to uncover the roots of such relational competences in monkeys and children, their implications for transitivity, seriation and classification in particular, and for cognitive growth in general.

## THE EMPIRICAL PROGRAMME

### Simple relational competences

Our work in this context began in earnest in 1970 when McGonigle and Jones (1975, 1978) investigated the relational competences of squirrel monkeys (*Saimiri scuireus*). Unlike the traditional one-step transposition paradigms which had until then yielded nothing but ambiguous results (Reese 1968), McGonigle and Jones used a training approach where one group of monkeys was first required to choose the larger of two stimuli so that given two pairs, AB and BC, B was chosen over A, and C was chosen over B. A second group was first required to choose B within both pairs. A long series of training episodes and transfer evaluations followed, both for size and for brightness relata (McGonigle and Jones 1978). The results were striking: in the simple relational (larger than) condition subjects consistently outperformed those who had either to conserve an absolute size value or solve by means of a rule for the "middle" relation. In fact, the performance of the relational monkeys was so robust that they resisted a whole host of stimulus transformations including a complete change of context (the stimuli were viewed in the dark and were self-illuminated) which perturbed the other encoding conditions run for comparison. So robust was the performance, and not merely superior to the others, that McGonigle and Jones (1978) interpreted the code as a primitive, not reducible to lower levels of processing, at least for squirrel monkeys. The profile for brightness was broadly similar.

Naturally at that time we were keen to pursue other aspects of relational

competence. An obvious extension was the relationship between the relations themselves and the part these played in important cognitive ordering
competences such as seriation. In the case of size relations, for example,
what is the natural order or "syntax" of relational acquisition? And is the
relation "bigger than" more fundamental than its inverse as suggested by
the lexical marking effects found in natural language (Clark 1969; Clark,
Carpenter and Just, 1973)? Would the "middle" rule be learnt by monkeys
only after they had mastered the basic comparatives? And if a "middle"
rule of relation was achieved, could monkeys seriate size as children do
(Inhelder and Piaget 1964)? Initially, production problems stood in the
way. Monkeys cannot manipulate blocks precisely enough to qualify for
the sorts of seriation tasks first developed by Inhelder and Piaget. However,
using a conditional rule-based technique, we were able to train monkeys to
solve a multiple size problem, initially with a test set of three objects; using
the "bigger than" rule, when the objects were all black, a "smaller than"
one when they were all white, and the "middle" one when they were all
red. In these initial phases, an effect similar to the lexical marking effect
was found (McGonigle and Chalmers 1980, 1986) reflecting a consistent
asymmetry between performance on the "bigger than" *versus* the "smaller
than" relational codes. Of significance also, were some of the selective
congruity effects we recorded. As reported for human subjects by Banks
(1977), we found that the fastest "bigger than" judgements were made
with the biggest stimuli in the set ("bigger" of the big stimuli was faster
than "bigger" of the small stimuli). However, the congruity effect was
asymmetrical: choosing the smaller of "big" items was also faster than the
"smaller" judgements for "small" items, indicating some derivation of the
inverse from the endpoint of the series representing "most" (bigness or
magnitude). These RT-based profiles persisted in a steady state and
remained long after successful acquisition of both rules. McGonigle and
Chalmers (1984) have reported similar and striking asymmetries in the way
size series are represented by children as old as nine years. Figure 14.1
shows a comparison of six-year-old children and monkeys on the simple
"choose larger"/"choose smaller" tasks for all binary comparisons within
a set of five items (monkeys) and seven items (children). (Children were
asked to compare animal sizes from memory, following questions such as
"which is bigger, a cat or a cow?") Of particular interest here for the
question of the ontology of relational competence, was the further finding
(McGonigle and Chalmers 1984) that it took six-year-old children less time
to deny that a small animal such as a mouse is "big" than it took them to
confirm that it is "small".

When monkeys were tested with three rules in operation, the middle-
sized (red-based conditional rule) one took by far the longest to acquire.
However, on extension to a five-item apparatus (McGonigle and Chalmers
1995b), which enabled us to include two more colour conditional-based

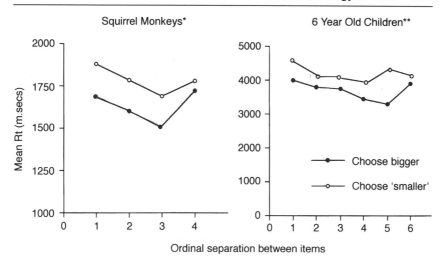

Figure 14.1 Relational asymmetries found during paired comparisons within multiple item sets

rules (if yellow, choose second biggest; if green, choose second smallest), the transfer performance of all monkeys showed that, whereas the biggest and the smallest rules transferred well to the five item set, the "middle" rule did not. Instead it appears to have been based on a default rule within the three stimulus set, i.e. as a "not the biggest or the smallest". Instead, we noted the acquisition of the three internal rules from the *smallest* stimulus: second smallest, followed by "middle-sized", followed by second biggest. From the standpoint of an ontology of relations, more-over, the contrast with one based on logical proof and justification could hardly be more striking. Instead of a co-ordination mechanism being the scaffold by which a number of ordinal values are established, it appeared from these results as if the converse is the case, the order of acquisition being : first the relation of bigger, then the denial of big to its inverse small, followed by a unidirectional calibration of the internal ordinal values. Results from (a) four-year-old children using identical stimuli and proce-dures to those used with monkey (McGonigle 1987), and (b) from five-year-olds using a touch screen version of the colour conditional task (Chalmers and McGonigle 1995) showed a more symmetrical error distribution round middle-sized, but again, clearly demonstrated that, in the context of five stimuli, "middle-sized" is not the "next" most easy rule after the end values. Instead, an end-inwards calibration of the series seems to occur. The strong marking effects in other tests with children, however, indicate,

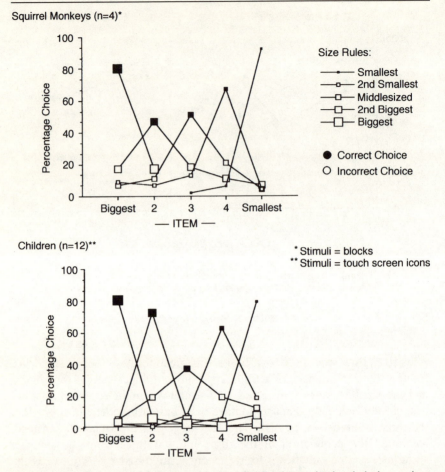

*Figure 14.2* Correct and incorrect choice distributions obtained during colour conditional training on size stimuli

that in common with monkeys, the big end of the series has primacy. Figure 14.2 illustrates the choice profiles obtained from both species, following training on the five size rules.

The conviction, if not the evidence, was growing that seriation and related ordinal competences are a prior stage and causal to relational co-ordinate mechanisms as used in middleness, and not *vice versa*. Our interest was more than captured, therefore, by the controversy which first surrounded the publication of the 5-term series' experiment by Bryant and Trabasso (1971) who claimed that once precautions were taken to ensure that young children could retain the premises they could make genuine transitive inference very well. Equally important, Bryant and Trabasso also catered for earlier fears (e.g. Smedslund 1966) that a positive result (one showing transitivity of choice) might arise from a simple labelling strategy (A is big; C is small), and extended the set of items to five (A>B; B>C; C>D; D>E), in which the crucial test comparison was now B $v$ D – the single comparison within the permutative set which could not generate labels biased towards a transitive outcome (see also Youniss and Murray 1970). False positives and false negatives thus catered for, the results of this study showed high levels of transitive choice even on the test item BD in children as young as four, and seemed to leave no alternative interpretation other than that subjects fully understood the predicates as relational statements and co-ordinated these to produce a conclusion as of *necessity*. Whilst protocols demanding justification – gauged in terms of (re) statements of the predicates – used to determine the conclusion (Glick and Wapner 1968) were not administered, the notion that the conclusions were based on necessary knowledge rather than some associative mechanism established in training was reinforced by a good fit the authors reported between the Cartesian product derived from the levels of retention of the predicates and the *levels* of transitive choice.

We were especially interested in two features of the work. First, its quasi-symbolic nature. McGonigle and Jones (1978) had already tested squirrel monkeys on a form of transitivity where monkeys immediately chose A in a triad ABC following relational training on A>B B>C. However, in those circumstances, the relations could be perceived directly. Under the conditions as specified by Bryant and Trabasso, they could not. Furthermore, McGonigle and Jones had already secured a profile on size relata for squirrel monkeys where it was clear that they could detect and exploit single asymmetric relations of size and brightness, but showed no competence within the same training conditions for co-ordinating them as demanded by a rule for middle. The tantalising question was, therefore, given a suitable adaptation to the 5-term series, would the monkeys' choices also be transitive? If so, would it be possible to sustain the argument that such choices derived *necessarily* from a mental representation of the predicates at an abstract level enabling, in turn, predicate co-ordination? In short, if choices were transitive would they also be *inferences*, drawn of necessity from the pairwise input?

**Transitivity**

In the first comparative study on transitivity, McGonigle and Chalmers (1977) trained monkeys on the Bryant and Trabasso (1971) five-term series problem. In line with Bryant and Trabasso's crucial (second) experimental condition which removed direct perceptual feedback, the task was made a quasi-symbolic one for the monkey. For the child this was achieved by the use of verbal instruction with no visual feedback. For the monkey, it was achieved by training the monkey selectively within each comparison to choose, for example, blue over green, red over blue, etc. To ensure a non-arbitrary relationship between the stimuli which could not be perceived directly, weight differences were introduced. Thus one stimulus (tin) would be heavy – filled with lead shot – the other light (empty). At that time a deliberate decision was made not to seriate the weights, as the monkey might have been able to associate a particular member of the five-term series with a particular weight value, and solve the problem on that basis alone (this possibility existed in the first experiment reported by Bryant and Trabasso (1971) where the subjects were given direct visual feedback of the size differences). However, as McGonigle and Jones had already discovered that squirrel monkeys much prefer relational to absolute judgments (although published in 1978 the research had been carried out between 1969 and 1973, and before the transitivity work), it seemed the best, and indeed the only compromise. Even if stimuli had been given labels as "heavy" and "light", the crucial B $v$ D comparison was designed (as it was in the case of children who might "convert statement of relation into statements of class membership" [Piaget 1928]) to thwart a double labelling strategy.

The results were striking: monkeys showed very high levels of transitive choice on all test comparisons including the crucial B $v$ D pair. In addition, as ten trials per subject were administered, it was discovered that all but one subject (out of eight)) were significantly transitive on the B $v$ D comparisons. In addition, strong serial position effects were observed during acquisition, regarded by Trabasso (1977) as the *sine qua non* of linear ordering. Given our previous results on "middle" size, the puzzle now was to adjudicate between a co-ordinate mechanism and an alternative account. Whilst on the surface, the data looked as compelling as Bryant and Trabasso's, the circumstantial evidence weighed against it. To help adjudicate, we used special post-tests . Based on the form of superlative as used initially by Piaget (1928) such as "which is the fair*est* (or dark*est*) Edith Susanne or Lilli?", we presented monkeys with all ten triadic combinations of items which derive permutatively from the five terms of the series. Our rationale was to probe specifically the possibility that monkeys co-ordinate the items paired during training to solve (binary) tests of transitivity. If B and C and D were featured simultaneously, we argued, memory for the predicates would be minimised, and a co-ordination mechanism enhanced or well supported by the sight of the relevant items. However, we found a significant decrement in the level of transitive choice from that obtained in binary tests, with a proportion of choices going to the other items in the triads.

Nevertheless the triadic choice data, whilst less transitive, were essentially well behaved, sufficient to enable models based on *individual* protocols to be developed (Chalmers and McGonigle 1984; Harris and McGonigle 1994; McGonigle and Chalmers 1977, 1986). The first, a binary sampling model, simply assumed that at the time of test the monkey used one pair of items to control its decision. Thus, stochastically, on any one triadic transitivity test, for example, only one pair is accessed from memory. To illustrate in the case of the triad BCD, the subject would randomly access BC or CD or BD. If each pair is sampled equally often, then each pair will be sampled in approximately 33 per cent of all trials. When sampling BC, C will be chosen 33 per cent of all choices (assuming that the chooser always chooses consistent with training); when sampling CD, D will be chosen 33 per cent, in the case of the novel configuration, BD, the assumption was that the chooser would choose each item equally often, so B and D would each receive approximately 17 per cent of all choices. Overall, the pattern for this triad would be B (17 per cent), C (33 per cent) and D (50 per cent) or a transitive outcome without any pair co-ordination or integration. The match to the data was reasonable, and showed interesting variations in accordance with the composition of the triads. In the case of ABC, for example, the projection from the model was A (0 per cent), B (33 per cent) and C (66 per cent). This followed because, even though AC is a novel pairing, when sampled from the triad ABC, A could always be avoided on the basis of training.

The triadic transfer profiles, therefore, were clear, and the stochastic interpretation compelling. However, it could be argued that the effects we produced with monkeys were only specific to these subjects. Critically, we needed to evaluate children on similar triadic post-tests. Here we had a number of options. One was to replicate the experimental conditions of Bryant and Trabasso (1971), adding the triadic phase in an attempt to determine the ages and stages at which children maximise choices within the triads as demanded by the rule of transitivity. Initial attempts, however, to administer the tests to four-year-olds without some form of direct perceptual feedback failed (Chalmers 1977, and see also Perner, Steiner and Staehlin 1981). In any event, even if such experiments had been successful, it would have left open the question of the child's response to the conditions as given to monkeys. Accordingly, five- and six-year-old children were given our own adaptation of the five-term series problem. Two groups of subjects were run. In the first, training was given as per the monkey experiment. Here the child had to discover which member of the pair hid a coloured plastic counter. No statements of relation were provided by the experimenter. To cater for the possibility that linguistic elaboration might serve some critical semiotic function, however, we also tested children in another, verbal condition. Here, the subject was explicitly asked to discover, e.g. the "heavy" and the "light" item within each pair. Once again, the results were striking and clear cut. Subjects from both groups exhibited significant levels of transitive choices. However, an equal and dramatic decrement in levels of transitivity occurred for both non-verbal (asymmetrical) and verbal (symmetrical) training conditions. As the pattern of results for children and monkeys was thus very similar, we concluded, therefore, that our original result was not a monkey-specific one. In both species, the triadic tests appeared to diminish the case for pairwise co-ordination as a mechanism underwriting transitivity, whether the series was trained in one or both directions.

Converging evidence on this interpretation was provided by Trabasso, Riley and Wilson (1977) using decision-time measures and expanding the five-term series to six, thus enabling more tests to be derived which excluded end-points. A striking feature of Trabasso's findings was that decision times for "inferences" were faster than the time it took subjects to retrieve the connecting predicates. The data were sufficiently regular, in fact, to show an inverse relationship between solution times to pairs of test items and their ordinal distance (a form of "symbolic distance effect" as first reported by Moyer 1973). Such a phenomenon would seem to rule out predicate co-ordination, at least at the time of test. This follows from the reasonable assumption that subjects could not possibly access remote pairs via co-ordination mechanisms without incurring considerable "costs" deriving from the need to first access each of the connecting predicates – so the greater the number which had to be accessed, let alone co-ordinated, the slower the inferences on this account. However, the SDE derives from decision time data which shows exactly the opposite.

Whilst Trabasso et al. (1977) interpreted their findings as reflecting the spatial paralogical device uncovered by de Soto, London and Handel (1965) in their work with human adults (see McGonigle and Chalmers 1986 for a full discussion) no direct evidence (from e.g. verbal protocols) has been provided from their experiments that children were mentally mapping predicates into some imagined vector. Instead Trabasso was content to use the linearity of the RT data (SDE) to provoke the implication that subjects form a linear representation of the series, ends-inwards. In any case, even if such protocols had established some mappings of this sort, it would not have resolved the problem of the causal role of (co-ordinate) premise integration mechanisms as a precursor to the SDE or whether, instead, the SDE and the ends-inwards mechanisms proposed, eschew the need for predicate co-ordination and are ontologically prior to such a competence.

In the monkey we seemed to have the ideal subject to evaluate the latter possibility experimentally. Apparently unable to co-ordinate the predicates, but able to acquire a five-term series and exhibit transitive choice patterns robustly over all novel combinations of test pairs, we now needed to evaluate the monkeys' decision times for evidence of an SDE. So in a second study with five of the original eight subjects, and with procedures modified to enable the recording of accurate decision times, McGonigle and Chalmers (1992) evaluated the status of the SDE in relation to monkey choice transitivity. Some 10 years after the original transitivity study, we re-trained the animals, taking care to establish very high levels of steady state performance on the four trained pairs. In their original work on "internal psychophysics", Moyer (1973), Paivio (1975) and others clearly showed that the SDE was a phenomenon arising in relation to items which were already well-known, well-rehearsed and, to all intents and purposes, equally easy to recall. Accordingly, monkeys were over-trained on the connecting pairs to very high levels of choice, targeting in particular the middle pairs, BC and CD, which contributed, as they do in human studies, to a pronounced serial position effect during the acquisition stage (Chalmers and McGonigle 1984). Binary transitive testing was then maintained in blocks of 10 observations per (test and training) pair. To cater for the possibility that the SDE might be a post-deductive phenomenon, the RTs for all pairs were analysed for any significant variance, and then and only then were the pairs collapsed across ordinal separation to see if this variance was due to an inverse linear relationship as per the SDE.

All monkeys showed individually significant inverse linear trends by the third block of test trials. No other trends emerged in the RTs. The SDE was now identified for the first time in a subject who appears not to use co-ordinate mechanisms when making transitive choices. One obvious possibility now suggested itself. Had monkeys (by now) "integrated" the items into a series? Once again, triadic post-tests immediately following the binary phase clearly indicated that this was not the case. Here a new feature was introduced to ensure that the reduction in transitive choice during triadic tests was not due simply to the novelty arising from having three items for choice. (It should be noted, however, that these subjects had prior experience of triads where the stimuli varied in size.) Now special (two-value) triads were used as training configurations, that is the "pairs" were given as triplets, AAB, ABB, BBC, BCC, etc., before three-value triads (e.g. BCD) were administered. Yet the transfer results were largely unchanged from the profiles established in 1977. The inclusion of decision time data, together with our triadic transfer tests in this later study, thus enabled us to eliminate predicate co-ordination *within the binary phase of the experiment*. This was important as it was possible to argue that "triads evaluate something else". Yet the congruity between the implications of the RT data and the triads is striking – both sets of data strongly exclude a co-ordination account of transitivity.

Co-ordination apart, a further and strong implication of Trabasso's interpretation of the SDE as a paralogical device is that a competence for linear ordering of items – where each item has a separate place within the representational device – should enable the subject to seriate the items quite explicitly in subsequent post-tests. Trabasso's interpretation of the SDE as a strong indicator of linear representation is challenged by these results. If the argument is that the SDE is an even stronger indicator of linear ordering than the choice profile alone, then we might have expected a positive relationship between the strength of the SDE and the level of overall transitivity within the triads. We did not find it. The implication is clear: the SDE has been over-interpreted as an indicator of linear ordering. One reason for this was discovered in a re-analysis of the RT data by McGonigle and Chalmers in their 1992 study. We found that four out of our five subjects showed a distinct directional asymmetry when ordinal distance functions were plotted separately from each "end" of the series (AB, AC, AD, AE as compared with DE, CE, BE, AE). Two monkeys were uniformly fast on the "E" comparisons; two on the "A" comparisons, and the difference in RT between these fast pairs and those involving the opposite end of the series was the biggest source of variance in the RT data (see Figure 14.3). In other words it was possible to account for the linearity found in the collapsed data, in terms of a statistical mechanism; the greater the ordinal separation, the more likely that one of the items would be from the "privileged" end of the series; hence the faster the decision time. Thus the (end-related) salience of the items rather than ordinal separation *per se* could produce the SDE. Where there is directional asymmetry, therefore, it can interact with ordinal separation to produce the appearance of linearity, without presuming anything more than a very crude classification of items into "good" and "bad". On re-analysis, Trabasso's own data (from Trabasso, Riley and Wilson 1977) show that such directional asymmetry is evident in the data of children as old as nine. As Figure 14.3 shows, the asymmetry is expressed, in this case, in terms of a consistent advantage for comparisons from the "long" endpoint of the series as compared with those from the "short" end, despite the fact that both linguistic comparatives were used as questions.

## A formal model

In summary, the SDE data, the transitive choice data and the triadic data tell a consistent story, and as far as we can tell, one which transcends species boundaries. The persistent problem seems to lie in the number of items which the subjects must explicitly seriate, not how the subject deals with remote versus adjacent pairs once trained to a high level of success. A formal analysis of these data, moreover, using a production system approach (Harris and McGonigle 1994), shows clearly why this should be the case. These investigators represented each item as a condition-action pair such as "If A then select (or avoid) A". Each item had a place in an overall stack, and each condition-action pair could be based on an "avoid" or a "select" value. Thus "If E then E (select)", could be followed in the stack by "If A avoid A", etc. Using this system, Harris and McGonigle were able to model each subject on both binary and triadic phases of both the original (1977) and the later (1992) study. An important discovery was that only a small subset of rule stacks (16 in all) could cope with the adjacent pairs of the five-term series from a total number of rule stacks of

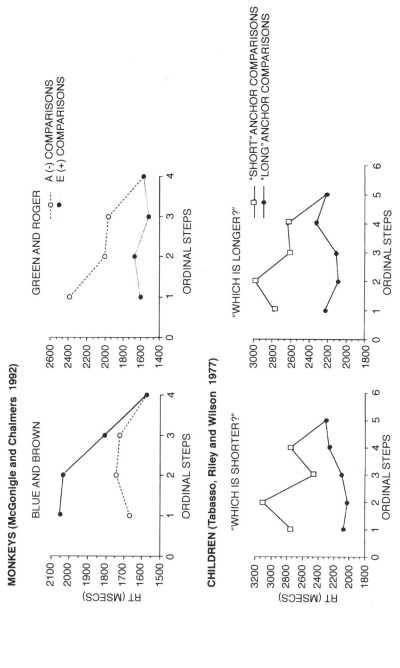

*Figure 14.3* "Wedge" functions obtained when the "Symbolic Distance Effect" is plotted from both ends of the series

1,920 which can be permutated with the only constraint that each rule refers to a different item. Equally crucial was the discovery that a property of this subset is that *all* stacks that perform correctly on the adjacent pairs also perform correctly on the remote pairs. This contrasts with other formal models such as the rank tensor product model of Halford (1993) in which a transitive decision about a remote pairing is higher-level and more complex than a decision concerning any of the adjacent pairings. In the Harris and McGonigle model, by contrast, only *triads* make extra demands on the subject; the rule stacks have to be augmented to deal with the triadic configurations.

In short, this model illustrates very clearly how a mechanism which could solve binary transitivity tests might fail at least initially to maintain equivalent levels of performance on triads. Clearly, we are now in a position to formally justify the behavioural data obtained already showing that transitivity under binary conditions is less complex than explicit seriation. On the formal assay we have provided, it would be difficult not to be transitive, in fact, once the connecting pairs have been encoded. This formal analysis identifies, furthermore, a mechanism for transitivity which, although rule-based, does not tautologically restate the conventional one based on a proof or justification for transitivity.

Formal models apart, the behavioural profile we report here is fully congruent with the many findings of transitivity in children very much earlier than explicit seriation. Bryant and Trabasso's claims for four-year-olds in transitivity tests, for example, are in contrast with Inhelder and Piaget (1964) demonstrations, that it is not until around six or seven years of age that children can construct a size series on a principled basis. This long-standing developmental phenomenon, well supported by other investigators (Baylor, Gascon, Lemoyne and Pothier 1973; Kingma 1984; Leiser and Gillieron 1990; Young 1976), is an ontological paradox when considered from logical accounts of transitivity in young children. That is, if children as young as four years are indeed able to understand the full implication of the comparatives used in transitivity tests and can integrate these "in the mind's eye" into a linear series, they ought to be able to place actual rods of different heights which they can see directly in front of them in an ordered row (see also failures in seriation post-tests following transitivity training reported by Riley and Trabasso 1974; Riley 1976).

One way of removing the paradox, of course, would be to claim that demonstrations of transitivity in young children derive from their use of associative or other non-logical procedures[2] provoked by the training conditions used to ensure premise retention. On this view, transitivity within the context of training studies as conventionally reported with young children requires only arbitrary relationships based on temporal chaining and paired association between items.

Whilst we would take issue with the view that *all* transitivity is explicable on the basis of simple learning mechanisms shared by many species (von Fersen, Wynne, Delius and Staddon 1992), it is nevertheless difficult to find experimental evidence to date which enables some clear *behavioural* arbitration between competences based on arbitrary "habit of mind" mechanisms and those based on the detection of relational invariances. Attempts to isolate "logical" connectivity have taken the form of violating the logical connectivity between the items to see if it makes any difference to the transitive outcome (de Boysson-Bardies and O'Regan 1973), or removing the temporal connectivity which conventionally links the pairs in a series congruent with the logical one (by first introducing the pairs to the subject in serial order from e.g. AB to DE), to see if transitivity depends on these serial connections (Adams 1978; Kallio 1982; Halford 1984). The problem with the first experimental strategy is that logical connectivity is not the only basis for making transitive choices and even adults will "connect" indeterminate relations in linear reasoning tests (McGonigle and Chalmers 1986). The problem with the second one is that presenting relational information in a way which is serially incongruent with the logical series can render training difficult or nearly impossible (Halford 1984). In any event, the fact that human adults can achieve high levels of transitivity where the connectives are entirely arbitrary (Siemann and Delius 1993) means that choice measures alone are unlikely to afford sensitive indicators of the levels of comprehension operating to produce success. So associative mechanisms cannot be differentiated readily from logical ones in such training studies. Whilst a good qualitative arbitrator between transitive choices and transitive inferences would undoubtedly be subjects' ability to justify their conclusions as declared in protocols or "think aloud" data (see Smith 1993), the use of justification as the sole criterion would eliminate linguistically immature subjects and thus overlook the study of potentially important precursor competences both in young humans and in other species. On the operating hypothesis that logical competences are not "all or none", moreover, it is crucial that we can devise criteria which can be adopted over as wide a range of subjects as possible – whatever the species.

## Seriation training

Confronted by these difficulties, one option is to abandon training altogether. Recently Pears and Bryant (1990) have produced convincing evidence of transitive choice based on height relations in children under five years. In a task which neatly avoids the need for training, subjects are simply asked to anticipate which block would be "higher" amongst the elements of a putative tower which could be built from them. Such methods are restricted to particular sorts of spatially-based ordering tasks, however. Another tactic is to train children according to very explicit ordering

*Table 14.1* General design of touch screen based serial tasks (ESRC project 1990–93)

| AGE | 5 years | | 7 years | |
|---|---|---|---|---|
| TASKS | arbitrary | connected | arbitrary | connected |
| CONNECTIVE | colour | size | colour | size |
| SET SIZE (no. of items) | 5  7 | 5  7 | 5  7 | 5  7 |

requirements. In our most recent developmental project[3] (Chalmers and McGonigle 1995; McGonigle and Chalmers 1993), we provided a training environment in which two fundamentally different types of ordering task were given to the same child (see Table 14.1). One of these was a size ordering task, which we varied in complexity and presented to five- and seven-year-old children, the other was entirely arbitrary (a sequence of colours), established exclusively via the temporal chaining amongst the items provided by during training. All tasks were presented on a computer-driven touch screen. Thus, rather than lift and replace items, as in the conventional seriation task, all the subject must do is to learn to touch each icon, irrespective of its position on the screen (which varies from trial to trial) in a serial order as demanded by the experimental condition. Following each touch, feedback is given in the form of a bleep for a correct response, or a buzz for an incorrect one, following which the subject continues to touch the icons until the correct one is found. Both conditions, therefore, are entrained via the temporal association linking one item to the next. Any difference in acquisition between the two tasks can therefore be interpreted in the light of what the size connectives afford the subject, either to aid or to hinder performance. Training measures, furthermore, can be used to interpret the sources of task complexity within and across tasks.

One measure of complexity which we used was sequence length, a crucial dimension to ordering and one which interacts with the subjects' ability to connect the items on a basis other than strict temporal succession alone. As Figure 14.4 shows, the permutations of sequences increases geometrically with sequence length and becomes a cognitively hostile number above five or so items.

That is, if an agent is to try and guess a particular sequence, and if there are seven or more elements, the inductive space is big enough to make it a serious computational problem. One option is to heavily constrain the problem by choosing one sequence and one sequence alone. This would appear to be our strategy in memorising all twenty-six letters of our alphabet. That is, in order to remember the letters, we impose, by convention, a fixed order relationship as in A,B,C etc. In the case of non-arbitrary

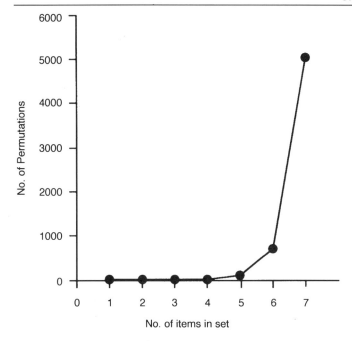

*Figure 14.4* Expansion of combinatorial possibilities as a function of set size

series, however, or more accurately, specific sorts of non-arbitrary sequence such as a monotonic scale in music, it can be seen that these are predictable and redundant and if properly assimilated by the agent will be data reducing. That is, once a consistent direction of change is detected, and the intervals between the items metricated (in the examples here we shall assume equal intervals – as indeed occurs in conventional seriation tasks), the subject will be able to predict, and thus generate, each legitimate successor on a principled basis. Using this procedure, an infinite set could be searched successfully without incurring extra memory demands.

Arbitrary sequences, by contrast, become progressively more difficult with increases in sequence length. From a computational standpoint, given the combinatorial explosion problem as represented here, it becomes inductively necessary either to limit the length of the sequence to some manageable number of components or to seriate using relationally based connectives. Outside the narrow inductive space of the optimal conditions for associative learning, the advantages, therefore, of the "quick fix" afforded by the spatio-temporal contiguity principle are now gone; instead, a competence based on relational perception offers the only secure prospect of constraining the order of moderate to large numbers of alternatives. In this, the detection of the relevant relations between constituents of a putative sequence is a necessary but not a sufficient condition for successful performance. As we have argued elsewhere (McGonigle and Chalmers 1993; Chalmers and McGonigle 1995), path selection and restriction through the combinatorial space is also required. And only monotonic paths will be of benefit.

The first testable derivation of this position is that the *number* of items used in a seriation task will be an important determiner of success. This follows from our combinatorial argument; in fact Figure 14.4 shows very clearly *why* the addition of an extra term or two beyond five items introduces, by the mere fact of the *geometrical* expansion in the potential series, a serious discontinuity in task difficulty which will not be recognised if one views the numbers of terms on a simple ordinal scale. As Figure 14.5 illustrates, five-year-olds who were able to acquire a five-term seriation task with relative ease were seriously disadvantaged, and two failed altogether when the series was extended by a mere two items to seven in all. This indicated that five-year-olds had not yet grasped the full strategic implications of a monotonic path through the size series, as on our argument, it requires a highly principled application of serial search procedures to maintain seriation with six or seven stimuli or more. This interpretation is reinforced by the fact that the same subjects showed a very similar profile on the arbitrary (colour) series as well. Seven-year-olds, by contrast, required little or no training on either of the monotonic size

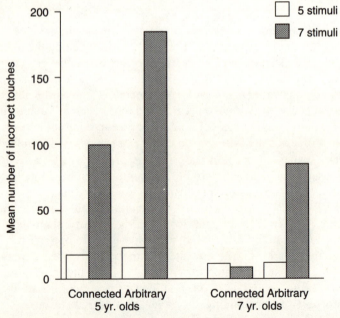

*Figure 14.5* Mean number of errors during acquisition of connected (size) sequences and arbitrary (colour) strings entrained on a touch screen

sequences, accommodating the set increase for size relations with no difficulty. The arbitrary sequence, by contrast, shows the effect on acquisition that a set size increase has on these subjects, when there is no object-based criterion for selecting an *a priori* route through the set.

The second testable derivation of our position is based on the notion that only some of the sequences which can be permutated from size relations are psychologically plausible. As we have argued already, these will be the "redundant", monotonic ones. The corollary is that other sequences will be difficult, if not impossible, to acquire. We tested this directly by training the same five- and seven-year-old children on five-term non-monotonic sequences such as "second biggest, smallest, middle-sized, second smallest, biggest" under exactly the same conditions as the monotonic sequences (see Figure 14.6). As Table 14.2 illustrates, many five-year-olds failed to learn such sequences even after 200 trials. On this occasion, seven-year-olds were also disadvantaged by these sequences, and when these were increased by just two items to seven, most subjects failed.

The pattern of results we obtained from what was a very extensive investigation (McGonigle and Chalmers 1993; Chalmers and McGonigle 1995) thus strongly indicates that size seriation is fundamentally a search problem. Motivated by the requirements to support a long sequence of sizes, the most economical method of doing so is surely to search the set from one pole consistently, and maximize the (potential) redundancy in the series by computing the same direction of change quite consistently. For such sequences, it can thus be seen that once redundancy is detected, memory resource demands materially diminish – so the older subject may succeed by making the task easier!

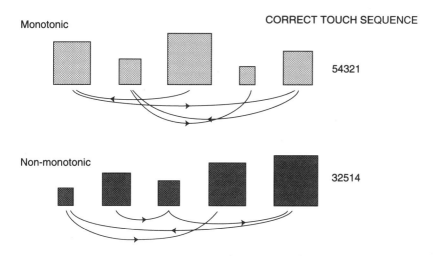

*Figure 14.6* Two types of size sequence entrained on the touch screen

*Table 14.2* Acquisition profiles for monotonic and non-monotonic size sequences

| | MONOTONIC | | | NON-MONOTONIC | | |
|---|---|---|---|---|---|---|
| | % Succ. Ss* | Mean trls.** | Range | % Succ. Ss* | Mean trls.** | Range |
| **5 items** | | | | | | |
| 5 yr. olds | 100 | 13.4 | 2–31 | 59 | 30 | 13–40 |
| 7 yr. olds | 100 | 4.0 | 2–9 | 91 | 24 | 8–38 |
| **7 items** | | | | | | |
| 7 yr. olds | 100 | 4.7 | 1–23 | 25 | 26 | 19–40 |

* those reaching a criterion of 80% completely correct sequences across 10 trials (within 40 trials).
** to the start of criterion run.

## Cognitive growth implications

Small wonder then that Piaget, just as seems natural, has conventionally represented the seriation task as a monotonic one, even though, of course, non-monotonic versions are equally legitimate. It now seems clear as well why ten items is an important number – safely into the region of lethal combinatorial explosion – in supporting the seriation task as an important indicator of cognitive growth.

If our analysis is on the right lines, moreover, one of its interesting implications is that operational seriation in particular, and cognitive growth in general, may be guided by a strong data-reducing economic principle (Klahr and Wallace 1970). Given that we are resource-limited agents, it would seem reasonable that affecting more powerful and, at the same time, more economic solutions would be a good (optimising) strategy to adopt, especially if the procedures involved could be routinised to deal with similar cases. The former outcome would emerge from cognitive regulators which selected for the least costly solutions. If routinised, moreover, such data-reducing procedures would afford a second form of redundancy, by leaving the system free to take on board new and challenging information which might otherwise overload it.

If cognitive economy is a primary motive for self-induced changes in information management as we suggest, then we need to be in an experimental position to determine the extent to which the *agent* can arbitrate between various solutions to a given on the basis of economy alone. For this we need new paradigms. In the case of supervised learning, for example, the subject may elect to choose an efficient solution on the basis of external tuition alone, yet fail to achieve the same solution spontaneously. On the other hand, the study of spontaneous production, whilst possible in some cases (Sinclair, Stambak, Lezine and Verba 1990), can be a long and drawn-out process where many of the crucial changes can occur outside the window of the laboratory (Bryant 1974). Accordingly we have devised new paradigms which enable us to take full experimental advantage of the central implication of our new characterisation. Once again, the touch-screen based methodology is crucial if not totally essential. Paradigms based on precisely this concept have been underway in our laboratory at Edinburgh for the past three years or more featuring both human and non-human primates.

## Self-regulation and search

Developed first with our *Cebus apella* (McGonigle, De Lillo and Dickinson 1992, 1994), the paradigm is deceptively simple. The task is merely to search all items on a touch-screen exhaustively. No selective reinforcement is applied throughout the subject's production. If exhaustive, i.e. all items have been interrogated by the subject, then the screen blanks out, and the subject is rewarded. The subject may of course reiterate throughout the search, in which case the only penalty is that more than the minimal number of responses is made, and reward is inevitably postponed. Our first experiment with adult, feral born *apella* and young children aged between two and four years was designed as a very simple first evaluation of these issues. At this stage, the icons were identical and varied in number from one to nine items. All the subject had to do was to ensure that all icons were touched once. When this condition was satisfied, the monkeys got a peanut, the children saw an icon with a man on a ladder going up a tree. With each trial, the man stepped further up the ladder towards some apples. This seemed to provide the children with as much incentive as peanuts did for monkeys!

The first issue is of course whether or not subjects will search all items at all, especially when the number of items increases to nine or more. At issue too is the extent to which *changes in the efficiency* of search are revealed by the subject over a succession of attempts, and in the absence of explicit differential feedback as to which particular route to search through the item space. For we would argue that changes over time which show the subject drifting or relaxing towards efficient search, objectively assessed as the equivalence between the items to be searched and the number of responses made, would provide the first ostensible index of the work of cognitive regulators working to some extent outside the scope of immediate environmental arbitration.

Children (from two years eleven months to four years six months) provided us with clear templates of failure and success (Figure 14.7). Older (four-year-old) children proved very efficient from the very first exposure. Their success was directly correlated with their using a spatial vector, usually the vertical one, and imposing a grid type organisation on

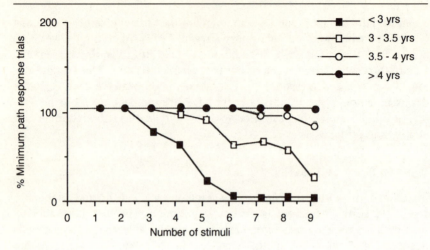

*Figure 14.7* Search performance of young children in tasks with increasing numbers of identical items

the array. Where this was not easy, as in the case of random configuration effects, particularly with items of less than seven in number, there was a consistent use of a proximity principle; only adjacent items were searched in turn. Such constraints on search, as exhibited by these older subjects, indicate to us the use of a data-reducing economy principle. In each case, these subjects kept a very simple record of what they had interrogated: stopped at any point along the search path, they could readily resume from the point of last contact. In contrast, younger children jumped, often at random, from one icon to another; as a consequence, perhaps, they rapidly lost track of where they had been, and began to reiterate. Worse still, within the larger sets particularly, they would get into search loops and persistently neglect an item or two. In this event, they were not only uneconomical; they also failed to satisfy the exhaustive search condition, and rapidly became demoralised. Under these conditions it was difficult to persuade them to continue, to see if they would improve with practice.

There was no such motivational difficulty with the *apella*, however. Over a period of months they worked with great commitment. Initially, they were not searching economically, however – at least in the case of sets greater than five to six items. This performance changed significantly, however, in the case of four out of six subjects working entirely without the selective feedback as given in conventional learning experiments. The only positive feedback they got was at the terminus of exhaustive search, when the screen went blank and the dispenser gave them a peanut. How they chose to search, however, was left entirely to them. That the majority were able to improve significantly their efficiency on the basis of search "experience" alone, suggests an important ability to *self-regulate* based on factors other than those provided by immediate environmental arbitration. How they achieved relatively high levels of search efficiency also converges on the strategies used by successful children. Here, too, seriation of the items followed an adjacency principle and approximated to vectorial constraint. A full analysis of the monkey data has been provided by De Lillo (1994), and an extensive account of the developmental and comparative data, including a study with pigeons, by McGonigle, De Lillo, Dickinson and St Johnson (1995). Significantly, pigeons we tested under comparable conditions were unable to search more than approximately four items without losing track of which stimuli they had interrogated, and thus failed to meet the exhaustive search criterion under these circumstances. Related deficits in birds even under quite specific training conditions have also been found (Terrace and McGonigle 1994).

## Classification and hierarchical cognitive architectures

In variations of this paradigm we have begun a long-term programme on both linear and hierarchical features of memory organisation. As the number of items to be encoded increases, memory will be severely taxed to the point where it will become hopelessly inefficient – at least as far as retrieval is concerned – unless some organisational schemes are elaborated to manage the data. Segmenting populations of objects and events into classes is one good data-management and data-reducing strategy which makes for more efficient retrieval.

Without some hierarchical device, however, even classes *per se* will not take an agent very far along the road of efficient information management – soon the number of classes will increase to a critical number and once again tax the system. Hierarchies are an efficient response to this problem. A core question, therefore, concerns the development of classes, and their related hierarchical structures over the course of evolution and ontogeny. The key issue here is the extent to which the subject will exploit classification schemes as a data-reducing principle and organise the elements into chunks. Figure 14.8 summarises what is essentially a shell to support the

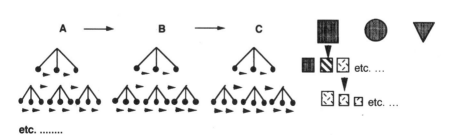

*Figure 14.8* McGonigle's classification paradigm

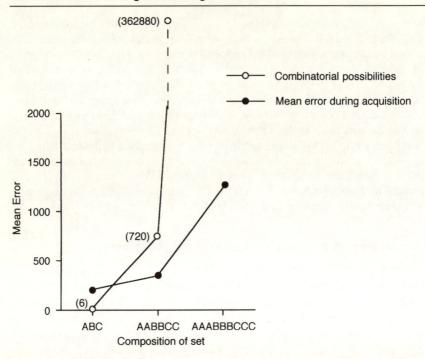

*Figure 14.9* Increase in error during acquisition by *Cebus apella* of 3,6 and 9 item sequences, composed of sub-classes A, B and C

design of several current experiments of this sort which derive from it, and which, critically, encompasses both classification and seriation within the one experimental assay.

Already it is clear that *Cebus apella* are organising sequences much longer than those previously reported; they can now achieve 12-item seriation, where there are opportunities for classification, and we have not reached the upper limits of their performance as yet. Preliminary analyses indicate that each class is the basis for a segment or chunk making it less likely that the items will migrate out of order (McGonigle 1987). This is first shown by the acquisition performance. As Figure 14.9 shows, the error following increases in sequence length from three to six and then to nine items does not follow the cost function expected were each unit of the sequence to be regarded as independent of all others, i.e. from an induction perspective, classification changes the combinatorial space from a nine-value problem (362880 possible sequences) to essentially a highly tractable one as can be seen in their performance recorded here.

A further feature of the paradigm which is of central importance is the way it enables us to evaluate the hierarchical nature of classification and how this may be evolved dynamically in interaction with our task. For this

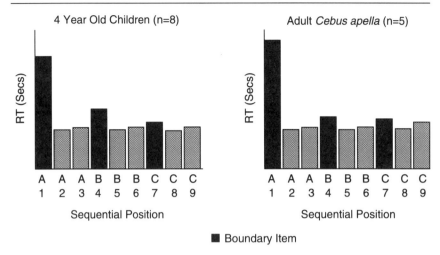

*Figure 14.10* Search times for 9 item sequences composed of three categories, each with three exemplars

we have turned to time measures with both species. With children (McGonigle and Jaswal 1993), analyses of the time it takes to respond to each item in turn within the sequence also shows strong classification effects (see Figure 14.10). These indicate a clear demarcation between the search times for items within a particular category once its ordinal position has been computed, and the time it takes to identify the ordinal rank of the categorical items within the sequence as a whole. It is much more costly (in time) to search for the first item in each category (e.g. Ai) than subsequent ones (e.g. Aii, Aiii, etc.); i.e. the first item within each class takes the longest time to identify and seems to act as a "prime" for others within the same class. When the category is exhaustively searched, however, the time it takes to search the first item of the successor category (e.g. Bi of BBB) suddenly increases and seems to be determined by the number of categories which remain (prospectively) to be searched within the remainder of the sequence. Extended analysis of the monkey data reveals similar characteristics.

In addition, as monkeys and young children are now showing that they can tolerate variations in the exemplars of each class, specific seriation requirements can be imposed within each class as well. That is, once subjects can show that they can tolerate size variation within a class by chunking the exemplars regardless of size and colour variation, then we can impose an ordering rule as a within-class requirement, i.e. the subject is then required to order each item within each class, as well as order each class in turn. In this way, seriation and hierarchical classification can be evaluated within the same subject in the same experiment. *Evidence for hierarchical organisation is based on the subject maintaining categorical boundaries between classes*, even under conditions where each item, whatever its category, has to be ordered. That is, if subjects turn the whole task into one long, linear sequence, there should be no reason to maintain the categorical boundaries, and indeed, sequencing breakdown is predicted.

A long-term programme, our monkey studies in particular – now running on paradigms such as these for the past three years or more with the same subjects – are enabling us for the first time to assess cognitive growth as it relates to classification and seriation through a full scale assessment of the role of task experiences *per se*, uncontaminated by developmental variables inevitable in similar longitudinal work with young children.

## DISCUSSION

A central question of our programme has been to help specify the important dimensions of change in cognitive (non-reactive), competence and cognitive regulation over the course of evolution and development. Here psychology is very much on trial. One tradition, based on what Harvey Carr, the American philosopher, once referred to as "the educated salivations of a Russian dog", still surfaces by extension as a "learning by association" approach. Based on a three-way contingency paradigm which keeps the temporal interval and the spatial separation between discriminandum, manipulandum and feedback as small as possible, its essential strength, both as a paradigm and as an adaptive mechanism, lie in the way in. which purely arbitrary connections can be established on the basis of regular association with what are otherwise completely unconnected objects and events. In this sense, there can be no special provision for any necessary connections based on a perceived material relationship such as size. And the procedures involved, designed to maximise rate of learning, minify the induction problem to such insignificant levels as to produce what Vygotsky has called a "levelling" effect. That is, species of whatever complexity show very similar profiles when assessed using these methods, an effect which McPhail has exploited as the "null hypothesis". Whilst the mechanisms reflected in these paradigms are "old" in evolutionary terms (Lashley 1960), they do not cater for the significant distinction between arbitrary and non-arbitrary connections between objects – nor do they (nor can they) specify how evolutionary systems invest in complexity, and become more powerful, both as engineered by evolution and as a consequence of their own individual life histories (Terrace and McGonigle 1994).

Another tradition derives from a cognitive endstate characterisation of human intelligence as rule-governed, based on a symbol-level representation which enables the agent to explicitly represent and mentally manipulate logical "objects". The epistemological benefits of such systems as expressed in mathematics and in the sciences to promote "strong inference" are clear. However, rule-based systems have been a poor launching pad from which to motivate programmes into the origins of necessary knowledge. Piaget's top-down ontology was designed to trace the competences of the "epistemic subject" (Smith 1993) to its ontogenetic antecedents (for the evolutionary process as a whole setting the lower ontological bound is a matter, as Piaget has rightly observed, of infinite regress). Intended to eschew nativism, a failure to identify – even to admit that there could be – "structures unpolluted by history and genesis", i.e. the cognitive primitives of the system – has left such approaches with the impossible task of trying to specify the transition within *ontogeny* from "habit of mind" or arbitrary to non-arbitrary and necessary knowledge. As a consequence there is remarkably little known about the possible mapping within ontogeny between hardwired design primitives and their epigenetic implementation which leads to the "high level" cognitive behaviours we recognise in (at least some) human adults. Primitives apart, the further problem is the lack of a consistent and coherent, principled hierarchy of organisation which has been used in these contexts on a purely informal basis . A plausible yet intuitive hierarchy is conventionally based on what might be considered as the level of abstraction at which the system operates; the higher the level of abstraction, the "higher" the cognitive process (Piaget 1970; Donaldson 1992; Karmiloff-Smith 1992). Unless a nativist one, this position is tied to the idea that evolution and development involves a serial unfolding of progressively abstract layers of cognitive competence: in addition, each later stage or layer of competence is a derivation of the previous one.

Instead, we adopt the position that different sorts of adaptive competences are *co-present* as lower-bound design primitives within a given agent, and not derived serially one from the other as one layer of an adaptive system hands over the baton to another. We support the proposition that in complex systems at least, a wide spectrum of high-level cognitive behaviours have hardwired underpinnings as *necessary preconditions* for their (ultimate) expression in later cognitive development. For us the evolutionary and in particular the comparative question centres initially on the design primitives themselves: the less rich and diverse the primitives, the more limited the system ontogenetically. The ontogenetic issue, by contrast, centres on the (epigenetic-based) development of design primitives over the life history of the individual. The richer the floor competences, on this view, the more promising the ontogenetic space of possibility, a proposition finding progressively more favour (Karmiloff-Smith 1991). However, both aspects of system investigation require a programme of investigation with very specific requirements, rarely met in developmental research alone, and certainly not catered for by the traditional short cross sectional "diagnostic" studies which have been the mainstay of the human developmental discipline so far. As Van Geert (1994) points out, "Unfortunately there is still only little longitudinal research, especially of the kind that a dynamic model requires, namely data with a high sampling frequency".

A major problem in this context, however, has been to establish task scenarios which both enable long-term assays of performance longitudinally and which keep the subject's interest. Rather than shallow assays which are merely psychometric, *post-hoc*, and "normative" in motivation, furthermore, we need tasks which enable us to achieve rich behaviour graphs of individual subjects (e.g. Young 1976). Equally crucially, these tasks must be capable of principled, *a priori*, and objective variation in their complexity, adapted to the subject's performance and progress. As we have focused on order, and ordering mechanisms as the major window on cognitive systems, we can define task complexity in terms of sequence length and sequence compositionality. This enables us to establish a principled task hierarchy of difficulty, thus affording a rich measurement space for both comparative and human developmental research. If Simon (1969) is correct, furthermore, that . . . "the apparent complexity . . . of behaviour over time is largely a reflection of the complexity of the environment", we need to manipulate that environment in a principled way, governed by far more than intuitive notions of complexity (some of these exemplified in the "levels of abstraction" school of thought which has bedevilled, in our view, so much comparative and developmental cognitive research to date). A significant aim of our programme, therefore, is to study at close range how cognitive systems "invest in complexity" – from what Simon (1969, pp. 25–26) has called the "intrinsic" characteristics of the inner environment – cultivated by initial experiences on tasks which can be calibrated in complexity. Crucially, over time, we can now study with our new procedures how the agent regulates "epigenetically" in the course of these task experiences. Crucially too, we can determine whether subjects can use their early task experiences to solve later problems of a new order of difficulty (initially, quite impossible for them to solve). In short, using the window of ordering as a regulative environmental influence, we can now study, over a wide range of species and almost all ages of human development, how agents grow as inductive systems, from "weak to strong".

## SUMMARY AND CONCLUSIONS

In conclusion, we have argued in this paper that the battlelines drawn up between associative, nativisitic and rationalist camps have obscured important ontological issues which first centre on the design primitives which provide the preontological underpinnings for individual agents of a species. In the context of the "rational" agent, we argue that an important first plank is based on a common currency of utility which links items not otherwise connected or connectable on a material scale. In the absence of material relationships between objects, a primitive bond can be established on the basis of spatial and temporal proximity. This makes for good inductive management: the smaller the temporal interval, and the closer the objects, the smaller the working inductive space, and thus the less "noise" in the computation of connectedness based on "habit of mind" mechanisms. However, while such mechanisms are extremely powerful and ubiquitous, within (now) well specified limits, the ability to connect objects on a material basis represents an important shift, in our view to a new, non-arbitrary domain. Here, the connection between objects is necessary and enforces a number of consequences which lead on to a progressively more powerful system. Quite apart from the necessary logical properties of such relata, the psychological consequences for the agent as a knowledge-gaining system are profound. This follows from our argument that once objects are materially connected, and once their numbers begin to exceed five or so, then some method of path restriction based on a detection of relational and necessary connectives must be found to overcome the combinatorial problem. As in the case of the alphabet, one way to do this is to impose the very same path through an arbitrary set (and in the ABC, etc. convention). However, as we have seen in the case of size relata, serial paths through sets of items so connected vary considerably in their psychological difficulty. Only monotonic ones have the qualities of predictability and data reduction. And this has brought us to a further psychological stage, derived entirely from relational competence – the stage of self-regulation by the agent where options within the combinatorial space afforded by the set of items to be connected are adjudicated more on the basis of an economy principle than on the basis of direct environmental feedback. If so, we propose that both linear and hierarchical structures as those which emerge in human cognitive systems are evolved as data-reducing structures, selected for on the basis of cognitive optimality; i.e. those structures which enable the agent to manage the most information for the least outlay in resource terms. If we are correct, then the new paradigms we have outlined will provide for a clear developmental and comparative differentiation between the agent's treatment of arbitrary and non-arbitrary connections between objects. Far from reifying the associative versus logical distinctions now so prevalent, we seek instead to study the consequences for learning and indeed for logic itself of what may seem at first only a minor change in the native endowment of a given species – to connect objects relationally. How individual agents chart a route epigenetically from such design primitives to more powerful knowledge-gaining structures remains to be fully explored, but for us, at least, it poses one of the most exciting if neglected empirical questions in psychology today.

## NOTES

1 The authors gratefully acknowledge project grant support from the Economic and Social Research Council, the Medical Research Council and NAW.
2 In the absence of materially based connectives, or in cases where the agent is incapable of identifying the material and necessary connection between objects under judgement, it would be important of course to have a common currency with which to judge and rank alternatives such that actions may be rational, consistent, and systematic. Models of precisely such mechanisms have been put forward by Tversky (1969) and Navarick and Fantino (1974) to cater for unidimensional stochastic types of choices where the subject must use some subjective scale to provide the common currency to weld the items together so that these can be ranked – indeed it was a possibility that we considered in precisely these terms when we first discovered choice transitivity in monkeys following five-term series training (McGonigle and Chalmers 1977). Berlyne (1965) and Bradbury and Nelson (1974) have also used a similar sort of notion based on aesthetic scales to evaluate colour preferences in very young children and to determine when their preferences become internally consistent, such that where a subject prefers blue over green and green over red that the same subject also chooses blue over red. Bradbury and Nelson refer to such a competence as pre-logical, and there is little doubt that there is a strong evolutionary pressure to enable agents to rank outcomes according to some sort of utility in order to maximise fitness (Edwards 1954).
3 ESRC project grant,"An Experimental Analysis of Ordering Skills in Young Children", 1990–93, awarded to B. McGonigle.

## REFERENCES

Adams, M. J. (1978) "Logical competence and transitive inference in young children", *Journal of Experimental Child Psychology* 25: 477–489.
Banks, W. P. (1977) "Encoding and processing of symbolic information in comparative judgments", in G. H. Bower (ed.) *The psychology of learning and motivation, Vol. II*, New York: Academic Press.
Baylor, G.W., Gascon, J., Lemoyne, G. and Pothier, N. (1973) "An information processing model of some seriation tasks", *The Canadian Psychologist* 14: 2, 167–196.
Berlyne, D. E. (1965) *Structure and direction in thinking*, New York: Wiley.
Bradbury, H. and Nelson, T. M. (1974) "Transitivity and patterns of children's preferences", *Developmental Psychology* 10(1): 55–64.
Bryant, P. E. (1974) *Perception and understanding in young children*, London: Methuen.
Bryant, P. E. and Trabasso, T. (1971) "Transitive inferences and memory in young children", *Nature* 232: 456–458.
Chalmers, M. (1977) "Transitivity and the representation of stimulus relations by young children", unpublished Ph.D. thesis, Edinburgh University.
Chalmers, M. and McGonigle, B. (1984) "Are children any more logical than monkeys on the five term series problem?" *Journal of Experimental Child Psychology* 37: 355–377.
Chalmers, M. and McGonigle, B. (1995) "Logical *versus* serial processes in the development of seriation", under review for *Cognitive Psychology*.
Clark, H. H. (1969) "Linguistic processes in deductive reasoning", *Psychological Review* 76: 387–404.

Clark, H. H., Carpenter, P. A. and Just, M. A (1973) "On the meeting of semantics and perception", in W. D. Chase (ed.) *Visual information processing*, New York: Academic Press.

de Boysson-Bardies, B. and O'Regan, K. (1973) "What children do in spite of adults' hypotheses", *Nature* 246: 531–534.

De Lillo, C. (1994) "The Logic of Memory Search in Non-human Primates (*Cebus apella*)", unpublished Ph.D. thesis, Edinburgh University.

de Soto, C. B., London, M. and Handel, S. (1965) "Social reasoning and spatial paralogic", *Journal of Personality and Social Psychology* 2: 513–521.

Donaldson, M. (1992) *Human Minds. An Exploration*, London: Penguin.

Donnett, J. G. and McGonigle, B. O. (1991) "Evolving speed control in mobile robots: From blindness to kinetic vision", *Vision Interface*: 35–41.

Edwards, W. (1954) "The theory of decision making", *Psychological Bulletin* 51: 380–417.

Fersen, L. von, Wynne, C.D.L., Delius, J.D. and Staddon, J.E.R. (1992) "Transitive inference formation in pigeons", *Journal of Experimental Psychology: Animal Behaviour Processes* 17: 334–341.

Geert, P. van (1994) *Dynamic systems of development. Change between complexity and chaos*, New York: Harvester Wheatsheaf.

Glick, J. and Wapner, S. (1968) *Child Development* 39: 611–620.

Halford, G.S. (1984) "Can young children integrate premises in transitivity and serial order tasks?" *Cognitive Psychology* 16: 65–93.

Halford, G.S. (1993) *Children's understanding. The development of mental models*, Hillsdale, NJ: Lawrence Erlbaum.

Harris, M.R. and McGonigle. B. O. (1994) "Modelling transitive inference", *The Quarterly Journal of Experimental Psychology* 47(B): 3, 319–348.

Inhelder, B. and Piaget, J. (1964) *The early growth of logic in the child*, London: Routledge & Kegan Paul.

Kallio, K.D. (1982) "Developmental change on a five-term transitive inference task", *Journal of Experimental Child Psychology* 29: 1–5.

Karmiloff-Smith, A. (1991) "Beyond modularity", ch. 6 in S. Carey and R. Gelman (eds) *The epigenesis of mind*, Hillsdale, NJ: Lawrence Erlbaum.

Karmiloff-Smith, A. (1992) *Beyond modularity: A developmental perspective on cognitive science*, London : MIT Press

Kingma, J. (1984) "Task sensitivity and the sequence of development in seriation, ordinal correspondence, and cardination", *Genetic Psychology Monographs* 110 (2): 181–205.

Klahr, D. and Wallace, J.G. (1970) "An information processing analysis of some Piagetian experimental tasks", *Cognitive Psychology* 1: 358–387.

Kuenne, M.R. (1946) "Experimental investigation of the relation of language to transposition behaviour in young children", *Experimental Psychology* 36: 471–490.

Lashley, K.S. (1960) "Persistent problems in the evolution of mind", in F.A. Beach, D.O. Hebb, C.T. Morgan and H.W. Nissen (eds) *The neuropsychology of Lashley*, New York: McGraw-Hill.

Lawrenson, W. and Bryant, P. E. (1972) "Absolute and relative codes in young children", *Journal of Child Psychology and Psychiatry* 12: 25–35.

Leiser, D. and Gillieron, C. (1990) *Cognitive science and genetic epistemology*, New York: Plenum.

McGonigle, B.O. (1987) "Non-verbal thinking by animals", *Nature* 325: 110–112.

McGonigle, B.O. (1990) "Incrementing intelligent systems by design", *Proceedings of Simulations of Animal Behaviour* 525–531, Paris: MIT Press.

McGonigle, B. O. and Chalmers, M. (1977) "Are monkeys logical?" *Nature* 267: 694–696.

McGonigle, B. O. and Chalmers, M. (1980) "On the genesis of relational terms: A comparative study of monkeys and human children", *Antropologia Contemporanea* 3: 236.

McGonigle, B. O. and Chalmers, M. (1984) "The selective impact of question form and input mode on the symbolic distance effect in children", *Journal of Experimental Child Psychology* 37: 525–554.

McGonigle, B. O. and Chalmers, M. (1986) "Representations and strategies during inference", in T. Myers, K. Brown and B. O. McGonigle (eds) *Reasoning and discourse processes*, London: Academic Press.

McGonigle, B.O. and Chalmers, M. (1992) "Monkeys are rational!", *The Quarterly Journal of Experimental Psychology* 45B (3): 189–228.

McGonigle, B.O. and Chalmers, M. (1993) "An experimental analysis of ordering skills in children. ESRC Project grant final report", British Lending Library.

McGonigle, B. and Chalmers, M. (1995a) *The growth of intelligence in complex systems: A cognitive analysis*, to be published by MIT Press.

McGonigle, B. and Chalmers, M. (1995b) *Multiple size relational rule learning by monkeys*, ms. in preparation.

McGonigle, B., de Lillo, C. and Dickenson, T. (1992) "Serial order induced search in children and monkeys", paper presented at the 5th European Conference on Developmental Psychology, Seville, Spain.

McGonigle, B., de Lillo, C. and Dickenson, T. (1994) "Classification to order : a comparative analysis of categorical seriation in monkey and man", paper presented at the XVth. Congress of the International Primatological Society, Bali, Indonesia.

McGonigle, B., de Lillo, C., Dickenson, T. and St Johnson (1995) *Serial search strategies and self-regulation in children, monkeys and pigeons*, submitted for publication.

McGonigle, B. and Jaswal, V (1993) "Categorical seriation in children", Laboratory for Cognitive Neuroscience, Edinburgh, technical report.

McGonigle, B.O. and Jones, B. (1975) "The perception of linear gestalten by rat and monkey: sensory sensitivity or the perception of structure?" *Perception* 4: 419–429.

McGonigle, B.O. and Jones, B. (1978) "Levels of stimulus processing by the squirrel monkey: relative and absolute judgments compared", *Perception* 7: 635–659.

Moyer, R.S. (1973) "Comparing objects in memory: Evidence suggesting an internal psychophysics", *Perception and Psychophysics* 13(2): 180–184.

Navarick, D.J. and Fantino, E. (1974) "Stochastic transitivity and unidimensional behaviour", *Psychological Review* 81: 427–441.

Nehmzow, U. and McGonigle, B. (1993) "Navigation mobiler roboter mittels Differential-Lichtkompass", *Workshop "Hybride und integrierte Ansatze zur Raumreprasentation und ihre Anwedung"*, Berlin (*German Journal for Artificial Intelligence, "KI"*), August.

Paivio, A. (1925) "Perceptual comparisons through the mind's eye", *Memory and Cognition* 3, 6: 635–647.

Pears, R. and Bryant, P. (1990) "Transitive inferences by young children about spatial position", *British Journal of Psychology* 81: 497–510.

Piaget, J. (1928) *Judgment and reasoning in the child*, London: Routledge & Kegan Paul.

Piaget, J. (1970) *Genetic epistemology*, New York: Columbia University Press.

Perner, J., Steiner, G. and Staehlin, C. (1981) "Mental representation of length and weight series and transitive inferences in young children", *Journal of Experimental Child Psychology* 31: 177–192.

Reese, H.W. (1968) *The perception of stimulus relations*, London: Academic Press.

Riley, C.A. (1976) "The representation of comparative relations and the transitive inference task", *Journal of Experimental Child Psychology* 22: 1–22.

Riley, C.A. and Trabasso, T. (1974) "Comparatives, logical structures, and encoding in a transitive inference task", *Journal of Experimental Child Psychology* 17: 187–203.

Siemann and Delius (1993) "Implicit deductive reasoning in humans", Naturwissenschaften 80: 344–366.

Simon, H.A. (1969) *The sciences of the artificial*, Cambridge: MIT Press.

Sinclair, H., Stambak, M., Lezine, R.S. and Verba, M. (1990) *Infants and objects. The creativity of cognitive development*, New York: Academic Press.

Smedslund, J. (1966) "Performance on measurement and pseudo-measurement tasks by 5–7 year old children", *Scandinavian Journal of Psychology* 7: 81–92.

Smith, L. (1993) *Necessary knowledge. Piagetian perspectives on constructivism*, Hove: Lawrence Erlbaum.

Terrace, H.S. and McGonigle, B. (1994) "Memory and representation of serial order by children, monkeys and pigeons", *Current Directions in Psychological Science* 3, 6: 180–185.

Trabasso, T. (1977) "The role of memory as a system in making transitive inferences", ch. 11 in R.V. Kail and J.W. Hagen (eds) *Perspectives on the development of memory and cognition*, Hillsdale, NJ: Lawrence Erlbaum.

Trabasso, T., Riley, C.A. and Wilson, E.G. (1977) "The representation of linear and spatial strategies in reasoning: A developmental study", in R. Falmagne (ed.) *Reasoning: Representation and process in children and adults* (pp. 201–229). Hillsdale, N.J: Lawrence Erlbaum.

Tversky, A. (1969) "Intransitivity of preferences", *Psychological Review* 76: 31–48.

Young, R.M. (1976) *Children's seriation behaviour – An artificial intelligence analysis of a Piagetian task*, Basel: Birkhauser.

Youniss, J. and Murray, F.B. (1970) "Transitive inferences with non-transitive solutions controlled", *Developmental Psychology* 2: 169–17.

# Chapter 15

# Children and arithmetic

*Peter Bryant*

**ABSTRACT**

The development of children's understanding of mathematical relations and of their grasp of the number system is described. It is discussed that children easily recognise one-way part–part relations but that the number system at first causes them difficulty. Children's relational understanding allows them to solve addition and subtraction problems fairly well when these deal with simple increases and decreases in quantity. It also helps them to make proportional judgements when these involve part–part relations. However, problems that involve reactions between parts and wholes are at first extremely difficult. The review also deals with the effects of context and shows the considerable aptitudes that are handed on to children in informal settings.

*Keywords*: Mathematics, logic, cognitive development

## INTRODUCTION

Relations are the stuff of mathematical development. Children must learn what it means to say that two numbers are equal or that one is more than the other. They have eventually to learn to deal with part–part relations (ratios) and with part–whole relations (fractions, for example). They must be able to co-ordinate separate relational judgements in order to measure and understand measurement (A = B, B = C, therefore A = C) and to understand an ordinal series (A > B, B > C, therefore A > C) properly. They have to learn about multiplicative relations. On top of all this they have to learn about the connections between these different relationships, if they are to acquire a coherent picture of the mathematics that they are taught at school and the mathematics that they use in their everyday life.

The research that psychologists have done on children's understanding of these mathematical relations falls quite neatly into three separate branches. Each of these asks its own distinctive questions, each has its own kind of theory and each employs its own empirical paradigms.

Although all three approaches have made a great deal of progress, particularly in recent years, the subject as a whole has suffered from a certain lack of connection between the three. There is no compelling theoretical or practical reason for this separation, and one of my main arguments in this chapter is that there is now an urgent need (by means mainly of longitudinal research and intervention studies) for us to bring the three together in order to understand how children learn mathematics as well as they do and why they learn no better than they do.

## THE THREE APPROACHES

### 1 Universal intellectual development and mathematical achievement

The first approach is concerned with intellectual development in general and in particular with the growth of the understanding of universal logical principles. The central idea entertained by those who adopt this approach is that young children's abilities increase and improve with age, and that this sequence of development is universal. It is the same everywhere, whether or not children go to school and are taught mathematics. Not only is the development universal, but so also are the truths that are understood as a result of this development. The link between children's intellectual development and their mathematical progress is simply that they need to reach a certain intellectual level in order to understand certain mathematical principles. Young children, it is argued, must surmount certain intellectual barriers before they can make any progress in mathematics.

Since the focus of interest here is on events which precede mathematics learning, the experimental paradigms that people have adopted to answer the questions posed by the first approach are usually a far cry from the sums and the word problems that children have to face in their mathematical lessons.

Piaget's theory (1952) and his experiments are the clearest example of this approach, but there are others too. In Piaget's view logic is the essential requirement and also at first a formidable barrier for the child learning mathematics. He argued that children's understanding of the counting system, their success with addition and subtraction and later with multiplication and division, their dealings with proportions, with measurement and with geometry, all depend on their ability to make various logical moves. So he and his colleagues, and later countless followers, gave children one-to-one correspondence, seriation and conservation tasks in order to see if they were ready for number, and transitivity tasks to see if they were in principle able to understand measurement.

## 2 Mathematical achievements and mathematical difficulties

The second approach tackles the child's experiences in the classroom head on. The main concern of those concerned with this approach is to find out what is happening when children solve mathematical problems, how they do so and why they make mistakes. Not surprisingly the empirical paradigms used here are tasks which are strikingly similar to those that the child is given in the classroom. The most common form of mathematical problem used by this group of researchers has been the word problem, in which sums are given in the form of brief and meaningful cameos ("Bill has three oranges: Sam has eight. How many more does Sam have than Bill?"), but there does not seem to be any particular theoretical reason for this preference, and it probably reflects the increasing use of word problems in mathematics lessons and in the work books which school children have to work through nowadays.

Although the hypotheses that different people have produced about children doing sums and solving various other mathematical problems are diverse, the form of the data that interest them is rather consistent. By and large they are interested either in the speed with which a child reaches a conclusion or in the mistakes that s/he makes on the way to a solution of a mathematical problem. Their concentration on actual mathematical problems has meant that they have little to say about the link between the way that a child solves a mathematical problem and the way that s/he solves any other problem. Their interests seem to stop at the classroom door, and thus the contrast between the two approaches that I have mentioned so far is stark. One group of researchers concentrates on abilities which affect many aspects of a child's life and can only speculate on their mathematical relevance: the other produces a great deal of data on children's mathematical achievements but cannot say anything for certain about the relevance of these to the child's intellectual life in general.

## 3 Mathematics and culture

The third approach concentrates on the transmission of knowledge. According to this view a considerable part of children's intellectual development is a direct result of the information that they are given and the intellectual tools that they acquire with the help of other people more experienced than themselves. What they learn about mathematics from other people is a valid part of this intellectual development, and it is valid in two ways. One is that the progress that children make in mathematics depends not only on the stage of intellectual development that they happen to have reached, but also quite considerably on the kind of mathematical instruction and mathematical experiences that they have both in and out of school. The second is that what they learn about mathematics may have in turn a formidable effect on their understanding of the environment. There is the possibility of a two-way connection: the children's intellectual level will affect their success in mathematics, but their growing mathematical success will play a part in their mathematical development.

Most of the psychologists who adopt this approach acknowledge Vygotsky (Vygotsky 1986; Vygotsky and Luria 1993) as their leader. It was he who proposed the idea of the "zone of proximal development", whereby children eventually manage to do on their own what at first they could only do with the help of an adult, and also the notion of the "cultural tool". He argued that people have devised effective tools (such as systems of measurement) over the centuries to help them to study and to control their environment, and have then handed these on across the generations, either in the classroom or in less formal settings: when a child masters such a tool not only is s/he more effective in an intellectual sense than before, but also their intellectual processes are transformed at the same time.

## THE FIRST APPROACH

### 1 Cardinal number

Piaget's influence (Piaget 1952; Piaget and Inhelder 1974; Piaget, Inhelder and Szeminska 1960; Inhelder and Piaget 1958) on our ideas about mathematical development is sometimes unacknowledged in current reviews of the subject, but it is still very strong. He posed most of the important questions which still dominate work on children's mathematics, and some of his answers are still quite plausible.

He can be counted as a sceptic as far as early mathematics is concerned. The idea of the development of reversibility – his central theoretical tenet – led him to the belief that young children acquire the appearance of being mathematical when in fact they have no real understanding of what they are doing and will not for several years.

Reversibility is the ability to perceive a change and at the same time to cancel it out subjectively by imagining the opposite change. In Piaget's theory reversibility lies at the heart of the understanding of all logic, and therefore, of all mathematics. A child whose intellectual processes are not reversible, according to Piaget, cannot understand the cardinal and ordinal properties of number, has no notion of the additive composition of numbers, is quite unable to reason about multiplication or division and cannot measure.

We can start with principle of cardinal number. This is that any set of a given number of objects will have the same quantity of objects in it as any other set with the same number in it. This is easy to show, because there is one-to-one correspondence between any two sets of the same number. For each object in one set there is an equivalent object in the other set and vice versa.

Suppose that the child is shown two parallel rows of objects and is asked to compare them numerically. A good way to accomplish the task would be to count the two rows. Another just as respectable way would be to compare the rows object by object, which is a strategy called one-to-one correspondence: see whether for every object in one row there is an equivalent object in the other and, for example, if there is and there are still some left over in the second row conclude that the second row is the more numerous one. A third, but thoroughly unreliable, way of making the comparison would be to judge the two rows on the basis of their lengths.

Young children adopt the third way, the unreliable way. Their spontaneous reliance on length is one of the most often repeated and most reliable phenomena in the history of empirical psychology. Children even choose this untrustworthy cue in the face of considerable inducement not to do so: there are two studies in which the one-to-one correspondence cues were emphasised by lines between the objects in each row, and even here many of the children still disregard one-to-one correspondence and went for length.

Reversibility, according to Piaget, is the key to the child's eventual discovery that one-to-one correspondence is a good cue and length a very bad one in comparisons of number. If a child who has reversible cognitive processes sees one of the rows being spread out s/he can work out that this has no effect on the actual number of objects in the row: they can now cancel out this change for themselves by imagining the inverse change and thus can realise that there has been no real change in number. Furthermore they can also see that changing the length of one of the rows does not alter the one-to-one correspondence between the two rows.

The child who thinks about quantity in an irreversible manner (the "irreversible" child) cannot do these things, and this leads him into some surprising errors. The most striking of these was illustrated first in some observations by Piaget himself (1952), and later in a provocative (though complex) experiment by Gréco (1962). Gréco noted that children still made the mistake of relying on length when they could already count objects quite well. He asked children both to count and to compare the quantity of two rows, one of which was longer than the other, though the two contained an equal number of objects. He found that many of the children counted the rows correctly, and said for example that there were five objects in one and five in the other, but nevertheless asserted that the longer row was more numerous.

Piaget and his colleagues reached two momentous conclusions on the basis of this and similar results. One was that children do not at first understand the cardinal properties of number: if they use length rather than one-to-one correspondence as a cue for quantity comparisons, and if they say that two rows both contain five objects and yet that one is more numerous than the other, they have no idea that two rows with the same number will be in one-to-one correspondence with each other and thus must be equal numerically. The other conclusion was that children at first do not know what they are doing when they count: a child who says that there are more objects in one row of five objects than in another row of five objects does not know the correct meaning of the word "five".

These two conclusions are difficult to fault. The evidence for the young child's mistaken reliance on the length cue and reluctance to turn to one-to-one correspondence with displays such as those we have described is hard and fast, and there is, as far as I know, no good evidence to refute Greco's claim that initially what the child says when s/he counts ("quotité") has nothing to do with what s/he thinks about the numerical quantities involved ("quantité").

However, there is at least one good reason for hesitating about the negative conclusion on one-to-one correspondence. It is that children often share, and sharing is an activity which on the face of it seems to depend on one-to-one correspondence. Three studies (Miller 1984; Desforges and Desforges 1980; Frydman and Bryant 1988) have shown that children as young as 4 share out numbers of things equally between two or more recipients rather successfully, and they usually do so on a repetitive "one for A, one for B" basis. Is this not a temporal form of one-to-one correspondence?

The answer must be "Yes", but then we have to consider the possibility that they share on a one-to-one basis without any idea why this is the right thing to do. Sharing, like counting, is a common activity which young children must witness quite often and may very well imitate. They may know that sharing in a one-to-one way is the appropriate action without having any good idea about the reason for it.

Olivier Frydman and I tried to find out more about children's understanding of sharing by devising a task in which children who share on a rote basis without understanding what they are doing would behave in one way, and children who understand the basis of one-to-one sharing would respond quite differently. We gave the children "chocolates" which were either single or double chocolates: in fact these were plastic unifix bricks, all of the same colour, which could be stuck together. We asked the children to share the chocolates out to two recipients, so that each recipient ended up with the same total amount. But we also told the children that one of the recipients only accepted doubles and the other only singles. So the child's problem was to work out that for every double that he gave one recipient, he now had to give two singles to the other one. We reasoned that a child who had shared on a one-to-one basis in a rote fashion would not be able to make this adjustment, whereas a child who understood the basis for one-to-one sharing would see the reason for changing to a one (double) for A, two (singles) for B pattern.

This study produced a very sharp developmental difference. Most of the 4-year-old children did not make the adjustment, and in fact the majority ended up giving the recipient who accepted doubles twice as many chocolates in all as the recipient who accepted singles. This was because these children continued sharing in a one-to-one manner, which meant that for every single that they gave one recipient they handed out a double to the other. In contrast, most of the 5-year-olds did manage to make the necessary adjustment. These children usually gave the double to one recipient and then immediately two singles to the other, and so on. The reason for the difference between the two age groups is unclear to us, but at the very least the study establishes that 5-year-old children have a clear and flexible understanding of the mathematical basis of one-to-one sharing.

What about the 4-year-olds? They had certainly hit a barrier in our new version of the sharing task, but we still had no idea how formidable that barrier was for them. So, in a later study we devised a new version of the singles/doubles task in which we introduced bricks of different colours. Our aim was to use colour cues to emphasise one-to-one correspondence. In this new task each double consisted of a yellow and a blue brick joined together, and half the singles were blue and half yellow. This was the only change, and yet it had a dramatic effect. Nearly all the 4-year-old children solved the problem, and they did so because they could now see how to use one-to-one correspondence to solve the problem. The typical pattern of sharing was to give a double (consisting of course of one yellow and one blue brick) to one recipient and then to give a yellow and a blue single to the other one. They adapted to one-to-one strategy successfully when the one-to-one cues were emphasised. They also learned a great deal from this experience, because when later on we gave the same children the single/doubles task with bricks of one colour only (as in the original experiment) these children did extremely well. They had surmounted the barrier that we identified in the first study, and we conclude from this that even 4-year-old children have a basic understanding of the reason why one-to-one sharing leads to equal quantities. It follows that they do have a respectable understanding of one-to-one correspondence and, therefore, a basis for understanding the cardinal properties of number.

But do they extend this understanding to number words? We looked at this question in another study. In this we took a group of 4-year-old children who could share quite well, and we asked them to share out some "sweets" (again unifix bricks) between two recipients. When this was done we counted out aloud the number of sweets that the child had given to one recipient, and then asked him or her how many had been given to the other recipient. None of the children straightaway made the correct inference that the other recipient had the same number of sweets even though they had meticulously shared the sweets out on a one-to-one basis: instead all of the children tried to count the second lot of sweets. We stopped them doing so, and asked the question again. Even then less than half the children made the correct inference about the second recipient's sweets.

Thus many 4-year-old children fail to extend their considerable understanding of sharing to counting. We conclude from this that young children do grasp the cardinality of number and yet do not at first apply this understanding to number words. Here, it could be said, is an example of quantite without quotite. The children do have quite a good grasp of one-to-one correspondence, but do not apply this knowledge to number words.

## 2 Counting

This last conclusion takes us directly to the question of young children's counting. The first point to be made about this extraordinary phenomenon is that it happens and that it happens at a very young age. From roughly the age of 2 years children begin to count. They count objects and actions and on occasion their counting is "abstract" in the sense that they simply produce their version of the number sequence without attaching the numbers to anything in particular. At first they make many mistakes and it is interesting to note that many of these seem to stem from their attempts to get to grips with the decade structure. Erroneous sequences like "twenty-nine, twenty-ten, twenty-eleven" are common (Fuson 1988) and show that it takes some time at least for children to grasp how the number sequence is punctuated by decades and, at a higher level, by hundreds and thousands.

The irregularity of our number words also seems for a while to be a serious problem. Most of the teen words "twelve, thirteen" and some of the decade words ("thirty", "fifty") are highly irregular in the sense that the words themselves do not denote their position in the decades structure at all well. Contrast the spoken number "one hundred and ten" with "eleven" and it is easy to see that in linguistic terms the former is much more clearly placed than the latter. The evidence that linguistic irregularities are stumbling blocks for children comes partly from data which show that teen numbers, where these irregularities are most striking, are particularly difficult for children who are learning to count, and partly from comparisons with children learning to count in other languages, like Chinese, in which the number words are not so capricious. I shall describe some of these studies in more detail later on in this chapter.

Nevertheless, even English-speaking children do count before they go to school, and by the time they get there, their knowledge of number words, though still imperfect, is quite considerable. What, we must now ask, is the significance of this achievement?

Two starkly different answers have been given to this question. The first is that pre-school counting is vacuous, that at first children mouth number words without understanding what these mean and that several years elapse between their first acquaintance with the number sequence and their understanding what this sequence actually means. Piaget (1952) took the most extreme version of this position. For him the evidence that children fail in one-to-one correspondence tasks and his consequent conclusion that they do not understand cardinality meant that they had a strikingly incomplete idea of the meaning of the number words which they so readily produce. A child who says that there are five counters in row A and five in row B and yet that row A is more numerous, does not know the correct meaning of the word "five".

A milder version of this position comes from the work by Frydman and myself on sharing. Our idea is that children do at first have a very poor idea of the meaning of number words, but that the stumbling block is the number system itself and not the principle of cardinality which, as the work on sharing shows, causes them few serious problems.

The starkly contrasting view (to Piaget's and to ours) of children's counting is that they grasp its essential principles right from the start. This is the conclusion reached by Gelman and Gallistel in their 1978 book on young children's counting and by Gelman and Meck (1983) in a later study of children's judgements of the correctness of a puppet's counting.

Gelman and her colleagues argued that children must grasp five basic principles in order to understand what they are doing when they count, and the main conclusion of these research workers is that children as young as 2 and 3 years do have this understanding even though they make many mistakes. The name that Gelman gives to this theoretical position is "principles before skills". Children understand the basic principles of counting right from the start, she argues: their mistakes are merely failures to put these principles into practice all the time, and this rests on skills which it takes them some time to acquire.

There are two main empirical bases for this theoretical position. One is some research, much of it done by Gelman's colleagues, which apparently shows that even babies can discriminate between numbers (Starkey and Cooper 1980; Strauss and Curtis 1981, 1984; Antell and Keating 1983; Starkey, Spelke and Gelman 1983; Cooper 1984; Starkey, Spelke and Gelman 1990). The other is Gelman's own work on counting in children between the ages of 2 and 5 years. In this chapter I shall deal only with the second set of studies.

The first three of the five principles are "how to count" principles. One is "the one-to-one principle". Here the requirement is that the child understands that he or she must count all the objects in a set once and once only: each one must be given just one number tag. This is quite a different requirement to Piaget's. For him one-to-one correspondence was about the relationship between members of different sets. For Gelman and her colleagues the one-to-one principle is about how to count one set of objects.

Another "how to count" principle is "the stable order principle", which means that one counts in a set order, and in the same set order each time. This principle is the nearest that Gelman and Gallistel get to ordinality, but again their requirement is different from and much less demanding than Piaget's because they are only concerned with the children's appreciation that they must count in a consistent sequence and not with their understanding that the sequence is a sequence of increasing magnitude.

The final how to count principle is "the cardinal principle", but despite its name it is a far cry from Piaget's notion of cardinality. In Gelman's terms the cardinal principle involves the understanding that the last number counted represents the value of the set. So a child who counts a set "one, two, three, four" must understand that "four", the last of these numbers, represents the number of objects in that set. The requirement falls short of Piaget's because it concerns the value of a single set and not the relation between sets of the same number.

Gelman's requirements involve two other principles. One is "the abstraction principle" which states that the number in a set is quite independent of any of the qualities of the members in that set: the rules for counting a heterogeneous set of objects are the same as for counting a homogeneous one. The other is "the order irrelevance principle": the point here is that the order in which members of a set are counted makes no difference, and anyone who counts a set, for example, from left to right will come to the same answer as someone else who counts it from right to left.

The main aim of Gelman's research on counting was to show that even very young children understand these principles at the time that they begin to count, and, therefore, know from the start what counting means. Gelman and Gallistel observed young children counting sets of objects and recorded whether the children always counted the same order and always counted each object once, and also whether they seemed to recognise that the last number counted signified the number of the set. Gelman and Meck (1983) also asked children to make judgements about a puppet which they saw counting: this puppet occasionally violated the one-to-one principle and the cardinal principle, and the aim of these experiments was to see whether the children could spot these violations. By and large the results of these studies supported Gelman's contention that the children did have some understanding of the three "how to count" principles as these were set out in her model.

So we end up with two entirely different answers to the question "Do children understand what they are doing when they count?", and it is worth spending some time considering what is the nature of this striking disagreement. It is certainly not a dispute about evidence, since the actual research of the two groups took an entirely different form. The fact is that Piaget and Gelman did different kinds of experiments because the criteria that each of them used for understanding counting were also quite different. Piaget opted for ordinality and cardinality, and Gelman for her five principles.

We have already noted that in some ways Gelman's requirements are less demanding than Piaget's, and this means that we should start by considering two possibilities. One is that Piaget's requirements are too strong, the other that Gelman's are too weak.

The first of these possibilities seems much more plausible than the second. Both models, for example, include cardinality, but they treat it quite differently. Piaget concentrated on the relationship between sets of the same number, and it is impossible to dispute his claim that a child will only understand the meaning of the word "six" if he or she also understands that a set of six objects is equal in number to any other set of six objects. Gelman, on the other hand, concentrated on the question of the child understanding that the last number counted represents the number of the set. It is true of course that the child must realise this, but it is also true that a child could grasp the fact that the last number is the important one without really understanding the quantitative significance of this number, at any rate as far as its relationship to other sets is concerned.

There is some striking evidence that young children who count quite proficiently still do not know how to use numbers to compare two different sets. Both Michie (1984) and Saxe (1979) have reported a remarkable reluctance in young children who have been asked to compare two sets of objects quantitatively to count the two sets. They knew the number sequence and so they were in principle capable of counting the objects and it would have been the right thing to have done, but they did not do it.

This reluctance to use number as a comparative measure was demonstrated even more clearly in a remarkable experiment by Sophian (1988) in which she asked 3- and 4-year-old children to judge whether a puppet who counted was doing the right thing. This puppet was given two sets of objects and was told in some trials to compare the two sets and in others to find out how many objects there were in front of it altogether. So in the first kind of trial the right thing to do was to count the two sets separately while in the second it was to count them together. Sometimes the puppet got it right but at other times it mistakenly counted all the objects together when it was asked to compare the two sets and counted them separately when it was asked how many objects there were altogether.

The results of this experiment were largely negative. The younger children did particularly badly (below chance) in the trials in which the puppet was asked to compare two different sets. They clearly had no idea that one must count two rows separately in order to compare them, and this suggests that they had not yet grasped the cardinal properties of the numbers that they counted.

This empirical evidence only serves to underline a conceptual point that Gelman's requirement for the understanding of cardinality was too undemanding. It is in principle possible for a child to understand that the last number counted is important and still have no idea about its quantitative significance. Fuson (1988) and Baroody (1992) have made the same point.

One of the most obvious differences between the two approaches is that Piaget is concerned above all with relations between sets while Gelman concentrates on children counting one set at a time. But there is even some evidence about young children counting single quantities that casts further doubt on Gelman's claims that children understand the cardinality of number words as soon as they begin to count.

An interesting study by Shipley and Shepperson (1990) shows that children find it quite difficult to count objects when these are broken up into different physical entities. When they were asked to count the number of forks and the forks themselves were physically separate entities, young children tended to count the physical bits, and not the actual number of complete forks. Also several studies (Wynn 1990; Frye, Braisby, Lowe, Maroudas and Nicholls 1989; Fuson 1988) have shown that when children are asked to give someone a certain number of objects ("Give me five bricks") they often fail to count and simply grab a handful of objects and the number that they had over is for the most part wrong. So, even when only a single set is involved, young children do not seem to understand the significance of counting. They may realise, when they do count, that the last number is the important one, but the fact that they do not seem to know exactly when to count suggests that they have no idea why counting is important. They have not grasped the cardinal properties of the number words that they know so well. Their performance fits the Piagetian picture of quotité without quantité very closely.

Much the same point can be made about the other two "how to count" principles. Children certainly have to know that they should count each object once and only once, but this is not the only form of one-to-one correspondence that they must understand. Piaget's point that children must also understand one-to-one correspondence between sets if they are to understand the quantitative significance of number words is surely right, and yet this is not part of Gelman's one-to-one principle.

Nor does Gelman's stable-order principle go nearly far enough. Numbers come in a certain order and it is certainly true that children have to understand this. But the reason for the order is that numbers are arranged in increasing magnitude and it is quite possible that a child who always produces numbers in the same sequence realises the quantitative significance of this sequence. Gelman's evidence is no help on this particular point, but much the same goes for the work of other interested psychologists. Piaget's evidence as we have seen is remarkably indirect since it concerns only continuous quantities and not number, and there does not seem to be any other clear work on young children's understanding of the ordinal properties of number. We simply cannot say whether children understand the ordinality of the number sequence or not.

My conclusions on this controversy about children's understanding of counting are simple. Of the two sets of requirements Piaget's are better than Gelman's. Children will only understand the quantitative significance of the number words that they learn when they have grasped both the cardinal and the ordinal properties of the number sequence. Most of the evidence suggests that children at first do not understand cardinality and Gelman's own work on the cardinal principle, as she defines it, throws no doubt on this suggestion. Our knowledge about children's understanding of ordinality is much less advanced, but again Gelman's work on the stable order principle does not in any way show that children understand the ordinal relations in the number sequence. There are good reasons for thinking that at first children are practising little more than a verbal routine when they count.

## 3 Ordinal number, inferences and measurement

The order of the words in the number sequence represents their magnitude (10 is more than 9, 23 more than 22), and as we have seen the difference between Piaget's assessment of children's understanding and Gelman's is as great over ordinality as over cardinality. We have seen that Gelman's more optimistic assessment is based on the children's evident ability to produce the same number words in the same order on different occasions, at any rate with small numbers.

The evidence to which Piaget appeals is typically a great deal less direct. Piaget's position is that young children are incapable of grasping the nature of a series that increases in quantity. He attributes this intellectual gap once again to a lack of reversibility. He argues that a child who does not possess this intellectual property is, as a result, incapable of handling the quantitative relations in even a simple series. So, faced with the series A > B > C, the "irreversible" child will be able to take in at one time that A > B and at another that B > C, but simply cannot grasp these two relations at the same time. He cannot do this because it is beyond him to understand that B can simultaneously be smaller than one quantity and larger than another.

The actual empirical studies which Piaget offers as evidence for this proposition are his well-known seriation and transitivity studies. In the seriation experiment children are asked to put sticks of different lengths in ordered series – ordered that is by their size. Young children fail to do this. The youngest behave randomly and slightly older children simply form two piles, one of the smaller and the other of the larger sticks, a pattern of responding which, according to Piaget, shows that they can take in single relations such as A > B at the same time, but have greater difficulty with a series in which a particular quantity is smaller than one and larger than another. More recently this position has received considerable support from an experiment by Perner and Mansbridge (1983) on children's memory for length. The task that they gave children was to learn about and remember the relations between three pairs of sticks of different colours and lengths. One group was shown a series of four sticks (A > B, B > C, C > D), and the other three pairs of disparate sticks (A > B, C > D, E > F), over a series of trials. The second group were much the more successful of the two groups: they learned better and they made fewer mistakes. Perner and Mansbridge quite plausibly attributed this difference to the fact that the first group had to deal with two-way relations (B larger in one pair and smaller in the other), and it is easy to see that this conclusion is at one with Piaget's view of children's difficulties with ordinality.

If the problem that children have with an ordered series is to be traced back to an inability to handle two-way relations, they should be equally out of their depth with transitive inferences. The premises in transitive inferences take the form of two or more quantitative relations (e.g. A > B, B > C) and the inference involves combining these in order to answer a question about the relation between the two quantities which are not directly compared (A?C). The idea that young children cannot make such an inference has more than one implication for their understanding of mathematics. The claim is relevant to the question of ordinality, of course, but it also implies that they should be unable to measure or to understand other people's measurements. If they cannot connect A and C by virtue of both having been compared to a common value (measure) B, then they will not see the point of taking a ruler to compare two lengths which cannot be compared directly.

The question about transitive inferences is one of the most vexed in studies of cognitive development. This is largely because the question imposes some formidable empirical problems for the researcher. In order to be sure that a mistake in a transitive inference task is a genuinely logical one (i.e. a failure to combine two premises to make an inferential judgement), one must be sure that the child can recall the two premises at the time that they are asked the inferential question (i.e. can they remember that A > B and B > C when asked the A?C question?). This was pointed out some time ago by Bryant and Trabasso (1971) and ever since we did so the most common empirical solution has been to make sure that the children learn the premises thoroughly before they have to face the empirical question.

But this leads to a new problem which was originally pointed out by Perner and Mansbridge (1983). It is that the experimenter might unwittingly be teaching the child something about ordinal relations during the learning period. If a child finds it difficult to remember that A > B and that B > C because he cannot appreciate that A can have different relations to different values, maybe repeated experience with these two pairs will eventually teach him that such two-way relations are possible.

The problem intensifies when one considers the empirical connotations of another requirement for transitive inference tasks for which Bryant and Trabasso (1971) were also responsible. We argued that such a task must involve at least five values rather than a minimum of three. We made the claim that an A > B, B > C (three value) task is inadequate. The child, we argued, could answer the eventual A?C inferential question in such tasks by remembering that A was larger when he last saw it or that C was the smaller. Thus the child could answer the question correctly, but illogically, merely by repeating one or both of these remembered values. If, however, one has a task with four premises (A > B, B > C, C > D, D > E) three of the quantities (B, C and D) are the smaller value in one of these pairs and the larger in another. Inferential judgements based on these quantities cannot be dismissed as mere parroting.

This requirement is now generally accepted, but unfortunately it makes the problem of ensuring that children remember the initial premises a much more daunting one. It is, as one might expect from Perner and Mansbridge's results, quite difficult for a 4-year-old child to learn and remember an A > B, B > C, C > D, D > E series. When we (Bryant and Trabasso) originally gave 4- and 5-year old children four such pairs to learn, we found that it took most of them many trials to do so. Thus our discovery that the children who remembered these pairs then made transitive inferences successfully is quite interesting, but we cannot rule out the possibility that we taught the children about ordinality in the first part of our experiment. Of course if that were true, it would be quite interesting too: one needs to know if it is so easy to teach young children about a logical principle in one single experimental session.

One way of getting round this empirical difficulty is to present children with the premises at the same time as they are asked the transitive question, but this is not so easy to do without at the same time providing so much information that the need for the inference actually disappears. Ros Pears and I (Pears and Bryant 1990) have managed an inferential task not with length but with relative position (up–down) in which no learning at all was necessary because the children could see the premises (pairs of different coloured bricks, one on top of the other) at the same time as they were asked the inferential question (the relative position of two of these bricks in a tower of five or six bricks) and we found that even 4-year-old children can make respectable transitive inferences, but since this is not a dimension of much importance in children's mathematics I will not dwell on the study any further.

We must pass on instead to the second mathematical implication of work on transitive inferences – measurement. If children need to understand transitive inferences in order to measure, then evidence that children can measure is evidence too that they can make transitive inferences. There is such evidence.

We ourselves (Bryant and Kopytynska 1976) gave 5-year-old children a simple measurement task in which they were faced with two blocks of wood each with a hole at the top, and were asked to compare the depths of the holes. The children also had a stick, and they used it systematically to measure these depths. Three different experiments of ours confirmed this result, and more recently Miller (1989) has reported an equivalent success with a similar but more meaningful task (working out which hole Snoopy must be hiding in). It is hard to see how young children could manage as well as they do in these tasks unless they understood the significance of transitive inferences.

Yet, we must still be cautious. Piaget's criteria for logical understanding were demanding, and the hardest criterion of all was his insistence on children grasping logical necessity. As Smith (1993) in a recent stimulating monograph on logical necessity has clearly shown, Piaget's position was that no one can be said to be making a genuinely logical judgement, even when it is the correct solution to a logical problem, unless that person also understands the properties which make this judgement necessarily true. "Necessary properties lay down both why something is, and has to be, what it is, and why it is not, and cannot be, anything else" (Smith 1993, p. 2). Piaget also thought that the only way that a person can show that he understands the necessity of a logical judgement is by justifying it logically. His position was that "a true, unjustified belief never amounts to knowledge" (Smith 1993, p. 65). The natural upshot of this is that children could not be said to understand transitivity, even when they solve transitivity problems, unless they can justify their inferences subsequently, and it needs to be said straightaway that none of the studies that I have just described fits that bill.

We are faced with an empirical question, which is how to establish not only the presence, but also the absence, of the understanding of logical necessity. It is perfectly plausible that someone who appeals to the logical necessity of a correct solution to a logical problem really does understand logical necessity, but one cannot, in my view, conclude that a person who fails to produce such a judgement therefore lacks this understanding. A child may have grasped logical necessity without being able to put it into words.

My rather hesitant conclusion about Piaget's hypothesis on ordinality and transitivity is that it is in the end rather unconvincing. Children may fumble in the seriation task, but they still seem to be able to work out that a quantity can have two values and to use this information in a measuring task. However, we certainly need more data on how they justify what they do in such tasks.

## 4 Addition and subtraction

The work that we have discussed so far shows that young children are able, at the very least, to take in simple quantitative relations like "same", "greater" and "smaller". It seems quite possible, therefore, that they can also cope with simple transformations which increase a quantity or decrease it (make it greater or smaller).

In fact children do naturally have a great deal of experience with increasing and decreasing quantities, and there is growing evidence that they may have some idea of the nature of addition and subtraction before they go to school.

Indeed psychologists' attempts to demonstrate the pervasiveness of the first two operations have now reached the cradle. Karen Wynn (1992) set out to see whether babies of 8 months old could work out the results of addition and subtraction. She used a measure of surprise (babies look longer at events which go against their expectations). She showed the babies either one or two Mickey Mouse toys which she then hid behind a screen. Then in full view of the child she either added a Mickey Mouse (1 + 1) to the one behind the screen or subtracted one from the two that were there (2 − 1). Finally she removed the screen. In every case either one or two Mickey Mouses were revealed: in half the trials the number there was the appropriate one (two Mickey Mouses in the 1 + 1 condition and one in the 2 − 1 condition), and in the other half it was not (one in the 1 + 1 condition and two in the 2 − 1 condition).

Wynn found that the babies looked longer at the inappropriate displays than at the appropriate ones, and she concluded that they could work out the results of simple additions and subtractions. However, she was quite rightly concerned that the babies might have simply responded as they did on the basis of expecting a change from the original number and finding no change in the appropriate displays (e.g. one in the 1 + 1 displays represents no change). So she ran another experiment in which she repeated the 1 + 1 condition with one alteration. When she finally removed the screen the babies either saw two Mickey Mouses (appropriate) or three (inappropriate). Thus both the appropriate and the inappropriate displays represented a change in number from the original amount.

Here too the babies looked at the inappropriate display for a longer time than at the appropriate one, and it is difficult to see how this impressive result can be interpreted in any other way than as evidence that even babies can work out the results of a 1 + 1 addition. [Whether they are as capable with subtraction is not yet certain (Bryant 1992).]

Given this striking result, it should not surprise us that other research with children who are considerably older, though still well within the preschool period, has also shown that they can work out the consequences of simple additions and subtractions. Starkey's (1983) study is a case in point. He gave children aged between 24 and 35 months two, three or four objects to put in a container. Then he either added or subtracted some objects himself or left the container untouched. The child was asked to remove all the objects from the container which was built in such a way that the child could only take out one object at a time.

Starkey's question was whether the children would reach into the box the right number of times (e.g. three times in a 3 − 1 trial), and he found that on the whole they did, at any rate when numbers less than four were involved. When the final sum was amounted to three or less the children were correct more often than would be expected by chance. Starkey concluded that pre-school children can work out the results of simple additions and subtractions, and, given Wynn's results, it is easy to accept this suggestion.

These, of course, are nonverbal tasks. Wynn's subjects knew no words: Starkey did not count or mention number in his experiment, and his measure (the number of reaches) was a nonverbal one. When number words are introduced, young children begin to make serious mistakes, but there is some interesting evidence that these errors are more frequent in some conditions than in others. In a rather similar task to Starkey's, Hughes (1986) also gave children (2–4 years in age) some bricks in a container and then added further bricks or subtracted some. Then he asked the children about the consequent number in the box. In fact the children managed quite well in this task but had considerable difficulty in another one which contained no reference to concrete material: the children were asked, for example, "what does one and one make?". This was a far more difficult task, and Hughes' contention, that children understand addition and subtraction, so long as these involve concrete material, seems a plausible one.

## 5 Conclusions – the first approach

It is, I think, a fair summary of the data on mathematics in the preschool period that it shows that children understand and use simple mathematical relations, and that they begin to learn about the number sequence, but that they have difficulty in combining these two very different types of mathematical achievement. One consequence of this disconnection is that young children often make mistakes about the meaning of the number words that they are learning. Piaget's doubts about their understanding of number words are justifiable: his reservations about their understanding of cardinal and ordinal relations, however, are far too pessimistic.

My thesis poses a causal question. What makes children so quick to grasp and use quantitative relations and yet so slow to come to terms with the basic meaning of number words? One possible explanation may lie in the informal instruction that they receive at home. A number of observational studies (Durkin 1993; Durkin, Shire, Riem, Crowther and Rutter 1986; Saxe, Guberman and Gearhart 1987) show how difficult it is for parents not to give ambiguous verbal information to their young children about actual numbers. However, a study by Riem (cited by Durkin 1993) suggests that mothers find it quite easy to encourage one-to-one correspondence, at any rate as far as counting is concerned, and sharing, as I have remarked, is an activity which is probably quite easy to imitate.

## THE SECOND APPROACH

The second approach is mainly sums. The people studied in this research are mostly schoolchildren, but in some cases they are adults. The mathematical problems that are given in these studies are school-like and they are often quite hard. They take the form mainly of word problems, which are problems embedded in a meaningful sentence or a passage of prose.

### 1 Counting and addition and subtraction

Hughes' conclusion, with which we ended the last section, is an encouragement to look again at counting and at number words. Abstract additions and subtractions which evidently cause young children so much difficulty are usually couched in number words. In fact, it is possible to reduce an addition to a simple count. You can solve 2 + 5 sum by counting up to 2 and then counting on by 5 from there. This is the most basic solution of all, and it is known as counting-all. It is, however, a relatively uneconomic way to solve an additional problem. After all, why go to the trouble of counting the 2? Why not start with 2 and count on from there? This justifiable shortcut is called the counting-on strategy and it is far more economic. But there is a still more sophisticated option which is (rather clumsily) called counting-on-from-larger. Given 2 + 5 the child could start with the larger number 5 and simply count on by 2 from there. To start with the larger number has the effect of reducing the amount that has to be added and thus makes the operation quicker and probably less prone to error.

There is ample evidence that children progress from counting-all to counting-on to counting-on-from-larger during their first 2 years at school. Furthermore, Groen and Resnick (1977) have shown that it is possible to hurry on this development by giving children concentrated experience with additions.

The apparently spontaneous realisation by young schoolchildren that the order of the addends is immaterial implies quite strongly that they have also understood one of the main properties of addition – its commutativity.

To treat 2 + 5 in the same way as 5 + 2 is surely to demonstrate an understanding that 5 + 2 and 2 + 5 are equivalent. So it seems quite likely that children who consistently count-on-from-larger will also understand the commutativity principle. Yet the evidence on this apparently highly plausible connection is rather disappointing. Baroody and Gannon (1984) claim that they have found children who have adopted the counting-on-from-larger strategy and yet do not seem to have any idea of the commutativity of addition. However, our own results (Turner and Bryant, submitted) fail to confirm this claim. In our sample all the children who counted-on-from-larger appeared to understand commutativity, though not vice versa.

One further point needs to be made about these counting strategies. They can be used as well for subtraction, and there is evidence (Woods, Resnick and Groen 1975) that children sometimes count down and sometimes count up to solve such problems. Indeed Woods *et al.* claim that experienced children use whichever of the two strategies is the more economical: given a sum like 9 − 2 where there is a small subtrahend and quite a large gap between the two numbers they count down (by 2, in this case): but with a sum like 9 − 7 where the subtrahend is larger and the gap smaller they count up (again by 2).

There is some debate, however, about the frequency and the value of these strategies. Woods *et al.* report that children count down frequently in subtraction problems, and that the strategy serves them well. Siegler (1987) on the other hand claims that the strategy is relatively infrequent and that it is error-prone. He reached this conclusion on the basis of a study in which he found that a large proportion of the children's subtraction errors occurred in problems in which they counted down.

Nevertheless the general readiness of young children to use their knowledge of counting to solve addition and subtraction problems is good evidence that, in spite of the initial difficulties which they have in understanding the nature of the number system in their first years at school, they are still able to use the counting system in an impressively flexible way to solve mathematical problems. These data also suggest that children understand a great deal about one property involved in addition – its commutativity. However, they tell us nothing about children's understanding of another essential mathematical property – the additive composition of number. For direct evidence on that we have to turn to another source of information about children's mathematical understanding – word problems.

## 2 Word problems

Word problems are sums that are embedded either in stories or at least in meaningful sentences. They play a familiar part in the mathematical exercise books that schoolchildren have to work their way through at school as they do in psychological studies of children's mathematical skills. Broadly speaking there are four kinds of addition and subtraction word problems, and these are:

a *Compare problems*
  Mary has six books, and John has four. How many more books does Mary have than John?
b *Equalise problems*
  John has five comics, and Mary has two. How many comics does Mary need to have the same as John?
c *Change problems*
  John has four marbles and is given two more. How many does he have now?
d *Combine problems*
  Mary has four apples, and John has two. How many do they have altogether?

The great interest of problems such as these is that different kinds of problem can contain exactly the same mathematical sums as each other but in a different context (Fayol 1992; de Corte, Verschaffel and de Win 1985; de Corte and Verschaffel 1987, 1988; Stern 1993). The different kinds of word problem simply represent the sum in different ways and in different contexts. Therefore, if one type of problem turns out to be much more difficult than another, the difference between the two should tell us something about the way in which children represent mathematical tasks to themselves. Here are some examples of such differences.

Compare problems are consistently harder than Equalise problems (Carpenter and Moser 1982; Riley, Greeno and Heller 1983; Cividanes-Lago 1993) even though a glance at the two examples above will demonstrate, that in mathematical terms the two are the same. The difference is quite pervasive too, for Cividanes-Lago (1993) has shown that it is almost as strong when continuous material (length) is used as when the problems are given in their usual numerical form. So we are dealing with a question about the representation of quantity in general, and not just of numbers.

One possibility is that it is a matter of young children's difficulty in understanding the additive composition of number. The most direct way to solve the Compare problem given above is to realise that the larger number – 6 – consists of the smaller number 4 plus some other number, which must, therefore, be $6 - 4$. To carry out this line of thought the child must realise that if $6 - 4 = 2$ then $4 + 2 = 6$. This in turn depends on an understanding (1) of part–whole relationships (6 consists of $4 + 2$ or $3 + 3$ or $1 + 5$) and (2) of the inverse relation between addition and subtraction, and it is worth noting that Piaget's theory predicts that both these forms of understanding are difficult, if not impossible, for children whose understanding of quantity is irreversible.

There is good evidence that the stumbling block in the difficult Compare problems is indeed the need to plot part–whole relationships. When Hudson (1983) managed to make these relationships more obvious, the performance of the young children that he was testing improved dramatically. His ingenious manoeuvre was to tell children about a certain number of birds who were looking for worms, when only a limited number of worms were available. How many birds, he asked, were unable to find a worm? The children found this version of the task considerably easier than a more typical Compare problem which involved exactly the same material. Evidently the new task was easier because the children were given a rationale for breaking up the larger number into two parts.

On the other hand the context of the Equalise problems probably helps the child by encouraging him to start with the smaller quantity and to count up to the larger. The context, therefore, helps the child to avoid the part–whole problem: the child does not have to break up the larger number: he simply has to increase the smaller one by a certain amount. Much the same analysis of the Equalise/Compare difference can be found in Riley, Greeno and Heller's theory about word problems.

## 3 Multiplication and division

It is generally recognised that multiplication and division are more difficult operations and are generally understood a great deal later by young schoolchildren than addition and subtraction. Indeed the relation between the easier and the more difficult operations is often portrayed in terms of conflict. There is considerable evidence that children often wrongly use an additive strategy when a multiplicative strategy is the appropriate one, and on the other hand Miller and Paredes (1990) have claimed that for a while children actually "learn to add worse" as a result of coming to grips with multiplication. However, it is also clear that children use their knowledge of the easier operations to help them with the more difficult ones. Children often resort to repeated addition to solve multiplication problems and to repeated subtraction to do division (Nunes, Schliemann and Carraher 1993).

It is often claimed that multiplicative relations are particularly difficult for children. The reason offered for the difficulty is that in multiplication the transformation depends on the size not just of the multiplier but also of the multiplicand. If you add 2 to 4 and 2 to 6, the change is the same in both cases: both numbers increase by 2. But if you multiply each of those numbers by 2 the transformation is quite different in either case. This particular difference between the two operations leads naturally to the question whether it is harder for children to understand multiplicative relations than additive ones.

There is no doubt at all that the answer is that it is a great deal harder. Multiplicative relations pose great difficulties even in late childhood in tasks devised by Inhelder and Piaget (1958) and reworked by others (Siegler 1976, 1978). It has also been claimed that children often treat a multiplicative relation as an additive one (Anderson and Cuneo 1978; Wilkening 1979; Wilkening and Anderson 1982).

The best example of the paradigm which has been used most frequently to support this claim is an experiment by Wilkening (1981). In this, children had to make judgements about time, speed and distance. They were given three animals who ran at quite different speeds (turtle, guinea pig, cat) and in different trials each of these animals ran for a certain period of time (the length of time that a dog barked). There were three periods of different lengths and that made nine trials in each task. In one of these tasks the child had to judge how far each animal would have run given the amount of time the dog barked at it. In another the child had to judge how long the dog had barked given the distance each animal had run. The question that Wilkening asked was whether the children's judgements would reflect the multiplicative relations in these tasks. For example, in the distance task would the children's judgements show that they realised that increasing the time would change the distance covered by the fast animal far more than the distance travelled by the slow one?          .

In fact in the Distance task the children's judgements did appear to be multiplicative, but Wilkening argued that this was probably an artefact. He observed that children tended to move their eyes along the track while the dog barked, and he guessed that they moved them at different speeds for the different animals. This is a perfectly respectable practical solution, but one that Wilkening dismisses as unmathematical. He laid more store by the results of the Time task which in the case of the younger children were essentially additive. The children recognised that the slower animals would take longer to travel a certain distance than a faster animal and that each animal took more time to travel a long than a short distance. But their judgements did not show that they had any idea that the difference in time taken to travel a short and a long distance was far greater for the slow than for the fast animal. On the other hand, the pattern of the older children's judgements appeared to represent the multiplicative relationship quite well. So, Wilkening concluded that younger children adopt an additive strategy for such tasks but, as they grow older, begin to recognise the multiplicative nature of situations like these.

These and other experiments which employ a similar design are elegant and their results are compelling in many ways. But there is a need for caution. After all, the children are not being asked to solve mathematical problems: the question is whether they recognise a multiplicative relation and it is quite possible that they may not see that this or that situation requires multiplication even though their judgements fall into the pattern that conforms with multiplicative relations.

Perhaps one should turn instead to word problems and to the kind of multiplication problems that children have to solve at school. Greer (1992) has proposed 10 different kinds of multiplication word problem and, though his list of categories is quite a complex one, it has the advantage of raising the possibility that different problems may mean quite different things to schoolchildren. Vergnaud (1983) has argued that this is the case but that there are in effect only two broad categories of multiplication problem, which, he claims, children treat in different ways. One type involves "isomorphism of measures", the other "product of measures".

Isomorphism of measures problems concern only two variables, and the proportion between them, such as: "If one box holds eight oranges, how many oranges would 18 boxes hold?" The question in isomorphism of measures problems is always about one of the original two variables (in this example oranges). In product of measures problems, two measures are multiplied to produce a third measure. Area problems are one example ("How many square inches is a table top with a length of 36 inches and a width of 18 inches?"), and Cartesian Product measures ("If a boy has seven different trousers and eight different shirts, what is the number of different outfits (trouser–shirt combinations) that he could wear?") are another.

Vergnaud's own research suggests that isomorphism of measures problems are a great deal easier for children than product of measures problems are. This may mean that isomorphism of measures problems are quite easy to represent, and particularly in terms of repeated addition.

There is, however, one known exception to the rule that isomorphism measures problems are easier than product of measure problems. Nunes and Bryant (1992) have shown that 10-year-old children from England and Brazil are more likely to grasp the principle of the commutativity of multiplication ($8 \times 3 = 3 \times 8$) with product of measures problems. In one study we posed several multiplication problems to each child and at the same time we made it possible for them to use a calculator if they wanted to. In the commutativity problems the children were readier not to use the calculator and to rely on the commutativity principle when the problems involved product of measures problems. Again this seems to be a matter of representation. It is quite easy to imagine changing a rectangular area measuring $8 \times 3$ feet to one measuring $3 \times 8$ feet. One simply needs to rotate the rectangle. On the other hand it is quite hard to make the imaginary transformation of eight oranges each in three boxes to three oranges each in eight boxes: that would involve an awful lot of juggling of imaginary oranges.

So, one important constraint in these multiplication problems is in the way that the children represent the multiplications. Another might be the kind of relations that they can cope with. This seems to be the case with proportional problems too. Proportions are pervasive – how full a glass is, how much of the day has passed, how much red and white paint to mix to make a particular pink. Yet most of the work on proportions seems to show that children under the age of 10 are completely at sea in proportional tasks and some demonstrate that many older children and even adults also find such tasks extremely hard. Bruner and Kenney's (1966) and Siegler and Vago's (1978) well-known studies of children's judgements about the relative fullness and emptiness of different sized glasses produced a dismally low performance in children below the age of 10, and Noelting's (1980a, b) attempt to find suitably proportional judgements about the ratio on concentrated orange juice to water ended in a similarly low result with children in this age range. Karplus and Peterson (1970) and Hart (1981) have found consistent errors in their proportional task in children as old as 16 years.

The most common explanation for these striking difficulties was originally provided by Inhelder and Piaget (1958). It is that proportional problems involve second order relations ("rapports de rapports"). To work out for example that one glass is proportionately fuller than another one has to look first at the proportion of liquid in each glass, and then to compare these two proportions. This last comparison – of a relation between relations – is what causes the difficulty according to Piaget and his colleagues.

There is another possibility. It is that children may be able to use their relational skills to work out some proportions but not others. In this case their difficulty would be in plotting individual proportions and not in comparing them. According to this analysis some proportions should be easier to work out than others.

A paper by Spinillo and Bryant (1991) took this view. The starting point was the evidence that children can take in and remember simple relations like larger and smaller, more or less. This means, we argued, that if an object is clearly divided into two parts the child should be able to register something about the relations between the two parts: for example, he should be able to work out that the two parts are equal in size, when they are, or that one part is bigger and takes up more room than the other. So the child should be able to compare quantities on the basis of their internal proportions in some cases. For example, if he remembers that there is more liquid than empty space in one glass (it's more than half full) that he has seen and then compares to another which has more empty space than liquid (less than half full) he should be able to work out that the relation between liquid and empty space is different in each container.

Notice that in this hypothetical example one container is more than half and the other less than half full. In fact the half boundary plays a crucial role in this analysis. Children should be able to make proportional discriminations which cross the half boundary (one glass more than half and the other less than half full) than when they do not (e.g. both containers more than half full, even though one is proportionately fuller than the other).

Our experiments with 5–8-year-old children supported this hypothesis. The task they were given was to recognise which of two boxes of white and blue bricks was represented in a much smaller picture. In the crucial comparison the bricks were in a different arrangement; the arrangement of the two sections in the picture was different from the arrangement in the two boxes (vertical vs. horizontal dividing line between the blue and white sections), which meant that the children could not solve the task on the basis of any shape or size cues. Yet the children did particularly well in judgements which crossed the half boundary (3/8 blue vs. 5/8 blue) and rather badly in comparisons which did not cross this boundary (e.g. 5/8 blue vs. 7/8 blue).

As far as we can see, the successful judgements were genuinely proportional ones, and the justifications which we recorded for these successful judgements bear this conclusion out. But it is worth noting that our idea is of part–part comparisons not of part–whole ones. The children, according to our hypothesis, were able to take in the relation between the blue and the white segments, but not between the blue section and the whole container. Otherwise they would be as successful in the comparisons that do not cross the half boundary as in those that do. Children of this age, it should be noted, would be at sea with the demand in Parrat-Dayan's task (Parrat-Dayan 1980, 1985; Parrat-Dayan and Vonèche 1992): "Give me half of the five apples." That task also involves part–whole relations.

## WHAT DOES THE CULTURE PROVIDE?

In the last decade there has been a remarkable shift in emphasis in psychologists' accounts of mathematical development. In the past most psychologists who dealt with the subject argued about children's abilities to do this and that, and paid very little attention to where these abilities came from. By and large they assumed that the culture in which the child lived played very little part in the development of these abilities. Piaget, for example, looked mainly to the child's informal interactions with his environment for the source of mathematical skills. Gelman argued that the basic "principles" behind counting, for example, are innate. These are disparate hypotheses, but both of them exclude the possibility of cultural influences.

There are now two lines of evidence which suggest that we should consider the role of culture very seriously. One concerns the nature of the number system, and the other the plain fact that the context in which a child deals with a mathematical problem can have a remarkable effect on the way that he tries to solve it.

Many of the psychologists who study children's counting, seem to treat the number system as a simple sequence. But our number system is not like that. It is a hierarchical structure based on decades. The decade structure makes it possible to count generatively. One does not have to remember that the next number after 1119 is 1120. We can generate these numbers on the basis of our knowledge of the structure of 10s, 100s and 1000s.

In the best, or at any rate the most regular, of all possible linguistic worlds one should be able to generate all the numbers up to 99 by knowing the rules and remembering the names for the numbers from 1 to 10. Chinese is actually one such language: the number words are entirely regular: thus the word for 11 is the equivalent of "ten–one" and for 24 "two–ten–four" and so on. However, there is a degree of irregularity in English number words, and particularly in the English teen words. The word "eleven", for example, gives nothing away, and "fifteen" is hardly better. Nevertheless the majority of English words for numbers greater than 20 do represent their position in the decade structure quite clearly.

This structure plays an important part in all but the simplest arithmetical operations: it is essential, of course, for the system of decimals: and it is also a necessary part of our daily lives since it is the basis for our currency and also for many of the measures that we use and talk about all the time. Not surprisingly, people who live in cultures which do not have this structure or any equivalent to it find it quite hard to do any but the simplest of mathematical calculations (Saxe 1991).

This structure, which lies at the heart of our mathematical lives, is a cultural invention. It was invented relatively late in the history of mankind, and it is not to be found in all cultures (Saxe 1981, 1991; Saxe and Posner 1983). It is not something that children will learn about spontaneously. It is handed on from generation to generation, and it would disappear if it were not taught either formally or informally to successive generations. These are important points for a developmental psychologist, because they mean that the decade structure perfectly fits Vygotsky's idea of a cultural tool. Cultural tools, Vygotsky argued, are inventions which increase the human intellectual power, and also transform humans' intellectual processes. The alphabet is one example, systems of measurement another, and the number system an obvious third.

Yet we still know relatively little about the way in which children learn about the decade system or about the effects that this learning has on their mathematical understanding. The best evidence is cross-linguistic. Miller and Stigler (1987) compared the way in which 4-, 5- and 6-year-old Taiwanese and American children counted and found quite striking differences. For the most part the Taiwanese children did a great deal better at abstract counting (i.e. just producing the numbers in the correct sequence) and there was a striking difference between the two groups in the counting of the teens which gave the American children a great deal more difficulty than it did the children from Taiwan. When the two groups counted objects, there was absolutely no difference between them in terms of their success in counting each object once (Gelman and Gallistel's one-to-one principle), but again the Taiwanese children did a great deal better in producing the right number words in the right order.

Miller and Stigler attribute the differences to the regularity of the Chinese system. One cannot rule out the possibility of differences in other factors, such as motivation, playing a part, but the Miller and Stigler explanation looks plausible and receives considerable support from subsequent comparisons by Miura, Kim, Chang and Okamoto (1988) of Japanese and American children's performance in simple mathematical tasks and by reports from Fuson and Kwon (1992a, b) of the considerable achievements of Korean children in complex addition tasks (the Japenese and the Korean number words are a great deal more regular than the English ones).

The differences originally reported by Miller and Stigler go far beyond success in counting. We (Lines, Nunes and Bryant unpublished data) recently compared Taiwanese and British children in a shop task which involved money. This shop task was originally devised by Carraher and Schliemann (1990), who asked children to buy certain objects and charged them certain amounts of money. In some cases the children could pay in one denomination (ones or tens), and in others they had to mix denominations (ones and tens) in order to reach the right sum. The condition which mixed denominations was easily the harder of the two, and Carraher and Schliemann rightly argued that this demonstrated that the children were having some difficulty in using the decade structure to solve mathematical problems, at any rate as far as money is concerned.

The Carraher/Schliemann study made an interesting developmental point about growth in the understanding of the decade structure, and our more recent project (the one by Lines, Nunes and Bryant) suggests that the nature of the linguistic system may have a considerable effect on the way that children become able to use the decade system. For we found not only that British children were worse at counting than Taiwanese children (a replication of Miller and Stigler) but also that, in the shop task, the Taiwanese/British difference in the mixed denominations condition was particularly pronounced. The Taiwanese were no better than the British children when the task was to pay for the purchases in ones, and not much better than the British group when they had to pay in tens. But when the children had to pay in a mixture of tens and ones (10p and 1p or $10 and $1) the superiority of the Taiwanese children was very striking indeed. It seems that the linguistic advantage helps the Chinese-speaking children not just to count more proficiently but also to grasp the relations between different levels of the decade structure and to use these relations to solve simple problems.

The number system becomes a cultural tool far earlier for them than for English-speaking children.

So the nature of the cultural tool affects the way that children learn about it, and so does the context in which they learn about this tool. Children learn about the decade structure at school but also outside it. The fact that money and other measures are organised in decades means that all children are bound to receive a significant amount of informal instruction about decades outside the classroom.

It is now clear that children can pick up quite different forms of mathematical knowledge in these two environments. The clearest evidence of this is the work by Carraher, Carraher and Schliemann (1985) with children who work in the informal economy in Brazil. These psychologists bought food from children who worked on market stalls, thus setting them problems which involved addition and multiplication (working out the price) and also subtraction (working out the change). Later Carraher *et al.* gave the same children equivalent problems in a more formal setting. These were either word problems or straight sums. The children were a great deal more successful in the market stall transactions than with the more formal problems. But the most striking result of the study was a qualitative difference between the calculations that the children made in the market and with the more formal calculations. In the market the children were remarkably flexible: they moved from addition to multiplication, in the same calculation, with no difficulty. In the more formal tasks they tended to stick to one algorithm, even when they realised that the answer that it produced for them was quite implausible.

The proficiency of children working in the informal economy in Brazil was later confirmed in a series of studies by Saxe (1988, 1991). Nunes, Schliemann and Carraher (1993) themselves went on to investigate the mathematical achievements in farmers, building foremen and fishermen who had received very little education, but had to carry out quite complex mathematical calculations in their work. These studies, and others of a similar genre (Gay and Cole 1967; Lave, Murtaugh and de la Rocha 1984; Lave 1988; Posner 1982; Scribner 1986; Schliemann and Nunes 1990; Nunes 1992) leave no doubt at all about the need to consider the situation in which people acquire mathematical knowledge and then use it. Ironically, mathematical achievements outside the classroom encourage us to think more about what is taught at schools. At the very least we must consider the reason for the psychological barrier, identified so clearly by Carraher *et al.* (1985) and by Nunes *et al.* (1993), that clearly exists between children's formal and informal mathematical experiences. Why do children make so little connection between the two?

# CONCLUSIONS

The study of children's mathematics is the study of their understanding of mathematical relations. This review has shown that very early on in their lives and well within the pre-school period children are able to detect and to remember simple one-way relations, and that their ability to do so allows them to do things which are genuinely mathematical. They share and they measure. These are relational activities: one involves a simple, one-to-one correspondence, relation between two quantities, and the other rests on a combination of two separate relational judgements. Furthermore, very early on they seem to grasp the way in which quantities can increase and decrease by addition and subtraction. The thesis that children's initial entry into the mathematical world is through their understanding of simple quantitative relations is actually quite an old one (Lawrenson and Bryant 1972; Bryant 1974).

In contrast, their pre-school encounters with numbers may not at first be of much importance, as far as their understanding of mathematics is concerned. This is probably because a true understanding of the number system almost certainly rests on a thorough grasp of the decade structure, and this must, in one way or another, be taught.

The relational understanding which children bring with them to school helps them in some ways, but is insufficient in others. It allows them to understand addition and subtraction fairly well, when these involve simple increases and decreases in quantity, and they soon are able to involve their growing understanding of counting to help them estimate the effects of these transformations by counting on or counting down. But problems which require some attention to the relations between parts and wholes continue to stump them. Much the same can be said about children's understanding of proportions. Their fairly rapidly acquired sensitivity to "half" is based on their ability to make part–part comparisons. Proportional judgements which involve part–whole calculations continue to elude them even in late adolescence.

For much the same reason multiplicative relations, as Piaget claimed a long time ago, are plainly much harder than additive relations for children to grasp, although we still need to find out a great deal more about this aspect of children's mathematical understanding.

Finally, the context in which children learn about and use their mathematics is a matter of great importance and great interest too. In particular the Brazilian work on "street mathematics" has demonstrated not only the significance of the considerable achievements which are handed on to children in informal settings, but also the worrying subjective barriers between children's formal and informal learning of mathematics. It is as if they live in two separate mathematical worlds with hardly a connection between the two. Surely we should find ways for them to bridge that gap.

There are other gaps for us to bridge. Although the broad outline of mathematical development is reasonably clear, or so it seems to me, yet there are still some formidable gaps in our research on the topic. In particular, we know very little about the connections between one mathematical achievement and another. There is a striking contrast here with work on children's reading, which has demonstrated, for example, many strong connections between children's pre-school abilities and their success in reading later on (Goswami and Bryant 1990). We have no such research in mathematics, and I cannot see why.

There are testable hypotheses here. One is that children's early experiences with relational comparisons, but not with the counting, are strongly connected to the progress that they make in learning about the four arithmetical operations at school. Another is that the real breakthrough in understanding the number system comes not through learning to count but through understanding the structure of the decade system. A third is that experience with part–part relations leads to an eventual understanding of part–whole relations, and hence to full proportional reasoning.

These are ideas which can be tested by a combination of longitudinal research and intervention studies, in just the same way as similar causal connections have been pursued and eventually discovered in work on children's reading. This should be our next move.

## REFERENCES

Anderson, N. H. and Cuneo, D. (1978) "The height + width rule in children's judgments of quantity", *Journal of Experimental Psychology – General* 107: 335–378.

Antell, S. E. and Keating, D. P. (1983) "Perception of numerical invariance in neonates", *Child Development* 54: 695–701.

Baroody, A. J. (1992) "The development of preschoolers' counting skills and principles", in J. Bideaud, C. Meljac and J.-P. Fischer (eds) *Pathways to number* (pp. 99–126), Hillsdale, NJ: Lawrence Erlbaum Associates.

Baroody, A. J. and Gannon, K. E. (1984) "The development of the commutativity principle and economical addition strategies", *Cognition and Instruction* 1: 321–339.

Bruner, J. S. and Kenney, H. (1966) "On relational concepts", in J. S. Bruner, R. R. Olver and P. Greenfield (eds) *Studies in cognitive growth* (pp. 168–182), New York: John Wiley & Sons.

Bryant, P. E. (1974) *Perception and understanding in young children*, London: Methuen.

Bryant, P. E. (1992) "Arithmetic in the cradle", *Nature* 358: 712–713.

Bryant, P. E. and Kopytynska, H. (1976) "Spontaneous measurement by young children", *Nature* 260: 773.

Bryant, P. E. and Trabasso, T. (1971) "Transitive inferences and memory in young children", *Nature* 232: 456–458.

Carpenter, T. P. and Moser, J. M. (1982) "The development of addition and subtraction problem solving", in T. P. Carpenter, J. M. Moser and T. A.

Romberg (eds) *Addition and subtraction* (pp. 10–24), New York: Lawrence Erlbaum Associates.

Carraher, T. N., Carraher, D. W. and Schliemann, A. D. (1985) "Mathematics in the streets and in school", *British Journal of Developmental Psychology* 3: 21–29.

Carraher, T. N. and Schliemann, A. D. (1990) "Knowledge of the numeration system among pre-schoolers", in L. P. Steffe and T. Wood (eds) *Transforming children's mathematics education* (pp. 135–141), Hillsdale, NJ: Lawrence Erlbaum Associates.

Cividanes-Lago, C. (1993) *Children's understanding of quantity and their ability to use graphical information*, unpublished DPhil thesis, University of Oxford.

Cooper, R. G. (1984) "Early number development: discovering number space with addition and subtraction", in C. Sophian (ed.) *The origins of cognitive skill* (pp. 157–192), Hillsdale, NJ: Lawrence Erlbaum Associates.

De Corte, E. and Verschaffel, L. (1987) "The effect of semantic structure on first graders' solution strategies of elementary addition and subtraction word problems", *Journal for Research in Mathematics Education* 18: 363–381.

De Corte, E. and Verschaffel, L. (1988) "Computer simulation as a tool in research on problem solving in subject-matter domains', *The International Journal of Educational Research* 12: 49–69.

De Corte, E., Verschaffel, L. and de Win, L. (1985) "The influence of rewording verbal problems on children's problem representations and solutions', *Journal of Educational Psychology* 77: 460–470.

Desforges, A. and Desforges, G. (1980) "Number-based strategies of sharing in young children", *Educational Studies* 6: 97–109.

Durkin, K. (1993) "The representation of number in infancy and early childhood", in C. Pratt and A. F. Garton (eds) *Systems of representation in children* (pp. 133–166), Chichester, U.K.: J. Wiley & Sons.

Durkin, K., Shire, B., Riem, R., Crowther, R. D. and Rutter, D. R. (1986) "The social and linguistic context of early number use", *British Journal of Developmental Psychology* 4: 269–288.

Fayol, M. (1992) "From number to numbers in use: solving arithmetic problems", in J. Bideaud, C. Meljac and J.-P. Fischer (eds) *Pathways to number* (pp. 209–218), Hillsdale, NJ: Lawrence Erlbaum Associates.

Frydman, O. and Bryant, P. E. (1988) "Sharing and the understanding of number equivalence by young children", *Cognitive Development* 3: 323–339.

Frye, D., Braisby, N., Lowe, J., Maroudas, C. and Nicholls, J. (1989) "Young children's understanding of counting and cardinality", *Child Development* 60: 1158–1171.

Fuson, K. C. (1988) *Children's counting and concepts of number*, New York: Springer-Verlag.

Fuson, K. C. and Kwon, Y. (1992a) "Korean children's understanding of multidigit addition and subtraction", *Child Development* 63: 491–506.

Fuson, K. and Kwon, Y. (1992b) "Learning addition and subtraction: effects of number words and other cultural tools", in J. Bideaud, C. Meljac and J.-P. Fischer (eds) *Pathways to number* (pp. 283–306), Hillsdale, NJ: Lawrence Erlbaum Associates.

Gay, J. and Cole, M. (1967) *The new mathematics and an old culture*, New York: Holt, Rinehart & Winston.

Gelman, R. and Gallistel, C. R. (1978) *The child's understanding of number*, Cambridge, MA: Harvard University Press.

Gelman, R. and Meck, E. (1983) "Preschoolers' counting: principles before skill", *Cognition* 13: 343–360.

Goswami, U. and Bryant, P. (1990) *Phonological skills and learning to read*, London: Lawrence Erlbaum Associates.

Gréco, P. (1962) "Quantité et quotité", in P. Gréco and A. Morf (eds) *Structures numériques élémentaires*, Paris: P.U.F.

Greer, B. (1992) "Multiplication and division as models of situations", in D. A. Grouws (ed.) *Handbook of research on mathematics teaching and learning* (pp. 276–295), New York: Macmillan.

Groen, G. and Resnick, L. (1977) "Can pre-school children invent addition algorithms?" *Journal of Educational Psychology* 69: 645–652.

Hart, K. (1981) *Children's understanding of mathematics*: 11–16, London: John Murray.

Hudson, T. (1983) "Correspondences and numerical differences between sets", *Child Development* 54: 84–90.

Hughes, M. (1986) *Children and number: difficulties in learning mathematics*, Oxford: Blackwell.

Inhelder, B. and Piaget, J. (1958) *The growth of logical thinking from childhood to adolescence*, New York: Basic Books.

Karplus, R. and Peterson, R. W. (1970) "Intellectual development beyond elementary school II: ratio, a survey", *School – Science and Mathematics* 70: 813–820.

Lave, J. (1988) *Cognition in practice*, Cambridge: Cambridge University Press.

Lave, J., Murtaugh, M. and de la Rocha, O. (1984) "The dialectic of arithmetic in shopping", in B. Rogoff and J. Lave (eds) *Everyday cognition*, Cambridge: Harvard University Press.

Lawrenson, W. and Bryant, P. E. (1972) "Absolute and relative codes in young children", *Journal of Child Psychology and Psychiatry* 12: 25–35.

Lines, S., Nunes, T. and Bryant, P. E. (unpublished paper) "Number naming systems in English and Chinese: linguistic effects on number understanding and basic mathematical skill".

Michie, S. (1984) "Why preschoolers are reluctant to count spontaneously", *British Journal of Developmental Psychology* 2: 347–358.

Miller, K. (1984) "The child as the measurer of all things: measurement procedures and the development of quantitative concepts", in C. Sophian (ed.) *Origins of cognitive skills* (pp. 193–228), Hillsdale, NJ: Lawrence Erlbaum Associates.

Miller, K. F. (1989) "Measurement as a tool for thought: the role of measuring procedures in children's understanding of quantitative invariance", *Developmental Psychology* 25: 589–600.

Miller, K. F. and Paredes, D. R. (1990) "Starting to add worse: effects of learning to multiply on children's addition", *Cognition* 37: 213–242.

Miller, K. F. and Stigler, J. W. (1987) "Counting in Chinese: cultural variation in a basic skill", *Cognitive Development* 2: 279–305.

Miura, I. T., Kim, C. C., Chang, A. and Okamoto, Y. (1988) "Effects of language characteristics on children's cognitive representation of number: cross-national comparisons", *Child Development* 59: 1445–1450.

Noelting, G. (1980a) "The development of proportional reasoning and the ratio concept, Part I – Differentiation of stages", *Educational Studies in Mathematics* 11: 217–253.

Noelting, G. (1980b) "The development of proportional reasoning and the ratio concept, Part II – Problem-structure at successive stages: Problem-solving strategies and the mechanism of adaptive restructuring", *Educational Studies in Mathematics* 11: 331–363.

Nunes, T. (1992) "Cognitive invariants and cultural variation in mathematical concepts", *International Journal of Behavioral Development* 15: 433–453.

Nunes, T. and Bryant, P. E. (1992) 'Rotating candy bars and rearranging oranges: a study of children's understanding of commutativity", paper presented at the annual PME conference at Amherst, MA.

Nunes, T., Schliemann, A.-L. and Carraher, D. (1993) *Street mathematics and school mathematics*, New York: Cambridge University Press.

Parrat-Dayan, S. (1980) *Etude génétique de la notion de moitié*, Geneva: J. L. de Rougemont.

Parrat-Dayan, S. (1985) "A propos de la notion de moitié: Rôle du contexte expérimentale", *Archives de Psychologie* 53: 433–438.

Parrat-Dayan, S. and Vonèche, J. (1992) "Conservation and the notion of half", in J. Bideaud, C. Meljac and J.-P. Fischer (eds) *Pathways to number* (pp. 67–82), Hillsdale, NJ: Lawrence Erlbaum Associates.

Pears, R. and Bryant, P. (1990) "Transitive inferences by young children about spatial position", *British Journal of Psychology* 81: 497–510.

Perner, J. and Mansbridge, D. G. (1983) "Developmental differences in encoding length series", *Child Development* 54: 710–719.

Piaget, J. (1952) *The child's conception of number*, London: Routledge & Kegan Paul.

Piaget, J. and Inhelder, B. (1974) *The child's construction of quantities*, London: Routledge & Kegan Paul.

Piaget, J., Inhelder, B. and Szeminska, A. (1960) *The child's conception of geometry*, London: Routledge & Kegan Paul.

Posner, J. (1982) "The development of mathematical knowledge in two West African societies", *Child Development* 53: 200–208.

Riley, M., Greeno, J. G. and Heller, J. I. (1983) "Development of children's problem solving ability in arithmetic", in H. Ginsburg (ed.) *The development of mathematical thinking* (pp. 153–196), New York: Academic Press.

Saxe, G. (1979) "A developmental analysis of notational counting", *Child Development* 48: 1512–1520.

Saxe, G. (1981) "Body parts as numerals: a developmental analysis of numeration among the Oksapmin in Papua New Guinea", *Child Development* 52: 306–316.

Saxe, G. (1988) "The mathematics of child street vendors", *Child Development* 59: 1415–1425.

Saxe, G. B. (1991) *Culture and cognitive development: studies in mathematical understanding*, Hillsdale, NJ: Lawrence Erlbaum Associates.

Saxe, G. P. and Posner, J. K. (1983) "The development of numerical cognition: cross-cultural perspectives", in H. Ginsburg (ed.) *The development of mathematical thinking* (pp. 292–318), New York: Academic Press.

Saxe, G., Guberman, S. R. and Gearhart, M. (1987) "Social and developmental processes in children's understanding of number", *Monographs of the Society for Research in Child Development* 52: 100–200.

Schliemann, A. D. and Nunes, T. (1990) "A situated schema of proportionality", *British Journal of Developmental Psychology* 8: 259–268.

Scribner, S. (1986) "Thinking in action: some characteristics of practical thought", in R. J. Sternberg and R. K. Wagner (eds) *Practical intelligence* (pp. 13–30), Cambridge: Cambridge University Press.

Shipley, E. F. and Shepperson, B. (1990) "Countable entities", *Cognition* 34: 109–136.

Siegler, R. S. (1976) "Three aspects of cognitive development", *Cognitive Psychology* 8: 481–521.

Siegler, R. S. (1978) "The origins of scientific reasoning", in R. Siegler (ed.) *Children's thinking: what develops?*, Hillsdale, NJ: Lawrence Erlbaum Associates.

Siegler, R. S. (1987) "Strategy choices in subtraction", in J. A. Sloboda and D. Rogers (eds) *Cognitive processes in mathematics*, Oxford: Clarendon Press.

Siegler, R. S. and Vago, S. (1978) "The development of a proportionality concept: judging relative fullness", *Journal of Experimental Child Psychology* 25: 371–395.

Smith, L. (1993) *Necessary knowledge*, Hove: Lawrence Erlbaum Associates.

Sophian, C. (1988) "Limitations on preschool children's knowledge about counting: using counting to compare two sets", *Developmental Psychology* 24: 634–640.

Spinillo, A. and Bryant, P. (1991) "Children's proportional judgements: the importance of 'half' ", *Child Development* 62: 427–440.

Starkey, P. (1983) "Some precursors of early arithmetic competencies", paper presented at the meeting of the Society for Research in Child Development, Detroit, MI: USA.

Starkey, P. and Cooper, R. (1980) "Perception of numbers by human infants", *Science* 210: 1033–1034.

Starkey, P., Spelke, E. and Gelman, R. (1983) "Detection of intermodal numerical correspondences by human infants", *Science* 222: 179.

Starkey, P., Spelke, E. S. and Gelman, R. (1990) "Numerical abstraction by human infants", *Cognition* 36: 97–128.

Stern, E. (1993) "What makes certain arithmetic word problems involving the comparison of sets so difficult?" *Journal of Educational Psychology* 85: 7–23.

Strauss, M. S. and Curtis, L. E. (1981) "Infant perception of number", *Child Development* 52: 1146–1152.

Strauss, M. S. and Curtis, L. E. (1984) "Development of numerical concepts in infancy", in C. Sophian (ed.) *The origins of cognitive skill* (pp. 131–156), Hillsdale, NJ: Lawrence Erlbaum Associates.

Turner, M. and Bryant, P. (unpublished paper) "Do children understand what they are doing when they add?"

Vergnaud, G. (1983) "Multiplicative structures", in R. Lesh and M. Landau (eds) *Acquisition of mathematics concepts and processes*, New York: Academic Press.

Vygotsky, L. (1986) *Thought and language*, Cambridge, MA: MIT Press.

Vygotsky, L. S. and Luria, A. R. (1993) *Studies on the history of behaviour: ape, primitive and child*, Hillsdale, NJ: Lawrence Erlbaum Associates.

Wilkening, F. (1979) "Combining of stimulus dimensions in children's and adult's judgement of area: an information integration analysis", *Developmental Psychology* 15: 25–53.

Wilkening, F. (1981) "Integrating velocity, time and distance information: a developmental study", *Cognitive Psychology* 13: 231–247.

Wilkening, F. and Anderson, N. H. (1982) "Comparison of two-rule assessment methodologies for studying cognitive development and knowledge structure", *Psychological Bulletin* 92: 215–237.

Woods, S. S., Resnick, L. and Groen, G. J. (1975) "An experimental test of five process models for subtraction", *Journal of Educational Psychology* 67: 17–21.

Wynn, K. (1990) "Children's understanding of counting", *Cognition* 36: 155–193.

Wynn, K. (1992) "Addition and subtraction by human infants", *Nature* 358: 749–750.

# Chapter 16

# Representation and reasoning in early numerical development

## Counting, conservation, and comparisons between sets

*Catherine Sophian*

The first experiment examined the developmental relation between counting and number conservation in the 3–6-year-old age range. Results indicated extended developments in both children's counting and their conservation reasoning, and a close relation between the two. Only the oldest children gave evidence of conserving, and they also differentiated appropriately between conservation and control problems in their use of counting. The second and third experiments extended the finding that children below 6 years of age do not conserve to conditions in which counting was precluded. These results provide evidence of protracted developments in young children's understanding of relational aspects of number.

Piaget (1952) viewed number development as an integral part of the development of logical reasoning, and that development as a product of very general properties of the child's interactions with the world. He and the many researchers who followed his lead found dramatic differences in the numerical reasoning of preschoolers versus older children, which they attributed to the dependence of a concept of number on concrete-operational structures that are not attained until around 6 or 7 years of age. Recently, however, interest has grown in a very different characterization of numerical development, one that emphasizes the primacy of representational uses of number, such as counting, rather than logical reasoning, and that correspondingly views young children as much more competent than Piaget believed (e.g. Gelman and Gallistel 1978; Wynn 1992).

This alternative conceptualization, and the research supporting it, has been heavily influenced by Chomsky's (1957) distinction between competence and performance, which inspired work in two directions. First, it led to the recognition that children may have a hypothesized concept or cognitive ability yet perform poorly on cognitive tasks assessing that ability for a variety of reasons. Thus, many researchers have argued that young children in fact understand number conservation but fail the standard Piagetian conservation problem because of linguistic difficulties, misleading social-interactional cues, or other performance factors (e.g. Bryant 1972; Gelman 1972; McGarrigle and Donaldson 1975; Rose and Blank 1974). Second, it led to the recognition that children may have implicit knowledge which is evident in regularities in their behavior even if they cannot express that knowledge explicitly (Gelman and Gallistel 1978). This insight led to extensive study of children's counting as a behavioral system in which implicit numerical knowledge might be revealed. Moreover, building on the idea that early counting is already conceptually based is the idea that later-developing numerical reasoning abilities, like conservation, are attained by gaining explicit access to the conceptual knowledge that was originally implicit in their counting: "Later developing number concepts often involve the accessing of implicit knowledge embedded in the structures which characterize early number concepts" (Gelman 1982, p. 217).

There are two potential difficulties for this characterization of number development, however – one pertaining to the general claim of early numerical competence and the other to the assertion that counting plays an important role in the development of conservation and related forms of numerical reasoning. The first stems from the double-edged nature of the competence-performance distinction: that is, if no task can directly tap children's underlying competencies, then data based on children's performance may overestimate as well as underestimate children's knowledge. Some evidence for the occurrence of such "false positives" comes from recent studies in which procedural modifications that were designed to increase conservation also increased the occurrence of conservation-like responses when they were not appropriate (e.g. Light and Gilmour 1983). Clearly, the conclusion that conservation and related forms of numerical reasoning develop much earlier than previously thought needs to be reevaluated in the light of this kind of evidence. The second difficulty stems from evidence of limitations on children's early understanding of counting, particularly their understanding of how counting can be used to compare two sets (Saxe 1977; Sophian 1987, 1988). It is precisely this use of counting that is most relevant to conservation problems. Thus this evidence seems to undermine proposals that young preschoolers attain conservation and related forms of reasoning on the basis of their proficiency in counting.

The principal evidence for the view that counting contributes to the development of conservation has come from training studies (e.g. Clements 1984; Gelman 1982; Gold 1978). For instance, Gelman taught children to count both sets before and after a conservation transformation and showed that children who received that training were subsequently more successful on conservation problems than children who had not received any counting experience or who had counted only one of the two sets. Evidence that a particular kind of experience *can* facilitate a particular development does not necessarily establish that it *does* contribute to that development in the normal course of development, however (Bryant and Bradley 1985). Minimally, to establish the latter claim we must also demonstrate that children normally receive the experience we hypothesize to be causal prior to, or at least concurrently with, the development of the abilities that by our hypothesis result from that experience. It is this antecedence that is called into question by the conjunction of findings of early conservation on the one hand, but relatively prolonged limitations on counting particularly *vis-à-vis* comparisons between sets, on the other.

Saxe (1979) directly compared the development of conservation and counting to compare sets and obtained findings that are compatible with the hypothesized causal role of counting in the development of conservation; that is, children were able to use counting to compare sets before they succeeded on the conservation test, and none of the children he studied were able to conserve without also being able to use counting to compare two sets. Baroody and White (1983) reported similar findings based on somewhat different counting tasks. However, the relatively late emergence of conservation in these studies is presumably at least partially a consequence of the use of standard Piagetian conservation problems, with all the attendant problems that have been so heavily criticized in the post-Piagetian era.

The present research reexamined the relation between children's counting and their reasoning about the effects of conservation transformations on the relation between two sets, using a conservation task that has elicited successful performance from young preschoolers in previous research (Bryant 1972). Bryant's primary concern was to eliminate potentially misleading length cues in the standard conservation problems; thus he asked children which of two unequally long rows had more, then moved the objects so that the rows were the same length, and asked children again which had more. Here length cues are neutralized because children must choose between rows that are the same length. Bryant found that children as young as 3 years of age conserved under these circumstances. The present research examined the developmental ordering between conservation on Bryant's task and the ability to count to compare sets. If children conserve before they can count to compare sets, then counting-based comparisons cannot be the basis for the discovery of the principle of conservation. On the other hand, if the two develop in tandem, or counting to compare develops first, that would be consistent with the hypothesis that counting contributes to the development of conservation.

A second and related question is: Does early conservation reasoning depend on how children have represented the sets in the first place? Since length of rows is in fact not conserved when objects are rearranged, it would be reasonable for children who have based their initial comparison between sets on length to fail to conserve their judgments across a conservation transformation. Bryant's data suggest that young children do conserve even length-based judgments. Nevertheless, it may be that conservation improves when children have found a sounder basis for their initial judgments. Such a result would provide further support for the notion that counting contributes to the development of conservation.

Two published papers have reported failures to replicate Bryant's findings of early conservation (Katz and Beilin 1976; Starkey 1981). The nonreplications are themselves open to criticism, however, on grounds that they did not make the connection between the pre- and posttransformation phase of the problems clear enough. If children view the posttransformation question as a new, self-contained, problem, of course, no conservation would be expected. Consistent with that interpretation, Starkey reports that children responded no differently to the posttransformation questions than to questions about the same arrays presented in a static (no-transformation) condition, and Katz and Beilin note that the majority of their subjects responded on the basis of cues such as color or position that likewise require no consideration of the pretransformation array. In the present research, a novel procedure of mounting stimuli on elastic strips was used so as to minimize the time needed to transform the arrays and, correspondingly, to maximize the continuity between the pre- and post-transformation phases of the problems.

Halford and Boyle (1985) argued that Bryant's results could be explained without crediting children with conservation knowledge. Instead, they suggest that children may have repeated their previous choice as a "default" strategy because they did not know how else to choose between rows that were equal in length. To control for this possible interpretation, the present research compared children's performance on conservation problems similar to Bryant's with their performance on substitution problems on which the sets might or might not be in the same numerical relation after the transformation as they were before it. If conservation-like responses reflect only perseveration, as Halford and Boyle suggest, they should occur as frequently on substitution problems as on conservation problems. On the other hand, a finding that children maintain their pretransformation judgments more following conservation transformations than following substitution transformations would clearly show that something more is involved than the default responses Halford and Boyle hypothesize.

## EXPERIMENT 1

### Method

*Subjects*

Twenty-two 3-year-olds (3 years, 6 months to 3 years, 11 months; $M = 3$–9), 20 5-year-olds (4 years, 10 months to 5 years, 3 months; $M = 5$–1), and 15 6-year-olds (6 years, 4 months to 6 years, 8 months; $M = 6$–5) participated in this experiment. There were approximately equal numbers of boys and girls in each group. Most of the children were Caucasian and middle class. The children lived in a rural academic community and were brought to a laboratory on campus for testing.

*Materials*

Four sets of identical small objects were used as materials: pink plastic fish, about 2.5 cm long; blue plastic fish, of the same size; yellow buttons, about 1 cm in diameter; and blue plastic bears, about 1 cm tall. The pink fish and the buttons always served as the set to be transformed (spatially or by replacement); the blue fish and the buttons always served as the stationary set. To facilitate rapid presentation and transformation of the arrays, the objects were sewn onto strips of elastic (for the sets to be transformed) or ribbon (for the stationary sets). There were eight elastic strips, one each of 3, 5, 11, and 13 pink fish and 3, 5, 11, and 13 buttons. There were four ribbon strips, one each of 4 and 12 blue fish and 4 and 12 bears. The objects were spaced unevenly on the strips so that the elements of the transformation and stationary sets would not be aligned with one another, whether the elastic was extended so as to be longer than the corresponding ribbon strip, unextended so as to be shorter, or partially extended so as to be the same length as the ribbon. In their extended position, the three-item and five-item strips of elastic measured 32.5 cm from the outer edges of the two endmost objects, and the 11-item and 13-item strips measured 52.5 cm. In their unextended position, the three-item and five-item strips of elastic measured 18 cm, and the 11-item and 13-item strips measured 30 cm. The four-item ribbon strips, and the three- and five-item elastic strips in their partially extended position, measured 24 cm from the outer edges of the two endmost objects; and the 12-item ribbon strips, and the 11-item and 13-item elastic strips in their partially extended position, measured 40.5 cm.

A long wooden board with nails in the appropriate places served to hold the strips in place. On one side of the board were pairs of nails to be used for small sets, and on the other side more widely spaced pairs of nails to be used for the large sets. The board was positioned with the nails for the small sets nearer the child when the small-set problems were administered, and with the nails for the large sets nearer the child when the large-set problems were administered.

*Procedure*

Each child received eight conservation problems and eight substitution problems. Within the substitution problems, four were substitution/same problems, which involved replacing the initial transformation set with the alternate set that had the same number of objects (e.g. replacing a strip of 11 pink fish with a strip of 11 buttons), and four were substitution/reversed problems, which involved replacing the initial transformation set with a strip composed of two more or two fewer of the alternate objects (e.g. replacing a strip of 11 pink fish with a strip of 13 buttons).

Within both the conservation and substitution problems, half began with the transformation set longer than the stationary set and half began with it shorter; and, crossed with that factor, half the time the longer row contained one more object than the shorter row and half the time it contained one fewer. In addition, half the problems involved small sets (three to five objects) and half involved large sets (11–13 objects).[1] Within the substitution problems, it was not possible to cross all of these factors completely with the two subtypes of problems (substitution/same vs. substitution/reversed) within the problems an individual child received. However, the total set of possible problems (including problems varying in which specific objects were used for the various sets) were divided into subsets in which all the factors were as fully crossed as possible, and different subsets were given to different children within each age and gender so that all of the possible permutations were represented about equally in the overall data set.

For each problem, the experimenter put a pair of strips in position on the nails so that the rows were horizontal to the child. During this initial, pretransformation, phase of the problems, the elastic strip was either in its fully extended position or in its unextended position and thus might be longer or shorter than the ribbon strip. The objects were positioned at varying intervals along the strips so that in either case there would not be any clear alignment between the objects on one strip and the objects on the other. The experimenter labeled the two sets and then asked the child which objects there were more of, saying, for example, "Here are some buttons and here are some blue fish. Are there more buttons or more blue fish?" The stationary set was always mentioned before the transformation set.[2] Children were not given explicit instructions either to count or to refrain from counting at this point or at any other point in the experiment.

Following the child's pretransformation judgment, the experimenter instructed the child to watch and then carried out the transformation. For the conservation transformation, she took the elastic strip and moved it to a new pair of nails that were exactly aligned with the nails on which the ribbon strip was placed. For the substitution transformation, she removed the elastic strip, put it out of view, and put a new one, composed of different objects (e.g. buttons instead of pink fish), onto the nails that were aligned with the ribbon strip. When the rows were in their posttransformation positions, they were exactly the same length and the objects at the ends of the rows were aligned with each other. However, there was still no clear alignment between the other objects on the two strips. Because exactly the same final array could result on the conservation problems, the substitution/same problems, and the substitution/reversed problems, differences across problems in children's judgments can only reflect the impact of what children saw before and during the transformation on children's judgments.

Following the transformation, the experimenter asked again which set had more. On two conservation problems, one substitution/same problem, and one substitution/reversed problem, she also asked the child why he or she thought that set had more. Because children's responses to these questions could not be scored reliably, however, this aspect of the data will not be reported here.

## Results

### Pretransformation performance

Children's strategies during the pretransformation phase of the problems were characterized in two ways: first in terms of whether or not there was observable counting and, second, in terms of the predominant choice they

*Table 16.1* Numbers of children at each age who counted and who showed different patterns of judgments during the pretransformation phase (Experiment 1)

|  | Consistently Chose More Numerous Row[a] | Consistently Chose Longer Row[a] |
|---|---|---|
| Consistently counted[a] | 0 3-year-olds<br>4 5-year-olds<br>7 6-year-olds | 0 3-year-olds<br>0 5-year-olds<br>0 6-year-olds |
| Counted intermittently | 0 3-year-olds<br>0 5-year-olds<br>5 6-year-olds | 0 3-year-olds<br>1 5-year-old<br>0 6-year-olds |
| Responded without observable counting[a] | 0 3-year-olds<br>0 5-year-olds<br>0 6-year-olds | 6 3-year-olds<br>6 5-year-olds<br>0 6-year-olds |

[a] On at least 13 of the 16 problems.

made. Individual classifications based on these two dimensions are summarized in Table 16.1. Children were classified as "length" responders if they chose the longer of the two rows on at least 13 of the 16 problems and as "number" responders if they chose the more numerous of the two rows on at least 13 of the 16 problems. This criterion represents a degree of concordance in children's responses that is statistically significant at the individual level, binomial $p = .01$. No children met equivalent criteria for consistently having chosen the shorter or the less numerous row. Independently, children were scored as having counted if they said two or more numbers either aloud or covertly but with identifiable lip movements.[3] For comparison to the response-based classifications, they were considered to be consistent counters if they counted on at least 13 of the 16 problems and as consistent non-counters if they gave no evidence of counting on at least 13 of the 16 problems. Intermediate cases were classified as mixed.

There was a marked association between counting and the predominant response children made. Children classified as consistent counters were substantially more likely than other children to be classified as number responders, $\chi^2(1) = 26.59$, $p < .001$. (All $\chi^2$ values are computed with a correction for continuity.) Likewise, children classified as consistent *non-counters* were substantially more likely than other children to be classified as length responders, $\chi^2(1) = 9.52$, $p < .01$. Likewise, there was a marked age-related increase in both counting and number responding. The 6-year-olds were significantly less likely to be consistent non-counters than either the 3- or 5-year-olds, $\chi^2$s$(1) \geqslant 8.19$, $ps < .01$, and they were significantly more likely to be consistent counters than the 3-year-olds, $\chi^2(1) = 11.99$, $p < .001$. They were also more likely than the 5-year-olds to be consistent counters, but not significantly so, $\chi^2 (1) = 3.16$, $p < .10$. Similarly, the 6-year-olds were significantly less likely to respond consistently on the basis of length, $\chi^2$s$(1) \geqslant 4.56$, $ps < .05$, and significantly more likely to respond consistently on the basis of number, $\chi^2$s$(1) \geqslant 10.13$, $ps < .01$, than either the 3- or 5-year-olds.

*Posttransformation judgments*

The proportion of problems on which children chose the same row after the transformation as they had chosen prior to it is summarized in Table 16.2. For comparability to the conservation problems, on the substitution problems if the child chose the to-be-transformed row before the transformation and the row that replaced it after the transformation, it was considered a "same" response. These data were analyzed in a 3 (age) $\times$ 2 (gender) $\times$ 2 (order) $\times$ 2 (problem type: conservation vs. substitution) $\times$ 2 (set size) analysis of variance. Significant main effects of age, $F(2, 45) = 4.64$, $p = .01$, problem type, $F(1, 45) = 15.11$, $p < .001$, and set size, $F(1, 45) = 5.64$, $p < .05$, were qualified by two-way interactions between age and problem type,

Table 16.2 Mean proportions of problems on which children chose the same row before and after the transformation (Experiment 1)

| | Conservation Problems | | Substitution Problems | |
| | Small Sets | Large Sets | Small Sets | Large Sets |
|---|---|---|---|---|
| **3-year-olds:** | | | | |
| Overall | .60 | .54 | .41 | .48 |
| No-count problems[a] | .53 (n = 21, t(20) = .38) | .54 (n = 22, t(21) = .55) | .40 (n = 20, t(19) = 1.24) | .51 (n = 22, t(21) = .18) |
| **5-year-olds:** | | | | |
| Overall | .65 | .54 | .53 | .54 |
| No-count problems[a] | .55 (n = 15, t(14) = .47) | .53 (n = 17, t(16) = .36) | .54 (n = 13, t(12) = .45) | .57 (n = 17, t(16) = .94) |
| **6-year-olds:** | | | | |
| Overall | .96 | .75 | .52 | .46 |
| No-count problems[a] | .91 (n = .13, t(12) = 5.28)*** | .77 (n = 13, t(12) = 2.74)** | .55 (n = 3) | .44 (n = 9, t(8) = .46) |

[a] Excluding problems on which child visibly counted during the posttransformation phase.

** significant $p < .01$

*** significant $p < .001$

$F(2, 45) = 4.13, p < .05$, and between problem type and set size, $F(1, 45) = 4.34, p < .05$. Simple effects tests comparing the problem types within each age group indicated that only the 6-year-olds maintained their pretransformation judgments more often on the conservation than on the substitution problems, $F(1, 45) = 8.84, p < .01$; for the younger age groups, $Fs(1, 45) \leqslant 1.55, ps > .10$. Age differences were significant within the conservation problems, $F(2, 45) = 5.86, p < .01$, but not within the substitution problems, $F(2, 45) = 1.29$. Newman–Keuls contrasts indicated that on the conservation problems the 6-year-olds maintained their pretransformation judgments significantly more often than either of the younger two groups ($ps < .01$), who did not differ from each other. Although the differences between the problem types were especially pronounced for small-set problems, simple effect $F(1, 45) = 18.76, p < .001$, they were significant even for the large-set problems, simple effect $F(1, 45) = 4.14, p = .05$.

Individual children were classified as consistent conservers if they maintained their pretransformation judgment in response to the posttransformation question on all or all but one of the eight conservation problems (regardless of counting; binomial $p = .035$). By this criterion, 11 of the 15 6-year-olds (73 per cent), compared with four out of 22 3-year-olds (18 per cent) and six out of 20 5-year-olds (30 per cent) consistently conserved.[4] Nonparametric contrasts confirmed a significant increase between 5 and 6 years of age in the proportion of children who consistently conserved, $\chi^2(1) = 4.83, p < .05$.

*Posttransformation counting*

Data concerning the proportion of problems on which children counted in the course of answering the posttransformation questions are presented in Table 16.3. A 3 (age) $\times$ 2 (gender) $\times$ 2 (order) $\times$ 2 (problem type) $\times$ 2 (set size) analysis of variance yielded significant main effects of age, $F(2, 45) = 11.33, p < .001$, problem type, $F(1, 45) = 46.67, p < .001$, and set size, $F(1, 45) = 17.13, p < .001$, which were qualified by two-way interactions of age $\times$ problem type, $F(2, 45) = 19.74, p < .001$, and problem type $\times$ set size, $F(1, 45) = 7.03, p = .01$, and by a three-way interaction of age $\times$ problem type $\times$ set size, $F(2, 45) = 4.71, p = .01$.[5] Differences between the two problem types were of primary interest, as evidence concerning children's sensitivity to the differential need for counting on substitution versus conservation problems. Since the interactions suggest that this differentiation varied across both age groups and set sizes, simple-effects tests examining the difference between substitution and conservation problems were conducted within each combination of age $\times$ set size. Simple effects of problem type were significant at 6 years for both the small-set, $F(1, 11) = 38.2, p < .001$, and the large-set problems, $F(1, 11) = 7.21, p < .05$, but they were not significant at 3 or at 5 years for either set size (3-year-olds:

Table 16.3 Mean proportions of problems on which children
counted during the posttransformation phase
(Experiment 1)

|  | Conservation Problems | Substitution Problems |
|---|---|---|
| 3-year-olds: | | |
| Small-set problems | .09 | .12 |
| Large-set problems | .00 | .04 |
| 5-year-olds: | | |
| Small-set problems | .41 | .55 |
| Large-set problems | .20 | .28 |
| 6-year-olds: | | |
| Small-set problems | .24 | .88 |
| Large-set problems | .25 | .54 |

$Fs(18) \leq 2.90$, $ps > .10$, 4-year-olds: $Fs(16) \leq 3.01$, $ps \geq .10$). The three-way interaction reflects the fact that the 6-year-olds differentiated more strongly between substitution versus conservation problems when the sets were small than when they were large (simple effect of problem type $\times$ set size: $F(1, 11) = 5.33$, $p < .05$), whereas the younger children showed similar patterns of counting across problem types regardless of set size (simple effects of problem type $\times$ set size: $Fs < 1$).

Posttransformation counting could have contributed to judgments that corresponded to the pretransformation judgment on conservation problems, because the numerical relation between the two rows in fact remained the same. Thus, further analyses were conducted to determine whether children's posttransformation judgments on the conservation problems corresponded to their pretransformation judgments even when they did not count the posttransformation array. The relevant means, along with the numbers of subjects on which they are based,[6] are presented along with the overall means in Table 16.2. Because missing data precluded comparison of all the problems to each other in an analysis of variance, a series of $t$ tests were performed comparing each age group's performance on each problem type to chance (.50, the proportion that would be expected to occur if children's posttransformation responses were independent of their pretransformation ones). Only two of these comparisons reached statistical significance – those for the 6-year-olds' performance on the small-set and large-set conservation problems (small-set problems: $t(12) = 5.28$, $p < .001$, large-set problems: $t(12) = 2.74$, $p < .05$, all other $t$ values $\leq 1.24$, $ps > .10$).

*Relations between pre- and posttransformation performance*

Two sets of analyses provided evidence that use of counting to compare the sets prior to the transformation was related to conserving in the posttransformation phase. The first analysis focused on subjects who showed very clear pretransformation strategies – either counting on at least 13 of the 16 trials ("counters": the four 5-year-olds and eight 6-year-olds represented in the top section of Table 16.1) or consistently choosing the longer row ("length responders": the six 3-year-olds and seven 5-year-olds in the right-hand column of Table 16.1). These two groups were then compared *vis-à-vis* how often they repeated their pretransformation judgment after a conservation transformation. In order to take into account age as well as pretransformation strategy, four separate groups defined by age as well as pretransformation strategy were compared to each other via a 4 (groups: 3-year-old length responders, 5-year-old length responders, 5-year-old counters, and 6-year-old counters) $\times$ 2 (set size) analysis of variance on children's posttransformation responses to the conservation problems. The effect of group was statistically significant, $F(3, 21) = 6.17$, $p < .01$. Post hoc contrasts indicated that the "counters" conserved significantly more ($Ms = .91$ at 5 years and .96 at 6 years) than the "length responders" ($Ms = .58$ at 4 years and .48 at 5 years), while children of different ages who used the same strategy did not differ from each other (Newman–Keuls tests, $p = .05$).

The second set of analyses examined the relation between the classification of individual children as consistent conservers or not and the classifications of pretransformation counting and pretransformation response patterns reported earlier (see Table 16.1). Of the 21 consistent conservers in the sample, 10 were also consistent "counters" during the pretransformation phase. In contrast, of the 36 children who were not consistent conservers, only two consistently counted in the pretransformation phase. The relation between conserving and pretransformation counting is significant, $\chi^2(1) = 12.09$, $p < .001$. Similarly, only four of the 21 conservers were classified as consistent noncounters during the pretransformation phase of the problems, versus 25 of the 36 nonconservers, $\chi^2(1) = 11.54$, $p < .001$. There was evidence that consistent conservation was developmentally prior to consistent pretransformation counting, in that there were more children who consistently conserved during the posttransformation phase of the conservation problems and yet had not counted consistently during the pretransformation phase than children who did not consistently conserve but had consistently counted during the pretransformation phase, 11 versus two children, McNemar's exact test, $p = .02$. However, when intermittent as well as consistent counting is considered, children are as likely to count as to conserve; 11 children counted either intermittently or consistently in the pretransformation phase but did not conserve consistently, while four children consistently conserved but did not count even intermittently, McNemar's exact test, $p = .06$.

There was also a significant association between consistent conserving during the posttransformation phase and children's patterns of judgments during the pretransformation phase. Of the 21 consistent conservers, 13 (three 5-year-olds and 10 6-year-olds) consistently chose the more numerous row prior to the transformation, while only two (one 3-year-old and one 5-year-old) consistently chose the longer row prior to the transformation, and six (three 3-year-olds and three 5-year-olds) showed a mixed pattern of pretransformation judgments. The conservers were significantly more likely to show a number-based pattern of pretransformation judgments than either a length-based pattern, $\chi^2(1) = 9.96$, $p < .01$, or a mixed pattern, $\chi^2(1) = 12.51$, $p < .001$.

Table 16.4 summarizes the relation between children's counting in the pre- and posttransformation phases of the problems. As can be seen, most of the 6-year-olds fit one of two coherent patterns. If they counted consistently during the pretransformation phase, then they also did so after the transformation, but predominantly on the substitution problems. Alternatively, they counted only intermittently in the pretransformation phase and also in the posttransformation phase, again primarily on substitution problems. Among the younger children, by far the dominant pattern was not to count during either portion of the problems. However, the instances in which these children did count consistently were quite evenly distributed across the different phases and types of problems.

## Discussion

Between 3 and 6 years of age there were marked changes in children's pretransformation judgments and the strategies by which they made those judgments, as well as in their posttransformation judgments and patterns of counting. Four closely interrelated developmental changes were observed. First, there was a marked increase in counting, particularly during the pretransformation phase and also in the posttransformation phase of the substitution problems. Second, presumably as a result of the increased counting, there was a marked increase in number-based pretransformation judgments and a decrease in length-based ones. Third, the 6-year-olds were much more likely than the younger children to carry over their pretransformation judgments to the posttransformation phase on the conservation problems, but not on the substitution problems. And fourth, the 6-year-olds, but not the younger children, showed selectivity in their use of counting during the posttransformation phase in that they were more likely to count on the substitution problems, on which there was no logical basis for making a judgment, than on the conservation problems, on which the relation between the rows could be inferred from information obtained prior to the transformation.

While these results confirm and extend previous evidence of developmental changes in young children's use of counting to compare two sets (Michie 1984; Sophian 1987), they fail to replicate Bryant's finding that

Table 16.4 Numbers of children who counted consistently on conservation and substitution problems (Experiment 1)

| Pretransformation Counting Classification and Age Group | Posttransformation: Conservation Problems | | | Posttransformation: Substitution Problems | | |
|---|---|---|---|---|---|---|
| | Consistently Counted[a] | Counted Intermittently | Responded without Observable Counting[a] | Consistently Counted[a] | Counted Intermittently | Responded without Observable Counting[a] |
| Consistently counted:[b] | | | | | | |
| 3-year-olds | 0 | 0 | 0 | 0 | 0 | 0 |
| 5-year-olds | 2 | 2 | 0 | 2 | 2 | 0 |
| 6-year-olds | 1 | 5 | 2 | 7 | 1 | 0 |
| Counted intermittently: | | | | | | |
| 3-year-olds | 0 | 2 | 1 | 0 | 3 | 0 |
| 5-year-olds | 1 | 4 | 1 | 1 | 5 | 0 |
| 6-year-olds | 0 | 2 | 5 | 0 | 6 | 1 |
| Responded without observable counting:[b] | | | | | | |
| 3-year-olds | 0 | 0 | 19 | 0 | 1 | 18 |
| 5-year-olds | 0 | 2 | 8 | 0 | 2 | 8 |
| 6-year-olds | 0 | 0 | 0 | 0 | 0 | 0 |

[a] On at least seven of the eight problems of a given type.
[b] On at least 13 of the 16 problems.

children as young as 3 years of age conserve information about the quantitative relation between two sets through a perceptual transformation. Two further experiments were conducted in an effort to resolve this discrepancy. These experiments will be briefly described, and then the implications of all three sets of results for the developmental relation between counting and conservation will be discussed.

An important difference between the present study and Bryant's was the inclusion of small-set problems in the present research. It seems unlikely that the use of small sets would interfere with early conservation, and indeed previous research has indicated that early conservation is if anything facilitated by the use of small sets (Cowan 1979; Winer 1974). However, the inclusion of small-set problems does appear to have encouraged children to count, an effect which carried over even to the large-set problems as indicated by substantial order effects. As a result, age differences in children's understanding of counting as a means of comparing two sets may have had a greater impact on children's conservation performance here than in Bryant's research. It is not clear how that could explain Bryant's evidence of significant conservation as early as 3 years of age, but it is possible that somehow the small set sizes altered the way children thought about the problems. For instance, the small sets might have elicited subitizing which provided an immediate basis for judgment and thus led children to rely less on earlier impressions they had formed about the two rows.

Thus, in Experiment 2, only large-set problems were presented, and counting was precluded. The primary goal was to examine the robustness of the age differences in conservation reasoning observed in the first experiment. If the age differences in conservation in Experiment 1 were due to older children's use of counting during the pretransformation phase, then the age differences should be reduced or eliminated when all children are prevented from counting and therefore must rely on perceptual comparison for their pretransformation judgments, as the younger children predominantly did in Experiment 1. On the other hand, if the age differences in Experiment 1 reflect differential understanding of the relation between the pretransformation and posttransformation arrays, there should still be substantial age differences even when counting is precluded and only large-set problems are presented.

## EXPERIMENT 2

### Method

*Subjects*

Twenty-two 3-year-olds (3 years, 7 months to 4 years, 0 months; $M = 3$–10), 21 5-year-olds (4 years, 11 months to 5 years, 4 months; $M = 5$–2), and

12 6-year-olds (6 years, 4 months to 6 years, 8 months; $M$ = 6–7) participated in this experiment. There were approximately equal numbers of boys and girls in each group. None of the children in this study had participated in Experiment 1. Most of them were Caucasian and middle class. They lived in a rural academic community and were brought to a laboratory on campus for testing.

## Materials

The 11-item, 12-item, and 13-item strips used in Experiment 1 were used again in this experiment, and they were displaced on the same wooden board as in Experiment 1. A cardboard screen, measuring 56 × 7.5 cm, was also used in this experiment.

## Procedure

Each child again received eight conservation problems, four substitution/same problems, and four substitution/reversed problems. All of the problems involved comparing a transformation set that contained 11 or 13 items with a comparison set of 12 items. Within each problem type, the problems varied in which row was longer initially and in whether the longer row contained one object more or one object fewer than the other row, as well as in the specific items that constituted the row.

The procedure for presenting the problems was identical to that in Experiment 1 except that the experimenter asked the child to answer without counting, and in order to further deter counting she gradually covered and uncovered the displays as she showed them to the child. The complete presentation procedure, which was terminated as soon as the child responded, was to give the child about 3 sec to look at the display initially, then begin to lower the screen, taking about 3 sec to lower it fully, then immediately begin to lift the screen again, once more taking about 3 sec to do so, then repeat the cycle two more times, ending with the screen in place after the child's third look, at which point it was not lifted again until the child had responded. As the experimenter began to uncover the objects for the child's third look she warned him or her that this would be his or her last look, and repeated the "Are there more" question. If the child had still not responded by the time she lifted the screen and replaced it once more, she repeated the question once again, leaving the screen in place. This procedure was used in presenting both the pretransformation and the posttransformation displays. No child in this experiment gave any evidence of counting either aloud or subvocally with identifiable lip movements.

Because it had not been possible to score children's responses to the why questions in Experiment 1 reliably, no such questions were included in Experiment 2. Instead, after children completed the main body of problems they were given four countersuggestion problems, on which the experimenter presented a simple rationale for choosing the opposite row and asked the posttransformation question again. The purpose of these countersuggestions was to assess the strength of children's conviction about their responses when they chose the same row they had chosen initially. If children were guessing, or carrying over their pretransformation responses for lack of another basis for responding as Halford and Boyle (1985) suggested, then they might be expected to be quite willing to agree to a different line of reasoning suggested by the experimenter, and they should be about equally willing to do so on conservation problems and on substitution problems. On the other hand, if they understood that conservation transformations cannot alter the relative numerosity of two sets, they may be more resistant to countersuggestions on conservation problems than on substitution problems.

Two of the countersuggestion problems involved a conservation transformation, one a substitution/same transformation, and one a substitution/reversed transformation. Prior to the presentation of the countersuggestion, these problems were identical to the problems in the main body of the experiment. The countersuggestion was attributed to a Raggedy Ann doll, and the rationale always referred to the transformation that had been performed. Thus, if the child had chosen the same row as before the transformation, the experimenter would say that Raggedy Ann thought that the other strip now had more, because this one had had more before but then one of the strips had been changed. If the child had chosen the opposite row from the one he or she chose before the transformation, the experimenter would say that Raggedy Ann thought that the strip the child chose initially had more because it had had more before and the strips had only been moved around.

## Results

### Pretransformation judgments

Six 3-year-olds (27 per cent), 10 5-year-olds (48 per cent), and two 6-year-olds (17 per cent) chose the longer row on 13 or more of the 16 pretransformation questions. Only one 3-year-old (5 per cent) and two 6-year-olds (17 per cent) chose the more numerous row on as many as 13 of the 16 pretransformation questions.

A 3 (age) $\times$ 2 (gender) $\times$ 2 (length: more numerous row longer vs. shorter) analysis of variance was conducted on the proportion of pretransformation questions to which children responded by correctly choosing the row with more items. This analysis produced significant main effects of age, $F(2, 49) = 3.79$, $p < .05$, and length, $F(1, 49) = 24.37$, $p < .001$, and a significant interaction between them, age $\times$ length, $F(2, 49) = 4.13$, $p < .05$.

There were significant age differences on the problems on which the more numerous row was shorter than the other, $Ms$ = .35, .26, and .57 for the three age groups, $F(2, 49)$ = 7.26, $p$ = .001, but not on the problems on which the more numerous row was longer than the other, $Ms$ = .68, .75, and .65, $F < 1$. On the former problems, the performance of the 6-year-olds was significantly better than that of either the 3-year-olds or the 5-year-olds, who did not differ (Newman–Keuls tests, $ps < .01$). The two younger groups chose the more numerous row significantly more often when it was also the longer row, $Ms$ = .68 at 3 years and .75 at 5 years, than when it was the shorter row, $Ms$ = .35 at 3 years and .26 at 5 years, indicating a substantial impact of length on their judgments (for the 3-year-olds: $F(1, 49)$ = 12.78, $p$ = .001, for the 5-year-olds: $F(1, 49)$ = 27.80, $p < .001$). In contrast, the 6-year-olds chose the more numerous row about equally often whether it was longer, $M$ = .65, or shorter, $M$ = .57, than the other row ($F < 1$). Across both subsets of problems, the 6-year-olds chose the correct row significantly more often than expected by chance, $t(11)$ = 2.33, $p < .05$, but the younger groups did not ($ts < 1$).

## Posttransformation judgments

The proportion of problems on which children chose the same row after the transformation as they had chosen prior to it was analyzed in a 3 (age) $\times$ 2 (gender) $\times$ 2 (problem type: conservation vs. substitution) analysis of variance. As in Experiment 1, for comparability to the conservation problems, responses to the substitution problems were considered "same" if the child chose the to-be-transformed row before the transformation and the row that replaced it after the transformation. The only significant effects in this analysis were a main effect of age, $F(2, 49)$ = 12.29, $p < .001$, and an age $\times$ problem type interaction, $F(2, 49)$ = 6.08, $p < .01$. The means corresponding to the age $\times$ problem type interaction are presented graphically in Figure 16.1. Simple effects tests indicated that the 6-year-olds were the only group whose performance varied significantly across the two problem types, $F(1, 49)$ = 6.63, $p$ = .01 (for the other age groups, $Fs \leqslant 2.32$, $ps > .10$), and the three age groups differed from each other only in their performance on the conservation problems, $F(2, 49)$ = 15.00, $p < .001$, for the substitution problems, $F(2, 49)$ = 2.08, $p > .10$. Pairwise comparisons among the age groups on the conservation problems indicated that the 6-year-olds performed significantly better than either of the other two groups (Newman–Keuls tests, $p < .01$), who did not differ from each other.

Individual children were considered to have maintained their pretransformation responses consistently during the posttransformation phase of the problems if they chose the same row they had chosen before the transformation on at least seven of the eight conservation problems (binomial $p$ = .035). None of the 22 3-year-olds, and only two of the 21

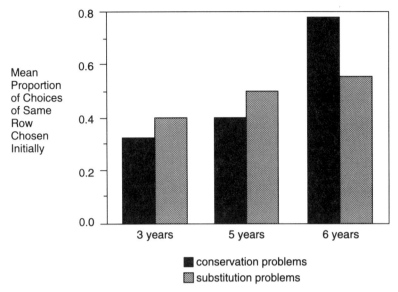

*Figure 16.1*   Mean proportions of problems on which children chose the same row (or one that had been substituted for it) after the transformation that they had chosen in the pretransformation phase (Experiment 2)

5-year-olds (10 per cent), but seven of the 12 6-year-olds (58 per cent) met this criterion. The increase between 5 and 6 years was statistically significant, $\chi^2(1) = 6.88$, $p < .01$.[7] None of the children who consistently conserved after the transformation showed a consistent pattern of choosing either the longer or the more numerous row before the transformation.

*Responses to countersuggestions*

On average, the 3-year-olds maintained their original responses in response to the countersuggestions on 48 per cent of the conservation problems and 43 per cent of the substitution problems; the 5-year-olds did so on 59 per cent of the conservation problems and 64 per cent of the substitution problems; and the 6-year-olds did so on 83 per cent of the conservation problems and 58 per cent of the substitution problems. A 3 (age) × 2 (gender) × 2 (problem type) analysis of variance on these data did not produce any significant effects, although the main effect of age approached significance, $F(2, 49) = 2.37$, $p = .10$. Although the interaction of age × problem type was not significant, $F(2, 49) = 1.85$, $p > .10$, simple effects tests were conducted to evaluate the age differences on each problem type separately because of the substantial age differences in the means for the conservation problems. Indeed, the age differences on the conservation problems were significant, $F(2, 49) = 3.32$, $p < .05$, whereas on the substitution problems they were not, $F(2, 49) = 1.13$, $p >$ .10. $T$ tests comparing the proportion of countersuggestion probes on which children maintained their original posttransformation response to a chance value of .50 were significant for the 6-year-olds on the conservation problems, $t(11) = 4.69$, $p < .001$, but not for either of the younger groups on those problems ($ts < 1$) nor for any age group on the substitution problems ($ts \leq 1.31$, $ps > .10$).

## Discussion

The results of this experiment parallel the findings of Experiment 1 in that only the 6-year-olds gave evidence of differentiating between conservation and substitution problems, and the younger age groups were substantially influenced by length in their pretransformation judgments. These results strengthen the conclusion that children do not understand the implications of a conservation transformation for the quantitative relation between two sets until about 6 years of age. They also suggest that the discrepancies between Bryant's (1972) results and the present results cannot be attributed to the inclusion of very small sets in Experiment 1 or to the propensity to count that those small sets apparently elicited.

An unusual feature of the present research was the mounting of the sets to be compared on strips of ribbon and elastic. This innovation, while designed to enhance continuity between pre- and posttransformation phases of the problems, could have contributed to the divergence between our results and those of Bryant (1972). For instance, the presence of the strips may have encouraged children to think in terms of the length of the strips rather than the number of objects in the sets. Since length is in fact not conserved when an elastic is stretched or relaxed, that could lead them to give less evidence of conservation reasoning than they might have shown if strips were not used. Experiment 3 therefore made one further effort to replicate Bryant's results using individual objects rather than sets mounted on elastic. The experiment focused on 5-year-olds because the findings for that age group in Experiments 1 and 2 present the greatest challenge to previous research suggesting that preschool children already have an understanding of conservation.

## EXPERIMENT 3

### Method

*Subjects*

Twelve 5-year-olds (4–11 to 5–4; $M = 5$–1), who had not participated in either of the two preceding experiments, were subjects. There were equal numbers of boys and girls. The children came from the same predominantly Caucasian, middle-class, rural community as those who participated in Experiments 1 and 2, and they were brought to the same laboratory for testing.

## Materials

The objects used in Experiment 2 were removed from their strips for Experiment 3. Otherwise, the materials were identical for the two experiments.

## Procedure

The procedure for Experiment 3 followed closely that used in Experiment 2, except that the objects were not attached to strips of ribbon or elastic. Instead, the experimenter positioned the objects individually, using different fingers to move several objects at a time so as to complete the transformations as quickly as possible. Although with this procedure it was still possible to carry out the transformations fairly quickly, it did take longer overall to present each problem in this experiment than it had in Experiments 1 and 2 (in part because of the time needed to position the sets at the beginning of the problems). As a result, it was necessary to reduce the total number of problems each child received in order to keep the testing session within the limits of the children's attention spans. Each child therefore was given six conservation problems, three substitution/same problems, and three substitution/reversed problems without countersuggestions in this experiment, followed by four countersuggestion problems as in Experiment 2. Within each problem type, the problems varied in which row was longer initially (the stationary row or the to-be-transformed row), in whether the more numerous row was longer or shorter than its counterpart, and also in the specific types of items that constituted the row. Although these variables could not be fully counterbalanced within the set of problems an individual subject received, they were varied as systematically as possible within subjects and they were fully counterbalanced across subjects.

Children's performance in this experiment was contrasted with that of the 5-year-olds in Experiment 2 in order to evaluate the degree to which mounting the objects on strips had affected children's performance in that experiment.

## Results

### Pretransformation judgments

Nine of the children in this experiment (75 per cent) chose the longer row in response to 10 or more of the 12 pretransformation questions. None showed that level of consistency in choosing the more numerous row prior to the transformation.

On average, children chose the more numerous row prior to the transformation on .93 of the problems on which that row was the longer row and on .13 of the problems on which it was the shorter one. A 2 (experiment) $\times$ 2 (gender) $\times$ 2 (length) analysis of variance comparing their performance to that of the 5-year-olds in Experiment 2 yielded a significant main effect of length, $F(1, 29) = 66.39$, $p < .001$, reflecting more correct choices when the more numerous row was also the longer one. The interaction of experiment $\times$ length approached significance, $F(1, 29) = 3.69$, $p = .06$. This result suggests that, if anything, the children tested with loose objects were even more strongly affected by length cues than those tested with strips of objects. Across the arrays where the more numerous row was longer versus shorter than the alternative, the 5-year-olds in this experiment were not significantly above chance in identifying the more numerous row, $t(11) = 1.77$, $p = .10$.

*Posttransformation judgments*

In response to the posttransformation questions, the children in this experiment chose the same row they had chosen before the transformation on .35 of the conservation problems, and on .51 of the substitution problems. A 2 (experiment) $\times$ 2 (gender) $\times$ 2 (problem type) analysis of variance comparing their performance to that of the 5-year-olds in Experiment 2 produced only a significant main effect of problem type, $F(1, 29) = 4.77$, $p < .05$. Children chose the row they had chosen initially significantly *less* often on the conservation problems than on the substitution problems. None of the effects of experiment approached significance, $Fs < 1$.

Individual children were considered to have conserved consistently if they chose the same row they had chosen before the transformation on all six of the conservation and/or substitution problems (binomial $p = .02$). By this criterion, two of the children in this experiment (17 per cent) consistently conserved on the conservation problems. One of those children also met the criterion for consistently choosing the longer row prior to the transformation, while the other showed a mixed pattern of judgments prior to the transformation. None of the children consistently maintained their pretransformation judgments on the substitution problems.

*Responses to countersuggestions*

The children in this experiment maintained their original posttransformation response after a countersuggestion on 46 per cent of the conservation countersuggestion problems and on 54 per cent of the substitution countersuggestion problems. A 2 (experiment) $\times$ 2 (gender) $\times$ 2 (problem type) analysis of variance comparing their performance in this respect with that of the 5-year-olds in Experiment 2 produced no significant effects, $Fs$ (1, 29) $\leq$ 2.49, $ps > .10$. The proportion of countersuggestion probes on which children in this experiment maintained their original posttransformation responses did not differ significantly from chance (.50) for either the conservation problems or the substitution problems, $ts(11) < 1$.

## Discussion

The results of this experiment again fail to replicate Bryant's (1972) report of conservation among children below 6 years of age, and they also provide no support for the idea that the use of strips of objects rather than loose ones in Experiments 1 and 2 might have increased children's reliance on length cues or decreased their tendency to conserve. While these findings do not bring us any closer to pinpointing the factors responsible for the divergence in results, they do show that the age differences in conservation observed in the present experiments are not chance occurrences nor are they restricted to an idiosyncratic method of testing.

## GENERAL DISCUSSION

The present research, then, indicates that both conservation reasoning and counting undergo a protracted development across the period from about 3 to 6 years of age. The two developments appear to be largely contemporaneous and closely connected. In Experiment 1, there was some evidence that conservation preceded counting to compare sets, in that children were more likely to conserve consistently on the conservation problems but not to count consistently on the substitution problems (or during the pretransformation phase of all the problems) than they were to count consistently but not conserve. However, the two tasks are asymmetrical in that on the conservation task, children would be expected to maintain their pretransformation judgments about half the time by chance alone, whereas it is unclear that counting is ever a chance performance, and it surely could not be expected to occur half the time by chance. For this reason, even occasional counting may indicate that a child has some understanding of counting as a means of comparing two sets, whereas only consistent conservation responses can be taken as evidence that the child understands conservation. Accordingly, it may be more appropriate to compare counting and conservation by looking at the relation between consistent conservation and at least occasional counting. This kind of comparison favors counting, although not significantly.

The close relation of both conservation and counting in Experiment 1 to age makes it difficult to disentangle their effects. Perhaps the most striking finding from Experiment 1 was that 5-year-olds who consistently counted during the pretransformation phase were much more likely to conserve even than their age-mates who responded to the pretransformation comparisons on the basis of length. Of course, since this is a correlational result, we cannot be sure that the pretransformation measure did not simply select out groups of 5-year-olds who differed from each other in a global way, such as intelligence or cognitive maturity. An alternative possibility, however, that warrants further investigation, is that children make a distinction between number-based comparisons and length-based ones in reasoning about the effects of a spatial transformation: They may expect numerical relations between sets to be conserved, but not length-based comparisons. Although counting was blocked in Experiment 2, the 6-year-olds still diverged from the younger children in that they did not base their pretransformation judgments on length, and they were apparently able to derive some veridical numerical information even from intermittent glimpses of the arrays, since their pretransformation judgments were significantly, albeit only slightly, above chance. Their success rate was far too low ($M = .61$) to support a requantification explanation for their tendency to conserve in the posttransformation phase of the conservation problems ($M = .78$), but it is consistent with the idea that they conserved because they were reasoning about a truly numerical, albeit inaccurate, representation of quantity rather than a spatially based one such as length.

Another possibility, not incompatible with that idea, is that developments in children's use of counting to compare sets, in their willingness to disregard length differences, and in their conservation of their pretransformation judgments all reflect a common underlying change in children's basic conception of numbers. Numbers are inherently relational, as Russell's (1919) classic definition of cardinal number as a class of classes illustrates: an essential part of what it means to say a set has three members, or any other number, is that it is equivalent to any other set of three in the specifically numerical sense that the elements of the two sets can be put into one-to-one correspondence. However, young children may think of numbers primarily as properties of individual sets, which is how they are typically used in counting. A developing appreciation of the relational character of numbers could account for all three of the co-occurring developments observed in this research.

This idea fits well with Elkind's (1967) distinction between identity conservation and equivalence conservation; Elkind noted that young children are much more successful in recognizing that a single quantity is still the same amount after a conservation transformation than at appreciating that the relation between two quantities remains invariant. Similarly, research on children's counting has found much greater competence among young children on problems involving just a single set than on problems involving relations between sets (Schaeffer, Eggleston and Scott

1974; Sophian 1987, 1988). Thus, both in representational activities like counting and in forms of reasoning like conservation children appear to follow the same developmental trajectory from an understanding of numerical properties of individual sets to an understanding of numerical relations between sets. Relational reasoning does not emerge at the same moment in all aspects of the child's numerical performance – a point which is well illustrated by the contrast in the present research between counting to compare sets, which was evident at 5 years of age, and conservation, which was not evident before 6 years – but it does on the whole characterize the tasks on which age differences are most apparent, as compared to those on which early competence is the norm.

One apparent exception to this generalization comes from Gelman's (1972) "magic studies," in which children learned to identify the "winner" between two small sets and they did so on the basis of numerical properties of those sets. This task looks relational because there are two sets involved and the child is choosing between them; yet it has become a classic demonstration of early competence, on which children as young as 3 years of age performed very well. The crucial question, however, is whether children were thinking of the "winner" in relational terms – for instance, as "the set with a larger number" – or whether they were simply focusing on properties of an individual set that made it a winner, for example, "it wins because it has three." Because Gelman was not seeking to resolve this question, her studies did not include the kinds of problems that would directly address the issue, that is, transposition problems in which the previous "winner" (e.g. a set of three in juxtaposition to a set of two) appeared in a different relational status (e.g. the set of three now juxtaposed with a set of four). Nevertheless, several aspects of the data support the view that children were considering the problems in terms of the properties of individual sets rather than the relation between them. For one thing, children were quite comfortable identifying the winner without even uncovering the second set: if the first set they saw had the "winning" number they accepted it as the winner. Moreover, when asked to explain why a set they had chosen was the winner, children typically counted the winning set but did not (so far as can be determined from the published report) refer to the contrasting numerosity of the losing set. Likewise, when problems were transformed so that there no longer was a winner, children expressed concern about the absence of a set with the desired numerosity (e.g. "Now where d'ya put the three's?" p. 84) but not about the change in the numerical relation between the two sets. According to Gelman and Gallistel (1978), some children even indicated that both sets could be "winners" (when they both had the previously winning numerosity).

The only evidence in the present research that children below 6 years of age distinguished between conservation and substitution transformations in reasoning about the relation between two sets was the finding that, in analyses combining the data from Experiments 2 and 3, the 5-year-olds were significantly less likely to repeat their pretransformation choice after a conservation transformation than after a substitution transformation. Surprisingly, this result suggests that 5-year-olds viewed the conservation transformation as indicating numerical change rather than invariance. It is possible that this is a spuriously significant finding, since no such trend was found in Experiment 1, and no significant effect emerged in the analysis of just the Experiment 2 data.[8] However, the result does bear a strong similarity to Katz and Beilin's (1976) finding that 3- and 4-year-olds performed *below* chance on conservation problems on which the two rows were the same length after the transformation. Although they attribute their finding to children's use of irrelevant cues such as position, it is unclear how, given counterbalancing, those cues could produce performance that differed from chance. A more plausible interpretation of children's tendency to reverse rather than conserve their initial judgments might be a social-interactional one that builds on the idea that children take the repetition of the comparison question as a cue that something important has changed, or that the child's original response is being doubted (Rose and Blank 1974). However, any such interpretation must somehow take into account the observation that children were not as likely to change their responses on substitution problems.

It might be argued that children responded differently to the repeated comparison question on conservation versus substitution problems precisely because they do, in some sense, understand the difference between the transformations. If they consider the substitution transformation to change the problem substantially, they will not view the posttransformation question there as a repetition of a question they have already answered; whereas, to the extent that they consider the conservation transformation irrelevant they will see the posttransformation question there as a repetition and thus perhaps a suggestion that their earlier answer was wrong. A difficulty for this interpretation, however, is that children were not especially likely to reverse themselves even on the countersuggestions, which directly challenged their earlier response; therefore it is unclear why interpreting the posttransformation question on the conservation problem as such a challenge should have led to a high rate of reversals.

An alternative account might be based on the idea that children look for social-interactional cues mainly when they do not understand the problem well enough to work out a solution for themselves. According to this interpretation, children understand substitution transformations well enough to know that they do not necessarily preserve or maintain numerical relations; interpreting the repeated comparison question in this context they draw the appropriate inference that they need to reevaluate their initial response but not necessarily to change it. On the other hand, lacking an understanding of the conservation transformation, they can only interpret the repetition of the comparison question on those problems as an indication that something important is different, and so they are inclined to change their response. This interpretation differs importantly from other accounts of social-interactional factors in the conservation task in that, far from maintaining that social-interactional factors mask children's understanding, it suggests that the impact of social-interactional cues is itself largely determined by limitations on children's understanding of the problems they are given.

The repeated finding from this series of experiments that young preschool children do not yet conserve number was unexpected in light of the widespread reports of early conservation in the post-Piagetian literature. Nevertheless, this negative evidence is compatible with a broader picture of children's developing numerical abilities that has been emerging from studies of children's counting as well as studies of their numerical reasoning, a picture that agrees in some respects with both Piaget's account of a relatively late-emerging, logic-based, concept of number and the post-Piagetian view of early, counting-based, numerical competence. Young children do display important numerical competences in their early counting, but those competences are for the most part restricted to assigning numerical values to individual sets. Protracted further developments are evident in children's understanding of numerical relations between sets, whether in a counting context or a conservation one.

## ACKNOWLEDGEMENTS

This research was supported by a grant from the Spencer Foundation. The author thanks Gloria Dobrydnio for her assistance with data collection.

## NOTES

1 The positions of the transformed and stationary sets were constrained by the positions of the nails on which the strips were placed. The rows were always horizontal to the child; thus one row was necessarily closer to the child than the other. The static set (mounted on ribbon) always occupied a middle position, and the to-be-transformed set (on elastic) was initially in an adjacent position, either closer to the child, if it was in its extended position (hence, longer than the ribbon row), or on the far side of the static set, if it was in its unextended position (shorter than the ribbon row). After the transformation, the transformed set was always placed on the far side of the static set from the child (just beyond the position used for unextended elastic strips during the pretransformation phase). The nails for this last position were precisely aligned with those for the static set.

2 This fixed order of mention might have created a bias toward the choosing the transformed set (because of recency). However, because the transformed set was equally often the larger and the smaller of the two sets (and equally often the initially longer and the initially shorter row) such a bias would only lead to

chance-level performance in terms of the relation between children's pretransformation and posttransformation choices.

3 This definition of counting corresponds to that used in previous research on
children's use of counting to compare two sets (Sophian 1987). In fact, in
general children's counting was quite standard. The accuracy of children's
counting was not systematically evaluated, because the focus of the research
was on the strategies children used and the relation between their pretransformation and posttransformation judgments rather than on the accuracy of either
judgment. However, previous research suggests that by $3\frac{1}{2}$ years of age (the
youngest age included in this research) almost all children can count sets of at
least four items accurately (Sophian 1987). Thus, we can assume that children at
all ages had the counting facility to quantify at least the small-set problems
accurately. In addition, the close relation between overt counting and number-
based judgments in the pretransformation phase (see Table 16.1) suggests that
when children counted they generally did so accurately.

4 For comparison, children's responses to the eight substitution problems were
also examined for patterns of consistent conservation-like responding. No 6-
year-olds, and only two 3-year-olds and one 5-year-old, consistently maintained
their pretransformation judgments on these problems. (Of these children, only
one – a 3-year-old – was among those who consistently conserved on the
conservation problems.) The difference between the number of 6-year-olds
who consistently conserved on conservation vs. substitution problems was
highly significant, 11 vs. 0, McNemar's exact test, $p = .001$.

5 Three additional interactions in this analysis involved order: problem type $\times$
order, $F(1, 45) = 4.59$, $p < .05$, age $\times$ set size $\times$ order, $F(2, 45) = 4.39$, $p < .05$,
and set size $\times$ gender $\times$ order, $F(1, 45) = 6.71$, $p = .01$. In general, these
interactions reflect the fact that children counted more often when the small-set
problems were presented first than when the opposite order was used, but this
effect only emerged for certain subsets of children on certain problems.

6 Only a subset of the subjects contributed data to each mean because some
children counted on every occurrence of one or more problem types.

7 A parallel analysis on the substitution problems identified no 3-year-olds, one 5-
year-old (5 per cent), and three 6-year-olds (25 per cent) who consistently
carried over their pretransformation responses. (All but one of these children,
a 6-year-old, also conserved consistently on the conservation problems.)

8 An analysis of just the Experiment 3 data likewise failed to corroborate a
significant difference between the conservation and substitution problems,,
$F(1, 10) = 2.95$, $p > .10$.

# REFERENCES

Baroody, A. J. and White, M. S. (1983) "The development of counting skills and
number conservation", *Child Study Journal* 13: 95–105.

Bryant, P. (1972) "The understanding of invariance by very young children",
*Canadian Journal of Psychology* 26: 78–96.

Bryant, P. E. and Bradley, L. E. (1985) *Children's reading problems*, Oxford: Basil
Blackwell.

Chomsky, N. (1957) *Syntactic structures*, The Hague: Mouton.

Clements, D. H. (1984) "Training effects on the development and generalization of
Piagetian logical operations and knowledge of number", *Journal of Educational
Psychology* 76: 766–776.

Cowan, R. (1979) "Performance in number conservation tasks as a function of the number of items", *British Journal of Psychology* 70: 77–81.

Elkind, D. (1967) "Piaget's conservation problems", *Child Development* 38: 15–27.

Gelman, R. (1972) "Logical capacity of very young children: Number invariance rules", *Child Development* 43: 75–90.

Gelman, R. (1982) "Accessing one-to-one correspondence: Still another paper about conservation", *British Journal of Psychology* 73: 209–220.

Gelman, R. and Gallistel, C. R. (1978) *The child's understanding of number*, Cambridge, MA: Harvard University Press.

Gold, R. (1978) "On the meaning of nonconservation", in A. M. Lesgold, J. W. Pellegrino, S. D. Fokkema and R. Glaser (eds) *Cognitive psychology and instruction*, New York: Plenum.

Halford, G. F. and Boyle, F. M. (1985) "Do young children understand conservation of number?" *Child Development* 56: 165–176.

Katz, H. and Beilin, H. (1976) "A test of Bryant's claims concerning the young child's understanding of quantitative invariance", *Child Development* 47: 877–880.

Light, P. H. and Gilmour, A. (1983) "Conservation of conversation? Contextual facilitation of inappropriate conservation judgments", *Journal of Experimental Child Psychology* 36: 356–363.

McGarrigle, J. and Donaldson, M. (1975) "Conservation accidents", *Cognition* 3: 341–350.

Michie, S. (1984) "Why preschoolers are reluctant to count spontaneously", *British Journal of Developmental Psychology* 2: 347–358.

Piaget, J. (1952) *The child's conception of number*, New York: Norton.

Rose, S. A. and Blank, M. (1974) "The potency of context in children's cognition: An illustration through conservation", *Child Development* 45: 499–502.

Russell, B. (1919) *Introduction to mathematical philosophy*, London: Allen & Unwin.

Saxe, G. B. (1977) "A developmental analysis of notational counting", *Child Development* 54: 84–90.

Saxe, G. B. (1979) "Developmental relations between notational counting and number conservation", *Child Development* 50: 180–187.

Schaeffer, B., Eggleston, V. H. and Scott, J. L. (1974) "Number development in young children", *Cognitive Psychology* 6: 357–379.

Sophian, C. (1987) "Early developments in children's use of counting to solve quantitative problems", *Cognition and Instruction* 4: 61–90.

Sophian, C. (1988) "Limitations on children's knowledge about counting: Using counting to compare two sets", *Developmental Psychology* 24: 634–640.

Starkey, P. (1981) "Young children's performance in number conservation tasks: Evidence for a hierarchy of strategies", *Journal of Genetic Psychology* 138: 103–110.

Winer, G. A. (1974) "Conservation of different quantities among preschool children", *Child Development* 45: 839–842.

Wynn, K. (1992) "Evidence against empiricist accounts of the origins of numerical knowledge", *Mind & Language* 7: 315–332.

# Chapter 17

# Beyond competence and performance
## Children's class inclusion strategies, superordinate class cues, and verbal justifications

*Michael Chapman and Michelle L. McBride*

Seventy-two children from 4 to 10 years of age were given 2 class inclusion tasks in which the superordinate class was perceptually and linguistically marked or unmarked. A minor subclass question was also asked in order to estimate the rates of children's underlying solution strategies. The results indicated (a) that the performance of 4–6-year-olds was inflated by guessing, (b) that scores were higher in the marked task as compared with the unmarked task because of different rates of inclusion logic, and (c) that children's verbal justifications closely approximated their estimated true competence, contrary to common assumptions. The conclusion is drawn that the relation between verbal justification and intrapsychic inference is an important theoretical issue, not merely a question of measurement validity.

The origins of the class inclusion task can be traced to Piaget's (1921) early study on children's understanding of the concept of a part. Briefly, he found that children aged 10–14 years tended to misinterpret sentences in which one thing was said to be part of another. For example, some children were found to interpret a sentence such as "Part of my flowers are yellow" as meaning "My part of the flowers are yellow." In this early phase of Piaget's research, children's reasoning was studied on an entirely verbal level. In *Judgment and Reasoning in the Child* (Piaget 1924/1928), he argued that children's reasoning and logical thinking developed from their need to justify themselves in the context of interpersonal argument.

After his work on sensorimotor development during the 1930s, Piaget (e.g. 1964) came to believe that he had overestimated the importance of verbal factors in his earlier work and that the primary factor in the development of children's reasoning was the interiorization and coordination of actions (on the concept of interiorization in Piaget's theory, see Furth 1968). In Piaget's terminology, interiorized actions become operations as a consequence of their intercoordination, and he called them *concrete operations* to the extent that they bore on concrete objects and events. In *The Child's Conception of Number*, Piaget (1941/1952) reinterpreted the development of children's understanding of the inclusion of a subclass in a superordinate class in terms of his new theory. Class inclusion was now explained as the result of an intercoordination or grouping of operations having the form $A + A' = B$. This formula is usually interpreted as representing the union of two subclasses ($A$ and $A'$) in a superordinate class ($B$). However, it would be more consistent with the operational thrust of Piaget's theory to interpret the terms $A$ and $A'$ as representing operations of bringing individual objects together to form the corresponding classes, the term $B$ as representing the operation of collecting the same objects that are collected by $A$ and $A'$, and the plus sign as representing the reversible composition of the operations $A$ and $A'$. Thus, the formula $A + A' = B$ taken as a whole represents the fact that the composition of the operations $A$ and $A'$ is equivalent to the operation $B$. The reversibility of this composition consists in the fact that each term in the equation can be derived from the other two – $B$ from the composition of $A$ and $A'$, $A$ from $B$ ignoring $A'$, and $A'$ in like manner from $B$ ignoring $A$.

Consistent with this new theory, Piaget (1941/1952, ch. 7) studied children's understanding of class inclusion with respect to a collection of real objects rather than through verbal problems alone. In the original study, children were shown a certain number of wooden beads, most of which were brown and only a few of which were white. They were then asked if there were more brown beads or more wooden beads. In contrast with the verbal problems used by Piaget (1921), which were solved consistently by children only at the ages of 10–14 years, the new class inclusion task was solved by most children after the ages of 7–8 years on the average. Below that age, children tended to say that there were more brown beads than wooden ones. Their justifications of their judgments suggested that instead of comparing the brown beads with the superordinate class of wooden beads, they compared the major subclass of brown beads with the minor subclass of white beads. In other words, they extended the term *wooden* only to the wooden beads that remained once the brown beads were accounted for, rather than to all the wooden beads.

## LANGUAGE AND OPERATIONS

Although linguistic factors had no place in Piaget's conceptualization of concrete operational reasoning, he continued to use children's verbal justifications as criteria for such reasoning. This apparent discrepancy was noted by Braine (1959) in his influential monograph on the nonverbal assessment of Piagetian concepts. Braine argued that because verbal expression was not part of Piaget's definition of concrete operational ability, his use of verbal explanations as assessment criteria could only introduce an additional and extraneous source of task difficulty. His prescription was to remove the factor of verbal expression as much as possible from the assessment procedure. This approach was extended to the study of children's classification by Braine (1962). The relative validity of such nonverbal assessment methods was debated by Braine (1964) and Smedslund (1963, 1965, 1966) in the context of transitive reasoning. Gruen (1966) argued that the different results obtained in different studies of conservation could be accounted for by the use of verbal explanations as assessment criteria by some investigators but not by others.

The historically decisive argument in this debate was perhaps that delivered by Brainerd (1973, 1977), who argued that the use of children's verbal explanations as criteria for the presence of cognitive competence was a systematic source of false negative measurement error. In Brainerd's view, the use of verbal explanations as assessment criteria resulted in the underestimation of children's abilities because of the possibility that children could understand a given concept without being able to put it into words. His prescription for this problem was to use a judgments-only criterion and to control the kinds of strategies used by children to obtain those judgments through appropriate experimental procedures. Despite some attempts to qualify this conclusion (Reese and Schack 1974), researchers in the field of cognitive development found this general line of reasoning convincing, as reflected in the widespread use of nonverbal or other indirect assessment methods during the 1970s and into the 1980s (Miller 1976; Siegel 1978).

The fact that children generally have been found to pass typical Piagetian tasks at earlier ages with indirect assessment methods than with classical Piagetian procedures seemed to support Braine (1959) and Brainerd's (1973) skepticism regarding verbal explanations. In their view, such indirect methods are more sensitive indicators of cognitive competence and, accordingly, are better able to detect the presence of such competencies among younger children (Brainerd 1977; Siegel 1978). In an extensive review of class inclusion research, Winer (1980) listed the use of different assessment criteria by different investigators as one possible explanation for discrepancies in age norms obtained across studies, although he doubted that those discrepancies could be explained through such criterion artifacts alone. Other potential influences on class inclusion performance considered by Winer included perceptual salience, linguistic variables, and class content. Despite research findings supporting the efficacy of each of these factors, Winer concluded that none were sufficient for explaining all of the variations between studies.

The major outcome of the debate over assessment criteria has been the proliferation of some often very ingenious indirect methods for assessing children's cognitive competence (Gelman and Baillargeon 1983; Miller 1976; Siegel 1978). One such method is Hodkin's (1987) performance model analysis of children's class inclusion performance. Hodkin reasoned that at least three strategies were available to children for solving the class inclusion task.

Inclusion logic is the comparison between a subclass and the super-ordinate class that contains it. In other words, this strategy is what the class inclusion study is intended to assess. Barring simple errors of comprehension or production, it will always lead to a correct answer because a superordinate class is necessarily more than any of its proper subclasses.

Subclass comparison is a comparison between the major and minor subclasses, rather than between superordinate and subordinate classes. In the traditional class inclusion task, this strategy always leads to incorrect judgments. Since Piaget (1941/1952), subclass comparison has been assumed to be the major source of error in young children's class inclusion reasoning.

Guessing is defined as a *random choice between the two alternatives provided in the class inclusion question* (e.g. "Are there more brown ones or more wooden ones?"). As such, it should lead to approximately 50 per cent correct and 50 per cent incorrect answers. In practice, this category probably should be broadened to include all strategies based on uncertain choices that result in a 50–50 probability of correct and incorrect answers, even if those strategies are not perfectly random. For example, children who consistently choose the last-mentioned alternative in the inclusion question will have a 50 per cent probability of a correct answer if the order of the alternatives is counterbalanced. In effect, such children are guessing that the second alternative is correct, and a random distribution of answers is guaranteed by counterbalancing.

Against the usual assumption that a higher percentage of correct answers on a class inclusion task necessarily reflects more inclusion logic, Hodkin reasoned that the same result could occur in some cases through increased guessing. For example, if 40 per cent of a given population of children solving a class inclusion task used inclusion logic and the remaining 60 per cent used subclass comparison, then the overall rate of correct judgments would be 40 per cent (ignoring other potential sources of error). If two-thirds of the children using subclass comparison started guessing instead, then the pass rate would climb to 60 per cent (the 40 per cent who used inclusion logic plus half of the 40 per cent who have started guessing). Thus, the interpretation of the rate of correct judgments is inherently ambiguous, but this ambiguity could be eliminated if one could estimate the overall rate of guessing within the population.

As a means of estimating the guess rate, Hodkin (1987) gave children a minor subclass inclusion problem. In addition to the typical class inclusion question in which the superordinate class is compared with the major subclass ("Are there more *blue* things or more *triangles*?"), Hodkin also asked children an inclusion question in which the superordinate class was compared with the minor subclass ("Are there more *blue* things or more *circles*?"). The point of including this minor subclass question was that children using either inclusion logic or subclass comparison would answer it correctly; the only solution strategy that would lead to an incorrect answer would be guessing. Because guessing involves a 50 per cent chance of a correct answer, about half of the children who guessed would answer correctly and half would answer incorrectly. In other words, the overall guess rate would be twice the number of incorrect answers observed on the minor subclass inclusion question.

Hodkin reasoned that the rate of guessing should be approximately the same on the standard inclusion question as on the minor subclass question. Accordingly, the estimated guess rate obtained in the manner just described could be used to derive the estimated rates of inclusion logic and subclass comparison on the standard class inclusion problem. Because correct class inclusion judgments result only from inclusion logic and from randomly correct guessing, the estimated proportion of children using inclusion logic can be derived by subtracting half of the total guess rate from the rate of correct answers to the standard inclusion question. Similarly, the estimated rate of subclass comparison can be obtained by subtracting half of the guess rate from the rate of incorrect inclusion answers.

Given estimates of the three solution strategies, the researcher can determine whether the differences in performance observed in different versions of the class inclusion task are attributable to different rates of inclusion logic or to different rates of noninclusion strategies. To illustrate the utility of this method, Hodkin (1987) compared two versions of the class inclusion task: a standard version in which the classes were identified with verbal labels (*triangles*, *circles*, and *blue things*), and a reduced language version in which the same classes were identified by pointing to corresponding geometric symbols (a *white triangle*, a *white circle*, and a *blue rectangle*, respectively). According to the common interpretation derived from Braine (1959) and Brainerd (1973), verbal response measures involve systematic false negative measurement error. Therefore, reducing the linguistic demands of the task should result in higher levels of assessed competence.

Consistent with that hypothesis, Hodkin found that class inclusion judgments were more often correct in her reduced language task as compared with the standard task. The more important question, however, was whether this performance difference resulted from a real difference in the use of inclusion logic or only from a difference in the relative rates of guessing and subclass comparison. Contrary to the false negative measurement error hypothesis, Hodkin found no significant differences between tasks in the estimated rates of inclusion logic. Instead, children used more subclass comparison in the standard task and more guessing in the reduced language task. The overall difference in correct judgments across tasks resulted from the fact that subclass comparisons always yield incorrect judgments, but guessing results in about 50 per cent correct judgments. Hodkin reasoned that children might have guessed more frequently in the reduced language condition because they were confused by nonverbal representations of classes. In other words, the nonverbal assessment procedure made the task harder instead of easier.

## SUPERORDINATE CLASS CUES

The research reported in this chapter had two main goals. The first was to employ Hodkin's (1987) method to estimate children's underlying class inclusion strategies as a means of interpreting the effects of perceptual or linguistic cues used to mark the superordinate class (Brainerd and Reyna, 1990; Markman 1989; Tatarsky 1974; Wilkinson 1976; Winer 1980). In a frequently cited example of such effects, McGarrigle, Grieve and Hughes (1978) compared performance on a standard class inclusion task, in which the superordinate class was defined generically ("Are there more *cows* or more *black cows*?"), with that of a modified version in which the superordinate class was perceptually and linguistically marked ("Are there more *sleeping cows* or more *black cows*?" – with the sleeping cows placed on their sides). Consistent with the hypothesis that performance would be enhanced by increasing the salience of cues defining the superordinate class, McGarrigle *et al.* found a significantly higher rate of correct judgments on the second task as compared with the first. They interpreted this finding as an indication that superordinate class cuing can facilitate the understanding of hierarchical class inclusion.

However, other interpretations are possible. According to Winer (1980), Piagetian theorists might interpret superordinate class cuing effects as a reflection of nonlogical figurative or intuitive processes rather than as a facilitation of genuine class inclusion (cf., Dean, Chaubaud and Bridges 1981). Similarly, Hodkin (1987) suggested that the observed effects of superordinate class cuing could result not from any facilitation of inclusion logic but from a higher rate of guessing in the perceptually marked task. In the study reported in this chapter, the latter hypothesis was tested by giving children both versions of the class inclusion task used by McGarrigle *et al.*, one in which the superordinate class of cows was perceptually and linguistically marked by placing them on their sides and calling them sleeping cows and one in which the cows were left standing and were simply called cows. In both versions, Hodkin's minor subclass comparison question was asked in addition to the standard class inclusion question as a means of estimating children's rate of guessing. The issue to be decided was whether performance differences between the two tasks were the result of differences in the use of inclusion logic or of differences in the noninclusion strategies of guessing and subclass comparison.

The second major goal of this study was to compare the rate of inclusion logic as estimated from Hodkin's model with performance as assessed by two frequently used assessment criteria: judgments only versus judgments plus justifications. According to Brainerd (1973, 1977), the use of verbal justifications as an assessment criterion results in a significant underestimation of children's true cognitive competence relative to the use of a judgments-only criterion. Most researchers have accepted that argument as bordering on self-evident. However, given a method for estimating the rates of children's underlying inference strategies, it becomes an empirical proposition whether and to what extent children's verbal justifications underestimate their true competence relative to some other criterion. Hodkin's performance model would appear to be well suited for testing that proposition.

## METHOD

### Subjects

Seventy-two children from predominantly middle-class backgrounds were recruited from after-school day-care centers. This number included 12 boys and 12 girls in each of three age groups: 4–6-, 7–8-, and 9–10-year-olds. Mean ages of these groups were 5.1, 7.1, and 9.3 years, respectively.

### Materials and procedure

The children were tested individually in a quiet corner of the day-care center. Each child was asked to compare two versions of the class inclusion task in one 15- to 20-min sitting. The order of the two tasks was counterbalanced, and an irrelevant task (digit span) was administered between them to "break set" and to minimize possible carryover effects from one task to the other.

The materials used in the class inclusion tasks were seven plastic horses, five of which were brown and two of which were white. In the unmarked task, the horses were placed in a standing position, and the superordinate class was referred to simply as *horses*. In the marked task, the horses were placed on their sides, and the superordinate class was referred to as *sleeping horses*. In both tasks the major and minor subclasses were identified with the brown horses and the white horses, respectively. The order of the marked and unmarked tasks was counterbalanced.

In all other respects, the procedures followed in the two tasks were identical. First, children were familiarized with the materials through a series of questions in which they were asked to name all of the objects and their colors. Then, children were asked the standard class inclusion question in which the superordinate class was compared with the major subclass. In the unmarked task, the question was "Are there more *horses* or more brown horses?" In the marked task, it was "Are there more *sleeping horses* or more brown horses?" After replying to the inclusion question, children were asked to justify their answers. In addition, children also were asked which was more, the (sleeping) horses or the white horses. The latter question comparing the superordinate class with the minor subclass was used to estimate the amount of guessing according to Hodkin's (1987) model. The order of this minor subclass question and the standard class inclusion question was counterbalanced as specified by Hodkin.

## Coding

Children's judgments on the class inclusion tasks were scored as *correct* or *incorrect*, depending on whether the superordinate or subordinate class was said to be more. Their justifications of these judgments were classified into the following three categories:

1 Irrelevant answers included failures to provide justifications (e.g. "I don't know") as well as non sequiturs and nonsensical answers (e.g. "because they're under there").
2 Subclass comparisons included all justifications in which children compared the two subclasses rather than the superordinate class and major subclass (e.g. "because there are five brown ones and only two white ones").
3 The inclusion logic category included all justifications in which children stated that all of the objects belonged to the superordinate class (e.g. "because they're all sleeping") or otherwise referred to the hierarchical relation of inclusion between the superordinate and subordinate classes (e.g. "because they're all sleeping, but only two are white"; "because they're all sleeping, but they're not all brown"; "because the brown ones and the white ones together make all the horses").

For analyses involving the *judgments-plus-justification* criterion, the judgment and justification codes were combined in the following way: Children were judged as passing a given task if they supplied a correct judgment and an adequate justification in terms of inclusion logic. Conversely, they were judged as failing the task if they gave an incorrect judgment or an inadequate (irrelevant or subclass comparison) justification. The interrater reliability (percentage of agreements) was 97.6 per cent for the three justification codes and for the judgments-plus-justifications category.

In addition to the judgments-only and judgments-plus-justification scores, the estimated rates of class inclusion strategies (guessing, subclass comparison, and inclusion logic) were calculated according to Hodkin's (1987) method as described earlier. First, the overall estimated rate of guessing was obtained by doubling the rate of failure on the minor subclass question, then the estimated rates of subclass comparison and of inclusion logic were obtained by subtracting half of the rate of guessing from the total rate of correct and incorrect judgments, respectively.

## RESULTS

### Age and task

Children's performance by task (marked vs. unmarked) and age group is shown in Table 17.1 in terms of the percentage of children passing at each age for both judgments-only and for judgments-plus-justifications criteria. As indicated in the table, children's performance increased with age in all task × criterion categories. Log-linear tests of the interaction between age group and performance were significant for each category. For the judgments-only criterion, the $L^2(2)$ values were 21.22 for the marked task and 23.90 for the unmarked task (both $ps < .001$). For the judgments-plus-justifications criterion, the corresponding values were 21.96 and 25.45 (both $ps < .001$). No significant effects were found for the order in which the marked and unmarked tasks were presented.

In comparisons between tasks, tests of correlated proportions revealed that performance was significantly higher in the marked task for the judgments-only criterion, cum bin $p < .02$, but that the two tasks did not significantly differ for the judgments-plus-justifications criterion. (Because of small sample size, exact significance levels of all tests of correlated proportions were determined through the cumulative binomial distribution, see Hayes 1988.) To test the interaction of these comparisons with age, children were classified into three groups on each criterion: (a) those who passed the marked task and failed the unmarked task, (b) those who performed equally on both tasks, and (c) those who passed the unmarked

Table 17.1 Percentage correct by task, age group, and criterion

|  | Age group | | | |
|---|---|---|---|---|
| Task | 4–6 | 7–8 | 9–10 | Overall |
| Judgments only | | | | |
| Marked | 54.2 | 58.3 | 100.0 | 70.8 |
| Unmarked | 37.5 | 45.8 | 95.8 | 59.7 |
| Judgments plus justifications | | | | |
| Marked | 29.2 | 54.2 | 91.7 | 58.3 |
| Unmarked | 25.0 | 45.8 | 91.7 | 54.2 |

Note: $n$ = 24 in each age group

*Table 17.2* Percentage of justification categories by task and age group

| Task | 4–6 | 7–8 | 9–10 | Overall |
|------|-----|-----|------|---------|
| | | Age group | | |
| | | Irrelevant answers | | |
| Marked | 33.3 | 20.8 | 8.3 | 20.8 |
| Unmarked | 33.3 | 12.5 | 4.2 | 16.7 |
| | | Subclass comparisons | | |
| Marked | 37.5 | 25.0 | 0.0 | 20.8 |
| Unmarked | 41.7 | 41.7 | 4.2 | 29.2 |
| | | Inclusion logic | | |
| Marked | 29.2 | 54.2 | 91.7 | 58.3 |
| Unmarked | 25.0 | 45.8 | 91.7 | 54.2 |

*Note:* $n = 24$ in each age group

task and failed the marked task. The log-linear test of interaction between these task performance comparisons and age groups was significant for the judgments-only criterion, $L^2(4) = 9.75, p < .05$. As shown in Table 17.1, the difference between the two tasks tended to decrease with age. For the judgments-plus-justifications criterion, the interaction between age group and the marked–unmarked comparison was nonsignificant.

**Justification categories**

The percentages of children giving each type of justification is presented in Table 17.2 by task and age group. Tests of the interaction between age group and justification category were significant for both the marked and the unmarked tasks, $L^2(4) = 24.88$ and $L^2(4) = 27.16$, respectively (both $p$s < .001). In general, irrelevant answers and subclass comparisons declined, and inclusion logic increased with age.

Tests of correlated proportions comparing the marked and unmarked tasks within each justification type yielded no significant differences. Log-linear tests of the interaction between marked–unmarked comparisons and age group for each justification type yielded a significant effect only for subclass comparison, $L^2(4) = 9.90, p < .05$. The difference between the marked and unmarked tasks was greater for 7–8-year-olds than for either of the other age groups.

## Estimated class inclusion strategies

The estimated rates for each of three class inclusion strategies specified in Hodkin's (1987) model – guessing, subclass comparison, and inclusion logic – are presented in Table 17.3 by task and age. Log-linear tests of the interaction between age group and class inclusion strategies were significant for both marked and unmarked tasks, $L^2(4) = 31.31$ and 32.68, respectively (both $ps < .001$). As shown in the table, the frequency of guessing tended to decrease with age in both tasks, subclass comparisons increased slightly (marked task) or remained the same (unmarked task) from 4–6 to 7–8 years, then decreased in both tasks from 7–8 to 9–10 years, and inclusion logic increased steadily with age in both tasks.

Tests of correlated proportions comparing marked and unmarked tasks for each solution strategy collapsed over age group revealed that subclass comparison was significantly lower (cum bin $p < .02$) and inclusion logic significantly higher (cum bin $p < .005$) in the marked as compared with the unmarked task. In contrast, guessing was equally distributed across tasks, as shown in Table 17.3. A log-linear test of the interaction between the marked–unmarked comparison and age group for each solution strategy was significant only for guessing, $L^2(4) = 12.83$, $p < .05$. There was a slight tendency for guessing to be higher in the marked task among the 4–6-year-olds and in the unmarked task among the 7–8-year-olds, although neither comparison was significant within each of those age groups alone.

Table 17.3 Estimated percentages of class inclusion strategies by task and age group

| Task | Age group | | | |
| | 4–6 | 7–8 | 9–10 | Overall |
|---|---|---|---|---|
| | Guessing | | | |
| Marked | 41.7 | 8.3 | 0.0 | 16.7 |
| Unmarked | 33.3 | 16.7 | 0.0 | 16.7 |
| | Subclass comparisons | | | |
| Marked | 25.0 | 37.5 | 0.0 | 20.8 |
| Unmarked | 45.8 | 45.8 | 4.2 | 31.9 |
| | Inclusion logic | | | |
| Marked | 33.3 | 54.2 | 100.0 | 62.5 |
| Unmarked | 20.8 | 37.5 | 95.8 | 51.4 |

Note: $n = 24$ in each age group

## Assessment criteria

To compare the judgments-only and judgments-plus-justifications criteria with the estimated true rate of inclusion logic, the observed frequencies of passes and failures corresponding to the percentages shown in Table 17.1 were fit to the estimated frequencies of children using inclusion logic versus other strategies represented by the percentages in Table 17.3. In this analysis, the Hodkin estimates were assumed to reflect the underlying population parameters, and the 7–8- and 9–10-year-old groups were collapsed into one category to avoid the statistical problems associated with low cell frequencies (i.e. the low frequency of failures among 9–10-year-olds). The results of this analysis were clear: A good fit was found between the judgments-plus-justifications criterion and estimated inclusion logic for both the marked task, $L^2(1) = 0.65$, $p > .40$, and the unmarked task, $L^2(1) = 0.34$, $p > .50$, but rates of correct judgments were significantly different from the estimated rates of inclusion logic for both marked and unmarked tasks, $L^2(1) = 4.50$ and $L^2(1) = 3.87$, respectively (both $ps < .05$). The lack of fit in the case of judgments clearly reflected the inflated rate of correct judgments among 4–6-year-olds that occurred because of lucky guesses (cf., Tables 17.1 and 17.3).

Also of interest was the question of whether the frequencies observed for the three types of verbal justifications shown in Table 17.2 approximated those estimated for the three strategies shown in Table 17.3. In this analysis, irrelevant justifications were assumed to correspond to a strategy of guessing, under the assumption that children who were uncertain how to solve the task would have been likely both to guess and to give irrelevant justifications. Again, the two older age groups were combined. The results revealed a good fit between verbal justifications and class inclusion strategies for the marked but not for the unmarked task, $L^2(1) = 0.40$, $p > .50$, and $L^2(1) = 10.64$, $p < .005$, respectively. A comparison between Tables 17.2 and 17.3 suggests that the lack of fit between justifications and strategies for the marked task can be explained as the result of discrepancies between noninclusion justifications and the corresponding strategies rather than from differences between justifications and strategies involving inclusion logic.

## DISCUSSION

The foregoing results provide reasonably clear answers to the questions posed at the beginning of the chapter. With respect to the question of superordinate cues, the hypothesis that the superiority of the marked task would reflect a real difference in inclusion logic was supported over the alternative hypothesis that task differences in performance would reflect different rates of guessing. With respect to the question of assessment criteria, the rate of correct judgments was found to be artificially inflated by a high rate of guessing among 4–6-year-olds, but the judgments-plus-justifications criterion was not found to underestimate inclusion logic as might have been expected from widely accepted arguments against the validity of verbal assessment (Braine 1959; Brainerd 1973). Instead, a very good fit was found between the judgments-plus-justifications criterion and the estimated rate of inclusion logic. In addition, verbal justifications closely approximated the estimated rates of noninclusion strategies in the standard unmarked task, but not in the marked task.

Before considering the implications of these results, it is important to note that the distribution of class inclusion strategies obtained in this study was also remarkably consistent with those reported by Hodkin (1987) for comparable tasks and age groupings. In this study, the distribution of strategies among 4–6-year-olds in the unmarked task was as follows: 33.3 per cent guessing, 45.8 per cent subclass comparison, and 20.8 per cent inclusion logic (Table 17.3). In Hodkin's study, the comparable figures were 31.3 per cent guessing, 43.7 per cent subclass comparison, and 25.3 per cent inclusion logic (Hodkin 1987, Table 17.2, standard condition averaged over 4–6-year-olds). None of the differences between the respective percentages across studies was statistically significant. Although one cannot claim normative status for these figures, the close convergence between the two studies provides evidence for the replicability of results obtained with Hodkin's method. The convergence is particularly remarkable considering the different materials employed in the two studies.

## Superordinate class cues

In McGarrigle *et al.*'s (1978) study, the class inclusion performance of 3–5-year-olds was found to be significantly higher when the superordinate class was perceptually and linguistically marked rather than labeled simply with a generic name. Those authors interpreted their findings as a real effect of superordinate class marking on young children's understanding of hierarchical class inclusion. An alternate possibility is that higher levels of performance reflected differential distributions of noninclusion strategies, as in Hodkin's (1987) reduced language condition. The present results favored McGarrigle *et al.*'s original hypothesis over the alternative.

In drawing this conclusion, two caveats are necessary. The first is that the methods used in this study did not allow for testing the separate effects of linguistic and perceptual marking of the superordinate class. With the same manipulation (cows placed on their sides and labeled *sleeping*), McGarrigle *et al.* (1978, Experiment 2) found that neither perceptual nor linguistic marking alone significantly improved performance relative to a standard unmarked condition; only the interaction of the two was effective. In contrast, Brainerd and Reyna (1990, Experiment 6) found with other materials that the effects of perceptual and linguistic marking were additive, as long as the array of objects was visible. When the array was removed from view before the class inclusion question was posed, the combinations of perceptual and linguistic marking was found to inhibit performance. Brainerd and Reyna interpreted the latter effect in the following way: When asked about a linguistically marked class (e.g. "Are there more animals with hats or more cows?"), children assume the existence of an unmarked class (that there are some animals without hats), and they are unable to correct this assumption if the array has been removed. The discrepancy between the findings of McGarrigle *et al.* and Brainerd and Reyna can perhaps be explained by the fact that there is nothing particularly interesting or unusual about animals lying on their sides until they are labeled *sleeping*, but the sight of animals wearing hats may be salient in itself.

The second caveat is that Hodkin's (1987) definition of inclusion logic in fact includes any strategy leading to 100 per cent correct answers. According to some interpretations of Piagetian theory, the facilitation of class inclusion through superordinate class cues might result from intuitive or figurative processes, rather than from a truly logical solution (Winer 1980, p. 320). Part of the difficulty in resolving this issue consists in knowing what ought to count as a logical solution. In particular, researchers differ on the question of whether the logic involved in class inclusion pertains only to the use of a logical strategy leading to correct answers on class inclusion problems or, in addition, to an understanding of the necessity embodied in logical inferences. For example, Markman (1978) proposed that young children might compare the superordinate and subordinate classes empirically without understanding that the superordinate class necessarily contained more objects than the subordinate class, and Smith (1982) suggested such empirical comparisons might be facilitated when both classes were identified by a positive perceptual characteristic (as in the marked task in this study). If the understanding of necessity is required, then the further problem arises of how such understanding should be assessed (Acredolo and O'Connor, 1991; Miller 1986).

Although we acknowledge the possibility that the estimated rate of inclusion logic obtained in this study with Hodkin's method might include nonlogical strategies (however they are defined), we believe it is unlikely. If that were the case, the true rate of inclusion would be even lower than the estimates given in Table 17.3, hence lower than the pass rate according to the judgments-plus-justifications criterion. But then the latter would tend to overestimate children's logical competence rather than to underestimate it as is usually assumed. We believe that the judgments-plus-justifications criterion is unlikely to overestimate children's understanding of class inclusion logic because such understanding is generally understood to be manifest in a logical justification as defined in this study. In sum, we believe that the most parsimonious explanation of our results is that superordinate class cues result in a real facilitation of class inclusion logic and not merely in the use of successful but nonlogical strategies. One implication of this finding is that competence in class inclusion is not a fixed characteristic of individual children but can actually vary as a function of task conditions.

Although guessing was not a significant factor determining task differences in this study, the results nevertheless illustrate the usefulness of Hodkin's method for distinguishing among alternative explanations. As demonstrated in her original study (Hodkin 1987), performance differences between some versions of the class inclusion task can indeed occur as the result of differential rates of guessing. Testing that possibility is therefore important in interpreting such differences in performance levels. The same argument holds true for other tasks besides class inclusion. The two-alternative forced-choice response format is generally characteristic of most Piagetian cognitive tasks so that children have a 50 per cent chance of success through guessing. Hodkin's method allows one to estimate the specific contribution of guessing to performance levels in the case of class inclusion, and similar methods might be possible for other tasks as well.

## Judgments and justifications

The second major goal of this study was to compare estimates of the true rate of inclusion logic obtained from Hodkin's (1987) method with the pass rates according to judgments-only and judgments-plus-justifications criteria. Contrary to the widely accepted hypothesis that verbal methods underestimate children's true competence, the estimated rates of inclusion logic did not differ significantly from the judgments-plus-justifications pass rates. Instead, a remarkable good fit between verbal justifications and estimated class inclusion strategies was found, especially for the standard unmarked task. Before these results are interpreted, however, it is prudent to consider the possibility that the lack of evidence for differences between verbal justifications and inclusion logic might be explained in terms of deficiencies in Hodkin's method for estimating rates of class inclusion strategies or the model on which it is based.

*Critique of Hodkin's model.* The model would appear to be most vulnerable with respect to the following assumptions: (a) that the rate of guessing is the same in response to the standard inclusion question as to the subclass inclusion and (b) that the only solution strategies available to children in the class inclusion task are guessing, subclass comparison, and inclusion logic. Although we believe that one could imagine reasons for doubting those assumptions, we think that the interpretation of the results of this study are unlikely to be altered by realistic violations of either one.

Consider first the assumption that the rate of guessing is the same for the standard inclusion question as for the subclass inclusion question. We suggest that two types of guessing can be distinguished – impulsive guessing as a random choice before the relevant task information has been considered and reflective guessing as a random choice after some difficulty has been encountered and judged to be beyond one's means or beyond the effort one is willing to exert. Because impulsive guessing occurs before the task information has been considered, there is no reason to expect differences in this type of guessing to occur between the standard and subclass inclusion questions. In contrast, one might expect differences in reflective guessing between the two questions to the extent that such guessing is more likely to occur in more difficult tasks.

Of the two inclusion questions, however, the standard inclusion question is likely to be the more difficult as judged both by theoretical and empirical considerations. Theoretically, the standard question should be more difficult because it has two potential interpretations that lead to different answers (i.e. if the term *horses* is taken to refer to all of the horses, then there will be more horses than brown horses, but if *horses* is understood as referring only to the white horses, then there will be more brown horses than horses). In contrast, the same two interpretations of the minor subclass question both lead to the same answer, a concurrence that should result in less cognitive conflict and equivocation. Empirically, the standard question is indeed the more difficult one. For the marked task, the standard class inclusion question was answered correctly at a rate of 70.8 per cent as compared with 91.7 per cent for the minor subclass question. By the test of correlated proportions, that difference is significant, cum bin $p < .001$. For the unmarked task, the comparable figures were 59.7 per cent and 91.7 per cent, cum bin $p < .001$. If anything, the guess rate should be higher for the standard question, and Hodkin's method accordingly would underestimate the true rate of guessing. But if the rate of guessing were underestimated in this study, then the true rate of inclusion logic would be lower than the estimates obtained. Such an outcome would not alter the conclusion that the estimated rate of inclusion logic is not significantly higher than the judgment-plus-justification rate.

Consider next the second major assumption of the method – that the only types of solution strategies available to children are guessing, subclass comparison, and inclusion logic. Recall how those strategies were defined operationally in the Method section. What is assumed in those definitions is that three general types of strategies are available to children: (a) those that result in a random (i.e. 50–50) distribution of correct and incorrect answers, (b) those resulting in systematically incorrect responses, and (c) those resulting in systematically correct responses. Defined in this way, guessing may include any strategy having a 50 per cent probability of success (e.g. order preference with order counterbalanced), and subclass comparison is the only strategy known to result in systematically incorrect answers. However, other strategies besides true inclusion logic that presumably could lead to systematically correct answers have sometimes been proposed. As described earlier, the existence of such nonlogical strategies would mean that the rate of inclusion logic obtained with Hodkin's method would overestimate the true rate because true inclusion logic would not be the only strategy leading to systematically correct answers. But if the true rate of inclusion logic were even less than that estimated in this study, then the judgments-plus-justifications criterion would be even less likely to underestimate the true rate. In summary, violations of the major assumptions of Hodkin's model are unlikely to alter the major conclusions of this study.

*Justification and intrapsychic inference.* Perhaps the most important implication of these results is that the relation between children's verbal justifications and their strategies of intrapsychic inference may require some reconsideration. One should note in this connection that the underestimation of competence presumed to characterize verbal assessment has failed to materialize in other recent studies as well. For example, Strauss and Ephron-Wertheim (1986) found that children performed significantly better on a Piagetian version of the balance-scale problem than on Siegler's (1976) rule assessment version of that task, although the Piagetian version was based on a judgments-plus-justification criterion and Siegler's version on a judgment-only criterion. (Excluding children who were judged as unscoreable on one or the other measure, 14 children scored at a higher level on the Piagetian task than on Siegler's task, and none showed the opposite pattern, sign test $p < .001$.) In other studies, children's verbal justifications have been found to correspond with their inferred inference strategies. Chapman (1991) found that children's justifications predicted the pattern of their correct and incorrect judgments in a transitivity of weight task, and Chapman and Lindenberger (1992) found that the transitivity judgments of children giving justifications on the basis of a composition of premise relations were statistically dependent on their memory for those same premises – a result that would be expected only if children had both inferred and justified their judgments by composing the premise comparisons.

We do not interpret such results to mean merely that children's verbal justifications are accurate indicators of their competence in intrapsychic inference after all. Instead, we suggest that justification and intrapsychic inference are conceptually distinguishable competencies and that the foregoing results reflect a close empirical correspondence between them. Such a correspondence may be found under some task conditions and not others, as suggested, for example, by the fact that a good fit between justifications and strategies was found for the unmarked but not for the marked task. The problem is to explicate the nature of that correspondence when it does occur. The overall point is that the relation between verbal justifications and intrapsychic inference is an important theoretical issue, not merely a question of measurement validity. What requires further elucidation are the substantive processes linking the ability to provide logical justifications for one's statements with competence in intrapsychic inference.

Following this line of reasoning, we believe that Braine (1959) and Brainerd (1973, 1977) were correct in identifying inconsistencies between Piaget's theory and his use of verbal assessment methods but that they were wrong in advocating the abandonment of the latter. Piaget was inconsistent in using verbal justifications as assessment criteria in the absence of any theoretical explanation of the relation between such verbalizations and the coordinations of operations that he believed to underlie concrete operational reasoning (Chapman 1991; Siegel 1978), but the alternative is not necessarily to abandon the study of children's justifications. Instead, we suggest that verbal justifications can be a rich source of information as markers of the ability to provide reasons in support of one's statements.

Rather than abandoning the study of justification, a more useful approach might be to study the relation between justification and intrapsychic inference in search of the missing link between the operations presumed to underlie reasoning and the language used to express it (Chapman 1991). In such a research program, all the indirect methods invented by the critics of verbal assessment criteria would still have a place, but such methods would be used together with rather than instead of verbal assessment criteria. Both methods are necessary because the project of studying the relation between competence in intrapsychic inference and competence in verbal justification (or other discursive skills) presupposes that the competencies to be compared can be assessed independently of each other. In this study, for example, Hodkin's model was used as an indirect method of assessing children's use of inclusion logic independent from their verbal justifications. The long-range goal should be to elucidate the processes that link the two competencies with each other, as suggested, for example, in theories of the sociogenesis of human reasoning from interpersonal argumentation (Piaget 1924/1928; Vygotsky 1978; see also Chapman 1991, 1993).

## CONCLUSION

The results of this study suggest (a) that higher class inclusion performance results from the perceptual and linguistic marking of the superordinate class because of real increases in children's use of class inclusion logic rather than because of increased guessing and (b) that the children's verbal justifications might approximate their competence in intrapsychic inference more closely than researchers generally have assumed. However, we do not interpret such results merely as evidence for the validity of Piaget's original assessment methods. Instead, we argue that both competence in intrapsychic inference and competence in justification should be recognized as legitimate objects of empirical investigation with the goal of illuminating the developmental processes that link them to each other. In such research, the kinds of indirect assessment procedures suggested by critics of Piagetian verbal methods would be used in addition to children's verbal justifications, not as a replacement for them.

## ACKNOWLEDGEMENTS

This research was supported by Operating Grant OG0037334 from the Natural Science and Engineering Research Council of Canada.

We would like to thank Dare Baldwin for her comments on earlier drafts of the manuscript, Karla Dye for assistance in data collection, and Alexander von Eye for his statistical advice.

## REFERENCES

Acredolo, C. and O'Connor, J. (1991) "On the difficulty of detecting cognitive uncertainty", *Human Development* 34: 204–223.

Braine, M. D. S. (1959) "The ontogeny of certain logical operation: Piaget's formulation examined by nonverbal methods", *Psychological Monographs: General and Applied* 73(5, Whole No. 475): 1–43.

Braine, M. D. S. (1962) "Piaget on reasoning: A methodological critique for the presence of cognitive structures", *Psychological Bulletin* 79: 172–179.

Braine, M. D. S. (1964) "Development of a grasp of transitivity of length: A reply to Smedslund", *Child Development* 35: 799–810.

Brainerd, C. J. (1973) "Judgments and explanations as criteria for the presence of cognitive structures", *Psychological Bulletin* 79: 172–179.

Brainerd, C. J. (1977) "Response criteria in concept development", *Child Development* 48: 360–366.

Brainerd, C. J. and Reyna, V. F. (1990) "Fuzzy-trace theory and perceptual salience effects in cognitive development", *Developmental Review* 10: 365–403.

Chapman, M. (1991) "The epistemic triangle: Operative and communicative components of cognitive competence", in M. Chandler and M. Chapman (eds) *Criteria for competence: Controversies in the conceptualization and assessment of children's abilities* (pp. 209–228), Hillsdale, NJ: Erlbaum.

Chapman, M. (1993) "Everyday reasoning and the revision of belief", in J. Puckett and H. W. Reese (eds) *Mechanisms of everyday cognition*, Hillsdale, NJ: Erlbaum.

Chapman, M. and Lindenberger, U. (1992) "Transitivity judgments, memory for premises, and models of children's reasoning", *Developmental Review* 12: 124–163.

Dean, A. L., Chaubaud, S. and Bridges, E. (1981) "Classes, collections, and distinctive features: Alternative strategies for solving inclusion problems", *Cognitive Psychology* 13: 84–112.

Furth, H. G. (1968) "Piaget's theory of knowledge: The nature of representation and interiorization", *Psychological Review* 75: 143–154.

Gelman, R. and Baillargeon, R. (1983) "A review of some Piagetian concepts", in P. H. Mussen (ed.) *Handbook of child psychology: Vol. 3. Cognitive development* (pp. 167–230), New York: Wiley.

Gruen, G. E. (1966) "Note on conservation: Methodological and definitional considerations", *Child Development* 37: 977–983.

Hayes, W. L. (1988) *Statistics* (4th edn), New York: Holt, Rinehart & Winston.

Hodkin, B. (1987) "Performance model analysis in class inclusion: An illustration with two language conditions", *Developmental Psychology* 23: 683–689.

Markman, E. M. (1978) "Empirical versus logical solutions to part–whole comparison problems concerning classes and collections", *Child Development* 49: 168–177.

Markman, E. M. (1989) *Categorization and naming in children*, Cambridge, MA: MIT Press.

McGarrigle, J., Grieve, R. and Hughes, M. (1978) "Interpreting inclusion: A contribution to the study of the child's cognitive and linguistic development", *Journal of Experimental Child Psychology* 26: 528–550.

Miller, S. A. (1976) "Nonverbal assessment of Piagetian concepts", *Psychological Bulletin* 83: 405–430.

Miller, S. A. (1986) "Certainty and necessity in the understanding of Piagetian concepts", *Developmental Psychology* 22: 3–18.

Piaget, J. (1921) "Essai sur quelques aspects du développement de la notion de partie chez l'enfant" (Essay on some aspects of the development of the concept of part in children), *Journal de Psychologie* 18: 449–480.

Piaget, J. (1928) *Judgment and reasoning in the child*, London: Kegan Paul, Trench & Trubner. (Original work published 1924.)

Piaget, J. (1952) *The child's conception of number*, London: Kegan Paul, Trench & Trubner. (Original work published 1941.)

Piaget, J. (1964) "Comments": Attachment to L. Vygotsky, *Thought and language*, Cambridge, MA: MIT Press.

Reese, H. W. and Schack, M. L. (1974) "Comment on Brainerd's criteria for cognitive structures", *Psychological Bulletin* 81: 67–69.

Siegel, L. S. (1978) "The relationship of language and thought in the preoperational child: A reconsideration of nonverbal alternatives to Piagetian tasks", in L. S. Siegel and C. J. Brainerd (eds) *Alternatives to Piaget* (pp. 43–67), San Diego, CA: Academic Press.

Siegler, R. S. (1976) "Three aspects of cognitive development", *Cognitive Psychology* 8: 481–520.

Smedslund, J. (1963) "Development of concrete transitivity of length in children", *Child Development* 34: 389–405.

Smedslund, J. (1965) "The development of transitivity of length: A comment on Braine's reply", *Child Development* 36: 577–580.

Smedslund, J. (1966) "Performance on measurement and pseudomeasurement tasks by five- to seven-year-old children", *Scandinavian Journal of Psychology* 7: 81–92.

Smith, L. (1982) "Class inclusion and conclusions about Piaget's theory", *British Journal of Psychology* 73: 267–276.

Strauss, S. and Ephron-Wertheim, T. (1986) "Structure and process: Developmental psychology as looking in the mirror", in I. Levin (ed.) *Stage and structure* (pp. 59–76), Norwood, NJ: Ablex.

Tatarsky, J. H. (1974) "The influence of dimensional manipulations on class-inclusion performance", *Child Development* 45: 1173–1175.

Vygotsky, L. (1978) *Mind and society*, Cambridge, MA: Harvard University Press.

Wilkinson, A. (1976) "Counting strategies and semantic analyses as applied to class inclusion", *Cognitive Psychology* 8: 64–85.

Winer, G. A. (1980) "Class-inclusion reasoning in children: A review of the empirical literature", *Child Development* 51: 309–328.

# Chapter 18

# The development of metalogical understanding

*David Moshman*

Does logical reasoning develop? To answer this question, we must clarify precisely what we mean by logical reasoning and by deveopment, and we must come to grips with a confusing morass of literature on logical reasoning in children and adults.

In the first section of this chapter, I will consider the concepts of logical reasoning and development and then apply the resulting definitions to the reasoning literature to conclude that logical reasoning does indeed develop, at least through adolescence. My argument will rest on a critical distinction between *logic* (involving the application of unconscious inference schemata) and *metalogic* (involving metacognitive awareness of logic). I will argue that development beyond early childhood is primarily at the level of metalogic. Then, in the second section, I will distinguish two aspects of metalogic: *metalogical strategies* (involving relatively conscious coordination of inference schemata) and *metalogical understanding* (involving conceptions about the nature of logic).

The third section of the chapter will propose four stages in the development of metalogical understanding. Relevant evidence will be reviewed. The fourth section will, then, consider how the child moves through the proposed stages. A "knowing levels" approach (Campbell and Bickhard 1986) will be highlighted and, then, placed in the context of a broader "dialectical constructivism."

## DOES LOGICAL REASONING DEVELOP?

### Logical reasoning

Reasoning may be defined as a subset of thinking in which one's cognitive processes follow rules or principles so as to reach conclusions that, if not fully justified, are at least somewhat constrained. Although reasoning, thus, includes forms of thinking that may be less than fully rational, it does not encompass aspects of thinking such as free associating or daydreaming, where rationality is simply not relevant. The term, *logical reasoning*, will be used in this chapter to mean *deductive* reasoning – reasoning that, by following strict rules of deduction, reaches conclusions that are not merely plausible or likely but *logically necessary*. If, for examply, sprognoids are known to be either animals or plants, and you find out they are not animals, you can conclude not merely that they are *probably* plants but that they *must* be plants. The conclusion is not merely a reasonable *in*duction but a necessary *de*duction.

## Development

Numerous studies find age differences in performance on a variety of logical reasoning tasks. Most developmentalists find it useful, however, to define development as referring only to age-related changes that are, in some sense, progressive – that is, those that tend toward greater differentiation and hierarchic integration, toward better adaptation and organization, toward higher levels of equilibrium, or, with respect to reasoning, toward increasing rationality. Thus, logical reasoning develops if it changes systematically with age in a way that shows increasing rationality.

## Rationality in children and adults

Using this definition of development, it is not immediately clear that logical reasoning develops. One basis for questioning the reality of development is the very impressive performance of preschool children on simple inference tasks – that is, tasks involving premises from which a conclusion can be immediately deduced. Young children presented with premises representing diverse logical domains (e.g. transitivity, class logic, propositional logic) commonly reach the same correct conclusions reached by adults (e.g. Hawkins, Pea, Glick and Scribner 1984; see reviews by Braine and Rumain 1983; Thayer and Collyer 1978). A case might be made that, if logical reasoning develops at all, its development is essentially complete by age five or six.

Another basis for questioning the view that logical reasoning develops is evidence of pervasive illogicality in the performance of adults on a wide variety of reasoning tasks (e.g. Cohen 1981; Evans 1982, 1983). Many researchers have concluded that human reasoning is essentially a collection of heuristics and response biases. If adult reasoning is as irrational as this literature suggests, there is little basis for asserting that logical reasoning develops with age.

Although the preschool rationality literature and the adult irrationality literature both cast doubt on the development of logical reasoning, they also appear to contradict each other. The two literatures, taken together, do not simply contradict the view that logical reasoning develops but suggest the highly counterintuitive conclusion that the pinnacle of rationality is reached by age five and reasoning goes rapidly downhill after that.

A closer look suggests that the source of the paradox is that the two literatures use quite different tasks. The preschool rationality research assesses the ability to make direct deductions from simple premises under favorable circumstances. The adult irrationality research, by contrast, tends to require subjects not simply to make an inference but to show substantial awareness and coordination of various ongoing and potential deductions, often under difficult and unfamiliar circumstances. We can make sense of both literatures by distinguishing logic, involving the use of basic inference schemata, from metalogic, involving a more explicit, metacognitive awareness of one's logical reasoning.

## Logic and metalogic

Consider a child who is told that a hidden ball is either red or green and that it is not red. Even a preschooler is likely to conclude that the ball is green. It would be incautious, however, to propose that the preschooler understands the distinction between premises and conclusions, thinks about the process of deducing a conclusion from premises, or understands the logical necessity of deductions. A more conservative and justifiable conclusion is that the child has simply assimilated the given information to an unconscious schema that immediately transforms it into the conclusion. We might represent the schema, in this case, as $p$ or $q$; not $p$; therefore, $q$. Braine and Rumain (1983) have proposed what they consider the basic inference schemata used by human beings, and they conclude, from their review of the literature, that, with the exception of several indirect inference schemata, most of the major deductive schemata used by adults are used quite effectively by children by the time they are old enough to be meaningfully assessed. To a large extent, basic logic, involving competence with the basic human inference schemata, is established by age five or six.

The sorts of tasks commonly administered to older children and adults, however, require much more than a single, immediate inference. Intentionally or not, such tasks assess the ability to think about the nature and use of logic and to coordinate several inference schemata within a single problem. We may refer to this level of competence as metalogic. Research with a variety of complex reasoning tasks indicates that metalogical abilities continue to develop long after the establishment of basic logic. The adult irrationality literature notwithstanding, older children and adults do show metalogical competencies lacking in younger children (Braine and Rumain 1983; Byrnes and Overton 1986; Moshman and Franks 1986; O'Brien 1987; O'Brien and Overton 1980, 1982; Overton, Byrnes and O'Brien 1985; Overton, Ward, Noveck, Black and O'Brien 1987).

In other words, it appears that the preschool rationality literature has demonstrated genuine logical reasoning in preschool children, but this does not preclude further development of metalogical competencies. Similarly, the adult irrationality literature has indeed shown numerous instances of irrational *performance* by college students on a variety of tasks, but this does not disconfirm the existence of genuine metalogical *competencies* beyond anything observed in preschoolers. Although logical reasoning is neither absent in young children nor perfect in adults, it does appear to improve with age. Thus, logical reasoning does develop, not only in the weak sense of changing with age but in the stronger sense of progressing toward greater rationality (Moshman and Lukin 1989).

## TWO ASPECTS OF METALOGIC

I have argued that the locus of development of logical reasoning beyond age five or six is at the level of metalogic. It is, thus, important to consider in more detail what metalogic consists of and how it develops. I will propose, in this section, that metalogic can be divided into two aspects: metalogical strategies and metalogical understanding.

### Metalogical strategies

Metalogical strategies are strategies of reasoning that go beyond simply assimilating premises to unconscious inference schemata. They involve an explicit distinction between premises and conclusions and a purposeful use of inference to deduce the latter from the former. Such strategies are typically conscious, or at least accessible to consciousness. They include, for example, strategies for systematically generating multiple possibilities consistent with premises (Markovits 1984), actively seeking counter-examples to potential conclusions (Johnson-Laird 1983; Overton, Ward, Noveck, Black and O'Brien 1987), or coordinating several inference schemata to construct a line of argument (Johnson-Laird 1975).

Johnson-Laird's (1983) "mental models" theory may be construed as proposing a general metalogical approach that he believes underlies all deductive reasoning. The theory suggests that children as well as adults typically solve syllogisms by imagining a state of affairs consistent with the premises, formulating a conclusion consistent with this state of affairs, and then searching for alternative possibilities consistent with the premises that would refute that conclusion (Johnson-Laird, Oakhill and Bull 1986; see also discussions by Braine 1990; Scholnick 1990).

Unfortunately, for questionable reasons, this mode of solution is proposed as an alternative to the view that people use formal rules of deduction (i.e. inference schemata). It is probably better seen as a complementary view. On simple reasoning problems, such as determining the color of the hidden ball, above, there is no need to go through anything as complex as what Johnson-Laird has suggested. It is more likely that people simply apply basic inference schemata of the sort proposed by Braine and Rumain (1983). Johnson-Laird and his collaborators, however, have focused their research on complex syllogisms that cannot be solved by assimilation to simple inference schemata. On such problems, it is likely that older children and adults are capable of applying various metalogical strategies in increasingly conscious and systematic ways.

Another example of a metalogical strategy is the use of *reductio ad absurdum* arguments. In such arguments, one assumes the truth of what one is trying to disprove and, then, through deductions from that assumption, reaches a contradiction: This allows one to reject the assumed premise. Such a strategy is metalogical, in that it does not simply reach a conclusion by unconsciously assimilating presented information to an inference schema. Instead, it constructs a line of reasoning intended to reach a contradiction and, thus, to indirectly allow one to reach a conclusion that could not be reached directly.

Notice that, in the case of a strategy of this sort, the reasoning takes a noticeable amount of time, and the reasoner, if asked, could probably reconstruct some semblance of what she or he did, step by step, and why. Compare the individual who is told the hidden ball is red or blue and is not red. The conclusion that it is blue follows immediately. If asked to justify this, even an adult probably would say something like, :"Well, you said it's red or blue and it's not red, so it's blue." Notice that this really explains nothing – it simply restates the premises and conclusion. Inference schemas lend themselves to immediate unconscious inferences; metalogical strategies, by contrast, are more planful, temporally extended, and susceptible to introspection. Unlike simple inference schemata, metalogical strategies reflect genuine understanding about the nature of logic.

## Metalogical understanding

Metalogical understanding consists of conceptions about the nature of logic. Such conceptions appear to be distinguishable from (although related to) strategies. For example, to consciously employ a strategy to generate a conclusion from premises requires a metalogical understanding of the distinction between premises and conclusions. To take a more specific illustration, the mental models strategy may require grasping the metalogical concept that a conclusion must be consistent with all possible states of affairs permitted by the premises. Similarly, understanding the role of contradiction in logic may be critical to effective use of the *reductio ad absurdum* strategy. The remainder of this chapter will attempt to describe and account for the development of metalogical understanding.

## STAGES IN THE DEVELOPMENT OF METALOGICAL UNDERSTANDING

The task of this section is to describe four stages of metalogical understanding and show that they are consistent with relevant empirical evidence. The following section will then attempt to explain the transition from stage to stage.

### Stage 1: Explicit content–implicit inference

Consider the following argument:

1 Sprognoids are either animals or plants.
  Sprognoids are not animals.
  Therefore, sprognoids are plants.

A Stage 1 child, given the information that sprognoids are either animals or plants and that they are not animals, will conclude that they are plants. From an external point of view, we as psychologists can note that the child has deduced a conclusion from the premises and can infer the use of a disjunctive inference schema ($X$ is $p$ or $q$; $X$ is not $p$; therefore, $X$ is $q$). The child herself, however, is not thinking about premises, conclusions, or the process of inference. She is thinking about sprognoids, animals, and plants. In other words, the object of her thinking, what she is explicitly aware of, is *content*. The process of inference, including a distinction between premises and conclusion, is implicit in her reasoning but is not itself an object of explicit awareness. The product of reasoning, then, is seen by the Stage 1 reasoner not as a conclusion (deduced from premises via a process of reasoning) but simply as a new fact.

Available evidence suggests that this picture of the Stage 1 child is an accurate account of most preschoolers. Although very young children can make correct inferences from a wide variety of premises, they do not expressly distinguish conclusions from premises or think about the process of reasoning (Sodian and Wimmer 1987; Somerville, Hadkinson and Greenberg 1979). It appears that the preschool child *uses* inference to generate conclusions but does not think *about* inference or construe the conclusions *as* conclusions. Metalogical understanding is simply absent at this age.

### Stage 2: Explicit inference–implicit logic

Consider now another argument:

2 Sprognoids are animals or plants or machines.
  Sprognoids are not animals.
  Therefore, sprognoids are plants.

Given the premises of this argument, a Stage 1 child may conclude that sprognoids are plants or may conclude that sprognoids are machines, perhaps depending on what the word sounds like. A Stage 2 child, in contrast, is likely to realize that there is a problem here. Depending on the situation, the child may withhold judgment, conclude you cannot tell exactly what sprognoids are, or request further information. His or her behavior shows awareness that conclusions are based on premises and are reached by a process of reasoning from those premises. The key difference between Stage 1 and Stage 2 children is not in basic logical reasoning but in metalogical understanding.

Again, as psychologists, we can examine Stage 2 behavior and see more than this. The Stage 2 child appears to respond differently to cases where a particular conclusion is logically necessary than to cases where certain conclusions are merely reasonable, plausible, probable, or conventional (Moshman and Timmons 1982). We can infer that she or he is not simply applying inference schemas but is making quite sophisticated use of distinctions in logical form. The Stage 2 child apparently distinguishes cases such as Argument 1, in which the form is such that the conclusion is logically necessary ($X$ is $p$ or $q$; $X$ is not $p$; therefore, $X$ is $q$) from cases such as Argument 2, in which the form does not involve a relation of necessity ($X$ is $p$ or $q$ or $r$; $X$ is not $p$; therefore, $X$ is $q$). Thus, although there is no explicit awareness of logical form and the associated property of logical necessity, implicit intuitions of form and necessity do affect reasoning at this level.

Research suggests that implicit appreciation of logical necessity first appears about age six (Somerville *et al.* 1979) and, between then and age 10, becomes sufficiently consolidated and generalized to show on an increasingly wide variety of tasks (Bereiter, Hidi and Dimitroff 1979; Byrnes and Overton 1986; Cormier and Dagenais 1983; Fabricius, Sophian and Wellman 1987; Markman 1978; Miller 1986; Piéraut-Le Bonniec 1980). The possibility of gaining knowledge via inference (as opposed to direct observation) also begins to be understood about age six (Sodian and Wimmer 1987). Stage 2 reasoning is, thus, typical of elementary school-age children.

### Stage 3: Explicit logic–implicit metalogic

Consider another argument:

3 Elephants are either animals or plants.
   Elephants are not animals.
   Therefore, elephants are plants.

Children at Stages 1 and 2 would reject this argument. Elephants, they would note, are *not* plants, so the argument is clearly illogical. A Stage 3 individual, on the other hand, would respond differently. Because she is explicitly aware of logical form and understands its distinction from empirical truth, she can appreciate that the form of Argument 3 is identical to the form of Argument 1, although the conclusion to Argument 3 is empirically false. She not only distinguishes logical form from empirical truth but understands their subtle interrelationship. Given the form of Arguments 1 and 3, the conclusion in each case necessarily follows from the premises. This does not guarantee that the conclusion *is* empirically true but shows that it *would be* true if the premises were true. The Stage 3 explicit understanding of the necessity of the relationship between premises and conclusions allows the individual to appreciate validity of argument form: An argument is valid if, regardless of the empirical truth of its premises and conclusion, it has a logical form such that, *if* the premises were true, the conclusion would have to be true as well.

Thus, sophisticated grasp of the interrelated concepts of logical form and necessity, and of their subtle relation to the concept of truth, is summed up in comprehension of the concept of inferential validity. Explicit awareness of the form of propositions and arguments allows the Stage 3 individual to systematically distinguish internal logical structure from the truth or falsity of content. The reasoning of the Stage 3 individual can be interpreted by a psychologist as showing an ability to work within a formal logical system as distinct from a natural language. Some degree of metalogical understanding is implicit in this distinction between logic and language, but metalogic is not itself the object of reflection.

Research by Moshman and Franks (1986) indicates that Stage 3 thinking begins to appear about age 11. They found that 9- and 10-year-olds had great difficulty with Argument 3 and others of this sort. On a variety of tasks involving several different forms of argument, children that age sorted and ranked arguments on the basis of the empirical truth or falsity of the content and appeared to ignore validity of argument form. Even after careful definition of validity, examples distinguishing validity from truth, explicit instructions to use the concept of validity to evaluate arguments, and up to 40 trials with systematic feedback, very few 9- and 10-year-olds seemed to grasp the concept of inferential validity as distinct from empirical truth. In sharp contrast, many 12- and 13-year-olds in the same series of studies spontaneously distinguished arguments on the basis of validity. With appropriate definition, examples, instructions, and/or feedback, most were quite consistent in evaluating arguments on the basis of validity rather than on the basis of empirical truth.

It appears that, although children between ages 6 and 10 have sufficient metalogical understanding to recognize when a conclusion is logically necessary, they are still strongly influenced by content. Only beginning about age 11 or 12 is there sufficient attention to the form of arguments to recognize that certain forms are inherently valid – their conclusions necessarily follow from their premises regardless of the content. Of course, the Stage 2 child's ability to distinguish necessary from merely plausible conclusions does show an implicit awareness of logical form and the associated quality of logical necessity. Only at Stage 3, however, is awareness of form and necessity sufficiently explicit to distinguish valid from invalid arguments independent of the empirical truth or falsity of their content (Moshman and Timmons 1982).

Achievement of Stage 3 metalogical understanding has implications not only for deductive reasoning but, more broadly, for the development of natural epistemologies – that is, conceptions about the nature of knowledge. An explicit grasp of necessity allows one to distinguish logical from empirical domains. Logical knowledge includes propositions that are necessarily true (tautologies) or necessarily false (self-contradictions), whereas the truth or falsity of empirical propositions can only be determined on the basis of evidence external to those propositions.

Osherson and Markman (1975) investigated reactions to a variety of propositions, including tautologies (e.g. *either the chip in my hand is not red or it is red*), self-contradictions (e.g. *the chip in my hand is white and it is not white*), and empirical statements (e.g. *the chip in my hand is yellow*). Subjects were asked whether they could decide the truth or falsity of the statements without seeing the chip. Children ranging in age from 6 through 11 years typically saw a need for empirical information in all cases, whereas most adults distinguished logical propositions (which were necessarily true or false) from empirical propositions (which could not be evaluated without seeing the chip). Cummins (1978), replicating the study with some methodological refinements, found that sixth graders did significantly better than third graders, but most still had great difficulty with nonempirical propositions.

Komatsu and Galotti (1986) used a different methodology in which children (ages 6, 8, and 10) were asked about various social conventions (e.g. the school year begins in September), empirical regularities (e.g. banging on a pot makes a loud noise), and logical necessities (e.g. there cannot be more apples than fruit). The questions focused on whether each of the various truths could be changed by consensus or could fail to hold in a different culture or on a different planet. They found distinctions between social conventions and other phenomena even in the youngest participants and increasing grasp of these distinctions with age. Children at all three ages, however, had trouble with the distinction between empirical regularities (which cannot be changed by consensus but might fail to hold on another planet) and logical necessities (which must hold in any conceivable world). A comparison group of college students appeared to grasp the distinction between empirical and logical knowledge.

Evidence from diverse sources, thus, suggests that Stage 3 understanding is not seen in children before the age of about 11 but is fairly common in adolescents and adults.

## Stage 4: Explicit metalogic

The Stage 3 individual can reason about the logical form of arguments and propositions from the metalogical perspective of a formal logical system. Only the Stage 4 individual, however, can think *about* such a system – that is, take it as an object of understanding. She or he can think about the system *as a system*, and grasp its interrelationships with other formal systems and with natural language.

The work of logicians in formalizing systems of logic, exploring their interrelationships with each other and with natural languages, and devising metalanguages for the purposes of such research is clearly at least at this level. It seems likely that the great difficulty of some abstract reasoning tasks typically administered to college students (Cohen 1981; Evans 1982, 1983) is due to the very challenging conflicts (for the Stage 3 thinker) between logical and linguistic systems (Politzer 1986). The minority of undergraduates who succeed on such tasks may be those who have made progress toward Stage 4.

Consider, for example, the well-known "selection task" (Evans 1982, 1983; Overton *et al.* 1987). It may be postulated that a Stage 3 grasp of formal logical relationships is adequate for easier versions of the task. Spontaneous success on the more abstract versions, however, may require a Stage 4 explicit understanding of the relationship between material implication (a formal logical relationship embedded in the structure of the task) and the conditional "if . . . then" (a linguistic connective central to the expression of the problem). This would explain why most college students and many younger adolescents do well in easier versions but only a minority of college students spontaneously solve the more difficult versions. The fact that even the most difficult versions are accessible to some undergraduates, however, suggests that progress toward Stage 4 is not limited to professional logicians.

It is worth noting a theoretically interesting ambiguity in determining at what stage an individual achieves metalogical understanding. Consistent with my earlier suggestion that most development beyond age five or six is at the level of metalogic, one could reasonably argue that even the Stage 2 child is reflecting on logic and, thus, has achieved some degree of meta-logical understanding. The inferential processes such a child reflects on, however, have to do with logic only from the external viewpoint of the psychologist who understands the nature of logic and the course of later development. The Stage 2 subject's own point of view does not yet include explicit knowledge of the central logical concepts of form and necessity. Thus, a case can be made that genuine metalogic, in the sense of thinking about the nature of logic, does not appear until Stage 3. However, at Stage 3, metalogical understanding merely provides the framework of reasoning rather than being itself the object of explicit attention. Using a still stronger criterion, then, genuine understanding (as opposed to use) of metalogic is not present until Stage 4 and is probably never achieved by most people. From a developmental perspective, the key point here is not to decide the "correct" criterion for metalogic in order to determine at what age, if ever, metalogic is achieved. On the contrary, the key point is that development moves progressively through increasingly powerful levels of metalogical understanding.

Is Stage 4 the highest level? It may be postulated that the explicit metalogic of Stage 4 is understood only from the perspective of an implicit "metametalogic". Stage 5 may be defined as a reflective differentiation and reconstruction of that metametalogic.

## Summary

Available evidence supports a four-stage model of the development of metalogical understanding (see Table 18.1). Preschool children often make correct inferences but think about content rather than about the deduction of conclusions from premises. Beginning about age six, children show better understanding of the purpose of inference and the nature of conclusions as new propositions derived from and, thus, justifiable on the basis of premises. This can be seen, for example, in the ability to distinguish necessary from merely plausible conclusions. Beginning about age 11, there appears to be a more explicit grasp of logical form and the

*Table 18.1* Development of metalogical understanding

| Stage | Explicit Object of Understanding | Knowledge Implicit in Reasoning (Subject) |
|---|---|---|
| Stage 1 Explicit Content Implicit Inference | *Content* | *Inference*: Conclusion deduced and, thus, distinct from premises |
| Stage 2 Explicit Inference Implicit Logic | *Inference*: Conclusion deduced from and, thus, related to premises | *Logic*: Form of argument distinct from empirical truth of premises and conclusions (necessity) |
| Stage 3 Explicit Logic Implicit Metalogic | *Logic*: Relation of argument form and empirical truth of premises and conclusions (validity) | *Metalogic*: Formal logical system distinct from natural language |
| Stage 4 Explicit Metalogic | *Metalogic*: Interrelations of logical systems and natural languages | |

associated property of logical necessity. This is revealed in the ability to grasp the concept of inferential validity and distinguish logical and empirical propositions. Finally, some adults construct Stage 4 conceptions of logical systems and their relationship to natural languages.

## THE CONSTRUCTION OF METALOGICAL UNDERSTANDING

Having described four stages of metalogical understanding, the remaining task is to explain the transitions. Nearly all modern developmentalists are constructivist in their view of developmental change. Extreme empiricism, in which an active environment impresses itself upon a blank and passive mind, is now commonly referred to as "naive empiricism" and seen as just that – naive. Extreme nativism, in which mature knowledge is seen as encoded directly in the inherited genotype, is commonly called "preformationism" and seen by most biologists and psychologists as an equally untenable position (Moshman and Lukin 1989). Mature knowledge is generally construed as actively constructed by the developing mind.

There are, however, a wide variety of constructivist views, which can be usefully divided into three general categories: exogenous constructivism, endogenous constructivism, and dialectical constructivism (Moshman 1982). *Exogenous constructivism* includes a range of views derived from or related to the empiricist perspective. Although knowledge is constructed by an active mind, the course of development is primarily directed by the environment with which that mind interacts. This position includes modern social learning theory and most information processing theories. *Endogenous constructivism* includes a variety of views derived from or related to either nativism or Piagetian theory. Nativist variants suggest that development is an epigenetic construction involving continuing interaction between the genotype and the environment. Although the endpoint is not performed in the genotype, the process is, nevertheless, strongly guided by heredity. Piagetian variants stress determination of development by the active mind rather than by the genes but remain endogenous in emphasizing internal guidance of the constructive process and, thus, relatively predictable stages. Finally, *dialectical constructivism* proposes a more balanced interaction of internal and external factors in determining the direction of development. The three parts of this section will propose, respectively, exogenous, endogenous, and dialectical constructivist accounts of the development of metalogical understanding.

### An exogenous constructivist account

Theorists in this tradition would probably be disinclined to see metalogical understanding as a distinct domain. An exogenous constructivist might propose that the development of logical reasoning includes the learning of basic inference schemata and, later, of various metalogical strategies. The inference schemata are implicit in language (e.g. in the meanings of logical connectives such as *and*, *or*, and *if . . . then*) and are, thus, learned as part of the general process of learning language. Metalogical strategies are learned primarily in academic contexts. Some, such as how to use a *reductio ad absurdum* argument, may be explicitly taught (e.g. in a math or logic class). Others may be constructed by the child in the course of general schooling. Learning to write, for example, may orient the child toward combining inferences into extended arguments.

The exogenous theorist would propose that most metalogical concepts are reducible to learned strategies. The concept of inferential validity, for example, consists of one or more strategies (e.g. hypothetico-deductive reasoning) that are used to solve validity tasks. These strategies are learned, primarily in academic contexts, although such learning may involve active information processing rather than passive incorporation.

Language learning and later academic experience are indeed critical to the development of logical reasoning and specific theories within the exogenous framework may be useful in explaining the relevant processes. It is unlikely, however, that metalogical understanding is merely a collection of learned strategies (Moshman and Lukin 1989). In particular, exogenous constructivist theories have great difficulty explaining why, if all knowledge is learned from the environment, the child comes to see certain knowledge as logically necessary (Moshman 1979; Moshman and Timmons 1982).

## An endogenous constructivist account

In contrast to exogenous accounts, endogenous accounts typically emphasize the sorts of cognitions I have labeled metalogical understandings. They are likely to see specific strategies as less fundamental in that they are either spontaneous outgrowths of one's level of understanding or are learned techniques sharply constrained by one's level of understanding. Constructing an explicit concept of logical necessity, for example, might make it possible to engage in hypothetico-deductive reasoning, but it is the former that is more basic. Similarly, purposeful search for counterexamples – which, according to Johnson-Laird's (1983) mental models theory, is central to solving complex (two- and three-model) syllogisms – requires a metalogical understanding of the role of counterexamples in logic. Strategies learned before the requisite level of metalogical understanding is attained would be superficial techniques or empirical generalizations without a firmly grasped logical basis.

In accounting for the development of metalogical understanding, I will draw most heavily on a specific variant of endogenous constructivism that can be seen in Campbell and Bickhard's (1986) theory of knowing levels, Kegan's (1982) theory of personality development, and Piaget's (1985) concept of reflective abstraction. In this view, knowing can always be divided (from an external perspective) into subject and object. The object is what the subject is explicitly aware of. It is never, of course, reality itself, but rather a constructed object of consciousness. The subject consists of implicit knowledge that is used to know the object but that is not itself explicitly known (except to the psychologist studying the process).

Development, from this perspective, consists of the construction of new, higher levels of subjectivity. In each transition, the previously implicit knowledge of the subject now becomes an explicit object of understanding. But the construction of the new subject, of course, entails a new level of implicit knowledge. Development, thus, never escapes subjectivity but, nevertheless, moves toward increasing objectivity.

Reflective abstraction may be thought of as involving two closely interrelated and mutually facilitative processes: (a) the construction of a new subject at a higher level of abstraction and (b) reconstruction of the old subject as an object of understanding. The construction of the new subject involves abstraction of elements of the old subject and the production of new implicit differentiations. The reconstruction of the old subject involves a reflection on previously implicit differentiations to refine them and ultimately coordinate them at a higher level of integration. The result is that the old subject now becomes an object known from the perspective of the new subject. The knowledge implicit in the old subject is now explicitly known by the new subject, which includes an implicit knowledge that is itself knowable only from the next higher level. At higher levels, the constructive process includes anticipatory construction of possibilities such that reflective abstraction (unlike empirical abstraction, which relies on inductive generalizations) leads to a sense of logical necessity (Piaget 1986).

This theoretical perspective greatly clarifies the development of metalogical understanding (see Table 18.1). At Stage 1, *Explicit Content–Implicit Inference*, the child thinks about content. The fact that the child can reach appropriate conclusions from various sorts of premises leads the psychologist to suggest that the child is using a variety of inference schemata. Implicit in the use of such schemata is the concept of inference, involving the generation of a conclusion based on but distinct from a set of premises.

Reflection on the process of inference involves refinement of the distinction between conclusions and premises. As this differentiation becomes increasingly explicit, it becomes possible to coordinate conclusions and premises at a higher level, involving realization that the conclusion is derived from the premises by a systematic process of inference. The inference process is itself understood from the perspective of newly constructed logical systems (classification, seriation, arithmetic, and so forth) based on the form (as opposed to the content) of inferences. These systems themselves, however, are not known by the subject. On the contrary, they *are* the Stage 2 subject, the perspective from which inference is understood. Because of their formal nature, they include a sense of logical necessity. If, for example, one has completed the structure of elementary arithmetic, $4 + 2$ *must* $= 6$, or the entire structure (including $6 - 4 = 2$, $6 - 2 = 4$, etc.) becomes incoherent. The child does not think *about* necessity, but can think about inferences from the perspective of their necessity.

Stage 2 appreciation of the necessity of a conclusion relative to certain premises requires knowledge of the logical necessity of the formal relation between premises and conclusion. The psychologist can, thus, infer an understanding of logical form and necessity. This understanding, however, is only implicit in the child's behavior. The child *uses* a structured logic, including the necessity of certain logical forms, to recognize that certain conclusions are logically necessary, but is not explicitly aware of logical structure or of the associated necessity of the relations between premises and conclusions. In other words, explicit awareness of inference at Stage 2 is associated with implicit concepts of logical form and necessity embedded in the use of logical structures.

As equilibrium is reached between the Stage 2 subject (logic) and object (inference), further reflective abstractions become possible. By taking the necessary relations between accepted premises and their required conclusions as objects of further metacognitive reflection, the child increasingly grasps the distinction between these formal relations and the empirical truth or falsity of the premises and conclusions. As awareness of logical form becomes increasingly explicit, however, it becomes possible to reintegrate the concept of form with the concept of empirical truth from which it has now been sharply differentiated. It is understood that some logical forms are better than others in that they guarantee the empirical truth of the conclusions provided the premises are empirically true. Thus, explicit reflection on necessary formal relations between premises and conclusions (the Stage 2 subject) gives rise to the concept of inferential validity (the Stage 3 object). (For detailed presentation of a protocol illustrating this transition in a 13-year-old, see Moshman and Lukin 1989.) As Stage 3 achieves consolidation, the Stage 2 concept of a necessary conclusion (based on an implicit awareness of the form of the premise–conclusion relationship) becomes a special case of the Stage 3 concept of validity of inference (based on an explicit awareness of necessary form as distinct from, but subtly related to, truth or falsity of content). It now becomes possible to distinguish the domain of logic, in which truth is based on logical form, from the domain of empirical reality, in which truth is an inductive generalization and can never attain logical necessity.

Implicit in Stage 3 conceptions is a distinction between a formal logical system and a natural language. Further reflective abstraction can, of course, refine this differentiation and lead to Stage 4 coordinations, as the complex interrelations of logical systems and natural languages become objects of explicit reflection. There is no limit, in principle, to the number of stages that can be generated by the process of reflective abstraction, although there may be pragmatic constraints on the speed of the process and the highest stage attained due to biological limitations of the human information processing system.

## A dialectical constructivist account

The endogenous account suggests that the environment, by stimulating or discouraging reflection, may facilitate or hinder development, but that it has no impact on the direction of development (i.e. the stages through which one passes). With respect to the proposed stages of metalogical understanding, this is a plausible claim. In fact, it is difficult to see how else one can account for the emergence of a sense of logical necessity that goes beyond recognition of empirical regularities and social conventions.

It is much less likely, however, that the environment has such minor and indirect impact on the emergence of specific metalogical strategies. Such a conclusion can only be defended by asserting that metalogical strategies are relatively superficial extensions of metalogical understanding that either emerge spontaneously as metalogical understanding develops or are learned in a manner determined more by developmental constraints than by environmental influences. Evidence in many areas of cognitive development suggests that specific strategies and exogenous learning are far more influential than the endogenous perspective suggests (Flavell 1985).

It appears that the exogenous and endogenous accounts have complementary strengths and weaknesses. Exogenous constructivism better accounts for the learning of strategies than for the developing grasp of their logical nature, whereas endogenous constructivism better accounts for the emerging grasp of logical necessity but trivializes the learning of strategies as a superficial extension of this.

A dialectical view suggests a substantive role for both exogenous and endogenous factors, and stresses the continuing interplay between the two. Exogenous construction may be predominant in the acquisition of metalogical strategies, whereas endogenous construction may be predominant in the emergence of metalogical understanding. Moreover, strategies and understanding are seen as equally fundamental and as continually enriching each other. Endogenous construction of understanding may enrich one's grasp of the logic behind the reasoning strategies one has learned and facilitate refinement and coordination of these strategies, as well as the learning of additional strategies. Correspondingly, exogenous construction of strategies may sometimes constitute the leading edge of metalogical development, as the process of endogenous construction endeavors to coordinate and reconstruct learned strategies at a deeper level of understanding (Moshman and Timmons 1982). The disequilibrium inherent in these complex interactions may provide much of the motivation for further exogenous and endogenous constructions (Piaget 1985).

Consider, for example, the relation of the concept of validity and the strategy of hypothetico-deductive reasoning. An exogenous view might suggest that students learn hypothetico-deductive reasoning (e.g. in a math class), and this leads to a conception of what valid arguments are. An endogenous approach might suggest that the concept of validity is constructed out of Stage 2 precursors and then makes it possible to produce or learn hypothetico-deductive reasoning. The dialectical approach suggests that either the relatively endogenous construction of the concept of validity or the relatively exogenous construction of hypo-thetico-deductive reasoning may precede the other, but whichever comes first is likely to facilitate the other. A continuing pattern of mutual facilitation in which neither strategy nor understanding gets very far ahead is the typical pattern of development.

The dialectical account cannot replace the exogenous and endogenous accounts. Metalogical strategies are learned primarily through exogenous mechanisms, whereas metalogical understanding is more endogenously constructed. The dialectical perspective reminds us, however, that there is a complex interplay between these two facets of development – their separation as distinct aspects is less a reality of cognition than a useful theoretical fiction. Metalogic may be construed as a strategy/understanding continuum ranging from (a) specific, discrete logical techniques; through (b) more general, structured sorts of strategies; through (c) more abstract metalogical concepts, such as tautology and validity; through (d) core conceptions of logical necessity. Toward the strategy end of the continuum, exogenous forces tend to predominate – at the extreme, specific techniques may be learned by rote and applied with minimal conceptual understanding. Toward the understanding end, endogenous forces tend to predominate – at the extreme, general conceptions of necessity develop in a sequence virtually impervious to environmental variations. But most of metalogical development falls between the extremes, and it involves varying proportions and complex interactions of external and internal factors. Thus, accounts of the exogenous construction of strategies and the endogenous construction of understanding, although providing genuine insight, are each partial and approximate stories abstracted from a larger and more complicated picture.

## CONCLUSION

At the 1981 meeting of the Society for Research in Child Development, as discussant for a symposium on logical necessity, I concluded the session with the following limerick:

The child thinks you only can know
What the evidence happens to show
Till she cries out, "FORSOOTH!
There are logical truths
That *are* necessarily so!"

Although my general perspective has not changed since I penned those immortal lines, I can be a bit more specific in concluding this chapter.

To make sense of the literature on the development of logical reasoning, it is critical to distinguish basis logic (involving the ability to reach correct conclusions) from metalogic (involving metacognitive awareness of logic). It appears that basic logical competence is quite impressive even in preschool children, whereas metalogic develops at least through adolescence. Metalogic includes metalogical strategies (relatively conscious and systematic coordination of inference schemata) and metalogical understanding (conceptions about the nature of logic, including the concept of logical necessity).

The development of metalogical understanding can be divided into four stages:

Stage 1 A stage of implicit inference about content.
Stage 2 A stage of explicit inference based on an implicit logic.
Stage 3 A stage in which logical necessity is explicitly understood on the basis of implicit metalogical awareness.
Stage 4 A stage involving explicit reflection on metalogic.

Progess through these stages may be accounted for in terms of reflective abstraction, an internally-driven constructive process in which knowledge implicit at any given stage becomes an explicit object of understanding at the succeeding stage. This endogenous process cannot be fully understood, however, without considering its continuing dialectical interaction with the more externally driven process of learning metalogical strategies.

Therefore, we ask: Does logical reasoning develop? If logic consisted only of basic inference schemata, we might conclude that its development is largely complete by age five or six. Considering, in addition, a variety of exogenously learned metalogical strategies, we might make a case for substantial change through adolescence. Because the specific strategies one learns are a function of one's environment, however, this would not be development in the stronger sense of systematically progressive change. In fact, given that one can learn incorrect strategies as well as correct ones, reasoning might even become more and more irrational.

Fortunately, there is more to logical reasoning than inference schemata and metalogical strategies. There also appear to be endogenously constructed metalogical conceptions, or, more broadly, an internally directed metalogical understanding. This understanding moves systematically through a sequence of differentiations and reintegrations toward increasingly explicit logical and metalogical conceptualization of inference. Exogenously learned strategies are endogenously coordinated and reconstructed along the way, ensuring that they too will show increasing coherence. Thus, the individual becomes increasingly able to reach defensible conclusions and generate sophisticated justifications. Although the specific nature of mature reasoning depends in part on the particular strategies one has learned, the endogenous construction of metalogical understanding ensures that logical reasoning will develop, not only in the sense of changing with age, but in the theoretically more meaningful sense of moving systematically toward an increasingly self-reflective rationality.

# REFERENCES

Bereiter, C., Hidi, S and Dimitroff, G. (1979) "Qualitative changes in verbal reasoning during middle and late childhood", *Child Development* 50: 142–151.

Braine, M.D.S. (1990) " The natural logic approach to reasoning", in W.F. Overton (ed.) *Reasoning, necessity and logic: developmental perspectives* Hillsdale, NJ: Lawrence Erlbaum Associates.

Braine, M.D.S. and Rumain, B. (1983) "Logical reasoning", in J.H. Flavell and E.M. Markman (eds) *Handbook of child psychology: Vol. 3. Cognitive development* (pp. 263–340), New York: Wiley.

Byrnes, J.P. and Overton, W.F. (1986) "Reasoning about certainty and uncertainty in concrete, causal, and propositional contexts", *Developmental Psychology* 22: 793–799.

Campbell, R.L. and Bickhard, M.H. (1986) *Knowing levels and developmental stages*, Basel: Karger.

Cohen, L.J. (1981) "Can human irrationality be experimentally demonstrated?", *The Behavioral and Brain Sciences* 4: 317–370.

Cormier, P. and Dagenais, Y. (1983) "Class-inclusion developmental levels and logical necessity", *International Journal of Behavioral Development* 6: 1–14.

Cummins, J. (1978) "Language and children's ability to evaluate contradictions and tautologies: A critique of Osherson and Markman's findings", *Child Development* 49: 895–897.

Evans, J. St. B.T. (1982) *The psychology of deductive reasoning*, London: Routledge & Kegan Paul.

Evans, J. St. B.T. (ed.) (1983) *Thinking and reasoning: Psychological approaches*, London: Routledge & Kegan Paul.

Fabricius, W.V., Sophian, C. and Wellman, H.M. (1987) "Young children's sensitivity to logical necessity in their inferential search behavior", *Child Development* 58: 409–423.

Flavell, J.H. (1985) *Cognitive development* (2nd edn), Englewood Cliffs, NJ: Prentice-Hall.

Hawkins, J., Pea, R.D., Glick, J. and Scribner, S. (1984) " 'Merds that laugh don't like mushrooms': Evidence for deductive reasoning by preschoolers", *Developmental Psychology* 20: 584–594.

Johnson-Laird, P.N. (1975) "Models of deduction", in R.J. Falmagne (ed.) *Reasoning: Representation and process in children and adults* (pp. 7–54), Hillsdale, NJ: Lawrence Erlbaum Associates.

Johnson-Laird, P.N. (1983) *Mental models*, Cambridge, MA: Harvard University Press.

Johnson-Laird, P.N., Oakhill, J. and Bull, D. (1986) "Children's syllogistic reasoning", *Quarterly Journal of Experimental Psychology* 38A: 35–58.

Kegan, R. (1982) *The evolving self: Problem and process in human development*, Cambridge, MA: Harvard University Press.

Komatsu, L.K. and Galotti, K.M. (1986) "Children's reasoning about social, physical, and logical regularities: A look at two worlds", *Child Development* 57: 413–420.

Markman, E.M. (1978) "Empirical vs. logical solutions to part–whole comparison problems concerning classes and collections", *Child Development* 49: 168–177.

Markovits, H. (1984) "Awareness of the 'possible' as a mediator of formal thinking in conditional reasoning problems", *British Journal of Psychology* 75: 367–376.

Miller, S.A. (1986) "Certainty and necessity in the understanding of Piagetian concepts", *Developmental Psychology*, 22: 3–18.

Moshman, D. (1979) "To *really* get ahead, get a metatheory", in D. Kuhn (ed.) *Intellectual development beyond childhood* (pp. 59–68), San Francisco: Jossey-Bass.

Moshman, D. (1982) "Exogenous, endogenous, and dialectical contructivism", *Developmental Review* 2: 371–384.

Moshman, D. and Franks, B.A. (1986) "Development of the concept of inferential validity", *Child Development* 57: 153–165.

Moshman, D. and Lukin, L.E. (1989) "The creative construction of rationality: A paradox?", in J.A. Glover, R.R. Ronning and C.R. Reynolds (eds) *Handbook of creativity*, New York: Plenum.

Moshman, D. and Timmons, M. (1982) "The construction of logical necessity", *Human Development* 25: 309–323.

O'Brien, D. (1987) "The development of conditional reasoning: An iffy proposition", in H.W. Reese (ed.) *Advances in child development and behavior* (Vol. 20), Orlando, FL: Academic Press.

O'Brien, D. and Overton, W.F. (1980) "Conditional reasoning following contradictory evidence: A developmental analysis", *Journal of Experimental Child Psychology* 30: 44–60.

O'Brien, D. and Overton, W.F. (1982) "Conditional reasoning and the competence-performance issue: A developmental analysis of a training task", *Journal of Experimental Child Psychology* 34: 274–290.

Osherson, D.N. and Markman, E. (1975) "Language and the ability to evaluate contradictions and tautologies", *Cognition* 3: 213–226.

Overton, W.F., Byrnes, J.P. and O'Brien, D.P. (1985) "Developmental and individual differences in conditional reasoning: The role of contradiction training and cognitive style", *Developmental Psychology* 21: 692–701.

Overton, W.F., Ward, S.L., Noveck, I.A., Black, J. and O'Brien, D.P. (1987) "Form and content in the development of deductive reasoning", *Developmental Psychology* 23: 22–30.

Piaget, J. (1985) *The equilibration of cognitive structures: The central problem of intellectual development*, Chicago: University of Chicago Press.

Piaget, J. (1986) "Essay on necessity", *Human Development* 29: 301–314.

Piéraut-Le Bonniec, G. (1980) *The development of modal reasoning: Genesis of necessity and possibility notions*, New York: Academic Press.

Politzer, G. (1986) "Laws of language use and formal logic", *Journal of Psycholinguistic Research* 15: 47–92.

Scholnick, E.K. (1990) "The three faces it", in W.F. Overton (ed.) *Reasoning, necessity and logic: developmental perspectives*, Hillsdale, NJ: Lawrence Erlbaum Associates.

Sodian, B. and Wimmer, H. (1987) "Children's understanding of inference as a source of knowledge", *Child Development* 58: 424–433.

Somerville, S.C., Hadkinson, B.A. and Greenberg, C. (1979) "Two levels of inferential behavior in young children", *Child Development* 50: 119–131.

Thayer, E.S. and Collyer, C.E. (1978) "The development of transitive inference", *Psychological Bulletin* 85: 1327–1343.

# Chapter 19

# Judgements and justifications
## Criteria for the attribution of children's knowledge in Piagetian research

*Leslie Smith*

In empirical research, developmentalists attribute knowledge to children on the basis of performances on assessment tasks. Since knowledge is not itself observable, criteria are needed for reasonable decisions to be made about how to classify different intellectual states, such as false belief, empirically true belief, necessary knowledge. In Piagetian research, there are two distinct views about the selection of such "response criteria". One view states that knowledge can be attributed on the basis of children's judgements-alone (J-view). A contrary view states that such attribution requires children to justify their judgements (JJ-view). An objection to the J-view is discussed by consideration of the two dominant philosophical accounts as to the nature of knowledge, namely the foundationalist and causal accounts. It is argued, first, that the foundationalist account requires the elimination of the J-view with which it is incompatible through its failure to deal with cases of knowledge at all. It is argued, second, that the causal account places a limitation on the J-view which fails to deal with cases of necessary knowledge. Since one of the main problems in Piagetian research is the construction of necessary knowledge, only the JJ-view should be used when this problem is addressed. Developmental research which is based on the J-view alone could not, without circularity, be concerned with the substantive issues which are outside its conceptual scope.

In research on children's development, intellectual tasks are used so that an adult can gain evidence which licenses the attribution of epistemic states to children. This attribution has two components, one empirical and the other criterial. The empirical component concerns the responses which children make in performing the task. Although such responses are open to direct observation, the underlying epistemic states which are expressed in them are not. Criteria are therefore needed for the identification of such different epistemic states as necessary knowledge, true empirical belief, false belief, guessing and so on. Thus the attribution is based, in part, on the observation of children's responses and, in part, on the criteria which allow these responses to count as different epistemic states. A standard problem for developmentalists is that of selecting reasonable "response criteria".

This question has generated controversy, such as whether the criteria should be behavioural or cognitive (Skinner 1985), verbal or non-verbal (Wheldall and Poborca 1979), individualized or social (Newman, Griffin and Cole 1989). One major dispute has, however, centred on whether the criteria should bear upon children's judgements or upon justified judgements. It is this latter dispute which merits attention here.

The justified judgement (JJ) view states that it is reasonable to attribute knowledge to a child only in cases where the child has expressed a justified judgement. This view is supported by Piagetian theory in several ways. First, Piaget's theory states that the onset of concrete operational knowledge is one accomplishment of intellectual development. Yet any operation is a reversible, interiorized action which is defined interdependently, as a member of a set of such actions. Thus the diagnostic assessment of operational knowledge requires a child's judgement, in which any one operation appears to have been used, to be checked against that child's ability to use any other operation from the same set. As Piaget and Inhelder (1966/1969, p. 76) put it, such operations "are never isolated but are always capable of being coordinated into overall systems". On this view, the child has the ability to coordinate any and all of the five general actions, which are identified through the constitutive principles of a *groupement*, namely combinativity, reversibility, identity, associativity and tautology (Piaget 1983/1987, pp. 120–121). A judgement and its justification are taken to be displays of at least two of these general actions. The implication is that, unless the judgement is justified, there is no case for supposing that the corresponding judgement embodies operational knowledge. The requirement that a child should support one response (judgement) by making another (justification) follows from this definition of operational knowledge. Second, good evidence is available to show that some Genevan findings, which are based on the assessment of children's justified judgements, are highly replicable for all levels of operational understanding (Shayer, Demetriou and Pervez 1988). Third, the phenomena in the domain of Piaget's theory include spontaneous intelligence, intellectual productivity and the understanding of necessity (Bickhard and Campbell 1989). Such phenomena are complex and their psychological interpretation requires innovative research. The general claim made by Piaget and Inhelder (1968; translated in Smith 1991a) is that access to the full pattern of children's justifications is required in innovative research on complex phenomena, where the full range of patterns in children's thinking cannot be pre-specified. Finally, Piaget's (1975/1985) account of equilibration identifies a generative mechanism that is responsible for developmental progression. In an empirical exemplification of parts of this model, a causal role has been assigned to children's justifications for their judgements

(Piéraut-Le Bonniec 1990). This position requires a commitment to the JJ-view.

The contrary view has also been supported. According to the judgement (J) view, it is sometimes reasonable to attribute knowledge to a child solely on the basis of that child's judgement(s) in performing a task. Three features in the support for this view may be noticed. First, whilst developmentalists accept that Genevan findings are reliable, their interpretation is regarded as open to question (Gelman and Baillargeon 1983; Halford 1989). Piaget is sometimes credited with an account of children's understanding which is too negative. In turn, the main research aim is to design tasks which allow children to exhibit the competence which they are already presumed to have. Second, a distinction drawn by Smedslund (1969), between attributing to children knowledge which they do not possess (false positive) and not attributing to children knowledge which they do possess (false negative), has been influential. Although they are mindful of the symmetrical nature of this diagnostic snare, many developmentalists contend that the requirement that children should always justify their judgements is too restrictive in leading to "false negative" diagnostic error (Flavell 1982). Finally, an argument has been offered, purporting to show that the incidence of "false positive" error is zero-to-low in research which uses a judgement-alone criterion, unlike the high incidence of "false negative" error in research which uses a judgement-and-explanation criterion (Brainerd 1973). Taken together, developmentalists have, in practice, tended to allow a child's display of a relevant judgement-alone to warrant the reasonable attribution of knowledge. In short, it is the J-view which has prevailed in much research.

The main purpose of the present discussion is to discuss a conceptual objection to the J-view with special reference to its use in Piagetian research. Discussion of this objection will be in two steps and will be dependent upon two philosophical accounts of the nature of knowledge and their implications for intellectual assessment.

## PART I

The first step is to state the objection. The discussion will centre on two dominant accounts in philosophical epistemology about the use of the concept of knowledge. One is the foundationalist and the other is the causal account of knowledge. The objection is that both accounts lead to the same conclusion, that the J-view cannot be used by developmentalists who address questions about the construction of necessary knowledge.

### Foundationalist account

The foundationalist account is the classical account of the nature of knowledge. Its sponsors include Plato in his *Theaetetus* (Plato nd/1935, 201D) as well as contemporary philosophers (Ayer 1956, p. 35; Chisholm 1977, p. 102; Haack 1990, p. 199). According to this account, a person knows a proposition $p$ if and only if three conditions are met: (i) $p$ is true, (ii) the person believes $p$ and (iii) the person is justified in believing $p$. The explanatory value of this account can be gauged by consideration of three epistemic states which are used in the description of concrete operational knowledge (Piaget and Szeminska 1941/1952), namely false belief (level I), true belief (level II) and necessary knowledge (level III).

It is worth noting at the outset that the distinctions between these three Piagetian levels have a well-defined basis. Level I and level II epistemic states differ by virtue of their truth value. The propositions which specify the content of a belief can be either true or false. It is widely accepted that propositions do differ as to their truth value both in normative discussions (Chisholm 1977; Haack 1990) as well as in Piagetian research where questions about children's correct/incorrect reasoning are central (Gelman and Baillargeon 1983; Halford 1989; Smith 1991b). The distinction between level II and level III is also accepted, since two propositions with the same truth value may differ as to their modality. A necessarily true proposition is different from one which is possibly true. This difference is accepted both in philosophical discussions (Hughes and Cresswell 1972; Kripke 1980) and in Piagetian research (Piéraut-Le Bonniec 1980; Murray 1981). Both normative distinctions are reflected in Piaget's structuralist works. However, whilst the former distinction has been well recognized in Piagetian commentary, the latter distinction has not been given equal attention. Such oversight is important. The key question to ask about a level III epistemic state concerns not just its truth value (is it correct?) but also its modality (is it necessary?). Indeed, the modal character of conservation, transitivity and inclusion can be identified.

Thus the logical notion of identity is central to conservation. Logicians define identity as a necessary relation: whatever $x$ might be, it is necessarily the case that $x$ is $x$ (Hughes and Cresswell 1972, p. 190; Kripke 1980, p. 3). This logical principle is general in its scope since it is presupposed in the defining criteria of any concept. "Every concept comprises a set of relevant attributes that define it. Sets of irrelevant attributes that the concept excludes are often correlated and associated with the relevant attributes. When they are, they make concept acquisition more difficult" (Murray 1978, p. 420; see also Murray 1981, 1990). The defining criteria of a concept are such that any object which satisfies them is – and has to be – the object which is described by that concept. Further, any object which does not satisfy these criteria is not – and could not be – the object, so described. Using the logical notion of identity as applied to the notion of number, a question which developmentalists need to confront concerns children's acquisition and use of its defining criteria. The point to bear in mind is that children who misuse the defining criteria of a notion, such as that of number, are making a logical error. If it is necessary that $x$ is $x$ – whatever $x$ might be – then the mistaken use of the defining criteria result not merely in error but in contradiction. In cases of non-conservation, if the defining criteria of number are necessary and yet these criteria result in different answers to the initial and second (post-transformation) questions, then the two answers must be contradictory. This is because a necessary proposition and its denial are contradictions (Hughes and Cresswell 1972).

An interesting objection to this conclusion is the rejection of its applicability to children's development. This delimitation could occur in one of two ways. First, it could be objected that young children are not adult logicians and so they might not have used defining – and so necessary – criteria at all. Second, the objection could be that the children might have used one set of defining criteria in their first answer but changed these criteria in giving their second answer, for example by forgetting their first answer or simply changing their minds.

The reply to the former objection is that it is question-begging to the extent that it implies that a successful response is simply a level II, rather than a level III, epistemic state. The criteria of number which Piaget and Szeminska (1941/1952) invoke are based on Russellian defining criteria, which are necessary (Smith 1986). Thus it is legitimate to raise questions about the extent to which developing children do understand such criteria. The reply to the latter objection is that it is ineffective for reasons which were anticipated by Piaget and Szeminska (1941/1952, p. 10), who point out that children can evade the contradiction by making successive use of multiple criteria. Their contention is, however, that contradictions still arise, since such children use multiple criteria in application to the same array. The outcome is that the numerosity of the array changes with these criteria and so contradictory claims are made. This is because the numerosity of one-and-the-same array is judged to change. Yet that array is self-identical and so instantiates the same logical principle of identity. The fundamental reason is the same, namely that the defining criteria of a concept embody the necessary principle of identity. (For an illustrative review of contradiction arising from the use of multiple criteria, see Smith 1991a.)

Similar considerations apply to transitivity and class-inclusion. Thus a standard definition of transitivity reads: "a relation $R$ is *transitive* if, for any $x$, $y$, and $z$, if $R$ holds between $x$ and $y$ and between $y$ and $z$, then it holds between $x$ and $z$" (Lemmon 1966, p. 182; cf., Lipschutz 1964, p. 85). Again, a standard definition of the relation of inclusion reads: "a class $A$ is included in a class $B$ if all the members of $A$ are members of $B$" (Lemmon 1966, p. 207; cf., Lipschutz 1964, p. 3). The key point is that these definitions specify logical properties of relations and classes respectively. From a logical point of view, any transitive relation has the property specified by the former principle, just as any included class has the property specified by the latter principle. From a psychological point of view, questions arise as to how children use these principles in their relational and classificatory thinking. A child who displays relational thinking in this specified logical sense is in a position to make corresponding deductive inferences. Similarly, a child who displays classificatory thinking in this specified logical sense has the ability to make valid deductions. Thus the logical properties of relations and classes make possible deductive forms of reasoning in much the same way that inference-principles – such as *modus ponens* ($p$ and, if $p$ then $q$, implies $q$) – make possible propositional deductions. Since deductive inferences are necessary inferences, the previous argument applies. Contradictory thinking is manifest in cases where these logical properties are inaccurately or incompletely understood. (For discussion of the modal nature of transitivity and inclusiion, see Smith 1987 and 1982 respectively.)

With the distinction between truth value and modality in mind, consideration can now be given to the construal of the three epistemic states – false belief, true belief and necessary knowledge – which the foundationalist account provides.

First, consider false belief. In studies of intellectual development, the importance of false belief is shown in the demarcation of incorrect and correct responses. Whilst the correct responses which children make can be interpreted as expressions of their true beliefs, their incorrect responses can be equally interpreted as expressions of their false beliefs. This is because belief, unlike knowledge, can take either truth value. That is, although beliefs can be either true or false, criterion (i) of the foundationalist account excludes there being cases of false knowledge. For example, if today is Wednesday, then the proposition "today is Tuesday" is false and so cannot describe what a person knows on any day other than a Tuesday. Whilst a person can think, or entertain the idea, or suppose that today is Tuesday, that person cannot know this, given that today is Wednesday. Proponents of the foundationalist account would say "Well, you might believe this but you don't know this" or "You think you know but you only believe this". In short, this account disqualifies false propositions as objects of knowledge. Since much research on intellectual development is concerned with charting the development of knowledge (Piaget 1950) or children's competence, i.e. correct understanding (Gelman and Baillargeon 1983), this is a welcome consequence of the foundationalist account.

Second, consider the distinction between true belief and knowledge. This distinction is also a central feature of the foundationalist account and is marked by criterion (ii) which states that possession of a true belief is necessary for cases of knowledge. That is, the absence of true belief means the absence of knowledge. But a necessary condition is not a sufficient condition. Just because the absence of true belief means the absence of knowledge, it does not follow that the presence of true belief means the presence of knowledge. For example, if possession of a first degree is a necessary condition of the possession of a doctoral degree, then it follows that non-graduates do not have doctoral degrees, even though it does not follow that all graduates do have doctoral degrees. According to the foundationalist account, true belief is related to knowledge in this way, presumably because a true belief could be due to a guess, or intuition, or association of ideas, or based on the irrelevant strategy, and so on. Thus the true belief "Tuesday is the first day of the year 1991" is not a case of knowledge, if it is a guess. The foundationalist account captures this point by the requirement that knowledge is a true belief which is justified. Evidently, some such distinction, between true belief due to guessing and true belief which is based on justification, has been drawn by developmentalists in early (Piaget 1926/1929) and more recent (Smedslund 1969) discussions. The level II epistemic states of Piaget and Szeminska (1941/1952) can be classified as cases of true belief.

Third, the foundationalist account can be used in the identification of knowledge, which is defined as true, justified belief. Cases of necessary knowledge (level III) would be dependent upon children's capacity to provide a relevant justification for their judgements with due attention to issues of modality. (See Piéraut-Le Bonniec 1980, for a review of such issues.) By its insistence on relevance and justification, the foundationalist account presupposes that a belief counts as knowledge only if it meets some standard of epistemic validity (Kitchener 1987).

Two objections might arise here, one about the nature of level II responses and the other about their demarcation from level III responses:

First, it might be objected that Piaget and Szeminska (1941/1952, p. 13) provide cases of true belief which are taken by them to amount to knowledge. In consequence, the foundationalist account leads to inappropriate classification and so should be rejected. This objection raises an important question of exegesis, since Piagetian level II states are not homogeneous. Even so, this objection begs the question at issue. The issue here concerns the defining criteria of knowledge and, according to the foundationalist account, knowledge always requires justification. A strict consequence is that a true, unjustified belief never amounts to knowledge.

Second, it might be objected that the foundationalist account provides grounds for contrasting true, unjustified belief and true, justified belief, which is knowledge. Yet the Piagetian position previously outlined was that true belief (level II) is different from necessary knowledge (level III). Thus the foundationalist account is based on one distinction (belief/knowledge), whilst the Piagetian position requires another distinction (empirical/ necessary) to be drawn as well. This objection is well taken. In reply, it is sufficient at this point in the discussion to notice that the two distinctions are related in that the second one presupposes the first. The second distinction concerns the subdivision of knowledge into empirical vs.

necessary knowledge. This distinction presupposes that knowledge can be distinguished from other epistemic states, of which true belief is one. Since the foundationalist objection to the J-view is based on the first (belief/knowledge) distinction alone, consideration of the second (empirical/necessary) distinction can be postponed, pending its elaboration in discussion of the causal account.

If the conditions stated in the foundationalist account are jointly necessary and collectively sufficient, two consequences follow. First, all cases of knowledge are cases where these three conditions are satisfied. Second, the only cases of knowledge are cases where the three conditions are satisfied. One main problem in philosophical epistemology is to evaluate this account by checking on whether there are other conditions, whether necessary or sufficient, which have to be satisfied for a case to be a case of knowledge. This philosophical problem is difficult to resolve just because both consequences have been rejected. In turn, this means that the foundationalist account seems to merit either revision, because the three conditions are not sufficient, or replacement, because they are not necessary.

*Revision: sufficiency conditions*

The claim that the three conditions are sufficient is the claim that all cases of knowledge are cases where a person has a true and justified belief. The counter-claim is that there are cases in which the three conditions are satisfied (the person has a true, justified belief) but which are not cases of knowledge (Gettier 1963). The occurrence of even one counter-example is incompatible with the claim that the three conditions are sufficient, and Gettier has provided at least one counter-example where the conditions are satisfied due to accident and coincidence. Thus the philosophical question for those who wish to retain the foundationalist account in its strong version, namely that the three conditions are sufficient, is the search for an argument which shows how the "Gettier objection" can be neutralized. Opinion is divided. One view is that the foundationalist account should be accepted as it stands, including the sceptical consequence which is the denial that there actually are cases of knowledge in ordinary life (Kirkham 1984). A second view is that the foundationalist account can be repaired by the addition of further conditions which defeat the "Gettier problem" (Chisholm 1982).

This dispute can be noted and set aside for present purposes. This is because the parties to this dispute are concerned about the sufficiency but not the necessity of the three conditions. That is, the parties to this dispute agree both that the only cases of knowledge are cases where a person has a true justified belief and that any case where a person does not have a true justified belief is not a case of knowledge.

So construed, the foundationalist account of the concept of knowledge is incompatible with the J-view in three respects: (a) condition (iii) of the foundationalist account could be interpreted categorically, as the claim that no judgement which is not justified is a case of knowledge. The J-view cannot meet this condition since, according to the J-view, a child can acquire knowledge even when a judgement is not justified; (b) condition (iii) could be interpreted hypothetically, as the claim that a judgement is a case of knowledge if, on request, it is justified. The suggestion is that the person who has knowledge would, if requested, always be able to justify a true belief, not that anyone actually does justify all true beliefs. Proponents of the J-view deny the legitimacy of such requests. By failing to make such a request, however, there is no way of discriminating cases where a justification is present from cases where it is absent. Thus retention of the J-view leads to a consequence which is incompatible with the foundationalist account, since the latter case (justification absent) would not be a case of knowledge; and (c) the foundationalist account requires that a justification should be valid by providing objective epistemic support for a true belief. A rationalization or a subjective justification which the person happens to have are inadequate. Such a requirement cannot be accommodated by the J-view, since no justification is deemed to be necessary nor *a fortiori* an objective justification.

By contrast, the foundationalist account is compatible with the JJ-view. On that view, a child is required to provide a justification for an expressed judgement. Second, a specific request is always made to elicit a child's justification. Third, the justification must be valid since only those justifications which have certain formal features are acceptable (Piaget and Inhelder 1966/1969; Voyat 1982).

*Replacement: necessity conditions*

The necessity of the conditions stated in the foundationalist account has also been challenged. Such a challenge is fundamental just because foundationalists see their task as that of providing more stringent conditions, over and above those contained in the classical account. Doubting whether this task will ever be successfully completed, some philosophers have stated an alternative causal account. Effectively, a challenge to the necessity of the three conditions is the rejection of the foundationalist account.

Before considering the challenge, there is a conclusion to carry from this discussion of the foundationalist account. If the three conditions in the foundationalist account are accepted as necessary, the J-view must be rejected. The present argument has the consequence that no intellectual state which has been assessed by the use of the J-view alone could, in principle, be a case of knowledge.

## Causal account

The starting-point of the causal account is a commitment to provide an account which has a better descriptive adequacy than the foundationalist account, manifest in a capacity to be in accord with the psychology of human cognition. The argument is that normative questions in epistemology are concerned with idealized rationality (Cherniak 1979) and, as such, are concerned with what human rationality ought to be like. Using the Kantian principle that "ought implies can", the argument is that normative questions cannot be answered independently of what human rationality is in fact like (Kornblith 1985). Naturalized epistemology is also concerned with the biological origins of human knowledge at the evolutionary level, including its emergence from lower forms of animal life (Radnitzky and Bartley 1987). Significantly, Piaget's (1967/1971) genetic epistemology makes a similar commitment. Although some Piagetians notice that Piaget's genetic epistemology provides a constructivist rather than a neo-Darwinian model of development (Gillièron 1987), it is evident that evolutionary and genetic epistemology are similar because of the common concern with descriptive adequacy. A central assumption, then, is that if naturalized (empirical, genetic) epistemology "is to construct the best possible theory of knowledge, it is incumbent upon it to make use of the best theories available" (Maffie 1990, p. 282). This is a significant admission, because the causal account is one manifestation of naturalized epistemology. The implication is that the causal account could be preferred because of its empirical backing. Such backing would be important on condition that there is agreement amongst psychologists as to which methods and which theories are the appropriate ones to use in gaining an acceptable psychology of human cognition. Yet as Maffie (1990, p. 290) also remarks, there are areas of potential weakness in naturalized epistemology due to the presence of disputes as to which scientific disciplines, theories and methods may be legitimately employed. In short, there is a prima facie case that an account of knowledge in terms of its causal origins could be explanatory of the procedures used in diagnostic assessment of children's knowledge on Piagetian tasks. However, a prior condition is that the causal account cannot be used to settle differences between different, empirical theories of intellectual development.

Using Goldman's account as a reference-point, the aim in this part of the discussion is to characterize the conditions which show when a person's belief counts as knowledge. There is an explicit denial both that a person should be able to justify a judgement as a condition of its acquisition, possession or display and even that there should be such a justification at that person's disposal (Goldman 1979, p. 2). Rather, a judgement is justifiably accepted by virtue of its causal ancestry. That is, proponents of the causal account deny that justification is a necessary condition of knowledge, i.e. they deny condition (iii) of the foundationalist account. From their perspective, it is quite possible for someone to hold a belief, which is not justified by that person, provided that belief has an acceptable causal formation in that person's mind. Goldman's task, then, is to specify more exactly the commitments which are embodied in the intuition that knowledge has a causal origin. His proposal is that at least two conditions should be met, first that the judgement should be the outcome of reliable cognitive processes and, second, that there should be no other cognitive processes which would have resulted in that person not forming that judgement (Goldman 1979, p. 20). It is clear that Goldman's proposal does have some purchase on adult (developed) cognition. Indeed, both common sense and cognitive psychology are viewed as a resource for the articulation of a more fine-grained description of correct and incorrect human intellectual functioning (Goldman 1978).

In short, developmentalists who accept the J-view could claim that the causal account is better suited to their purpose. They could concede that it may be desirable, in certain circumstances, to invite children to justify their judgements when performing Piagetian tasks. Yet they could still deny that this is necessary in the sense that justifications must be provided in all cases as a condition of the acquisition or possession of knowledge. Using the terminology of belief which Goldman prefers, the developmental sequence is stated to be a transition from false belief (level I), to true belief (level II), leading to necessary belief (level III).

The causal account is open to objection in its application to the diagnostic assessment of children's intellectual development. The objection is that the causal account is stated to be congruent with the psychology of human cognition. It follows that the causal account cannot be used, without circularity, to settle disputes within the psychology of human cognition. Yet the dispute between proponents of the J- and JJ-view is a dispute within psychology, since the parties to this dispute do make psychological commitments. This objection will now be elaborated with reference to the differentiation of necessary belief (level III) and true belief (level II).

The remaining discussion in Part I concerns two statements of the main objection. First, the objection could state that the causal account is too weak since it conflates the distinction between true and false belief. Second, the objection could state that the causal account is too weak because it could never cover cases of necessary belief. The latter is the stronger objection to the causal account.

In the first place, the objection might be that the causal account is too weak because it is insensitive to the distinction between false (level I) and true (level II) belief. This supposition could arise from the admission which is made by Goldman (1979) that all beliefs, including false beliefs, have a causal origin. This seems to be an embarrassing admission, one which obliterates the distinction between level I and level II beliefs. The suggestion is that the causal account treats true beliefs in the same way as false beliefs, in that each has a causal origin. The implication is that the distinction between children's incorrect and correct responses would collapse, if the causal account is retained.

To see why this is not a valid objection to the causal account, consider a case where a false belief may have an acceptable origin. Suppose two flocks of birds pass overhead. In estimating their size, the judgement might be "50", when there are in fact 50 birds in the first flock. This true belief would have an acceptable causal origin, if there were insufficient time to count all the birds in the flock and a correct estimate, which reflected previous successful experience in quantifying the size of flocks of birds, was made. In estimating the size of the second flock, the judgement might be "The same – 50", when there are in fact 49 birds in that flock. Even though this second belief is false, it has a similar causal origin. Further, it has the added advantage of being based on a transitive inference. According to the causal account, the formation of any belief is acceptable, provided that it arises in accordance with the conditions which the causal account sets out. Thus both judgements have an identifiable causal origin and there were no other processes which could have been used to generate a correct judgement. Thus the conditions of the causal account seem to have been satisfied in both cases, each of which would amount to cases of knowledge. Yet in the first case the judgement was correct, whilst in the latter it was incorrect.

It is important to see what is at issue. At issue is the conceptual question as to whether both, one or none of these two cases amounts to knowledge. This issue can be resolved either by recourse to intuition or by reference to an account which provides defining criteria of knowledge. According to the foundationalist account, the case where an incorrect judgement is made about the size is not a case of knowledge since only truths may be known. By contrast, the causal account does not seem to exclude such a possibility since its conditions may be satisfied even in cases where false judgements are made.

This interesting epistemological question will not be pursued since such cases do not arise in research on intellectual development. In such research, the tasks are usually well-structured, closed tasks with processes and procedures whose successful use allows children to display correct responses (cf., Gelman and Baillargeon 1983; Halford 1989). In a simple case, the tasks are designed so that children who use one intellectual process will make incorrect judgements whilst children who use a different process will make correct judgements. Although the beliefs of the former children will have an identifiable origin, there are other processes which they could have used to make the latter (correct) response. In developmental tasks, there usually are alternatives since the tasks are designed precisely to differentiate false belief (level I) from true belief (level II). For example, in conservation of number tasks, a level I belief may have an origin in terms of the perceptual salience of the transformed array. But this false belief would have been different if all of the information in the array had been used. Thus Goldman's second condition would not have been met since there were processes which could have been used to override both the formation and display of false belief.

Thus in the context of research on children's intellectual development, the causal account is sensitive to the difference between false and true belief. Moreover, Goldman's strategy of securing an account of knowledge which is congruent with the psychology of cognition is also secure. A central aim in research on intellectual development is to provide a better description of the conditions and processes leading to children's understanding and misunderstanding. Such descriptions could be added to the stock of common sense processes such as "confused reasoning, wishful thinking, reliance on emotional attachment, mere hunch, guesswork, and hasty generalization" (Goldman 1979, p. 9) or to cognitive models of memory and reasoning (Goldman 1978).

In the second place, the objection might be that the causal account is too weak since it is insensitive to the distinction between true (level II) and necessary (level III) belief. A level II belief is a true belief whose formation is due to the available information. By contrast, a level III belief requires some understanding of necessity. To see why this is a valid objection to the causal account, the distinction between truth value and modality requires clarification. The first step in the clarification is to show what this distinction amounts to. The second step is to show why this distinction cannot be drawn on the basis of the causal account.

The difference between truth value and modality has been discussed by philosophers from Plato (nd/1941) onwards. One way in which propositions differ is with respect to their truth value: a true proposition is different from one which is false. But truth value does not determine modality, since propositions also differ with respect to the manner in which they are true or false. Crucially, a true proposition could be one which is necessarily true or one which is contingently true, i.e. it is a possibly, not necessarily, true proposition. Given that today is my birthday, both of the following are true propositions, namely "today is today" and "today is my birthday". Yet their modal status is different since the latter is a proposition which could have been false, namely on any day other than today, unlike the former which could not be false, i.e. it is a necessarily true proposition. The distinction between truth value and modality has been explicitly drawn in logical (Hughes and Cresswell 1972) and psychological (Piéraut-Le Bonniec 1980) discussions. Quite simply, the conditions for the causal production of belief are distinct from the conditions for the epistemic validity of belief (Kitchener 1987). An acceptable belief may well have a causal origin but its acceptability will also depend upon normative principles, such as those of modality, which are constitutive features of an intellectual domain.

The distinction between truth value and modality has a special application to mathematical truths, notably in Frege's (1888/1980, paras. 7–8) rejection of Mill's claim that mathematical truths are completely definable in empirical terms by reference to observable facts. Frege's denial that a number can be defined in this way is supported by the rhetorical question as to which facts are asserted in the definition of the number 77,864. The implication is that this question is empirically unanswerable since there is no set of facts which provides the necessary and sufficient conditions of this number. Again, Frege raises the question as to which observations have to be carried out for someone to state that $1,000,000 = 999,999 + 1$, or which facts have to be observed in the definition of the number 0. Frege's conclusion is that mathematical truths are necessary truths and so their definition could never be stated in physical terms, which are never necessary in this sense.

It is no doubt for this reason that Piaget and Szeminska (1941/1952, p. 184) state that "number is the fusion of class and asymmetrical relation into a single operational whole" (p. 184). The three key notions in this definition are inclusion, transitivity and conservation, where each of these is given a genetic analysis in which necessity of understanding, and not merely correctness in understanding, is asserted to be important. This is because it is not merely a brute fact that number is invariant to spatial transformation; rather, this is a necessary truth (cf., Murray 1990). It is not merely correct that two elements which are equal to the same are equal to each other; rather, this is necessarily so (cf., Campbell and Bickhard 1986). It is not merely the case that the membership of a superordinate class which includes two non-empty subordinate classes is greater than that of one of its subordinate classes; rather, this has to be the case (Cormier and Dagenais 1983).

Significantly, the distinction between truth value and modality has been used by Piaget from his earliest studies. Thus Piaget (1924/1928, pp. 26, 56) contrasted the ability to provide a valid, logical justification with the ability to provide a causal, or psychological, justification, which may be invalid. Their non-differentiation was taken to result in contradictory thinking (p. 254), a corrective to which is reasoning based on necessity, when logical consequences are derived from relevant premises (p. 1). Piaget maintained the distinction in more recent discussions, such as his contention that "general and necessary categories such as causality are never found in ready made form, especially at initial stages" (Piaget 1967/1971, p. 269). This is because any such category "goes far beyond observation and the merely inductive and experimental regularity which arises from probability or factual determinism" (Piaget 1967, p. 424/1971, p. 306; my amended translation). On this view, observable knowledge arising from experience is fundamentally different from its coordination in necessary knowledge (Piaget 1975/1985, p. 8). This is because necessary knowledge transcends the limits of observable knowledge, whether physical or social (Piaget 1970/1983).

In general, Piaget argued that the psychological investigation of necessity would have to make use of models of intensional logic of necessity for the explication of meaningful thinking (Piaget 1977/1986; Piaget and Garcia 1987/1991, p. 3). This is because his genetic (empirical) epistemology addressed:

> . . . (one fundamental problem which is) to understand how the mind succeeds in constructing necessary relationships, which appear to be "independent of time", if the instruments of thought are only psychological operations that are subject to evolution and are constituted in time.
>
> (Piaget, 1950, p. 23; my translation)

The importance of this problem has been restated as the claim that genetic epistemology must address the question of how to explain "the passage from temporal construction to atemporal necessity" (Piaget and Garcia 1983/1989, p. 27; my translation). It is noted that the structuration of necessity will embody a logic of meaning, including the process of signifying implication (cf., Piéraut-Le Bonniec 1990). Intensional logic is taken to provide a model of this process, whose empirical identification will require innovative research into children's ability to use a system of thinking which combines implications of meaning, which are necessary, with their negations, which are contradictions (Piaget and Garcia 1987/1991, pp. 3–4).

This central problem cannot be appreciated, still less resolved, unless the distinction between truth value and modality is respected. Quite simply, the causal account could not be explanatory of the formation of necessity and, in that sense, is insensitive to the distinction between true (level II) and necessary (level III) belief. The reason why the causal account obliterates this distinction is apparent in the dispute between Hume and Kant. Despite their philosophical differences, both philosophers accepted that necessary truths could not, in principle, be empirically grounded. According to Hume, empirical (contingent, possible) truths have negations which are not self-contradictory, and so are not impossible, unlike necessary truths whose negations are self-contradictory, and so are impossible. In consequence, Hume (1739/1965, p. 165) contrasted two questions which can be raised about a necessary belief. One question concerns its causal origin and empirical formation in experience. The other question concerns the notion of necessity which does not owe its origin to causal experience. Even though a belief – including a belief in necessity – may have a causal origin in past experience, the content of that belief makes use of the notion of necessity and that notion does not have a similar origin. Whilst it is always possible for an empirical regularity to have exceptions, this is never possible with necessary truths. Thus there is no empirical basis for exceptionless, necessary truths. On this issue, Kant adopted the same position, manifest in his claim that "experience does indeed teach me what exists and what it is like, but never that it must necessarily be so and not otherwise" (Kant 1783/1953, p. 52). According to Kant, the notion of necessity will have its formation in experience even though it could not be derived from experience. The notion of necessity could not be derived from experience since it is not an empirical notion.

In short, the distinction between an empirically true belief and a necessary belief cannot be drawn solely on the basis of observable facts in the physical or social world. Whilst a level II belief can have a causal origin, owing its formation to past contingencies in the physical domain, a level III belief which is necessary is not solely based on its causal formation. From the fact that something is the case, it does not follow that it must be the case. Similarly, although the social world in which children develop may be contributory in the transmission of true (level II) beliefs, necessary (level III) beliefs do not have their basis in social experience. Even if there is social agreement that something is the case, it does not follow that it must be. Thus the causal account is insensitive to the fundamental difference between empirical and necessary truth.

The relevance of this argument to the dispute about whether children should be required to justify their judgements is that, following Goldman (1978), the causal account should be congruent with the psychology of human cognition. Yet there is a family of disputes over which developmentalists are currently divided. Besides the dispute about which methods to use in diagnostic assessment, two substantive disputes can be mentioned. One substantive difference concerns the stock of problems to be addressed. Following Laudan (1977), different theories can be identified by reference to the problems, and proposed solutions to those problems, which lie within their domain. For more than a decade, Murray (1978, 1981) has noted that Piaget's preferred method for the assessment of conservation explicitly requires a check on children's justifications as an integral feature of the development of modal understanding. Many critics, who accept the J-view, are typically concerned with the development of correct understanding. A natural extension of Murray's claim states that an account about the development of correct understanding is fundamentally different from an account of the development of necessary understanding (Murray 1990; Smith 1987). Thus a substantive difference is coupled with a difference about the methods appropriate to diagnostic assessment. A second substantive difference concerns the extent of young children's developing understanding. It turns out that many of the proponents of the J-view are those who also claim that young children are not as intellectually incompetent as Piaget's theory is taken by them to suppose (Brainerd 1978; Donaldson, Grieve and Pratt 1983; Gelman 1978). This is one position about intellectual development but not the only one on offer. According to other developmentalists, who accept the JJ-view, the ability to give a logical justification for a judgement is a logical competence whose use is essential to the formation of certain forms of reasoning (Chapman and Lindenberger 1988; Piéraut-Le Bonniec 1990). This latter position is substantively, and not merely methodologically, different from the former position.

In short, there are both methodological and substantive differences within the psychology of human cognition. It would be question begging to invoke the causal account of knowledge to settle these differences.

## PART II

The conclusion to draw from the discussion in Part I is that in philosophical epistemology there are two currently dominant accounts as to the nature of knowledge. Both accounts attempt to formulate conditions which can be used to classify cases of knowledge and other intellectual states. No attempt has been made to support one of these accounts to the exclusion of the other. Rather, both accounts have been examined so that their consequences for the assessment of children's intellectual development can be gauged. The specific issue concerns the implications of each account for the selection of reasonable "response criteria" in intellectual assessment.

The fundamentalist account specifies three conditions one of which is the ability to justify a judgement. One consequence of this acocunt is that the J-view does not provide reasonable "response criteria". This is because developmentalists who use the J-view do not require children to justify their judgements in their performance of a research task and so are never in a position to document cases where children acquire knowledge. By contrast, developmentalists who use the JJ-view in their research are able to meet this requirement and so are in a position to document cases where children acquire knowledge.

The causal account specifies conditions in terms of the causal origin of (true) beliefs. However, a belief in necessity, which has a causal origin, makes use of a notion which is not itself based on its causal origin. In consequence, none of the conditions stated in the causal account could be used in the documentation of cases where children acquire an understanding of necessity, unless psychological questions are begged as to which problems are worth addressing in research on children's intellectual development. Since one of the defining features of the causal account is its relaxation of the justification requirement made in the foundationalist account, developmentalists who use the JJ-view would not be affected by this negative consequence of the causal account.

In short, there are two accounts of knowledge. One account leads to the elimination of the J-view, with which it is incompatible. The other account leads to a limitation on the J-view, which could never deal with certain cases of knowledge. If Piagetian research is to engage with problems which are central to developmental theory, that research will have to use the JJ-view in the selection of reasonable "response criteria". Piagetian research which makes use of the J-view alone either fails to provide cases of knowledge altogether, or fails to address certain cases of knowledge which are central to developmental theory.

There are several ways of responding to this conclusion by developmentalists who use the J-view in their research. Six such responses are now briefly surveyed:

(1) It could be objected that the conclusion is empirically irrelevant, since it is a nice example of pointless philosophical disputation. Developmentalists should base their case on the available evidence, including evidence which has been gained, where appropriate, by the use of the J-view. This objection is simply misconceived. The question at issue is not the extent of the evidence but rather the nature of that for which it is evidence. A criterial question concerns the conditions for description of cases. If evidence is gained in the documentation of a case, the question to ask is: "a case of what?". Whilst the criteria of many notions are straightforward, philosophical accounts are needed to resolve disputes with problematic criteria. The concept of knowledge is problematic in just this sense. Significantly, explicit consideration of philosophical accounts permits rational decisions to be made about what sort of evidence is – and what sort of evidence is not – adequate in specific cases. Currently, there are two main accounts of the criteria of knowledge and both have been discussed in Part I.

(2) The converse objection could be stated, that the conclusion is not philosophical enough, since there are other accounts of knowledge. It follows that the main conclusions of the present discussion are provisional and even inconclusive. This objection is well taken. However, until some new (third) account has been presented, together with its implications for the selection of "response criteria", this objection is merely noted. Its strength cannot be decided *a priori*, in advance of the specification of that (third) account.

(3) It could be objected that it is in practice difficult to assess the understanding of young children, when their underdeveloped linguistic abilities mask underlying intellectual mastery. This objection begs the question, if a prior psychological commitment is made to the position that young children do have intellectual competence which has an incomplete linguistic expression. The point to notice is that the psychological question has already been begged, unless independent support for this preferred position has been given. Crucially, there is a rival position to consider here, namely that the ability to justify a judgement is itself an

intellectual, rather than a linguistic, ability. The basic intuition behind this latter position concerns the necessary connection which links a derived conclusion with its implying premises. If that conclusion embodies not merely a true proposition but also one which is deduced from relevant premises, the individual who has made that deduction should be able to express this connection in some appropriate way. The dispute between developmentalists, who support this objection and so who subscribe to the J-view, and their rivals, who subscribe to the JJ-view, is as much substantive as methodological. This dispute should not be settled in favour of one party by appeal to the merely practical difficulties arising from the position of the rival party.

(4) It could be objected that Piaget has given different answers to his "fundamental problem" which is the construction of necessity. In his structuralist works, the claim was made that the understanding of necessity is the hallmark of operational understanding which is manifest in middle-to-late childhood (Piaget and Inhelder 1966/1969). In his constructivist works, by contrast, the claim is that very young children have some understanding of necessity, well before the onset of operational under-standing (Piaget 1977/1986; Piaget and Garcia 1987/1991). The first point to make in reply is that this objection raises an important issue. The objection makes the valid point that, in some recent writings, an under-standing of necessity is attributed to very young children. However, the issue is not clear-cut since, in other recent studies, an understanding of necessity is confined to adolescents (Karmiloff-Smith 1990, pp. 123–124). Even though this question is important, the internal coherence of Piaget's position will have to remain unresolved in this discussion, which takes a neutral stance on the timing of the initial acquisition of modal understand-ing. This is because, second, the key issue here concerns the status of justifications as "response criteria". On this point, there is a unity to Piaget's position. In Piaget's recent accounts, interest still centres on the justifications of very young children with attention to their understanding of aspects of necessity. In fact, in both early (Piaget 1924/1928, p. 35) and recent (Piaget and Garcia 1987/1991, p. 59) studies the justified judge-ments of children aged 3 years are given. Thus Piagetian studies are uniform in this respect, namely in requiring children to justify their judgements.

(5) It could be objected that not all knowledge requires justification. Adapting the distinction due to Ryle (1949), knowing how is different from knowing that. This is because people can "intelligently perform some sort of operations when they are not yet able to consider any propositions enjoining how they should be performed" (Ryle 1949, p. 30). The sugges-tion is that adults have knowledge which they do not, and cannot, justify and this knowledge is shown in their activity. If this is true of adults, it would certainly hold good for children. Thus knowledge can be possessed

even in the absence of its justification. Even in infancy, similar cases are easy to find, including means–end behaviour, intentional activity and inferential search. Further, these cases embody some practical understanding of necessity, where justification is not required (Fabricius, Sophian and Wellman 1987; Wellman, Cross and Bartsch 1986).

This objection is valid. There are, however, two reasons why its force is limited. One reason is that a distinction should be drawn between practical intelligence and its representation. This distinction turns not on whether there are intellectual processes which underpin the mastery of skilled performances but rather on which intellectual processes underpin their conceptualized knowledge (Piaget 1974/1976). Although Piagetian tasks frequently make possible displays of practical "knowledge-how", the tasks relevant to the construction of operational knowledge are also reliant upon the formation of "knowledge-that", which is representational. The second reason is that there is a distinction to draw between the successful display of practical knowledge and an understanding of why that knowledge is the successful display which it is (Pinard 1986). Indeed, a standard issue which developmentalists confront arises from the demarcation of these two distinct forms of knowledge, namely how representational knowledge develops from the practical knowledge which precedes it (Karmiloff-Smith and Inhelder 1975). The difference between these two forms of knowledge is marked by the importance attached to the avoidance of "false positive" diagnoses of representational knowledge (Flavell 1982; Smedslund 1969).

(6) It could be objected that justification is not necessary provided appropriate methodological controls have been taken. Indeed, it is claimed that linguistic development does not require that (young) children should have *"consciously accessible verbally statable explanations"* (Karmiloff-Smith 1986, p. 86; her emphasis). In a review of metacognition, Brown, Bransford, Ferrara and Campione (1983) contend that this polymorphous notion embodies at least two meanings, one based on the consciousness of cognition and the other on the regulation of cognition. Crucially, their suggestion is that these two meanings are independent and so a metacognitive process could be subject to regulation but not available for conscious inspection. Again, accounts of the development of abstraction and reasoning contrast the implicit knowledge which is acquired during the earlier phases of development with explicit knowledge which is confined to later phases (Campbell and Bickhard 1986; Moshman 1990). Finally, developmentalists have shown an interest in the modal understanding of children during the early years of schooling (Markman 1978; Miller 1986; Russell 1983; Sophian and Somerville 1988). Provided the task has been designed appropriately, with due attention to proper experimental controls, it is permissible – so this objection runs – to use children's judgements, in the absence of justification, as expressions of their necessary knowledge.

The short reply to this objection is that, yes, methodological norms are important in psychological research – in fact, as important as other relevant norms. The argument in this chapter is that epistemic norms are also relevant norms to invoke in Piagetian research which is directed upon the construction of necessary knowledge. Norms include criteria of adequacy with distinct norms providing distinct criteria of adequacy. It follows that evidence which is accepted as adequate by reference to methodological norms will not thereby be equally adequate in relation to epistemic norms. Further, evidence which is accepted to be adequate by reference to an epistemic norm concerning truth value will not thereby be equally adequate in relation to an epistemic norm concerning modality. Epistemic norms are especially important in relation to the adequacy of evidence about the acquisition of necessary knowledge.

There is a distinction to draw between the acquisition and possession of knowledge. One main aim in Piagetian research is to chart the successive acquisition of different forms of knowledge. It is, however, worth noticing that philosophical accounts of knowledge are primarily accounts of the possession of knowledge. This difference is important, first, because the conditions which must be satisified for the possession of knowledge will have equal applicability to the acquisition of knowledge. This difference is also important because there may be other conditions – besides the conditions related to possession – which also have to be satisfied when questions about acquisition arise. For convenience, assume that developmental progression can be mapped on to a line such that spatial progression along the lines indicates progression in the development of knowledge. The line has a numerical scale such that, for any point $n$ on that scale, a lower point ($n-1$, $n-2$, . . . ) represents less advanced, whilst a higher point ($n+1, n+2, . . .$ ) represents more advanced, knowledge in the developmental sequence. A typical question which developmentalists address concerns that point on such a line which marks the initial onset of some specified knowledge.

If there is independent evidence that an individual has knowledge $K$ to level $n$, and if that evidence is adequate in relation to all relevant norms (both methodological and epistemic), then it is reasonable to use the J-view in empirical investigation which is directed upon the possession of that knowledge $K$ at that level $n$ and beyond, including its display in relation to experimentally controlled conditions. *Ex hypothesi*, there is independent and adequate evidence that the specified knowledge is possessed. According to the foundationalist account, justification is not required as a condition of the possession of knowledge. Rather, that account required that justification must always be available for inspection at reasonable request. Thus research which is reliant on methodological controls to elicit children's judgements – but not their justifications – is compatible with a commitment to the foundationalist account, if there is prior agreement that a specified level of knowledge is possessed. The presumption is that such justifications could have been invoked by the children, even though they were in fact by-passed. Further, adoption of the causal account leads to the same conclusion. If the specified knowledge has been antecedently acquired, then, *ex hypothesi*, the conditions of the causal account must have been satisfied. It would be reasonable, on methodological grounds, to bypass children's justifications and concentrate on their judgements, for example by investigation of the causal conditions for the production of that knowledge.

Yet much developmental research is concerned with the initial acquisition of knowledge. In such cases, different theoretically based predictions may abound with dispute arising about the extent to which there is evidence that knowledge $K$ at level $n$ is possessed. In the presence of such theoretical disputes, it is important that there is normatively adequate evidence about the acquisition of the specified knowledge. The argument presented in this chapter is that the implications of the two philosophical accounts are clear. If the foundationalist account is accepted, adequate evidence about the initial acquisition of knowledge should reveal children's justifications for their judgements. This is because the non-availability of such justifications at reasonable request is a reason for denying that that individual has the specified knowledge at all. If the causal account is accepted, adequate evidence about the acquisition of necessary knowledge should embody two features. One feature concerns the causal conditions which have to be open neither to conscious inspection nor to verbal expression. The other feature concerns the grounds on which the distinction between truth value and modality is drawn by the individual in some appropriate way. The argument in Part I stated that necessary knowledge could not merely be a causal outcome of determining conditions. It follows that it is not enough that an individual can make a reliable sequence of responses under controlled conditions. Lacking independent evidence about the possession of necessary knowledge, adequate evidence about its acquisition would have to ensure that the individual under investigation could distinguish truth from necessity. Failure to make this explicit is a reason for denying the validity of the claim that epistemic acquisition by that individual was, in fact, necessary knowledge.

The distinction between reliability and validity is well known in psychometric discussions (cf., Sternberg 1985). This distinction has equal applicability to Piagetian research. Whilst methodological norms have an obvious role to play in ensuring that studies are reliable, epistemic norms have an analogous role to play when questions of validity arise. Developmental tasks which are designed to be adequate may not in fact make similar demands with consequential implications for their validity. Reviews of Piagetian research are testimony to such disputes (Gelman and Baillargeon 1983; Halford 1989, Smith 1991*b*). Even so, consideration about the epistemic adequacy of the tasks used in such studies – especially in relation to norms of modality – is quite rare. This oversight is compounded by a pervasive commitment to the J-view. The argument presented here is that the JJ-view is the appropriate view to use in relation to questions about the initial acquisition of necessary knowledge.

In short, knowledge is knowledge, even when it is qualified as "procedural", "implicit", or "self-regulated metacognitive" knowledge. The argument here is that the acceptability of such attributions is dependent upon their adequacy in relation to relevant epistemic norms which lay down the defining criteria of knowledge. This argument is not a denial that some form of modal understanding may be acquired during the early phases of intellectual development. On the contrary: it was noted in reply to the fourth objection above that the early acquisition of modal understanding has been investigated in Genevan studies. Rather, the argument is that, in the absence of independent evidence, any study which states such a position will have to make some use of the JJ-view.

## CONCLUSION

Piagetian research which is directed upon the investigation of modal understanding could return differing answers to several issues. Implicit in the main argument is the view that these are important issues, which should be confronted. However, the present argument offers no resolution of these issues. Rather, the aim has been to forestall the premature formation of positions in relation to them.

Two issues have been already mentioned. One concerned the priority given to correctness over modality of understanding. Another concerned the priority given to early, rather than later, development of intellectual competence. It is interesting to speculate on whether these priorities would remain valid in empirical research where both the J-view and JJ-view were used systematically as experimental controls.

A third issue concerns the construction of better knowledge from lesser knowledge. There are many ways to ground the demarcation of lesser-advanced from better-advanced knowledge. Doubtless, any way of doing this is preferable to plain assertion. Some developmentalists (cf., Gelman, and Baillargeon 1983) have retained a structuralist commitment, whilst rejecting the specifically logical models which Piaget (1972) outlined. But structuralist positions are static unless they are accompanied by a constructivist model as to how structural progress, however specified, takes place. Piaget's (1970/1983, 1975/1985) account of equilibration could make some contribution here. If modal understanding is important, then an account of the construction of necessary knowledge is indispensable (cf., Piaget 1950). Experimental studies which assign priority to antecedent variables beg the substantive question of whether equilibration is a separate, but interdependent, factor in intellectual growth. If equilibratory change occurs, it does so on the basis of an interplay between necessary and contradictory aspects of a process which is internal to thinking itself (Murray 1990; Piéraut-Le Bonniec 1990; Smith 1987).

A fourth issue concerns developmental progression. Piaget has been credited with the view that development is a process leading from absence-to-presence of ability (Gelman 1978). From this perspective, the aim is to trace the course of sequences, leading from "not in competence to first in competence" (Flavell and Wohlwill 1969) or, indeed, to identify the earliest instances of intellectual understanding for inclusion in some *Jeunesse Book of Records*. As an aid to experimental design and analysis, children's responses are typically viewed dichotomously, as correct/incorrect, in experimental studies, such that a correct response at any age is viewed as the outcome of its previous absence. Yet this is not the only view, since Piaget has also been credited with the view that development is a process of differentiation and integration (Kohlberg 1987; Piaget 1983/1987; Smith 1991a). According to this interpretation, development occurs as the progressive change in understanding, which consists in the reduction of its lacunary, contradictory and irrelevant aspects. So viewed, intellectual development is not so much the absence of correct understanding but is rather initial misunderstanding whose present aspects are open to modification. Misunderstanding, which is manifest as incomplete, or contradictory, or redundant understanding contains elements which are the basis for its fundamental revision.

In short, research into children's intellectual development, using the J-view, can be legitimately undertaken. Such research can address its own stock of questions and make use of methods which are acceptable to those who subscribe to its conventions. Such research should not, however, be solely used in Piagetian research when central questions are begged. Even if a genetic epistemology is an empirical epistemology, it does not follow that conceptual (non-empirical) questions are of little relevance. On the contrary, the assessment of Piaget's theory is, and has to be, concerned with conceptual issues. Further, conceptual assessment does not require a commitment to Piaget's position, since a range of critical responses, including elaboration (Kitchener 1986; Overton 1990), reinterpretation (Chapman 1988; Smith 1991a) and revision (Bickhard and Campbell 1989; Campbell and Bickhard 1986), have been recently displayed.

## ACKNOWLEDGEMENTS

This chapter has been much improved in response to commentary from referees – my thanks are due to them.

## REFERENCES

Ayer, A. J. (1956) *The problem of knowledge*, Harmondsworth: Penguin.
Bickhard, M. and Campbell, R. (1989) "Interactivism and genetic epistemology", *Archives de Psychologie* 57: 99–121.

Brainerd, C. (1973) "Judgements and explanations as criteria for the presence of cognitive structures", *Psychological Bulletin* 79: 172–179.

Brainerd, C. (1978) *Piaget's theory of intelligence*, Englewood Cliffs, NJ: Prentice-Hall.

Brown, A., Bransford, J., Ferrara, R. and Campione, J. (1983) "Learning, remembering and understanding", in P. Mussen (ed.) *Handbook of child psychology*, vol. 3, New York: Wiley.

Campbell, R. and Bickhard, M. (1986) *Knowing levels and developmental stages*, Basel: Karger.

Chapman, M. (1988) *Constructive evolution*, Cambridge: Cambridge University Press.

Chapman, M. and Lindenberger, U. (1988) "Functions, operations and décalage in the development of transitivity", *Developmental Psychology* 24: 542–551.

Cherniak, C. (1979) "Minimal rationality", *Mind* XC: 161–183.

Chisholm, R. (1977) *Theory of knowledge*, Englewood Cliffs, NJ: Prentice-Hall.

Chisholm, R. (1982) *The foundations of knowledge*, Brighton: Harvester.

Cormier, P. and Dagenais, Y. (1983) "Class inclusion developmental levels and logical necessity", *International Journal of Behavioural Development* 6: 1–14.

Donaldson, M., Grieve, R. and Pratt, C. (1983) *Early childhood development and education*, Oxford: Blackwell.

Fabricius, W., Sophian, C. and Wellman, H. (1987) "Young children's sensitivity to logical necessity in their inferential search behaviour", *Child Development* 58: 409–423.

Flavell, J. (1982) "On cognitive development", *Child Development* 53: 1–10.

Flavell, J. and Wohlwill, J. (1969) "Formal and functional aspects of cognitive development", in D. Elkind and J. Flavell (eds) *Studies in cognitive growth*, New York: Oxford University Press.

Frege, G. (1888/1980) *The foundations of arithmetic*, Oxford: Blackwell.

Gelman, R. (1978) "Cognitive development", *Annual Review of Psychology* 29: 297–232.

Gelman, R. and Baillargeon, R. (1983) "A review of some Piagetian concepts", in P. Mussen (ed.) *Handbook of child psychology*, vol. 3, New York: Wiley.

Gettier, E. (1963) "Is justified true belief knowledge?" *Analysis* 23: 121–123.

Gillièron, C. (1987) "Is Piaget's 'Genetic epistemology' evolutionary?" in W. Callebaut and R. Pinxten (eds) *Evolutionary epistemology*, Dordrecht: Reidel.

Goldman, A. (1978) "Epistemics: The regulative theory of cognition", *Journal of Philosophy* LXXV: 509–523.

Goldman, A. (1979) "What is justified belief?", in G. Pappas (ed.) *Justification and knowledge*, Dordrecht: Reidel.

Haack, S. (1990) "Recent obituaries of epistemology", *American Philosophical Quarterly* 27: 199–212.

Halford, G. (1989) "Reflections on 25 years of Piagetian cognitive developmental psychology 1963–88", *Human Development* 32: 325–357.

Hughes, G. and Cresswell, M. (1972) *An introduction to modal logic*, 2nd edn, London: Methuen.

Hume, D. (1739/1965) *Treatise on human nature*, Oxford: Oxford University Press.

Kant, I. (1783/1953) *Prolegomena*, Manchester: Manchester University Press.

Karmiloff-Smith, A. (1986) "From meta-processes to conscious access: Evidence from children's metalinguistic and repair data", *Cognition* 23: 95–147.

Karmiloff-Smith, A. (1990) "Un cas particulier de symmétrie inférentielle", in J.

Piaget, G. Henriques and E. Ascher (eds) *Morphismes et catégories*, Lausanne: Delachaux et Niestlé.

Karmiloff-Smith, A. and Inhelder, B. (1975) "If you want to get ahead, get a theory", *Cognition* 3: 195–212.

Kirkham, R. (1984) "Does the Gettier problem rest on a mistake?" *Mind* XCIII: 501–513.

Kitchener, R. (1986) *Piaget's theory of knowledge*, New Haven, CT: Yale University Press.

Kitchener, R. (1987) "Is genetic epistemology possible?" *British Journal for the Philosophy of Science* 38: 283–299.

Kohlberg, L. (1987) *Child psychology and childhood education*, London: Longman.

Kornblith, H. (1985) *Naturalizing epistemology*, Cambridge, MA: Bradford Books.

Kripke, S. (1980) *Naming and Necessity*, Oxford: Blackwell.

Laudan, L. (1977) *Progress and its problems*, Berkeley, CA: University of California Press.

Lemmon, E. J. (1966) *Beginning logic*, London: Nelson.

Lipschutz, S. (1964) *Set theory and related topics*, New York: McGraw-Hill.

Maffie, J. (1990) "Recent work on naturalized epistemology", *American Philosophical Quarterly* 27: 281–293.

Markman, E. M. (1978) "Empirical versus logical solutions to part–whole comparison problems concerning classes and collections", *Child Development* 49: 168–177.

Miller, S. (1986) "Certainty and necessity in the understanding of Piagetian concepts", *Developmental Psychology* 22: 168–177.

Moshman, D. (1990) "The development of metalogical understanding", in W. Overton (ed.) *Reasoning, Necessity and Logic*, Hillsdale, NJ: Erlbaum.

Murray, F. (1978) "Training strategies and conservation training", in A. Lesgold, J. Pellegrino, S. Fokkema and R. Glaser (eds) *Cognitive psychology and instruction*, New York: Plenum Press.

Murray, F. (1981) "The conservation paradigm", in I. Sigel, D. Brodzinsky and R. Golinkoff (eds) *New directions in piagetian theory and practice*, Hillsdale, NJ: Erlbaum.

Murray, F. (1990) "The construction of necessary knowledge", in W. Overton (ed.) *Reasoning, Necessity and Logic*, Hillsdale, NJ: Erlbaum.

Newman, D., Griffin, P. and Cole, M. (1989) *The construction zone*, Cambridge: Cambridge University Press.

Overton, W. (1990) *Reasoning, necessity and logic*, Hillsdale, NJ: Erlbaum.

Piaget, J. (1924/1928) *Judgment and reasoning in the child*, London: Routledge & Kegan Paul.

Piaget, J. (1926/1929) *The child's conception of the world*, London: Routledge & Kegan Paul.

Piaget, J. (1950) *Introduction à l'épistémologie génétique*, vol. 1, Paris: Presses Universitaires de France.

Piaget, J. (1967/1971) *Biologie et connaissance*, Paris: Gallimard/*Biology and Knowledge*, Edinburgh: Edinburgh University Press.

Piaget, J. (1970/1983) "Piaget's theory", in P. Mussen (ed.) *Handbook of child psychology*, vol. 1, New York: Wiley.

Piaget, J. (1972) *Essai de logique*, Paris: Dunod.

Piaget, J. (1974/1976) *The grasp of consciousness*, Cambridge, MA: Harvard University Press.

Piaget, J. (1975/1985) *Equilibration of cognitive structures*, Chicago: University of Chicago Press.

Piaget, J. (1977/1986) "Essay on necessity", *Human development* 29: 301–314.

Piaget, J. (1983/1987) *Possibility and necessity*, vol. 2, Minnesota: University of Minnesota Press.

Piaget, J. and Garcia, R. (1983/1989) *Psychogenesis and the history of science*, New York: Columbia University Press.

Piaget, J. and Garcia, R. (1987/1991) *Toward a logic of meaning*, Hillsdale, NJ: Erlbaum.

Piaget, J. and Inhelder, B. (1966/1969) *The psychology of the child*, London: Routledge & Kegan Paul.

Piaget, J. and Inhelder, B. (1968) "Préface à la deuxième édition" *Le développement des quantités physiques chez l'enfant*, 3rd edn, Neuchâtel: Delachaux et Niestlé.

Piaget, J. and Szeminska, A. (1941/1952) *The child's conception of number*, London: Routledge & Kegan Paul.

Piéraut-Le Bonniec, G. (1980) *Modal reasoning*, London: Academic Press.

Piéraut-Le Bonniec, G. (1990) "Logic of meaning and meaningful implication", in W. Overton (ed.) *Reasoning, necessity and logic*, Hillsdale, NJ: Erlbaum.

Pinard, A. (1986) " 'Prise de conscience' and taking charge of one's own cognitive functioning", *Human Development* 29: 341–354.

Plato (nd/1935) *Plato's theory of knowledge*, London: Routledge & Kegan Paul.

Plato (nd/1941) *The Republic*, Oxford: Oxford University Press.

Radnitzky, G. and Bartley, W. (1987) *Evolutionary epistemology, rationality, and the sociology of knowledge*, La Salle, IL: Open Court.

Russell, J. (1983) "Children's ability to discriminate between different types of proposition", *British Journal of Developmental Psychology* 1: 259–268.

Ryle, G. (1949) *The concept of mind*, London: Hutchinson.

Shayer, M., Demetriou, A. and Pervez, M. (1988) "The structure and scaling of concrete operational thought: Three studies in four countries", *Genetic Social and General Psychology Monographs* 114: 309–375.

Skinner, B. (1985) "Cognitive science and behaviourism", *British Journal of Psychology* 76: 291–301.

Smedslund, J. (1969) "Psychological diagnostics", *Psychological Bulletin* 71: 237–248.

Smith, L. (1982) "Class inclusion and conclusions about Piaget's theory", *British Journal of Psychology* 73: 267–276.

Smith, L. (1986) "Children's knowledge: A meta-analysis of Piaget's theory", *Human Development* 29: 195–208.

Smith, L. (1987) "On Piaget on necessity", in J. Russell (ed.) *Philosophical perspectives on developmental psychology*, Oxford: Blackwell.

Smith, L. (1991) "Age, ability and intellectual development in Piaget's theory", in M. Chapman and M. Chandler (eds) *Criteria for competence*, Hillsdale, NJ: Erlbaum.

Smith, L. (1992) *Jean Piaget: Critical assessments*, London: Routledge.

Sophian, C. and Somerville, S. (1988) "Early developments in logical reasoning", *Cognitive Development* 3: 183–222.

Sternberg, R. J. (1985) *Beyond IQ*, Cambridge: Cambridge University Press.

Voyat, G. (1982) *Piaget systematised*, Hillsdale, NJ: Erlbaum.

Wellman, H., Cross, D. and Bartsch, K. (1986) "Infant search and object permanence: A meta-analysis of the A-not-B error", *Monographs of the Society for Research in Child Development*, serial no. 214, vol. 51, no. 3.

Wheldall, K. and Poborca, B. (1979) "Conservation without conversation?" *British Journal of Psychology* 71: 117–134.

# Chapter 20

# The cognitive basis of uncertainty

*James P. Byrnes and Harry Beilin*

**KEY WORDS**

Certainty · Classification · Equivalence classes · Indeterminacy · Inference · Necessity · Possibility · Reasoning · Uncertainty

**ABSTRACT**

The present chapter offers a review and analysis of studies of children's understanding of certainty and uncertainty. It proceeds first by proposing requisite skills needed for insight into uncertainty. Additional skills needed for specific inferences are then considered. It is argued that discrepancies in the literature regarding the apparent age of onset of the ability to discriminate certain from uncertain inferences are partly due to the fact that different inferential skills are tapped by different tasks. The acquisition of a key skill, the withholding of judgment in insufficient-information contexts, is argued to derive from children's ability to form equivalence classes.

A growing number of researchers have begun to investigate children's understanding of certainty and uncertainty (Acredolo and Horobin 1987; Byrnes and Overton 1986; Fabricius *et al.* 1987; Horobin and Acredolo 1989; Miller 1986; Piéraut-Le-Bonniec 1980; Scholnick and Wing 1988; Somerville *et al.* 1979; Sophian and Somerville 1988). In particular, it has been of interest to determine the age at which children can distinguish between (a) a conclusion that must be true since it is the only possibility (certainty), and (b) a conclusion that is only possibly true since other conclusions may also be drawn (uncertainty). In this respect, certainty derives from the necessity of a single possibility and uncertainty derives from multiple possibilities.

Children's understanding of uncertainty is an important topic for three primary reasons. The first concerns the role that possibilities and certainty play in decision-making behavior. As Fodor (1975, pp. 27–33) points out, every major cognitive theory of decision-making describes a knower who

(a) mentally represents alternative strategies for attaining a desired outcome, and (b) assigns "values" or weights to each alternative indicating the strength of belief that each solution will bring about the desired outcome. The first component can be characterized as the consideration of possibilities, while the second involves making certainty judgments. These components are common to such varying perspectives as Simon's (1955) classic account of decision-making, Bruner's (1966) theory of cognitive growth, Anderson's (1983) ACT model, Bransford and Stein's (1984) IDEAL problem solver, and Sternberg's (1986) triarchic theory of intelligence.

A second reason concerns the orienting role that uncertainty plays in learning contexts. Ever since Berlyne's (1960) early work on curiosity, numerous psychological and educational theorists have proposed that the introduction of an element of uncertainty (an unusual or unexpected event) arouses curiosity in the learner. This event in turn motivates the learner to explore reasons for its occurrence.

A third reason concerns the role that certainty plays in knowledge maintenance and change. In studies examining such disparate kinds of knowledge as self-schemata (Markus 1977), points of balance (Karmiloff-Smith and Inhelder 1977), causal relations (Kuhn *et al.* 1988), and transitivity (Murray and Armstrong 1976; Piaget 1981), particular conceptualizations held by subjects appear to be highly resistant to change even after outcomes contradictory to these conceptualizations are encountered. It is not one's knowledge per se that causes resistance to change, but one's *certainty* that particular conceptualizations are correct.

The present chapter provides a review and analysis of recent research on children's ability to discriminate between certain and uncertain inferences. We proceed by first proposing requisite skills that children must possess in order to comprehend certainty and uncertainty in any of the tasks employed within the studies reviewed. We also consider additional skills needed for subsets of tasks. Finally, we propose an explanation of age trends and contrast it with alternative accounts.

## TASK STRUCTURE AND REQUISITE SKILLS

The studies to be reviewed have employed a variety of tasks that, on the surface, appear to be formally similar but in fact pose distinct problems for children. For this reason, the age at which an above-chance number of children have been claimed to have unambiguous insight into uncertainty has ranged from 4 (Sophian and Somerville 1988) to 10 years of age (Piéraut-Le Bonniec 1980). To illustrate similarities and differences among tasks in the skills required, we first describe one version of a task used by Sophian and Somerville (1988), and then describe progressive modifications of this task that entail particular requisite skills.

Sophian and Somerville's (1988) basic task involves 4 identical cups mounted on a board. The board can be tilted, thereby spilling out the contents of all cups simultaneously. Out of the child's view, a toy is placed in one of the cups. The child is told a toy is in one of the 4 cups. In the child's view, the experimenter takes a second "partner" toy in her closed hand and sequentially places her hand in 2 of the 4 cups. The child is told that she will leave the second toy with the hidden toy if one of the cups she "visits" contains the hidden toy. Therefore, after the cups have been visited, "empty hand" implies that one of the visited cups contains the hidden toy, while "toy still in hand" implies that neither cup visited contains the hidden toy. After observing the experimenter's actions and inspecting her empty hand, children are asked to place small blankets beneath those cups that may contain the hidden toy, in order to cushion its fall. Comprehension of possibility is defined as placing blankets only under cups visited by the experimenter in the "empty hand" condition.

## Categorization and representation of possibilities

Adequate performance on the "4-cups" task (our label) requires two skills: (a) categorizing locations as being of particular *kinds* and (b) acknowledging at least two possibilities. The first requisite skill is itself composed of component skills. First, in assuming a categorization process, we assume de facto that each of the 4 cups must be *mentally represented* in terms of at least a short-term-memory encoding. Second, this categorization requires the *ascription of criterial properties* to some but not all of the cups. In the 4-cups task, this property is determined by the experimenter's actions: "visited" vs. "not visited". Hence, the locations are categorized into two kinds: "visited cups" (possess the criterial property) and "not-visited cups" (lack the criterial property). Because "visited" is not an inherent property of cups, we assume that a short-term-memory encoding must be involved. The third component of categorizing is the *integration* of locations sharing the same property within a single category. It is the creation of categories that creates the dichotomy between "possible" vs. "impossible" locations.

The need to form categories is true of all uncertainty tasks, whether arbitrary locations (e.g. cups, holes, houses) or, alternatively, causal relations (Byrnes and Overton 1986) are involved. Byrnes and Overton (1986), Horobin and Acredolo (1989), and Piéraut-Le Bonniec (1980) all used a "box task" in which objects of various diameters could be inserted into holes in the top of a box. In the Byrnes and Overton (1986) and Piéraut-Le Bonniec (1980) studies, the box contained two holes – one that permitted a thin stick to just pass through, and a larger one that also permitted a marble to pass through. The subject must infer which hole an object passed through, based only on knowledge of the object's identity. Certainty and uncertainty derive from the fact that only the stick can pass through the small hole and uncertainty derives from the fact that both the stick and the marble can pass through the larger hole. The relevant categories here are "small-hole objects" and "large-hole objects". The version of the box task used by Horobin and Acredolo (1989) involved three holes (small, medium, large) and three objects (small, medium, and large balls). In this case, three categories must be formed – "small-hole objects" (small ball only), "medium-hole objects" (small and medium balls), and "large-hole objects" (small, medium, and large balls).

In sum, then, comprehension of possibility entails in every study the requisite skill of categorizing locations or objects as being of particular kinds. However, all investigators besides Sophian and Somerville (1988) assessed something *in addition* to comprehension of possibility. If this were not true all studies would be likely to have shown approximately the same age of onset. Instead, the different requirements of the various tasks have contributed to the discrepant age trends referred to earlier. However, when one solely assesses comprehension of multiple possibilities, as Sophian and Somerville (1988) have, one finds very strong evidence of the requisite categorical skill in 4-year-olds. By 4 years of age, children are fully capable of creating the dichotomy between possible and impossible location.

In addition to forming categories, a second requisite skill is the representation of at least two possibilities. Patently, if a child consistently reasons in all contexts that only one possibility exists (e.g. one location), then the child cannot have insight into uncertainty and will believe that all inferences can be made with certainty. Given our earlier arguments, this would occur if a child failed to form categories, thereby treating all locations as discrete, nonintegrated entities. Sophian and Somerville (1988) report that whereas their 4-year-olds showed clear evidence of considering at least two possibilities, 2- and 3-year-olds often responded as if they considered only one location as a possibility. Somerville and Wellman (1987) suggest that very young children appear to consider only one possibility due to an overgeneralization of an object permanence belief that an object can occupy only one location at a time.

In sum, the first two requisite skills are clearly present by age 4. In the next section, we consider an additional skill required in some tasks: discriminating between sufficient-information and insufficient-information contexts.

## Discriminating informational contexts

In order to illustrate this skill, we can progressively modify Sophian and Somerville's (1988) original 4-cups task. First, we can include two kinds of trials – those in which the experimenter visits only one cup and those in which he or she visits 2–4 cups. On all trials, children are shown an empty hand after the cups are visited, indicating that the partner toy was left in one of the cups visited. Next children are posed the following question: "Do you know for sure which cup I placed the toy in, or would you have to look inside the cups to be sure?" On those trials in which only one cup is visited (certainty trials), an appropriate answer would be "I don't have to look since it has to be in the cup that you put your hand in". On those trials in which the experimenter visits 2–4 cups (uncertainty trials), an appropriate answer would be "I'd have to look in the cups, since you put your hand in both of these cups". This modified task, then, requires the additional ability of distinguishing between situations in which information is sufficient to draw an inference (certainty trials) from those in which it is not (uncertainty trials). With this change, the 4-cups task becomes formally analogous to the box task employed by Byrnes and Overton (1986), Horobin and Acredolo (1989), and Piéraut-Le Bonniec (1980), referred to earlier.

In examining this ability to discriminate between sufficient-information and insufficient-information contexts, we first consider studies that find a relatively late onset and then studies demonstrating an earlier onset. We then attempt to account theoretically for the discrepant age trends.

## Later onset

Piéraut-Le Bonniec (1980) gave the box task to children ranging from 4 to 10 years of age. During a pretest, each time a child gave a response, a counterexample was posed. For example, when told that a stick was being placed in the box, a child might incorrectly say, "I don't have to look (to determine which hole). It's in the little hole". The counterexample consisted of passing the stick through the large hole, and showing this outcome to the child. On test trials, Piéraut-Le Bonniec reported 4 response patterns. The first pattern, indicating lack of comprehension of the task situation, was found among 50 per cent of the 4-year-olds. Here, children often argued that they would have to look on all trials. (Hence, information is always insufficient.) A second pattern that frequently occurred at ages 4 (50 per cent) and 5 (48 per cent) was to argue that it was never necessary to look. Here, subjects said that they were sure which objects were placed in particular holes on both certainty and uncertainty trials. Children often justified their judgments on uncertainty trials by saying, for example, that the stick always went into the small hole because "It fits the slot" or "That is its hole". While erring on uncertainty trials, these subjects were correct on most certainty trials. At ages 6 (40 per cent), 7 (40 per cent) and 8 (60 per cent), the most common response was again to err mostly on uncertainty trials. However, these subjects attempted to find some way to resolve the uncertainty. Some adopted a systematic alternation strategy on uncertainty trials. If they incorrectly guessed the "small hole" on an uncertainty question, they would guess the "big hole" on the next encounter with this same question and justify this response by saying, "Last time it was the small hole". By ages 9 (50 per cent) and 10 (90 per cent), the most frequent response was complete success on all trials. On uncertainty trials, subjects argued that the box had to be inspected because "One could not know" (as opposed to "I don't know") which object had been selected.

Horobin and Acredolo's (1989) age trends were generally consistent with those of Piéraut-Le Bonniec (1980). In addition to including a third hole and object, Horobin and Acredolo (1989) further modified the task by asking children to point to possible objects or holes, displayed on memory aids, in addition to answering the certainty and uncertainty questions. Addition of the third hole allowed the construction of fully determinate (unambiguous) items (only one ball could fit in the hole), partially determinate problems (two of the three balls could fit; one could not), and completely indeterminate problems (all three balls could fit). The latter two problems involve ambiguity. Horobin and Acredolo (1989) found that, across the uncertainty trials, the percentages of correct responses were 3, 27, and 68 per cent, for 7-, 9- and 12-year-olds, respectively.

Piéraut-Le Bonniec's (1980) and Horobin and Acredolo's (1989) data thus demonstrate that discriminating between situations in which there is sufficient information to draw an inference and situations in which there is not is a much later acquisition than that of categorizing locations into "possible" versus "impossible". This 5-year gap is particularly striking considering that recognizing the insufficiency of information would appear to be an *immediate*, obvious conclusion, whenever there are two or more possibilities. Clearly, there is an additional step in the inference process, contributing to these trends. After considering 4 studies that demonstrated the ability to discriminate between sufficient-information and insufficient-information contexts in younger children, we propose our own explanatory model, which posits the additional inferential steps required, thereby accounting for the age gap that has emerged.

**Earlier onset**

Four studies show an earlier onset of the ability to discriminate between sufficient-information and insufficient-information contexts than shown in the studies by Piéraut-Le Bonniec (1980) and Horobin and Acredolo (1989). Each study we describe shows a progressively earlier age of onset, and therefore a decreasing age gap between the requisite skills and this additional skill.

Byrnes and Overton (1986) modified the original box task in two ways. First, instead of presenting contradictory feedback (counterexamples) only on pretest trials, like Piéraut-Le Bonniec (1980), feedback was given on all 4 pretest and 8 test trials. Second, two forms of feedback were used. In addition to showing the object opposite of the child's selection, as Piéraut-

Le Bonniec (1980) did, children were also given verbal feedback (e.g. "I guess the *best* thing to say is that you'd have to look inside since the stick can go in *both* holes"). In contrast to Piéraut-Le Bonniec (1980) and Horobin and Acredolo (1989), Byrnes and Overton found that the ability to discriminate between sufficient-information and insufficient-information contexts was apparent in 76 per cent of their 8-year-olds and 96 per cent of their 10-year-olds. It would appear that the use of two forms of feedback across all trials significantly lowered the apparent age of onset of this ability. This claim is supported by the fact that Horobin and Acredolo (1989) did not use a pretest phase in which contradictory feedback was given, and their subjects performed somewhat more poorly than did Piéraut-Le Bonniec's (1980) subjects. Moreover, Byrnes and Overton (1986) found that the ability to recognize the insufficiency of information was not limited to the box task; the correlation between the box task and a formally analogous multisufficient causality task, after partialling age, was 0.78.

In a similar study, Byrnes and Beilin (1987) found a still earlier onset. Children were sequentially shown cards depicting one of two causes leading to the same effect (e.g. a mother scolding and dog barking, each making the same boy cry). All outcomes consisted of a child expressing either a positive or negative emotion. Each sequence was described using a short story such as:

> This story is about a little boy. One day he forgot to clean up his room, so his mother scolded him. He didn't like being yelled at, so he began to cry.

After the second card (e.g. involving the barking dog) was presented and described, the experimenter pointed out how both causes could produce the same outcome (e.g. "So you see that his mother scolding made him cry and this big dog made him cry. They *both* do"). In addition, prior to asking certainty and uncertainty questions identical in form to those used by Piéraut-Le Bonniec (1980), children were told about "the way questions work". Specifically they were told:

> There are really two kinds of questions. One type of question is the kind when you really know the answer *for sure*. You know your answer has to be right. For example, can you tell me what color my shirt is? (waits for answer). That's right. That's the kind of question where you had to be right and you were really sure. The *other* kind of question is when you *don't* know the answer for sure. You have no idea what the answer is, and you'd be just guessing. For example, do you know what my middle name is? (waits for answer). That's right, you wouldn't know for sure. Guessing wouldn't help because we'd be here all day. Okay, with that in mind, let me ask you some questions about these first two stories.

Subjects were asked both certainty and uncertainty questions. For uncertainty questions, subjects were given the common outcome as the clue (e.g. "The picture shows a boy crying. Do you know for sure what made him cry?"). As in the Byrnes and Overton (1986) study, two forms of corrective feedback were given on all trials.

Consistent with prior studies, subjects performed significantly better on certainty than uncertainty questions. However, 70 per cent of the 7-year-olds who participated showed a statistically reliable ability to discriminate between sufficient- and insufficient-information contexts. This percentage is similar to that found among Byrnes and Overton's (1986) 8-year-olds, and substantially higher than that found among Piéraut-Le Bonniec's (1980) and Horobin and Acredolo's (1989) 9- and 10-year-olds. Moreover, correct performance was evident either immediately (zero or one feedback trial needed) or not at all.

A third study demonstrating a still earlier onset is one by Somerville *et al.* (1979). The task consisted of pairs of toy houses that either could or could not be discriminated as to which was a fictional character's house, based on the nature of the objects in front of each house. During a training phase, children learned which objects indicated which person's house (e.g. a white dog indicated a boy's house). Then, during a test phase, two objects were placed in front of each house. The pairing of objects created the distinction between sufficient-information (certainty) trials and insufficient-information (uncertainty) trials. For example, an insufficient-information context might be: House 1 (white dog, red chair) vs. house 2 (white dog, blue chair). Children were then asked questions such as "Do you think you can choose which one is the boy's house, or would you have to ask somebody because you can't tell?". As in the Byrnes and Overton (1986) study, feedback was given and correct responses were explained to children during a training phase. Somerville *et al.* (1979) found that whereas 29 per cent of 5-year-olds demonstrated success on one or both kinds of insufficient-information trials, 74 per cent of 6-year-olds were correct on one or both of these trials. This high level of success in 6-year-olds is similar to that found in the present authors' 7-year-olds.

Finally, Fabricius *et al.* (1987) presented preschoolers with three cut-out paper houses and asked them to find the house that matched a particular description. Each house had two doors that could be opened and inspected. One door was always larger than the other. The larger door either had a drawing of a grown-up behind it or was empty. The smaller door either had a child behind it or was empty. Selecting a house to match a description (e.g. "no one home") constituted the inference, and what was shown in the first door opened on a given house determined the sufficiency or insufficiency of information. When the information provided by opening the first door was insufficient, opening the second door provided the opportunity to gain further information. For example, if the child was looking for a house with no one home and the first door opened was empty, then the second door should be inspected in order to confirm whether it too was empty. Fabricius *et al.* found that on sufficient-information trials, 72 per cent of 3- and 5-year-olds from a university-based preschool drew the correct immediate inference and did not search the second door. Across insufficient-information trials, they correctly searched the second door on an average of 75 per cent of trials. However, only 28 per cent of the 3-year-olds and 44 per cent of the 5-year-olds reliably distinguished sufficient- from insufficient-information trials. A second experiment showed that whereas 25 per cent of a second group of non-university-based 5-year-olds made a reliable discrimination between trial types, 69 per cent of 7-year-olds did.

In sum, these studies collectively demonstrate that the ability to discriminate between sufficient-information and insufficient-information contexts is initially evident by age 5, and demonstrable in the majority of 6-year-olds. We need to explain, however, *why* the 5-year age gap could be reduced to 1 year and also identify how 5- and 4-year-olds still differ.

## EXPLAINING DISCREPANT AGE TRENDS

Before offering our own explanations, we consider two classes of alternative explanations that we label competence-performance and differentiation explanations.

### Competence-performance explanations

Compentence-performance explanations are based on the assumption that specific factors mask inferential competencies in young children and have a lessening effect with age. Differentiation explanations are based on the view that development in inferential skills derives from the progressive differentiation of component notions.

Competence-performance explanations hold that factors such as memory limitations, verbal task demands, and response biases mask young children's ability to withhold judgment in insufficient-information contexts. Those who argue for memory limitations would have to suggest that children forget all but one possibility. However, the ability to remember two or more locations is clearly evident in 4-year-olds (Sophian and Somerville 1988). Furthermore, most studies employ a pretest learning phase in which memory for locations has to be established prior to testing, and the systematic alternation strategy requires that a child remember his or her most recent response. Moreover, Somerville *et al.* (1979) demonstrated empirically that memory for possibilities is not sufficient for correct performance.

Regarding verbal task demands, it is true that the ability to withhold judgment has not been tested via nonverbal means. Sophian and Somerville

(1988) and Fabricius *et al.* (1987) used a nonverbal response criterion, but did not assess the ability to withhold judgment in the face of uncertainty. One could perhaps use a nonverbal game format in which children gain points by electing not to choose an alternative on uncertainty trials. However, there is indirect evidence that verbal comprehension failures do not explain age differences. Byrnes and Duff (1989) found that a majority of 4- and 5-year-olds possessed significant comprehension of the modal auxiliaries "have to", "might", "can't" and "might not". Modal auxiliaries are used in natural languages to express notions of possibility and necessity (Lyons 1977). Similarly, Shatz *et al.* (1983) found comparable performance in preschoolers who used terms such as "know" and "think" in natural discourse. These terms likewise indicate a child's assessment of the certainty of his or her knowledge.

Braine and Rumain (1983) have suggested that children's poor perfor-mance on the box task results from a bias they have against the "can't tell" response. However, only Somerville *et al.* (1979) explicitly used the "can't tell" alternative, and their subjects performed much better than Piéraut-Le Bonniec's (1980) subjects who did not have this explicit response option. Typically, the response required is "I'd have to look inside to be sure". Fabricius *et al.* (1987) have shown that young children will make analogous "I don't know" judgments under some circumstances. Finally, investigators using repeated feedback (Byrnes and Beilin 1987; Byrnes and Overton 1986) have found that all but one or two children who withhold judgment do so after a single feedback trial (usually on the pretest). In light of these findings, the response bias explanation is not very compelling.

Another response bias proposed by Fabricius *et al.* (1987) is based on the notion of referential ambiguity. Children are said to be sensitive to infor-mation insufficiencies and often try to resolve the ambiguity by seeking clarification. Research on referential ambiguity has shown that when the inadequacy of information is reduced through the addition of clarifying factors, young children show referential communication skills not revealed by standard tasks. Fabricius *et al.* argued that since in Somerville *et al.*'s (1979) houses task no additional information is available, children may resolve the ambiguity by choosing one of the alternatives. Fabricius *et al.* modified the houses task in a way that permitted obtaining additional information. However, their modified task no longer required children to *withhold judgment* in the face of uncertainty. Therefore, their data cannot be used to explain development in this skill.

In sum, there is good reason to believe that performance factors do not adequately explain children's acquisition of the ability to withhold judgment in the face of insufficient information. We shall contend that age differences are better accounted for by appealing to changes in competence.

## Differentiation explanations

Two differentiation explanations of age trends have been proposed. Piéraut-Le Bonniec (1980) presented a variety of tasks besides the box task to children between the ages of 3 and 12 to assess their knowledge of three kinds of modality – pragmatic (i.e. the possibility of making things), epistemic (i.e. discriminating between knowing that something is the case and not knowing whether it is the case or not), and alethic (i.e. constructing formal hypotheses and reasoning based on them). Acquiring insight into each kind of modality consists of the construction of opposite and contrary relations, as well as the differentiation of related notions. Piéraut-Le Bonniec presents data suggesting that the order of acquisition of insight into these forms of modality is pragmatic at ages 6–7, epistemic at ages 8–9, and alethic at ages 10–11.

A second differentiation hypothesis is offered by Horobin and Acredolo (1989). They posit three stages in the ability to "avoid premature closure". In the first stage, children are said to be unaware of ambiguity in that they identify a single solution to each problem and assign a non-zero probability to only one alternative. At the second stage, children recognize ambiguity more readily, but nevertheless still typically endorse only one possible alternative. Here, notions of multiple possibilities are said to be undifferentiated from a subjective sense of the most likely outcomes. That is, only the solution that children believe is the most probable is identified as possible. At the third stage, children are said to clearly recognize ambiguity, readily endorse multiple possibilities, and assign non-zero probabilities to alternatives. In fact, even though they consider certain alternatives to be more likely than others, this assignment does not influence their recognition of which alternatives are possible. Hence, "possibility is finally differentiated from probability" (Horobin and Acredolo 1989, p. 200).

In the case of both Piéraut-Le Bonniec's (1980) and Horobin and Acredolo's (1989) explanations, the empirical data are consistent with their accounts. However, there are two principal problems with their views. First, a differentiation hypothesis requires that a single undifferentiated complex be present at some early point and become differentiated over time into two distinct concepts, presumably as a result of interactions with the environment. This means that there should be some symmetry in confusions. We know of no evidence in this regard. The second difficulty, admitted by Piéraut-Le Bonniec (1980, p. 153), is that a differentiation view is only a description "of observable steps" and does not constitute an explanation. Put another way, that certain concepts seem to be confused does not explain why they are confused at one point but not at some later point.

## Reinterpreting age-trend explanations

We do not, then, ascribe to any of the competence-performance or differentiation explanations. Rather, we argue that the discrepant age trends arise from two sources. The first involves a persistent cognitive tendency to find some way to resolve indeterminacy. Virtually all children (including 10-year-olds) are found to respond with certainty on their first encounter with an uncertainty trial. That is to say, children know that there are at least two possibilities (requisite skill) but respond as if there were only one possibility in insufficient-information contexts. Some have called this tendency "premature closure" (Acredolo and O'Connor 1991; Lunzer 1978) and others have called it a "response bias" (Braine and Rumain 1983).

In order to perform well on insufficient-information (uncertainty) trials, children need to "accept the lack of closure" (Lunzer 1978), i.e. they need to actively inhibit a cognitive tendency or predisposition towards closure. Put another way, they need to recognize that the task situation in and of itself cannot be used to resolve indeterminacy, despite their inclinations to do so.

In all four box task studies discussed, a significant number of children demonstrated knowledge of possibilities but responded with certainty nonetheless. Close analysis of the response patterns and justifications shows that these children appealed to inconsequential aspects of the task situation to find a basis for resolving the indeterminacy. The systematic alternation strategy, for example, found by Piéraut-Le Bonniec (1980), by Byrnes and Overton (1986), and by Byrnes and Beilin (1987) is reminiscent of the "gambler's fallacy". In the box task, children believe that finding the stick in the small hole makes finding it in the large hole very likely on the next trial. Additionally, the perceptual covariation between stick and small hole, and marble and large hole, provides a convenient pattern on which a tendency towards closure might be based. Finally, a number of children who failed to appreciate indeterminacy on multicause tasks argued that one cause was more powerful and, therefore, more likely than another.

It is therefore not surprising that Somerville et al. (1979) found the earliest age of onset of the ability to withhold judgment in insufficient-information contexts because their task stimuli provided very little basis for finding some way to resolve the indeterminacy. In particular, (a) the houses employed were identical; (b) there was no perceptual covariation between features of the house and inhabitants (e.g. size); and (c) the objects placed in front of the houses did not systematically relate to the houses in any way. Thus, the choice of stimuli can either minimize or encourage premature closure. In spite of the fact that such features were minimized, Somerville et al. reported that 12 per cent of children first said that they had to ask somebody on uncertainty trials, then selected one house anyway. It is also not surprising that Fabricius et al. (1987) found evidence of correct responding even in 3-year-olds, since their task provided children with the opportunity to obtain more information and did not require them to withhold judgment in the face of insufficient information. In contrast, all of the studies discussed in the present section except the Fabricius *et al.* study actually assessed the ability to withhold judgment in the face of uncertainty, a skill that we claim has as its prerequisite the ability to discriminate between sufficient-information and insufficient-information contexts.

The second explanation for discrepant age trends concerns the extent to which researchers explained response options and provided children with contradictory feedback. Horobin and Acredolo (1989) provided the least feedback and reported the latest onset. Piéraut-Le Bonniec (1980) provided one kind of feedback and found a somewhat earlier onset. Byrnes and Overton (1986) and Byrnes and Beilin (1987) provided two forms of feedback and found an earlier onset than either Piéraut-Le Bonniec or Horobin and Acredolo. Finally, the present authors added a description of "how questions work" to the two forms of feedback and found an even earlier onset. Whereas Somerville *et al.* (1979) only provided feedback during training, they also minimized seductive stimuli features as described previously.

Although one can reduce age differences by minimizing task demands, there still is a qualitative difference between 5-year-olds and younger children, i.e. the 5-year-olds are able to withhold judgment when information is insufficient. What is responsible for this change? In the next section we propose an account based on equivalence classes.

## EQUIVALENCE CLASSES AND UNCERTAINTY

In order for children to understand that they should not draw an inference when they have insufficient information, they need to engage in the following deduction: "Since both alternatives *could* be the case, and I do not know which is the case, I conclude that *one could not know*". Children who withhold judgment in indeterminate situations may differ from children who do not in that the concept "both alternatives could be the case" means something different to the two groups of children. In particular, children who draw inferences in insufficient-information contexts fail to understand that each alternative is *equally a possibility*. Instead, they believe that one alternative is more likely than another. We argue that children who withhold judgment, on the other hand, place both alternatives within an *equivalence class*.

In an equivalence class, all instances of the class are considered to be representatives of the class by virtue of conforming to a set of defining criteria (Bruner *et al.* 1956; Piaget and Inhelder 1964; Scholnick 1983; Smith and Medin 1981; Vygotsky 1962). Individual differences among members of the class are effectively ignored, such that members achieve equal status or representativeness due to possession of the defining criteria. It is for this reason that any member can be substituted into frames such as "X is a Y", and the truth value of the proposition is preserved. For example, robin, hawk, and ostrich can all equally be substituted for "X" in "X is a bird", and the statement remains true (Quine 1950).

To see how placing alternatives within an equivalence class might lead a subject to withhold judgment, consider a task in which an experimenter has a robin, hawk, and ostrich behind a screen and tells the subject that "It's a bird". The subject's recognition of the insufficiency of this information for identifying the particular bird is very much contingent upon his or her construction of an equivalence class. The knowledge of which bird is more prototypical, frequent, or highly valued in a probabilistic sense does not help the subject at all. All of the instances are representatives of the class, and any of them could be selected. Such a task is a clear illustration of Osherson and Smith's (1981) claim that prototypes are involved in the cognitive process of perceptual identification, whereas core concepts with defining criteria (i.e. equivalence classes) are needed for reasoning.

We make the claim, then, that children who withhold judgment do in fact integrate possibilities into a categorical representation, but this representation is not an equivalence class. In contrast, children who have insight into the insufficiency of the information construct an equivalence class of alternatives in which the likelihood of each alternative is effectively equated. We do not mean that subjects equate alternatives in a true mathematical sense, but rather, in the sense of both being possible.

Thus, we argue that representational change underlies the observed developmental trends. Our assumptions regarding equivalence classes, of course, have their roots in Piagetian theory, in particular concrete operational classes, which Piaget claimed to be based on defining criteria (Piaget and Inhelder 1964). However, we by no means imply that attaining Piaget's stage of concrete operations is what is responsible for insight into uncertainty. The argument we are making can be made without introducing the theoretical assumptions of stage theory.

In support of our account regarding equivalence classes are the findings that preschoolers seem to organize their concepts around prototypes (Rosch 1978), and that there occurs a "characteristic-to-defining shift" in classification between the ages of 5 and 9 (Keil and Batterman 1984; though see Keil 1989, for qualifications regarding this shift). Keil and Batterman found kindergarteners more likely to use characteristic features as membership criteria (e.g. "gray hair" for "grandfather"), whereas older children were more likely to use defining features (e.g. "father of my parent").

Byrnes and Beilin (1987) asked children to sort the 8 causal sequence pairs employed in their study. Results showed that when children formed 4 piles, they invariably used the common outcome as the basis for grouping. Moreover, children who were able to form higher-level hierarchical classes were significantly more likely to recognize the insufficiency of information on uncertainty trials. Of course, since we did not measure the ability to construct equivalence classes per se, these data are only highly suggestive. Additional studies that directly assess the claim that the construction of equivalence classes underlies correct performance on the box task and other uncertainty tasks are clearly in order.

What kind of study would provide definitive evidence in favor of our claim? Presumably it would be one that employs a task similar in kind to Keil and Batterman's (1984) task and is used to assess the ability to construct equivalence classes. It would also employ a task requiring the ability to withhold inferences in insufficient-information contexts. Ideally, one would use the same stimuli for both tasks and correlate performance on the two among a group of subjects on the same age. An alternative to this correlational methodology would be one in which children were trained to form categories based on defining features, to determine whether training improves inferential performance. Those sceptical of the validity of tasks such as Keil and Batterman's that rely on verbal responses might prefer a task in which children are asked to give objects to an experimenter after prompts of the form, "Give me all the Xs". The order in which objects are given could be informative as to whether categories are based on high-frequency, characteristic features or defining features. In any case, additional data are needed to assess the validity of our proposal.

Before drawing conclusions, we might add that we did not discuss two further skills related to uncertainty due to space limitations: (a) discriminating between situations in which one can and one cannot obtain additional information when information is insufficient (i.e. resolvable vs. unresolvable uncertainty), and (b) constructing sets of unactualized, hypothetical possibilities. To assess the former skill, Scholnick and Wing (1988) devised a task that represents a merger of Fabricius et al.'s (1987) task and the box task. Regarding the latter skill, Byrnes (1988) summarizes the research on hypothetical possibilities.

## CONCLUSION

In sum, we have argued that the following skills are entailed in comprehension of uncertainty: (a) categorization of locations or objects as being of particular kinds; (b) recognition of at least two possibilities; (c) discrimination between sufficient- and insufficient-information contexts; and (d) withholding of judgment in insufficient-information contexts. The variety of apparent ages of onset for the heretofore unrefined notion of "comprehension of uncertainty" is largely due to the fact that different tasks have required only subsets of the above skills and that the tasks used have features that either facilitate or hinder the expression of nascent inferential skills. In this way the present review serves to impose order on a confusing array of studies.

It should be clear that there is a very important difference between possession of the first three skills and possession of the fourth. At every age from 4 to 10 years, one finds two groups of children who differ in terms of the skill of withholding judgment in insufficient-information contexts, but who do not differ in other relevant ways, such as school grades (Byrnes and Beilin 1987), and the proportion of children who have the ability to withhold judgment, of course, increases with age.

We argue that acquiring this fourth skill is highly adaptive because it contributes significantly to knowledge growth in many conceptual domains. Consider, for example, that in their daily lives children are constantly confronted with outcomes in need of explanation. Such circumstances are prototypical insufficient-information contexts. Children who possess only skills a–c will consider only a few familiar causes as possible and will assume with certainty that one of these causes was at work without gaining further information. Children who also possess skill d, in contrast, are likely to attempt to gain additional clarifying information and will often discover that a new, unfamiliar cause produced the outcome. In this way withholding judgment in insufficient-information contexts may contribute significantly to growth in knowledge of causal relations. It is easy to show how this skill might contribute in an identical way to advances in spatial knowledge (locations, etc.), or indeed any knowledge that can be organized hierarchically. Hence, we believe that investigations of the role of uncertainty judgments in the growth of knowledge and conceptual change will prove a highly fruitful avenue of research.

## ACKNOWLEDGEMENTS

The research described in this chapter was partially supported by NICHD training grant 5T32HD07196 awarded to the Developmental Psychology program of the City University of New York/Graduate Center. Portions of this research were presented at the biennial meeting of the Society for Research in Child Development, Baltimore, 1987. The authors thank Sister Rita Dorn of St. Pius X school (Baltimore, Md.), Mary Anne Filano of Our Lady of Fatima school (Secane, Pa.), Leverett Kelley of the Abbott school (Ann Arbor, Mich.) and Barbara Wasik for their help.

## REFERENCES

Acredolo, C. and Horobin, K. (1987) "Development of relational reasoning and avoidance of premature closure", *Developmental Psychology* 23: 13–21.
Acredolo, C. and O'Connor, J. (1991) "On the difficulty of detecting cognitive uncertainty", *Human Development* 34: 204–224.

Anderson, J.R. (1983) *The architecture of cognition*, Cambridge, MA: Harvard University Press.

Berlyne, D.E. (1960) *Conflict, arousal, and curiosity*, New York: McGraw-Hill.

Braine, M.D.S. and Rumain, B. (1983) "Logical reasoning", in P. Mussen (ed.) *Handbook of child psychology*, vol. 3 (pp. 263–340), New York: Wiley.

Bransford, J.D. and Stein, B.S. (1984) *The IDEAL problem solver*, New York: Freeman.

Bruner, J.S. (1966) *Toward a theory of instruction*, Cambridge, MA: Belknap Press of Harvard University Press.

Bruner, J.S., Goodnow, J.J. and Austin, G.A. (1956) *A study of thinking*, New York: Wiley.

Byrnes, J.P. (1988) "Formal operations: A systematic reformulation", *Developmental Review* 8: 1–22.

Byrnes, J.P. and Beilin, H. (1987) *The relation between causal and logical thinking in children*, paper presented at the biennial meeting of the Society for Research in Child Development, Baltimore, MD.

Byrnes, J.P. and Duff, M.A. (1989) "Young children's comprehension of modal expressions", *Cognitive Development* 4: 369–387.

Byrnes, J.P. and Overton, W.F. (1986) "Reasoning about certainty and uncertainty in concrete, causal, and propositional contexts", *Developmental Psychology* 22: 793–799.

Fabricius, W.V., Sophian, C. and Wellman, H.M. (1987) "Young children's sensitivity to logical necessity in their inferential search behavior", *Child Development* 58: 409–423.

Fodor, J.A. (1975) *The language of thought*, Cambridge, MA: Harvard University Press.

Horobin, K. and Acredolo, C. (1989) "The impact of probability judgments on reasoning about multiple possibilities", *Child Development* 60: 183–200.

Karmiloff-Smith, A. and Inhelder, B. (1977) "If you want to get ahead, get a theory", *Cognition* 3: 195–212.

Keil, F.C. (1989) "Commentary: Conceptual heterogeneity versus developmental homogeneity (on chairs and bears and other such pairs)", *Human Development* 31: 35–43.

Keil, F.C. and Batterman, N. (1984) "A characteristic-to-defining shift in the development of word meaning", *Journal of Verbal Learning and Verbal Behavior* 23: 221–236.

Kuhn, D., Amsel, E. and O'Loughlin, M. (1988) *The development of scientific thinking skills*, Orlando, FL: Academic Press.

Lunzer, E.A. (1978) "Formal reasoning: A reappraisal", in B.Z. Presseisen, D. Goldstein and M. Appel (eds) *Topics in cognitive development: Vol. 2. Language and operational thought* (pp. 47–76), New York: Plenum.

Lyons, J. (1977) *Semantics, Vol. 2*, Cambridge: Cambridge University Press.

Markus, H. (1977) "Self-schemata and processing information about the self", *Journal of Personality and Social Psychology* 35: 63–78.

Miller, S.A. (1986) "Certainty and uncertainty in the understanding of Piagetian concepts", *Developmental Psychology* 22: 3–18.

Murray, F.B. and Armstrong, S.L. (1976) "Necessity in conservation and non-conservation", *Developmental Psychology* 12: 483–484.

Osherson, D. and Smith, E.E. (1981) "On the adequacy of prototype theory as a theory of concepts", *Cognition* 9: 35–58.

Piaget, J. (1981) *Experiments in contradiction*, Chicago: University of Chicago Press.

Piaget, J. and Inhelder, B. (1964) *The early growth of logic in the child*, New York: Basic Books.

Piéraut-Le Bonniec, G. (1980) *The development of modal reasoning: Genesis of necessity and possibility notions*, New York: Academic Press.

Quine, W.V.O. (1950) *Methods of logic*, New York: Holt, Rinehart & Winston.

Rosch, E. (1978) "Principles of categorization", in E. Rosch and B.B. Lloyd (eds) *Cognition and categorization*, Hillsdale, NJ: Erlbaum.

Scholnick, E.K. (1983) "Why are new trends in conceptual representation a challenge to Piaget's theory?", in E.K. Scholnick (ed.) *New trends in conceptual representation: Challenges to Piaget's theory?*, Hillsdale, NJ: Erlbaum.

Scholnick, E.K. and Wing, C.S. (1988) "Knowing when you don't know: Developmental and situational considerations", *Developmental Psychology* 24: 190–196.

Shatz, M., Wellman, H.M. and Silber, S. (1983) "The acquisition of mental verbs: A systematic investigation of the first reference to mental state", *Cognition* 14: 301–321.

Simon, H.A. (1955) "A behavioral model of rational choice", *Quarterly Journal of Economics* 69: 99–118.

Smith, E.E. and Medin, D.L. (1981) *Categories and concepts*, Cambridge, MA: Harvard University Press.

Somerville, S.C., Hadkinson, B.A. and Greenberg, C. (1979) "Two levels of inferential behavior in young children", *Child Development* 50: 119–131.

Somerville, S.C. and Wellman, H.M. (1987) "Where it is and where it isn't: Children's use of possibilities and probabilities to guide search", in N. Eisenberg (ed.) *Contemporary topics in developmental psychology* (pp. 113–137), New York: Wiley.

Sophian, C. and Somerville, S.C. (1988) "Early developments in logical reasoning: Considering alternative possibilities", *Cognitive Development* 3: 183–222.

Sternberg, R.J. (1986) *Intelligence applied*, New York: Harcourt Brace Jovanovich.

Vygotsky, L.S. (1962) *Thought and language*, Cambridge, MA: MIT Press.

# Chapter 21

# Proof construction

## Adolescent development from inductive to deductive problem-solving strategies

*Carol Foltz, Willis F. Overton and Robert B. Ricco*

Inductive and deductive approaches to the construction of problem-solving proofs were examined using a task that requires the discovery of a geometrical figure hidden behind a series of covers. It was proposed that during adolescence, with the acquisition of a formal reasoning competence (as measured by Overton's [1990] version of Wason's selection task), there would be a transition from inductive to deductive proof construction strategies. One hundred adolescents were assessed on both the problem-solving proof task and the reasoning competence selection task. The results demonstrate that a formal level of reasoning competence is associated with taking a deductive approach to proof construction. Formal reasoners tend to construct a proof based on the use of a falsification strategy as demonstrated by their search for disconfirming instances. A nonformal level of competence on the other hand is associated with inductive approaches. In this situation nonformal subjects tend to employ a verification strategy as demonstrated by the generation of redundant information. Results support the hypothesis that there is a cognitive developmental progression from an inductive approach to the construction of proofs to a deductive approach.
(Piaget, J., 1987, "Preface", in J. Piaget, P. Mounoud and J.-P. Bronkart (eds) *Psychologie*, Paris: Gallimard)

Solving a problem and establishing a proof for that solution can proceed from one of two bases. On the one hand, one can move in a general inductive fashion by starting with particular observations that culminate in a hypothesis, and the hypothesis is verified by further observations. On the other hand, one may proceed deductively. In this case a working hypothesis or a set of hypotheses are first formulated and inferences drawn from these are tested observationally. When the deductive path is followed the proof involves issues of logical necessity. The inductive path involves levels of probability and hence degrees of experienced certainty, but not logical necessity (Overton 1990).

These two paths are not, of course, mutually exclusive. A hypothesis, for example, can be arrived at through induction, while a proof is deduced. Or a hypothesis may be derived from other general propositions, while the proof is induced. Similarly, an examination of the development of problem solving may reveal that inductive processes are primary during one phase, deduction at another, and some combination at still another phase.

In the present study we focus on an exploration of the developmental progression during adolescence in constructing a proof. Specifically, we examine the question of whether, during adolescent development, there is a transition from a primarily inductive mode to a deductive mode of proof construction. Although the literature on the development of problem solving is large (e.g. Bruner, Goodnow and Austin 1956; Bruner, Olver and Greenfield 1967; Eimas 1969; Gholson 1980; Kemler 1978; Klahr and Dunbar 1988; Klayman and Ha 1989; Koslowski and Maqueda 1993; Kuhn, Amsel and O'Loughlin 1988; Small 1970; Tschirgi 1980; Tumblin and Gholson 1981), there are little empirical data that focus on the development of proof construction. A formal proof involves the establishment of a logically necessary conclusion. Logical necessity or entailment is a situation where it is absolutely impossible to find an argument with true premises and a false conclusion. Such proofs are characterized by their validity, and thus they directly implicate deductive reasoning (Ohmer 1969; Overton 1990). Proof construction differs from problem solving in that the subject not only searches for the single correct solution but also does so in the fewest moves possible and with absolute certainty. Thus, in proof construction, but not in problem solving, the subject must select moves that are individually necessary and jointly sufficient in order to meet the demands of the situation.

Piaget (1987) has suggested that the development of proof construction follows a stage-like sequence which moves toward logical necessity. In his exploratory study, Piaget assessed logical necessity in terms of the integration of necessary and sufficient conditions. Very young children were unable to establish the evidence which was a necessary condition for a conclusion; hence, their attempts at proofs were insufficient. Elementary school-aged children, on the other hand, generated logical proofs. These were, however, limited by a failure to recognize the sufficient characer of the proof. That is, these children seemed to believe that by identifying more and more verifying instances they could achieve a greater degree of certainty. As a consequence, these children generated redundant information or evidence. This reflects an inductive approach to proof construction. Finally, during adolescence, subjects not only began to give a proof necessary for a conclusion but also appreciated that when this evidence is considered jointly, it is sufficient for an absolutely certain conclusion. Piaget (1979, 1986, 1987) has suggested that it is only with the development of a deductive system in adolescence that the necessary conditions are integrated into a whole and the proof is then justified as being sufficient.

While the investigation of Piaget establishes an important empirical starting point, the conclusions of this work are limited by the study's descriptive character. One important problem is that the ability to reason in a formal deductive fashion was never directly assessed in the study. Subjects were assumed to possess a certain logical reasoning competence based solely on age. Given this confound between age and logical reasoning competence, a strong conclusion cannot be drawn about the role of logical reasoning in proof construction. Another significant limitation of this investigation is that it introduced no clear cut or specific internal criteria to distinguish presumably inductive and deductive approaches.

Diagnosing inductive and deductive approaches to constructing a proof is complicated by the issue of the relationship between logical necessity and the experience of certainty. To say that a conclusion is logically necesary is to say that it is absolutely impossible to find situations in which the argument has true premises and a false conclusion. Thus, the premises provide absolutely conclusive evidence for the truth of the conclusion and this is independent of any particular set of empirical observations or experience of certainty. On the other hand, the observation of an empirical regularity yields a contingent truth and perhaps a very strong feeling of certainty regarding the occurrence of this phenomenon. It does not, however, yield logical necessity because the premises provide only probably evidence for the truth of the conclusion. While feelings of certainty have mistakenly been used as definitive evidence for logical necessity in some studies (e.g. Miller 1986), others have pointed out that a claim of complete certainty regarding a conclusion is an inadequate operationalization of a deductive approach (e.g. Murray 1990; Overton 1990).

In the present study inductive and deductive approaches are assessed according to several criteria. A primary criterion is the developing individual's employment of verification and/or falsification strategies during proof construction. An inductive approach is characterized by a verification strategy (Wason and Johnson-Laird 1972). That is, inductive hypothesis testing is based on the assumption that proof is established by finding confirming instances of the hypothesis; hence, the degree of certainty regarding a conclusion increases in proportion to the number of confirming instances. Confirming instances are themselves reflected in the subject's search for redundant information. The production of redundant information serves as a primary measure of a verification strategy.

In contrast to the verification strategy of the inductive approach, a deductive approach is characterized by a falsification strategy (Wason and Johnson-Laird 1972). That is, a deductive approach recognizes that a hypothesis cannot be proven conclusively and that hypothesis testing necessarily involves discovering disconfirming instances. Disconfirming instances are themselves reflected in the search for information which is inconsistent with one or more hypothesis. The elimination of hypotheses from a larger set of hypotheses or solutions serves as a primary measure of a falsification strategy.

For a deductive approach, falsification must also proceed by systematically narrowing the larger set of possible solutions until only one hypothesis is left (Piaget 1979). A systematic search for disconfirming evidence not only involves the elimination of hypotheses from the larger solution set but also attempts to maximize the number of hypotheses to be eliminated by each disconfirming instance. A systematic falsification procedure allows one to keep track of hypotheses already eliminated, which in turn permits the sufficient character of proof to be recognized; thus, this strategy is characterized by its efficiency (Bruner *et al.* 1956). Thus, maximizing the number of hypotheses eliminated each move serves as a second measure of a falsification strategy.

The general hypothesis in this study is that there will be a developmental progression from inductive to deductive approaches to proof construction. While some researchers prefer to conceptualize inductive and deductive strategies as individual differences (e.g. Klahr and Dunbar 1988), the efficiency and absolute certainty inherent in a deductive approach makes it reasonable to propose that a deductive strategy is a developmental advancement over an inductive strategy. It is further expected that the development to a deductive approach presupposes the acquisition of a formal deductive reasoning competence. Because this hypothesis proposes that cognitive competence rather than age mediates the type of approach taken, a measure is needed that will directly assess the developmental status of the individual's formal logical competence independently of the confounding effect of chronological age. In a number of earlier investigations (Byrnes and Overton 1986, 1988; Overton 1990; Overton, Ward, Noveck, Black and O'Brien 1987; Reene and Overton 1989; Ward and Overton 1990) it has been demonstrated that a modified version of Wason's (1966) selection task successfully assesses available formal deductive competence. The case for a developmental transition from an inductive to a deductive approach to proof construction is strengthened to the degree that those who have an available formal deductive competence construct proofs using an eliminatory strategy. Because contemporary research (Byrnes and Overton 1986, 1988; Overton *et al.* 1987; Ward and Overton 1990) demonstrates that deductive competence becomes available in adolescence, early adolescents are assessed in the present study.

In summary, this study explores the development of proof construction in adolescence. Adolescents are assessed on a logical reasoning task (the selection task) and a proof construction task to explore the hypothesis that, with the acquisition of a formal reasoning competence, there is a transition from inductive to deductive proof construction strategies.

# METHOD

## Subjects

Subjects were 55 fifth-graders (28 males, 27 females) and 45 eighth-graders (21 males, 24 females). The mean age for fifth-graders was 10.5 ($SD = .37$), and the mean age for eighth-graders was 14.0 ($SD = .40$). The subjects were drawn from several middle schools in the suburban Philadelphia area. They were predominantly white and socioeconomic status predominantly middle- to upper-middleclass.

## Tasks and procedures

### General procedure

Each subject was tested individually at their middle school. Subjects were administered Overton's (1990) version of Wason's selection task and then asked to construct a proof. The selection task was always completed first.

### Selection task

The selection task is composed of a series of conditional propositions ("If p, then q"). In order to claim a formal deductive understanding of an implication ("If p, then q"), it must be recognized that particular instances of the antecedent and consequent clauses of the sentence are permissible, that other instances are not permissible, and that still others are indeterminate. This is not possible unless deductive reasoning is systemically available. Systemic availability refers to the fact that deductive reasoning involves a network of inferences rather than being limited to only one or two specific types of inferences. For example, it may be the case that inductive reasoners understand some form of the inference "if p, then q; p; therefore q;" as a promise or a causal sequence. Evidence of deductive systemic availability occurs when this sequence becomes the valid *modus ponens* inference, and this in turn operates as part of a network of inferences.

The selection task is clearly a deductive reasoning task and one that requires coordination among the permissible and impermissible instances that define implication. Although each problem focuses on the certainty of the *modus tollens* inference, it involves the recognition and coordination of several inference forms. Thus, it is well suited for evaluating the systemic availability of deductive competence.

Test booklets were constructed containing an instruction page, one warm-up problem, and nine conditional reasoning problems. Each problem was presented on a separate page and all problems were in an "if p,

*Table 21.1* Selection task conditional propositions

| Statement |
| --- |
| * If a person is swimming in the public pool, then a lifeguard is present. |
| If a person is drinking beer, then the person is 21 years of age. |
| If a person is driving a motor vehicle, then the person must be over 16 years of age. |
| If a student is caught running in the halls, then the student must be punished. |
| If a person is retired from work, then the person is over 55 years of age. |
| If a student strikes a teacher, then the student is suspended. |
| If a person has a handgun, then the handgun must be registered. |
| If a drunken driver kills someone, then the driver must be charged with murder. |
| If a child with aids attends school, then the child has the community's approval. |
| If a girl under 14 years old has an abortion, then she must have her parents' permission. |

* Warm-up problem.

then q" form (see Table 21.1). Using the lifeguard problem as an example, the format of each page was as follows: At the top of the page were four response alternatives presented in rectangular boxes. These response alternatives corresponded to the affirmation of "p" (i.e. swimming), the affirmation of "q" (i.e. lifeguard), the denial of "p" (−p; i.e. sunbathing), and the denial of "q" (−q; i.e. no lifeguard). Below these alternatives were the following instructions: "Each of the above cards has information about four different people at the public pool. On one side of the card is the person's behavior at the pool. On the other side of the card is whether or not a lifeguard is present. Here is a rule: IF A PERSON IS SWIMMING IN THE PUBLIC POOL, THEN A LIFEGUARD IS PRESENT. Select the card or cards that you definitely need to turn over to determine whether or not the rule is being broken." Space was provided below the boxes for the subject's choice.

The correct solution to each problem consisted of the selection of the "p" alternative (yielding a "p" and possible "−q") in conjunction with the "−q" alternative (yielding a "−q" and possible "p"). The reason for this is that these alternatives and only these two alternatives could possibly yield the "p and not q" falsification instance. That is, the card "swimming" ("p") might yield "the absence of a lifeguard" ("−q") on the other side, thus giving a necessary falsification of the rule. Similarly, the card "no lifeguard" ("−q") might yield "a person swimming" ("p") on the other side, again showing the necessary falsification instance.

The instruction page informed the subject that the booklet contained several problems and that each presented a rule. Subjects were further informed that for each problem, they were to determine whether the rule was being broken. The experimenter read aloud the instructions while the subject read along silently. Subjects were then presented with a single warm up conditional reasoning problem which was followed by verbal feedback concerning the correct responses (feedback was *not* given on test trials). Verbal feedback consisted only of pointing out the correct responses. The feedback did not involve a discussion of the answers. Testing was conducted individually. The order of response alternatives was randomized across problems, and the problem order was randomized across subjects – except for the standard warm-up problem.

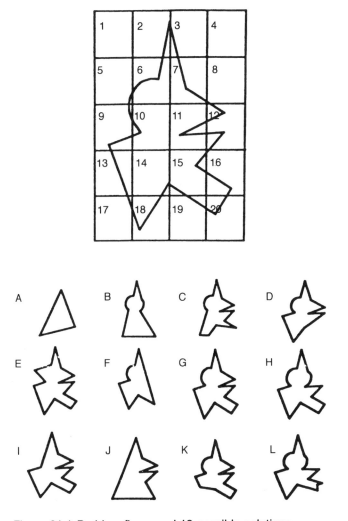

*Figure 21.1* Problem figure and 12 possible solutions

*Construction of a proof*

The problem figure was a large and irregular closed 13-sided outline shape (32 × 47.5 cm inscribed on a 40 × 60.2-cm canvas board – see Figure 21.1). Construction of this figure is described by Piaget (1987). The figure was hidden from view by 20 (10 × 10 cm) rectangular covers. Twelve small irregular closed shapes (9.3 × 14 cm), 1 identical in form and 11 similar in form to the problem figure, were also placed in front of and in view of the subject. The subject was instructed that only one of these small figures was identical to the hidden large figure and that the task was to discover which one of the figures was hidden under the covers.

Subjects were instructed that they would remove covers, one by one, until they arrived at a solution. They were informed that once a cover was removed, it would not be replaced. They were also informed that they were free to make any notes they believed would be helpful on a pad provided by the experimenter. Specific instructions emphasize that the goal of the problem is to discover the identical figure in the *fewest moves possible* while being *absolutely certain* it is the correct figure. They were told that the fewest possible choices to solution by a subject thus far was five. In fact, the problem can be solved with absolute certainty in four choices.

Prior to the removal of a specific cover, subjects were asked to state the reason for the choice of that cover. Following removal of a cover, they were asked how the new information helped them arrive at a decision. These questions were used to assess confirmatory (inductive) and eliminatory (deductive) strategies.

A number of questions were also asked in order to assess the necessity of a conclusion. First, subjects were asked to state whether the solution was a guess and then whether the solution could possibly be any other figure. Finally, subjects were requested to indicate how certain they were regarding their solution by picking a number from 1 to 100, with 100 being absolutely certain.

## Scoring

*Selection task*

The correct logical response is the selection of the "p" and the "−q" alternatives and not selecting the "q" and the "−p" alternatives. This selection combination – the complete falsification solution – was given a score of 1 for each of the nine problems. Any other combination of selections was given a score of 0.

Confidence that an individual possesses formal deductive reasoning increases to the extent that the individual is consistent in presenting logical solutions; therefore, each subject's performance was assessed for how consistently the complete falsification solution was selected across the nine problems. A subject's reasoning was classified as formal deductive if the complete falsification solution was given on any six or more of the nine problems. This criterion follows that introduced by Overton and his colleagues (Overton *et al.* 1987; Reene and Overton 1989; Ward and Overton 1990) and is based on the notion that an individual should solve a majority of the test problems correctly if formal reasoning competence is available.

## Construction of a proof

Several scores were developed for this task:

1 *Number of choices to solution.* A concept of sufficiency would be indicated by a strategy that does not yield redundant information. This is characteristic of an eliminatory strategy that minimizes the number of choices to solution as compared to a confirmatory strategy yielding redundant information and hence an inflated score.

2 *Necessity-sufficiency classification.* All subjects claimed to be absolutely certain about their solution. Consequently, a method was needed for assessing necessity in conjunction with sufficiency independent of verbal conclusions. This Necessity-Sufficiency classification of subjects was developed as follows: The top row of covers numbered one to four were not considered in this score (these covers were not included in this scoring system because each of these covers contains a feature common to all the smaller figures, thereby revealing useless information) and the remaining 16 covers were divided into four quadrants (see Figure 21.1). Quadrant one consists of covers numbered 5, 6, 9 and 10 in the upper left corner; quadrant two consists of covers numbered 7, 8, 11 and 12 in the upper-right corner; quadrant three consists of covers numbered 13, 14, 17 and 18 in the lower-left corner; and quadrant four consists of covers numbered 15, 16, 19 and 20 in the lower-right corner. Each quadrant contains one piece of information that is necessary for the correct solution: (a) the curve in quadrant one (i.e. the shape under covers 5, 6, 9, 10), (b) the upper triangle in quadrant two, (c) the lower appendage in quadrant three, and (d) the rectangular form in quadrant four. Although each quadrant contains four covers, the removal of only one cover from each quadrant is jointly sufficient (i.e. for necessary conditions) to establish the logical necessity of a correct solution. Thus, a solution can be achieved with four specific choices by identifying a necessary condition from each quadrant and in turn recognizing that these conditions are jointly sufficient for an absolutely certain conclusion. The removal of additional covers from a quadrant yields redundant information. For example, if cover number six is removed, partially revealing the circular edge, it would be redundant to then remove cover number five, which also partially reveals the circular

edge, and hence, cover number five does not eliminate any other possibilities. Of course, an inductive reasoner would consider this redundant information useful because it provides a confirming instance of the hypothesis.

A subject who arrived at the correct solution in four and only four choices was thus classified as demonstrating a necessity-sufficiency concept (deductive approach). A subject who chose more than one cover per quadrant, regardless of the number of choices to solution, was classified as demonstrating a concept of empirical necessity (inductive approach).

(3) *Elimination of potential solutions*. This score reflects whether the subject maximizes the number of solutions (hypotheses) eliminated on each move. The maximum is considered achieved if the subject chooses a cover that eliminates a number of figures equal to or greater than any other unremoved cover. For each move, a 0 is assigned if the subject chooses a cover that maximizes the number of eliminated figures (given the figures [solutions] still remaining). Each move where the subject does not maximize the number of eliminated figures 1 point is recorded. The final score consists of a tally of all points awarded on individual moves. A lower score indicates the elimination of a greater number of solutions. A subject who systematically applies a falsification strategy would identify covers that maximize the number of solutions to be eliminated, whereas an inductive reasoner would not demonstrate a preference for such covers. Only deductive reasoners should possess the competence to anticipate the complete set of results of a particular move and thereby maximize the number of potential solutions to be eliminated. Therefore, deductive reasoners should score lower than inductive reasoners on elimination.

(4) *Classification of verbal justifications as eliminatory, confirmatory, a combination elimination/confirmation, or a guess*. An eliminatory strategy reflects deductive reasoning. That is, it reflects recognition that a specific cover can yield one of at least two shapes. Thus, regardless of the outcome elimination reduces the set of solutions. For example, cover number nine might yield a rounded edge, an angle, or a straight line and depending on which shape is revealed, figures without that specific shape would be eliminated. After this cover is removed and the subject is asked how this information facilitates a conclusion, the subject mentions that this information eliminates or narrows down a set of solutions. In summary, subjects who offer eliminative justifications proceed by narrowing down the set of total possibilities until they arrive at the only figure possible.

A confirmatory strategy, on the other hand, reflects inductive reasoning. That is, the subject has a specific hypothesis in mind and selects a cover to develop further empirical instances of that solution. For example, a subject chooses cover number nine because it might show a rounded edge. If the cover yields a rounded edge, they feel proof has been established for the particular figure or shape. For example, when asked how this information helps him or her, a subject responds that now he or she knows it is in fact a rounded edge. Falsification would only occur if this cover did not reveal a rounded edge. In such an instance, subjects announce that they are wrong and switch to another specific hypothesis.

Moves phrased as an eliminatory strategy but yielding redundant information were considered a pseudoeliminatory strategy and were categorized as a confirmatory strategy. A combination score was assigned when a subject responded with a confirmatory response to the first inquiry and shifted to an eliminatory response on the second inquiry. For example, subjects expect to discover a specific shape before the removal of a cover. However, once their expectation is invalidated, they realize the solution not only has to be another possibility but could be one of many. A fourth category was a default category for cases of nonverbalization or guesses. Percentages of eliminatory responses and confirmatory responses were computed from the above classifications.

Inter-rater reliability for the four response categories was computed using Cohen's $\kappa$ ($\kappa = .800$, $p < .001$). The $\kappa$ statistic reflects the percentage of agreement between raters after controlling for chance. A $\kappa$ value of 0 indicates no agreement, whereas a $\kappa$ value of 1 indicates perfect agreement (Cohen 1960). Therefore, it appears that a substantial level of category agreement was observed between the two independent raters.

## RESULTS

A preliminary analysis was computed on the selection task to determine whether there were any age differences in deductive reasoning ability for the two age groups tested. A 2 × 9 (Grade × Problem) analysis of variance, with repeated measures for problem, was computed using the complete falsification solution as the dependent measure. No significant differences were found for grade, $F(1, 98) = 2.12$, $p = .149$. This was consistent with earlier research for the grades selected (see Overton 1990). That is, while the literature demonstrates an age effect between 4th and 12th grades, no significant age effects have been found between the 5th and 8th grades, although the mean score for 8th-graders ($M = 5.02$) was higher than the mean score for 5th-graders ($M = 4.15$). There was a main effect for problem, $F(8, 91) = 7.89$, $p = .0001$. Post hoc analysis revealed that the beer, driving, gun, aids, and abortion problems were easier to solve than the murder, teacher, and hall problems, and that the beer, driving, and gun problems were easier to solve than the murder, teacher, hall, and retire problems. Interaction effects were not significant, $F(8, 91) = 1.00$, $p = .4384$.

The finding of no age differences supports the grouping of subjects across grades into categories of formal reasoning, transitional reasoning, and nonformal reasoning. This grouping removes any possible Age ×

*Table 21.2* Subject's level of reasoning competence, mean problem-solving choices, and percentage of eliminatory-confirmatory proof strategy

| Reasoning level | Number of choices to solution | Information eliminated per card choice* | Percent eliminatory strategy | Percent confirmatory strategy |
|---|---|---|---|---|
| Formal | 4.83 | 2.63 | 66.39 | 17.78 |
| Transitional | 5.32 | 3.32 | 53.74 | 27.84 |
| Nonformal | 5.83 | 3.68 | 41.80 | 38.38 |

* Lower score = more information eliminated.

Reasoning Level confound. Subjects who gave six or more out of the nine possible complete falsification solutions were classified as formal reasoners, subjects with four or five complete falsification solutions were classified as transitional reasoners, and subjects with three or fewer complete falsification solutions were classified as nonformal reasoners. Forty subjects were classified as nonformal (21 males and 19 females), 19 as transitional (8 males and 11 females), and 41 as formal (20 males and 21 females); the mean age for each reasoning group was: Nonformal, $M = 12.0$, $SD = 1.75$; Transitional, $M = 11.6$, $SD = 1.70$; Formal, $M = 12.4$, $SD = 1.82$.

The reasoning level classification was then used as a grouping variable for exploring the relation between level of formal reasoning and the ability to construct a logical proof. A 3 × 2 (Reasoning Level × Gender) analysis of variance was computed on the total number of choices to solution for the proofs task (see Table 21.2). All subjects achieved the correct solution within 11 choices and scores ranged from 4 to 11 choices. There was a significant effect for reasoning level, $F(2, 94) = 4.94$, $p = .0091$. Because the variances between the formal and nonformal reasoning groups were not equal, a special post hoc procedure was used to adjust for this violation of a basic assumption of an $F$ distribution (Marascuilo and Serlin 1988). The Welch post hoc analysis revealed that the formal reasoning group made significantly fewer moves to solution than the nonformal reasoning group, $t = 3.119$, $p < .05$. Neither group was significantly different from the transitional group, although the transitional mean is consistent with a linear prediction, $F = 9.20$, $p = .002$. Because having fewer moves to solution suggests a subject is employing an eliminatory strategy, these findings support the developmental hypothesis that the presence of a formal reasoning competence predicts the use of an eliminatory strategy and hence a deductive approach to logical proof construction.

There was a significant effect for gender, $F(1, 94) = 9.26$, $p = .003$. Regardless of reasoning level, males ($M = 4.88$) made significantly fewer moves to solution than females ($M = 5.75$). The interactions were not significant, $F(2, 94) = .47, p = .625$. Thus, males employed an eliminatory strategy significantly more often than females.

The next analysis specifically examined the relationship between reasoning level and the demonstration of a logical necessity-sufficiency concept. A Loglinear analysis was computed to test the linear prediction anticipated between reasoning level and necessity-sufficiency classification: Formal deductive reasoners were expected to achieve a necessary and sufficient conclusion in four choices. Nonformal reasoners were not expected to achieve a necessary conclusion in four choices (that is, an insufficiently established conclusion). No specific predictions were made for transitional subjects. Twenty-two formal reasoners, 7 transitional reasoners, and 10 nonformal reasoners achieved a necessary and sufficient solution in four moves, while 19 formal reasoners, 12 transitional reasoners and 30 nonformal reasoners did not construct such a solution. A maximum-likelihood analysis of variance was conducted on this contingency table in order to examine whether the obtained frequencies are compatible with a linear prediction. The results suggested that an unrestricted model (an unrestricted model predicts no significant relationship between the predictor and predicted variables) ($\chi^2 = 6.75$) was not significantly different from a restricted model (a linear prediction) (likelihood ratio, $\chi^2 = .01, p = .91$). The lack of a significant difference between models indicates that a linear prediction is compatible with the data.

The results of this analysis suggest that individuals who have acquired a formal deductive level of reasoning competence do identify the necessary information needed from individual quadrants and in turn recognize the sufficient character of this proof. Thus, it appears that to the degree that one has acquired a formal deductive competence one is able to integrate necessary and sufficient conditions.

A third analysis was computed for a 3 × 2 (Reasoning Level × Gender) analysis of variance using number of figures eliminated per move as the dependent measure (see Table 21.2). It will be recalled that this is a measure of a systematically applied eliminatory strategy. There was a significant effect for reasoning level, $F(2, 94) = 4.01, p = .021$. Tukey's post hoc procedure revealed that the formal reasoning group maximized the number of eliminated figures more often (a lower score indicates the subject maximized the number of potential solutions eliminated across moves) than the nonformal reasoning group. Neither group was significantly different from the transitional group, although the transitional mean is consistent with a linear prediction, $F = 7.48, p = .004$. Thus once again, these findings support the hypothesis that the presence of formal reasoning competence is predictive of the use of a systematic eliminatory strategy.

There was also a significant effect for gender, $F(1, 94) = 7.47, p = .008$. That is, males ($M = 2.71$) maximized the number of eliminated solutions across moves more often than females ($M = 3.63$). The interaction effects were not significant $F(2, 94) = .26$, $p = .78$. This finding suggests that males systematically employ an eliminatory strategy significantly more often than females.

A similar set of analyses was conducted on two dependent measures based on subjects' verbal justifications. First, a 3 × 2 (Reasoning Level × Gender) analysis of variance was computed for the percentage of eliminatory justifications, which is characteristic of a deductive approach to hypothesis testing. There was a significant effect for reasoning level, $F(2, 94) = 6.15$, $p = .003$. Tukey's post hoc comparisons revealed that the formal reasoning group used eliminatory justifications significantly more often than the nonformal reasoning group. Neither group was significantly different from the transitional group, although the transitional mean is once again consistent with a linear prediction, $F = 11.90$, $p = .0004$. There was no significant effect for gender, $F(1, 94) = 2.29$, $p = .134$, nor were the interactions significant, $F(2, 94) = 1.92, p = .152$. These findings demonstrate that individuals possessing a formal level of reasoning competence present a verbal eliminatory justification with greater frequency than do other reasoning groups.

The second of these two analyses was a 3 × 2 (Reasoning Level × Gender) analysis of variance computed for the percentage of confirmatory justifications, which is characteristic of an inductive approach to hypothesis testing. Once again, there was a significant effect for reasoning level, $F(2, 94) = 8.27, p = .001$. Tukey's post hoc comparisons revealed that the non formal reasoning group presented confirmatory justifications significantly more often than the formal reasoning group. Neither group was significantly different from the transitional group, although the transitional mean is consistent with a linear prediction, $F = 16.41$, $p = .0001$. There was no significant effect for gender, $F(1, 94) = 2.14$, $p = .147$ or for the interactions, $F(2, 94) = .84, p = .436$. The findings support the hypothesis that inductive reasoners construct proofs using a confirmatory strategy significantly more often than deductive reasoners.

## DISCUSSION

As predicted, the findings of this study support the general conclusion that there is a developmental progression from inductive to deductive approaches to the construction of logical proofs. Further, this development is related to the acquisition of a formal level of reasoning competence (Overton 1990). The findings demonstrate that individuals who lack formal reasoning competence tend to construct proofs using a confirmatory strategy, whereas those who have an available formal reasoning competence tend to construct proofs using an eliminatory strategy.

The fit between formal reasoning competence and a deductive approach to proof construction is, of course, not perfect. A few false positives with respect to a necessary and sufficient proof and formal reasoning did occur. As would be expected on the basis of chance selection of highly informative covers in the proof task, a few scores suggest an integrated concept of necessity and sufficiency without the prerequisite formal reasoning.

The findings of this study and those of earlier investigations (e.g. Byrnes and Overton 1986, 1988; Overton 1990; Overton, Ward, Noveck, Black and O'Brien 1987; Reene and Overton 1989; Ward and Overton 1990) support the view that the selection task successfully taps formal reasoning competence. However, it should be noted that some have claimed that the selection task assesses merely pragmatic reasoning or permission schemes. This controversy is discussed in detail by Overton (1990). Recent Rasch scaling analysis (Mueller, Reene and Overton 1994) has provided further evidence that the version of the selection task used in this study forms a unidimensional construct and no more than two problems can be accounted for by reasoning other than formal reasoning.

The findings of the study provide strong evidence of an association between formal reasoning competence and approaching a problem-solving task in a deductive style. However, the evidence is essentially in the form of convergent validity. What is needed in future studies, is not only further convergent validity, but also evidence that will increase the divergent validity of this measure. For example, such studies would have to demonstrate that some other measure, such as IQ, or verbal or spatial ability, does not relate as strongly to a necessary and sufficient conclusion as does performance on the selection task.

An unexpected finding was the gender difference on the number of moves to solution and the number of possibilities eliminated per move. Regardless of reasoning level, males use an eliminatory strategy and systematically apply this strategy significantly more often than females as indicated by the fewer moves to solution and the greater number of possibilities eliminated per move by males. Because the problem solving task has some obvious spatial features, this effect may be accounted for by the consistent gender difference on spatial tasks found in the literature (Liben and Downs 1993; Linn and Peterson 1985).

The present study also points to the importance of distinguishing between a logically necessary conclusion and the experience of certainty. Originally, it was expected that deductive and inductive reasoners would express different degrees of certainty regarding solutions. However, all subjects claimed absolute certainty when asked to indicate how certain they were about their solution. In fact, when subjects were asked to judge how certain they were regarding their solution on the scale ranging from 1 to 100, most subjects chose 90 or greater. Inductive and deductive reasoners could not be differentiated even within the 90 to 100 range. This finding is not particularly unexpected given the fact that even conclusions arrived at inductively can yield strong feelings of certainty.

In conclusion, the present findings support the general hypothesis that there is a developmental progression from inductive to deductive approaches to problem solving in proof construction. While evidence of divergent validity is still needed in order to strengthen the claim that formal reasoning is a prerequisite for achieving a necessary and sufficient proof, it appears that this developmental progression is meaningfully associated with the presence of a formal deductive reasoning competence. This competence allows for the distinction between logically necessary conclusions and empirically certain conclusions, a distinction which is critical for adequate and consistent performance on formal reasoning tasks.

## ACKNOWLEDGEMENTS

The authors express their appreciation to Nora Newcombe, Michael Tucker, Mary Winn, Ulrich Mueller, and Michele Reimer for their helpful comments on earlier drafts of this chapter. We also thank the students, teachers, and administrators at Abington Friends School, Lower Merion Elementary, Nazareth Academy, and Waldron-Mercy Academy for their assistance and cooperation.

## REFERENCES

Bruner, J. S., Goodnow, J. J. and Austin, G. A. (1956) *A study of thinking*, New York: Wiley.

Bruner, J. S., Olver, R. and Greenfield, P. (1967) *Studies in cognitive growth*, New York: Wiley.

Byrnes, J. and Overton, W. (1986) "Reasoning about certainty and uncertainty in concrete, causal, and propositional contexts", *Developmental Psychology* 22: 793–799.

Byrnes, J. and Overton, W. (1988) "Reasoning about logical connectives: A developmental analysis", *Journal of Experimental Child Psychology* 46: 194–218.

Cohen, J. (1960) "A coefficient of agreement for nominal scales", *Educational and Psychological Measurement* 20: 37–46.

Eimas, P. D. (1969) "A developmental study of hypothesis behavior and focusing", *Journal of Experimental Child Psychology* 8: 160–172.

Gholson, B. (1980) *The cognitive-developmental basis of human learning: Studies in hypothesis testing*, New York: Academic Press.

Kemler, D. G. (1978) "Patterns of hypothesis testing in children's discriminative learning: A study of the development of problem-solving strategies", *Developmental Psychology* 14: 653–673.

Klahr, D. and Dunbar, K. (1988) "Dual space search during scientific reasoning", *Cognitive Science* 12: 1–48.

Klayman, J. and Ha, Y. (1989) "Hypothesis testing in rule discovery: Strategy, structure, and content", *Journal of Experimental Psychology* 15: 596–604.

Koslowski, B. and Maqueda, M. (1993) "What is confirmation bias and when do people have it?" *Merrill-Palmer Quarterly* 39: 104–130.

Kuhn, D., Amsel, E. and O'Loughlin, M. (1988) *The development of scientific thinking skills*, New York: Academic Press.

Liben, L. S. and Down, R. M. (1993) "Understanding person-space map relations: Cartographic and developmental perspectives", *Developmental Psychology* 29: 739–752.

Linn, M. and Peterson, A. (1985) "Emergence and characterization of sex differences in spatial ability: A meta-analysis", *Child Development* 56: 1479–1498.

Miller, S. (1986) "Certainty and necessity in the understanding of Piagetian concepts", *Developmental Psychology* 22: 3–18.

Mueller, U., Reene, K. and Overton, W. F. (June 1994) *Rasch analysis of a deductive reasoning task*, paper presented at the annual symposium of the Jean Piaget Society, Chicago, IL.

Murray, F. (1990) "The conversion of truth into necessity", in W. F. Overton (ed.) *Reasoning, necessity and logic: Developmental perspectives* (pp. 183–203), Hillsdale, NJ: Erlbaum.

Ohmer, M. (1969) *Elementary geometry for teachers*, Massachusetts: Addison-Wesley.

Overton, W. F. (1990) "Competence and procedures: Constraints on the development of logical reasoning", in W. F. Overton (ed.) *Reasoning, necessity and logic: Developmental perspectives* (pp. 1–32), Hillsdale, NJ: Erlbaum.

Overton, W., Ward, S., Noveck, I., Black, J., and O'Brien, D. (1987) "Form and content in the development of deductive reasoning", *Developmental Psychology* 23: 22–30.

Piaget, J. (1986) "Essay on necessity", *Human Development* 29: 301–314.

Piaget, J. (1987) *The role of necessity in cognitive development*, Minneapolis: University of Minnesota Press.

Piaget, J. and Voyat, G. (1979) "The possible, the impossible, and the necessary", in F. Murray (ed.) *The impact of Piagetian theory: On education, philosophy, psychiatry, and psychology* (pp. 65–86), Baltimore, MD: University Park Press.

Reene, K. and Overton, W. F. (1989) *Longitudinal investigation of adolescent deductive reasoning*, paper presented at the biennial meeting of the Society for Research in Child Development, Kansas City, MO.

Small, M. Y. (1970) "Children's performance on an oddity problem as a function of the number of values on the relevant dimension", *Journal of Experimental Child Psychology* 9: 336–341.

Tschirgi, J. E. (1980) "Sensible reasoning: A hypothesis about hypotheses", *Child Development* 51: 1–10.

Tumblin, A. and Gholson, B. (1981) "Hypothesis theory and the development of conceptual learning", *Psychological Bulletin* 90: 102–124.

Ward, S. and Overton, W. (1990) "Semantic familiarity, relevance, and the development of deductive reasoning", *Developmental Psychology* 26: 488–493.

Wason, P. C. (1966) "Reasoning", in B. Foss (ed.) *New horizons in psychology* (pp. 135–151), Harmondsworth, England: Penguin Books.

Wason, P. C. and Johnson-Laird, P. N. (1972) *Psychology of reasoning: Structure and content*, Massachusetts: Harvard University Press.

# Conclusion

## Piaget's epistemology: psychological and educational assessment

*Leslie Smith*

### PIAGET'S EPISTEMOLOGY

A useful place to start is Piaget's (1987c) intellectual epitaph shown at the outset of this volume about the future of his own work and scientific theory generally (translation in Smith 1992d, p. 464). This is an instructive passage on at least three counts. First, it clearly signals the fact that Piaget took his work to be a contribution to epistemology or the theory of knowledge. This is unsurprising since the title of several books makes this crystal clear, notably his *chef d'oeuvre* (Piaget 1950) as well as companion texts (Piaget 1972). Second, although epistemology is epistemology, psychology has some role to play in Piaget's epistemology for two reasons. One is that Piaget's epistemology is a genetic, or developmental epistemology whose main aim is to replace the *a priori* question "What is knowledge?" with the empirical question "How does knowledge develop?" (Piaget 1950, p. 13; 1983, p. 127). Since this latter question is empirical, psychology could be in a position to provide an answer by reference to the growth of knowledge in children. The other reason is that genetic epistemology is regarded as the inter-disciplinary study of the growth of knowledge, both at its inception (Piaget 1918) and in recent overviews (Piaget 1979). Piaget was not the first genetic epistemologist (Baldwin 1911). And cognitive science is now widely regarded as a comparable study (Hunt 1989; Karmiloff-Smith 1992), where psychology occupies a distinctive, though not unique, place. This is because biology, sociology and logic also have an analogous place. An answer to Piaget's empirical question "How does knowledge develop?" could arise from these disciplines as well. Third, although Piaget believed that his position was on the right lines in its outline form, he also believed that it was incomplete and so required development into some better successor (Piaget 1976, 1980a).

This stance is based on three assumptions. One is that there are *good cases of knowledge* which can be identified. This assumption is non-trivial since it is a denial of scepticism, according to which human knowledge is never possible (Ayer 1956; Hookway 1990). This assumption requires that knowledge does occur, that there are experts for each knowledge-domain in which knowledge occurs, and that the experts can recognise paradigm examples of knowledge in the domain. The second assumption is that cases of *good knowledge* can be identified. This assumption too is non-trivial since it is an assertion that knowledge can be ranked on some scale of intellectual value. It is not required that there should be some one unitary scale (Piaget 1950, 1995a). There is a commitment to the development of, and not merely the evolution of, knowledge such that cases of knowledge which fall in any domain can be ranked, where any such case can be judged in relation to "success criteria" (does this case meet the minimum standard in this domain?), and where any such case can be evaluated as well (is this a case of good knowledge in this domain; is it better than other cases; does it amount to best knowledge?). The third assumption is that all knowledge requires a subject. Again, this is a non-trivial assumption since an epistemology without a knowing subject is a consequence of the view that there is a logic of justification but no logic of discovery (Popper 1979). This third assumption requires that there must always be a subject whose knowledge develops in a principled way (Piaget and Garcia 1989). Armed with these assumptions, Piaget is in a position to address the empirical question "How does knowledge develop?" with attention to the principles by which it is possible for a subject to acquire and develop novel knowledge on the basis of available knowledge.

In short, Piaget's epistemology is distinctive for the reason given in the citation to his APA Distinguished Scientist award: "he has approached questions up to now exclusively philosophical in a resolutely empirical manner and has made epistemology into a science separate from philosophy, but related to all the human sciences" (quoted in Piaget 1972, p. 15). Piaget realised that his work provided a *tertium quid* (third alternative), notably by using a scientific methodology to address philosophical problems. This stance had implications notably for the nature–nurture problem in psychology (Smith 1993a, sect.7; Vidal 1994). Intellectual development, human intelligence, and cognitive style are typically studied in psychology as phenomena in their own right, leading to a psychology of the person. The proposal from genetic epistemology is that the growth of knowledge can also be studied in its own right. Piaget's *tertium quid* is just such a study.

Thus *intellectual development* during childhood is ambiguous. This could be the study of *knowledge* which develops in children's minds. Alternatively, it could be the study of *children* in their development through the life-span. Whilst Piaget's (1950, p. 17) epistemology is concerned with the former, developmental psychology has interests in the latter (Flavell *et al.* 1993). After all, there are multiple respects in which children are worthy of psychological study quite independently of their knowledge. Piaget's epistemology does not require that the psychological study of children should be converted into the epistemological study of their knowledge. But it does require that this difference should be respected in that conclusions from neither type of study should be prematurely generalised to the other. The distinction between the psychological and epistemic subject is drawn to demarcate the difference (Piaget and Inhelder 1969; Inhelder and Piaget 1980, Inhelder and Cellérier 1996). The issue for Piaget is not to collapse the psychological into the epistemic subject but is rather to show how the functioning of the psychological subject *hic et nunc* (in the here and now) is generative of rationally legitimate knowledge. Piaget's main point is that since knowledge does develop, the natural question to ask concerns how this happens.

Knowledge really does develop: this phenomenon is not in doubt. What is in doubt is its explanation. The doubts are shown in two ways. First, there are multiple explanations, most of which are in competition with the others (Case and Edelstein 1993; Demetriou *et al.* 1992; Flavell *et al.* 1993; Kuhn 1990; Siegler 1991; Wellman and Gelman 1992). Second, persistent challenge to the adequacy of any one principal contender arises. There are two levels of challenge to Piaget's work. The dominant version of the challenge is that any (epistemological) account should also be informed by psychological theory which will build on Piaget's legacy in such a way that "allows the achievements of general cognitive psychology to be applied to it" (Halford 1992, p. 212). This version does not require the elimination of Piaget's legacy but nor does it require the retention of any of its specific features. An alternative version of the challenge is to regard Piaget's position as a "view of development so fundamental that it will always find a place among theories of development (possibly as) a contending presence in the free-for-all that defines current psychological theorising" (Beilin 1992a, pp. 191–2). But if there are two versions of the challenge, which is the one to use?

The approach to be followed here inclines to the alternative version. Arguably, it makes sense to make a minimal theoretical commitment and so use Piaget's work as a default position. Arguably as well, it makes sense to make a maximal methodological commitment. One is through rational investigation directed on the critical assessment of principles and criteria. The other is through empirical investigation with attention to hypothesis-testing and evidence. Each type of investigation should complement the other.

## EQUILIBRATION AND EQUILIBRIUM

One of the aims in rational investigation is to identify, and then to give a rationale for, criteria to be satisfied in any minimally adequate account of the development of knowledge. Two criteria were stated by Piaget (1950, pp. 34, 50), one concerning coherence and the other novelty. Coherence is required in that available knowledge provides one touchstone for the development of knowledge. Since development depends on change, can any case of knowledge remain self-consistent through transformation? This criterion does not amount to an epistemology of the stone-age, whereby past knowledge is preserved as an enduring fossil. To the contrary, some level of consistency is a precondition of rational disagreement in science itself (Piaget 1995a, pp. 91, 230). There can be degrees of consistency and new standards of consistency due to new systems of knowledge. The second criterion concerns novelty: does the development of knowledge lead to knowledge which is better than currently available knowledge? "The central problem of a constructivist epistemology is the problem of the construction or creation of something which did not exist before" (Piaget and Voyat 1979, p. 65). This criterion requires that the creation of new knowledge must always remain open, whether that knowledge is merely new to the developing individual or novel to a society of rational minds. The open nature of intellectual development *qua* the growth of knowledge has frequently been cited by Piaget (1971, 1986) as a criterial attribute. This criterion leads to a relational conception of knowledge in that all knowledge can be linked both to its more primitive antecedents as well as to its more advanced consequences.

It is Piaget's central argument that the development of consistent knowledge which has the capacity to generate novel and so better knowledge requires a constructivist explanation. It is a strict consequence that the development of knowledge could not be viewed as a unitary sequence with fixed start- and end-points, since novel knowledge cannot be fixed in advance and since the origins of knowledge are heterogeneous (Piaget 1986, 1995a). Thus the analogy of development as a staircase (Case 1991) or ladder (Bidell and Fischer 1992) could not fit Piaget's constructivist account. The negative rationale for constructivism is that available explanations in terms of nature and nurture could not fit the facts. Is it really supposed that the theories of Cantor or Einstein are encoded in the genome or in Western European culture (cf., Piaget 1980c, p. 150 and 1995a, p. 188 respectively)? A positive rationale is based on the concepts of equilibration and equilibrium, which Piaget regarded as central to, and necessary for, any such explanation (Smith 1993a, sect. 23). This creates something of a paradox in that, despite the massive attention accorded by developmentalists to the evaluation of Piaget's work, these concepts are typically passed over in silence. Divergent evaluations of Piaget's equilibration accounts are prevalent. On the one hand, some developmentalists regard Piaget's position as fundamentally flawed (Hamlyn 1978; Haroutunian 1983). Others have argued that even if there are specific deficiencies in Piaget's accounts, his general contention is fundamentally valid (Brown 1985;

Chapman 1988; Moessinger 1978; Smith 1992d, pp. 460–63; Smith 1993a, sect. 23).

There are several reasons why Piaget's three equilibration accounts, which are reviewed elsewhere (Chapman 1988), have been regarded as problematic. One reason is due to translation. The first two accounts are available only in French texts, whilst only the last one has been translated (Piaget 1978), and re-translated (Piaget 1985) into English, no doubt for the reason given by Smith (1993a, p. xiv). A second reason is that since Piaget's accounts are tied to his *tertium quid* approach to the nature–nurture problem in the psychology, there is ample scope for reductionism, possibly as an obvious way to offset perceived obscurity. Piaget's own claim is that equilibration is a separate factor which coordinates other factors in nature and nurture. But that claim is liable to be reduced to the claim that equilibration is nothing but the interaction of factors in nature and nurture, i.e. is not a separable factor as such. A third reason is that Piaget's (1985) equilibratory models do not seem to generate testable predictions. Experimentally minded developmentalists might view this as decisive in their rejection of Piaget's account. But testability is not the sole criterion to use in scientific evaluation. Here's why.

Consider a scientific theory P which generates a prediction Q which is disconfirmed in experimental testing. The choice is then clear, is it, for reasons given by Popper (1979): we should abandon the theory P which generated these empirical findings? Matters are not so clear-cut on two counts. First, Popper's account assigns an absolute priority to theory which is tested through predictions extracted from it. But this is not the only account in the philosophy of science and Laudan (1984) has argued that a reticulated model, whereby value, theory or method may each have priority, provides a better fit with scientific practice. Thus it is possible that the negative testing was due to the values and methods used, and not merely to theory. Any research-programme is a complex which includes an axiology, ontology and methodology (Lakatos 1974; Laudan 1977). To which of these is the negative testing due – all, some, or just one? This is reinforced by a second argument concerning falsification based on *modus tollens* (Popper 1968). *Modus tollens* is determinate only when it deals with simple propositions. Suppose you say that yesterday was Friday, so today is Saturday. You then check today's newspaper and see that today is Sunday. So you infer that yesterday was not Friday. So much is clear with simple propositions. Matters are indeterminate when *modus tollens* deals with complex propositions. Piaget's research-programme has at least four elements, covering epistemological principles and psychological tasks, criteria and methods which, taken together, lead to an empirical prediction. Even if the prediction is disconfirmed, it is an open question which elements of the antecedent should be replaced – all four members of the quartet, or some, or just one (Smith 1992a, p. xxii; 1993a, sect. 9).

The argument of Jacques Vonèche (this volume) is that equilibrium is a principle relating a system with an environment whereby certain conditions of the existence of the system are maintained as constants through adjustment in the system to the environment. Piaget's commitment to some version of this principle puts him in good company, since at least six major psychologists have made similar commitments. It is Vonèche's view that any evaluation could only benefit from consideration of Piaget's (1918) first account in *Recherche* (see also Vidal 1994). Equilibrium could not – in principle – be defined in a domain-dependent manner since it is the coordination of factors operative in other domains. At issue in Vonèche's discussion are criterial aspects of organisation in a system or organism, based on Piaget's first account. One such aspect concerns conservation, or preservation, of parts and whole. There is a link to forge here with the sense in which deductively valid arguments are truth-preserving. Another is the distinction between constituting-constituted reason since a fertile system is less a completed system than an organization which is capable of unlimited development in line with its own principles. A third is the modal aspects of Piaget's account in which necessary knowledge is one principal outcome of intellectual growth with an application not merely to the actual world but also to any possible world as well. Finally, the biological basis of Piaget's account is evident by virtue of Piaget's adaptation of Bergsonian ideas, which run counter to those in evolutionary epistemology.

There are two reactions to problematically competing evaluations of an account. One is to ignore the account. The other is to check out its origin. The latter is Vonèche's stance which is supported by the unavailability of alternatives. There is no acceptable evolutionary explanation of the growth of knowledge (Kesselring 1994). Indeed, any putative neo-Darwinian explanation would amount to its own *reductio ad absurdum* (Nagel 1986, pp. 78–9). Thus Piaget's constructivism, with its focus on equilibration leading to successive forms of partial equilibrium, is an interesting *faute de mieux*. One attractive feature of Piaget's (1950, p. 38; cf., Chapman 1988) account is the commitment to a gradual convergence of the growth of new knowledge on a limit which is never in fact attained. The line taken by Vonèche is not to endorse Piaget's first account, which could well lead to problems about the internalisation of knowledge (Vonèche and Vidal 1985), but rather to contribute to its conceptual revision. (See also Tryphon and Vonèche 1996.)

A complementary argument in favour of an equilibrium account is offered by Ernst von Glasersfeld (this volume) with special reference to the question: in virtue of what is knowledge true? Realism offers a classical answer to this question in terms of truth by correspondence to reality (cf. Smith 1993a, sect. pp. 8–10, 15–21). Such a view requires there to be not merely particular objects in the actual world but also abstract objects. Realists would say that the truth of 7 + 5 = 12 is due to a correspondence with the abstract objects which are the corresponding numbers. These abstract objects are universals which have an independent existence quite separate from particular objects in the actual world. Piaget's epistemology, von Glasersfeld contends, provides an alternative to realism in radical constructivism. The central contention is that the outcome of development is a constructed object whose origin is due to an intellectual process which is different from adaptation and learning. Adaptation concerns survival in some environment due to a genetically available potential, whilst learning concerns skills built up in action and thought over experience. The argument is that there is a distinct process which is a type of learning directed upon adaptation. This process of radical construction has elements of both but is reducible to neither, which is one defining property of equilibration. On this view, the detection of disturbances manifests as intellectual conflict and a system's resulting modes of self-organization in response to them are all constructions. In turn, an understanding of the world depends not on a match, which can never be established, between knowledge and reality but rather on the construction of a viable stock of intellectual tools. Any organism may construct a viable set of intellectual tools which "work" for that organism in a certain range of environments without excluding the possibility of an alternative or even better construction in others. It is made clear that radical constructivism requires some revision to psychological theory and to educational practice due to the unacknowledged commitment to realism and truth by correspondence. The central task – at all levels of knowledge from the amoeba to Einstein – is not merely to show how learners acquire available knowledge but rather to show how new knowledge can be developed at all from the knowledge available to the learner. Further elaboration of his general argument is offered elsewhere by von Glasersfeld (1995), who makes it clear that radical construction does not exclude social equilibrium.

Empirically minded psychologists might say that they have no need of any such hypothesis, or at least no need to be concerned with such abstract issues. On such a view, neither realism nor constructivism is an issue in developmental psychology. But agnostic psychologists would be incapable of giving a principled answer in the following example which is artificial but not an artefact (APU 1991; Nunes *et al.* 1993; Saxe 1991). One child says that, in the context of street-trading, $7 + 5 = 32$, but that, in a classroom context, $7 + 5 = 12$. Another child says the converse: $7 + 5 = 12$ in street trading but $7 + 5 = 32$ in the classroom. Which of these is the true response? And why is this so? The point is that we know which answer is the true one. And this is not a matter of authority or conformity, still less convention. Mathematical truths are true. Children do develop a mathematical understanding of such truths. Is it seriously supposed that the truth of $7 + 5 = 12$ is on a par with the proposition that Snow White met seven dwarfs? The only way to give a principled answer is by addressing the question which is the starting-point of von Glasersfeld's discussion. (See *Modal knowledge* below for further discussion of the problem of knowledge of universals.)

Social equilibrium is rarely mentioned, much less analysed, in the social critique of Piaget's work and divergent evaluations continue to appear (Chandler and Chapman 1991; Light and Butterworth 1992; Smith 1992c; Tryphon and Vonèche 1996; Wozniak and Fischer 1993). The starting-point of Richard Kitchener's (this volume) argument is that Piaget's social account has suffered considerable neglect on the part of sociologists, not to mention psychologists. His paper is a commentary based on the French text of one paper in Piaget's (1995a) main work which assigns a central place to social equilibrium applied to values, rules and signs. One claim is that conservation applies to cultural values and norms as equally as to number. But values are constitutive elements of culture and society. Thus the question to ask about cultural transmission is not whether it occurs but rather under what conditions it is successful, i.e. what are criteria of value exchange. For example, partners to an exchange usually accept an intellectual value such as truth, so the question arises as to how such a value is reciprocally understood. The real point about conservation is that both partners should accept the self-identical value as a condition of a rational meeting of minds. This is not a proposal for conformity but rather for autonomy. Kitchener sets out to show that Piaget does have a model of how common values are essential to human exchanges. A second claim arises from Kitchener's review of these criteria in relation to comparable positions in recent discussions. Piaget is taken to have a distinctive account in which human rationality has a social basis. This is because the norms and values which make communication possible have one and the same psycho-social application. This position has an evident relevance to education which is typically concerned with their transmission and development (see also Kitchener 1993). The central point made by Kitchener is not, of course, that Piaget's model of social exchange is acceptable as it stands but rather that it is distinctive and important since it addresses a fundamental problem. As such, it merits attention, deployment and improvement.

Evidently, the same issue is central to von Glasersfeld's discussion of constructivism and Kitchener's discussion of social equilibrium, namely how the concept of truth, and similarly fundamental concepts and values, are understood by a human mind at all (Smith 1995a). This parallelism is important for reasons due to Vygotsky (1994, p. 344; cf., Smith 1995a, 1996a) and the distinction between unity-identity of operations in social interaction. Truth is self-identical in all its instances, whether these occur in an individual's mind or in some cultural setting. But the knowledge in a social unit may be differentially shared. One implication of Kitchener's discussion is the reminder that the problems of the development of rational knowledge and objective values are not resolved simply by reference to culture and society. There is, however, a rational challenge at this point about the concept of rationality. A denial that the concept of rationality is intrinsically flawed has been outlined in relation to philosophy (Nagel 1986), psychology (Cohen 1981) and sociology (Gellner 1982). Even so, the counter-case, that this concept is problematic, continues to be pressed (see Margolis 1986; Gergen 1994; Barnes and Bloor 1982 respectively). This important dispute can be noted and side-stepped since there is the prior question as to how anyone could acquire the concepts which are central to this dispute in the first place, such as the distinction between truth and falsity, coherence and incoherence, and similar values.

Truth and coherence are epistemological values. Indeed, the Cartesian commitment to the mind's search for truth (Williams 1978, p. 36) is accepted by Piaget (1995a, p. 184). But this commitment is also modified in that a higher priority is assigned to the mind's search for coherence (Piaget 1985, pp. 13, 139). But the obvious question to ask concerns the origin of these values. Indeed, are values constructed and, if they are, how does this occur? There are two interpretations of Piaget's position here and it is Terrance Brown's (this volume) argument that Piaget changed his position as to which was preferable. One interpretation is that only episte-mological values are objective, where truth and necessity are the paradigm cases. In consequence, all other values are due merely to affectivity which energises, without transforming, activities. One disastrous consequence of this view, Brown points out, is that intelligence is defined by Piaget as goal-directed action but that unanticipated goal-selection is not intelligent. The other interpretation is that values are implicated at every level and permeate every domain by providing the goals, guidance and guarantees that make objective knowledge possible at all. This interpretation has its basis in several statements that action is the basis of knowledge and, as such, is always value-laden (cf., Piaget 1953, pp. 8–13; 1983, p. 104). The difficulty for this interpretation is that it is problematic unless elaborated and this is something that Piaget (1981) did not carry through. It is Brown's argument that affectivity provides an essential, but theoretically neglected, mediating link. This link has a basis, in part, in Piaget's (1985) equilibra-tion account and, in part, in the elaboration of complementary ideas, one of which is that affectivity supplies heuristics with varying levels of power and fit. As such, affectivity is a surrogate between biology and rationality in that affect transforming schemes give direction to action and so to knowledge. (See also Brown 1995; Brown and Weiss 1987.)

There is a comment and a question here. The comment concerns the practical problems of identifying the operative values in any individual. In turn, these practical problems are coupled with theoretical inadequacy about how the construction of rational values and objective knowledge can be carried through. It is pretty clear that Piaget took there to be rational values, such as autonomy and equity (1995a), as well as objective knowledge tied to truth and necessity (1986). Although the explanation of rational construction is a daunting task generally, it is not a unique difficulty for Piaget's account. Indeed, there is current interest in the elaboration of a unified account which does equal justice to affective, motivational and social, and not merely to intellectual, issues in learning and development (Levine and Resnick 1993; Pintrich et al. 1993; Tobias 1994). What remains open from Brown's argument is the use of Piaget's equilibration account, or some developed version of it, in providing a reconciling explanation. The question concerns an ambiguity in Piaget's (1980a, p. 40) stated concern with the development of a "feeling of necessity", for example the feeling arising in successful deduction. There is a dilemma here. Any such feeling could also arise when invalid inferences are made and several empirical studies indicate the prevalence of such cases. On the other hand, if the feeling is authentic, it is no longer a merely subjective feeling. This is because valid deductions are truth-preserving. Which other feelings have that property? This issue is taken up later (see *Modal knowledge* below). It may be that this dilemma illustrates Piaget's main point about equilibration, namely its coordinating character in unifying into one coherent account what appear to be separate dimensions of the mind. If the origins of subjective belief lie in subjective feelings and values, their objective counterparts may be a generative factor in objective knowledge.

## EDUCATION AND SOCIAL DEVELOPMENT

Questions about values are central to education since "to educate is to adapt the child to an adult, social environment . . . there are, therefore, two terms in the relation constituted by education: on the one hand the growing child; on the other the social, intellectual and moral values into which the educator is charged with initiating that individual" (Piaget 1970a, p. 137). Thus the principal aims of education are twofold, namely the transmission of values from society to the individual and the construction of values by the individual. Such aims are a commonplace (Case 1985). But they are frequently interpreted consecutively with transmission preceding construction. What is distinctive about Piaget's position is that the attainability of such aims requires transmission through concurrent construction. On this view, transmission is effective only if what is transmitted is understood in terms of a constructed system. This is, of course, the main point about equilibration, namely that transmission makes sense to an individual only if that individual has available a system of understanding which coordinates what is transmitted into a coherent system of knowledge which is generative of novelty. Piaget (1980a) was dismissive of the "American question" about whether children's progress along developmental sequences can be accelerated (Gelman 1972; Ginsburg 1981). But neither did he rule this out since transmission is acknowledged to have a part to play in the acquisition of knowledge (Piaget 1995a, pp. 37, 57, 291). In fact, Piaget (1932, p. 414) made it clear that the educational application of his work is an empirical issue just in case its constructivist tenets are respected. Is, then, the use of his work in educational and social settings still a promising line to take? A general argument in favour of a positive reply to this question is available elsewhere (Smith 1992c; 1993a, sect. 21). Three papers are relevant to this same issue, one about intervention, another about cooperation, and a third about argumentation. They lead to a fourth paper which deals with an issue about microgenetic method.

Educational intervention is central to the work of Philip Adey and Michael Shayer (this volume), who set out a positive answer to their "British question", namely can intervention make an educationally significant difference? The reported gains in an adolescent sample are reflected in national examinations across three core (English, mathematics, science) subjects. Despite the presence of an unexpected age–gender interaction, this outcome is taken to be novel and an advance over comparable studies (for example, Feuerstein *et al.* 1981). What is made evident is that educational intervention could be shown to be effective only if certain conditions are met. These conditions include population data about the sequence of understanding (Shayer *et al.* 1976); an intervention design with longitudinal and experimental elements which separate effects due to the programme and those due to its implementation by teachers; and a planned sequence of teaching tasks together with an intervention programme with a basis in Genevan (Inhelder and Piaget 1958) work relevant both to the acquisition and transfer of general thinking skills (Adey and Shayer 1994). It is rare to find a demonstration that a proposed educational intervention actually is effective. That such a demonstration has a Piagetian basis runs counter to the prevalent view that Piaget's work has a meagre educational pay-off. Even so, questions of interpretation arise. One concerns Piaget's (1995a) exchange model (cf., Kitchener, this volume) which was not invoked by Adey and Shayer who instead state that their programme has a social dimension, taken by them from Vygotsky's work. Another issue concerns the internalisation of knowledge which is a prerequisite of transfer. The interpretation of this process is problematic (Smith 1996a); or at least, as Vygotsky (1978, p. 57) put it, still unresolved. A third issue concerns modal knowledge which was not specifically investigated even though it is embodied in the mathematics and science sequences of the National Curriculum (Smith 1993b, c).

Cognitive conflict is one of several mechanisms which are taken by Adey and Shayer to contribute to intellectual development. Cognitive conflict is one manifestation of mental disequilibrium, yet "the transition from disequilibrium to coherence is what must be explained" (Piaget 1985, p. 13). Even if cognitive conflict occurs in the minds of individuals, that still leaves open the extent to which this is also, or instead, a social process. Vygotsky (1994) is committed to the joint presence of initially social and later individual internalisation. Others regard internalisation as an intrinsically social process (Harré 1986). At any event, Piaget has sometimes been credited with an account which excludes any such social process. But this attribution is simply false for reasons given by Kitchener (this volume; see also Smith 1993a, sect. 21; 1995a, 1996a). An empirical version of this criticism concerns cognitive conflict as it occurs between cooperating partners (Doise *et al.* 1975; Schubauer-Leoni *et al.* 1989). This leads to the question of whether social cooperation typically results in progression, non-progression or regression (Russell *et al.* 1990; Tudge 1990).

The study due to Christine Howe, Andrew Tolmie and Catherine Rodgers (this volume) is an adaptation of a standard task in which children aged eight to twelve years were selectively and systematically grouped so that differences in their understanding could be detected in relation to four levels of social grouping and three intellectual levels. At issue was the question of whether cooperative work where participants held divergent beliefs about a scientific concept, in this case motion down an incline, leads to progress at the individual level. Overall, the results were mixed with progression manifest only in certain groupings at certain levels. In turn, this means that the general answer about the outcomes of cooperation is non-progression, i.e. progression happens in some cases but not in others. (See also Howe 1993.) In one way, this is a welcome finding which matches a comparable claim made about Vygotskian perspectives, that social class or social context are variable – not invariant – in their effects (van der Veer and Valsiner 1994). In another way, the finding is not welcome in that it is evidently possible for members of a group to reach a joint decision which is not comprehensively accepted or understood by each member. Vygotsky's (1994, p. 344) unity-identity distinction can apply to classroom groupings with a vengeance, for example when inert learning or even copying arise from learning directed upon identification with more advanced peers rather than upon grounded identity in points of view. It therefore raises all the questions about valid forms of intellectual exchange and autonomy (Piaget 1995a).

Piaget (1995a, pp. 154–5) regarded the exclusive disjunction "individual or social" as over-simplified since the same rational standards fit both individual operations and social cooperation. An independent argument which is compatible with Piaget's stance is due to Deanna Kuhn (this volume). Her concern is with human argumentation directed upon real-world problems. Her contention is that there is a fundamental unity between rhetorical arguments, where premises function as the reasons for a conclusion, and dialogical argument, where individuals offer arguments for their beliefs (conclusions) and offer counter-arguments against the rival beliefs of others. In turn, one main focus in Kuhn's study is reasoning *qua* the justifications used by individuals for and against the rival positions. Her case is that there is a family of reason-giving skills which can be identified as they arise in real-world reasoning contexts. Not surprisingly, these skills, which are open to construction (Kuhn *et al*. 1988), are differentially available to participants, who in this study ranged from adolescents to middle-aged adults. A central claim made by Kuhn is that argumentation embodies skills which have both social and individual instantiations. Arguably, the development of these skills in adolescence is compatible with some interpretation of the account of formal operations (cf., Kuhn and Brannock 1977) as well as through Piaget's exchange model interpreted through identity across communicative interactions, such as argumentation (Smith 1995a). But there are differences as well. First, there is an explicit concern with aspects of argumentation, such as evidence and rebuttals. Second, the subjects were given real-world social problems in the expectation that they would have prior beliefs, familiarity and interest in the problems under discussion, and so would have their own lay theories about content-specific problems. Third, although education and schooling are plainly not synonymous, Kuhn's educational study has evident implications for schooling directed upon the teaching of thinking and reasoning (cf., Coles 1993; Kuhn 1990).

A question about methods arises at this point. Robert Siegler and Kevin Crowley (this volume) outline a case for regarding microgenetic studies as complementary to two standard (cross-sectional and longitudinal) methods. Their key point is that since change is a constitutive feature of development, the two standard methods based on pre-planned and well-controlled studies may be insensitive to developmental changes, for example when these arise in a variable and non-predicted manner. The implication is not that this will always happen but rather that only a microgenetic approach could be sensitive to such changes when they do happen. Thus in microgenetic studies, the density and duration of observations will be geared irregularly over time and directed upon the specific case under investigation. Thus this method requires a suspension of experimental control with an expected gain in validity. There are respects in which an example of microgenetic study is to hand (Kuhn, this volume). Some of the multiple origins of the microgenetic approach are reviewed by Siegler and Crowley, including its basis in Genevan work (Inhelder 1989; Inhelder and Cellérier 1995). A notable omission in their discussion pertains to Piaget's work. Yet it is pretty clear that microgenesis is compatible with Piaget's "critical method", notably in the key contention that the over-reliance on experimental studies and standardisation thereby excludes the detection of novel knowledge (cf., Smith 1993a, sect. 11). It is also clear that Piaget did use microgenetic methods in his infancy studies (Piaget 1953, 1954, 1962) and that his "critical method" embodied the main elements of microgenetic methods. Within any interview, variability is evident with respect to its duration and density of questions posed as well as their range and quality.

## REASONING AND DEVELOPMENT

The classical definition stated that man is a rational animal (Aristotle 1987). But this definition leaves open the number of cases which fall under it. Although the concept *horse* has multiple instances, the concept *unicorn* has in fact none, and the concept *round square* could have none. Is *rationality* similar to *horse*, *unicorn* or *round square*? Two questions arise here. One is raised by Rousseau (1974): what if "childhood is the sleep of reason"? A second is due to Piaget (1950): what if the mind wakes up to reason gradually?

It is one thing to reason and quite something else to reason successfully. The human mind can be as easily satisfied by pseudo-logic as by logic (Pareto 1963, sect. 972; cf., Smith 1995a, p. 4). Yet the relation between logic and psychology continues to generate major disputes. Although Frege (1888/1980) has shown that logic has nothing to learn from psychology, Macnamara (1994) has pointedly argued that the converse does not follow at all, since psychology actually does have a lot to learn from logic. This conclusion leaves open what this "lot" amounts to. There are at least two reasons why this could never be nil. First, if psychology has nothing to learn from logic, then observers would never be in a position to distinguish logical from illogical thinking, contradiction from coherence. Thus logic provides assessment criteria in reasoning. Second, if psychology has nothing to learn from logic, then the thinker would never be auto-nomous: an inference which in accordance with the laws of logic is not thereby an inference due to those laws. Autonomy in logical thinking is central to Piaget's (1966, pp. 135, 143; 1995a, p. 138) epistemology. Both Aristotle (1953, bk. 6, ch. 13) and Kant (1948, sect. 25) have argued that action in accordance with a moral rule is not thereby action due to that rule. Both arguments apply to logical rules and so a correct response which is compatible with some logical principle is not thereby a response which is due to it. Quite simply and for assessment purposes, non-autonomous logical thinking may not be logical thinking at all. In fact, Isaacs (1951) regarded Piaget's work as a signal contribution to psycho-logic, or the study of normative facts. On this view, logic has an essential part to play in providing a model of the mind at work. The use of a logic as a model of the mind has in fact been one distinctive feature of Piaget's approach, manifest in his use of operational logic, category theory and entailment logic (Smith 1993a, p. 177).

Piaget's model of operational logic has attracted criticism (Bynum *et al.* 1972; Ennis 1976) and counter-criticism (Apostel 1982; Bond and Jackson 1991). This critique continues. Mays (1992) has argued in some detail that the criticism of Piaget's operational logic due to Ennis is invalid. It does not fit Piaget's interests which lay not in logic but in psycho-logic, and so the question as to how anyone develops an understanding of propositional logic in the first place. It is false in logic, since it accepts uncritically Russell's (1919) view that propositional logic is prior to class logic against the equally acceptable converse position (Couturat 1965). By failing to separate these two positions, Ennis attributes to Piaget's logic the existential commitments which pertain to propositional logic (Russell's view), when the class logic used by Piaget makes different existential assumptions (Couturat's view). In short, Mays has argued that Piaget's (operational) logic is intelligible and, as such, is exactly what Piaget (1967) took it to be, namely a logic.

Trevor Bond (this volume) arrives at a similar conclusion. His argument is that the psychological critique of Piaget's operational logic is dependent on the assumption that tasks which are designed to be equivalent are actually shown to be equivalent but that this assumption is honoured in its breach. The point is that the equivalence assumption is an assumption which strictly requires objective support. His specific argument is in three steps. Following Shayer, Demetriou and Pervez (1988), the first step is that the techniques of Rasch analysis can measure equivalence stringently. The second step concerns evidence from a study of adolescent performances on several tasks of formal operational thinking (cf., Bond 1995). These tasks were designed in relation to essential properties of formal operational thought. The reported outcome is that, using Rasch measures directed upon both person-ability and item-difficulty, these performances are equivalent and thus can be used in an empirical elaboration of Piaget's notion of a *structure d'ensemble*. This is the third step of Bond's argument, namely that questions about valid measurement of performances on psychological tasks inform, but do not determine, epistemological theory. Although no epistemological interpretation is on offer, there is a realisation that a further level of analysis is required in any adequate evaluation of Piaget's position. An epistemological interpretation of the notion of *structure d'ensemble* in terms of universal knowledge – that is, knowledge of universals, not the generalisation or transfer of knowledge – is sketched below.

There is a different approach to take since Piaget has used multiple logical models. It is thus possible to by-pass one model, such as operational logic, in favour of another, such as category theory, whose psychological (Davidson 1988; Halford 1992; Hoffman 1981) and epistemological (Apostel 1982; Wittman 1975) merits are discussed elsewhere. Category theory is used as a logical model in two Genevan studies (Piaget *et al.* 1977; Piaget *et al.* 1992) and is attractive on two counts. One is heuristic in that Piaget's research-programme permits the use of any available analytic tool and especially those with a rationale in current work in the disciplines forming the "spiral of the sciences" (Piaget 1918, 1979). The other is substantive in that category theory is taken by Piaget to offer a unitary model of knowledge at all operational levels, including early forms of rationality. It turns out that explicit use of Piaget's logical models is rare and his early practice, where logic serves merely as an assessment criterion, is widely followed instead.

Children's analogical reasoning provides a test case. A traditional view states that analogical reasoning is difficult and so rarely accomplished prior to adolescence. The study due to Usha Goswami and Ann Brown (this volume) addresses this issue so as to provide evidence that children can reason by analogy and not merely by association. In their study, analogies are presented to children aged four to nine years in a series of three pictures together with a blank, rather than by the written word. Further, the four picture options were always planned to cover three forms of (incorrect) association and only one (correct) analogy. Three types of evidence support their central claim. One is evidence about the picture actually selected. A second type is evidence based on children's predictions on seeing the analogy problem prior to the four possible answers. A third type is evidence based on justifications, including the denial that any other answer is correct. Their main conclusion is elaborated primarily in terms of a knowledge-based account of analogical reasoning in a range of companion studies. (See also Brown 1990; Brown et al. 1996; Goswami 1992.)

Two questions arise here. One question to ask concerns the relation between their position and Genevan positions. It seems to be compatible with claims made both by Inhelder and Piaget (1964, ch. 6) and by Piaget (1977, ch. 6), in that children across the same age range are reported to be similarly successful on a comparable set of picture-based tasks. There is an evident opportunity to see whether a model of reasoning based on category-theory is explanatory of young children's thinking in as much as comparison and transformation are the principal functions of rational creation (Piaget et al. 1992, p. xvii; cf., Halford 1992). However, Goswami and Brown's position is incompatible with Lunzer's (1970), according to which "full" analogical reasoning requires the capacity to think in terms of relations between relations in one integrated act of thought. This capacity is taken by Lunzer to be characterisable in terms of Piaget's formal operational thinking. There are two respects in which Lunzer's study is open to challenge. One is the conversion of claims about the sequence of understanding into claims about the chronological onset of understanding (see the criterion-indicator distinction in Smith 1993a, sect. 18). However, this distinction may be equally relevant to Goswami and Brown's position. The other is that Lunzer's tasks generate merely one set of right/wrong answers, unlike Piaget's tasks which are used to pin-point a range of difference across a sequence of levels of understanding (see the distinction between minimal-maximal levels of ability in Flavell et al. 1993). And this relates to a second question about the sequence of levels in analogical reasoning: is "lower level" (analogical) reasoning itself generative of "higher level" reasoning? This question is a direct implication of Piaget's epistemology, that new knowledge does develop from available knowledge. It is not clear how the (Goswami and Brown) knowledge-based account can deal with this issue. Thus it is not clear how analogies in cartoons (Feuerstein *et al.* 1981) or proverbs (Binet 1915; Piaget 1959) emerge from prior understanding of picture-based analogies such as spider–web/bee–beehive. Interestingly, there is a reply to hand with respect to the continuity between analogical and proportional reasoning (see *Number development* below).

Another line is the investigation of early rationality with regard to fundamental concepts, which are such that, in their absence, objective experience is impossible and, by their presence, reality is constituted. It is well known that such concepts as space and object permanence were central to studies of infancy (Piaget 1954) and childhood (Piaget and Inhelder 1956). It is Eugene Subbotsky's (this volume) argument that Piaget's studies did not go far enough and a test case is provided by object-permanence which could still be problematic in representational understanding during childhood and even in adult life. Subbotsky's strategy is to focus on a defining property of object permanence which is then manipulated in a "magic task" to ascertain whether a contrary principle (in this case, object non-permanence) underlies performance. His results are interpreted to show that such contrary principles do not simply disappear but rather re-emerge in the responses of children and adults. (See also Subbotsky 1992, 1994.)

Arguably, this conclusion is compatible with Piaget's account of egocentrism since Subbotsky's evidence is testimony to the variable proportion of egocentric responses in different subjects through the life-span. The variable proportion of children's egocentric responses in different contexts is explicit in several discussions (Piaget 1959, p. 37; 1995a, p. 308; 1995b). The prevalence of egocentric error in adult life is a central thesis of Piaget's (1995a) social account, and his account of the history of science (Piaget and Garcia 1989). But Subbotsky's studies also focus upon a neglected aspect of rational thinking, namely its vulnerability to the prevalence of magical thinking. Note, however, that Piaget (1995a, pp. 201, 243) was specifically aware that magical thinking – in adults in primitive societies or in childhood – is different from autonomous rationality and indeed regarded their demarcation as a major issue in his epistemology.

Carl Johnson and Paul Harris (this volume) take up this issue, developing a case elaborated in previous studies (Harris 1989; Harris *et al.* 1991). Their aim is to show that the distinction between ordinary and magical events is understood by children aged four years and that this understanding can be reliably assessed. A consequential aim is to ascertain whether children believed that magical events can occur in actuality. Their evidence is taken to support the conclusion that credulity is manifest in some children who apparently infer from an imagined event that a real event had taken place. The conclusion drawn by Johnson and Harris that "the imagination is a breeding ground for magical fantasies" is evidently compatible with Piaget's account of egocentrism, interpreted as non-differentiation (Smith 1993a, sect. 25). The conflation of an actual event with a possible (imagined) event is a modal conflation. Even if, as the classical dictum has it, *ab esse ad posse valet consequentia* (the inference from what is the case to what can be the case is valid), the converse does not follow at all since the actual is merely a subset of the possible. The children in this study seem to have conflated the valid principle with its invalid converse. As such, this is a modal conflation. It is also evident that Johnson and Harris' conclusion is compatible with Piaget's own definition of egocentrism as "essentially the non-differentiation of the subjective and the objective . . . (Using Wallon's formula) *'The child thinks in the optative rather than in the indicative'*" (Piaget 1962, p. 285 – my amended translation and emphasis).

Logical reasoning is such that the formal properties of logic can never be directly observed as such but must always be instantiated through non-logical properties. In consequence, there is every opportunity to conflate the former (logic) with the latter (context). Thus the (correct) claim that formal operations permit the detachment of logic from its context is converted into the (incorrect) claim that this detachment permits the operation of logic in a context-free manner (Smith 1993a, pp. 155–7). At any event, the pervasive effect of contextualisation on performances on reasoning tasks is well documented, leading to the conclusion that individuals do not use context-free rules of logic, even when they are performing at advanced levels (Lawson 1992; Lawson *et al.* 1978; Wason 1977). Disputes continue as to how to explain contextual effect. One proposal is in terms of "mental models", which is the term used by Johnson-Laird and Byrne (1991) to describe their own account in their rejection of the so-called "mental logic" account of formal operations (Inhelder and Piaget 1958). Matters are not so clear-cut for reasons given by Smith (1993a, sect. 19; 1994) and by Bonatti (1994). The companion case due to Henry Markovits (this volume) is that contextual effects themselves are subject to developmental change. This case is an elaboration of previous work which sets out to infuse a mental model with a modal component generative of alternative possibilities (Markovits 1993; Markovits and Vachon 1990). There are two predictions about fantasy contexts in relation to rationality: first, such contexts would increase correct true responses on valid argument forms with false premises and, second, decrease correct uncertainty responses on invalid forms with true premises. The evidence available in his study is taken to support both predictions. One consequence, drawn from this study, is that the interaction between reasoning and context is not undertaken globally on an all-or-none basis but is instead a variable interplay, since fantasy contexts can be helpful and harmful with different reasoning rules.

There is, however, a question to raise about reasoning in fantasy contexts, and so about magic contexts as well: are fantasy contexts extensional at all? There are two grounds for this question, one concerning assessment criteria and the other reasoning models.

The question about assessment criteria is an adaptation of a remark by Putnam (1972) who denies that fantasy propositions are extensional. Recall that a context is extensional just in case a proposition is either true or false, permitting the application of well-founded rules of reasoning (Sainsbury 1991). Putnam's argument appears to be that, by definition, a fantasy context is unique and capricious so only its author or designer can ascertain what is true, false and uncertain in that context. In consequence, imaginativity rather than extensionality prevails. In such contexts, a reasoning rule such as *modus placens* ($p ==> p \lor -p$: this is the whimsical rule "anything goes" which states that any proposition entails itself or its own negation) may be just as applicable as *modus ponens* ($p -> q \ \& \ p ==> q$: this rule states that the consequent of a conditional is entailed by that conditional together with its antecedent). Fantasy and magical contexts may be like modal and mental contexts, in which principles of extensional logic are accepted not to have an application (cf., Quine 1963).

There is a second matter, concerning reasoning models. The disjunctive syllogism ($p \lor q \ \& \ -p ==> q$: this rule states that a contradiction or any proposition together entail that proposition) is accepted as a valid reasoning rule in New York "mental logic" (Braine and O'Brien 1991) but is restricted in Genevan "mental logic" (Piaget and Garcia 1991, pp. 153–8). This dispute is important since it parallels a dispute in modal logic about the status of the disjunctive syllogism (see the example in Smith 1993a, p. 26). Further, *modus ponens* can be defined disjunctively ($-p \lor q \ \& \ p ==> q$) for reasons given by Haack (1978). This means that the choice of a reasoning model is important, since there are differences between the two versions of "mental logic".

The issue to confront is the same in relation to assessment criteria and to reasoning models. One is whether fantasy and magic contexts are extensional or not. The second is whether an uncertain response is the correct response on all such tasks, if such contexts are not extensional.

## NUMBER DEVELOPMENT

Piaget (1952, p.184) stated that "number is the fusion of class and asymmetrical relation into a single operational whole". This claim has its basis in Russell's (1919) definition of number. Second, it is taken by Piaget to fit the facts of children's development of numerical knowledge.

A celebrated definition of number was given by Russell (1919) who explicitly rejected any definition of number based on counting for two reasons. One is that the putative definition would be circular: counting is successful only in virtue of number. The second is that counting can lead to contradictions unless guided by clear classification. Things counted as one can be many depending on categorisation, as in this dialogue: "How many did you say?" "One soccer team and eleven players". "I see, twelve". Classification has to be well founded and binding on both partners to an exchange, otherwise numerical error, as in this example, can arise, or even vicious contradiction in its own right, as in Russell's paradox (1919, p. 136; see Smith 1993a, sect. 5.2) whose implications for children's development have not gone unnoticed (Quine 1974, pp. 95–6). Declining to define number in terms of counting, Russell proposed to explicate number solely in terms of logic and it is for this reason that his account is a logicist account of number. According to Russell (1919, p. 18 – his emphasis), "*the number of a class is the class of all those classes that are similar to it*. Thus the number of a couple will be the class of all couples. In fact, the class of all couples will *be* the number 2, according to our definition . . . and it is not difficult to prove that numbers so defined have all the properties that we expect numbers to have". This elegant claim is a massive under-estimation since the proof in question required the extensional logic of *Principia mathematica* (Whitehead and Russell 1962). Such a logic was expected to capture all of the core properties of number and so of mathematical reasoning. An evaluation of this logicist programme is offered by Korner (1960). Note well that Russell's definition presupposes some stance on the problem of universals. Declining to follow the realism of Frege (1888/1980), Russell regarded nominalism as the outcome of his position which in this case is the reduction of number to logic. Piaget's constructivism is an alternative stance to both realism and nominalism about number as a universal (von Glasersfeld, this volume).

Russell's account captures three important properties of number (Smith 1993a, p. 72). One property is equivalence, since $9 = 6 + 3$. This property is respected since the class which is 9 is the same as the logical sum of the class which is 6 and the class which is 3. Further class properties are also evident, notably class inclusion, since the class 9 includes the class 6 and the class 3. A second property is the transitivity of number since the relation between the three classes 9, 6 and 3 is asymmetric and forms a transitive series. A third property is that inferences about number are truth-preserving: if $9 = 6 + 3$, then $6 = 9 - 3$. To say that inference about number is truth-preserving is just to say that conservation is a property of number.

In short, Piaget's (1952) study of conservation, transitivity and class inclusion is an attempt to outline an account which both captures the spirit of Russell's definition of number and which is in accord with the facts of numerical development during childhood. Such an account would be relevant to children's mathematical reasoning and so to the development of novel knowledge in mathematics. Previous research on each of these three notions was reviewed elsewhere (Smith 1992b) with four further contributions here which deal with number development, conservation, classification and transitivity.

Piaget's account of the development of number has generated major disputes (Bideaud 1992). One consequence has been the emergence of several approaches to this important aspect of human development (Cobb 1994; Solomon 1989, 1996). Central to Peter Bryant's (this volume) chapter is the outline of a unifying scheme which sets out to exploit the convergences in three research traditions on children's mathematical development. His main strategy is not to collapse the differences but rather to establish connections arising from experimental studies. Piaget's work is directly discussed in two areas. One area concerns logic and mathematics. Bryant's main conclusion is that young children acquire a correct but non-quantitative understanding of numerical relations and sequences. Both rational and empirical issues are implicated here, including the criteria to be used in attributing a specified level of understanding of a mathematical principle and the design of causal studies to establish their efficacy. The second area concerns mathematics problems typically encountered in classrooms. A special case is proportionality. Bryant's review captures the *leitmotif* of a range of studies with due attention to his own study dealing with the half boundary. This study provides a bridge, linking both Genevan and British research as well as the age range from pre-schooler (Goswami and Brown, this volume) to adolescence (cf., Karplus 1981; Noelting 1980). It also contributes to the continuity between analogical reasoning and the quantification of proportions. The third area is culture where research on mathematics in the street and the school leads to the question of why children have a limited ability to combine their formal and informal experiences. This is, of course, a difficult question which is pursued by Nunes and Bryant (forthcoming).

Mathematical truths are regarded as a paradigm example of necessity (Ayer 1956; Korner 1960; Haack 1978). A truth such as $7 + 5 = 12$ is a necessary truth, in that no number other than 9 could be the answer to the proportionality question 4:6::6:? Although this aspect of mathematical knowledge has been noticed in relation to psychology (Murray 1990) and education (Smith 1993b), it has attracted insufficient attention. It could be said: this is because the current stock of problems is marked by insufficient consensus and convergence. Indeed, this is exactly the starting point to Bryant's paper. The issue is, however, a general one and it will resurface later in the distinction between correctness and necessity.

The status of conservation in the development of number provides a test case. Although Bryant's (1974) own past research has been influential, in making the claim that children aged three to four years can conserve number, that claim has generated two sorts of riposte. In Bryant's (see this volume) own subsequent work, interest has centred on numerical equivalence and the onset of proportional reasoning. Note that both require conservation, since the number which is the relation between 4 and 6 is the same as the number which is the relation between 6 and 9. So this research builds upon the earlier studies. But the earlier study generated a second type of reply, notably in the counter-claim made by Halford and Boyle (1985) that Bryant's conservation study amounted to a false-positive since the correct responses could be explained other than through conservation. Catherine Sophian (this volume) has reassessed this dispute. A related aim of her study is the reassessment of the claim that counting is the basis of conservation as well as number (Gelman 1972; Gelman and Gallistel 1978). The evidence available in Sophian's study is based on conservation and substitution tasks. Both types required a transformation, the former where length cues could result in non-conserving responses and the latter where a counting strategy would be required to ensure numerical equivalence. The evidence reported is taken to provide both a strong denial that conservation is present in very young children and a weaker assertion that conservation precedes counting. Whilst noting that the development of counting and of conservation is shown still to be complex, and so not well understood, Sophian allusively invokes in her conclusion Russell's (1919) definition of number. *Plus ça change.*

Research on intellectual development has to confront two issues about consistency in children's understanding. One issue concerns Piaget's criterion about coherence in knowledge systems. This issue concerns children's abilities to think consistently at all and also to develop new standards of consistency. The other issue concerns regularities and the extent to which children can respond in the same way on different tasks with equivalent designs. The former is a criterial issue. The latter is empirical. The point is that, in Sophian's study and many others like it, different tasks are used with an equivalent design. Thus the empirical issue is central. But this still leaves open the issue of coherence as a criterion in one and the same mental act. If different tasks generate different mental acts, it might be desirable to find that coherence is the norm *qua* intellectual value. But is this an essential consequence of the accounts under investigation, since degrees of irregularity may be normal?

Classification is a fundamental element in human understanding. The extensive work on the development of classification in children is reviewed elsewhere (Markman 1989). The starting point of Piaget's study of classification was in logic for two reasons. First, all classification has some logical element. This logical element in classification may be inductive

(Lopez *et al.* 1992), or logical criteria relevant to natural and nominal kinds (Keil 1989). The logical element may also be evident as deductive classi-fication, which was central to Piaget's (1921) early work. Second, Russell's (1919) definition of number requires an understanding of class inclusion, and not merely class membership, since Russell defined number as a class of classes. Class membership is a relation between a class and its instances, for example the class *flower* and the class *daisy* both apply to the same instance, such as an actual daisy growing in a garden. Class inclusion is a relation between one class and another class, for example between *daisy* and *flower*. A consequential issue concerns necessity. Even if there is an actual daisy in the garden, things could have been otherwise – it could have been a pansy, perhaps not even a flower at all. But if the actual object in the garden is a daisy, it must be a flower. And this could not have been otherwise, i.e. it is a necessity. Note that Russell's (1919) extensional logic was restricted to mathematics where, of course, all truths are necessary. In extensional logic, the issue of necessity is side-stepped by Russell with an incipient reduction of entailment to material implication (von Wright 1957). However, Piaget was well aware that the truth-functional relation of material implication is not the same as the logical relation of entailment (Smith 1993a, sect. 26). And he further realised that necessary truths may well be learned empirically (Kripke 1980). An argument is set out else-where (Smith 1982, 1993a, sect. 24) to show that this aspect of intellectual development is captured by Piaget's (1952) distinction between responses at level 2 (correct understanding) and level 3 (necessary understanding). In short, it is Piaget's claim that mathematical reasoning and the development of novel knowledge require children to understand class inclusion relation-ships and to understand deductive relationships in classification.

There is evidence in support of Piaget's logical inference model of class inclusion (Campbell 1991). This model states that a specified level of logical understanding is essential to numerical reasoning and so mathema-tical quantification is not required as a prerequisite. Note that this argument fits the logical model in Piaget's (1952) account with its developmental sequence at global, intensive, extensive and metric levels of numercial understanding (Smith 1993a, p. 166). A rationale is available due to the two meanings of quantification, one in mathematics and the other in predicate logic. Logical quantification does not require mathematical quantification (Sainsbury 1991). Further, it is Piaget's argument that children understand class logic in advance of propositional and so predicate logic (Mays 1992).

In their chapter, Michael Chapman and Michelle McBride (this volume) address the issue concerning the incidence of guessing in the assessment of inclusion reasoning (cf. Hodkin 1987). Their study illustrates Chapman's (1988, 1991) central contention that methodological issues implicate sub-stantive issues. The evidence reported by Chapman and McBride suggests that the younger children, aged four to six years, are more liable to respond on the basis of guessing and so not on the basis of deduction. Guessing and deduction are, of course, exclusive opposites. Their further suggestion is that the older children in their study (up to ten years) were able to justify their responses and thus were in a position to reason deductively. It is, however, evident that their study does not directly identify explicit criteria relevant to necessary understanding based on deduction (cf., Cormier and Dagenais 1983). This is an intriguing omission.

The inspiration for Piaget's study of transitivity is the work of Burt (1919), notably the task "If Edith is lighter than Susan and Edith is darker than Lily, who is the darkest?" Piaget (1921; cf., 1928, ch. 3 sect. 4) was stunned by the fact that even adolescents gave incorrect responses on such tasks (a protocol is summarised in Smith 1993a, p. 116), leading him to deny that children's understanding of logic is the same as adults' understanding. Piaget's question is not about whether children are logical – that is, whether children use a logic – since it is his claim that they always are. Rather, his question is about which logic this is (Smith 1992b, p. 1; Smith 1993a, sect. 8.5). His positive answer is that logical understanding develops in a distinctive way. In his studies of infancy, Piaget (1954, Obs. 66) reported evidence to show that infants aged eighteen months have developed a behavioural mastery of transitive relationships with a representational understanding arising later during childhood. The primary reason for this developmental lag was due to children's difficulites in understanding the logic of relations (Piaget 1952, ch. 6).

Piaget's case is based on the point that each and every relation must be transitive, intransitive or non-transitive (Lemmon 1966, pp. 179–87). Note that these are mutually exclusive and collectively exhaustive properties. This is a pretty reasonable requirement – as reasonable as the requirement that any natural number is either odd or even but not both. Armed with the critical assumption that the terms of a direct relation are in the same relation as the terms of its converse – the relation of A and B is the same in *A is longer than B* as in *B is shorter than A* – Piaget's explanation is that anyone who infers that Lily is the darkest on Burt's task does not understand the transitivity of the relation *darker than*. So his proposal is that incorrect responses are due to children's use of a logic other than adults' logic of relations.

An alternative explanation was offered by Bryant and Trabasso (1971) in terms of children's difficulties in remembering the premises from which a deductive inference is made. Their task required prior training which generated controversies (Chapman and Lindenberger 1988). A variant task was used by Pears and Bryant (1990) where prior training was not required. Their findings have been confirmed, leading to further questions about children's understanding of relations (Markovits *et al.* 1995).

The explanation in terms of memory of premise information could appear in two forms. One version is that the non-use of adults' logic is not the only way in which children could draw the incorrect conclusion in a transitivity task, since memory difficulties could be equally responsible. The other version is that children who remember the premise information are thereby in a position to use adults' logic. Both versions rest on the assumption that the logical coordination of premise information is not only important in its own right but also essential for transitive understanding. This assumption is questioned by Brendan McGonigle and Margaret Chalmers (this volume). They do not question the importance of logical coordination but they do question its necessity as a mechanism responsible for transitive choices. Central to their case is the methodological commitment to comparative research. Their argument is that if the origins of knowledge lie in biology, rational knowledge can arise in non-human species, for example squirrel monkeys (Chalmers and McGonigle 1984). In turn, if rational responses are evident in non-human species, two questions arise. One is whether simian and human rationality is the same. A second concerns the mechanism responsible for intellectual mastery in either case. Drawing on a comprehensive range of studies of monkeys and children with tasks designed in terms of recent controversies about transitive understanding, their answer is a qualified "yes" to the first question. The parallelism is taken to be shown by the "symbolic distance effect", manifest as a decrease in reaction times with an increase in the ordinal distance between items in an ordered array on triadic tasks (monkeys) and five-term tasks (children). To the second question, the answer is that logical coordination is not the only way to make transitive choices and that relational mastery is due instead to intellectual search procedures. This leads to their main conclusion which is based on principles of cognitive economy, rather than on logical principles, in the explanation of how cognitive systems invest in complexity. (See also McGonigle and Chalmers 1995.)

In one way, this conclusion is compatible with Piaget's (1971, 1979) epistemology which has the clear implication that if knowledge develops, its origins lie in biology. There is a further compatibility in that the intellectual mechanism identified by McGonigle and Chalmers is viewed as a proto-logical form of understanding. It is therefore possible that this distinct and independent mechanism could also contribute to a logical understanding of transitivity. In another way, their conclusion is incompatible with Piaget's epistemology which set out to show how logical coordination arises. There are at least two ways in which a correct relational understanding can be present. One is through ordering comprehensively all of the terms of the several instances of a relation (such as *heavier than*) in an array. Another is through realising the logical property instantiated in those terms (for example, the transitivity of this relation). The first is necessary for the second but not, of course, sufficient. Yet the second is required for an understanding of the logic of transitive relations. The counter-argument, then, is that mastery of the terms of a relation, which is transitive, is an essential (necessary) accomplishment but it is not the same as a realisation that a relation is transitive and so necessary.

## MODAL KNOWLEDGE

Central to Piaget's epistemology is the celebrated question "How is knowledge possible?" The kernel to Kant's (1933, B4) answer was in terms of universal and necessary knowledge in that "necessity and universality are . . . sure criteria of a priori knowledge". Piaget transformed Kant's question into an empirical counterpart "How does knowledge develop?" But in doing so, he saw the need to retain a place for the Kantian twin criteria of universality and necessity. Thus the issue for Piaget is to show how the development of universality and necessity in human understanding makes rational knowledge possible at all. Note that the Kantian tower analogy (quoted in Smith 1993a, p. vi) fits Piaget's epistemology: one unitary tower reaching to the heavens is unrealistic. By contrast, there may well be scope for multiple more humble dwellings instead.

It might be objected: Piaget is offering a depressing account of children's minds since this development could never happen. It could just as easily be replied: Piaget is actually offering a promising account of children's minds since development really does happen. Universality is intelligible to school children, as shown by Eus who explains both that whatever you do to two containers with different quantities of liquid *"you can never make them the same"* and that two containers with the same quantity *"are always the same"* (Piaget 1952, p. 18; my amended translation). School children also have some understanding of necessity which captures Aristotle's (1987) definition in *De Interpretatione* (18b): anything whose negation is impossible is necessary. Phi, aged five years, is shown a cube whose five visible sides are white and is asked the colour of the rear, invisible side: *"the box is all white so the back can't be any other colour"* (Piaget 1987a, p. 31). This is a questionable inference leading to an erroneous conclusion and yet it contains the core properties of Aristotle's definition. Piaget defined knowledge through transformation since it is his claim that the acquisition of knowledge is always tied to psycho-social activities (Piaget 1983, p. 104; 1995, pp. 70–1). The development of deductively necessary knowledge offers a test-case.

First, deduction is defined through validity (Sainsbury 1991). Valid arguments not merely do not have, but rather could not have, true premises and a false conclusion (Haack 1978). The relation linking the premises and conclusion of a valid argument is entailment (von Wright 1957).

Second, deduction is truth-preserving but not truth-producing (Sainsbury 1991). Deduction is truth-preserving since

1  All men are mortal
2  Socrates is a man

together entail

3  Socrates is mortal

In this classic argument, each proposition is true and (1) and (2) together entail (3), which is true. So deduction is truth-preserving. By contrast, although

4  All women are immortal
5  Socrates is a woman

together entail

6  Socrates is immortal

each of (4), (5) and (6) is false. So deduction is not truth-producing.

Third, all entailments are necessary (Anderson and Belnap 1975), and so all deductions are necessary. A valid argument is such that, if its premises are true, its conclusion must also be true.

Fourth, necessity is a modal concept which is defined through other members of the same modal family. The inter-definability of modal notions is well known (Haack 1978; Kneale and Kneale 1962; Sainsbury 1991): anything whose negation is impossible is necessary, just as anything whose negation is not necessary is possible (Smith 1993a, p. 172). This means that any one notion within a modal family is understood only through some other member of that same family.

Fifth, there are several distinct families of modal concepts (Hintikka and Hintikka 1989; Piéraut-Le Bonniec 1980). Necessity and possibility belong to the family of alethic modality. Other modal families are different. Thus epistemic modality covers certainty and supposition. Deontic modality covers obligation and permission. The properties of these families are isomorphic and so can be defined in a comparable way to necessity and possibility (von Wright 1951; cf., Smith 1993a, p. 172). All modalities are distinct from truth-functionality. The deontic modality of morality is exemplary of the other families. The question of which moral judgment to make is different from the question of the manner or modality of that judgment. Thus the mere statement of the moral judgment "tell the truth" leaves open whether this is a moral obligation (you should do this) or a moral permission (you may do this). Analogous ambiguity extends to other modal families, including alethic modality. Quite simply, anyone who has the true belief that $7 + 5 = 12$ may believe that this is a necessity or that it is merely true in fact, i.e. a possibility.

There are two consequences of this review of deductive understanding and modality for accounts of intellectual development. One concerns the distinction between correctness and necessity. The other concerns necessity, certainty and obligation which are members of different modal families.

The first consequence concerns correct understanding and the understanding of necessity on deductive tasks. Many developmentalists have been, rightly, concerned with children's ability to make correct deductive inferences. Yet it has to be shown both that the correct response is not due to extra-logical factors and that the correct response is due to modal knowledge. Yet this distinction has been typically by-passed in Piagetian research (Murray 1978; Smith 1982, 1992b). A similar objection applies to research on formal reasoning (Smith 1993a, sect. 19; 1994; cf., Johnson-Laird and Byrne 1994). The implication is that conclusions aimed at the elimination of Piaget's account are undermined by the reduction of necessity to correctness. This is because the construction of necessary knowledge is Piaget's principal problem (Smith 1993a, p. 1). As such, it is central to deductive reasoning and mathematical knowledge. But this epistemological problem is not resolved through a psychological account about the development of correct understanding.

The distinction between correctness–necessity and its relevance to developmental sequences is central to the argument of David Moshman (this volume). His main argument is that the understanding of necessity occurs over time in that children gradually awake from Rousseau's (1974) "sleep of reason" level by level. Each of his four levels are illustrated by reference to current research on intellectual development. His further case is that distinctive processes contribute to this construction. Just because the mechanism is unknown, it makes sense to draw upon available positions. Moshman's discussion is a timely contribution to a principal but unresolved issue and the reconciling spirit of his argument is exemplary since he sets out to draw upon research in psychology generally and upon Piaget's equilibration accounts. Yet there seems to be at least two problems. One is that psychological research on modal knowledge has been typically undertaken independently of Piaget's equilibration account, and so their integration can be expected to be problematic. It leads straight to the divergent stances identified at the outset of this chapter taken by Halford (1992) and Beilin (1992a) about Piagetian principles. Further, Piaget has several equilibration accounts relevant to affective, social and intellectual domains (1981, 1995, 1985 respectively). The integration of these accounts has yet to be carried through systematically. In short, there are major problems in carrying through an explanation of the development of necessary knowledge. Yet the unavailability of any such explanation is itself a matter of concern, since the relevance of current studies of modal knowledge is left wide open.

Here is a test case. Does the development of modal knowledge have its origin in infancy? A paradigm example concerns infants' physical reasoning (Baillargeon *et al.* 1985). In a typical study (Baillargeon *et al.* 1985), infants aged five months were presented with physically possible or impossible events which are occluded so that attention may centre on the amount of time the infants look at these two distinct types of event. Thus it seems that modal mastery occurs during infancy. Such studies show considerable ingenuity. But they lead straight to unanswerable questions: exactly what is the object of the recognitive capacities of the infants in such studies? First, are the infants responding to the defining or to the characteristic properties of modal concepts? Keil (1989) has shown that children have problems in keeping these properties distinct for many concepts and so infants could well be expected to have similar problems with modal concepts. Second, do the infants distinguish between what is not the case and what could not be the case? Children find the distinction between actuality and possibility is difficult to draw (Miller 1986; Murray 1978). Infants may be expected to have comparable problems. Third, physical and logical impossibility are distinct, and also problematic in children's minds (Braine and Rumain 1983). Why should infants find this an easy distinction to draw? These infancy studies are simply indeterminate about the origins of modal knowledge. No possibility is open to direct observation nor, a fortiori, is an impossibility (Piaget 1987a, p. 3). It is an open question as to whether the infants in such studies are responding to characteristic properties of events which do not in fact occur. This is quite different from responding to the defining properties of events which could not occur, even if they could in principle occur. Without an account of the development of modal knowledge, the relevance of such studies remains in doubt.

In research on intellectual development, it is well known that valid assessment should avoid the twin dangers of false-positive and false-negative error in diagnosis (Flavell *et al.* 1993). Thus a diagnosis would be invalidated both if a child is credited with knowledge, when this is false since the knowledge is absent, and if the child is not credited with knowledge, when this is false since the knowledge is present. Brainerd (1973) has argued that an individual may have acquired knowledge which cannot be expressed, and so judgments provide a parsimonious criterion in the assessment of children's knowledge. The strict implication of Brainerd's position is that justifications are irrelevant in such assessment. There is a counter-case to consider in that methodological norms are not the only norms at issue in assessment since epistemological norms are implicated as well. The point is that certain concepts generate normative disputes and so cannot be settled empirically. One example concerns the origin of life: does human life begin at conception, actual birth or at some point in between? Again, it is von Glasersfeld's (this volume) argument that one analysis of the concept of truth (truth as correspondence) is suspect and should be replaced by a rival analysis (truth as construction). Note that empirical investigation cannot settle such disputes which require rational investigation instead (other examples are given in Smith 1993a, sect. 4.2). The concept of knowledge is problematic in that competing analyses of this concept continue to be given by philosophers. One strategy is to survey the major analyses of any concept under dispute. With necessary knowledge in mind (Smith, this volume), two rival analyses of the concept of knowledge are the foundationalist and causal accounts. The argument is that justifications are required in the assessment of necessary knowledge, whichever account is invoked. The implication is not that justifications are required for a judgment to be made at all, but rather that both accounts require that there should always be some independent evidence based on justifications about the initial acquisition of necessary knowledge.

The argument that justifications are required to document novel cases of necessary knowledge may well have one benefit. The actual reasons given by an individual in their reasoning provide the royal road to rationality. "The role of reason is thus to introduce new necessities in systems where they were merely implicit or remained unrealised" (Piaget 1980b; see also Moshman 1994; Piéraut-Le Bonniec 1990). There is a penalty as well: even if the general argument is accepted, that still leaves open its fit in specific cases. Without specific criteria, the empirical problem remains, namely how to identify actual instances of modal reasoning. This problem in turn leads to the general question about the operationalisation of Piaget's logical models.

The second consequence concerns necessity, certainty and obligation which are members of different modal families. An individual may be in different epistemically modal states with regard to an alethic modality. Suppose someone learns by trial and error that the sum of the interior angles of Euclidean triangles equals 180 degrees and is then presented with a mathematical proof. The proof yields a necessity (alethic modality) which in tender minds is often coupled with doubt and uncertainty (epistemic modality). Note that Descartes (1931) in the *Meditations* entertained sceptical doubts (epistemic modality) about propositions regarding the existence of the external world, which he regarded as alethically necessary. Further, certainty may be directed upon non-necessity. A supreme optimist will buy a lottery ticket in the full certainty of winning the jackpot, even though the winning sequence of numbers is not a necessity. And Wittgenstein (1969, sect. 250, 418) regarded the philosophical enterprise of giving a proof of the external world as self-defeating since a proposition such as "Here is one hand" – as in Moore's putative proof – is beyond reasonable doubt and so as certain as any proposition made available in its support. In short, certainty is not necessity and conversely, necessity is not certainty.

If distinct modal concepts are distinct, even though their properties are isomorphic, they should not be run together. If Piaget's (1980a, p. 40) "feeling of necessity" has an objective basis, it may instantiate concepts from different modal families. In the argument above about immortal women, the inference of (6) from (4) and (5) may well be the experience "it has to be" in much the way that a moral action out of duty can be accompanied by a feeling charged with moral obligation (Wright 1981). Any feeling of necessity may instantiate concepts from other modal families and so it may be coupled with a conviction of certainty. But this does not mean that certainty is the same as necessity, any more than logical necessity is the same as moral obligation. Yet claims are made about certainty (epistemic modality) in the explanation of necessity (alethic modality), for example in some of Piaget's (1987a, ch. 3) studies. Other developmentalists appear to have followed suit by posing certainty questions about necessities (Miller 1986), or by treating undecidability as possibility (Acredolo and O'Connor 1991, p. 210). Further, comparable claims are made in cognitive psychology in explanation through pragmatic reasoning schemas based on the deontic logic of permission (Cheng and Holyoak 1985; Cosmides 1989). But the deontic relation of obligation–permission and the alethic relation necessity–possibility are isomorphic. Thus the proposal is effectively that the problems in one modal family can be explained in terms of another modal family. And this simply pushes the main problem one step back (Smith 1997).

There is a counter-case. It could be said in reply that there is no confusion of distinct modal concepts but rather a focus on inter-dependent phenomena. It is the children who run separate modal notions together despite the fact that investigators refrain from following suit, as is shown in some of Piaget's (1987b, ch. 8) studies. It is for this reason that certainty can and should be investigated in the same context as necessity. Indeed, there are several studies in this volume where certainty is investigated concurrently with deduction and necessity. A good indication of the difficulties here is provided by the discussion due to James Byrnes and Harry Beilin (this volume), who explicitly acknowledge that there are different modal families but nonetheless regard epistemic modality as jointly productive with alethic modality in knowledge hierarchies. In a review of available studies, their main conclusion is that the understanding of uncertainty, manifest as the demarcation of alternatives, is present in children at the outset of schooling. This finding cries out of course for explanation and their second argument concerns two principles. One is the tendency to accept closure prematurely. The other is the availability of feedback generative of modality, for example feedback which contradicts a previous response. Their third argument concerns the formation of equivalence classes over alternatives, which in turn requires the identification of classes of possibilities, impossibilities and necessities within an integrated system. Thus their case is that members of the two modal (epistemic and alethic) families must be inter-linked for modally coherent knowledge to develop. (See also Beilin 1992a, b.)

If the proposal concerns the inter-dependence of these two modalities, this case is attractive. The trouble is that if the members of each modal family have isomorphic properties, there is a temptation to push the main problem one step back. The main problem is to explain how necessity, say, is constructed. The reason why this is a problem is that the world is the totality of facts and so there is no necessity in the world (Wittgenstein 1972). By parity of argument, there is neither certainty nor obligation in the world. Yet the actual world is the starting-point for children's development. So the problem is to show how our knowledge due to the actual world is generative of knowledge of "possible worlds". The construction of certainty from supposition, or of obligation from permission, is just as problematic as is the construction of necessity from possibility. But since the problem is the same in these cases, where is the advance to explain construction in one family by reference to construction in another family where the same problem arises?

A different approach is taken by Carol Foltz, Willis Overton and Robert Ricco (this volume). Their argument is that the development of necessary knowledge merits its own explanation since the growth of such knowledge can occur both inductively and deductively. Although the children, aged ten and fourteen years, in their study were asked to rate the certainty of their beliefs about necessities, this criterion turned out not to be useful since all the children expressed very high certainty levels irrespective of the alethic status of their beliefs. In turn, their proposal is to track the development of proof construction using a Genevan task (Piaget 1987b). One difference is that versions of the selection task were used to assess children's understanding rather than a formal operational task (Overton *et al.* 1987). One finding was that there were no grade, even though there were gender, differences. Note that gender differences are well known in educational settings (APU 1991; cf., Adey and Shayer, this volume) but are less evident in research on reasoning (cf., Markovits, this volume). Further, their claim is that some evidence is on offer to show that reasoning level and proof construction are associated. Their interpretation of this association is in terms of a transition from inductive to deductive approaches. (See also Overton and Palermo 1994; Ricco 1993.) This is an enterprising study, if only because Piaget's constructivist studies have received far less attention than his structuralist studies (see Beilin 1992a for this classification). However, there are differences as well. The interpretation of proof construction in Piaget's study was asserted, but not actually shown, to be in terms of the structuralist levels. The use of versions of the selection task in attempting to remedy this deficiency leads to the question of which levels of understanding are tapped by this family of tasks (Smith 1993a, sect. 19).

Recall that necessity is defined in terms of possibility: anything is necessary whose negation is impossible (Kneale and Kneale 1962; Sainsbury 1991). But what does this mean? A version of the problem of universals arises at this point, since modal concepts are standardly defined through "possible worlds" (Kripke 1980). The actual world is familiar enough. But things could have been otherwise in unlimited ways, each of which is a "possible world". Reverting to necessity, a proposition is necessary just in case it is impossible for its negation to be true in any possible world. What exactly is a "possible world"? There are three views on offer in response to this intractable question in philosophical logic. One is modal realism, according to which there are an infinite number of possible worlds which exist in much the way that the actual world exists (Lewis 1986). The second is modal nominalism, according to which possible worlds are fictions in much the way that the characters in fairy tales are fictions (Rosen 1990). The third view is modal representationalism according to which possible worlds are constructions (Kripke 1980). Note that a comparable problem arises about the status of number. Realists say that any number exists as an abstract object (Hale 1994). Nominalists say that a number is a fiction (Field 1980). Intuitionists say that a number is a construction (Korner 1960). The main objection to realism is its ontological slum since it seems preposterous to suppose that each and every possible world exists just like the actual world (Quine 1963). The main objection to nominalism is its relativism (Putnam 1972): is the truth of 7 + 5 = 12 really no different from that of Snow White meeting seven dwarfs? The main objection of constructionism is its fallibilism (Haack 1978): how are we to tell which constructions can be carried through? The problem is that these are the major accounts on offer in philosophy and so the decision to reject them all is to court non-rationality.

This problem in philosophy is transformed in Piaget's epistemology into the problem of how anyone develops any knowledge of possibility and necessity. How is access to a possible world acquired at all (Smith 1993a, sect. 3.2)? On this interpretation, the issue is less a matter of deciding which of the *available* positions in philosophy is right but rather of showing how the key notions that define these positions were *acquired in the first place*. This issue is not about universal assent to necessary truths, whether in mathematics or deductive reasoning. It is rather about access to universals which are abstract objects with attendant necessary properties. Such access requires the construction of a system of knowledge which matches the two criteria of intellectual development, namely coherence and novelty. Any such system must be coherent since a possible world must be a consistent world. Further, new knowledge is made possible by the use of such a system, for example the realisation that the actual is merely a subset of the possible. A paradigm example of such a system is a *structure d'ensemble* (over-arching structure; cf., Piaget 1995a) which provides successively better levels of synthesis of the actual, the possible and the necessary (Inhelder and Piaget 1958, p. 251). *Universal knowledge* is therefore an ambiguous notion. It is here interpreted as the developing knowledge by the human mind of a universal. It is quite separate from the capacities whereby knowledge is then open to transfer and generalisation on possession (Smith 1995a, 1996a, b).

## CONCLUSION

Optimism about a scientific theory can appear in two senses. In one sense, the theory is widely endorsed. In the other sense, the theory generates new problems which merit attention. The stance taken here is optimistic in this second sense. Thus to Piaget's (1987c) question about the future of his work, it is opportune to adapt his own answer to a companion question about how he saw the future of psychology: "with optimism. We see new problems every day" (Piaget 1970b). In short, Piaget's epistemology is a considerable intellectual resource which has raised, and which continues to raise, good questions in psychology and education. The reason why Piaget's epistemology is an intellectual resource is because it provides a bridge which links a priori questions in philosophy with empirical issues across "the spiral of sciences" (Piaget 1918, 1979). Philosophical questions are always fundamental questions. Three such questions with a direct relevance to rational knowledge have been central in this discussion. They concern universality, identity and necessity.

Universals are the common currency in a rational meeting of minds. If all knowledge is particularistic, tied to unique contexts and defined through its own peculiar character, experience will be ineffable, or at least incommunicable. The constructivist interpretation of universals which is presented here attaches importance to the question of how any universal is understood on the basis of initial experience based on the actual world, which is particularistic, highly contextualised and possessing its own specific character. The epistemological point behind this position is less to identify a fixed stock of universals assent to which is binding on all minds but is rather to elaborate principles through which access to any universal is acquired in the first place. The construction of knowledge directed upon a universal requires the continual breaking of the bounds of experience. Such construction is never complete since universal knowledge in this sense is a limiting case which is never actually attained.

Identity is a relation which is required for two cases of knowledge – perhaps in one mind, perhaps in the minds of two different individuals – to count as the same. A universal such as truth is self-identical in all of its instances. But individuals have differential access to any such universal, since lively minds, rich cultures and variegated societies provide an unending source of diversity. The construction of universal knowledge is always charged with mental, cultural and social elements. These essential mediators provide both an opportunity and a challenge. They make development possible and so that is the opportunity. They provide a challenge as well due to the presence of elements which can and do defeat rational construction. Identity in knowledge is not a prescription for rigid conformity but is rather a prerequisite for rational disagreement and eventual intellectual advance.

Necessity is the touchstone of rationality. Necessary knowledge is important less because of its unrevisability but rather because it provides a sure criterion of what could not be otherwise. The paradigm examples of necessary knowledge occur in deductive reasoning and mathematical knowledge. Such knowledge is universal knowledge in the strict sense that it is universally accessible. It is self-identical knowledge which is common to all of its cases. Finally, it is necessary and true in any possible world. Necessity provides both a guarantee that good knowledge is to hand as well as a goal in the development of new knowledge which is in advance of available knowledge.

It is pretty clear that Piaget's optimism about his work is well founded in that this trinity continues to hold central but problematic notions. It is also pretty clear that there are engaging accounts in psychology and education with a relevance to these same problems. These accounts are testimony to the interesting, important but also problematic nature of intellectual development.

## REFERENCES

Acredolo, C. and O'Connor, J. (1991) "On the difficulty of detecting cognitive uncertainty", *Human Development* 34: 204–223.

Adey, P. and Shayer, M. (1994) *Really raising standards*, London: Routledge.

Anderson, A.R. and Belnap, N. (1975) *Entailment: the logic of relevance and necessity*, Princeton, NJ: Princeton University Press.

Apostel, L. (1982) "The future of Piagetian logic", *Revue Internationale de Philosophie*, 142–3, 612–35. (Reprinted in L. Smith (ed.) (1992) *Jean Piaget: Critical assessments, vol. 4*, London: Routledge.)

APU (1991) *APU mathematics monitoring*, London: HMSO.

"Aristotle" (1953), in J. Thomson (ed.) *The ethics of Aristotle*, London: Allen & Unwin.

"Aristotle" (1987), in J. Ackrill (ed.) *A new Aristotle reader*, Oxford: Oxford University Press.

Ayer, A. J. (1956) *The problem of knowledge*, Harmondsworth: Penguin.

Baillargeon, R. (1995) "A model of physical reasoning in infancy", in C. Rovee-Collier and L. Lipsitt (eds) *Advances in infancy research*, vol. 9, New Jersey: Ablex.

Baillargeon, R., Spelke, E. and Wasserman, S. (1985) "Object permanence in five-month-old infants", *Cognition* 20: 191–208. (Reprinted in L. Smith (ed.) (1992) *Jean Piaget: Critical assessments, vol. 1*, London: Routledge).

Baldwin, J. M. (1911) *Thought and thinking*, London: George Allen.

Barnes, B. and Bloor, D. (1982) "Relatavism, rationalism, and the sociology of knowledge", in M. Hollis and S. Lukes (eds) *Rationality and relativism*, Oxford: Blackwell.

Beilin, H. (1992a) "Piaget's enduring contribution to developmental psychology", *Developmental Psychology* 28: 191–204.

Beilin, H. (1992b) "Piaget's new theory", in H. Beilin and P. Pufall (eds) *Piaget's theory: Prospects and possibilities*, Hillsdale, NJ: Erlbaum.

Bideaud, J. (1992) *Pathways to number*, Hillsdale, NJ: Erlbaum.

Bidell, T. and Fischer, K. (1992) "Cognitive development in educational contexts: implications of skill theory", in A. Demetriou, M. Shayer and A. Efklides (eds) *Neo-Piagetian theories of cognitive development*, London: Routledge.

Binet, A. (1975) *Modern ideas about children*, New York:

Bonatti, L. (1994) "Why should we abandon the mental logic hypothesis?" *Cognition* 50: 17–39.

Bond, T. (1995) "Piaget and measurement I: the twain really do meet", *Archives de Psychologie* 63: 71–87.

Bond, T. and Jackson, I. (1991) "The Gou protocol revisited: a Piagetian contextualisation of critique", *Archives de Psychologie* 59: 31–53. (Reprinted in L. Smith (ed.) (1992) *Jean Piaget: Critical assessments, vol. 1*, London: Routledge.)

Braine, M. and O'Brien, D. (1991) "A theory of *if*: a lexical entry, reasoning program, and pragmatic principles", *Psychological Review* 98: 182–203.

Braine, M. and Rumain, B. (1983) "Logical reasoning", in P. Mussen (ed.) *Handbook of child psychology, vol. 3*, New York: Wiley. (Reprinted in L. Smith (ed.) (1992) *Jean Piaget: Critical assessments, vol. 2*, London: Routledge.)

Brainerd, C. (1973) "Judgements and explanations as criteria for the presence of cognitive structures", *Psychological Bulletin* 79: 172–179. (Reprinted in L. Smith (ed.) (1992) *Jean Piaget: Critical assessments, vol. 2*, London: Routledge.)

Brown, A. (1990) "Domain-specific principles affect learning and transfer in children", *Cognitive Science* 14: 107–33.

Brown, A., Metz, K. and Campione, J. (1996) "Social interaction and individual understanding in a community of learners: the influence of Piaget and Vygotsky", in A. Tryphon and J. Vonèche (eds) *Piaget–Vygotsky: The social genesis of thought*, Hove: Erlbaum.

Brown, T. (1985) "Foreword", in J. Piaget *Equilibration of cognitive structures*, Chicago: University of Chicago Press.

Brown, T. (1996) "Values, knowledge and Piaget", in E. Reed, E. Turiel and T. Brown (eds) *Values and knowledge*, Hillsdale, NJ: Erlbaum.

Brown, T. and Weiss, L. (1987) "Structures, procedures, heuristics and affectivity", *Archives de Psychologie* 55: 59–94. (Reprinted in L. Smith (ed.) (1992) *Jean Piaget: Critical assessments, vol. 4*, London: Routledge.)

Bryant, P. and Trabasso, T. (1971) "Transitive inferences and memory in young children", *Nature* 232: 456–58. (Reprinted in L. Smith (ed.) (1992) *Jean Piaget: Critical assessments, vol. 2*, London: Routledge.)

Burt, C. (1919) "The development of reasoning in school children", *Journal of Experimental Pedagogy* 5: 68–77.

Bynum, T., Thomas, J. and Weitz, L. (1972) "Operational thinking: Inhelder and Piaget's evidence", *Developmental Psychology* 7: 129–32. (Reprinted in L. Smith (ed.) (1992) *Jean Piaget: Critical assessments, vol. 1*, London: Routledge.)

Campbell, R. (1991) "Does class inclusion have mathematical prerequisites?" *Cognitive Development* 6: 169–94.

Case, R. (1985) *Intellectual development*, London: Academic Press.

Case, R. (1991) *The mind's stair-case*, Hillsdale, NJ: Erlbaum.

Case, R. and Edelstein, W. (1993) *The new structuralism in cognitive development theory: Theory and research on individual pathways*, Basel: Karger.

Chalmers, M. and McGonigle, B. (1984) "Are children more logical than monkeys on the five-term series problem?" *Journal of Experimental Child Psychology* 37: 355–77. (Reprinted in L. Smith (ed.) (1992) *Jean Piaget: Critical assessments, vol. 2*, London: Routledge.)

Chandler, M. and Boutilier, R. (1992) "The development of dynamic system reasoning", *Human Development* 35: 121–37.

Chandler, M. and Chapman, M. (eds) (1991) *Criteria for competence*, Hillsdale, NJ: Erlbaum.

Chapman, M. (1988) *Constructive evolution*, Cambridge: Cambridge University Press.

Chapman, M. (1991) "The epistemic triangle: operative and communicative components of cognitive competence", in M. Chandler and M. Chapman (eds) *Criteria for competence*, Hillsdale, NJ: Erlbaum.

Chapman, M. and Lindenberger, U. (1988) "Functions, operations and *décalage* in the development of transitivity", *Developmental Psychology* 24: 542–51. (Reprinted in L. Smith (ed.) (1992) *Jean Piaget: Critical assessments, vol. 2*, London: Routledge.)

Cheng, P. and Holyoak, K. (1985) "Pragmatic reasoning schemas", *Cognitive Psychology* 17: 391–416.

Cobb, P. (1994) "Where is the mind? Constructivist and sociocultural perspectives on mathematical development", *Educational Researcher* 23(7): 13–20.

Cohen, J. (1981) "Can human irrationality be experimentally demonstrated?" *The Behavioural and Brain Sciences* 4: 317–70.

Coles, M. (1993) "Teaching thinking: principles, problems, and programmes", *Educational Psychology* 13: 333–44.

Cormier, P. and Dagenais, Y. (1983) "Class inclusion developmental levels and logical necessity", *International Journal of Behavioural Development* 6: 1–14. (Reprinted in L. Smith (ed.) (1992) *Jean Piaget: Critical assessments, vol. 2*, London: Routledge.)

Cosmides, L. (1989) "The logic of social exchange: has natural selection shaped how humans reason? Studies with the Wason selection task", *Cognition* 31: 187–276.

Couturat, L. (1965) *L'algèbre de la logique*, Hildesheim: Georg Olms.

Davidson, P.M. (1988) "Piaget's category-theoretic interpretation of cognitive development: a neglected contribution", *Human Development* 31: 225–44. (Reprinted in L. Smith (ed.) (1992) *Jean Piaget: Critical assessments, vol. 4*, London: Routledge.)

Demetriou, A., Shayer, M. and Efklides, A. (eds) (1992) *Neo-Piagetian theories of cognitive development*, London: Routledge.

Descartes, R. (1931) *Philosophical works, vol. 1*, New York: Dover.

DeVries, R. (1987) *Programs of early education*, New York: Longman.

Doise, W., Mugny, G. and Perret-Clermont, A. (1975) "Social interaction and the development of cognitive operations", *European Journal of Social Psychology* 5: 367–83.

Ennis, R.H. (1976) "Children's ability to handle Piaget's propositional logic: a conceptual critique", *Review of Educational Research* 45: 1–41. (Reprinted in L. Smith (ed.) (1992) *Jean Piaget: Critical assessments, vol. 1*, London: Routledge.)

Feuerstein, R., Miller, R., Hoffman, M., Rand, Y., Mintzker, Y. and Jensen, R. (1981) "Cognitive modifiability in adolesence", *Journal of Special Education* 15: 269–87. (Reprinted in L. Smith (ed.) (1992) *Jean Piaget: Critical assessments, vol. 3*, London: Routledge.)

Field, H. (1980) *Science without numbers*, Oxford: Blackwell.

Flavell, J., Miller, P. and Miller, S. (1993) *Cognitive development*, 3rd edn, Englewood Cliffs, NJ: Prentice-Hall.

Frege, G. (1888/1980) *The foundations of arithmetic*, Oxford: Oxford University Press.

Gellner, E. (1992) *Postmodernism, Reason and Religion*, London: Routledge.

Gelman, R. (1972) "Logical capacity of very young children: number invariance rules", *Child Development* 43: 371–83. (Reprinted in L. Smith (ed.) (1992) *Jean Piaget: Critical assessments, vol. 3*, London: Routledge.)

Gelman, R. and Gallistel, R. (1978) *The child's understanding of number*, Cambridge, MA: Harvard University Press.

Gergen, K. (1994) "Exploring the postmodern: perils or potentials?" *American Psychologist* 49: 412–16.

Ginsburg, H. (1981) "Piaget and education", in I. Sigel, H. Brodzinsky and R. Golinkoff (eds) *New directions in Piagetian theory and practice*, Hillsdale, NJ: Erlbaum. (Reprinted in L. Smith (ed.) (1992) *Jean Piaget: Critical assessments, vol. 3*, London: Routledge.)

Glasersfeld, E. von (1995) *Radical constructivism*, London: Falmer.

Goswami, U. (1992) *Analogical reasoning in children*, Hove: Erlbaum.

Haack, S. (1978) *Philosophy of logics*, Cambridge: Cambridge University Press.

Hale, B. (1994) "Is platonism epistemologically bankrupt?" *The Philosophical Review* 103: 299–325.

Halford, G. (1992) "Analogical reasoning and conceptual complexity in cognitive development", *Human Development* 35: 193–217.

Halford, G. and Boyle, F. (1985) "Do young children understand conservation of number?", *Child Development* 56: 165–76. (Reprinted in L. Smith (ed.) (1992) *Jean Piaget: Critical assessments, vol. 2*, London: Routledge.)

Hamlyn, D.W. (1978) *Experience and the growth of understanding*, London: Routledge & Kegan Paul.

Haroutunian, S. (1983) *Equilibrium in the balance*, New York: Springer.

Harré, R. (1986) "Social sources of mental content and order", in J. Margolis, P. Mancias, R. Harré and P. Secord *Psychology: Designing the discipline*, Oxford: Blackwell.

Harris, P. (1989) *Children and emotion*, Oxford: Blackwell.

Harris, P., Brown, E., Marriott, C., Whittall, S. and Harmer, S. (1991) "Monsters, ghosts and witches: testing the limits of the fantasy–reality distinction in young children", *British Journal of Developmental Psychology* 9: 105–23.

Hintikka, J. and Hintikka, M. (1989) *The logic of epistemology and the epistemology of logic*, Dordrecht: Kluwer.

Hodkin, B. (1987) "Performance model analysis in class inclusion", *Developmental Psychology* 23: 683–9. (Reprinted in L. Smith (ed.) (1992) *Jean Piaget: Critical assessments, vol. 2*, London: Routledge.)

Hoffman, W. (1981) "Mathematical models of Piagetian psychology", in S. Modgil and C. Modgil (eds) *Toward a theory of psychological development*, Windsor: NFER.

Hookway, C. (1990) *Scepticism*, London: Routledge.

Howe, C. (1993) "Piaget's theory and primary school physics", *Child Development and Care* 95: 23–39.

Hunt, E. (1989) "Cognitive science: definition, status, and questions", *Annual Review of Psychology* 40: 603–30.

Inhelder, B. (1989) "Bärbel Inhelder", in G. Lindzey (ed.) *A History of Psychology in Autobiography*, vol. VIII, Stanford, CA: Stanford University Press.

Inhelder, B. and Cellérier, G. (1995) *Pathways of discovery in the child*, Hillsdale, NJ: Erlbaum.

Inhelder, B. and Piaget, J. (1958) *The growth of logical thinking*, London: Routledge & Kegan Paul.

Inhelder, B. and Piaget, J. (1964) *The early growth of logic in the child*, London: Routledge & Kegan Paul.

Inhelder, B. and Piaget, J. (1980) "Procedures and structures", in D. Olson (ed.) *The social foundations of language*, New York: Norton.

Isaacs, N. (1951) "Critical notice: *Traité de logique*", *British Journal of Psychology* 42: 185–8. (Reprinted in L. Smith (ed.) (1992) *Jean Piaget: Critical assessments, vol. 4*, London: Routledge.)

Jean Piaget Archives (1989) *Jean Piaget Bibliography*, Geneva: Jean Piaget Archives Foundation.

Johnson-Laird, P. and Byrne, R. (1994) "Authors' response", *The Behavioural and Brain Sciences* 17: 775–77.

Kant, I. (1933) *Critique of pure reason*, 2nd edn, London: Macmillan.

Kant, I. (1948) *Groundwork of the metaphysics of morals*, in H. Paton (ed.) *The moral law*, London: Hutchinson.

Karmiloff-Smith, A. (1992) *Beyond modularity*, Cambridge, MA: MIT Press.

Karplus, R. (1981) "Education and formal thought – a modest proposal", in I. Sigel, H. Brodzinsky and R. Golinkoff (eds) *New directions in Piagetian theory and practice*, Hillsdale, NJ: Erlbaum. (Reprinted in L. Smith (ed.) (1992) *Jean Piaget: Critical assessments, vol. 1*, London: Routledge.)

Keil, F. (1989) *Concepts, kinds and cognitive development*, Cambridge, MA: MIT Press.

Kesselring, T. (1994) "A comparison between evolutionary and genetic epistemology", *Journal for General Philosophy of Science* 25: 293–325.

Kitchener, R. (1993) "Piaget's epistemic subject and science education: epistemological vs. psychological issues", *Science and Education* 2: 137–48.

Kneale, W. and Kneale, M. (1962) *The development of logic*, Oxford: Oxford University Press.

Kohlberg, L. and Mayer, R. (1972) "Development as the aim of education", *Harvard Educational Review* 42: 449–96. (Reprinted in L. Smith (ed.) (1992) *Jean Piaget: Critical assessments, vol. 3*, London: Routledge.)

Korner, S. (1960) *The philosophy of mathematics*, London: Hutchinson.

Kripke, S. (1980) *Naming and necessity*, Oxford: Blackwell.

Kuhn, D. (1990) *Developmental perspectives on teaching and learning thinking skills*, Basel: Karger.

Kuhn, D., Amsel, E. and O'Loughlin, M. (1988) *The development of scientific thinking skills*, New York: Academic Press.

Kuhn, D. and Brannock, J. (1977) "Development of the isolation of variables scheme in experimental and 'natural experiment' contexts", *Developmental Psychology* 13: 9–14. (Reprinted in L. Smith (ed.) (1992) *Jean Piaget: Critical assessments, vol. 1*, London: Routledge.)

Lakatos, I. (1974) "Falsification and the logic of scientific research programmes", in I. Lakatos and A. Musgrave (eds) *Criticism and the growth of knowledge*, corrected edn, Cambridge: Cambridge University Press.

Laudan, L. (1977) *Progress and its problems*, Berkeley, CA: University of California Press.

Laudan, L. (1984) *Science and values*, Berkeley, CA: University of California Press.

Lawson, A. (1991) "Is Piaget's epistemic subject dead?" *Journal of Research in Science Teaching* 28: 581–89.

Lawson, A. (1992) "What do tests of 'formal' reasoning actually measure?", *Journal of Research in Science Teaching* 29: 965–83.

Lawson, A.E., Karplus, R. and Adi, H. (1978) "The acquisition of propositional logic and formal operational schemata", *Journal of Research in Science Teaching* 15: 465–78. (Reprinted in L. Smith (ed.) (1992) *Jean Piaget: Critical assessments, vol. 1*, London: Routledge.)

Lemmon, E. (1966) *Beginning logic*, London: Nelson.

Levine, J. and Resnick, L. (1993) "Social foundations of cognition", *Annual Review of Psychology* 44: 585–612.

Lewis, D.K. (1986) *On the plurality of possible worlds*, Oxford: Blackwell.

Light, P. and Butterworth, G. (1992) *Context and cognition*, New York: Harvester.

Lopez, A., Gelman, S., Gutheil, G. and Smith, E. (1992) "The development of category based induction", *Child Development* 63: 1070–90.

Lunzer, E. (1970) "Problems of formal reasoning in test situations", in P. Mussen (ed.) *European research in child development*, Chicago: University of Chicago Press.

Macnamara, J. (1994) "Logic and cognition", in J. Macnamara and G. Reyes (eds) *The logical foundation of cognition*, New York: Oxford University Press.

Margolis, J. (1986) *Pragmatism without foundations: Reconciling realism and relativism*, Oxford: Blackwell.

Markman, E.M. (1989) *Categorization and naming in children: Problems of induction*, Cambridge, MA: MIT Press.

Markovits, H. (1993) "The development of conditonal reasoning: a Piagetian reformulation of mental models theory", *Merrill-Palmer Quarterly* 39: 133–60.

Markovits, H. and Vachon, R. (1990) "Conditional reasoning, representation, and level of abstraction", *Developmental Psychology* 26: 942–51.

Markovits, H., Dumas, C. and Malfait, N. (1995) "Understanding transitivity of a spatial relationship: a developmental analysis", *Journal of Experimental Child Psychology* 59: 124–41.

Mays, W. (1992) "Piaget's logic and its critics: a deconstruction", *Archives de Psychologie* 60: 45–70.

McGonigle, B. and Chalmers, M. (1995) *The growth of intelligent systems: A cognitive analysis*, Cambridge, MA: MIT Press.

Miller, S. (1986) "Certainty and necessity in the understanding of Piagetian concepts", *Developmental Psychology* 22: 3–18. (Reprinted in L. Smith (ed.) (1992) *Jean Piaget: Critical assessments, vol. 2*, London: Routledge.)

Moessinger, P. (1978) "Piaget on equilibration", *Human Development* 21: 255–67. (Reprinted in L. Smith (ed.) (1992) *Jean Piaget: Critical assessments, vol. 4*, London: Routledge.)

Moshman, D. (1994) "Reason, reasons, and reasoning", *Theory and Psychology* 4: 245–60.

Murray, F. (1978) "Teaching strategies and conservation training", in A. Lesgold, J. Pellegrino, S. Fokkema and R. Glaser (eds) *Cognitive psychology and instruction*, New York: Plenum Press. (Reprinted in L. Smith (ed.) (1992) *Jean Piaget: Critical assessments, vol. 2*, London: Routledge.)

Murray, F.B. (1990) "The conversion of truth into necessity", in W. Overton (ed.) *Reasoning necessity and logic*, Hillsdale, NJ: Erlbaum Associates.

Mussen, P. (ed.) *Handbook of child psychology*, vol. III, New York: Wiley.

Nagel, T. (1986) *The view from nowhere*, New York: Oxford University Press.

Noelting, G. (1980) "The development of proportional reasoning and the ratio concept. Part I – differentiation of stages", *Educational Studies in Mathematics* 11: 217–53. (Reprinted in L. Smith (ed.) (1992) *Jean Piaget: Critical assessments, vol. 1*, London: Routledge.)

Nunes, T. and Bryant, P. (1996) *Children doing mathematics*, Oxford: Blackwell.

Nunes, T., Schliemann, A. and Carraher, D. (1993) *Street mathematics and school mathematics*, Cambridge: Cambridge University Press.

Overton, W., Ward, S., Black, J. and O'Brien, D. (1987) "Form and content in the development of deductive reasoning", *Developmental Psychology* 23: 22–30. Reprinted in L. Smith (ed.) *Jean Piaget: Critical assessments*, vol. 1, London: Routledge.

Overton, W. and Palermo, D. (1994) *The nature and ontogenesis of meaning*, Hillsdale, NJ: Erlbaum.

Pareto, V. (1963) *A treatise on general sociology*, 4 vols, New York: Dover.

Pears, R. and Bryant, P. (1990) "Transitive inferences about spatial position by young children", *British Journal of Psychology* 81: 497–510. (Reprinted in L. Smith (ed.) (1992) *Jean Piaget: Critical assessments, vol. 2*, London: Routledge.)

Piaget, J. (1918) *Recherche*, Lausanne: La Concorde.

Piaget, J. (1921) "Essai sur quelques aspectes du développement de la notion de partie chez l'enfant", *Journal de Psychologie Normale et Pathologique* 18: 449–80.

Piaget, J. (1923) "La psychologie et les valeurs religieuses", in *Association Chrétienne d'Etudiants de la Suisse Romande* (ed.) Sainte-Croix 1922, pp. 38–82.

Piaget, J. (1932) *The moral judgment of the child*, London: Routledge & Kegan Paul.

Piaget, J. (1950) *Introduction à l'épistémologie génétique, vol. 1, La pensée mathématique*, Paris: Presses Universitaires de France.

Piaget, J. (1952) *The child's conception of number*, London: Routledge & Kegan Paul.

Piaget, J. (1953) *The origins of intelligence in the child*, London: Routledge & Kegan Paul.

Piaget, J. (1954) *The construction of reality in the child*, New York: Basic Books.

Piaget, J. (1959) *Language and thought of the child*, 3rd edn, London: Routledge & Kegan Paul.

Piaget, J. (1962) *Play, dreams and imitation in childhood*, London: Routledge & Kegan Paul.

Piaget, J. (1966) "Part II", in E. Beth and J. Piaget *Mathematical epistemology and psychology*, Dordrecht: Reidel.

Piaget, J. (1967) "Logique formelle et psychologie génétique", in CNRS (ed.) *Les modèles et la formalisation du comportement*, Paris: Centre National de la Recherche Scientifique.

Piaget, J. (1970a) *Science of education and the psychology of the child*, London: Longman.

Piaget, J. (1970b) "A conversation with Jean Piaget", *Psychology Today* 3: 25–32.

Piaget, J. (1971) *Biology and knowledge*, Edinburgh: Edinburgh University Press.

Piaget, J. (1972) *The principles of genetic epistemology*, London: Routledge & Kegan Paul.

Piaget, J. (1976) "Postface", *Archives de Psychologie* 44: 223–8.

Piaget, J. (1977) *Recherches sur l'abstraction réfléchissante, vol. 1*, Paris: Presses Universitaires de France.

Piaget, J. (1978) *The development of thought*, Oxford: Blackwell.

Piaget, J. (1979) "Relations between psychology and other sciences", *Annual Review of Psychology* 30: 1–8.

Piaget, J. (1980a), in J-C. Bringuier (ed.) *Conversations with Jean Piaget*, Chicago: University of Chicago Press.

Piaget, J. (1980b) "La raison en tant qu'objectif de la compréhension", unpublished paper.

Piaget, J. (1980c) "The psychogenesis of knowledge and its epistemological significance", in M. Piattelli-Palmarini (ed.) *Language and learning*, London: Routledge & Kegan Paul.

Piaget, J. (1981) *Intelligence and affectivity*, Palo Alto, CA: Annual Reviews.

Piaget, J. (1983) "Piaget's theory", in P. Mussen (ed.) *Handbook of child psychology, vol. 1*, New York: Wiley.

Piaget, J. (1983) "Piaget's theory", in P. Mussen (ed.) *Handbook of child psychology, vol. 1*, New York: Wiley.

Piaget, J. (1985) *Equilibration of cognitive structures*, Chicago: University of Chicago Press.

Piaget, J. (1986) "Essay on necessity", *Human Development* 29: 301–14.

Piaget, J. (1987a) *Possibility and necessity, vol. 1*, Minneapolis: University of Minnesota Press.

Piaget, J. (1987b) *Possibility and necessity, vol. 2*, Minneapolis: University of Minnesota Press.

Piaget, J. (1987c) "Préface", in J. Piaget, P. Mounoud and J-P. Bronkart (eds) *Psychologie*, Paris: Gallimard.

Piaget, J. (1995a) *Sociological studies*, London: Routledge.

Piaget, J. (1995b) "Commentary on Vygotsky's criticism", *New Ideas in Psychology*.

Piaget, J. and Garcia, R. (1989) *Psychogenesis and the history of science*, New York: Columbia University Press.

Piaget, J. and Garcia, R. (1991) *Toward a logic of meanings*, Hillsdale, NJ: Erlbaum.

Piaget, J., Grize, J-B., Szeminska, A. and Bang, Vinh. (1977) *Epistemology and psychology of functions*, Dordrecht: Reidel.

Piaget, J., Henriques, G. and Ascher, E. (1992) *Morphisms and categories*, Hillsdale, NJ: Erlbaum.

Piaget, J. and Inhelder, B. (1956) *The child's conception of space*, London: Routledge & Kegan Paul.

Piaget, J. and Inhelder, B. (1969) *The psychology of the child*, London: Routledge & Kegan Paul.

Piaget, J. and Voyat, G. (1979) "The possible, the impossible and the necessary", in F. Murray (ed.) *The impact of Piagetian theory*, Baltimore: University Parks Press.

Piéraut-Le Bonniec, G. (1980) *The development of modal reasoning*, New York: Academic Press.

Piéraut-Le Bonniec, G. (1990) "The logic of meaning and meaningful implication", in W. Overton (ed.) *Reasoning, necessity and logic*, Hillsdale, NJ: Erlbaum. (Reprinted in L. Smith (ed.) (1992) *Jean Piaget: Critical assessments, vol. 2*, London: Routledge.)

Pintrich, P., Marx, R. and Boyle, R. (1993) "Beyond cold conceptual change: the role of motivational beliefs and classroom contextual factors in the process of conceptual change", *Review of Educational Research* 63: 167–99.

Popper, K. R. (1968) *The logic of scientific discovery*, London: Hutchinson.

Popper, K. R. (1979) *Objective knowledge*, 2nd edn, Oxford: Oxford University Press.

Putnam, H. (1972) *Philosophy of logic*, London: Allen & Unwin.

Quine, W. (1963) *From a logical point of view*, 2nd edn, New York: Harper.

Quine, W. (1974) *The roots of reference*, La Salle, IL: Open Court.

Ricco, R. (1993) "Revising the logic of operations as a relevance logic", *Human Development* 36: 125–46.

Rosen. G. (1990) "Modal fictionalism", *Mind* 99: 327–54.

Rousseau, J-J. (1974) *Emile*, London: Dent.

Russell, B. (1919) *Introduction to mathematical philosophy*, London: Allen & Unwin.

Russell, J., Mills, I. and Reiff-Musgrove, P. (1990) "The role of symmetrical and asymmetrical social conflict in cognitive change", *Journal of Experimental Child Psychology* 49: 58–78. (Reprinted in L. Smith (ed.) (1992) *Jean Piaget: Critical assessments, vol. 3*, London: Routledge.)

Sainsbury, M. (1991) *Logical forms*, Oxford: Blackwell.

Saxe, G. (1991) *Culture and cognitive development*, Hillsdale, NJ: Erlbaum.

Schubauer-Leoni, M-L., Bell, N., Grossen, M. and Perret-Clermont, A-N. (1989) "Problems in assessment of learning: the social construction of questions and answers in the scholastic context", *International Journal of Educational Research* 13: 671–84. (Reprinted in L. Smith (ed.) (1992) *Jean Piaget: Critical assessments, vol. 3*, London: Routledge.)

Shayer, M. and Adey, P. (1981) *Towards a science of science teaching*, London: Heinemann.

Shayer, M., Demetriou, A. and Pervez, M. (1988) "The structure and scaling of concrete operational thought: three studies in four countries", *Genetic, Social and General Psychology Monographs* 114: 309–75. (Reprinted in L. Smith (ed.) (1992) *Jean Piaget: Critical assessments, vol. 3*, London: Routledge.)

Shayer, M., Kuchemann, D. and Wylam, H. (1976) "The distribution of Piagetian stages of thinking in British middle and secondary school children", *British Journal of Educational Psychology* 46: 164–73. (Reprinted in L. Smith (ed.) *Jean Piaget: Critical assessments, vol. 1*, London: Routledge.)

Siegler, R. (1991) *Children's thinking*, 2nd edn, Engelwood Cliffs, NJ: Prentice Hall.

Smith, L. (1982) "Class inclusion and conclusions about Piaget's theory", *British Journal of Psychology* 73: 267–76.

Smith, L. (1987) "On Piaget on necessity", in J. Russell (ed.) *Philosophical perspectives on developmental psychology*, Oxford: Blackwell. (Reprinted in L. Smith (ed.) *Jean Piaget: Critical assessments, vol. 4*, London: Routledge.)

Smith, L. (ed.) (1992a) *Jean Piaget: Critical assessments, vol. 1, Understanding and intelligence*, London: Routledge.

Smith, L. (ed.) (1992b) *Jean Piaget: Critical assessments, vol. 2, Children's thinking*, London: Routledge.

Smith, L. (ed.) (1992c) *Jean Piaget: Critical assessments, vol. 3, Education and society*, London: Routledge.

Smith, L. (ed.) (1992d) *Jean Piaget: Critical assessments, vol. 4, Intellectual development*, London: Routledge.

Smith, L. (1993a) *Necessary knowledge: Piagetian perspectives on constructivism*, Hove: Erlbaum.

Smith, L. (1993b) "The development of necessary knowledge: psychological and educational issues", *Early Child Development and Care* 95: 3–22.

Smith, L. (1993c) "Good accounts of good practice", *Education 3–13* 21 (3): 38–45.

Smith, L. (1994) "Mental models and modality", *The Behavioural and Brain Sciences* 17: 774–75.

Smith, L. (1995a) "Introduction to *Sociological studies*", in J. Piaget *Sociological studies*, London: London: Routledge.

Smith, L. (1995b) "Universal knowledge", paper presented at the Jean Piaget Society Annual Symposium, Berkeley, CA.

Smith, L. (1996a) "The social construction of rational understanding", in A. Tryphon and J. Vonèche (eds) *Piaget–Vygotsky: The social genesis of thought*, Hove: Erlbaum.

Smith, L. (1996b) "With knowledge in mind: novel transformation of the learner or transformation of novel knowledge", *Human Development* (forthcoming).

Smith, L. (1997) "Necessary knowledge and its assessment-criteria in intellectual development", in L. Smith, J. Duckrell, P. Tomlinson (eds) *Piaget, Vigotsky and Beyond*, London: Routledge.

Solomon, Y. (1989) *The practice of mathematics*, London: Routledge.

Solomon, Y. (1996) *The development of mathematical skills*, London: Routledge.

Sophian, C. and Somerville, S. (1988) "Early developments in logical reasoning: considering alternative possibilities", *Cognitive Development* 3: 183–222.

Subbotsky, E. (1992) *Foundations of the mind: Children's understanding of reality*, Hemel Hempstead: Harvester Press.

Subbotsky, E. (1994) "Early rationality and magical thinking in preschoolers: space and time", *British Journal of Developmental Psychology* 12: 97–108.

Tobias, S. (1994) "Interest, prior knowledge and learning", *Review of Educational Research* 64: 37–52.

Tryphon, A. and Vonèche, J. (1996) *Piaget–Vygotsky: The social genesis of thought*, Hove: Erlbaum.

Tudge, J. (1990) "Vygotsky, the zone of proximal development and peer collaboration", in L. Moll (ed.) *Vygotsky and education*, Cambridge: Cambridge University Press.

Veer, R. van der and Valsiner, J. (1994) "Introduction", *The Vygotsky reader*, Oxford: Blackwell.

Vidal, F. (1994) *Piaget before Piaget*, Cambridge, MA: Harvard University Press.

Vonèche, J-J. and Vidal, F. (1985) "Jean Piaget and the child psychologist", *Synthèse* 65: 121–38.

Vygotsky, L. (1978) *Mind in society*, Cambridge, MA: Harvard University Press.

Vygotsky, L. (1994), in R. van der Veer and J. Valsiner (eds) *The Vygotsky reader*, Oxford: Blackwell.

Wason, P. C. (1977) "The theory of formal operations – a critique", in B. Geber (ed.) *Piaget and knowing: studies in genetic epistemology*, London: Routledge & Kegan Paul. (Reprinted in L. Smith (ed.) (1992) *Jean Piaget: Critical assessments, vol. 1*, London: Routledge.)

Wellman, H. and Gelman, S. (1992) "Cognitive development: foundational theories of core domains", *Annual Review of Psychology* 43: 337–75.

Whitehead, A. and Russell, B. (1962) *Principia mathematica to *56*, Cambridge: Cambridge University Press.

Williams, B. (1978) *Descartes: The project of pure enquiry*, Harmondsworth: Penguin Books.

Wittgenstein, L. (1969) *On certainty*, Oxford: Blackwell.

Wittgenstein, L. (1972) *Tractatus logico-philosophicus*, corrected edn, London: Routledge & Kegan Paul.

Wittman, E. (1975) "Natural numbers and groupings", *Educational Studies in Mathematics* 6: 53–75.

Wozniak, R. and Fischer, K. (1993) *Development in context*, Hillsdale, NJ: Erlbaum.

Wright, D. (1981) "The psychology of moral obligation", in L. Smith (ed.) (1992) *Jean Piaget: Critical assessments, vol. 1*, London: Routledge.

Wright, G.H. von (1951) *An essay in modal logic*, Amsterdam: North-Holland.

Wright, G.H. von (1957) *Logical studies*, London: Routledge & Kegan Paul.

# Index